CURATIVE
ASPECTS
OF
MENTAL
RETARDATION

CURATIVE
ASPECTS
OF
MENTAL
RETARDATION

Biomedical and Behavioral Advances

edited by

FRANK J. MENOLASCINO, M.D.
University of Nebraska Medical Center
Omaha, Nebraska

RONALD NEMAN, PH.D.
Association for Retarded Citizens of the United States
Arlington, Texas

JACK A. STARK, PH.D.
University of Nebraska Medical Center
Omaha, Nebraska

·P A U L·H·
BROOKES
PUBLISHING CO.
Baltimore • London

Paul H. Brookes Publishing Co.
Post Office Box 10624
Baltimore, Maryland 21204

Copyright 1983 by Paul H. Brookes Publishing Co., Inc.
All rights reserved.

Typeset by Brushwood Graphics, Baltimore, Maryland.
Manufactured in the United States of America by
Universal Lithographers, Inc., Cockeysville, Maryland.

Library of Congress Cataloging in Publication Data
Main entry under title:
Curative aspects of mental retardation.

  Bibliography: p.
  Includes index.
  1. Mental deficiency—Treatment—Addresses, essays,
lectures. 2. Psychobiology—Addresses, essays, lectures.
I. Menolascino, Frank J., 1930–   . II. Neman, Ronald
III. Stark, Jack A., 1946–   . [DNLM: 1. Mental retardation—
Therapy—Congresses. WM 300 C975 1980]
RC570.C87 1983   616.85'8806   82-17787
ISBN 0-933716-29-X

Contents

Contributors

Gershon Berkson, Ph.D.
Professor, Department of Psychology
University of Illinois at Chicago
Box 4348
Chicago, IL 60680

Sidney W. Bijou, Ph.D.
Adjunct Professor of Psychology and
    Special Education
The University of Arizona
College of Education
Department of Special Education
Tuscon, AZ 87521

Michael D. Browning, Ph.D.
Department of Pharmacology
Fellow, Bush Center in Child Development
    and Social Policy
Yale University School of Medicine
333 Cedar Street
New Haven, CT 06510

Earl C. Butterfield, Ph.D.
Professor of Education
University of Washington
406 Hall Health, GS-27
Seattle, WA 98195

Verne S. Caviness, Jr., M.D.
Director, Southard Laboratory
Eunice Kennedy Shriver Center for Mental
    Retardation
200 Trapelo Road
Waltham, MA 02154

Kenneth L. Davis, M.D.
Chief, Psychiatry Services
Bronx Veterans Administration Medical
    Center
130 West Kingsbridge Road
Bronx, NY 10468
    and
Associate Professor of Psychiatry
Mt. Sinai School of Medicine of the City
    University of New York
One Gustave Levy Place
New York, NY 10029

Park S. Gerald, M.D.
Chief, Clinical Genetics Division
Children's Hospital Medical Center
300 Longwood Avenue
Boston, MA 02115

Mary Jo Harrod, Ph.D.
Associate Professor
Division of Clinical Genetics
Department of Obstetrics and Gynecology
The University of Texas Health Science
    Center at Dallas
5323 Harry Hines Boulevard
Dallas, TX 75235

Abba J. Kastin, M.D.
Professor, Department of Medicine
Tulane University School of Medicine
    and
Chief of Endocrinology
Veterans Administration Medical Center
New Orleans, LA 70146

Gary Lynch, Ph.D.
Professor and Chairman
Department of Psychobiology
University of California
Irvine, CA 92717

Frank J. Menolascino, M.D.
Professor of Psychiatry and Pediatrics
University of Nebraska Medical Center
42nd & Dewey Avenue
Omaha, NE 68105

**Aubrey Milunsky, MB.B.Ch., D.Sc.,
F.R.C.P., D.C.H.**
Professor of Pediatrics and Obstetrics &
Gynecology
Director, Center for Human Genetics
Department of Pediatrics
Boston University School of Medicine
80 East Concord Street
Boston, MA 02118

Ronald Neman, Ph.D.
Association for Retarded Citizens of the
United States
Research and Demonstration Institute
Box 6109
Arlington, TX 76011

**A.K. Ommaya, M.D., F.R.C.S.,
F.A.C.S.**
Former Chief, Applied Research in
Surgical Neurology
National Institute of Neurological and
Communicative Disorders and Stroke
National Institutes of Health,

Chief Medical Advisor
Biomechanics Research
National Highway Traffic Safety
Administration,
and
Clinical Professor of Neurosurgery
George Washington University Medical
Center
Washington, DC

Dominick P. Purpura, M.D.
Dean of Medical School
Stanford University
Stanford, CA 94305

Curt A. Sandman, Ph.D.
Professor of Psychiatry and Human
Behavior
University of California, Irvine
and
Director of Research
Fairview Hospital
2501 Harbor Boulevard
Costa Mesa, CA 92626

Jack A. Stark, Ph.D.
Associate Professor of Medical Psychology
Departments of Pediatrics and Psychiatry
University of Nebraska Medical Center
42nd & Dewey Avenue
Omaha, NE 68105

Roger S. Williams, M.D.
Neuropathology
Eunice Kennedy Shriver Center for Mental
Retardation
200 Trapelo Road
Waltham, MA 02154

Preface

MENTAL RETARDATION IS A WIDESPREAD handicapping condition that afflicts from 1% to 3% of the population, according to varying estimates. Many billions of dollars are expended annually in the ongoing care and habilitation of retarded individuals. The more disabling forms of retardation can involve a lifetime care cost for a single individual that exceeds $300,000. The social and economic impact of research leading to a reversal of conditions associated with mental retardation could consequently be enormous.

For years, research in mental retardation has centered on either prevention or amelioration. This focus is due in large part to the fact that retardation has traditionally been viewed as irreversible. Irreversibility has, in fact, been used as a means of distinguishing mental retardation from the phenomenon of mental illness. However, as a result of tremendous progress in the biomedical and engineering sciences in the last two decades, a reconsideration of the incurable nature of mental retardation is now merited.

As a first step toward reassessing the extent to which mental retardation can be considered irreversible, the Association for Retarded Citizens of the United States (ARC–US) sponsored, through its Research and Demonstration Institute, a major national conference entitled "Mental Retardation: The Search for Cures." Its purpose was to assess research endeavors in several disciplines in order to produce a volume that would provide a rallying point for a new direction in mental retardation studies: the elucidation and application of curative approaches to the symptom of mental retardation.

An examination of current research reveals that we have already crossed the threshold of utilizing cures for mental retardation. However, the ARC–US sensed the need for a catalyzing event such as the Cure Conference that would initiate this process by assembling researchers from diverse disciplines to examine how present knowledge can be coupled with future research efforts that are specifically directed toward cures. It has become abundantly clear that the nature of mental retardation demonstrates that efforts to reverse it require a multidisciplinary focus.

Until ARC–US adopted the search for cures as one of its major organizational goals, little attention had been paid to this area of endeavor. With mental retardation long regarded as hopelessly irreversible, scientists have not actively pursued research efforts toward cures. It is hoped that this book will initiate a significant change in the thinking about this major social problem, and hasten the day when the announcement, "Your child is mentally retarded," is no longer so dreaded and devastating an event.

The scope of this "Cure Project" involved the scientific objective of identifying and commissioning prominent scientists from different disciplines to prepare in-depth overviews of research in key areas in which definitive advances in the treatment of mental retardation have been accomplished. These key areas included the potential for nerve cell regeneration in the central nervous system—including grafting and transplants; pharmacological agents that function as memory and learning enhancers; metabolic approaches, including advances in the cure of inborn errors of metabolism; the impact and effectiveness of early childhood stimulation; and future vistas in chromosomal and genetic engineering.

Mental retardation is characterized by unusual difficulty in learning and in applying what is learned to the problems of ordinary life. There are over 350 known conditions and disorders that produce the symptom of mental retardation, varying from the expressions of genetic and chromosomal abnormalities to the untoward effect of exposure to toxic substances, from brain impairment sustained during birth to severe personal-social and environmental deprivation. The consequences of these multiple causative factors may not only produce the symptom of mental retardation, but also be accompanied by impaired sensory and motor abilities.

Amelioration, one of the initial and ongoing goals of ARC–US, was initially approached by ARC–US and its member units through attempts to enhance the developmental potentials of retarded citizens (e.g., through operating Early Opportunity Centers, pressing for improvement in public institutions, pushing for early multidisciplinary diagnostic evaluations that ideally led to specific treatment interventions, and the rapid establishment of local systems of supportive services). These efforts have spurred the evolution of a full spectrum of modern, developmentally oriented services that have already significantly altered the attainments of retarded children and adults. For example, two decades ago it was commonplace for professionals to view children with Down syndrome as ''helpless and hopeless,'' and textbooks on mental retardation referred to the usual developmental expectancy of these individuals as falling within the severely retarded range. Yet, it is now recognized that when infants with Down syndrome have had the opportunity to benefit from early and specifically structured infant stimulation in the home, as well as from early entry into developmental centers and modern special education programs, they often function at the mildly retarded level of mental retardation! Thus, the implementation of modern ameliorative methods—which ARC–US has so aggressively advocated—has dramatically raised the horizons of possible intellectual-social adaptive growth for these retarded citizens.

Similarly, the persistent demand that early diagnostic efforts be immediately followed by specific and active treatment interactions has erased many of the secondary motor, special sensory, seizure, and emotional handicaps that formerly hampered the developmental attainments of mildly retarded individuals. When these secondary handicaps are specifically ameliorated, there is often noted a marked improvement in the degree to which these persons function as mentally retarded individuals—or above the mentally retarded range!

Each of these examples of ameliorative efforts reflects the ARC–US's persistent search for increasingly more complex developmental goals for retarded children and adults: goals that embrace progressively helping mentally retarded persons—to a maximal degree—toward the near-normal or normal level of intellectual and social-adaptive function. Thus, what started out as attempts on the part of ARC–US to raise developmental expectations has increasingly brought results that suggest the strong possibility that amelioration may be too limited a goal and that an allied challenge—cure—can be realistically aspired to during this century.

The *second goal* that has been a hallmark of the ARC–US movement since its inception has been a strong commitment to research activities aimed at preventing mental retardation in future generations. In 1958, ARC–US, with assistance from the National Institutes of Health, commissioned a book entitled *Mental Subnormality* (Masland, Sarason, & Gladwin, 1958) that contained an overview of previous research activities on the multiple causes of mental retardation and outlined promising areas for future research. For the first time, the extant knowledge about mental retardation was assimilated into one volume. Its publication had a revolutionary impact and led to the establishment of mental retardation as a major research focus for scientists worldwide. The book became the clarion call for the ARC–US's governmental affairs activity in encouraging extensive efforts by the federal government to invest in research on behalf of retarded citizens. The President's Panel Report (1963) and the resulting specific recommendation for establishing the Mental Retardation Research Centers and University Affiliated Facilities ensued. At the state and local levels, ARC–US continued its energetic efforts to apply the fruits of research by lobbying state legislatures to establish newborn screening efforts (i.e., for inborn errors of metabolism), and supporting professional and public awareness and educational thrusts concerning needed prevention programs at all levels of society. These prevention efforts continue as a vital central goal of the national parent movement in this country.

The major progress in mental retardation that has been achieved since publication of the *Mental Subnormality* book should not be underestimated. Nevertheless, today, an urgent need exists to assess the current status of those areas of biomedical and behavioral research that hold promise for extending the prevention vistas to meet the ARC–US's third challenge: exploring the spectrum of cures for mental retardation.

Lest the concept of cure seem too grandiose a goal at this time, it should be noted that modern treatment of mental retardation has become a more encouraging area of endeavor owing to numerous basic and applied research studies that clearly document what can be done. Indeed, we can now speak of prevention (primary prevention) for some retarded persons, cures (secondary prevention) for a few individuals, and treatment or habilitation (tertiary prevention) for all retarded persons.

Primary prevention removes the causative factors for the initial occurrence of a disorder. Direct application of basic research findings has provided dramatic eradication of some potential causes of mental retardation (e.g., through the widespread utilization of iodized salt, rubella vaccination, and maternal desensitization in Rh— factor blood incompatibility). In addition, amniocentesis has permitted the early diagnosis and active treatment (*in utero*) of a few of the inborn errors of metabolism. Unfortunately, there is still a wide gap between current knowledge and the application of existing primary prevention technology. The major challenge in actively utilizing this increasing body of knowledge lies in the area of public education. For example, the causative-preventive mechanisms of both rubella and Rh— disease are well understood. Yet, the direct application of this knowledge depends on whether the prospective parent is immunized and/or desensitized. Thus, there is a continuing need for broad dissemination of health information to primary and secondary school students, professionals, and the general public.

The primary prevention of mental retardation has been and is one of ARC–US's key organizational goals, and continuing priority has been given to research in this area. More research is needed into the mechanisms by which social, environmental, infectious, immunological, nutritional, traumatic, and psychogenic social factors impair intellectual performance. Special emphasis must also be directed at unraveling the variables responsible for the well-known over-representation of mildly retarded persons in the most socially and economically disadvantaged segments of our society. In addition, primary prevention could be fostered as a result of better understanding of basic neurological and perceptual processes. Relatively little is known about the workings of the brain and billions of neurons and synapses. Likewise, research is desperately needed on attention, perception, and memory. Although progress *is* being made in the primary prevention of mental retardation, it is proceeding, as might be expected, through a succession of small dramatic breakthroughs across a broad front of basic research endeavors.

Secondary prevention/treatment involves attempts to substantially reduce or remove (i.e., to *cure*) the symptom of mental retardation. In the past, the usual examples of secondary prevention were the very early diagnoses and energetic treatments of hypothyroidism as well as some of the inborn errors of metabolism such as phenylketonuria and galactosemia in the early months of life, and surgical treatment for hydrocephalus and the premature closing of the cranial sutures. Today, secondary prevention is increasingly focused on altering the external manifestation of known genetic disorders and the active treatment of secondary handicaps (e.g., motor, sensory, emotional, and seizure phenomena). An ongoing secondary prevention research focus relates to altering the negative influences of abnormal genes. For example, current research in genetics is directed at understanding the missing or lower level of essential body substances and supplementing these substance enzymes (e.g., via enzyme replacement, induction, or co-enzyme functions)—both in the fetus and in the newborn. Developmental enrichment programs for both parents and the "at risk" child are showing great potential for altering the early manifestations of mental retardation in culturally-familially and psychosocially-economically deprived youngsters. These programs (e.g., the Milwaukee Project), which are still few in number, offer great promise for both primary and secondary prevention in the largest grouping of mentally retarded persons: those who are mildly handicapped.

Advances in emergency care procedures and rehabilitative approaches have lessened the intellectual impairment residuals of victims of trauma. Similar medical advances in the management of toxemia (i.e., treatment of the pregnant mother's borderline hypertension condition), and pretesting of the child immunization substances before routine administration (i.e., the pertussis vaccinations) have all reduced the frequency of residuals of intoxication as a cause of mental retardation. Early and definitive treatment of infectious causes of mental retardation, such as meningitis, is now increasingly more successful. The intensity and quality of active treatment of other severe infections such as toxoplasmosis or cytomegalovirus in the newborn period can spell the difference between a "past infection" or a "current cause" for the symptom of mental retardation.

ARC–US has made great gains over the past 30 years in providing long-term developmental, educational, and rehabilitation programs for the nation's retarded citizens. These basic elements of *tertiary prevention* are well known and will not be discussed in detail.

Given the advances that have been made in primary and tertiary prevention, ARC–US, while continuing its commitments to these important areas, is now focusing increased attention on a critical facet of secondary prevention: total reversal of conditions and disorders that produce the symptom of mental retardation. The ARC–US Research and Demonstration Institute directly addresses this challenge through the contents of this volume.

Frank J. Menolascino, M.D.

REFERENCES
Masland, R.L., Sarason, S.B., & Gladwin, J.T. *Mental subnormality*. New York: Basic Books, 1958.

Acknowledgments

THE OPPORTUNITY TO PARTICIPATE in a 4-year effort to define and identify curative approaches to mental retardation has been challenging and exciting. The Association for Retarded Citizens of the United States (ARC–US) and the President's Committee on Mental Retardation were the primary national forces in planning and sponsoring a national conference entitled "Mental Retardation: The Search for Cures." This conference marked the beginning of a lengthy process in assembling the latest scientific knowledge available on the curative findings in mental retardation. Appreciation is extended to the contributing scientists who, in their respective activities in the key research areas reviewed in this book, have made major contributions to the field of mental retardation. Their contributions will serve as a clear beacon for current-future curative approaches on behalf of mentally retarded citizens. The ongoing support of the membership of ARC–US and that of its key executive officers, Drs. Philip Roos and Brian McCann, was invaluable, along with assistance from the staff and volunteer members of the ARC–US Research and Demonstration Institute. Thanks is due to Vivian Strampe for her assistance in the preparation of this manuscript and to Terry Barton for his interpretative editorial contribution. The academic support extended by the Nebraska Psychiatric Institute and the Meyer Children's Rehabilitation Institute—components of the University of Nebraska Medical Center at Omaha—is deeply appreciated.

Most important, without the generous contributions of Andrea Knight and her close friends, the above-noted conference and this book would not have been possible. All of these efforts symbolize the synergistic essence of the parent movement on behalf of retarded citizens, the ongoing commitment of professional colleagues to understand the basic and applied research parameters of the symptom of mental retardation, and the ever-widening cadre of human services staff members and citizens who daily serve mentally retarded citizens and their families.

Frank J. Menolascino, M.D.
Ronald Neman, Ph.D.
Jack A. Stark, Ph.D.

themes and overviews

The Search for Cures of Mental Retardation

Jack A. Stark, Ph.D.
University of Nebraska Medical Center
Omaha, Nebraska

A S WE TRAVEL THROUGH THE INFINITY OF TIME, we continue to make new discoveries not only about ourselves, but about the cosmos that surrounds us. In the past 100 years, an explosion of knowledge has enabled the human race to accomplish awesome feats, from drilling oil wells 5 miles deep, to sending rockets through space. We can now cook, launder our clothes, and wash the dishes—all automatically; we can entertain ourselves through such marvels as television; we can use computers to figure our bank balance, control the energy flow in our homes, and play chess. And at our beckoning is a host of other miracles. Technically, indeed, we live in a magical world.

Perhaps, though, the acquisition of knowledge may be likened to a luxury liner plowing through the ocean. Inevitably, the detritus of the sea collects on the hull and eventually the ship must be dry-docked to have that hull cleaned. It is almost axiomatic that as we gather knowledge, we also tend to acquire burdensome myths, stereotypes, and dogmas. Thus, though we make progress, we become at the same time prisoners of the past, struggling to overcome the rigidities and confusion of thought created by those myths, stereotypes, and dogmas.

The area of mental retardation is a typical example of our tendency to become encumbered by faulty concepts of the past. In our approach to treating mental retardation, we have too often allowed ourselves to be entrapped by the twin curses of "helplessness" and "hopelessness," complete with negative, self-fulfilling prophecies that find their expression in such terms as "subtrainable," "custodial," and "irreversible." It is time we brought the vessel to dry-dock and scraped away the mythology, the stereotyping, and the dogma that impede our progress.

One may at this point legitimately ask, "Our progress toward what?" We may legitimately respond, "Our progress toward cure."

Cure. A powerful word that makes clinicians and researchers alike recoil. A word that in the area of mental retardation raises the specter of fear that millions of parents of mentally retarded children will be given false hope. Cure embodies, indeed, the philosophy of hope. It is a word and a philosophy that can and must be faced now. For if not now, when?

We cannot now claim to possess many cures for mental retardation, but we do have some. Clearly, we need to redirect some of our ongoing research efforts toward the areas of most

1

promise. We are not holding out false hope to parents; we are investing in the future through careful interpretation of our present knowledge and a new posture toward the implications of current findings.

Certainly there is no search in progress for the "magic pill." With 350 known causes for the symptom of mental retardation, there can be no single cure. There are many potential cures, just as for cancer, heart disease, and mental illness. We must continue to seek them out. Not to make the attempt would amount to an appalling abandonment of our most basic obligation toward our fellow human beings.

The manner in which mental retardation is now universally defined may cause some mental retardation professionals to regard the concept of cure as invalid. The prevailing definitional concept of mental retardation requires the presence of both significantly subaverage measured intelligence and significantly subaverage social adaptation. In turn, both of these criteria have intentionally been conceptualized and defined operationally so as to require no further assumptions as to their cause other than the proviso of developmental onset.

It is linguistically and scientifically valid to speak of the *cure of diseases* that lead to damage of the structure of the brain or the impairment of its functioning. However, not all brain impairment leads to the symptom of mental retardation. It is also legitimate to pursue the partial or full *reversal* of the symptom of mental retardation insofar as this might be achieved either by a cure of the disease that has impaired the brain (and which in turn has impaired global cognitive behavior) or by improved social adaptation or measured intelligence. These latter two "scores" (theoretically, that is all they are) can be improved by a variety of social means even in adults of superior functioning. Yet, it would be considered absurd to speak of curing superior levels of global intellectual functioning by achieving even greater superior global intellectual functioning. However ridiculous that may seem, it is well worth thinking about. Who knows what it could lead to?

Professionals in the field of mental retardation emphasize that our posture toward seeking more cures in mental retardation can be accomplished more scientifically and less controversially by means of our existing constructs and language. Specifically, we define "cure" as *significantly increasing the current level of intellectual functioning and the concomitant level of social adaptation*. This definition and its application in this book are schematically illustrated in Figure 1.

If the word "cure" seems idealistic, grandiose, or unattainable, consider this: Applied research in the past 25 years has already led us to a point where we can realistically speak of the *primary prevention* of over 40 disorders that can produce mental retardation (see Chapter 1); the *secondary prevention* (or cure) of a rapidly increasing number of the causes of mental retardation; and outstanding advances in developmentally oriented treatment and habilitation to maximize the lives of all retarded persons (*tertiary prevention*). As described in Figure 2, much has been

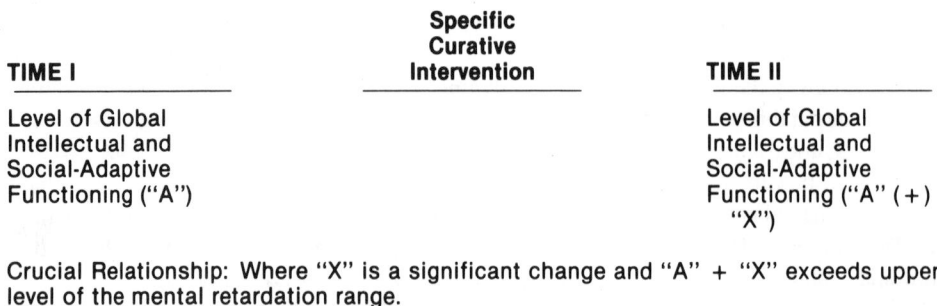

TIME I	Specific Curative Intervention	TIME II
Level of Global Intellectual and Social-Adaptive Functioning ("A")		Level of Global Intellectual and Social-Adaptive Functioning ("A" (+) "X")

Crucial Relationship: Where "X" is a significant change and "A" + "X" exceeds upper level of the mental retardation range.

Figure 1.   Definition of a curative approach.

Primary Prevention (i.e., Total prevention of the handicapping condition):

- Rubella vaccination

- Rho-Gam for Rh (−) mothers following first pregnancy

- Vitamin B_{12} treatment of pregnant mothers with an amniocentesis positive fetus (methylmalonic acid deficiency)

- Intrauterine fetal surgery: Hydrocephaly

- Maternal serum alpha-protein determination during early pregnancy: Neural tube disorders

Secondary Prevention (i.e., Very early diagnosis and reversal to normal state — cure):

- Craniostenosis

- Congenital hypothyroidism

- Phenylketonuria

- Lead intoxication

- Galactosemia

- Maple syrup urine disease

- Homocystinuria

- Early and comprehensive treatment of meningitis and encephalitis

Tertiary Prevention (i.e., Minimizing residual handicaps and maximizing future development):

- Enhanced seizure management

- Parental support and guidance

- Effective psychiatric care

- Infant and child development programs

- Special sensory treatment and/or prognosis

- Physical therapy and/or prosthesis for motor handicaps

Figure 2.   Accomplishments in primary, secondary, and tertiary prevention of mental retardation.

accomplished already in the areas of *primary* and *tertiary* prevention. But is it possible to enhance efforts in *secondary* prevention and find "cures" not just for the few but for many of the six million retarded citizens in our country? The three areas of prevention (primary, secondary or cure, and tertiary) emphasize the different timing aspects of treatment intervention. Typically, professional research has emphasized the investigation of the primary and intrinsic secondary (i.e., beyond the timing aspect of possible treatment intervention) aspects.

It was not until 1977 that the search for cures was adopted as a major policy by the Association for Retarded Citizens (ARC). Prior to that time, mental retardation was, for the most part, viewed as an irreversible phenomenon. The ARC recognized the need to overcome this deeply entrenched parental and professional view by developing a new posture that clearly recognized that there is an empirical basis for optimism. The initial response by some parents and professionals was understandably negative. They were wary that false hopes would be raised that a medical model (of causality and treatment) was being embraced rather than the developmental model, and they were quick to point out that mental retardation was not a single entity that could be cured like a ''disease.''

Subsequent position papers, developed and published by the ARC, addressed these and similar valid concerns, but the scientific findings that would underscore the cure thrust remained to be coalesced. Accordingly, a conference, titled ''Mental Retardation: The Search for Cures,'' was organized in 1980 to examine the frontiers of research efforts directly or indirectly aimed at mental retardation, with a specific focus on those efforts that might offer realistic opportunities for cures. It was hoped that this gathering would serve as a catalyst for bringing significant change in national thinking about this major societal challenge—reversing the symptom of mental retardation. Underscored at the conference were the increasing prospects for curative interventions in the symptom of mental retardation in contrast to the prevailing national postures of prevention and amelioration. To millions of parents of mentally retarded sons and daughters there was at last a realistic basis for hope for a changed future for their children. By the year 2000, it may be possible to look back at the 1980 conference as the gathering that significantly changed the course of scientific inquiry into mental retardation. It is from that original conference that this book has evolved over the last few years.

As demonstrated by the chapters in this book, the research in progress is already wide-ranging. Studies like those of Dr. Verne S. Caviness, director of the Southard Laboratories of the Eunice Kennedy Shriver Center for Mental Retardation in Boston, on the cellular events critical to the normal development of the cerebral cortex, and research projects like that being conducted by Dr. Earl C. Butterfield, formerly research training director for the Kansas Center for Research in Mental Retardation and currently professor of education at the University of Washington, on significantly improving cognitive skills of mildly mentally retarded persons, are but a part of the multidisciplinary efforts in the search for cures of the causes of mental retardation. Based on the presentations here, it is indeed reasonable to anticipate startling advances during the next two decades in the secondary prevention, or cure, of the symptom of mental retardation.

While the optimism generated by the possibilities is compelling, caution must temper the flush of anticipation. It must be remembered that the majority of these scientific activities are in various stages of research development. Direct clinical applications to date have been minimal. And, while it is not unreasonable to expect continuing scientific breakthroughs, one must bear in mind that the number of causes is myriad and the range of accompanying challenges broad. The complexity of mental retardation with its polycausal aspects will necessitate ever closer collaborative research efforts between biomedical and behavioral researchers in both basic and applied research.

The interdependence of research efforts in mental retardation is noted in Figure 3, which demonstrates both the basic processes leading to curative approaches and key intervention strategies of biomedical and behavioral researchers. Figure 3 also represents a synopsis of major topical research areas discussed in this volume.

In addition to the work of these chapter authors, hundreds of other prominent biomedical and behavioral researchers, although not directly involved in mental retardation research, continue to add to the enormous growth of data that carries potentially profound implications for mentally retarded individuals. One notable example is the work of Dr. Norman Anderson, head of the Molecular Anatomy Program at the Argonne National Laboratory. Dr. Anderson has proposed an innovative approach to biomedical knowledge, envisioning ''molecular anatomy''—which is a detailed understanding of human anatomy at the molecular level. He proposes

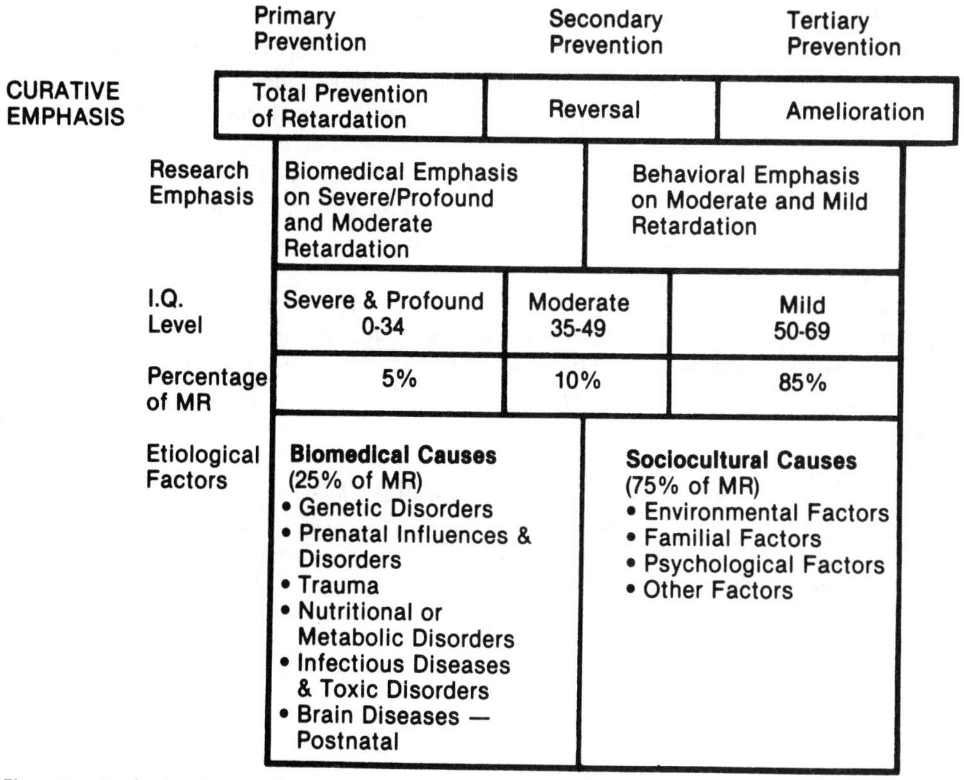

	Primary Prevention	Secondary Prevention	Tertiary Prevention
CURATIVE EMPHASIS	Total Prevention of Retardation	Reversal	Amelioration
Research Emphasis	Biomedical Emphasis on Severe/Profound and Moderate Retardation	Behavioral Emphasis on Moderate and Mild Retardation	
I.Q. Level	Severe & Profound 0-34	Moderate 35-49	Mild 50-69
Percentage of MR	5%	10%	85%
Etiological Factors	**Biomedical Causes** (25% of MR) • Genetic Disorders • Prenatal Influences & Disorders • Trauma • Nutritional or Metabolic Disorders • Infectious Diseases & Toxic Disorders • Brain Diseases — Postnatal	**Sociocultural Causes** (75% of MR) • Environmental Factors • Familial Factors • Psychological Factors • Other Factors	

Figure 3. Professional research interests and levels of retardation.

the development of a Human Protein Index, a comprehensive roster of every variety of protein in the human body. There are an estimated 30,000 different kinds of proteins, of which only 1% to 2% are known (not counting the immunoglobulins). Compilers of this roster anticipate that it will list all of the proteins, including their function and location in the body, the exact effect of certain genes (which dictate proteins' manufacture), and the location of these genes on specific chromosomes. This index should prove of inestimable value to medical science, since virtually every disease is involved with proteins in some way. In addition, nearly every variety of disease and injury results in damaged tissues that can be typed through the protein leakage that occurs with such insults. In essence, using the proposed Index, diseases could be more clearly understood at the molecular level and—it is hoped—effectively treated. It is the promise in such research proposals as the Human Protein Index and the growing body of empirical data generated by work such as that reported in this volume that underpin the thrust toward finding more ''cures'' to mental retardation.

Plaguing the research endeavors in mental retardation, however, are major funding problems. Both a general lack of financial support and discontinuities in grant awards hinder the continuation of significant research studies on curative interventions. It is an issue that will not easily be resolved—but rather than dwell on the dilemmas of our current national economic status, it should be noted that the research efforts reviewed herein have all benefited from ongoing national financial support. Indeed the President's Committee on Mental Retardation, a major coordinating effort concerning mental retardation efforts in the federal government, has had the active support of every president since its founding in 1960. Our presidents, ARC-US, and researchers themselves *are* aware of the critical need for funds to further our progress toward curative interventions for our mentally retarded citizens. We believe research funding in this area *will* continue to receive high priority. Truly, rapidly emerging curative approaches can and will have major impacts on the lives of many retarded citizens. These considerations make such research support deserving of a wide national commitment and investment.

To traverse the terrain of known-unknown knowledge, with its research and clinical challenges, and to solve, as well, the knotty issues surrounding interdisciplinary cooperative efforts will not be easy. Certainly, the exchange of knowledge and views across and among disciplines, as demonstrated by the chapters in this book, will continue to be essential as both basic explorative and clinically applied research efforts pursue more energetically the possibilities for curing complex deficits in human development. It is clear that curative approaches to mental retardation will increasingly move from possibility to probability to actual treatment intervention. The vast sea of the unknown in mental retardation *has* finally yielded us specific ventures in wisdom, and we have only to plumb its depths anew to reap further mental benefits for retarded persons in the near future.

Curative Aspects of Mental Retardation:
Biomedical and Behavioral Advances
edited by Frank J. Menolascino, M.D., Ronald Neman, Ph.D., and Jack A. Stark, Ph.D.
Copyright 1983   Paul H. Brookes Publishing Co., Inc.   Baltimore · London

section I

GENETIC AND DEVELOPMENTAL ASPECTS OF MENTAL RETARDATION

Introduction

FRANK J. MENOLASCINO, M.D.
University of Nebraska Medical Center
Omaha, Nebraska

T HE FIRST SECTION OF THIS BOOK deals with the work of six scientists in genetics and cellular neurobiology. Each of these scientists has made significant contributions in the ongoing struggle against mental retardation.

A traditional approach to reviewing the causes of the symptoms of mental retardation has been to examine abnormalities that stem from genetic disorders. These abnormalities can produce minor or major problems in the manner in which the body as a whole, or a small metabolic dysfunction can come about secondary to the known autosomal recessive, autosomal dominant, or sex-linked genetic disorder. Conclusions about the possible origins and causes of genetic disorders have, unfortunately, often resulted in the attaching of negative stigmas (e.g., "An uncle blighted the family tree"), as well as the adoption of defeatist attitudes (e.g., "It is a genetic disorder, which is too bad because we cannot fight the genes"). In the three chapters on genetics by Drs. Aubrey Milunsky, Park S. Gerald, and Mary Jo Harrod, these and similar misperceptions are viewed from a far more modern and optimistic posture. Prevention, cure and exciting vistas on future research possibilities are all detailed.

In Chapter 1, Dr. Milunksy focuses on current progress in reversing genetic disorders, before and after birth. He notes that medicine has progressed to the point that 30 to 40 inborn errors of metabolism (i.e., genetic disorders that lead to mental retardation) can now be *cured*. Technological advances in prenatal diagnosis hold great possibilities for reversing genetic disorders during pregnancy. The reader should note that the *in utero* treatment and cure of certain inborn errors of metabolism represent a major advance over the past and current treatment practice of waiting until the birth of the child, which exposes the child unnecessarily to a lengthy period of intrauterine damage. Early diagnosis and treatment and the production of a cure have been clearly demonstrated in a number of these disorders. Surely the prospect of finding other cures should not seem as "impossible" to us as it did a scant decade ago! The rewards include a tremendous potential for active treatment and cure of once believed "hopeless" disorders—to the betterment of a multitude of born and unborn children.

In Chapter 2, Dr. Gerald contends that body and central nervous system malformations—though they originate *in utero* from genetic causes—do, in fact, continue to be active postnatally (i.e., metabolically) and therefore offer the possibility of positive intervention and reversal (cure) shortly after birth. Dr. Gerald states that the traditional stance is that genetic disorders express themselves biochemically (e.g., via atypical or abnormal intermediary metabolism based on the gene/enzyme aberration(s) involved). Viewed from this perspective, disorders such as Down syndrome should therefore be as therapeutically "approachable" as the well-known

9

inborn errors of metabolism such as phenylketonuria. Dr. Gerald's refreshing and compelling views give credence to the ARC–US's thrust in seeking a hopeful posture toward curative approaches—even in the "dreaded" area of genetic causes of mental retardation. He also focuses on intervention studies on one chromosomal disorder, the fragile-X syndrome, as an example of a comparative line of research that may be directly relevant to the search for a cure of another major chromosomal cause of mental retardation: Down syndrome. The cytogenetic treatment techniques for blocking or altering abnormal gene/enzyme activity are rapidly being perfected and will likely first be applied as an intervention technique to the fragile-X chromosome syndrome, believed to be a primary cause of mental retardation in males (Gerald, 1980).

For example, utilizing gene substitution/insertion techniques, we can now locate, isolate, and substitute abnormal gene/enzyme configurations. Such "genetic engineering," as this work is popularly called, may in the near future be directly applied to the phenomenon of Down syndrome. Through specific chromosome bonding/staining techniques and enzyme action studies, the extensive knowledge concerning the areas of chromosome 21 that we are gathering (via enzyme-function/clinical symptom and behavioral correlates) may allow us to make selective gene/enzyme sequence substitutions within this abnormal chromosomal matrix and begin to utilize secondary prevention (i.e., curative) approaches to this syndrome. This existing blueprint of future possibilities for attacking Down syndrome could lend striking success to one of our key national research efforts—since persons with this disorder constitute the largest grouping of the mentally retarded, cause massive amounts of family mental anguish, and a societal investment of millions of service delivery dollars!

In Chapter 3, Dr. Harrod presents programmatic data for preventing genetic disorders through genetic screening and counseling. This service approach will be essential in developing a curative posture as we perfect the technology outlined by Drs. Milunsky and Gerald.

Closely allied to the genetics challenges, both in terms of traditional approaches to study and in "negative clouds of the past" that must be dispelled, are the topics of malformations or malfunctioning of the brain. Drs. Verne S. Caviness, Dominick P. Purpura, and Roger S. Williams review these areas in the second part of Section I. The authors discuss a wide spectrum of the known causes of the symptom of retardation: genetic, anatomical, neurophysiological, effects of infection, decreased oxygenation, toxic factors, trauma, hormone disturbances, etc. This diversity of the possible causes of central nervous system malfunctioning does not demonstrate that it consists of a *singular* etiological factor. Nevertheless, the authors state that though our knowledge base in these areas is limited, we *do* have sufficient information to know where to look and how to try to help—and thus illuminate future roads to curative approaches. For example, one needs to be exceedingly cautious in forecasting any immediate curative effect deriving from peripheral and central nervous system brain tissue transplants. Still, the fact that cellular grafts and neuron transplants have been successfully accomplished, particularly in animal models, represents considerable progress, and the era of the major neurological "rebuilding of the brain" may be upon us.

In Chapter 4, Drs. Caviness and Williams stress that a major series of highly complex cellular events takes place as the human brain develops *in utero*. A clear understanding of the timing and the nature of these events is essential before consideration can be given to intervention in instances where brain development has gone awry. One can currently predict possible intervention tactics based on the demonstrable lesions that outline both the stages of brain maturation and when the developmental interruption occurred. Defining the nature of possible corrective factors or treatments awaits the time when the brain yields more of its secrets. Yet, by identifying the precise developmental stage at which damage occurred, we can now pinpoint the specific causative agents that threaten or may threaten the developing brain.

Chapter 5, by Dr. Purpura, examines some allied problems further down the path of brain development research. His research focuses on a fuller understanding of the possible disorders that selectively destroy brain cells, as well as on the development of a clearer picture of *what* occurs (i.e., the nature of the disease process). How the disease process occurs (i.e., how it is explained) is also coming into clearer focus (for example, in the selective destruction of the Purkinje's cells in the brain, where a "rosary" effect is noted). Knowing the "what" and "how" of a wide variety of brain destructive processes then allows more specific study of possible operative mechanisms. Thus, a continuous causal process is established of clarifying the known causes as a prelude to focusing on unknown causes. An analogous area of research is Alzheimer's disease (a specific and progressive destruction of brain tissue that produces what is commonly termed "senility" in elderly individuals), in which individual early researchers were unaware that they were working on the *same* process of brain destruction. More recently, it has become clear that the underlying processes in Alzheimer's disease are identical in "severity" and are secondary to specific nerve cell damage (the "how"); soon, it is hoped, we will understand the "why" of the disease. Further research on the "why" dimension will lead to possible treatment interventions to reverse this process of brain destruction and/or mal-development.

An exciting perspective was the recurring theme by Drs. Caviness, Williams, and Purpura that the study of brain malformation has become a dynamic area of research activity. Gone is the dry cataloging of brain sections for "holes in the brain" that were regarded as telltale signs of "hopelessness." The indefinite "fevers" approach has also passed, in which nonspecific clinical manifestations (e.g., early changes in behavior, an elevated body temperature, or semi-coma status) were equated with "brain fever" and attributed to even more nebulous possible causative factors (e.g., "It seems to run in the family").

Knowing the exact stage of brain development that the damage occurred can at least narrow the focus of possible operative causes and, more important, can lead to direct intervention strategies and curative approaches. An example from another perspective was the deduction in 1941 of the Australian ophthalmologist, Dr. Norman Gregg, who noted a series of young children with small eyes (cataracts) from a region of Australia. Knowing that the eye forms embryologically during the first 3 months of pregnancy, he studied what factors could have similarly affected these children during this period of intrauterine life. The clear association of a rubella epidemic in Australia during the time these children's mothers were pregnant eventually led to a major research breakthrough in the understanding of one specific cause of the symptom of mental retardation.

The research of Drs. Caviness and Williams is directed to the internal points of brain cell development where known syndromes (e.g., brain malformations) occur. Increased knowledge in this area will help us focus more sharply on possible internal-external causes of brain malformations—leading, it is hoped, as with rubella, to the discovery, study, and eventual prevention of other major causes of mental retardation. The era of the scientific study of the biological basis of the symptom of mental retardation has truly arrived! Emphasis on the specific processes of illness will lead to further understanding and, eventually, curative milestones.

REFERENCES

Gerald, P. S. X-linked mental retardation and an X-chromosome marker. *New England Journal of Medicine,* 1980, *303,* 696–697.

Curative Aspects of Mental Retardation:
Biomedical and Behavioral Advances
edited by Frank J. Menolascino, M.D., Ronald Neman, Ph.D., and Jack A. Stark, Ph.D.
Copyright 1983   Paul H. Brookes Publishing Co., Inc.   Baltimore · London

part A

GENETIC ASPECTS OF
MENTAL RETARDATION

part A

GENETIC ASPECTS OF
MENTAL RETARDATION

chapter 1

Genetic Aspects of
Mental Retardation

From Prevention to Cure

Aubrey Milunsky, MB.B.Ch., DSc., F.R.C.P., D.C.H.
Boston University School of Medicine
Boston, Massachusetts

Use of the word "cure" with reference to mental retardation has been, and perhaps still is, inappropriate. Recent advances in molecular biology and genetics, however, make it at least reasonable to enage in discussion that could ultimately lead to the formulation of an overall research perspective on this subject. The advent of biotechnology, which has facilitated many of the advances that characterize the "new genetics," should not obscure important other measures now being used either to prevent the occurrence of certain types of mental retardation or to alleviate specific treatable disorders. This chapter, then, will first briefly assess the status of the prevention of mental retardation; second, consider extant therapeutic strategies; and third, discuss the theoretical implications of the "new genetics" as it relates to the "cure" of mental retardation.

PERSPECTIVES ON THE
ETIOLOGY OF MENTAL RETARDATION

Any effort to prevent, treat, or ultimately even cure disorders causing mental retardation requires as the first step a clear perception of the etiology of the disorder. Mere inspection of the tabulated known causes of mental retardation fosters an immediate realization of the broad extent of conditions leading to irrevocable mental handicap (Milunksy, 1975). Most disturbing, however, is the observation that the cause of mental retardation is frequently not known. Moser and Wolf (1971), in a study of 1,077 retarded patients with IQs less than 50, discerned no etiological diagnosis in 34% of their cases. In his study of 800 severely retarded institutionalized patients, Berg (1963) observed a definite cause or distinct syndrome in only one-third of those carefully studied cases. Experience at the developmental evaluation clinic at the Children's Hospital Medical Center in Boston revealed that no cause for the diagnosis was established in 27% of 1,058 children with variable hereditary types of mental retardation (Milunsky, 1975). Others have emphasized that uncertainty about the cause is even greater in patients who are less severely affected (Crome & Stern, 1972).

15

Table 1.   Etiological classification of mental retardation

Type	Example
Genetic	
Chromosomal abnormalities	Down syndrome, trisomy 18, trisomy 13
Disorders of amino acid metabolism	Phenylketonuria, maple syrup urine disease
Disorders of mucopolysaccharide metabolism	Hunter's or Hurler's syndrome
Disorders of lipid metabolism	Tay-Sachs disease
Disorders of carbohydrate metabolism	Fucosidosis, galactosemia
Disorders of purine metabolism	Lesch-Nyhan syndrome
Miscellaneous inborn errors of metabolism	I-cell disease
Consanguinity, incest, etc.	
Hereditary degenerative disorders	Schilder's disease, retinal degeneration, etc.
Hormonal deficiency	Congenital hypothyroidism, pseudohypoparathyroidism
Hereditary syndromes or malformations	Primary microcephaly, X-linked hydrocephalus
Neuroectodermatoses	Tuberous sclerosis
Unknown	
Acquired	
Prenatal	
Infection	Rubella, toxoplasmosis, cytomegalic inclusion disease
Irradiation	Microcephaly
Toxins	Ethyl alcohol, mercury
Unknown	Malformations, placental insufficiency
Perinatal	
Prematurity	
Anoxia	Birth injuries, hypoglycemia
Cerebral damage	Hemorrhage, trauma, infection
Infection	Meningitis, encephalitis
Postnatal	
Brain injuries	Accidents, hemorrhage from coagulation defects or other cerebrovascular accidents, thrombosis, ruptured aneurism
Infection	Meningitis, encephalitis, brain abscess
Anoxia	Cardiac arrest, hypoglycemia, respiratory distress syndrome
Poisons	Lead, mercury, carbon monoxide
Hormonal deficiency	Hypothyroidism
Metabolic	Hypernatremia, hypoglycemia
Postimmunization encephalopathy	Rabies, pertussis, smallpox
Sociocultural	Deprivation
Kernicterus	
Epilepsy	

Reprinted by permission from: Milunsky, A.(ed.). *The Prevention of Genetic Disease and Mental Retardation*. Philadelphia: W.B. Saunders Co., 1975.

Inspection of Table 1 reveals the considerable contribution of acquired causes (about one-third) to the development of mental retardation. It becomes readily obvious also that effective therapy or even cure of mental retardation established from an acquired condition is, and will probably remain, extraordinarily unlikely.

Perhaps it is somewhat unexpected that opportunities for prevention, therapy, or even cure appear much more likely for those disorders resulting in mental retardation of genetic origin. Table 1 is instructive (and disturbing) in communicating how disparate the genetic causes are. The hereditary causes range through numerical or structural chromosomal anomalies, specific enzymatic deficiencies, disorders affecting cell membranes, hormonal deficiencies, malformation syndromes, and hereditary multisystem diseases whose fundamental defects have as yet largely resisted research inquiry.

Subtle causes of developmental delay are probably not yet fully recognized. Only recently, for example, has the effect of maternal smoking during pregnancy been recognized as affecting adversely the developing fetal brain, with consequences such as learning disorders later in childhood. Similar observations have implicated alcohol ingestion during pregnancy and have expanded the understanding of the fetal alcohol syndrome to include the more subtle learning defects now recognized in association. The effects of many different medications taken during early pregnancy may alone or synergistically affect the developing fetal brain. The term *behavioral teratogenesis* is now used to refer to behavioral aberrations resulting from environmental insults such as drug ingestion in early pregnancy (Golub & Golub, 1981).

Clearly, total prevention of a disorder or avoidance of its consequences by prompt diagnosis and treatment (e.g., phenylketonuria) is the optimal direction. Attempts to reverse acquired and probably irrevocable mental retardation are unlikely to meet with any significant success. When considering either care or cure, a clear comprehension of the fundamental mechanisms causing mental retardation must be achieved. A more basic antecedent step would of course be the development parri passu of research leading to an understanding of *normal* brain function. Unfortunately, neuropathological correlation in the less severe forms of mental retardation (and even in some severe forms of mental handicap) has not been rewarding. The recent morphological observations of anatomical abnormality noted in the brain of a dyslexic child are an important exception.

THE CURRENT STATUS OF APPROACHES TO THE PREVENTION OF MENTAL RETARDATION

Strategies aimed at preventing mental retardation or genetic disease (Figure 1) must of necessity be initiated by the recognition of causality. From the foregoing it should be clear that thus far, for one-third to two-thirds of patients with mental retardation, a clue to the cause has not been discovered. Despite our knowledge of some causes of mental retardation, our efforts at remedying them is still remarkably inadequate.

While progress, for example, has been made in the prevention and certainly the treatment of prematurity, this remains a major contributor to acquired mental handicap. In addition, even as the decade of the 1980s began, 20%–40% of women in the urban ghettos of the United States did not come for antenatal care prior to 20 weeks of gestation. The importance of immunization against childhood illnesses such as rubella furthermore receives insufficient emphasis in the public health area, the public acting as though oblivious of the rubella epidemic not so long ago. Between 5%–10% of young women in their childbearing years are susceptible to rubella. As another example, obvious screening opportunities for conditions such as congenital hypothyroidism are still not fully utilized in the United States. The frequency of this disorder is one in every 4,000–5,000 newborns. Affected infants have an easily diagnosable and treatable disorder in which mental retardation could be averted by the early initiation of lifelong therapy. Yet the absence of a nationwide screening program serves to illustrate our collective impotence in moving rapidly to establish such an important health-maintenance measure.

While we continue to perform poorly in the prevention of acquired conditions leading to mental retardation, our record in the prevention of genetic disorders has been equally unimpressive. Despite the availability of genetic counseling, I estimate that close to 90% of individuals who will benefit from such counseling do not seek it or do not have it recommended to them. Certainly there are data to suggest that even in the face of high risk and the provision of genetic counseling pointing up such risks, some couples may not be deterred from pursuing further offspring (Milunsky, 1975). However, there are studies that do demonstrate that couples receiving genetic counseling are more often deterred

Recognition of Causes

Development of Attitudes Toward Prevention

Education — professional/ public

Birth control; steriliza-tion; artificial insemina-tion; adoption

Attention to ethical/legal imperatives

Early antenatal care

Government support of service programs

Support and encourage-ment of research

Genetic counseling

Control of infectious dis-eases, e.g., Rubella

Carrier detection

Removal of environmental causes, e.g., lead

Prenatal genetic diagnosis

Prevention of prematurity

In utero or postnatal treatment

Remediation of socio-economic problems

Newborn homozygote screening

Early intervention programs

Early, accurate diagnosis & treatment (PKU, galactosemia, congenital hypothyroidism, Wilson's disease)

Family-oriented medical record systems; genetic registers

Multidisciplinary Regional Service and Research Centers

Prevention of Genetic Disease

Prevention of Mental Retardation

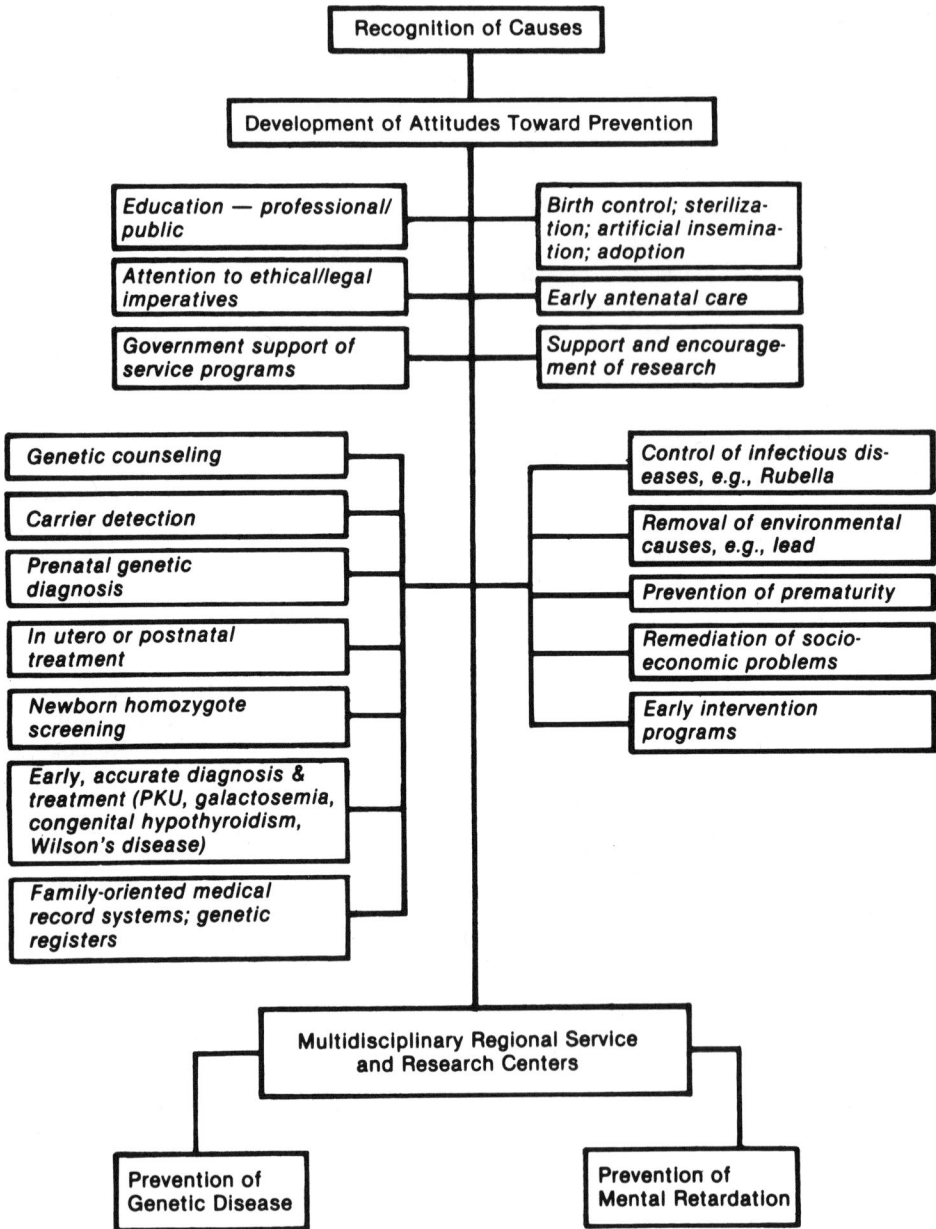

Figure 1.   Strategies for the prevention of mental retardation and genetic disease. (Reprinted by permission from: Milunsky, A. (ed.), *The Prevention of Genetic Disease and Mental Retardation*. Philadelphia: W.B. Saunders Co., 1975.)

from assuming high risks in subsequent preg-nancies. It should be emphasized that the goal of genetic counseling is not to deter individ-uals from childbearing but rather to enrich procreative autonomy by providing all the necessary information upon which rational decisions can be made.

The detection of carriers of specific genetic disorders is now increasingly possible (Mil-unsky, 1975). Once again efforts to offer tests for carrier detection prior to pregnancy have been moderately successful among Ashke-nazi Jews (Tay-Sachs disease), unsuccessful among blacks (sickle cell anemia), and hardly initiated for those of Mediterranean extraction (Thalassemias). Homozygote screening for inborn errors of metabolism (e.g., phenylketonuria and galactosemia) has been extremely successful in some states such as Massachusetts and not well organized in other states such as California. Genetic screening for homozygotes had been regarded as important where treatment may follow diagnosis. Unfortunately the rarity of some of these conditions, such as galactosemia, has raised all forms of cost-benefit discussions. Even the availability of maternal serum alpha fetoprotein screening for neural tube defects has yet to become a reality in the U.S., even though its clinical usefulness was discovered almost 9 years ago.

The advent of prenatal genetic diagnosis in the mid-1960s represented the most significant advance ever in the prevention or avoidance of mental retardation. Currently the potential of prenatal diagnosis is the early detection of all chromosomal anomalies, the management of over 200 sex-linked disorders through fetal sex determination, the early diagnosis of over 100 different biochemical disorders of metabolism, and the detection of certain major anatomical malformations, such as neural tube defects (Milunsky, 1979). The main indication for prenatal diagnosis is advanced maternal age. Nevertheless, there are only a few states in which more than 20% of pregnant women at risk (35 years and over) have amniocentesis and the necessary studies. There are three major reasons for this remarkable underutilization of an important technology that has been available for over 12 years. The first is the lack of awareness of the indication for studies by physician and patient alike. Second, the cost of the laboratory studies has been too great for some. Third, antipathy toward abortion even of a defective fetus has disinclined others. While treatment *in utero* has succeeded only rarely (e.g., methylmalonic aciduria), that avenue remains open for further progress, which could well be slow. Meanwhile, efforts to educate the public about the prevention of genetic disease should be encouraged (Milunsky,

1977). We now know that about four times more children are born because of the availability of prenatal diagnosis as compared to the number of pregnancies terminated. This diagnostic approach should be viewed as a life-saving, not a life-taking technique.

HEALTH "BEHAVIOR"

Behavioral actions to prevent or avoid genetic disease are not very different from measures taken to avoid other diseases. Rosenstock (1979) defines preventive health behavior as any activity undertaken by a person who believes himself to be healthy, for the purpose of preventing disease or of detecting disease in a presymptomatic stage. He points out that for the prevention of genetic disease certain educational goals must be met:

1. Individuals must first be motivated in a manner that makes them receptive to information about genetics. Schools, for example, should teach not only genetics, but create awareness about the importance of genetic health. Couples planning to have children need to understand that a prime responsibility of prospective parents is to *Know Your Genes* (Milunsky, 1977).

2. Everyone should be aware that he or she possesses a few harmful genes that may lead to the birth of a child with a genetic disorder. Rosenstock emphasizes that all of us need to recognize our personal susceptibility to having genetic disease or transmitting it.

3. It is necessary for individuals to comprehend and believe that their harmful genes may cause genetic disease in themselves or their offspring; furthermore, that such disease may be burdensome in its severity.

4. All prospective parents should be educated to understand that there are methods to prevent or avoid the effects of genetic disease. Again, Rosenstock emphasizes that recognition of the ben-

efits of such techniques is an important key to promoting health motivation.

5. Individuals or prospective parents need to be educated to understand that any economic or psychological barriers against taking preventive health actions are reasonable.

Clearly the perception by the public at large that genetic disease is an important health dimension in their own lives should facilitate steps toward motivating the population to more vital health behavior.

CURRENT THERAPEUTIC STRATEGIES IN THE MANAGEMENT OF GENETIC DISEASE

Despite our present inability to cure genetic disease, there are impressive therapeutic techniques available for treating genetic disease or avoiding its complications (Rosenberg, 1979).

Avoidance

The clinical complications of certain genetic disorders can be avoided either completely or to a significant degree by preventing exposure to certain substances or conditions. For example, in the common glucose-6-phosphate dehydrogenase deficiency, avoiding the ingestion of sulfonamides (and certain other drugs) will prevent the development of a severe hemolytic anemia. Those individuals genetically deficient in pseudocholinesterase activity will not suffer prolonged or irreversible apnea from succinylcholine given as an adjunctive muscle relaxant during anesthesia. Skin malignancies might be avoided in xeroderma pigmentosum if sunlight could be avoided.

Restriction

The most common example of this technique is the restricted diet (excluding phenylalanine) used in the management of phenylketonuria. A similar approach using diets that exclude lactose for the management of lactase deficiency has been in use for many years. In both these and other disorders that can be managed by dietary restriction, the basic genetic condition remains unaffected. It is the clinical consequences that may be mitigated by such treatment, most commonly exemplified by the prevention of mental retardation that otherwise results from untreated phenylketonuria.

Replacement

A number of genetic disorders are known in which specific substances are genetically deficient. Among the most common is diabetes mellitus (not always genetic) in which insulin is deficient. Another common genetic disorder, hemophilia, is characterized by a deficiency of antihemophilic globulin. In both these and other conditions, administration of the deficient substance provides a critical treatment for the patient but not a cure. Other conditions in this category include cortisol deficiency in congenital adrenal hyperplasia and thyroxine deficiency in congenital hypothyroidism.

Efforts have been made repeatedly to replace deficient enzymes, for example, in some of the lipid storage diseases. In Gaucher's disease, Brady, Pentchev, Gal, Hibbert, and Dekaban (1974) have administered the specific enzyme (glucocerebrosidase) intravenously into affected patients. While some biochemical evidence of effective uptake of these enzymes was demonstrated, major problems still exist. The essential difficulty in the replacement strategies is our inability to transfer active enzymes into the very cells where they are required, such as in the brain.

Supplementation

Certain biochemical genetic disorders are characterized by clinical signs that result from defective synthesis or transport because of the lack of a small molecular weight compound. Such inherited deficiencies can now in some 20 different genetic disorders effectively be tackled by supplementing with physiological or pharmacological amounts of the deficient product or catalyst. Hence administration of co-balamin (vitamin B_{12}) can overcome the deficiency of transcobalamin resulting in methylmalonic acidemia. Pyridoxine-dependent seizures can possibly be obviated by the use of pyridoxine (vitamin B_6).

Drug Therapy

A number of different genetic metabolic disorders are known in which the clinical signs result as a consequence of the deposition of specific substances in body tissues. The treatment goal is to enhance the excretion of these stored substances or to actually prevent their deposition. Hence, in Wilson's disease, in which excess copper is deposited in both liver and brain, penicillamine is used to chelate copper and increase its urinary excretion. In hemochromatosis, the excess accumulating iron can be chelated and its excretion increased by using the drug desferrioxamine. Once again the genetic disorder remains unaffected while the clinical complications may be diminished or removed.

Enzyme Induction

About 15 years ago investigators demonstrated that the activity of certain microsomal enzymes could be induced by administration of certain drugs. For example, the administration of barbiturates to infants with jaundice due to deficiency of glucouronyl transferase activity led to a decrease in serum bilirubin concentrations. This barbiturate-induced synthesis of a deficient enzyme opened up a new therapeutic strategy, which unfortunately has yielded no further successful examples thus far.

Plasma Exchange

The removal of excessive accumulating metabolic products in the body not unexpectedly spawned a technique of selective removal. Plasma exchange, or plasmapheresis, has been used repeatedly and successfully in the management of hereditary familial hypercholesterolemia. This technique effectively controls hypercholesterolemia, with the plasma exchange procedures being done for the removal of lipoproteins on a one- to two-week continuous schedule.

Surgical Strategies

Three surgical approaches have been used in the treatment or management of genetic disease.

1. *Excision:* It is usually appropriate to speak in terms of cure after excision of the genetically induced retinoblastoma, for example, excision of other tumors in association with other genetic disorders (for example, brain tumors in association with tuberous sclerosis) may also on occasion save the patient's life, but not affect the actual genetic condition. Removal of the spleen in certain genetic conditions (such as Gaucher's disease) is often necessary to avert secondary complications, but does not affect the disease itself.

2. *Surgical correction:* Acquired or inherited hydrocephalus, or hydrocephalus associated with spina bifida, is usually treated by placing an intracranial shunt to dissipate any accumulating pressure from cerebrospinal fluid not draining through blocked channels. Indeed, recently the placement of a shunt within the brain of a fetus with hydrocephalus was achieved by ultrasonic guidance. While mental retardation was not averted in this case (Birnholz & Frigoletto, 1981), the technical feasibility of this approach was demonstrated. Once again, however, the basic genetic disorder remains untouched.

3. *Transplantation:* Various types of transplantation have been tried in efforts to both treat or cure genetic diseases (Table 2). Some efforts have been particularly successful, such as the complete correction of the Wiskott-Aldrich syndrome, achieved by allogeneic bone marrow transplantation (Parkman, Rappeport, Geha, Belli, Cassady, Levey, Nathan, & Rosen, 1978) and for a 5-

Table 2. Examples of genetic disorders in which transplantation techniques have been attempted

Transplantation	Disorder	Reference
	Wiskott-Aldrich syndrome	Parkman et al., 1978
	Severe combined immunodeficiency	Buckley et al., 1976
Bone Marrow	Infantile malignant osteopetrosis	Coccia et al., 1980
	Chronic granulomatous disease	Foroozonfar et al., 1977
Renal	Fabry's disease	Desnick et al., 1972
	Gaucher's disease	Groth et al., 1979
Splenic	Gaucher's disease	Groth et al., 1971
Liver	Neimann-Pick disease	Daloze et al., 1977
Cultivated Skin Fibroblasts	Sanfilippo A syndrome	Dean et al., 1981

month-old girl with the autosomal recessive form of severe infantile osteopetrosis (Coccia, Krivit, Cervenka, Clawson, Kersey, Jim, & Nesbit, 1980). Similar success has been achieved with bone marrow transplantation in a child with chronic granulomatosis (Foroozonfar, Hobbs, Hugh-Jones, Humble, James, Selwyn, Watson, & Yamamura, 1977). In the absence of suitable bone marrow donors, a successful effort was made to correct severe combined immunodeficiency by administering fresh fetal liver cells directly by intraperitoneal infusions (Buckley, Whisnant, Schiff, Gilbertson, Huang, & Platt, 1976). In one of the two attempts as this mode of treatment, the fetal liver cells reversed the immunodeficiency.

ADVANCES TOWARD CURE

Genetic diseases result from a host of complex, poorly understood mechanisms. For the relatively common chromosomal disorders, such as trisomy 21, it is not at all clear why or how mental retardation occurs. It is uncertain, for example, whether a fundamental defect causes the trisomic condition and at the same time leads to cellular dysfunction and the typical phenotypic features of the disorder in question. In other words the extra chromosome 21 in Down syndrome may simply be a phenotypic effect and a reflection of a more fundamental defect that initially led to nondisjunction. Indeed there are data to show that nondisjunction itself may be familial.

Genes that code for specific enzymes may malfunction in some way, leading to enzymatic deficiencies with resultant errors affecting catabolism or synthesis of complex glycoproteins. Exactly how mental retardation evolves from increasing complex lipid accumulation in, for example, the lipid or mucopolysaccharide storage disorders, remains obscure. Similarly, endocrine deficiencies (such as thyroxine in congenital hypothyroidism) affect the development of intelligence by mechanisms that are again unclear. Other genetic diseases result from structural protein abnormalities that affect cerebral function by mechanisms presently not understood either. For the vast majority of genetic disorders causing mental retardation, there is no knowledge of the fundamental genetic defect and of course no clue as to why mental retardation occurs. Indeed we still lack a definitive biological and biochemical understanding of how intelligence, memory, and other complicated brain functions develop.

Clearly the *cure* of any genetic disorder, whether it be chromosomal, monogenic, or even polygenic in origin, represents an awesome task. The realities are that for chromosomal disorders, cure of the living child is at present an untenable concept. For well-defined enzymatic deficiencies, provision of the deficient enzyme to all those cells requiring correction would be theoretically feasible. However, the difficulty of transferring the necessary enzymes, continuously and correctly targeted (for example, to every brain cell) in a stable functional form, poses another formidable goal. The transplantation techniques may still offer an important dimension of therapy in this field.

Dramatic advances have occurred in the last few years in molecular biology with special reference to DNA. One critical methodological development that opened a new approach to the analysis of DNA was the discovery of enzymes called restriction endonucleases. These restriction enzymes were able to digest or cut DNA molecules into specific fragments in the same way that specific proteolytic enzymes are able to fragment proteins. As more and more restriction endonuclease enzymes were discovered, it was realized that specific cleavage-recognition sites occur along the length of the DNA. It now appears that even these cleavage-recognition sites are genetically determined.

Following cleavage of DNA by restriction endonucleases, the obtained fragments could be further studied by electrophoretic fractionation. The technical finesse to recombine, clone, or amplify DNA segments soon followed. Very recently, rapid methods for determining nucleotide sequences have been developed, thereby ultimately enabling a technique that would allow the detection of sequences in which mutation has occurred. In fact, site-directed *in vitro* mutagenesis has now become possible, allowing for the creation of specific experimental mutations.

The synthesis of polydeoxynucleotides of predetermined sequences opens up the possibility of introducing cloned functioning genes into human cells. Certainly the ability of cultivated mammalian cells to take up exogenously added DNA has been shown. In addition, gene expression in these cells has also been documented. While there is no doubt that gene sequences can easily be introduced into living cells, their intracellular organization and function cannot yet be controlled.

Recent experiments have employed micro-injection techniques in which DNA was successfully introduced directly into the nuclei of cultivated cells. In addition, through a novel form of gene transfer in mice, the prevention of fatal genetic anemia was achieved. The technique used was microinjection of normal hematopoietic stem cells directly into the fetal placenta, from which organ the cells entered the fetal circulation. The allogeneic normal fetal liver cells that were microinjected were later recognized as pluripotential for both white and red blood cells. The animals remained immunologically tolerant of the donor cells and no graft vs. host reaction was observed (Fleischman & Mintz, 1979). As a consequence the expected fatal macrocytic anemia did not develop.

This remarkable microinjection technique clearly presents potential opportunities for the cure of genetic disorders involving the hematopoietic system. Certain hematopoietic cells also contain lysosomal enzymes (for example hexosaminidase) that would be deficient in specific hereditary storage disorders (e.g., Tay-Sachs disease). The theoretical problem, which may be insuperable, is to effect the entrance of specific functional lysosomal enzymes directly *into* all brain cells in particular. Only by achieving normal lysosomal enzyme action *within* brain cells can we reasonably hope to "cure" or, better still, prevent the development of mental retardation.

Efforts have already been made to transfer genes into embryonic cells of mice. If these genes can be shown to function and participate in embryo formation, a system will surely evolve for introducing genes directly into mice. Recombinant DNA has already been introduced into fertilized mouse embryos by microcapillary injection (Gordon, Scangos, Plotkin, Barbosa, & Ruddle, 1980). These embryos were reimplanted in pseudopregnant mice. Clearly if exogenously introduced genes can be preserved through embryonic development, and if gene expression can be obtained, a vital new horizon with the potential for gene therapy will have been opened.

The advent of gene therapy introduces a host of ethical considerations (Mercola & Cline, 1980). These issues ought to be addressed now in an effort to anticipate problems that could be obviated. The exploration of these issues is beyond the scope of this chapter.

Certain inherent difficulties exist when considering gene therapy as a tool to prevent disease. For example, there is a need to establish a prenatal diagnosis in the *embryonic* phase of pregnancy. Quite possibly, genetic cures may have to wait for technological refinements that allow the sampling of a few or even single embryonic cells. Only then, with diagnoses made just prior to or immediately after implantation, will active intervention with "gene therapy" provide an opportunity for the successful prevention of mental retardation due to genetic causes. In addition, important questions about gene therapy still have to be answered. Will the added gene function? or will it be able to act only in concert with other genes not provided? Will a higher frequency of birth defects of malignancy be associated with such manipulations? With what certainty and precision will individual genes be tailored so that not only their structure but also their function is retained?

When we consider the current irreversibility of mental retardation and the suffering it causes, yet contemplate, as well, the extraordinary advances in genetics that we hope will continue, we look with great hope toward cure and prevention, remembering Robert Browning's exhortation, "Ah, but a man's reach should exceed his grasp/Or what's a Heaven for?" (*Andrea del Sarto*).

REFERENCES

Berg, J.M. Proceedings of the 2nd International Congress of Mental Retardation. Part I. Basel, Switzerland: S. Karger, 1963.

Birnholz, J.C., & Frigoletto, F.D. Antenatal treatment of hydrocephalus. *New England Journal of Medicine*, 1981, *302*, 1021.

Brady, R.O., Pentchev, P.G., Gal, A.E., Hibbert, S.R., & Dekaban, A.S. Replacement therapy for inherited enzyme deficiency. Use of purified glucocerebrosidase in Gaucher's Disease. *New England Journal of Medicine*, 1974, *291*, 989.

Buckley, R.H., Whisnant, J.K., Schiff, R.I., Gilbertson, R.B., Huang, A.J., & Platt, M.D. Correction of severe combined immunodeficiency by fetal liver cells. *New England Journal of Medicine*, 1976, *294*, 1076.

Coccia, P.F., Krivit, W., Cervenka, J., Clawson, C., Kersey, J.H., Jim, T.H., & Nesbit, M.E. Successful bone-marrow transplantation for infantile malignant osteopetrosis. *New England Journal of Medicine*, 1980, *303*, 701.

Crome, L., & Stern, J. *The pathology of mental retardation*. Baltimore: Williams & Wilkins Co., 1972.

Daloze, P., Delvin, E.E., Glorieux, F.H., Corman, J.L., Bettez, P., & Toussi, T. Replacement therapy for inherited enzyme deficiency: Liver orthotopic transplantation in Niemann-Pick disease Type A. *American Journal of Medical Genetics*, 1977, *1*, 229–239.

Dean, M.F., Muir, H., Benson, P.F., & Button, L.R. Enzyme replacement therapy by transplantation of HLA-compatible fibroblasts in Sanfilippo A syndrome. *Pediatric Research*, 1981, *15*, 959.

Desnick, R.J., Allen, K.Y., Simmons, R.L., Allen, K.Y., Woods, J.E., Anderson, C.F., Najarian, J.S., & Krivit, W. Correction of enzymatic deficiencies by renal transplantation: Fabry's Disease. *Surgery*, 1972, *72*, 203.

Fleischman, R.A., & Mintz, B. Prevention of genetic anemias in mice by microinjection of normal hematopoietic stem cells in the fetal placenta. *Proceedings of the National Academy of Sciences* (U.S.A.) 1979, *76*, 5736.

Foroozonfar, N., Hobbs, J.R., Hugh-Jones, K., Humble, J.G., James, C., Selwyn, S., Watson, J., & Yamamura, M. Bone-marrow transplant from an unrelated donor for chronic granulomatous disease. *Lancet*, 1977, *i*, 210.

Golub, M.S., & Golub, A.M. Behavioral teratogenesis. In: A. Milunsky, E.A. Friedman, & L. Gluck (eds.), *Advances in perinatal medicine*, Vol. 1. New York: Plenum Publishing Corp., 1981.

Gordon, J.W., Scangos, G.A., Plotkin, D.J., Barbosa, J.A., & Ruddle, F.H. Genetic transformation of mouse embryos by microinjection of purified DNA. *Proceedings of the National Academy of Sciences* (U.S.A.), 1980, *77*, 7380.

Groth, C.G., Collste, H., Dreborg, S., Hakansson, G., Lundgren, G., & Svennerholm, L.

Attempt at enzyme replacement in Gaucher disease by renal transplantation. *Acta Paediatrica Scandinavica,* 1979 *68,* 475.

Groth, C.G., Hagenfeldt, L., Dreborg, S., Lofstrom, B., Ockerman, P.A., Samuelsson, K., Svennerholm, L., Werner, G., & Westberg, G. Splenic transplantation in a case of Gaucher's disease. *Lancet,* 1971, *1,* 1260.

Mercola, K.E., & Cline, M.J. The potentials of inserting new genetic information. *New England Journal of Medicine,* 1980, *303,* 1297.

Milunsky, A. *The prevention of genetic disease and mental retardation.* Philadelphia: W.B. Saunders Co., 1975.

Milunsky, A. *Know your genes.* Boston: Houghton Mifflin Co., 1977.

Milunsky, A. *Genetic disorders and the fetus: Diagnosis, prevention, and treatment.* New York: Plenum Publishing Corp., 1979.

Moser, H.W., & Wolf, P.A. The nosology of mental retardation: Including the report of a survey of 1,378 mentally retarded individuals at the Walter E. Fernald State School. *Birth Defects,* 1971, *7,* 117.

Parkman, R., Rappeport, J., Geha, R., Belli, J., Cassady, R., Levey, R., Nathan, D.G., & Rosen, F.S. Complete correction of the Wiskott-Aldrich syndrome by allogeneic bone-marrow transplantation. *New England Journal of Medicine,* 1978, *298,* 921.

Rosenberg, L. Therapeutic modalities for genetic diseases: An overview. In: C.J. Papadatos & C.S. Bartsocas (eds.), *The management of genetic disorders.* New York: Alan R. Liss, 1979.

Rosenstock, I.M. Patterns of health behavior. In: Y.E. Hsia, K. Hirschhorn, R.L. Silverberg, & L. Godmilow (eds.), *Counseling in genetics.* New York: Alan R. Liss, 1979.

Curative Aspects of Mental Retardation:
Biomedical and Behavioral Advances
edited by Frank J. Menolascino, M.D., Ronald Neman, Ph.D., and Jack A. Stark, Ph.D.
Copyright 1983   Paul H. Brookes Publishing Co., Inc.   Baltimore · London

chapter 2

Chromosomal Derangement and Treatment Prospects

Park S. Gerald, M.D.
Children's Hospital Medical Center
Boston, Massachusetts

CHROMOSOMAL ABNORMALITIES ARE generally associated with overt congenital abnormalities and with mental retardation. This fact leads naturally to the supposition that the mental retardation component is the result of a congenital malformation of the brain. This view can be substantiated in a few instances—for example, as trisomy 21 (Down syndrome) and trisomy 13—in which anatomical defects of the brain are known to occur. It is then an easy step from this generalization to the conclusion that mental retardation resulting from congenital malformation of the brain is the result of events completed before birth and is therefore unassailable after birth. This chapter challenges this *fait accompli* attitude and suggests an approach whereby the development of treatment regimens might be possible.

POSTNATAL ACTIVITY OF SOME CONGENITAL MALFORMATIONS

In considering the concept that genetic changes that cause congenital malformations affect processes that occur only before birth, one could hypothesize that if these genetic changes were to act after birth as well, then some of the morbidity of congenitally malformed, mentally retarded children might be attributable to the postnatal action of these genetic changes. If true, an attack upon this postnatal action might ameliorate a portion of the total morbidity, including mental retardation, of the congenitally malformed child.

Kartagener's Syndrome

Evidence of this possibility is presented with regard to study of an inherited malformation complex known as Kartagener's syndrome (KS) (Kartagener, 1933). This condition is inherited as an autosomal recessive disorder. Affected individuals typically exhibit situs inversus totalis, bronchiectasis, and sinusitis. (The absence of mental retardation in KS does not diminish the relevance of this condition to this discussion.) A few years ago, a major advance in our knowledge of this disorder was achieved through the study of

This work was supported in fact by a program project grant from the National Institute of Child Health and Human Development (HD–04807) and by the Mental Retardation Research Program (HD–06276).

sperm from two KS males (Eliason, Moss-berg, Camner, & Afzelius, 1977). The sperm were examined not because the patients had KS, but because they sought medical assistance for infertility. The sperm in both patients were found to be abnormal in a unique way—the sperm tails were immotile even though the sperm were otherwise normal and metabolically active. Electron micrographs of the sperm tails demonstrated the cause of the immobility—the cross-sections showed the absence of dynein arms (see Figure 1). Since the dynein arms are believed necessary for generating the energy required for tail motion (they have ATPase activity) (Gibbons & Rowe, 1965), their absence would be expected to lead to immotility.

The explanation for the connection between sperm immotility and the triad of findings that characterize KS, however, requires an additional piece of information. The cells of the respiratory epithelium (and certain other types of epithelium) have numerous cilia on their surfaces. In cross-section, each cilium closely resembles a sperm tail, including the presence of dynein arms. It has been found that all cilia from KS patients lack

dynein arms. This is true for both male and female patients. (Variant forms of KS, with different abnormalities of the cilia, however, are now being found [Schneeberger, McCormack, Issenberg, Schuster, & Gerald, 1980]). The defect in cilia is at present the best diagnostic test for this syndrome. As predicted, these defective respiratory cilia are immotile when examined under the phase microscope. It is reasonable to assume that the respiratory components of KS (the sinusitus and bronchiectasis) are the consequence of the ciliary immotility, since accumulation of secretions secondary to the immotility is a reasonable cause of the infections. Unfortunately, we do not have a ready explanation for the connection between the dynein arm defect and the situs inversus, although a speculative explanation has been ventured (Afzelius, 1976).

KS serves as a model for demonstrating the continued activity after birth of a genetic defect that produces a congenital malformation (situs inversus totalis). Since the situs inversus does not usually produce symptoms, the postnatal activity of the genetic defect (the aberration in the dynein arms) clearly is responsible for almost all the mor-

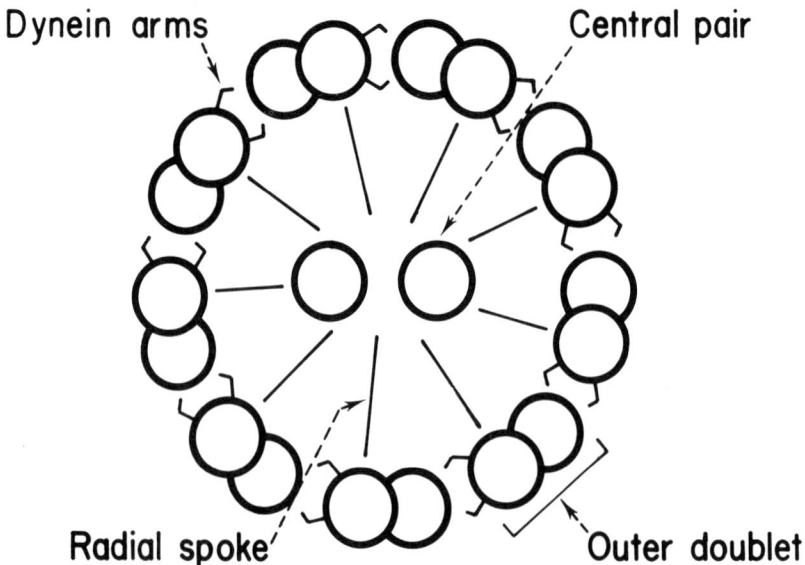

Figure 1.   Schematic diagram of the cross-section of a sperm tail or a cilium. Several components of the structure are identified, particularly the dynein arms—the structures that are missing in most patients with Kartagener's syndrome.

bidity associated with this disease. If a means of therapy for the postnatally occurring morbidity could be developed, these patients would be essentially symptom-free.

Gene Dosage

Kartagener's syndrome is not the only known example of the postnatal activity of genes associated with congenital malformations, although it is the most clear-cut. A number of other illustrations can be chosen from known chromosome disorders. Before discussing these, it is necessary to discuss the concept of gene dosage. When there is extra or missing chromosome material (conditions respectively known as trisomy and monosomy), the number of genetic loci present necessarily changes. Since the autosomes are essentially the only chromosomes of importance in this discussion, the alteration results in either three representations of a given locus (in trisomy) or a single occurrence of the locus (in monosomy), in contrast to the pairs of loci found in the normal, diploid state. When either a single or a triple representation of a given locus is present, instead of the normal pair, it is necessary to determine if there is a corresponding change in the amount of product controlled by these loci. That is, is there a decrease or increase in the amount of messenger and associated protein product to correspond with the number of loci? If a correlation does exist, gene dosage is said to occur.

The search for gene dosage began soon after the discovery of chromosome disorders in humans. Initially, it was assumed that gene dosage would occur invariably in conjunction with chromosome disorders and that a consistent increase in the activity of a particular enzyme in individuals trisomic for a given chromosome would be evidence that the gene for the enzyme was located on that chromosome. This optimistic expectation was quickly dispelled when it became known how many other factors affected enzyme activity. For a time, gene dosage fell into disrepute. The subject was re-opened, however, when alternative means for assigning genetic loci to

individual chromosomes were developed (more will be said about this later). Once it became known that a particular gene was located on a given chromosome, the assessment of gene dosage for this locus could be analyzed more critically. The more recent studies of enzyme activity (or protein) for a number of different loci have shown that a direct relation generally exists between the number of representations of a given locus and the amount of protein produced (Francke, 1981).

In view of the frequency of trisomy 21 (Down syndrome), it is appropriate to explore in detail here the question of gene dosage for chromosome 21. The enzyme superoxide dismutase (the cytoplasmic form, E.C. 1.15.1.1, which is symbolized as SOD-S) is now known to have its locus on chromosome 21 (Tan, Tischfield, & Ruddle, 1973). This enzyme is not believed to have any relevance to the mental retardation accompanying trisomy 21. Assays for the activity of SOD-S, as well as quantitation of the protein itself, show an approximate 50% increase in patients with trisomy 21 (Summitt, 1981). In some patients who have only a portion of the long arm of chromosome 21 extra (this is sometimes referred to as "partial trisomy 21") there is also an increased amount of SOD-S. Those patients with partial trisomy of chromosome 21 and an elevated level of SOD-S are trisomic for a common segment of the long arm of chromosome 21. Patients trisomic for other segments of chromosome 21 do not show the elevation in SOD-S. The SOD-S locus clearly exhibits gene dosage. The patients who were trisomic for various segments of chromosome 21 were also examined for their clinical appearance. In nearly every instance, the patients with an elevation of SOD-S also exhibited the phenotype of Down syndrome, while those who lacked the increased enzyme activity also lacked the typical Down syndrome phenotype. Many other patients with partial trisomy for chromosome 21 have been examined for their clinical phenotype alone (without SOD-S studies). These patients provide evidence that trisomy

Partial Trisomy 21

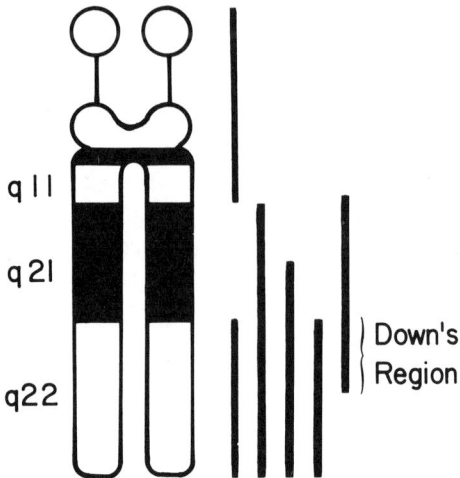

q 11

q 21

q22

} Down's
} Region

Figure 2.   Schematic representations of the portions of chromosome 21 that have been present as extra genetic material in patients presenting with the clinical features of Down syndrome. Only the small region indicated is common to all these patients. This implies that this small region contains all the genes that must be present in triplicated amount for the clinical features of Down syndrome to develop. The remaining portion of the chromosome presumably contributes relatively little to the development of Down syndrome. (Illustration redrawn from Summitt, 1981.)

for a small segment of q 21 may be sufficient to produce the major manifestations of the Down syndrome phenotype (Figure 2).

Since studies of gene dosage have focused, for technical reasons, on enzymes that are easily quantified, the current evidence is selective and may not be representative of loci in general. There is one published study whose methodology avoids this bias. In this study, the messenger RNAs produced in cultured fibroblasts by genes on chromosome 21 were shown to be elevated in cells trisomic for chromosome 21 (Kurnit, 1979). Although this study is the only one of its kind, its findings are consistent with the belief that most genetic loci exhibit gene dosage.

It should be remembered that gene dosage studies have generally been performed on postnatal tissues. This provides support for the notion that the postnatal action of genes may contribute to the morbidity of patients with chromosome abnormalities. Blocking or altering this aberrant genetic activity might ameliorate the patient's morbidity. Indeed, techniques that will make the desired advances in this area possible are now being perfected. These techniques are discussed below in relation to X chromosome aberrations. The first mental retardation syndrome that this author hopes will be cured as the result of these developments is the fragile-X syndrome.

Fragile-X Syndrome

Since the fragile-X syndrome has only recently received much attention, a brief review of this disorder is appropriate. In 1969, Herbert Lubs described a family with four retarded males occurring in three generations (Lubs, 1969). Each of the affected males exhibited a peculiar change in his X chromosome in a portion (15% to 50%) of his cells. This change appeared to result from a thinning of the chromosome, so that the portion of the chromosome distal to the region of thinning appeared to be attached to the main body of the chromosome only by a fine thread (Figure 3). The region of thinning was constant in its location in all individuals. The consistency of the cytogenetic findings and the X-linked pattern of its inheritance suggested that the mental retardation and the X abnormality were different aspects of the same phenomenon. Because the thinned region is highly susceptible to rupture, the condition became known as the fragile-X syndrome. Only about one-third of women who are obligate heterozygotes will show the fragile X, and even then it is displayed only in a small fraction of their cells (Sutherland, 1979a). The limited expression of the cytogenetic aberration in both males and females is in part determined by culture conditions. Hydrogen ion, serum protein, folate, and thymidine concentration all influence the proportion of metaphases exhibiting the fragile X (Sutherland, 1979b). Finally, while the frequency of this condition is still uncertain, some indirect evidence suggests that several percent of retarded males may have the fragile-X syndrome.

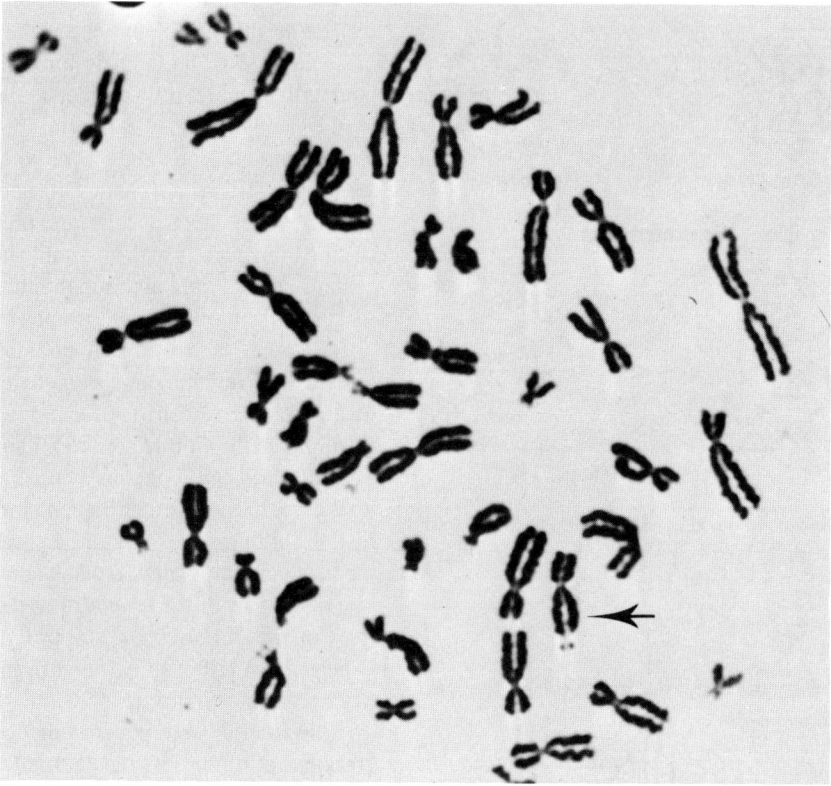

Figure 3. Photomicrograph of a metaphase from a male with the fragile-X syndrome. The arrow points to an abnormal X chromosome with two small "satellites" attached by narrow threads to the ends of the long arms. The abnormal chromosome in such metaphases is identified as an X chromosome by restaining the metaphases and verifying that the chromosome has the characteristic banding pattern of an X.

Consider now how the recently developed tools of genetics and molecular biology could be used to develop a cure for the fragile-X syndrome. This discussion will assume that the genetic change producing the fragile-X site is the "cause" of the mental retardation and that it exerts its effects by altering the action of a normal gene (or genes) at that site. A cure ought to be possible if the altered gene action is restored to normal, but to do that the nature of the gene(s) that is altered by the fragile-X phenomenon must first be determined.

It now appears feasible to isolate segments of the human X chromosome by combining the techniques of recombinant DNA and somatic cell hybridization. It has been possible for several years to isolate random segments of human DNA through the use of recombinant DNA. This is accomplished by fragmenting total human DNA, chemically uniting each fragment with the DNA of bacterial virus, and using the human-viral recombinant DNA to infect bacteria. (This can be done in such a way that the entire human genome is contained within the pool of recombinant DNA segments. This pool is often referred to as a "library.") This procedure is schematically illustrated in Figure 4. Each bacterium in one's final library will contain no more than one piece of human DNA (combined with the bacterial virus). Simple bacterial procedures can then be used to isolate populations of bacteria derived from a single bacterium. In this way, a large volume of bacteria, each bacterium containing the identical human-viral DNA segment, can be prepared. From this material, numerous copies of a human DNA fragment can be obtained.

Once a single piece of human DNA has been randomly isolated, how can one determine if it is derived from the X chromosome?

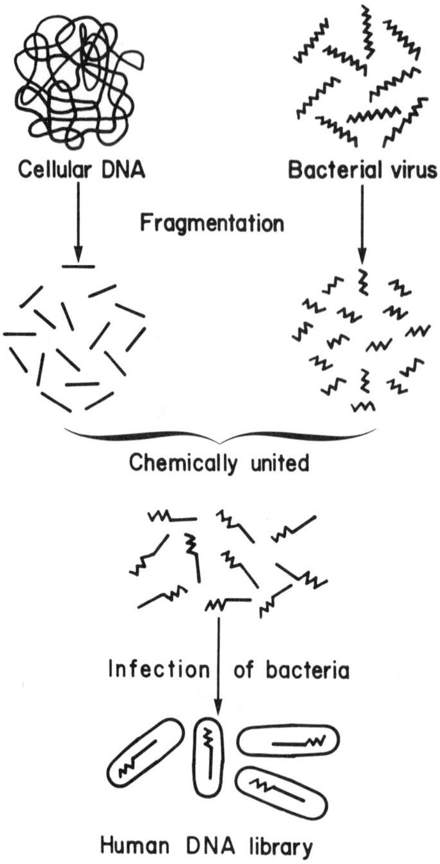

Figure 4. Schematic illustration of the formation of a DNA "library." The DNA from a human cell and from a bacterial virus are cut into pieces by an enzyme (endonuclease). The several pieces are then ligated together to produce molecules of recombinant DNA. The fragment of bacterial virus present confers upon the recombinant molecules the ability to multiply in a bacterial host. When a single bacterium is isolated, a single recombinant molecule is simultaneously isolated. Both the bacterium and the recombinant virus then multiply at the same time. The result is a large amplification of the single original human fragment. The human fragment can then be isolated and analyzed or utilized.

Somatic cell hybrids provide a solution to this problem. Before describing their use, a simple account of the preparation of hybrid cells is in order. Two different cell populations are fused together to yield cells, each of which has two different nuclei. If one of the two types of nuclei comes from a cell type that is adapted to rapid growth in tissue culture (that is, it comes from an established cell line), then it will begin to divide in the fused cell. The other nucleus within the cell will also respond to the signals for cell division and will concomitantly divide. The end result will be a population of cells with single nuclei containing chromosomes from both parental cell types. This is a somatic hybrid cell population. When hybrid cells are prepared by fusing human cells with an established line of rodent cells, an additional phenomenon occurs—the human chromosomes are rapidly lost, leaving a hybrid cell population with only a very few human chromosomes in any cell (Weiss & Green, 1967). It is possible to manipulate the culture conditions so that each of the hybrid cells contains a human X, but so that essentially no other human chromosome is present. This X-containing hybrid cell can be further manipulated so that it contains only the distal part of the long arm of the X. This part of the X corresponds approximately to where the fragile site is found in males with the fragile-X syndrome.

The hybrid cell populations containing various portions of the normal X chromosome are the tools needed to determine both if the randomly isolated recombinant DNA segment is derived from the X chromosome and from which region of the X. The technique used in these determinations depends upon the fact that DNA is comprised of two complementary DNA chains. The sequence of DNA bases in each chain is related to the sequence in the other chain, so that corresponding bases in the two chains pair together through hydrogen bonding. This characteristic of the chains permits the use of a radioactively labeled DNA sequence to identify a homologous DNA fragment (Figure 5). The radioactively labeled sequence used in this fashion is known as a probe.

The segment of human DNA that was isolated by recombinant DNA technology as earlier described can be radioactively labeled and employed as a probe. The probe is first used to examine the DNA of a hybrid cell population that contains an intact human X chromosome and no other human chromosome. If the probe is able to bind to one of the DNA segments from the hybrid cells, but

```
-AGTTAC-        -GGCTAA-
-TCAATG-        -CCGATT-

-TTTGGG-        -CTCTCT-
-AAACCC-        -GAGAGA-
```

DNA Fragments

+

```
      * * * * * *
    -TTTGGG-        Probe
    -AAACCC-
      * * * * * *
```

↓

```
  * * * * * *
-TTTGGG-              -TTTGGG-
-AAACCC-              -AAACCC-
                       * * * * * *
```

Identified Fragments

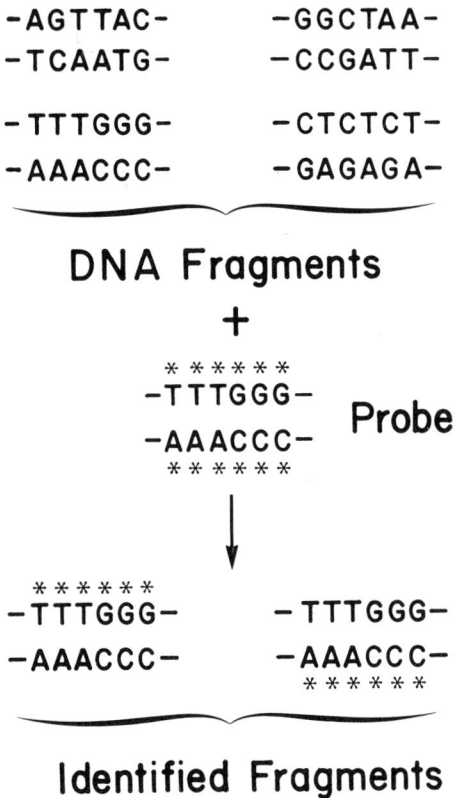

Figure 5. Schematic illustration of the hybridization together of DNA chains that permits the use of a segment as a probe to identify a similar segment. All DNA fragments consist of two DNA chains that pair together. The two chains are complementary, that is, As are always opposite Ts and Gs opposite Cs. This pairing process results in a high affinity of a chain for its partner and complementary chain. The fragment that is to be used as a probe is radioactively labeled. The probe and the fragments to be examined are caused to separate into individual chains. The chains are mixed together and the original conditions restored so that pairing of the chains occurs again. In this case, only the fragment with chains complementary to the probe can thereby be identified.

is unable to bind to DNA from hybrid cells without the X, then the probe is likely to be derived from the X chromosome. The process can be repeated with DNA from hybrid cells containing various portions of the X, and in this way any isolated human fragment that is derived from the X can be assigned to a specific portion of the X.

As marvelous as these new techniques obviously are, they are not sufficient in themselves to attain our goal. It is unlikely that any

reasonable number of isolated human DNA segments will contain the one piece that corresponds to the fragile-X site. This follows from the fact that the X chromosome is approximately 150 million base pairs long (a unit of length of a DNA sequence is known as a base pair or bp) and each isolated segment is no longer than 20,000 bp. A method for fine "gene mapping" must be employed so that the DNA segments may be placed in order in relation to one another and especially in relation to the fragile-X site. This can be done by exploiting the recently discovered phenomenon of DNA polymorphism.

Again, some background information is necessary. One way to fragment DNA is to digest the DNA with an enzyme (one of a class of enzymes known as "restriction endonucleases") that cleaves the DNA at a relatively limited number of sites— approximately once every 4,000 bp. Cleavage occurs only at a particular DNA sequence so that a reproducible set of fragments is produced. If the DNA fragments are separated from one another by electrophoresis, a consistent pattern is produced that depends upon the specific restriction endonuclease used.

In actuality, each enzyme cleaves human DNA into a million or more fragments, so that the electrophoretic pattern is too complicated to be examined directly. The probe concept may be used to highlight specific fragments, however, and to render the analysis of an electrophoretic pattern very precise. A solution containing the probe is layered over an electrophoretic pattern. The probe will adhere to any complementary sequences and nowhere else. After the excess probe is washed away, the electrophoretic pattern is examined by autoradiography to reveal the electrophoretic band to which the probe has adhered (Figure 6). In general, no more than a few bands will appear in the autoradiogram. Because of the consistency with which the restriction endonuclease cleaves the DNA, an identical pattern will be obtained from each sample of human DNA, unless the DNA sequence is altered. If the DNA sequence at

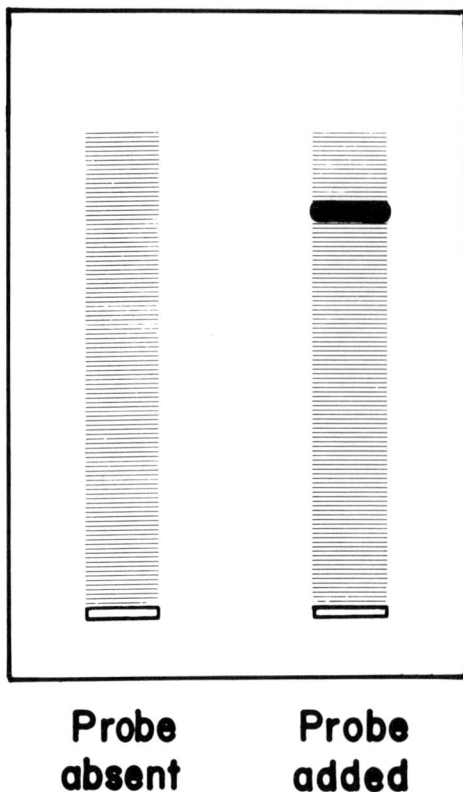

Probe absent   Probe added

Figure 6. DNA from human cells is digested with enzymes (endonucleases) that release a reproducible set of fragments. The fragments are then separated by electrophoresis. In the absence of a probe, the millions of fragments present yield a pattern too dense to permit identification of individual bands. The probe is layered over the pattern and the chains separated to permit the probe to react with any complementary sequence. After the excess probe is washed off, the residual radioactivity reveals the site at which the complementary sequence is located.

associated with disease or any other phenotypic change. They are conveniently referred to as polymorphisms in DNA sequence. Since these polymorphisms are variations in DNA sequences, they are inheritable. As with any other genetic polymorphism (e.g., blood group polymorphisms) they can be traced through a family and used for linkage analysis.

DNA fragments that have been assigned to the distal portion of the long arm of the X can be used as probes to search for DNA polymorphisms of the X. It can be expected that at least some of the probes will identify relatively common polymorphisms. These polymorphisms may be followed through families and their relative order on the chromosome determined by the pattern of their inheritance. The transmission of these polymorphisms in families with the fragile-X syndrome could be used to identify any DNA probe that is close to the fragile-X site. That particular DNA segment could then be used to search for adjacent (overlapping) DNA segments from the human DNA library. By identifying a series of overlapping segments, it may be possible to "walk" along the X chromosome until the region on the fragile site is reached. (It is assumed here that the fragile site is the result of an alteration in DNA sequence. If this is found to be true, this will greatly facilitate the site's identification.)

The preceding paragraphs have outlined the general approaches that this author believes will be successful in defining the DNA defect that presumably underlies the fragile-X abnormality. The next step will be to determine how that defect leads to the clinical picture we call the fragile-X syndrome. It is not clear at present how this will be accomplished, but the following conjectures can be made.

When a sequence of DNA exerts an action, the DNA sequence is considered a gene. Currently, it is assumed that genes exert their action through the production of messenger RNA (mRNA). Messenger RNA in turn is used by the machinery of the cell to specify the production of a particular protein. Since the mRNA is copied from the DNA, the two

one of the digestion sites is changed, the enzyme will be unable to cleave at that site and the size of the fragment released will be changed. By using different restriction endonucleases—each of which cleaves a different DNA sequence—in combination with various DNA probes, it should be possible to search quite effectively for DNA sequence alterations. The searches for variations in human DNA sequence that have been published indicate that such variations may occur with remarkably high frequency (Jeffreys, 1979). It should be noted that these variations in DNA sequence are generally not substances are very similar in structure. This structural likeness means that the DNA and RNA have an affinity for one another (that is, they can hybridize together). The DNA region that contains the hypothetical DNA alteration referred to earlier (which characterizes the fragile-X change) will hybridize with the messenger RNA that it produces. This property will allow the messenger to be isolated. The sequence of the isolated mRNA will suggest the sequence of the amino acids in its protein product. Once the amino acid sequence has been inferred, it should be possible to synthesize a protein fragment representing a portion of that sequence. This protein fragment could be used to generate an antibody, and the antibody could be used to study the distribution of the protein among cells, tissues, etc. The information obtained from such studies will, it is hoped, lay the

necessary groundwork so that we can determine how the protein functions, both in normal and in fragile-X individuals. Finally, after all these "ifs," we might be able to correct the defect in our fragile-X patients, perhaps by replacing the defective protein or by inserting the normal gene into the cells.

Clearly, these plans for the future require the development of many new approaches. This should not be surprising, since recombinant DNA techniques are providing us with many opportunities that have never been available before. We are, indeed, exploring new ground. Nevertheless, we may be greatly reassured by the extraordinary rapidity with which accomplishments in the field of recombinant DNA have been achieved. This rapid progress is certain to continue and will enable us to achieve cures for at least some types of mental retardation.

REFERENCES

Afzelius, B.A. A human syndrome caused by immotile cilia. *Science*, 1976, *193*, 317–318.

Eliason, R., Mossberg, B., Camner, P., & Afzelius, B.A. The immotile-cilia syndrome. *New England Journal of Medicine*, 1977, *297*, 1–6.

Francke, U. Gene dosage studies in Down syndrome. In: F. de la Cruz & P.S. Gerald (eds.), *Trisomy 21 (Down syndrome): Research perspectives*. Baltimore: University Park Press, 1981.

Gibbons, I.R., & Rowe, A.J. Dynein: A protein with adenosine triphosphates activity from cilia. *Science* 1965, *149*, 424–426.

Jeffreys, A.J. DNA sequences variants in the gamma, agamma, delta and beta globin genes of man. *Cell*, 1979 *18*, 1–10.

Kartagener, M. Bronschiectasien bei situs viscerum inversus. *Klin Tuberk*, 1933, *83*, 489.

Kurnit, D.M. Down syndrome: Gene dosage at the transcriptional level in skin fibroblasts. *Proceedings of the National Academy of Sciences, USA*, 1979, *76*, 2372–2375.

Lubs, H.A. A marker X chromosome. *American Journal of Human Genetics*, 1969, *21*, 231–244.

Schneeberger, E.E., McCormack, J., Issenberg, H.J., Schuster, S.R. & Gerald, P.S. Heterogeneity of ciliary morphology in the

immotile-cilia syndrome in man. *Journal of Ultrastructure Research*, 1980, *73*, 34–43.

Summitt, R.L. Chromosome 21 specific segments that cause the phenotype of Down syndrome. In: F. de la Cruz & P.S. Gerald, (eds.), *Trisomy 21 (Down syndrome): Research perspectives*. Baltimore: University Park Press, 1981.

Sutherland, G.R. Heritable fragile sites on human chromosomes III. Detection of fra(X) (q27) in males with X-linked mental retardation and in their female relatives. *Human Genetics*, 1979a, *53*, 23–27.

Sutherland, G.R. Heritable fragile sites on human chromosomes I. Factors affecting expression in lymphocyte culture. *American Journal of Human Genetics*, 1979b, *31*, 125–135.

Tan, Y.H., Tischfield, I., & Ruddle, F.H. The linkage of genes for the human interferon-induced antiviral protein and indophenol oxidase-B traits to chromosome G-21. *Journal of Experimental Medicine*, 1973, *137*, 317.

Weiss, M.C., & Green, H. Human-mouse hybrid cell lines containing partial complements of human chromosomes and functioning human genes. *Proceedings of the National Academy of Sciences, USA*, 1967, *58*, 1104–1111.

Curative Aspects of Mental Retardation:
Biomedical and Behavioral Advances
edited by Frank J. Menolascino, M.D., Ronald Neman, Ph.D., and Jack A. Stark, Ph.D.
Copyright 1983   Paul H. Brookes Publishing Co., Inc.   Baltimore · London

chapter 3

Genetic Screening
and Counseling

MARY JO HARROD, PH.D.
The University of Texas Health Science Center at Dallas
Dallas, Texas

I NEVITABLY, DURING THE EVALUATION of a child with mental retardation, come the moments when the conclusions must be presented to the parents and an attempt made to explain just what the findings mean. Explaining "just what the findings mean," however, is a time that can be as frustrating as it is painful for counselors and parents alike.

When a chromosomal abnormality is diagnosed, a genetic counselor may likely show the parents photographs of their child's chromosomes and point out that an extra chromosome is present, for example, or a part of a chromosome is missing or duplicated. The question the counselor usually hears next is, "Well, what does that chromosome do?" Despite the counselor's education and experience, his or her response is usually limited to, "Unfortunately, we really don't know exactly what it does, but we do know that an extra copy or a missing piece of it causes a lot of different problems." If the disorder is relatively common, the counselor can resort to statistics and talk about reported findings in a series of patients in an attempt to answer parents' more important questions, "What does this mean? Will our child live? How

much will he be able to learn? What will this do to our family?"

TECHNOLOGICAL ADVANCES

As techniques of performing chromosome studies have improved, however, genetic counselors often face a situation where even statistics do not exist, because many chromosomal disorders are rare, or at least have not been frequently described. Often a counselor and the medical profession in general simply does not know enough about a particular disorder to help a family anticipate the future. Researchers in mental retardation have always assumed that chromosomal abnormalities, which must involve hundreds and hundreds of genes along the length of a chromosome, always cause mental retardation—with perhaps the exception of some of the sex chromosome abnormalities—and that the degree of retardation is generally severe. However, with the new chromosome study techniques and with recognition of smaller and smaller structural abnormalities in the chromosomes, geneticists are realizing that not all chromosomal abnormalities cause profound mental retardation, and that some abnormalities are associated with what we have described as "learning disabilities" in some children or with specific verbal disabilities. Increased recognition of these clinical syndromes will inevitably help counselors in informing families and telling them what to expect of the child—which may well include the news that the situation is not as hopeless as once would have been thought just a few years ago. A vast amount of information about different chromosomal disorders is necessary before conclusions can be drawn, however—information that can only come from studying children with abnormalities, testing them, and conducting regular follow-ups to chart what happens to them as they get older.

DIAGNOSTIC CONSIDERATIONS

The situation is even more difficult for the counselor when the diagnosis involves not a chromosomal abnormality, which can at least be visualized by showing the karyotype, but a genetic disorder due to the presence of a single abnormal gene or a pair of genes. The diagnosis may be based completely on physical findings or on biochemical abnormalities; it is almost always extremely difficult to explain that all of the child's different problems are due to this abnormal genetic material and are somehow related. Chapter 2 provides examples of two single gene disorders with diverse effects that are presumably the result of a single gene operating in different cells within the body. The chapter offers an interesting clue for looking at many other sorts of disorders. We researchers sometimes focus on a one-organ system, without thinking what that gene might be doing in other organs. We do not think imaginatively enough about what the ultimate result of that gene product might be to enable us to recognize some of these pleiotropic effects. The fragile-X syndrome discussed in Chapter 2 provides an intriguing introduction to possible uses of new research techniques to isolate this abnormal gene. Once the particular DNA sequence is iso-

lated, it may be possible to determine not only what causes individuals with fragile-X syndrome to be mentally retarded, but also what causes such things as minor malformations. Affected individuals do not have the same physical appearance, but they tend to have some common minor abnormalities. What protein is being coded by that sequence of DNA that affects not only the development of the brain, causing mental retardation, but the ears, so that they stick out, and the testes, so that in some of these individuals they are larger than they should be?

Why is it that having an extra chromosome, whether it be a 21, an 18, a 13, or one of the others, causes that incredibly complex entity that we recognize as a clinical syndrome? Not only mental retardation but certain physical abnormalities are characteristic of each of these extra chromosomes. If a way could somehow be found to turn off that extra dose of the chromosome after birth, would this make a difference? Obviously such a procedure could not restructure an abnormal brain that is the result of trisomy 13. Could some of the postnatal effects be altered, however? The answers to the above questions must await breakthroughs in our knowledge of just how human genes and chromosomes function and how these functions are controlled in human beings.

TREATMENT PROBLEMS

Another inevitable question that clinicians dread is, "What can you do about this condition now that you have made the diagnosis?" Frequently, the answer is painful for all involved. As was pointed out in Chapter 1, some associated medical complications of a disorder can be treated, some physical and intellectual limitations can be overcome with intensive educational effort, and support and concern can, of course, be offered the child and his or her family. Rarely, however, can the word "cure" be mentioned in a positive sense. Nevertheless, with all of the technology and talent that is available to us at the University of Texas Health Science Center at

Dallas, for example, parents often cannot understand why an engineer and a computer cannot between the two of them "reprogram" their child's genes. If only the matter were that simple!

Chapter 1 emphasizes that prevention of mental retardation is a more accessible goal at present than is its cure. Clinical genetic services such as genetic counseling and prenatal diagnosis are among the most effective means of prevention available, but are underutilized. Their effectiveness depends upon their availability and the public's awareness of the existence and the need for such services.

Funding for services is not popular. The United States has a national genetic disease control act that provides about four million dollars a year to "stamp out" genetic disease. That does not go far. Not only is it inadequate to allow geneticists to provide the service we are capable of right now, but it will be even less adequate if we succeed in our attempts to educate the general public and the medical profession to the important role genetics can play in the prevention of mental retardation.

Molecular biology, genetic engineering, neurobiology—all of the fields that are concerned with mental retardation are tremendously diverse, complex, and require highly specialized training. A major concern of many geneticists is the fact that basic biomedical research is not being encouraged to the extent that it should be. Bright young people who express an interest in such research are being channeled instead into applied research. After all, "Who is going to hire you once you get your degree?" By not encouraging Congress and the current administration to support training in basic biomedical research, our nation threatens to fall behind in the expertise and knowledge that in the past has enabled scientific discoveries benefiting human beings worldwide. It is not only a question of adequate funding, so that research careers are more economically attractive, but also a matter of education, of encouraging the curiosity and talent of students from the beginning of their school years so they will view a career in science as desirable. Certainly the breakthroughs that may come about in the fight to prevent and cure mental retardation are among the more difficult and exciting possibilities of genetic research.

Curative Aspects of Mental Retardation:
Biomedical and Behavioral Advances
edited by Frank J. Menolascino, M.D., Ronald Neman, Ph.D., and Jack A. Stark, Ph.D.
Copyright 1983   Paul H. Brookes Publishing Co., Inc.   Baltimore · London

part B

BRAIN DEVELOPMENT
AND FUNCTION
Relationships to
Mental Retardation

chapter 4

Normal and Pathological Development of the Cerebral Cortex

Cytogenesis and Histogenesis

VERNE S. CAVINESS, JR., M.D.
ROGER S. WILLIAMS, M.D.
Eunice Kennedy Shriver Center for Mental Retardation
Waltham, Massachusetts

T HE DEVELOPMENTAL PERIOD IS one of unequaled hazard to human life and health (Niswander & Gordon, 1972). The mortality rate of gestation is 20%. Most fetuses that do not survive gestation are aborted during the first trimester. However, the mortality rate between the 20th week of gestation and the end of the first postnatal month remains as high as 3.5%, which is eight times the mortality rate of the general population.

The overall morbidity of the developmental period in man is approximately 5% of all live births (Kurland, Kurtzke, & Goldberg, 1973). Disorders of the central nervous system (CNS) are between two and three times as frequent as those of the cardiovascular and gastrointestinal systems, the second and third most frequently affected systems (Saxen & Rapola, 1969). In the United States alone, approximately five million people, 3% of the general population, are afflicted with developmental disorders of the CNS. In most instances, disability is moderate (i.e., IQs ranging from 50 to 70, defects in speech, cognition, or epilepsy). However, between one and two million people in this country are severely handicapped by cognitive, motor, or perceptual abnormalities (Holmes, Moser, Halldorsson, Mack, & Maltzilevich, 1972; Niswander & Gordon, 1972).

These statistics inform us that the causes and consequences of developmental failure are among the most pressing confronting our society. The search for the mechanisms that govern the development of the nervous system and that offer attack points for disease must be viewed as among the most critical challenges and responsibilities of biomedical science.

THE CEREBRAL CORTEX

A Major Challenge

No level of the central nervous system—the cerebral hemisphere, the cerebellum, the brain stem, or the spinal cord—is exempted from attack by developmental disease. However, it is particularly the neocortex that demands the attention of the developmental pathologist. Diseases that strike the cerebral cortex and the underlying fiber systems of the central white matter are associated with devastating abnormalities of cognition, language, memory, and complex motor functions. Furthermore, the cerebral neocortex appears to be particularly vulnerable to the pathological processes that strike during the developmental epoch. The remarkable complexity of events through which this organ develops, its large size, and the long duration of its developmental cycle may be only the most obvious factors that confer a heightened vulnerability to disturbances of the maternal support system, i.e., infections, hydrocephalus, and a host of other less well understood disease processes.

Cellular Organization of the Cerebral Cortex

The overt behavior of the individual, particularly in relation to intelligence, language, and skilled motor performance, is directed in large measure by the aggregate function of the millions of nerve cells, that comprise the cerebral neocortex. This vast population of nerve cells is divisible into multiple classes—each with its characteristic shape, relative position, and pattern of connections with other cells. These connections are the basis for the nerve cells' functional role in neural circuits. It is a remarkable architectural feature of the neocortex that the component neurons are ordered according to their cell class into five successive, parallel planes or laminae. These lie below an outer or "molecular" layer that contains axons and dendrites of cells but few cell bodies. Neocortical layers II and III are formed of small and medium-sized pyramidal cells, respectively, which give rise to the majority of connections between cortical regions within the same and between the two hemispheres (Jacobson & Trojanoski, 1974). A dense population of small granular cells inhabits subadjacent

layer IV. These are "local circuit" neurons; that is, their axons are distributed only to a small territory near their cell bodies. In most regions of the cortex, layer V contains larger pyramidal cells that give rise to all projections of the neocortex that descend below the thalamus to brain stem and spinal cord (Gross, Ewing, Carter, & Coutler, 1978). Finally, the polymorphic neurons of layer VI are the origin of connections between the neocortex and the thalamus (Jacobson & Trojanoski, 1975; Wise & Jones, 1977).

The overall sequence of events through which the cerebral cortex develops may be divided into two broad epochs: 1) a period of cytogenesis and histogenesis, and 2) a period of growth and differentiation. A very different succession of cellular events occurs during these two epochs.

THE CELLULAR EVENTS OF DEVELOPMENT—AN OVERVIEW

Cytogenesis and Histogenesis

Cytogenesis refers to the formation of cells; histogenesis refers to the events through which cells are assembled into the individual tissue components of the nervous system. In the majority of regions of the human fetal nervous system, including the cerebral neocortex, these events are compressed into the first two trimesters of pregnancy (Sidman & Rakic, 1973; Dobbing & Sands, 1973). They extend well into the first year of postnatal life in the cerebellum. At the end of the second trimester, when cytogenesis and histogenesis of the cerebral hemispheres are largely complete, the weight of the entire brain is only 100 grams, or less than one-third of its weight at term.

It is essential to keep in mind that these early dramatic events in the formation of the cerebral cortex are paralleled by equally critical events in the formation of supporting tissues. The blood vascular system, the choroid plexus at the margins of the ventricles, and mesenchymal membranes around the nervous system and the skull are also formed during this period. Normal development of the cerebral hemisphere is dependent upon adequate vascular perfusion and the normal formation of circulation of cerebrospinal fluid. In addition to their "nutritive and waste disposal" functions, these two circulatory systems probably provide a balance of hydraulic forces necessary for proper support and molding of the developing nervous system (Desmond & Jacobson, 1977).

The glial cells of the cerebrum, unlike the neurons, are relatively inconspicuous at this stage of development. An exception is the specialized radial glial cell that differentiates very early and, as we note later, plays a major role in the development of young neurons within the cortex (Schmechel & Rakic, 1979).

Differentiation and Growth

Once committed to their definitive positions and having achieved their basic cellular configurations, neurons enter a period of growth (Marin-Padilla, 1970; Purpura, 1975). During this second epoch, their axonal and dendritic surfaces become linked together to form a stable pattern of innerconnections that are the basis for functional neuronal circuits. Far more young neurons are probably generated than will eventually inhabit the adult nervous system (Jacobson, 1978). Cells that are not recruited into stable connections die and are eliminated. In the human brain, the second epoch has an extended period that continues through the second half of pregnancy, the first postnatal decade, and perhaps beyond. Cells increase greatly in size and come to assume their characteristic adult shapes. Multiple glial cell species proliferate. Astrocytes differentiate and acquire the ability to elaborate fibrous processes in response to injury. The oligodendroglial cells elaborate the myelin sheath essential to the function of multiple axonal systems. The brain increases in size approximately 15-fold to reach its adult weight of approximately 1,500 grams. The blood vascular system and cerebrospinal fluid pathways achieve their definitive configurations and physiological

characteristics. Maturation of the investing mesenchymal structures is marked, finally, by closure of the boney sutures of the skull.

Each of these two developmental epochs is associated with a quite different range of neuropathological disorders. The remainder of this chapter is concerned with the normal and pathological events of cytogenesis and histogenesis in the cerebral cortex. Chapter 5 focuses upon the epoch of growth and differentiation.

Cytogenesis and Histogenesis— Normal Development

The normal sequence of events through which cells are generated and assembled into the complex laminated architecture of the cerebral cortex is extremely complicated (Sidman & Rakic, 1973). The task might be simpler if neurons were born and developed in situ. Neurobiologists have known for nearly a century, however, that the actual sequence of events is much more intricate. Nerve cells are, in fact, generated by an epithelium that lines the ventricular cavities lying deep within the cerebral hemispheres and remote from the cortex itself. Once the young neuron has completed its last cell division, it must undergo an extended migration in order to reach its final destination within the cortex. Particularly in the human and other primate brains, this distance may be many times the length of the cell itself, and the migratory terrain a dense thicket of axons and other cellular processes (Rakic, 1975).

The mechanism that induces the young neuron to undertake its seemingly impossible journey to the cortex is unknown. Whatever the mechanism, cells seem to be guided in their course by ascending along the radially extended processes of the radial glial cells (Rakic, 1975). In some way, young postmitotic cells appear to recognize these glial fibers and turn to them for guidance in their ascent to the developing cortex. The cell body of the specialized glial element lies also near the ventricular lining. Its elongate radial processes ascend fully to the outer margin of the cerebral wall where a terminal expansion contributes to the limiting glial membrane of the central nervous system (Schmechel & Rakic, 1979).

Migrating cells are radially elongated with tapered leading and trailing processes. Although they are still in a relatively undifferentiated state and resemble each other very closely, it is probable that these cells are already committed to become members of specific neuronal classes even before reaching the cortex. For many, some degree of differentiation actually begins before entering the cortex, as evidenced by the elaboration of an axonal process from the inferior pole of the cell (Shoukimas & Hinds, 1978).

After the young neuron enters the developing cortex, it still has difficult and essential maneuvers to make in order to achieve its appropriate position in the complex architectural pattern. The task might be easier if the young neuron simply migrated until it encountered a cell that had preceded it. This is not the case. On the contrary, the cerebral neocortex is assembled in an "inside-out" sequence; that is, as the structure is finally constituted, cells lying in the deepest layers are the earliest formed, whereas those directed to progressively more superficial layers arise at successively later times in development (Rakic, 1975). This is because each migrating cell in its turn migrates fully to the molecular layer before it stops migration. It appears to do so along the intracortical segment of the ascending radial glial fiber. Therefore, it is probably essential that the young, relatively undifferentiated migrating cell be able to bypass earlier arrivals in the course of its ascent.

Once migration is completed, the young cell appears to become firmly fixed to adjacent cellular elements with the possible exception of the radial glial fiber itself (Caviness, Pinto-Lord, & Evrard 1981). Neurons that are generated from a continuous zone of the germinal matrix and that migrate along the same radial glial fiber probably come to be grouped together in a radial cellular column. Since many cells of the same class are generated at roughly the same time, they eventually occupy the same relative positions on adjacent radial columns. Thus, cells of the same class occupy a series of tangential planes accounting for the characteristic laminar pattern of cortical structures (Evrard, Caviness, Prats-Vinas, & Lyon, 1978).

Once in position, the young postmigratory neuron finds itself in an environment that influences profoundly the basic form that its dendritic arbor will develop. The immature cortex is actually a three-tiered fibrocellular scaffolding (Marin-Padilla, 1970). Specifically, the molecular layer is, in part, a stratum of axons; in the depths of the cortex a zone, referred to as the "subplate" (Kostovic & Molliver, 1974), includes another stratum of axons. The majority of immature postmigratory neurons come to be tightly packed in the cell-rich zone or cortical plate bracketed by these fiber-rich strata. Early in the course of cellular differentiation, dendritic growth appears to be outward, with branching occurring only within these axon-rich strata, rather than toward the cell bodies of other cells (Pinto-Lord & Caviness, 1979). With regard to the pyramidal cell classes, at least, it appears that the characteristic precocious development of the terminal portion of the apical dendrite is induced in some way from the leading migratory process as it enters the molecular layer. Similarly, the sprouting of dendrites from the cell soma appears to be induced later as the cell comes into relation with the fiber stratum of the subplate. Beyond this stage, the emphasis in cortical development shifts to the more extended process of growth and differentiation and the construction of connections between cells.

Disorders of Cytogenesis and Histogenesis

Disorders that intercept development during the early phases of cytogenesis and histogenesis are usually grave in their consequences. Most are associated with miscarriage in the first trimester (Creasy & Alberman, 1976). Even if the fetus survives to term, the disorder is likely to be lethal in the perinatal period or in the first few postnatal months. Survival is associated with profound psychomotor retardation.

It is certain that multiple, diverse pathologic processes act to disrupt cytogenesis and histogenesis of the human cerebrum. These include intercurrent necrotizing and metabolic diseases on the one hand, and the consequences of complex chromosomal rearrangements or gene mutations on the other. Their effects upon the course of development are expressed in a wide spectrum of grossly apparent malformations of the cerebrum. The majority of these have been recognized uniquely in man. Few have been produced in experimental animals by teratologic means; few are the issue of single gene mutations or chromosomal rearrangements occurring in species other than man. For these reasons, current concepts of pathogenesis in this domain of human developmental neuropathology are, in large measure, hypotheses derived from morphological analysis of the malformation themselves. The salient features of an instructive selection of these are described below. All but the first described, anencephaly, are extremely rare.

Anencephaly In anencephaly virtually the entire forebrain as well as varying portions of the brain stem and cerebellum are absent (Lemire, Beckwith, & Warkany, 1978). This malformation is one of the more commonly encountered in the miscarried or stillborn infant (Creasy & Alberman, 1976). It has been produced in experimental animals by teratologic agents directed against the generative epithelium, resulting in cell death and failure of the neural tube to close. A variety of cytotoxic agents directed against the human fetus at the end of the first month of gestation, when neural tube closure should occur, probably cause this malformation in man.

Holoprosencephaly In this malformation, the telencephalon, normally represented by the two cerebral hemispheres, forms a single cerebral vesicle (Figure 1). The olfactory bulbs, normally components of the basal region of the cerebral hemispheres, are absent. Whereas those cortical regions that occupy the lateral and posterior aspects of the normal cerebral hemispheres may be bilaterally present in the holoprosencephalic vesicle, those occupying the rostromedial aspect of the normal cerebral hemispheres may be absent (Yakovlev, 1959). It is as though the sector of the rostral neural tube, which is normally the origin of structures forming the anterior-medial wall of the two

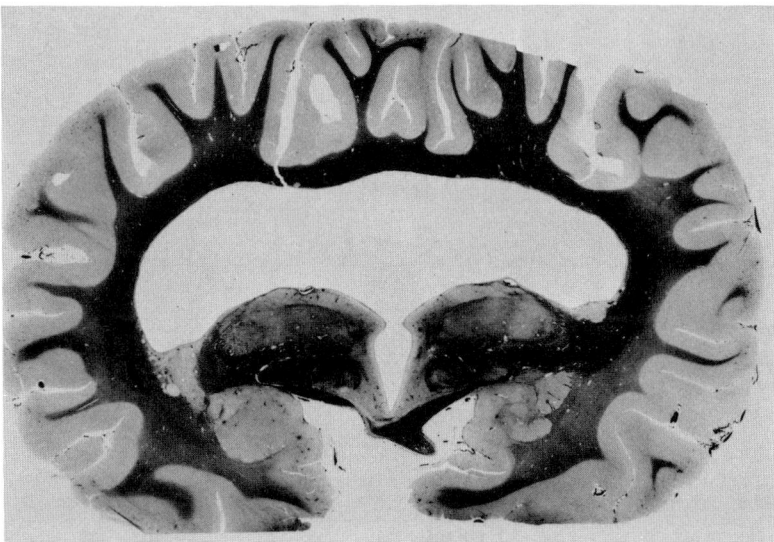

Figure 1.   Coronal section of a holoprosencephalic brain stained for myelin. There is a single cerebral vesicle; diencephalic and subthalamic structures are normally paired.

cerebral vesicles, had been destroyed, and continuity between the remaining portion reestablished in some way. Consistent with this view—that the malformation is caused primarily by a necrotizing process—is the observation that the anterior diencephalon may be replaced by a fibrovascular scar in typical cases. The process must occur before the fifth week of gestation, that is, before the two cerebral vesicles evaginate at the rostral extremity of the neural tube, but soon after closure of the tube. In confirmation of the inference, a typical example of this malformation has been discovered in an aborted fetus at the seventh week of gestation (Mall, 1917).

Microcephaly Microcephaly is a general term meaning a brain that is more than three standard deviations smaller than the norm. For the purposes of this chapter, the term is reserved for malformations confined to the

cerebral hemispheres in which there has been no obvious tissue destructive process (Friede, 1975). The convolutional pattern of the cerebral hemispheres is usually relatively simple. The cytologic features of the cerebral cortex are generally abnormal (Figure 2). Typically, the cortical cell population is dominated by neurons characteristic of layers V and VI of the normal brain. Often these appear clustered to an exaggerated degree into radially aligned columns (Williams, 1979). By contrast, cells typical of layers II through IV of the normal cortex are reduced in number, and may be absent altogether. As a rule, such cells are not found in heterotopic positions below the cortex, suggesting that the disorder does not reflect a disturbance in neuronal migration.

From the previous review of the histogenetic sequence of the cerebral cortex, it is apparent that the cortex in the microcephalic

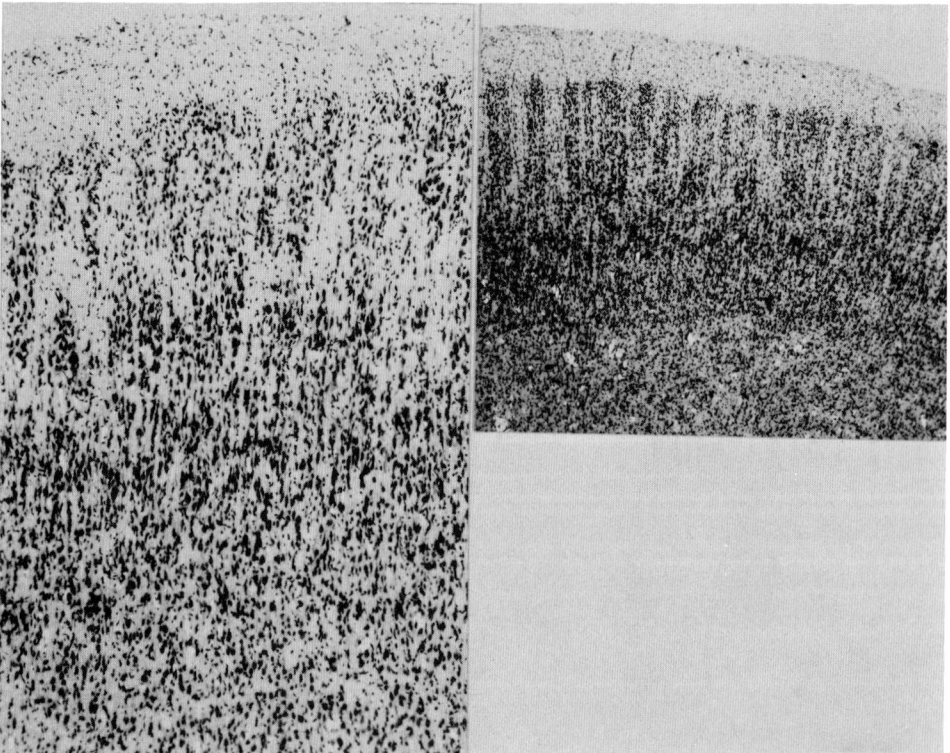

Figure 2.   Neocortex from an infant with microcephaly. The exaggerated columnar grouping of neurons is obvious at low magnification (right). A variable but marked reduction in the number of neurons of layers II–IV is evident at higher magnification on the left. (Courtesy of Professor Gilles Lyon.)

malformation is populated by the earliest formed neurons. The latest formed neurons may be virtually absent. There is no histologic evidence that these late-formed cells have been destroyed en route to the cortex or subsequent to their arrival at the end of migration. It appears more likely that the central generative zone of the developing brain does not produce the neuronal classes that are normally the last formed. Typical examples of the disorder have been transmitted by autosomal recessive inheritance. The role of the mutated gene in the pathogenesis of the developmental disorder is unknown.

Lissencephaly This malformation receives its name from the fact that the cerebral convexity is smooth, with profound reduction in the number of fissures and gyri. The medial and inferior aspects of the hemisphere, by contrast, may have a relatively normal convolutional pattern (Figure 3). As with microcephaly vera, the neuronal population of the cortex may be limited to those characteristic of layers V and VI of the normal brain (Stewart, Richman, & Caviness, 1975). For the most part, these appear to be relatively normal in their cytologic features, and in relatively normal position with respect to each other and to the overlying molecular layer. By contrast, many medium to large pyramidal neurons of the incomplete cortex are inverted 180° in polarity, so that their primary dendrites point away from the pial surface (Caviness & Williams, 1979). Just below the cortex, there is a narrow laminar zone containing few cells, an appearance that suggests the effect of a necrotizing process. Below the cell-poor laminar zone is a wide field of heterotopic neurons. These are dominated by cells most characteristic of the normal superficial cortical layers, but they are not ordered into laminae by class, as they would be in the normal cortex.

In this disorder, evidently, the earlier formed neurons complete their migrations in normal fashion; the migrations of later formed neurons, by contrast, appear to be interrupted by a necrotizing process, directed rather focally at the level of the subplate.

Such a process would presumably destroy the immediately subcortical segments of radial glial fibers. Conceivably, it is this mechanism that leads to arrest of cell migration in the lissencephalic malformation.

The Zellweger Malformation This complex systemic metabolic disorder, associated with abnormality of brain development, is also transmitted by autosomal recessive inheritance (Volpe & Adams, 1972). There is an abnormality in the surface gyral pattern of the cerebral hemisphere that occurs bilaterally in the centro-Sylvian regions (Evrard, Caviness, Prats-Vinas, & Lyon, 1978) (Figure 4). The gyri in the Sylvian region are smaller than normal, whereas those more medially in the central region are wider than normal. The cell pattern of the cortex is also abnormal, especially in the region of the gyral anomaly (Figure 5). Although the five principal cellular layers are explicitly present, they are narrower than normal and contain a reduced complement of cells. This is particularly true of the most superficial layers, a disparity accentuated in the wide-flat gyri of the central region.

In this respect, the cortical anomaly bears a superficial resemblence to that of lissencephaly and microcephaly described above. Unlike these latter, however, a large contingent of neurons is distributed in heterotopic position throughout all levels of the cortex, extending deeply into the subcortical white matter. Among these neurons in heterotopic position are cells of all neuron classes, that is, cells normally destined for all of the neocortical layers. The cell pattern analysis suggests that the malformation is a consequence of a disorder of migration that is partial in degree. Thus, it affects only a limited proportion of neurons, but this includes cells that undergo their migrations throughout the entire period of migration (Evrard et al, 1978). Possibly the general metabolic abnormality associated with the Zellweger mutation causes a nonspecific disruption of cell metabolism that interferes with the ability of the cell to migrate. Alternatively, the mutation may target more specifically some as-

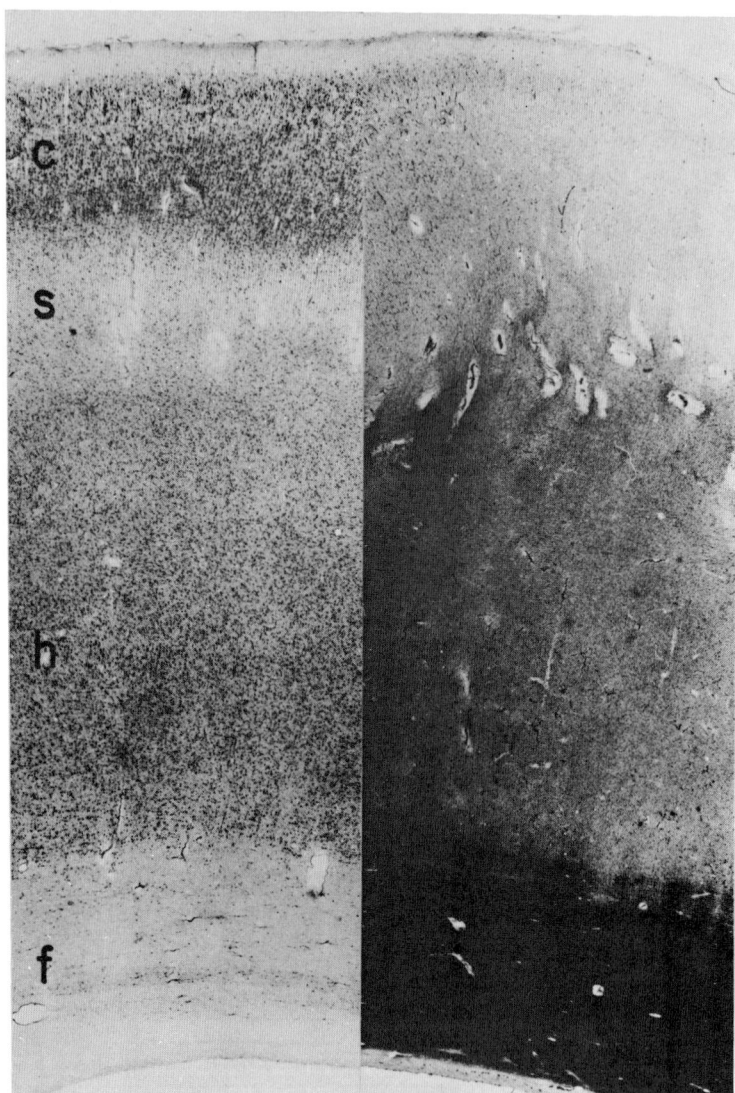

Figure 3.   The cerebral wall of a lissencephalic brain is viewed in adjacent cell (left) and myelin stains (right). The laminae of the cortex (c) resemble layers I, V, and VI of the normal brain. Cell numbers are greatly reduced in a laminar zone (s) immediately below the cortex. Below is a broad field of heterotopic neurons (h), which are aligned radially with each other, but which are not segregated by subclass into discrete tangential laminae. (Reprinted from Caviness & Williams, 1979, with permission from the publisher.)

pect of the mechanism that permits neurons to ascend along the radial glial fiber.

Driftwood Cortex This malformation, apparently transmitted by autosomal recessive inheritance, is unique among malformations in man in that large axon fascicles are directed to the most superficial plane of the cortex (Rebeiz, Wolf, & Adams, 1968). In this respect, at least, ''driftwood cortex''

in man is similar to the reeler neocortical malformation in mice, which also occurs consequent to autosomal recessive mutation (Caviness, 1977). In the mutant mouse, the abnormality of axon trajectory appears very early as the cortical plate emerges. Monoaminergic axons are among the first to establish this abnormal fiber trajectory (Caviness & Korde, 1980). The mechanism for this

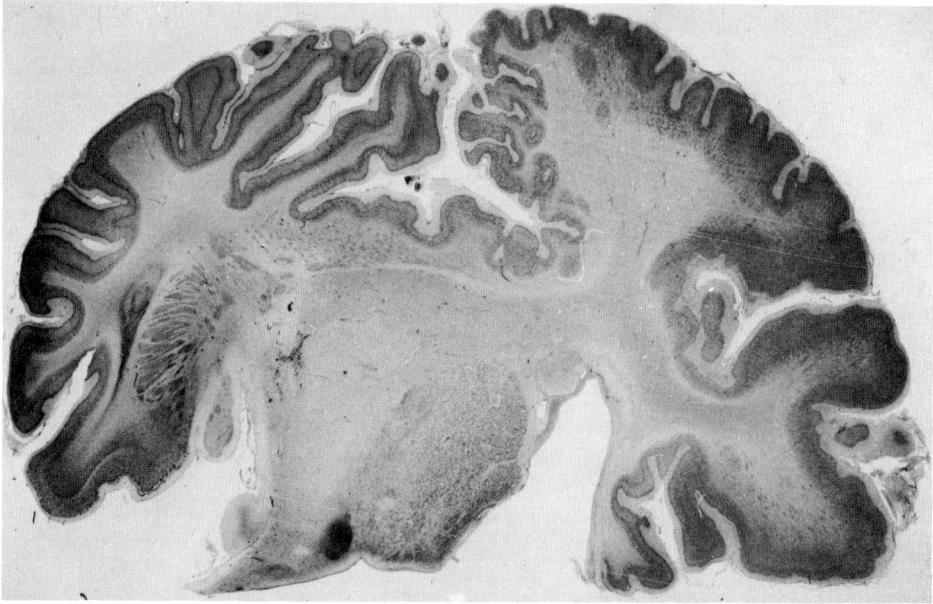

Figure 4. A coronal section through the cerebral hemisphere of a brain with the Zellweger malformation demonstrates the characteristic convolutional abnormality in the centro-Sylvian region. Gyral width is increased dorsomedially and reduced laterally. Heterotopic neurons lie subjacent to the malformed cortex. (Reprinted from Evrard et al., 1978, with permission from the publisher.)

process is unknown, as is the developmental history of the human malformation.

Extracerebral Ectopia A heterogeneous group of cerebral malformations may be associated with neuronal ectopias, that is, neuronal masses located within the meninges and extrinsic to the cerebral hemisphere (Caviness, Evrard, & Lyon, 1978). This anomaly has been associated with the "fetal alcohol" syndrome (Jones, Smith, Ulleland, & Streissgath, 1973) but is probably not specific to any teratogenic agent.

The illustrated example (Figure 6) is associated with what appears to have been a relatively mild injury directed to the most superficial part of the developing cortex, that is, to the interface of the mesenchymal membranes and the molecular layer. In points where damage has occurred, a mesenchymal-neuroglial scar has formed. Young nerurons, presumably already in position at the most superficial level of the cortex when the injury occurred, have apparently resumed their migrations subsequent to the event. Many have migrated beyond the limits of the central

nervous system to establish a large colony of cells in the subarachnoid compartment. This malformation in man underscores the critical role of the molecular layer and pial-glial membrane as factors controlling the positions of young neurons at the end of migration.

Agenesis of the Corpus Callosum The largest commissure of the forebrain, the corpus callosum, is absent. The fibers that normally form this commissure are routed instead into an anomalous fiber bundle that courses in rostrocaudal direction, parallel to the cingulate bundle. Otherwise, the cerebral hemispheres may appear normal. This disorder is known to be transmitted by autosomal recessive inheritance in the mouse and may be seen with chromosomal disorders in man. It appears to reflect a failure of axons of the commissural system, arising from cells of the cerebral cortex, to establish their normal trajectory through the lamina reuniens (Rakic & Yakovlev, 1968). Normally the corpus callosum begins to form at the end of the first trimester, and increases in bulk throughout the entire developmental period. This rare

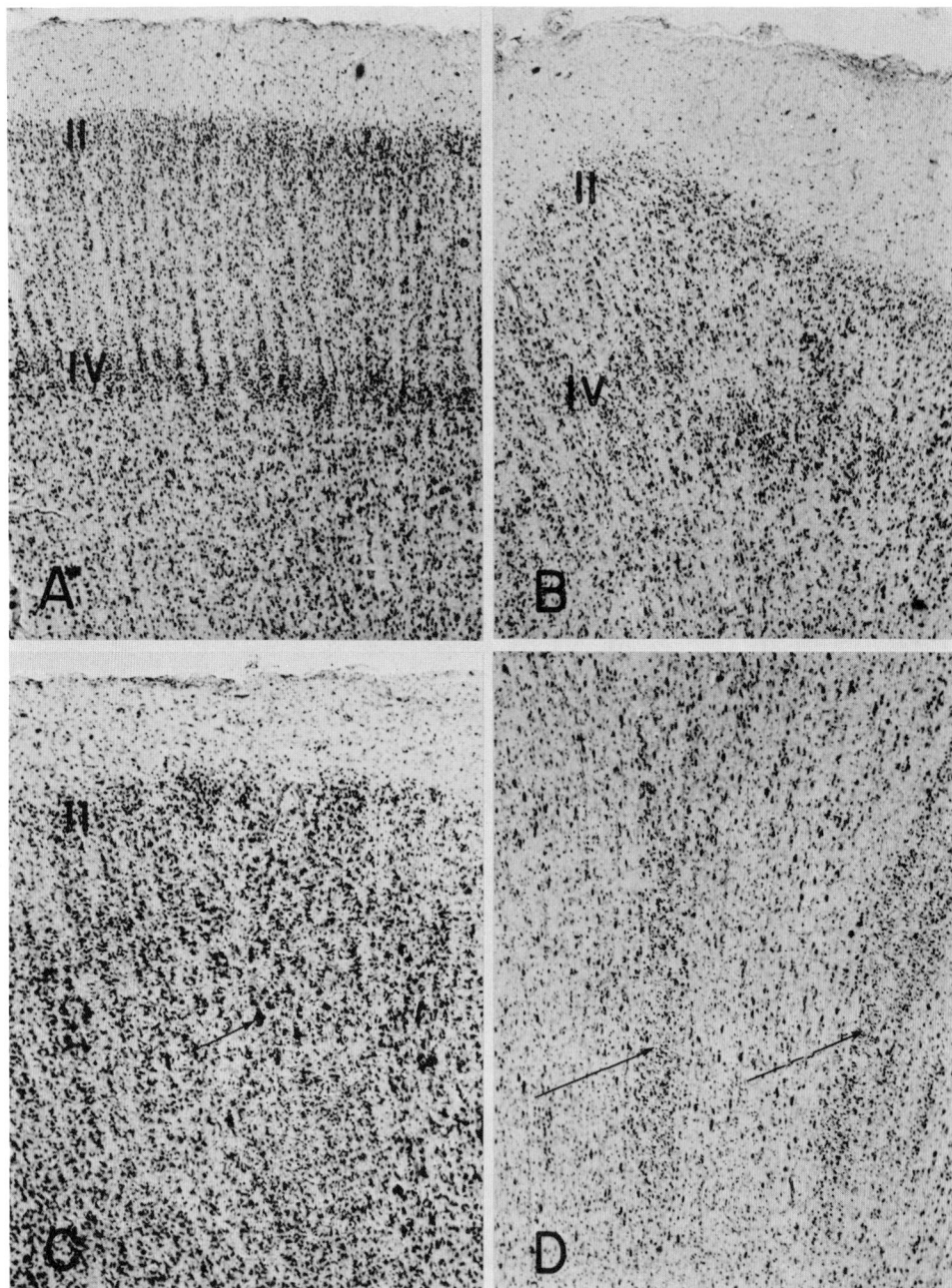

Figure 5. Neocortex that is normally (A), excessively (B), and less than normally (C) convoluted in the Zellweger malformation. Roman numerals identify layers that would correspond to laminae II and IV in the normal brain. Particularly in cortical sections of excessive gyral folding, the cells of these laminae are imperfectly aligned. The arrow in C designates a large pyramidal neuron, characteristic of normal layer V, in anomalous superficial position. Heterotopic neurons (D) lie subjacent to the malformed cortex. Clusters of "granular" neurons typical of cortical layer IV, are marked by arrows. (Reprinted from Evrard et al., 1978, with permission from the publisher.)

malformation should be distinguished from more common developmental disorders in which the corpus callosum has been des-

troyed by a variety of necrotizing processes (von Monakow, 1899).

Megalencephaly Essentially the con-

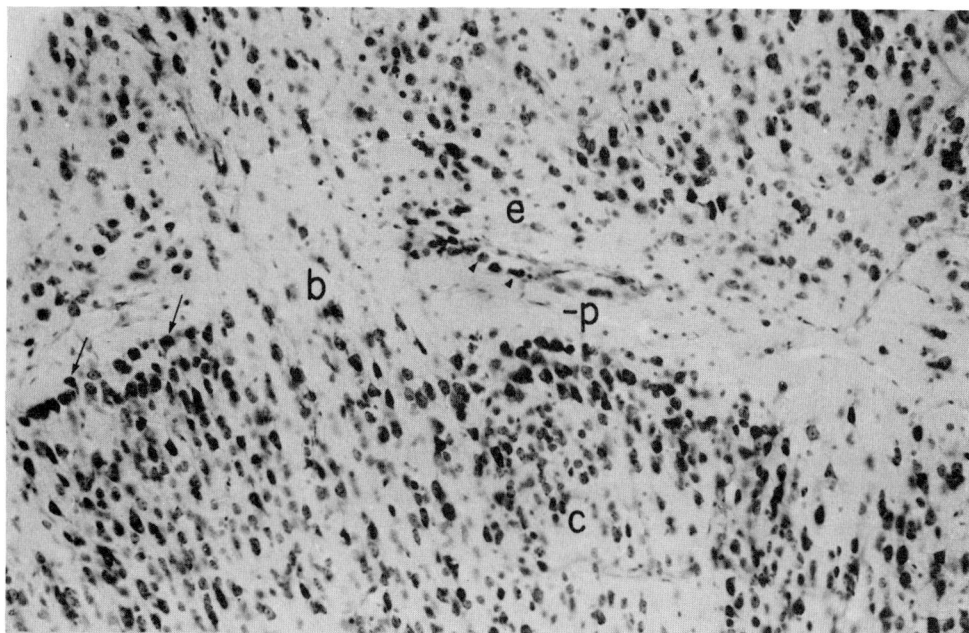

Figure 6.   High power photomicrograph of a neuronal ectopia. Neurons have migrated into the normally cell-poor molecular layer (c), subjacent to the pial-glial barrier (p). A bridge of neurons and glial tissue (b) extends through a breach in the pial-glial barrier, forming a neuron-glial ectopia within the subarachnoid space (e). (Reprinted from Caviness et al., 1978, with permission from the publisher.)

verse of microcephaly, megalencephaly is applied to brains that are more than three standard deviations greater than the norm in weight. The gyral pattern may be normal or anomalously excessive (Friede, 1975). The cortical laminar pattern is usually normal, but subcortical heterotopias are occasionally present. Excessive brain size has been attributed to a greater than normal number of neurons and glial cells in the brain, as well as to a greater than normal size of the individual cellular elements. To the extent that this observation is correct, the malformation may reflect abnormal control of cell numbers through the process of cell death. This process, essential to the fine regulation of the number of cells recruited into neurocircuits, may be disordered by mechanisms that are completely unknown.

FUTURE DIRECTIONS

The above observations direct our attention to the dramatic succession of cellular events through which the cerebral neocortex of man is constructed. Further, they orient our search toward an understanding of the mechanisms that control the cellular interactions governing these events and that may be disrupted with disastrous consequences by a host of disease processes. We understand the cellular events of development only in their broadest outlines; major questions are unresolved relating to their molecular mechanisms and genetic regulation.

Malformations reviewed in this chapter identify important unsolved problems to which future research should be directed. Particular areas for future study are the developmental mechanisms that control the number of cells in the central nervous system; that determine cell class; that assure cell migration along the radial glial fiber; and that dictate cell positions in the cortex after migration is accomplished. Other areas for future inquiry include the nature of interaction between developing dendrites and axonal strata that regulate dendritic development and lead to the formation of interneuronal connections.

Although the study of human pathology is an indispensable base from which to pose questions, it promises no answers. For these, analytical experiments must be conducted in animals. However, we must recognize the sobering reality that there are few genetic or teratologic paradigms for study of the majority of pathological processes affecting cytogenesis and histogenesis in man. Therefore, new teratologic models must be devised, and suitable mutant animals sought.

We are also challenged to develop and apply new methods. General cell and fiber stains, Golgi impregnations, and transmission electron microscopy have made essential contributions to our comprehension of the cellular events through which development proceeds. These "traditional" methods tell us nothing, however, of the molecular mechanisms that control these events and that must be attack points for many diseases affecting development. The focal plane of analysis must now shift, then, from the appearance of cells and their processes to an inquiry into the molecular constituents of the membranes of cells. It is through these constituents that all cells must communicate with each other and thereby direct each other's movements and modulate each other's growth and differentiation. An entirely new wave of methods, including immunocytochemistry, lectin cytochemistry, and autoradiography, are now available to make such inquiries possible. Such methods offer, thereby, enormous implications for developing curative approaches to mental retardation.

REFERENCES

Caviness, V.S., Jr. Reeler mutant mouse: A genetic experiment in developing mammalian cortex. *Society for Neurosciences Symposia*, 1977, *2*, 27–46.

Caviness, V.S., Jr., Pinto-Lord, M.C., & Evrard, P. Development of laminated pattern in the cerebral neocortex; comparative studies in normal and reeler mouse. In: L.L. Brinkley, B.M. Carlson, & T.G. Connelly (eds.), *Morphogenesis and pattern formation: Implications for normal and abnormal development*. New York: Raven Press, 1981.

Caviness, V.S., Jr., Evrard, P., & Lyon, G. Radial neuronal assemblies, ectopia and necrosis of developing cortex. *Acta Neuropathologica*, 1978, *41*, 67–72.

Caviness, V.S., Jr., & Korde, M. Monoaminergic afferents to the neocortex: A developmental histofluorescent study in normal and reeler mouse embryos. In preparation, 1980.

Caviness, V.S., Jr., & Williams, R.S. Cellular pathology of developing human cerebral cortex. In: R. Katzman (ed.), *Congenital and required cognitive disorders*. New York, Raven Press, 1979.

Creasy, M.R., & Alberman, E.D. Congenital malformations of the central nervous system in spontaneous abortions. *Journal of Medical Genetics*, 1976, *13*, 9–16.

Desmond, M.E., & Jacobson, A.G. Embryonic brain enlargement requires cerebrospinal fluid pressure. *Developmental Biology*, 1977, *57*, 188–198.

Dobbing, J., & Sands, T. Quantitative growth and development of the human brain. *Archives of Disease in Childhood*, 1973, *48*, 757–767.

Evrard, P., Caviness, V.S., Jr., Prats-Vinas, & Lyon. The mechanism of arrest of neuronal migration in Zellweger malformation: An hypothesis based upon cytoarchitectonic analysis. *Acta Neuropathologica*, 1978, *41*, 109–117.

Friede, R.L. *Developmental neuropathology*. New York: Springer-Verlag, 1975.

Gross, W.P., Ewing, L.K., Carter, C.M., & Coulter, J.D. Organization of corticospinal neurons in the cat. *Journal of Comparative Neurology*, 1978, *143*, 393–419.

Holmes, L.B., Moser, H.W., Halldorsson, S., Mack, C., & Matzilevich, B. *Mental retardation, an atlas of diseases with associated physical abnormalities*. New York: MacMillan Publishing Co., 1972.

Jacobson, M. *Developmental neurobiology*, (2nd ed.). New York: Plenum Publishing Corp., 1978.

Jacobson, S., & Trojanoski, J.Q. The cells of origin of the corpus callosum in the rat, cat and rhesus monkey. *Brain Research*, 1974, *74*, 149–155.

Jacobson, S., & Trojanoski, J.Q. Corticothalamic neurons and thalamocortical terminal fields: An investigation in rat using horseradish proxidose. *Brain Research*, 1975, *85*, 385–401.

Jones, K.L., Smith, D.W., Ulleland, C.N. & Streissgath, A.P. Pattern of malformation in offspring of alcohol mothers. *Lancet*, 1973, *1*, 1267–1271.

Kostovic, I., & Molliver, M.E. A new interpretation of the laminar development of the cerebral cortex: Synaptogenesis in different layers of the neopallium of the human fetus. *Anatomical Record*, 174, *178*, 395.

Kurland, L.T., Kurtzke, J.F., & Goldberg, I.D. *Epidemiology of neurologic and sense organ disorders*. Cambridge, MA: Harvard University Press, 1973.

Lemire, R.J., Beckwith, J.B., & Warkany, J. *Anencephaly*. New York: Raven Press, 1978.

Mall, F.P. Cyclopia in the human embryo. *Contributions to Embryology of the Carnegie Institution*, 1917, *5*, 33–45.

Marin-Padilla, M. Prenatal and early postnatal ontogenesis of the human motor cortex: A Golgi study. I. The sequential development of the cortical layers. *Brain Research*, 1970, *23*, 167–183.

Niswander, K.R., & Gordon, M. *Women and their pregnancies*. Philadelphia: W.B. Saunders Co., 1972.

Pinto-Lord, M.C., & Caviness, V.S., Jr. Determinants of cell shape and orientation: A comparative Golgi analysis of cell-axon interrelationships in the developing neocortex of normal and reeler mice. *Journal of Comparative Neurology*, 1979, *187*, 49–70.

Purpura, D.P. Normal and aberrant neuronal development in the cerebral cortex of human fetus and young infant. In: N.A. Buchwald & M.A.B. Brazier (eds.), *Brain mechanisms in mental retardation*. New York: Academic Press, 1975.

Rakic, P. Timing of major ontogenetic events in the visual cortex of the rhesus monkey. In: N.A. Buchwald & M.A.B. Brazier (eds.), *Brain mechanisms in mental retardation*. New York: Academic Press, 1975.

Rakic, P., & Yakovlev, P.I. Developmnt of the corpus callosum and cavum septi in man. *Journal of Comparative Neurology*, 1968, *132*, 45–72.

Rebeiz, J.J., Wolf, P.A., & Adams, R.D. Dys-topic cortical myelinogenesis ("Driftwood Cortex"). A hitherto unrecognized form of developmental anomaly of the cerebrum of man. *Acta Neuropathologica*, 1968, *11*, 237–252.

Saxen, L., & Rapola, J. *Congenital defects*. New York: Holt, Rinehart & Winston, 1969.

Schmechel, D.E., & Rakic, P. A Golgi study of radial glial cells in developing monkey telencephalon: Morphogenesis and transformation into astrocytes. *Anatomy and Embryology*, 1979, *156*, 115–152.

Shoukimas, G.M., & Hinds, J.W. The development of cerebral cortex in the embryonic mouse: An electronmicroscopic serial section analysis. *Journal of Comparative Neurology*, 1978, *179*, 795–830.

Sidman, R.L., & Rakic, P. Neuronal migration with special reference to the developing human brain: A review. *Brain Research*, 1973, *62*, 1–35.

Stewart, R.W., Richman, D.P., & Caviness, V.S., Jr. Lissencephaly and pachygyria: An architectonic and topographical analysis. *Acta Neuropathologica*, 1975, *31*, 1–12.

Volpe, J.J., & Adams, R.D. Cerebro-hepato-renal syndrome of Zellweger: An inherited disorder of neuronal migration. *Acta Neuropathologica*, 1972, *20*, 175–198.

von Monakow, C. Über die misbildungen des central nervensystems. *Erq. Path. Anat.*, 1899, *6*, 513–581.

Williams, R.S. Golgi and routine microscopic analysis of congenital microcephaly ("Microcephaly vera"). *Annals of Neurology*, 1979, *6*, 173.

Wise, S.P., & Jones, E.G. Cells of origin and terminal distribution of descending projections of the rat somatosensory cortex. *Journal of Comparative Neurology*, 1977, *175*, 129–158.

Yakovlev, P.I. Pathoarchitectonic studies of cerebral malformations. III. Arrhinencephalies. *Journal of Neuropathology and Experimental Neurology*, 1959, *18*, 22–55.

Curative Aspects of Mental Retardation:
Biomedical and Behavioral Advances
edited by Frank J. Menolascino, M.D., Ronald Neman, Ph.D., and Jack A. Stark, Ph.D.
Copyright 1983   Paul H. Brookes Publishing Co., Inc.   Baltimore · London

chapter 5

Cellular Neurobiology of Mental Retardation

Problems and Perspectives

Dominick P. Purpura, M.D.
Stanford University
Stanford, California

MENTAL RETARDATION DENOTES a condition of significant intellectual impairment that is manifest during the developmental period. It encompasses a wide range of intellectual deficits varying from mild mental subnormality to profound neurobehavioral failure. Although at least 200 factors, either alone or in various combinations, have been identified or suspected as causative agents in the genesis of mental retardation, little is known concerning the mechanism by which any developmental perturbation results in mental deficiency. All that can be said with some degree of certainty is that mental retardation is a consequence of faulty central nervous system activities. This fact has guided basic research efforts in mental retardation toward the attainment of three specific aims: a) the understanding of the morphophysiological mechanisms underlying the development of normal brain function, b) the identification and analysis of pathogenetic factors producing aberrant neurobehavioral development and, c) the definition of strategies for preventing or ameliorating mental retardation.

Much of the effort to date in mental retardation biomedical research has been directed toward the identification of specific causative factors of, for example, hypothyroidism, genetic abnormalities, phenylketonuria (PKU), and other inborn errors of metabolism. While this important area of inquiry has generated significant programs for detection and prevention, few attempts have been made to understand the mechanisms and processes by which these insults impact upon the developing brain. It is of great importance that phenylketonuria can be identified in the neonate and that dietary measures can be taken to prevent significant mental impairment as a result of this metabolic error. The fact that enzyme deficiencies of neuronal storage disorders such as Tay-Sachs disease can be identified antenatally or that thyroid replacement therapy, if initiated in time, can prevent mental deficiency, underscore the remarkable accomplishments of past research. What must be addressed now is the fundamental question of *mechanism*. How does PKU result in mental retardation? Why does the storage of metabolites in neurons cause them to function improperly? What role does thyroid hormone play in the maturation of brain function? What is the effect of gene dosage in Down syndrome on the development of cognitive function? Finally, if mild mental subnormality is largely a consequence of social and economic disadvantage, how do these multifactorial extrinsic perturbations modify developmental programs of functional maturation of the brain?

The emphasis in these questions on basic processes derives from the well-established principle that in the long run the most cost-effective health science research is that aimed at the acquisition of fundamental knowledge concerning basic mechanisms. With regard to mental retardation research, it will be necessary to pursue the study of basic mechanisms at cellular, neuro-integrative, and socio-behavioral levels of organization. This is the major objective sought in the research programs summarized in this chapter, all of which focus on high-priority areas of inquiry that can be productively explored in the next 5 years with realistic expectations for success.

NORMAL AND
ABNORMAL BRAIN MATURATION

During the course of human brain development, approximately 200 billion cells differentiate into neurons, become organized into different systems and make appropriate functional connections with sensory organs and muscles. The process of brain development begins in the earliest stages of embryonic life and extends well into the second decade. With the exception of the cerebellum, a structure concerned largely with coordination of movement, the brain *probably* acquires its full complement of neurons prior to birth in the human infant and perhaps as early as the beginning of the last trimester of gestation. Why probably? The answer, simply stated, is that while excellent data are available regarding the time or origin of many of the neurons in the monkey brain, nothing is known concerning the schedules of generation or the numbers of neurons produced in the embry-

onic and early fetal stages of human brain development. Since one of the primary requirements for normal brain function is a sufficient number of neurons (whatever this number may be) it follows that identification of the genetic and epigenetic factors regulating the formation of the ''correct'' number of neurons is of critical importance. One approach to this problem must be sought in the pursuit of *in vivo* laboratory animal and cell culture studies of developing neuron systems to define regulatory factors of neurogenesis and process formation in early differentiating neurons.

While neurons constitute the fundamental information-processing unit of the brain, they are outnumbered by the supporting cells or glia that play several crucial biological roles in facilitating neuronal operations and processes. In the mature brain, glia far outnumber neurons, but the period of maximal glial proliferation occurs somewhat later than the growth spurt period for neurons. What factors determine the relative numbers of glia and neurons and the extent to which early mechanisms of intercellular communication play a role in signaling functions in glia-glial and neuron-glial relations are unknown. Neurochemists and immunologists have made great progress in identifying ''marker'' molecules on the outer or plasma membranes of isolated neurons and glia that suggest a number of biochemical mechanisms underlying cell specificity. These studies are in the earliest stages of development, but they hold great promise for answering some of the most important questions in developmental neurobiology, namely: How does a neuron tell the difference between itself and other neurons; How does it recognize neurons it wants to contact, while avoiding others; and finally; How do neurons and glia know when to turn on metabolic reactions that unite them in functional units? These questions deserve the highest priority of consideration in any forward-looking research plan.

Neurons once formed must sometimes travel or migrate relatively great distances in the developing brain to reach their correct addresses in the neuronal subsystem for which they were originally specified by genetic programs. Research over the past decade has provided clues to at least two mechanisms of neuronal migration. Newly formed neurons at early stages in embryonic development produce long processes that arise from the ends of their cell bodies. One process anchors itself to the lining of the primitive ventricular cavity immediately subajacent to the germinative layers, while the other process grows into the wall of the developing pallium (primitive cerebrum) until it makes contact with the outer surface membrane. In this way primary polar processes serve to anchor the primitive neuron to a particular site. There follows, then, a process whereby the cell body with its nucleus migrates intracellularly to assume a position remote from its place of origin. Intracellular migration of the cell body can also occur by the cell body moving away from the early processes it emits. Both forms of neuronal migration must involve complex, temporospatial regulation of intraneuronal cytoskeletal elements that aid in the extension and directed growth of processes. In addition, there must be continued incorporation of newly synthesized surface membrane constituents during the growth of processes. Once the correct address has been attained, extended processes must be reabsorbed or transformed into other elements such as dendrites or axons during the subsequent phase of neuronal differentiation.

The phenomenon of neurite or process formation in primitive neurons introduces another set of critical neurobiological issues. Process formation and extension structures and other components that constitute the cytonet and cytoskeleton of neurons. The production of microtubule proteins, their assembly and disassembly, and the incorporation of plasma membrane constituents at the growing ends (growth cones) of developing processes are problems of fundamental importance that will require considerable attention. This point is given further emphasis below.

At a later stage of development, newly formed neurons undergo "free" migration to attain their correct position in the brain. Neurons destined for the cerebral cortex are aided in the migratory process by the presence of long radial processes of specialized glial cells that span the thickness of the primitive pallium. The phenomenon encompasses a variety of progressively more complex problems: First it is clear that the time a neuron is formed is a determinant of the position in the cerebral cortex the neuron will eventually attain. Time of origin is also related to neuron typology, i.e., what kind of neuron the differentiated element will be. The relationship between the neuron and glial cell must be specified in some way, but how?

Recent research has provided evidence that the plasma membrane of neurons is a mosaic of charged macromolecules consisting of glycolipids, glycoproteins, and glycoaminoglycans. Are the electrochemical signals resulting from different configurations of charged surface macromolecules matched by the complementary macromolecules associated with different but related cells? What factors guide the neuron to its proper location? For many years it has been argued that gradients of "chemical" signals in the external milieu of developing processes can influence directed growth by inducing the cytoskeletal system of the neuron to extend processes in the direction of increasing potency of the "signal." In the case of neurons migrating in close relationship to glial radial fibers, what are the chemical signals exchanged during the "contact guidance" mechanism? It is now known that faulty migration of neurons related to the loss of effective guidance by specialized glial cells is associated with disorganization and even neuronal attrition in subsystems involved in complex cortical functions.

The orderly development of some parts of the brain and spinal cord not only depends upon the production and proper location of a specified number of neurons, but also on the elimination of a variable proportion of neurons after much of the circuitry of the nervous system has been established. In recent years, much evidence has accumulated to the effect that programmed neuronal death is a prominent feature of developmental processes. Why are more neurons generated in some sites than appear necessary to carry out a particular function? What factors concerning the relations of these neurons with their target sites or with the activity they exhibit determine neuronal death? Do some neurons in the cerebral cortex exhibit early cell death because of similar determinants? Answers to these questions are clearly within the scope of current neurobiological research efforts and should continue to be supported.

EXPLORATIONS AT
THE CELLULAR LEVEL

In general, the processes of neuronal proliferation and migration are early developmental events in the human brain usually occupying the first half of gestation. Beyond the 20th week, neuronal differentiation, i.e., the development of dendrites and axons, and the formation of synaptic connections, dominates the developmental process. The extensive dendritic systems of pyramidal neurons of the cerebral cortex will eventually serve as receptor surfaces for a variable synaptic input from other neurons. In the human infant, dendritic branching patterns of most types of neurons in the cerebral cortex are established by the time of birth, but increases in segment length and terminal branching continue throughout the first and second year and perhaps longer. Since dendrites of pyramidal neurons, the predominant cell type of the cerebral cortex, provide 95% of the available membrane surface area for synaptic contacts, it follows that factors that influence dendritic growth and development will significantly modify the functional activity of the cerebral cortex. Overt alterations in dendritic branching patterns and dendrite/soma volume ratios have been documented in immature laboratory animals in experimental hypothyroidism, phenylalanine loading, lead intoxication, various genetic mutations, and environmental deprivation. These perturbations also exert a profound impact on the number, morphology, and distribution of dendritic spines, the small protuberances of dendrites that serve as postsynaptic targets for presynaptic axons of neighboring and distant neurons.

A significant set of observations reported in recent years points to the vulnerability of dendritic spines in a wide variety of neurobehavioral developmental disorders associated with mental retardation. What must be understood is the fundamental mechanism regulating dendritic spine formation. Dendritic spines with postsynaptic membrane particles indicative of receptor-like elements can exist in the absence of presynaptic processes. But how does the loss of previously established synapses involving dendritic spines alter spine morphology and function? One of the striking observations relating to dendritic spine morphology has been made in examination of cortical neurons in a number of cases of developmental failure with profound mental retardation. In these cases the major abnormality involves structural features of dendritic spines, many of which retain fetal-like characteristics. Such observations demonstrate the need to examine the full range of processes governing dendritic spine maturation and the establishment of spine synapses.

A closely related problem has been disclosed in the recent discovery that severely retarded infants and children whose cortical neurons exhibit abnormal dendritic spines also show varicose transformations in dendrites that take on a string-of-beads appearance beginning with the most distal dendrite segments. Correlated electron microscope studies of these varicose dendrites disclose a prominent disarray of microtubules with swirls of these elements in the varicosities. Evidently a disorganization in the mechanisms of alignment parallel to the long axis of dendrites may be an important factor in the genesis of the dendritic varicosity, with subsequent alteration in dendritic spines and the loss of integrative property of dendritic systems. This is the most likely explanation for progressive developmental failure. Again, these observations point to elementary biological mechanisms involved in microtubule polymerization and depolymerization and the factors that could impact upon processes for regulating neuronal geometry and dendritic morphophysiological properties.

The problem of defining the fundamental mechanisms of neuron-neuron and neuron-glial recognition was noted above in relation to neuronal migration and process formation. This problem is in fact the central issue of developmental neurobiology and for this reason alone requires additional comment with respect to mechanisms of synaptogenesis.

When it is realized that each neuron of the 200 billion neurons in the brain is destined to make and receive about 10,000 contacts with other cells (although some neurons make or receive up to 200,000 synaptic contacts) the problem of elucidating the rules and principles guiding the establishment of this astronomical number of synaptic connections in the normal mature brain becomes awesome indeed. There are no definitive answers to the major enigma of neurobiology, i.e., how do neurons make and maintain appropriate connections? There have, however, been abundant and heuristically valuable speculations based for the most part on "chemoaffinity" theories of one kind or another as noted above. Since the fundamental secrets of brain development remain shrouded in this problem, its solution will greatly facilitate an understanding of the impact of developmental perturbations on synaptogenesis.

Regulatory mechanisms in synapse formation and operation are being studied in a wide variety of biological preparations and even some artificial membrane systems. It is now appreciated that the nature of the target sought by a presynaptic element not only defines the number of synapses, but also the functional type of connections and the nature of the chemical transmitter that operates the synapse. It is now more than a quarter of a century since the first definitive nerve growth factor for the development of sympathetic ganglia was identified in salivary glands and other tissues. Since then, growth factors in

heart muscle, glial tumors, epidermal tissues, other neurons, etc., have been shown to play important roles in regulating the metabolic machinery for cell differentiation, neurite growth, transmitter synthesis, and synapse formation. The vast amount of work in the field of "trophic" agents raises the question of whether there are specific growth factors capable of influencing neuronal differentiation and synaptogenesis in the human cerebral cortex. Concerning this question, recent studies of neuronal storage diseases, in which morphological methods for demonstrating neurons in their entirety have been employed, have revealed the presence of neuritic growth and secondary but aberrant dendritic differentiation on mature human cortical neurons laden with gangliosides and other complex metabolites. It is now evident from these observations that neuronal storage disorders must be viewed as derangements of cell surface membrane regulation. What is more intriguing, however, is that findings of secondary dendritic growth and differentiation in neurons in these inborn errors of metabolism point to the role of gangliosides and probably other glycolipids and glycoproteins in the establishment of neuronal interrelations. It should be emphasized that neuronal diseases are invariably associated with mental retardation and in many instances progressive neurobehavioral deterioration and death. Hence the mechanisms of neuronal geometry distortion, new neurite and synapse formation, and other factors that alter neuronal function in these metabolic disorders must be clarified.

Research procedures for studying morphogenetic events at the light and electron microscopical levels are now sufficiently advanced to permit detailed analysis of immunofluorescent-labeled cell surface antigens, membrane particles, and a host of subcellular organelles related to neuronal and glial processes. There is, however, a paucity of data on the changing functional properties of immature neurons and their synaptic organizations, due in large part to inherent difficulties of obtaining viable preparations for *in vivo* studies at very early stages of ontogenesis. It must be emphasized that the basic business of the nervous system is information processing, and its currency is electrical signals of varying complexity. Such signals are generated across the plasma membrane and involve different ionic species and processes at different sites in dendrites, cell body axon, and pre- and postsynaptic components of synapses.

BIOCHEMICAL FRONTIERS

The pioneering studies of the early 1950s on the ionic basis of the nerve impulse and postsynaptic potentials served to uncover a wealth of mechanisms with which excitable cells generate different electrical activities. Early views of the physiological basis of the nerve impulse based on sequential changes in sodium and potassium permeabilities controlled by variations in the electrical field across the membrane have now been expanded to include consideration of gating mechanisms by which such fields open or close transmembrane ion channels. Many laboratories throughout the world are concerned with the problems of how different transmembrane ion channels are influenced by drugs, synaptic transmitter agents, and a host of other naturally occurring biologically active agents. The role of calcium in a variety of electrogenic as well as secretory and metabolic processes of neurons has been of special interest in view of the extent to which transmembrane as well as intracellular calcium ion kinetics determine transduction of sensory processes, the release of synaptic transmitter agents, and postsynaptic electrogenic and metabolic events triggered by activation of various cyclic nucleotides.

Unfortunately, virtually nothing is known about the factors that regulate or determine the number and distribution of different ion channels sensitive to membrane voltage or chemical transmitters in developing neurons. Data obtained from mature neurons and single axons point to an unequal distribution of sodium and potassium channels on the cell body surface and at different sites in axons. Calcium channels are ordinarily concentrated at presynaptic terminals. However, their presence in the dendrites of certain classes of central neurons, including dendrites of Purkinje cells of the cerebellum, and pyramidal neurons of the hippocampus, an old cortical structure, is now highly likely. Quite remarkably, the growth of dendrites of Purkinje cells is accompanied by the appearance of electrical responses that are dependent in part on calcium. While action potentials dependent upon sodium are normally found in the cell body and axons of Purkinje cells, dendrites make use of voltage sensitive changes in calcium permeability to generate a significant proportion of their electrical signals. There is also good evidence obtained in the past few years that calcium spikes in dendrites of hippocampal pyramidal cells may underlie the extraordinary excitability of these cells. Slow inward currents caused by calcium can activate newly discovered potassium currents that can repolarize the neuron and prepare it for cyclic excitability surges. It is imperative that more information be obtained on developmental factors regulating membrane electrogenesis, since it is evident that abnormalities in electrical signaling in neuronal subsystems can wreck havoc with normal synaptic transaction. One clue that this area of inquiry will yield important data relevant to basic mechanisms is the observation that in early states of neuronal maturation, pyramidal neurons of the cerebral neocortex exhibit partial and full spikes in dendrites, whereas dendritic spikes are not normally observed in mature neurons. Development in this instance is apparently accompanied by a redistribution or loss of ion channels or other processes regulating impulse generation in dendrites of these cells. An intriguing problem in this regard is the extent to which the changing electrical properties of dendritic membrane is related to the ontogenesis of dendritic spines, synapses, and other synapses on the dendritic shaft.

It is now well-established that at the developing nerve-muscle junction, there is a great change in the acetylcholine sensitivity of the muscle membrane surrounding the site at which the nerve makes synaptic contact with the muscle. Evidently at this time receptors for the transmitter are diffusely distributed, but at a later stage such receptors are concentrated at the synapse. Injury to the nerve, muscle tendon, or inactivity can result in a return of this diffuse chemosensitivity. Striking changes in dendritic excitability with retraction of synapses can also be observed in spinal motoneurons following damage to the axon. Do these alterations in membrane properties occur also in cortical neurons as a consequence of damage to synaptic pathways or functional inactivity? To answer this question will require new knowledge on the nature, turnover, and distribution of receptors and receptor-ionophores (i.e., molecules controlling ion channels in the membrane) in different parts of the neuron, the identity and mode of action of chemical agents that bind to these receptors, and how they modify the actions of other drugs and transmitters on synaptic and nonsynaptic membrane. Such information will bring us closer to answering how synapses are formed, influenced by neighboring synapses, and stabilized during development. This would be particularly pertinent knowledge, since it has recently been shown in several developing systems that more synapses are formed initially by different axons than is necessary for a particular function. One hypothesis is that chemical information is exchanged between pre- and postsynaptic elements that selectively stabilizes one type of connection at the expense of others. This important developmental process of 'synapse sculpturing' must undoubtedly play a role in shaping the functional circuitry of the maturing brain.

THE BRAIN AS THE MASTER GLAND

Much of the foregoing discussion of fundamental mechanisms in neuronal signaling has emphasized the role of neurosecretory processes, i.e., the release of chemical agents by neurons, in the overall functional activity of the brain. Since the synthesis, transport, release, postsynaptic action, and inactivation of chemical synaptic messengers are complex interacting events, it is little wonder that the study of identified and suspected synaptic transmitters or modulators of neuronal activity has become a major biological "growth industry." The hope that mental deficiency may be ameliorated by administration of specific chemicals or drugs capable of improving cognitive functions never flags. But expectations must be tempered by reality lest valuable research resources be dissipated in unsound therapeutic fads. There are encouraging signs that manipulation of the brain's chemical machinery may be a productive future strategy in the biomedical management of mental retardation. Such signs have emerged from new knowledge that the brain manufactures, stores, and distributes a wide variety of chemical agents of potential importance as transmitters or synapse modulators. That the brain is indeed the Master Gland—not the pituitary, as was once taught—is now abundantly clear from findings that a score of peptide releasing and release-inhibitory factors regulating pituitary hormones are located in neurons at the base of the brain in the hypothalamus. These neurons are in turn influenced by synaptic pathways whose neuron cell bodies and axons are rich in biogenic amines, amino acid transmitters, other peptides, and acetylcholine. In the past decade the number of such suspected transmitter/modular agents has nearly quadrupled—so that at least 30 distinct chemical entities are considered "putative transmitters."

The use of discrete microbiochemical techniques and parallel immunocytochemical and autoradiographic methods for detecting suspected transmitter/modulator agents has resulted in establishment of a new field of neuroanatomy involving the mapping of neuronal pathways and connections by biochemical and pharmacological probes. In fact, these new methods, which also make use of the fact that neurons can take up precursor or marker molecules and thereby light up different pathways, has resulted in the discovery of brain circuits that could not be visualized (or imagined) previously! The past decade of exciting discoveries promises to be surpassed by the prospects of the next decade as neuroscientists focus on the biochemical pharmacology of the brain. What findings are likely to impact upon research efforts in mental retardation? A few examples follow.

It is known that the biogenic amine pathways from the brain stem are among the earliest to invade the developing forebrain and primitive cerebral cortex. How do these newly discovered systems influence cortical development? Do the transmitters released by biogenic amine pathways produce effects that are fundamentally different from the classical effects of transmitters such as acetylcholine at the neuromuscular junction? What role do these amines play in producing long-term changes in synaptic activities at different stages of development?

Certain biogenic amines have been implicated in mechanisms of behavioral modification, particularly in animals with relatively simple nervous systems whose behaviors can be studied in precise morphophysiological detail. In the case of sensitization, a process whereby an animal learns to increase a given response to novel (or injurious) stimuli, it has been shown at a cellular level that sensitization involves the action of a biogenic amine, serotonin, that serves to increase cyclic AMP that in turn increases calcium influx and thereby enhances transmitter release at the sensitized synapse. These findings, which begin to relate overt specific behaviors to molecular events at the synapse, raise questions as to the role of biogenic amines, peptides, and other putative transmitters in the most complex operations of the human brain.

THE INTERDEPENDENCE
OF FORM AND FUNCTION

It has been known for many years that, although much of the neuronal circuitry of the brain is established via genetic instructions, the use to which this circuitry is put, as well as the disuse it suffers, can markedly alter the

normal functional, and in some instances, the structural integrity of the circuitry. The most outstanding example of this is seen in the visual system, in which depriving the brain of visual input from one eye early in development reduces the number of cortical neurons that receive input from both eyes when animals are tested sometime after the period of deprivation. Pharmacological manipulations of the biogenic amine innervation of the visual cortex during the deprivation period have been reported to markedly influence and even prevent the disuse effects, suggesting that such pathways can modulate trophic interactions between competing synaptic pathways. Do the functional changes in synaptic efficacy in developing cerebral cortex brought about by variations in sensory input in the laboratory animal bear upon the issue of functional retardation in the socially and educationally disadvantaged child? Only a great deal of additional research at all levels of neuronal organization in studies aimed at defining mechanisms of functional validation of developing synaptic pathways will provide an answer to this intriguing question.

A final point of possible relevance of transmitter agents to mental retardation research arises from recent studies on the relationship of dietary factors to amino acid precursors of amine transmitters in the brain. Evidently blood and brain levels of two important biogenic amine precursors, tyrosine and tryptophan, can be significantly manipulated by diet. Choline, a precursor of acetylcholine, another important brain transmitter, can also be modified by dietary intake. Since acetylcholine and the biogenic amines are believed to be important in motivational systems and learning and memory processes, it is not unlikely that deficits in these higher nervous functions could be due to or influenced by the availability of transmitter precursors. Further research along these lines in addition to the studies required on developmental mechanisms of synthesis, storage, release, and synaptic actions of transmitter/modular agents are of central importance in mental retardation research.

The final stage in the development of the

competent brain is the transformation of relatively slowly conducting pathways to high-speed conductile systems in accordance with specific requirements for rapid input-output information processing. This is accomplished by proliferation of oligodendroglia and their activation to produce the insulating myelin that ensheaths axons except at bare sites called nodes, at which sodium and potassium channels are concentrated. At myelinated segments between these nodes there is little or no current flow; hence the conducted impulse speedily "jumps" from node to node. The study of myelin with its complex proteins, lipids, glycoproteins, and glycolipids is still a major problem whose complexity increases annually. Myelination is known to be delayed or disorganized by a host of factors including malnutrition, hypothyroidism, and inborn errors of metabolism, all of which are associated with mental retardation. It is now strongly suspected that axons must engage in some sophisticated signal interaction with oligodendroglia for the latter elements to wrap extended portions of their cytoplasm around a number of different axons. What are these signals and how are they regulated? What mechanisms control the formation of nodal membrane in the axon with its high density of transmembrane ion channels? These questions, along with previous issues concerning the role of astroglia in the production of radial fibers for aiding neuronal migration implicate glia in some of the fundamental mechanisms of brain maturation. It would be difficult to envision a developmental disorder leading to severe mental retardation that did not impact upon the biological integrity of glial cells.

At this juncture in mental retardation research it is appropriate to shift the focus from basic membrane, cellular, and synaptic processes to the wider purview of aggregate neuronal operations distributed in different synaptic organizations. Despite intensive study, the problems of defining the morphophysiological substrate of sensation, perception, or the mechanisms underlying even the simplest volitional movements remain unresolved. There is a great need to explore further the sensory transduction process at different types of receptors, particularly for audition and vision, and to employ new anatomical marker techniques for identifying neurons at various way stations that are subjected to extensive physiological study in behaving animals. Multiple microelectrode recording techniques for simultaneous registration of electrical signals and on-line computer-assisted methods of data analysis must be further refined to allow for the investigation of event-related activities at several sites. In this way, clues may be forthcoming on the significance of distributed activities in different subsystems involved in particular sensorimotor functions, as well as memory and learning.

Computer-assisted methods of recording and analyzing evoked potentials in human subjects are now available that permit detection of potential changes localized to relatively small portions of the brain. In several studies, signals have been recorded that relate to language functions in auditory and visual modalities in normal and perceptually impaired subjects. Attempts are also being made to employ these techniques to provide objective neurophysiological measures of behavioral competency as an adjunct to neurological and behavioral assessment of preterm infants at risk for mental retardation. Continued exploration of these tactics for early detection of neurobehavioral deficits may permit development of intervention strategies for prevention of later cognitive disabilities in a population of high-risk preterm infants.

While much important research on the development of normal and aberrant perceptual and cognitive processes in the human infant can be anticipated with the sophisticated computer-based electrophysiological and behaviorial techniques noted above, a wide range of more basic issues concerning the organization of the cerebral cortex and its related structures requires continuing consideration. Genetic factors in cortical organization can be profitably examined in morphophysiological, biochemical, and immunobiological studies of mutants and various hybrid strains of mice (chimeras). These studies have already yielded abundant data on determinants of cellular architecture and organization in different types of cortex and other laminar structures, and can be expected to be continuously productive. Other animal models of metabolic disorders that mirror in all respects inherited deficiencies in human infants should also be utilized more widely. For example, feline G_{M1} and G_{M2}-gangliosidosis is a superb model of human storage diseases such as Tay-Sachs disease and offers strong likelihood of providing basic date on the mechanisms of brain dysfunctions in a wide range of neuron storage diseases.

Models of abnormal brain function have also been developed over several decades with various surgical or chemical techniques for the production of discrete lesions. Much information on the response of the immature brain to the loss of basal ganglia structures and related systems has been obtained in recent studies employing both surgical and neurotoxin techniques. The use of such neurotoxins including kainic acid and other toxic analogues of putative transmitter agents to eliminate specific pharmacologically distinct components of complex pathways should provide critical data on the contributions of different systems to overt behavioral abnormalities. Several heuristic models of neurobehavioral ''retardation'' in rats with selective neurotoxin-induced lesions of biogenic amine pathways produced in the neonatal period are already yielding data on possible mechanisms of mental retardation.

IS THE BRAIN MODIFIABLE?

This brief survey of problems and perspectives of mental retardation research would be incomplete without consideration of the most intriguing question in contemporary neuroscience: Is the brain modifiable? The immediate answer to this of course is: Whose brain and what is meant by modifiability? It has long been known that lower vertebrates such as fish and amphibia possess a remarkable potential for regenerating different parts of the central nervous system. Recovery of function following damage to the motor system in immature monkeys is rapid and virtually complete in contrast to similar damage in adult animals, but why this is so has escaped adequate explanation. In the past decade remarkable ''plasticity'' of neural pathways has been demonstrated in young and even in adult mammals. Whereas neuroscientists were previously busy detailing the reasons why brain neurons could *not* regenerate or sprout new axons and synapses, now they are recording all the conditions in which axonal sprouting and new synapse formation can be achieved. The question is no longer, ''Why don't mammalian central neurons regenerate axons and synapses?'', but rather, ''What are the factors preventing axonal regrowth after injury?'' The turnabout in conceptualization augers well for mental retardation research, for advantage must be taken of every opportunity to disclose the factors preventing or restricting synaptogenesis and regeneration of damaged axons if, as it is currently suspected, some forms of mental retardation are associated with faulty synaptogenesis.

The problem of brain modifiability is not exclusively a problem of damaged axons sprouting new collaterals and synapses. For example, recovery from frontal cortex lesions in infant monkeys is associated with new connections that form between intact cortex and certain subcortical structures. It has also been shown that training infant monkeys before they sustain frontal cortical lesions can greatly facilitate recovery of functions involving the damaged cortex. Here behavior is in some fashion facilitating mechanisms of functional recovery. Whereas the neurobiological dogma was once: ''Neurons make synapses and synapses make behavior'', now it may have to be added that ''Behavior modifies synapses!'' Are there ''motivational'' systems that employ the vast biogenic amine, peptidergic, etc., projection pathways of the neuraxis that are capable of facilitating (or restricting) synaptogenesis and recovery of function? Clearly every avenue of approach dealing with the cellular and integrative neurobiology of restitution and modification of brain function should be high-priority mental retardation research.

CONCLUSION

Clearly, the neurosciences have begun to make significant inroads into answering basic questions concerning the mechanisms that produce the symptom of mental retardation. These basic research efforts have focused on three specific areas:

1. The understanding of the morpho-physiological mechanisms underlying the development of normal brain function

2. The identification and analysis of pathogenetic factors producing aberrant neurobehavioral development

3. The definition of strategies for preventing or ameliorating mental retardation

The pace and richness of current neuroscience research efforts augers well for the further elucidation of the impaired or faulty maturation of the central nervous system's mechanisms that produce the symptom of mental retardation.

Curative Aspects of Mental Retardation:
Biomedical and Behavioral Advances
edited by Frank J. Menolascino, M.D., Ronald Neman, Ph.D., and Jack A. Stark, Ph.D.
Copyright 1983   Paul H. Brookes Publishing Co., Inc.   Baltimore · London

chapter 6

Neuropathological Abnormalities

Search for Causative Agents

ROGER S. WILLIAMS, M.D.
Eunice Kennedy Shriver Center for Mental Retardation
Waltham, Massachusetts

As ELUDED TO IN CHAPTER 5, it is axiomatic in scientific medicine that treatments and cures are predicated upon precise
diagnoses. In turn, precise diagnoses are
based upon specific information about underlying pathophysiological mechanisms. Although the theme of this book is cures, the
truth is that few cures are today available in
most cases of mental retardation, due to the
paucity of information about causative factors.

The dilemma of the neuropathologist is
largely technical. In cases of *intrauterine*
disease the neuropathologist is generally presented with brain material that is in poor
condition, coming from abortuses or stillborn
infants long dead. Even in cases of survival
after intrauterine insult, brain material comes
to the pathologist late, long after the disease
process was active. Therefore our ability to
define causes in individual human cases is
extremely limited.

NEUROPATHOLOGICAL APPROACHES

The new approaches to neuropathology, reviewed in Chapters 4 and 5, are unique and

potentially powerful. The approach outlined
in Chapter 4 uses conventional histological
methods that have been available to pathologists for almost 100 years to systematically
reexamine the histology and topography of
brain pathology, utilizing contemporary concepts of developmental neurobiology. Such
an approach permits more precise estimates
as to *when* during development the pathological process was maximally active. Further, the neuropathologist can formulate hypotheses, based upon established pathological principles, as to which disease states
may reasonably account for the observed
changes. These hypotheses can in turn be
tested by clinical epidemiology or by the
development of appropriate animal models.

An impression gained repeatedly from
neuropathological examination of human developmental disorders, such as those outlined
in Chapter 4, is that many seem to arise
secondary to acquired destructive processes.
When an etiology can be defined, particularly
for those disorders arising during the second
half of gestation, it is congenital infection or
cerebral perfusion failure (Friede, 1975). Maternal hypoxia, diabetes, hypotension and

69

hypertension, premature placental separation or excessive infarction, and premature delivery are all known to be potentially significant in this regard.

A case reported recently by Adams, Prod'hom, and Rabinowicz (1977) highlights the need for further research. They examined the brain of an infant born with severe generalized hypotonia and respiratory insufficiency. Death occurred a few hours after birth and neuropathological examination revealed widespread nerve cell loss and a prominent inflammatory response, dating the pathology to at least a week before birth. There was no evidence of congenital infection or placental pathology. In retrospect the mother was aware that fetal movement had seemed less just prior to delivery, but her health was judged to be excellent and no other adverse factors were identified.

Experiments with fetal monkeys merit further investigation in this connection (Myers, 1975; Myers & Myers, 1979). The Myerses have developed surgical techniques whereby monkey fetuses can be removed temporarily from the uterus while appropriate monitoring devices are applied, then returned to the uterus for the remainder of gestation. When the pregnant monkeys are later restrained for testing, unanesthetized mothers become fearful and exhibit appropriate autonomic responses. Although maternal blood pressure and pulse rise appropriately, the cerebral circulation of the fetus may fall substantially, sometimes to levels compatible with tissue destruction. Placental and fetal cerebral circulation are protected, however, when the pregnant monkey is lightly anesthetized. Experiments of this type may provide new insights into the pathophysiology of placental and fetal cerebral circulation which, when combined with improved antepartum care and noninvasive techniques of fetal monitoring, could result in earlier detection and prevention of ischemic encephalopathies.

The second innovative approach, outlined in Chapter 5, carries the level of analysis to individual nerve cells, their processes, and subcellular organelles. Investigation of nerve cell pathology relies heavily upon high resolution cytological methods, that is, electron microscopy and Golgi impregnations. Unfortunately, the high resolution afforded by the electron microscope makes it extraordinarily susceptible to artifactual changes resulting from suboptimal fixation. The Golgi impregnations are very old methods that have been resurrected for use in clinical neuropathology with gratifying results. The silver and mercury chromate impregnations, developed by Golgi almost 100 years ago, allow the neuropathologist to entirely analyze the surface area of individual cells. Golgi methods are also relatively high resolution, and are therefore susceptible to artifacts resulting from poor fixation, but the requirements for optimal fixation are less stringent than for electron microscopy (Williams, Ferrante, & Caviness, 1978). The selection of appropriate cases for study by brain biopsy makes the technical limitations inherent in these methods more relative than absolute. Conventional cell and fiber stains, the Golgi methods, and electron microscopy all have unique capabilities and, when used together, permit the best possible opportunity for defining the locus and distribution of cellular pathological changes in human neurological disorders. Unfortunately, electron microscopy is seldom of benefit when applied to postmortem brain tissue obtained at the time of autopsy.

When brains judged to be "normal" by conventional histological methods are examined in Golgi impregnations, many are found to have abnormalities of dendritic structure of potential significance for the neuronal malfunction that characterizes them (Huttenlocher, 1974; Marin-Padilla, 1976; Purpura, 1974). Golgi analysis has also provided important new insights into the evolution of cerebral malformations (Caviness & Williams, 1979; Williams, Ferrante, & Caviness, 1976) such as the prenatal origin of nerve cell pathology in sex-linked copper malabsorption syndrome (Williams, Caviness, Marshall, & Lott, 1978) and the cellular pathology of spongiform encephalopathies (Landis, Williams, & Masters, 1981). Golgi and electron microscopic analyses of cerebral cortical neurons in lipid storage diseases confirm that changes in axonal and dendritic structure appear in response to the accumulation of intracytoplasmic lysosomal inclusions long before evidence for frank nerve cell degeneration, leaving open the possibility that appropriate therapy may arrest the process before irreversible changes occur.

Despite these exciting advances, the brains of some individuals with severe mental retardation and behavioral abnormalities still defy pathological classification even when examined by all the methods mentioned above (Huttenlocher, 1974; Williams, Hauser, & Purpura, 1980). In part, this may be because the geometry of nerve cells is exceedingly complex and subtle and significant changes in the branching complexity of their neurites may go unrecognized by the unaided eye of the neuropathologist. Quantitative morphometric techniques are being employed currently to facilitate examination of these cases (Buell & Coleman, 1981; Matthysee & Williams, 1980; Paldino & Purpura, 1979).

RESEARCH IN THE NEUROSCIENCES

It is also probable that some cases of mental retardation result from abnormalities at a molecular level that are pejorative to nerve cell function but are beyond the resolution even of the electron microscope. Recent technological advances in the neurosciences are being adapted increasingly for application to the human brain and hold great promise for expanding the frontiers of neuropathological investigation in the near future. It is now feasible, for example, to take small pieces of brain tissues obtained from humans at biopsy or post mortem for quantitative analysis of neurotransmitters and their enzymes. This approach has resulted in important insights into the molecular pathology of schizophrenia and the neurodegenerative disorders of late life (Bird, 1980). Mass spectrophotometry may also be used to survey body fluid, such as the spinal fluid and small cellular fractions from selected brain regions, for biochemical differences of potential importance for mental retardation. Immunocytochemical techniques have recently been applied successfully to human postmortem tissue and can demonstrate the cellular location and regional distribution of neuropeptides (Zalneraitis, Marshall, & Landis, 1981). It is now possible to separate individual neuronal populations from human brain tissue post mortem for precise analysis of structural proteins (Selkoe, 1980), and to isolate and sustain their ribosomes and other subcellular organelles *in vitro* to identify and analyze the activity of short-lived cytoplasmic enzymes of importance for normal cellular regulation (Gilbert, Brown, Strocchi, Bird, & Marotta, 1981).

In summary, it is hoped that application of these and other technological advances to the investigation of human mental retardation can be expected to result in a better understanding of the etiology and pathogenesis of disorders and improved strategies of prevention, treatment, and curative approaches in the future.

REFERENCES

Adams, R.D., Prod'hom, L.S., & Rabinowicz, T. Intrauterine brain death: Neuro-axial reticular core necrosis. *Acta Neuropathologica,* 1977, *40,* 41–49.

Bird, E.D. A brain tissue resource center to promote research in schizophrenia. In: C. Baxter & T. Melnechuk (eds.), *Perspectives in schizo-* *phrenia research.* New York: Raven Press, 1980.

Buell, S.J., & Coleman, P.D. Quantitative evidence for selected dendritic growth in normal aging but not in senile dementia. *Brain Research,* 1981, *214,* 23–41.

Caviness, V.S., Jr., & Williams, R.S. Cellular

pathology of the developing human nervous system. In: B. Katzman (ed.), *Congenital and acquired cognitive disorders,* ARNMD. New York: Raven Press, 1979.

Friede, R.L. *Developmental neuropathology.* New York: Springer-Verlag, 1975.

Gilbert, J.M., Brown, B.A., Strocchi, P., Bird, E.D., & Marotta, C.A. The preparation of biologically active messenger RNA from human post-mortem brain tissue. *Journal of Neurochemistry,* 1981, *36,* 976–984.

Huttenlocher, P.R. Dendritic development in neocortex of children with mental defect and infantile spasms. *Neurology,* 1974, *24,* 203–210.

Landis, D.M.D., Williams, R.S., & Masters, C.L. Golgi and electron microscopic studies of spongiform encephalopathy. *Neurology,* 1981, *31,* 538–549.

Marin-Padilla, M. Pyramidal cell abnormalities in motor cortex of child with Down's Syndrome: A Golgi study. *Journal of Comparative Neurology,* 1976, *167,* 63–82.

Matthysee, S., & Williams, R.S. Quantitative neurohistology with a computer microscope. In: C. Baxter & R.T. Melnechuk (eds.), *Perspectives in schizophrenia research.* New York: Raven Press, 1980.

Myers, R.E., Four patterns of perinatal brain damage and their condition of occurrence in primates. In: B.S. Meldrum & C.D. Marsden (eds.), *Primate models of neurological disorders.* New York: Raven Press, 1975.

Myers, R.E. & Myers, S.E. Use of sedative, analgesic, and anesthetic drugs during labor and delivery: Bane or boon? *American Journal of Obstetrics and Gynecology,* 1979, *133,* 83–104.

Paldino, A.M., & Purpura, D.P. Quantitative analysis of the spatial distribution of axonal and dendritic terminals of hippocampal pyramidal neurons in immature brain. *Experimental Neurology,* 1979, *64,* 604–619.

Purpura, D.P. Dendritic spine dysgenesis and mental retardation. *Science,* 1974, *186,* 1126–1128.

Selkoe, D.J. Altered protein composition of isolated human cortical neurons in Alzheimer's disease. *Annals of Neurology,* 1980, *8,* 468–478.

Williams, R.S., Caviness, V.S., Jr., Marshall, P.C., & Lott, I.T. The cellular pathology of Menke's steely hair syndrome. *Neurology,* 1978, *28,* 575–583.

Williams, R.S., Ferrante, R.J., & Caviness, V.S., Jr. The cellular pathology of microgyria: A Golgi analysis. *Acta Neuropathologica,* 1976, *36,* 269–283.

Williams, R.S., Ferrante, R.J., & Caviness, V.S., Jr. The Golgi-rapid method in clinical neuropathology: Morphologic consequences of suboptimal fixation. *Journal of Neuropathology and Experimental Neurology,* 1978, *37,* 13–33.

Williams, R.S., Hauser, S.L., & Purpura, D.P. Autism and mental retardation, neuropathologic studies performed in four retarded persons with autistic behavior. *Archives of Neurology,* 1980, *37,* 749–753.

Zalneraitis, E.L., Marshall, P.C., & Landis, D.M.D. Immunocytochemical studies of neuropeptides in Huntington's Disease. *Neurology,* 1981, *31,* 63.

Curative Aspects of Mental Retardation:
Biomedical and Behavioral Advances
edited by Frank J. Menolascino, M.D., Ronald Neman, Ph.D., and Jack A. Stark, Ph.D.
Copyright 1983   Paul H. Brookes Publishing Co., Inc.   Baltimore · London

Conclusion

FRANK J. MENOLASCINO, M.D.
University of Nebraska Medical Center
Omaha, Nebraska

A REVIEW OF THE TOPIC OF PREVENTION of genetic diseases that cause mental retardation reveals a large number of causes of genetic disorders. Yet, recognizing the cause, in cases where that is possible, is only the beginning. Dr. Hugo Moser, in his recent review examined whether it was, in fact, possible to apply the tools we already have to prevent genetic disease and mental retardation (Moser, 1982). He concluded that if we utilized all that we currently know, we might be able, in the near future, to prevent some 30% of the major causes of severe mental retardation. Certainly that is a reachable goal. In reviewing the causes of mental retardation and the variety of mechanisms involved, one must start at the *initial* cause. Whether that cause is genetic or acquired, it becomes clear that, as one discusses cures in mental retardation, it is much more instructive to look first at the genetic aspects of mental retardation.

GENETIC ASPECTS OF MENTAL RETARDATION

It is currently difficult to imagine a cure for vascular or other phenomena that cause global or semi-global damage in the brain. Cures for serious genetic disease can be envisaged, however, if one looks at the variety of mechanisms already known. These mechanisms can—either singly or together—be the initiating insult to the brain.

Gene mutations, chromosomal breaks, or nondisjunctions might appear at the same time, be sequential in the same case, or later lead in a multiple fashion to the developing problem. All these basic aspects of cause (including excessive or reduced cell death, a cell failing its coded directions to reduce the synthesis of a variety of different substances, etc.) might ultimately be narrowed down to a final common pathway. After all, the organism can respond in only so many ways. If one is sick, for example, one may vomit and have diarrhea. There are over a hundred causes of each of these symptoms, but ultimately the symptoms are the common endpoint that the body displays and that are seen clinically in the sick person. In the same manner, a common pathway of a genetic disease might be manifested in essentially too few cells or cell products to affect the localized formation of tissues, maturation of tissues, function of tissues, or may cause other imbalances in that evolvement. The final product is the symptom of mental retardation. Thus, a variety of insults, acting singly or together, can follow a common or uncommon pathway to a final defect.

Chemical changes that might occur, whether from radiation, drugs, viruses, etc., may alter the sequence in the cellular DNA molecule. Again, a variety of possible effects exist, so the change in the cellular DNA molecular sequences could affect a single base pair, it could affect long segments, it could produce all kinds of changes in the DNA, and open up an entire arena of problems. All of these possible problems lead, if these insults occur at a germinal phase, to inheritable disorders, or to those that we think are simply sporadic in nature (i.e., affecting somatic cells as opposed to the germinal cells).

When one considers environmental insults, there is a critical need to assess the stages of gestation at which the insult occurs. These are fairly well recognized in terms of organ formation and malformation. For example, if the insult occurs between the 21st day and the 45th day of gestation, then the fetus's heart, eyes, limbs (etc.) may be affected, and one may ascertain with reasonable certainty when a particular defect occurred. This process is especially well-noted in the diethylstilbestrol as well as the thalidomide experiences (i.e., in thalidomide, the mother must ingest it at a particular stage of gestation, while beyond that critical point malformations do not appear secondary to its presence). Unfortunately, these processes are not so easily understood because, for example, it has been documented that twins exposed to thalidomide at the same time have been affected in quite different ways: one was severely retarded while the other was only mildly retarded—in an identical twin pregnancy!

In the genetic determination of abnormality, either from mutational or truly genetic origin, certain processes may influence cell proliferation, the migration of cells, and the organization of cells in an organ or other systems. Consider, for example, that in the formation of the fingers and the digits that they initially form as a clump, and that there is initially programmed cell death in the development and migration of cells along an axis so as to form a complete hand. Chemotaxic events can interfere with the actual programming of cell death to form the fingers of the hand so that these stepwise events are interrupted. Thus, on either a hereditary or a sporadic basis, very short fingers, extra fingers, etc., might form. Furthermore, the kinds of causative agents that cross the placenta, whether they be teratogenic or mutagenic, can cause all kinds of effects besides malformations.

The concept of behavioral teratogenesis, which is now increasingly recognized, was first exemplified by experiments in which the administration to pregnant rats of substances like chlorpromazine (Thorazine) would cause, in subsequent generations, learning deficits. Exposed pregnant rats have offspring who ultimately are unable to learn (e.g., tasks such as maze learning)—all deficits induced by the chlorpromazine. In the human, we know virtually nothing about the agents that can cause these behavioral phenomena, whether they be learning deficits or perhaps even mild mental retardation syndromes.

One of the most disconcerting factors about intrauterine exposure is the delayed effects. We now know much about the effects of X rays and diet. We also know, for example, that regarding smoking in pregnancy, the birth weight is directly associated with the amount of smoking (i.e., the higher the number of cigarettes smoked, the lower the birth weight), and, furthermore, that it is now also reasonably well established that learning deficits are more common among offspring of women who have smoked considerably in pregnancy. The questions are how? why? Is it simply a transfusional oxygen phenomenon because of the interference with perfusion of the embryo or the fetus, or does something else interfere with the synaptic and other developments in the developing brain?

Concern should also be directed to other factors that overlie both the development of malformation and cancer. We know, for example, that if pregnant rabbits or pregnant rats are exposed to nitrosic urea compounds (which are carcinogenic) the offspring develop cancers (often brain tumors) with a frequency approaching 100%. Of further concern is that these cancers develop about 6 months *after* the birth of the rat that has been exposed *in utero,* which is equivalent to about 17 or 20 years in human terms. Also, we now know that if one takes mice who have been exposed to these compounds (i.e., in the uterus when the mother was exposed) and reexamine sequential generations of the offspring of such mice, we notice with alarm that subsequent generations show a higher frequency of tumor formation or cancers. We suddenly begin to note the evolvement of a kind of genetic propensity toward cancer.

Turning to the questions of causes and mechanisms of mental retardation within the organ systems and the chromosomes, single gene disorders, and polygenic disorders, we find problems that exemplify why it is so difficult to produce basic approaches to cures in mental retardation. For example, if one looks at the chromosomal section of chromosome number 13 or 18, the dogma and current conventional wisdom would suggest that just because there is an extra chromosome, as in trisomy 21, or an extra 18 present, that the extra chromosome is the cause of the malformation. Though it is appealing to think that way, we may ultimately be trapped by such a narrow interpretation, for it is also possible that the extra chromosome (e.g., chromosome 21), is simply only a reflection of the fundamental insult and is itself only a part of the body appearance resulting from the chromosomal defect. That is, in the child with Down syndrome who has an extra chromosome number 21, the fundamental genetic insult may be at the cell's surface, not allowing appropriate cell-to-cell interactions or interfering with cell-to-cell communications or recognition of other signals that are implicit in the formation of tissues. Thus, the extra chromosome may be only another bodily manifestation (at the tissue level) of the still unknown cause of Down syndrome, and not its cause!

It is also recognized that within the same family there may be enormous differences in the severity of the expression of a genetic disorder. For example, in neurofibromatosis some infants have only a few skin spots, while others are severely affected. We have only recently begun to recognize that in the pregnant mother who is herself affected—as compared to where there is no family history—the offspring of the affected mother has neurofibromatosis that is more frequently and severely involved. What is it in the maternal uterine milieu that makes for this excess suppression of the underlying genetic disorder?

We also do not know why the father's age should relate to the development of a series of genetic disorders. The role of advanced paternal age in the occurrence of achondroplasia was perhaps among the earlier genetic disorders that have been recognized in that association. Nor do we know why advanced maternal age necessarily is associated with the increased frequency of chromosome disorders like Down syndrome. There is much speculation about nondisjunction being due to stickiness of the "odd" chromosomes, etc. These conditions are not related to the nondisjunction phenomenon in chromosomes.

There is the classical challenge of the storage diseases exemplified by the child who is physically normal for an entire year, but has had the biochemical enzymatic deficiency evident at 14 weeks of gestation (if not before that time). These children are born perfectly normal and attain all of the milestones at 1 year, but then they deteriorate gradually and become severely retarded from metachromatic leukedystrophy or one of the other storage disorders. If one observes the embryonic fluid cells under the electron microscope in these storage disorders, one notes cell inclusions that clearly signal the presence of the metabolic disorders *in utero*. We are also faced, in the same group of inborn metabolic disorders, with the clear recognition that there are different forms of the same disorder: infantile forms that are severe, less-severe, and later-onset types of these disorders. This finding implies either different enzyme mutation, subunit mutations, or some other change in the basic enzyme disorder that is allowing for a long-term evolution of the disorder. These types of causes of enzyme deficiency convey some idea of the difficulty in approaching the question of cure.

A disease that develops as a consequence of, for example, failure of intestinal absorption of copper provides an opportunity to think of causes of mental retardation that arise as a consequence of problems distant from the brain. Many of these conditions are exemplified by the diabetic mother who has a higher frequency—perhaps double the frequency—of bearing infants with congenital malformation. What is it in the diabetic milieu that produces this higher rate? Is it the general metabolic milieu, or is it the genes? One is not sure.

TECHNIQUES IN PREVENTION

The above examples demonstrate how problematic it is simply to view the end product of the symptom of mental retardation and talk about cure. What is being done about prevention? Though we continue efforts in genetic counseling, potential parents continue to make subsequent decisions (i.e., secondary to genetic counseling visits) that defeat the major intents of counseling. High risk people should deter. Drs. Aubrey Milunsky and Mary Jo Harrod, in Chapter 1 and 3 respectively, emphasized that genetic counseling is underutilized and that individual awareness of risk needs to be increased. We are not now reaching enough of the parents of the potential patient. Perhaps this is because we most frequently approach genetic counseling with a nondirective slant; we do not—and should not—tell people what to do with their reproductive autonomy.

What have we done about prenatal detection? The message essentially is that we have made a relative shambles of our efforts to provide ethnic or other carrier-detection systems. For Tay-Sachs disease, screening works reasonably well, but there are ethnic couples still marrying in the U.S. without having had a carrier-detection test. Artificial insemination by donor is an extremely important option in the management of couples who have high risks for conceiving infants with associated disease. More than 10,000 infants a year are born in this country as a consequence of artificial insemination donors. We have done screening for inborn errors, even though detection rates are sometimes infinitesimally small, and there are questions as to whether this is a cost-beneficial activity. State legislatures and other public concerns are also demanding cost-benefit analyses for screening efforts since the basic message is: "With the tools we have, we should be able to do very well."

The requisites for effective enzyme therapy are enormously demanding and provide serious obstacles to the easy manipulation or administration of enzymes that might benefit an individual. The question arises as to when an embryo or child should be submitted to this kind of enzyme supplementation. We know from the lipid storage disorders that if the neuropathology of the brain is examined at 14 weeks' gestation, stored gangliosides and other changes are already found to be present. There is the allied problem of the blood-brain barrier as a roadblock for enzyme therapy. How does one direct enzymes, provided either by lysosomes or other techniques, into the area where they are needed? Genetic diseases have been treated in various ways: we have tried avoidance as, for example, avoiding the galactose in galactosemia; we have tried restriction, as restricting protein in the urea cycle disorder; we have tried replacement, as in pancreatic enzymes in cystic fibrosis; allied techniques in Wilson's disese; supplementation of vitamin D, and many other kinds of supplementation. On balance, and despite its remarkably poor utilization, we have perhaps succeeded most with prenatal diagnosis. However, even in its widest context, prenatal diagnosis has only a relatively narrow application in the ultimate prevention of mental retardation.

We know that in people of advanced maternal age (i.e., age 35 and over) there are risks that lead to the recommendation of amniocentesis studies. In some states, amniocentesis is utilized for almost 10% of pregnant mothers who are "at risk." There are over 100 different inborn errors of metabolism that we can diagnose today through amniocentesis, but we need to answer a specific question: Was there a previously affected child? Without that information there is no way of doing a profile or running a diagnostic test on a particular embryonic fluid or cells therein.

For the polygenic disorders, such as anencephaly or spina bifida in the fetus of about 18 weeks' gestation, Dr. Milunsky in Chapter 1, reviewed his experiences with 20,000 cases from around the nation as to the alpha fetoprotein determination. As he has noted (Milunsky, personal communication, 1981):

> We are faced with the fact that if we examine all "at-risk" pregnancies, we note that about 1 in 10 of all the offspring of these pregnancies end up with a neurotube defect (i.e., hydrocephaly). We should only be examining this 10%—but 9 out of 10 babies who are born with neurotube defects are born to women who have not previously had an affected child. For that reason fetal serum protein testing has actively evolved. Its detection efficiency approximates 90%. But now we find that nationwide there is little money to pursue this testing. . . .

Other diagnostic tools are available, such as the angiogram, the sonogram that illustrates that we can diganose hydrocephalus in a 16 or 18 week fetus, fetoscopy that allows not only the visualization of fetal defects inside of the pregnant uterus, but also the opportunity to obtain blood samples and make diagnoses such as sickle cell anemia and thalassemia.

Looking to the future, the chromosome analysis of 1990 will almost certainly cause people to look back and say, "What an unbelievably rough and unsophisticated method they had in 1983 to distinguish one chromosome from another only by its individual bands." Ultimately we will be using the cell sorter literally to pull out of the mothers' blood the fetal cells that are circulating (rather than obtain them via the currently more costly and technologically involved amniocentesis procedure). These fetal cells contain the whole sample for genetic-DNA material. (Incidentally, the reason why the cell sorter has not succeeded to date is that the fetal cells that circulate into the mother's blood cannot be induced to divide, i.e., to go into metaphase, probably because they are not true lymphocytes. Nevertheless, these fetal cells that the cell sorter finds contain the DNA that is required for making an analysis and study.) We know from past experiments that, in bacteria, we can take DNA and isolate it, literally chop it up with enzymes called restriction endonucleases, and these chopped up segments of DNA can be placed on special polyacrylamide gels. Ultimately one can develop cleavage maps—of how to specifically chop up the DNA into specific fragments. There are several hundred specific cleavage enzymes by now that allow for specific chopping off of DNA segments. One can imagine the residents of 2010 referring to a booklet provided by the regional genetics laboratory that says that if one wants to test for x disease, this is what must be sent to the laboratory. A doctor may say which chromosome he or she wants, because the various DNA loci would already be known by specific gene mapping. And individuals will be told, of course, that at the site of specific cleavages on the DNA some of the newly ordered fragments can easily be recombined and the remaining DNA fragments in a patient under one's care can be amplified upon. One will be able, for example, to sequence in a row the specific nucleotides received from the regional genetic laboratory and determine what sequence should be investigated for the treatment or cure of a specific cause of mental retardation. Ultimately, we will have the ability to synthesize the nucleotides of predetermined sequences and then take those sequences and inject them into the human ovarian follicle, and perhaps directly influence fertilization by introducing these particular sequences at the appropriate time. It is exciting to contemplate and speculate upon the advances that lie ahead.

Many professionals concerned with genetics note that we must talk more to general audiences, rather than to other experts. They see communication among the specialities as one of the greatest stumbling blocks in past and current genetic research efforts. Each of us can speak to colleagues in our particular specialty and make ourselves readily understood; but the problem is that when we try to listen to colleagues in other settings, then they forget that we haven't the slightest idea what an obscure nerve is! So we must promote the notion of ongoing interchanges of our information bases; and, in that way, a subject as diffuse as the multiple manifestations of retardation can be more properly advanced.

POSTNATAL TREATMENT OF CHROMOSOME ABNORMALITIES

The frequency with which chromosome abnormalities are found in the developing fetus and infant is not easily determined. To begin with, there is the gray period subsequent to pregnancy—which is about 2 weeks after conception—since until implantation has occurred, pregnancy is not generally recognized by the woman who bears the pregnancy itself. We know almost nothing about the first 2 weeks of the postconceptional period. It was pointed out that chromosome abnormalities in the human are extraordinarily common—far more common than was ever appreciated prior to the reports of clinical studies. The frequency of the role of chromosomal abnormalities in the newborn population is really *only* because nature has seen fit to eliminate the vast majority of chromosomal abnormalities prior to the delivery period. Accordingly, as we increasingly improve the health status of the fetus *in utero,* we might have a greater survival of individuals who have very serious and basic abnormalities. Thus, chromosomal abnormalities are numerically—including the first recognized chromosomal abnormalities *in utero*—perhaps the largest types of disease to which human beings are prone! Even though most of these disorders are currently "eliminated" via spontaneous abortion, we do have approximately *one in every 200 births* with chromosomal abnormalities. Approximately half of those are silent abnormalities, in that they cannot be recognized in the newborn infant. These are largely with sex chromosomal abnormalities that are more manifest at adolescence than in infancy or childhood.

The chromosomal disorders that we do recognize are serious ones such as trisomy 21 (or Down syndrome). A key point to be stressed is that in the past it has been assumed that since these chromosomal disorders originated in the *in utero* period (i.e., they are congenital in origin), and occur at the time of conception, that it is impossible to cure such disorders if we begin our attack at the time of the newborn period. In Chapter 2, Dr. Park S. Gerald presented compelling evidence that this postnatal nontreatability thesis is invalid. Indeed, we may soon be able to proceed with efforts to effectively treat or ameliorate these chromosomal conditions in the infant, if not truly effect a cure. Dr. Gerald examined the nontreatability thesis by first discussing the concept that a congenital malformation, particularly one typified by a chromosomal abnormality such as Down syndrome, is necessarily something that takes its total course of damage *in utero, prior* to the time at which we customarily begin to attack problems of a disease state. He elected a different chromosomal abnormality than Down syndrome to make his point, and stated that the example was a prototype that directly relates to the postnatal treatment of chromosomal abnormalities. The disease he discussed was Kartagener's syndrome; individuals with this syndrome have chronic lung and respiratory airway disease (bronchiectasis) and situs inversus totalis (i.e., individuals who have their internal organs literally reversed from one side to the other—though the heart is normally on the left side, in these individuals their hearts are on the right side of the chest, etc.). Aside from the major body organ position displacement (which really causes these individuals essentially no difficulty unless a surgeon tries to remove an appendix from the right side when it is really on the left) these people do suffer primarily from respiratory disease, sinusitis, and recurrent ear infections. In the earlier studies of Kartagener's syndrome it was not at all clear *how* having organs on the wrong side of the body would lead to respiratory disease, although there were a number of individuals who attempted contorted explanations, such as the suggestion that the twisting of the lungs around (during embryonic life), caused the bronchi of the respiratory tree to become kinked and led to accumulation of secretions and the resultant sinusitis and lung infections. However, except for the reversal of organ placement, people with Kartagener's syndrome were thought to be as normal as nonaffected individuals. A new insight into this particular disease came when two patients (both males), independent of one another but relatively concurrent in time, sought help in infertility clinics in Scandinavia. In line with the emphasis on infertility studies in Scandinavia, these two individuals were studied extensively and were tested as to their sperm count and shape (i.e., morphology) and sperm viability and motility. Sperm in normal male individuals are extremely fast-moving cells that are constantly in motion. Thus, it was startling to see that the sperm from these two males were totally immotile. The sperm were not dead—they were completely metabolically normal—but their tails were absolutely straight instead of being in violent motion. Sperm motility has been a subject of great interest to geneticists and electron microscopists for a number of years, and the detailed anatomy of the sperm is well known: Internal microtubules are arranged in a series of nine doublets, each of which has a central microtubule and a pair of smaller central microtubules that the electron microscopy abbreviates to the nine plus two description; the other components are entities called radial spokes, which appear necessary to keep this ordered configuration and, finally, entities known as dynein arms—"dyne" meaning "a force" and "ein" is the typical suffix meaning "protein." It has been found from studying sperm of lower organisms that the structure of the sperm is so stable that sea urchin sperm exhibit essentially the same configuration as human sperm. Indeed, by working with sea urchin sperm, one can extract a portion of the proteins of the configuration and leave most of the configuration intact. When the protein is extracted differentially so as to remove it only from these dynein arms, then one can make a study solution of that protein alone. Further research has shown that the high enzyme sugar metabolism system in the body (including high energy phosphorus) is able to provide the energy necessary for the continuous and rapid motility of the sperm tail. Therefore, those studying the two men with Kartagener's syndrome were extremely interested to discover that their sperm tails were also missing the arms. This anatomical finding fits perfectly with the expectation that this type of sperm would be unable to move.

How does the structure of sperm relate to the bronchiectasis and to the situs inversus? It turns out that the nine plus two configuration, and all the allied details noted in the sperm cell, are *exactly* what we see in cilia cells located on the surface membranes of the lungs, sinuses (etc.) in an individual with Kartagener's syndrome. An allied detail is that the offset individual's cilia is also missing the dynein arm, and its omission is another reason that cilia do not move—and hence, secretions are not moved along the lung's membranes, but, instead, they pool, become infected, and produce bronchiectasis. So the respiratory symptomatology of Kartagener's syndrome was given a perfectly reasonable explanation but as yet we still have not accounted for the situs inversus. Dr. Gerald deliberately chose this syndrome because it is an autosomal recessive disease characterized primarily at birth by the situs inversus (which is a congenital malformation). Yet the symptomatology that troubles the patient is related to a respiratory disease that is strictly a postnatal, not an antenatal, event. Here then, is evidence of a continued action of genes that—although they do cause congenital malformations—have a disease process that occurs postnatally, not antenatally, and results in symptomatic disorders clearly separate from the particular inherited entity. This prototype indicates unqualifiedly that just because there is a congenital malformation due to a chromosomal disorder, it *does not mean that the disease process was all initiated and completed prior to birth.* Indeed, a disease such as Down syndrome, for instance, could well be due to the postnatal action of the genetic disorder caused by the extra chromosome.

An allied question discussed in Chapter 2 was that of how do genes in chromosomal disorders act after birth? This question introduced the subject of gene dosage. Given three chromosomes instead of two (as in trisomy 21, Down syndrome) so that chromosomes are represented as *three* of a kind instead of a single *pair,* do all those genes exert an action? If so, what is that action? If there are three chromosome genes instead of two is there 150% of the normal product of those genes, in which case these genes would be said to "overdose"? Similarly, if there is only one gene instead of two, is there only 50% of the gene product?

Findings in gene dosage indicate that genes *do* indeed overdose! As far as we know, and as far as has been estimated and assayed, all genes that occur in triplicate instead of the normal duplicate *do* show 150% of the normal gene product.

There is an enzyme known as superoxide dismutase, whose gene has been located on chromosome 21, and when individuals are trisomic for this entire chromosome, one finds 150% of the normal activity for this enzyme. In individuals who are trisomic for only a portion of the known chromosome disorder, in some instances an elevation of a given enzyme level is found and in other instances, no elevation. We can thus assume that the locus for the enzyme superoxide dismutase actually resides in a specific region of chromosome 21, which is that site common to all instances where the 150% activity is noted. So we can show not only that gene dosage occurs, but also offer some insight into where the genes are located on a given chromosome. Though the enzyme superoxide dismutase is present in excess in Down syndrome, it is not associated, as far as we know, with any of the symptomatology of the syndrome; so we still do not have a specific answer to the question of how Down syndrome is caused. However, when we look at individuals who are trisomic, or have trisomy 21 in particular, and then look at their phenotype, we find that those who show the phenotype of Down syndrome do have in common this particular region, which by the way, is perfectly coincident with that which causes the increased activity of the enzyme. So we can hypothesize that this portion of chromosome 21 is responsible for the primary phenotype of Down syndrome and also for the enzyme super-oxide dismutase. This suggests, *not proves,* that possibly the real attributes of Down syndrome are the result of a very limited number of genes in triplicate, and may not be due to a whole extra chromosome. Indeed, perhaps only a few genes are primarily responsible for the expression of Down syndrome.

We can extrapolate from the superoxide dismutase story that the involved genes caused the difficulty by virtue of their dosage action. If we accept that thesis, which is speculative, then what is needed in order to cure Down syndrome—or at least those aspects of it that are due to postnatal action of the specific chromosome 21 genes—is to selectively isolate all of the known enzymes-genes so as to elucidate what they are doing, and then reverse the negative aspects of their activity. As we know, this is not a a small task, but it is also not unconquerable! In fact, it is actually imminent. The processes for genetically mapping, pooling, and substituting genetic components—as in chromosome 21—were clearly illustrated by the discussion in Chapter 2 on the approach to understanding the fragile-X syndrome. Accordingly, a rational attack plan to further explore and begin to alter the components of the fragile-X syndrome (and by corollary, Down syndrome) can lead to future curative treatment plans for these clinical syndromes that produce mental retardation. The theoretical basis and a specific treatment alternative is currently available and there is great promise that this major clinical challenge—the cure of the fragile-X syndrome, Down syndrome, and a variety of allied chromosomal disorders—will be attained before the end of the 1980s.

DEVELOPMENTAL NEUROBIOLOGY

The overriding focus in Chapters 4 and 5, on the early development and function of the brain, was the hemispheres of the human brain, and particularly the cerebral cortex. The brain is the source of those functions that are most precious to us in regard to the many dimensions of personality, learning, memory, and the integration of sensory modalities and fine motor functions—all of which are so characteristically human. The brain structure, particularly its outer cortical shell, is in fact a community of billions of nerve cells. As noted by Drs. Verne S. Caviness and Roger S. Williams in Chapter 4, there has been an ongoing historical scientific study of the way in which the nerve cells of the central nervous system are initiated, grow, and gain maturity in the complex overall surface of the brain. As one looks closely at this ribbon of cerebral cortex, one sees the distinct layers of cells and their characteristic architectural appearance. Getting a closer look at these cells, by impregnating them with silver via the Golgi method, one can see the complex and elegant structure of the individual nerve cell.

The most characteristic cell of the cerebral neocortex is, of course, the pyramidal cell. This cell has a large, tear-formed body, a spherical elaboration of receptive processes from its body, and an apical dendrite that seems to thrust itself down through the molecular layer. One can recognize cells of this configuration at all levels of the cortex, and see that there is also a systematic change in their size. The pyramidal cell has a profusion of dendrites that go in all directions, and that send messages outside of the cortex. There are smaller pyramidal cells (called interneurons) that apparently take care of "local" messages in the cortical circuit. Indeed, the function of the cerebral cortex and the brain must ultimately be understood in terms of the mass aggregate, the function of all these cells as they communicate with each other through their connections. The developmental history of the cerebral cortex, and indeed the brain, must be understood as the developmental history of these individual cellular elements, and particularly as they interact with each other (i.e., adapting to each other) to form the final structure.

As noted by Drs. Caviness and Williams, the developmental history of the neocortex is usually subdivided into two broad epochs: 1) An early epoch of cell formation, and histogenesis (i.e., the assembly of cells once formed into the various structures of the brain), and 2) a later epoch of growth and differentiation. As far as the neocortex is concerned, the first phase has a rather compressed period: the first two trimesters of pregnancy (e.g., the first 6 months). The latter phase has a *very* extended period running through the third trimester of pregnancy, through the first decade of postnatal life and even beyond. The first phase generates a brain that weighs almost 100 grams. During the second phase, the period of growth differentiation and the formation of connections, the brain expands from 100 g to virtually 1,500 g. The cellular events that occur during these two epochs are quite different. Similarly, the disease processes to which these two epochs are vulnerable also have markedly different consequences.

Drs. Caviness and Williams concentrated on the first of these two epochs, that of early cell formation and histogenesis. Dr. Dominick P. Purpura followed in Chapter 5 with a review of the developmental processes and vulnerabilities of the second epoch.

Chapter 4 noted that early growth starts in layers (i.e., mantels) and that as the cells divide and generate, they must make an extraordinary journey—as freely motile elements—starting where they are formed and ending with their positional destiny. The cells get themselves into position and then elaborate into the principal axons or systems that will bind them as a functional unit with the cell populations around the remainder of the central nervous system. A remarkable event! Cells once generated arrive at their definitive position by crossing a distance that is many, many times, perhaps many hundred times, their own diameter. The terrain they cross is an extraordinarily complex thicket. The cells do it by forming an alliance with a neighbor cell population that is quite different in its functions. An interaction between the young neurons and this other type of cell that serves as the neuron's guide ensues. These guide cells are the so-called radial glial cells (the precursor of the standard astrocytes that differentiate early). The radial glial cell has its own cell body very deep within the cerebral wall, and an elongated process that ascends radially all the way to the surface. This radial glial fiber—serving as the guiding friend—gets the neocortex neuron from its place of origin to its final destination. Once the neuron completes the migration and reaches the developing cortical zone, its problems are not over, however. It still has to make a critically complex maneuver in relation to other cells, as follows: Each cell in its turn migrates up to the molecular matter, stops, digs in, and fixes itself into position. The next cell comes along, bypasses the earlier cell, and lifts the early neocortex outer layer up a little further. Each cell must therefore bypass the cell that got there before it, reach the roof, and push it up a little more. This is not a random pattern, but a columnal stacking, one cell on top of the other, with the radial glial fiber probably serving as an axial organizing structure. Once in position, the axon cell of the neocortex maintains its relative position and then begins to elaborate the fundamental details and architecture of its dendritic pattern. At this point, there is ushered in the period of growth differentiation, and the formation of connections begins.

These early development events are vulnerable to the action of a variety of disease processes, each in its turn having quite a different impact upon the developing brain. In reviewing the spectrum of the types of disorders that strike the developmental process right at the "bedrock" level, one of these disorders is termed anencephaly—the absence of major portions of the brain altogether. A variety of processes can strike the generative cell layers of the brain and destroy them. Thus, the origin of the term *anencepaly,* since there is virtually no brain—just a vascular mass in the place where the brain ought to be.

The disorders that can strike the developing generative layer are not all so generalized. For example, the baby who is noted in the first few days of life to have a very small head often has a brain that weighs about 250 g, very much less than the normal 800 to 1,000 g that it should weigh. This is called microcephaly and there are many examples of this disorder. In this malformation, there is characteristically no evidence of an intercurrent destructive process, or evidence that the early cells did not migrate or complete their migration. Instead, it is as though some process prevented the generation of cells from forming (and this can be due to viruses such as rubella; radiation; genetic factors; etc.).

Later, the formed populations of neurons can be subjected to attack during the migratory process itself. In the malformation called lissencephaly the outer surface of the brain is smooth, and when one looks at the cell pattern in this malformation there is a cortex, but it turns out to be formed from the earliest of the cells. It is as though some intercurrent process struck the brain during the period of cell migration and isolated cells before they completed their migration—perhaps by sheering off the radial glial fibers that would normally guide them to their position—leaving them normally formed below, but in an abnormal cortical form or position in which they are simply unable to participate in normal function.

Chapter 4's survey of malformations that can strike the early developmental epoch revealed that this group of disorders can be devastating. Where survival occurs, it is in the face of major functional disability. Some of the disorders are due to genetic mutations but, as was also noted in Chapter 1, the majority are probably the consequence of disease processes that strike the developmental unit of mother and fetus. Many of these are probably relatively commonplace diseases such as infections, or perhaps immune diseases. Certainly toxic substances (including drugs) that the pregnant female might be taking also play a role. As we look at the challenge of therapy in this area, it is obvious that we must think of our responsibilities of treating the combined maternal-developing fetal unit. The most appropriate treatment in these disorders is that directed in anticipation, against the acute diseases as they might strike, thus preventing their destructive access to the developing nervous system.

Dr. Purpura, in Chapter 5, noted that since a research strategy implies that one is trying to assess the progress being made in a specific research field, in his case neurobiology, then according to this strategy one can ask, is it reasonable to expect that on the basis of available knowledge, one can begin to ask whether we can effect curative approaches and reversibility in the area of mental retardation? Dr. Purpura noted that the neurobiology-science community probably is not ready to accept the notion of cure as a serious challenge, the reason generally stemming from the enormous insecurity in the field about what we know about this complex organ called the brain. In the final analysis, it is the complex activity of the brain for which we are most concerned, since mental retardation is defined in terms of intellectual capacity, which generally develops during the period of early life.

Chapter 5 reviewed ways of looking at brain development challenges and provided some understanding of where we are and the specific areas we need to focus upon. Obviously, if we consider the full range of what we don't know about the developing brain, it would be very depressing! Instead, the national Association of Retarded Citizens and the National Institutes of Health in Bethesda, Maryland, are concerned with the challenge of developing potentially helpful research strategies (i.e., strategies that enhance the potential of applied treatment endeavors). Several major studies and task forces have already generated hundreds of recommendations for research in this area—all of which deserve funding, of course, if only we had infinite resourses. What are the priority areas? Dr. Purpura (personal communication, 1981) has stated:

> I believe it is time for a clearer understanding, even in a simplistic way, of how we get this enormously complex picture of human behavior. We have an important dogma in neuroscience that, simply stated, says that neurons are at the basis of behavior, and not necessarily blood vessels, or the liver, or the kidney; and that these neurons make connections—synapses—and the synapses make behavior. Very simple. In fact, it is so outrageously simple that it seems to imply some degree of ignorance. But this is an important dogma, and it has provided one major advance in the fundamental neurosciences: From this dogma we have generated several hundred recommendations as to the kind of information we need to know to more directly approach the understanding—and possible cure—of mental retardation.

Significantly, Dr. Purpura has a long history of conducting research on the period of human brain development between the 25th and 32nd weeks, the period during which many babies are born prematurely, as such. Dr. Purpura's research has direct relevance to the study of perinatal programs, the low birth weight infant, etc. During the last 4 or 5 years we have obtained clear information of what the brain's cortex looks like in 25-week-old, preterm infants (weight about 600 g), who are now surviving in newborn intensive care units. What do their brains look like? Dr. Purpura noted that many of these infants' cortical cells are still in the stage of growth of their dendritic structure. This is the stage of beginning dendritic differentiation, many of the cells are correctly arranged in place (as Drs. Caviness and Williams indicated in Chapter 4) and their final functional positions have been established. This is a significant point in growth since all the brain cells that we will ever have in our brain (at least in the neocortex) are present at about 26-27 weeks—and no more neurons will be added later in life. Dr. Purpura has identified the period between the 26th and 33rd weeks as the major period of dendritic growth in terms of the rate of increment of dendritic growth in the human cortex. Not only is there great dendritic growth during this time, but the spines of the dendrites also make their major appearance. In addition, the density of synapses is attained. This density maintains itself, increases slightly in the postnatal period, and drops off by about the age of 12 or 14 years to reach a lower density. This remarkable situation indicates something that we have not been sufficiently attuned to: *That the newborn baby brain has enormous amounts of synaptic machinery in place, ready to go!* And maybe the machinery has been operating much earlier than that. This finding emphasizes new challenges for the antenatal and early postnatal clinical problems we confront. It also provides a rational basis for our national commitment to early infant education!

Dr. Purpura noted that his recent findings as to the "rosary" effect in the dendrites of pyramidal cells may occur in many of the currently unknown causes of retardation. He believes that the "rosary" effect finding is a critical point in the biology of the neuron. The effect deals with the dendritic system, with the synapses, and in some way with the biophysical properties of the message-cable system that the dendrite is supposed to represent. Something fundamental in cell biology is happening in terms of the cytoskeleton that maintains the integrity of the dendritic tree—keeps the diameters correct, keeps the relationship between the spine and its input branch sites at a proper ratio through experience, and underlines the operation and usage patterns of the brain. Accordingly, the kind of research strategies that must be developed must begin by a knowledge of what is going on in the brains of retarded individuals. Dr. Purpura has asked the question, What is it that is a *common* basis for all of the cognitive defects one sees in mentally retarded individuals? To begin to form an answer, he examined further the changes in dendrites in retarded persons as well as his recently discussed "rosary" pattern. In developing a strategy from a dendritic damage standpoint, he noted that neuroscientists must realize that their work derives from the vast knowledge in neurobiology and cell biology that has already accumulated and to which basic research has already started to provide more basic clues. Thus, his findings as to the "rosary" effect have led him to emphasize this aspect of the cell biology of the central nervous system—rather than only the synapses and spines of the pyramidal cell. He has noted (Purpura, personal communication, 1981):

> What are some of the fundamental issues? I think we must decide what are the fundamental defects. We cannot, in fact, go after 300 disparate causes. Instead, we must focus on what are the common nodal points, and the nodal points repeatedly reported in recent experimental work—study after study—come back to the questions of, How do the synapses work? How do they change? How are they modifiable? and How do they operate on such elements as the adjacent cortical neurons? This is where the neuroscience view currently stands, and this is where we need to focus the bulk of our future research.

Lastly, the clear delineation of the high state of synaptic maturity of the newborn infant is a tremendously exciting parameter of Dr. Purpura's studies. This finding brings much credence to the work of colleagues such as Dr. Alice Hayden and Dr. Norris Haring regarding their program on very early developmental-educational stimulation of Down syndrome infants and young children. Herein, ongoing neuroscience research has provided a strong understanding for an environmentally oriented treatment-curative approach. Truly, in this instance, basic and applied research efforts on the symptom of mental retardation have crossed the line from initial findings to early treatment-management trials—a powerful illustration of how research has always been the eternal fountain for new treatments that can enhance the lives of citizens.

REFERENCES

Moser, H. *Future directions and challenges*. Paper presented at the President's Committee on Mental Health, Atlanta, September, 1982.

section II

EFFORTS TOWARD
UNDERSTANDING AND REPAIRING
BRAIN FUNCTION

Introduction

FRANK J. MENOLASCINO, M.D.
University of Nebraska, Medical Center
Omaha, Nebraska

F OR A LONG TIME IT WAS THOUGHT that the brain was incapable of repair following injury or disease trauma. A considerable body of evidence now suggests otherwise. Techniques to repair brain damage include both chemical and surgical interventions. In addition, there is growing evidence indicating that a recovery from brain injury in early life is not necessarily spontaneous and that environmental factors may provide potent stimulation. Much research lies ahead, but findings thus far hold promise for the future.

MEMORY AND LEARNING MECHANISMS

Chapter 7, by Dr. Frank J. Menolascino, discusses research considerations for assessing how the developmental dimensions of memory and learning functions can be studied in humans. The chapter focuses specifically on research elements that must be incorporated into studies in this area and outlines criteria for judging the efficiency of such research elements.

The research implications discussed in Chapter 7 are pertinent to the mechanisms described by Dr. Gary Lynch in Chapter 8, which focuses on the hippocampus area of the brain. This area of the brain clearly possesses the capacities for storing and processing learning behaviors, since it has been shown that direct stimulation (chemically and electrically) of the hippocampus produces lasting physiological and structural changes. Dr. Lynch's research stresses that the hippocampus may well be the neurological base for human learning, displaying all the components of a microcosm of the learning process. In addition, the developmental growth pattern of the hippocampus region suggests that it may well play a role in synthesizing-integrating sensory inputs from the peripheral nervous system with the association network processing of the central nervous system such as the temporal lobes and the prefrontal and frontal areas. More importantly, Dr. Lynch's animal experiments have definitely shown that learning experiences (e.g., developmental stimulation) consistently produce new cell branching in previously damaged areas of the hippocampus. These documented changes suggest the existence of potent biochemical mechanisms that may prove quite different from the well-studied processes associated with electrical transmission in the central nervous system and the regulation of membrane physiology in the rest of the body. The next step for researchers is to attempt to identify in human models the probable anatomical sites of learning ''brain circuits'' that have so far been found in animals. Similarly, the studies on regenerative potentials in the hippocampus cast serious doubt on the long-held belief that only peripheral nervous system components can regenerate. Obviously, the documented findings of regeneration of the hippocampus (which is a central nervous system component) indicate that chemical stimulation or other stimuli should be studied further.

NERVE CELL REGROWTH

Dr. A. K. Ommaya, in Chapter 9, reports on his and a number of other investigators' studies into nerve cell regrowth (in animals). Dr. Ommaya's research centers on a process of neurosurgical procedures used to "fuse" completely severed spinal cords via a myelin sheath graft. Although at present the principal problem has been the amount or degree of regrowth across the severed spinal cord, these preliminary findings are very positive. Similarly, Dr. Ommaya reports on brain tissue transplants that can be selectively placed into the brain of a rat, grow, and become neurochemically active (i.e., the brain tissue transplants secrete brain chemicals necessary for nerve cell transmission). The ability of these brain tissue transplants to permanently affect behavior or to become fully integrated into the surrounding brain structures is now actively being studied. For example, recent procedures (in humans) have underscored the efficacious role of transplanting equivalent brain tissue into those portions of the brain affected by parkinsonism. Rather than a chemical replacement substitute such as the use of L-dopa, this neurological procedure implants actual secreting cells into the affected parkinsonian patient.

Together with the outstanding work of Dr. Michael D. Browning, whose studies of synaptic plastity and the potential for enhancing brain function are reported in Chapter 10, Dr. Ommaya's focus on transplants offers additional great potential for reversing the symptom of mental retardation (in those with selected focal damage). The enhancement of intrinsic brain development via transplants is further complimented by the prospect of introducing additive components into the brain via new tissue.

Attempts at intrinsic enhancement of brain functioning as illustrated in Chapter 10 provide a hypothesis for the cure of mental retardation by studying the biological bases of learning. Dr. Browning's research has concentrated on a brain process called long-term synaptic plasticity (LTP), which he considers to be the neural substrate of all learning.

In sum, the interplay of intrinsic and extrinsic enhancement and the treatment-cure potentials we see discussed in Chapters 7–10 offer clear encouragement in the effort to ameliorate or reverse the basic mechanisms that have traditionally been viewed as "immutable" factors in mental retardation.

Curative Aspects of Mental Retardation:
Biomedical and Behavioral Advances
edited by Frank J. Menolascino, M.D., Ronald Neman, Ph.D., and Jack A. Stark, Ph.D.
Copyright 1983   Paul H. Brookes Publishing Co., Inc.   Baltimore · London

chapter 7

Developmental Interactions of Brain Impairment and Experience

Prospects and Roadblocks for Curative Approaches

Frank J. Menolascino, M.D.
University of Nebraska Medical Center
Omaha, Nebraska

THE CRITICAL IMPORTANCE OF early and ongoing sets of developmental experiences and transactions with the environment for maturation of the central nervous system (CNS) and the orderly development of intelligence and personality in normal individuals has been clearly documented (Goldman, 1976; Rosenzweig, 1971). In recent years it has become equally clear that such developmental experiences are also central to the nature and extent of recovery following brain impairment in early life (Rutter, 1981). For example, in their book *Environments As Therapy for Brain Dysfunction,* Walsh and Greenough (1976) reviewed the firm, clinical research evidence relating to the effects of experience on recovery of central nervous system function. In contrast to previous rather fatalistic opinions concerning potentials for even minimal recovery, it has been clearly noted that the potential for recovery is both rendered more positive and is dependent upon the provision of ongoing opportunities for developmental stimulation with the exter-

nal interpersonal environment (both prior to and after brain impairment). The recent recognition of the role of environmental stimulation as an essential dimension of the compensatory capacity following brain impairment raises new hope for the treatment and cure of resulting disorders such as mental retardation.

This chapter therefore is a brief overview of the basic questions concerning mechanisms by which functions can be restored in a person with an impaired central nervous system. It provides a framework for analyzing the manner in which external-internal sets of experiences can and do influence the recovery process.

It should be noted that although the focus here is on specific aspects of the processes that lead to recovery in altered brain functioning, we now know that the success of these processes makes the traditional professional posture of passively awaiting changes in brain functioning after the brain has been altered no longer tenable. Indeed, such a

viewpoint assumes an undue reliance on internal mechanisms for brain repair, in contrast to findings that definitely underscore the
importance of environmental stimulation to
both the initiation and persistence of indices
of enhanced brain functioning—whether in
the damaged or nondamaged individual.

Furthermore, to view the external processes discussed here as subservient to intrinsic factors is to sorely overlook the need for a
major focus on the nature, extent, and quality
of input that the individual receives from
ongoing environmental experiences. One is
reminded of the early studies of the role of
muscle-relaxant, pharmacological agents in
cerebral palsied (especially spastic) children.
The children remained in their cribs while
they were administered the pharmacological
agents and assessed for possible improvement. Yet, the phenomenon of spasticity is
noted primarily when the anti-gravity
muscles are called into play; if opportunities
for upright body activities are not provided,
then the mechanisms for musculature activity
are not elicited. Obviously, one cannot view a
supine child—in a crib—as a reliable candidate for assessing the purported therapeutic
value of such drugs—whether they worked or
not! Similarly, it has been shown that specific
efforts to reverse cerebral impairments in the
child or adult must simultaneously assure that
a high level of environmental stimuli/
involvement *is* provided—lest the lack of
external activities or involvement override or
obliterate intrinsic improvements in the status
of central nervous functioning. For example,
the studies on infantile marasmus have
clearly demonstrated the devastating effects
of lack of external activation. Accordingly,
though the role of specific intrinsic factors is
discussed in this chapter, the reader must
continually recall that these processes do not
occur in an interpersonal vacuum. Indeed, the
ever present envelope of interpersonal stimulation may still be a poorly understood aspect
of the complex supportive framework that is
necessary to enhance our clinical efforts
aimed at maximizing recovery potentials in
the central nervous system.

RECOVERY OF CENTRAL NERVOUS SYSTEM FUNCTION FOLLOWING SURGICAL INTERVENTIONS

Surgical lesions on the brain of young animals and the documented effects of experience thereafter have been closely studied. A
pivotal study that related early experience to
the symptomology noted following surgically
induced brain impairment was reported by
Hebb in 1949. Hebb had been impressed by
the finding that global intelligence scores
often remained normal in humans who had
undergone neurosurgical procedures, especially frontal lobotomies. His findings suggested that the aspects of global intelligence
that permitted the human to approach problem solving *differently* following neurosurgical procedures were the product of sets
of experiences during early development, and
thus were relatively resistant to brain impairment. Similar findings were noted by
Goldberger (1971) on rats that had undergone
cortical lesions as infants or as adults, and had
been placed (postoperatively) for prolonged
periods in enriched environments. Goldberger noted that such sets of experiences in
the infants would greatly ameliorate the expected intellectual and behavioral deficits.
Follow-up studies compared the effects of
such cortical lesions in rats raised under im-
poverished conditions with those in rats
raised in enriched environments. These studies have been replicated and strongly support
the thesis that enriched developmental rearing (as to external conditions) greatly amelio-
rates the expected learning and behavioral
deficits following surgically induced brain
impairments.

A number of studies on adult animals,
however, have pointed to a nonspecific function for the postoperative enriched developmental environment. Of interest are findings
that rats with hypothalamic lesions recover
their normal feeding behavior more quickly if
exposed to daily 1-hour episodes of low-level
electrical stimulation through electrodes
(Harrell, Raubeson & Balagura, 1974).

Likewise there is evidence that recovery of visual-motor functions can be enhanced by CNS-activating drugs given postoperatively (Glassman, 1971; Meyer, Horel & Meyer, 1963; Ward & Kennard, 1942). Such studies provide important evidence of a general level of central nervous system activation in providing resilience to brain impairment. However, since age of subject, type and size of lesion, rearing history, and behavioral task are all confounded in the research that has been conducted to date, an evaluation of the features of experience that are critical for protecting against (induced) brain impairment awaits further research.

Experimental studies of the role of early experience (i.e., before the onset of the brain impairment) in recovery from local brain impairment have supported the view that these experiences and environmental stimulation can strongly counteract the degree of brain impairment (Will, Rosenzweig, Bennett, Herbert, & Morimoto, 1977). Nevertheless, the environmental-experience effects noted from these studies have not been striking. Recently, more clear-cut evidence that early experience may have profound effects on the course of recovery from brain impairment has been obtained in research on rhesus monkeys. Since the cerebral organization, developmental parameters, and potential for complex behaviors of rhesus monkeys are similar to those of humans, these studies are pivotal. Major findings from these studies are:

1. The return of some abilities after brain impairment in early life depends heavily upon previous experience. Monkeys that underwent surgical prefrontal cortical impairments as adults typically exhibited severe deficits on spatial tests (Goldman, 1976; Mishkin, 1964). However, monkeys given the same surgical impairments as infants can perform as well as normal monkeys when they reach 2 years of age—if they have received prior training on a series of cognitive tasks during their earlier development (Goldman & Mendelson, 1977). Interestingly, without these earlier experiences with cognitive tasks, monkeys who had similar surgically induced cortical impairments as infants failed to learn the spatial task when they reached 2 years of age. If equivalent postoperative experience is provided for monkeys operated on as infants or as adults, recovery of function is exhibited only by those operated on as infants. Accordingly, the recovery effect appears to be an all-or-nothing phenomenon, and thus the effectiveness of extrinsic developmental experiences in promoting recovery appears to be related to the age at which it is given.

2. If brain impairment is extensive or includes critical brain areas, recovery will not occur despite opportunities for extensive postoperative test experiences (Goldman, 1976). For example, monkeys who had large portions of the entire lateral prefrontal cortex and orbital cortex surgically removed, are unable to learn spatial tasks at maturity, even when given the same kind and amount of experience as that which induces recovery following the surgical removal of the prefrontal cortex alone. Such findings indicate that the lateral prefrontal area is a critical brain area for facilitating the environmentally induced recovery of function postsurgically; if impairment is severe, no recovery occurs.

3. The positive effects of experience on recovery after brain impairments are not solely caused by the training experiences. Again, Goldman (1976) ruled on the *specific* content of early experiences by assessing prefrontal lobotomies and unoperated controls who had been trained on a nonspatial task as infants and examined on both a spatial and nonspatial task as juveniles. The performance of the experienced monkeys was compared to that of operated and unoperated monkeys who had not received the early training. Performance

on both classes of tasks was predictably impaired by orbital lesions; however, postoperative training in infancy beneficially aided the spatial but not the nonspatial deficits caused by the prefrontal lesions. Thus, the evidence that recovery of spatial functions can be obtained following a variety of earlier training experiences indicates that previous experience acts *nonspecifically* to offset deficits caused by specific brain damage in monkeys.

Though further investigations are needed to clearly understand the parameters of experience that encourage restitution of function, current evidence from studies on both rodents and monkeys indicates that extrinsic environmental factors play a major role in minimizing the behavioral effects of specific brain injury in early life. The studies on monkeys, in particular, suggest that experience can be powerful and may produce its beneficial effects by providing a lengthened general level of stimulation rather than by reactivating previously trained specific habits. This nonspecific, facilitatory function of past experience suggests some of the central nervous system mechanisms that are involved in neurobehavioral plasticity following central nervous system impairments.

EFFECTS OF EARLY
EXPERIENCE ON BRAIN
STRUCTURE AND BIOCHEMISTRY

The effects of early environmental experience on a variety of brain structural and biochemical measures have been thoroughly studied (Levitan, Mushyinski, & Ramirez, 1972; Mistretta & Bradley, 1978; Sperry, 1961). In a classical study, Rosenzweig, Krech, Bennett, and Diamond (1962) noted that the cerebral cortex of rodents that had been reared in enriched environments was heavier and thicker than the cortex of rodents reared under less stimulating conditions. This overall difference in enriched rodents has been attributed to increased glial cell number (Rosenzweig, Bennett, & Diamond, 1970), enlarged cell bodies and their nuclei, and

increased dendritic branch and spine formation (Schapiro & Vukovich, 1970). These dramatic anatomical changes imply considerable activation of ribonucleic acid (RNA) and protein synthesis in the brains of rodents exposed to enriched environments. Research findings have confirmed higher brain RNA content and increased RNA diversity in the enriched rodents (Rosenzweig, Bennett, & Diamond, 1970; Uphouse & Bonner, 1975). Further, Levitan, Mushyinski, and Ramirez (1972) reported that the incorporation of essential amino acids, i.e., leucine, into the brain was increased in enriched rodents. These studies only begin to suggest the profound nature of possible metabolic effects of enriched experience on the central nervous system, whereas the anatomical studies have clearly shown increased protein synthesis in the brain.

The strongest evidence for distinct extrinsic environmental influences on brain development has been noted in studies of selective stimulation (or deprivation) in a single special sensory modality. Although neuronal (and behavioral) parameters have been shown to be changed by stimulation/deprivation of all the senses, the most clear-cut results are found in studies of the visual system, where the anatomical and functional modifications resulting from alteration in the visual input have been documented (Blakemore, 1974; Greenough, Fass, & DeVoogd, 1976; Pettigrew, 1974). An early demonstration of the effects of visual deprivation was a study that noted that the retinal ganglion cells of the chimpanzee degenerate following their early development in dark-rearing environments (Chow, Riesen, & Newell, 1957). There exists similar overwhelming evidence that the early visual environment can modify the structure and function of connections in various regions of the mammalian visual system (Grobstein & Chow, 1975).

In summary, there is anatomical, physiological, and biochemical evidence for alteration of brain tissue in animals that have been subjected to a variety of environments during development. As will be noted, this developmental information has implications for mechanisms by which experience could significantly affect the outcome of brain injury.

THEORIES OF RECOVERY

Cognitive and behavioral recovery after known brain impairment has been explained in both psychological-behavioral and physiological modes. These explanatory modes are frequently noted to be antithetical to one another. The psychological-behavioral explanatory approaches to central nervous system recovery stress the ability of brain-impaired organisms to learn a variety of alternate approaches to complete a given task. The straightforward nature of this explanation, which is popularly referred to as "substitution theory" (Teuber, 1974), has never been subjected to extensive experimental study, although many observations relevant to the reported effects of experiences during earlier developmental stages (i.e., before the injury) tend to facilitate psychological-behavioral recovery. These observations have been related to the range of opportunity an organism has had to form new problem-solving strategies (i.e., a developmental model approach). A physiological explanation of central nervous system recovery—along the "substitution theory" approach—does provide some basis for inferring a regression to earlier modes of central nervous system organization modes that can (via training) become more completely developed. This point of view (i.e., the non-dichotomous nature of the behavioral-physiological theme of central nervous system recovery) can explain why adolescents or adults can fail to benefit from extrinsic experiences, while the exposure of infants can be more effective. In other words, the exposure to extrinsic stimulation early in development, while the organism is more flexible, can enhance the central nervous system at the tissue level. Any explanation as to the possible mechanisms by which experience significantly alters an organism's response to brain impairment must account for these boundary conditions.

The physiological explanations of psychological-behavioral recovery after brain impairment tend to focus on the phenomenon of diaschisis (i.e., the disappearance of biochemical or electrical signs of activity in anatomically intact tissue). Although the neurophysiological basis of diaschisis is not currently understood, it has been delineated as a distinct finding in humans (Meyers, Shinohara, Kanda, Ericsson, & Kok, 1970). The disappearance of diaschisis (i.e., the reappearance of electrical or biochemical activity in previously damaged brain tissue) could physiologically account for behavioral recovery, including recovery that is secondary to extrinsic stimulation. The reactivation of damaged neurons has been noted to occur secondarily to subsequent partial regeneration of brain cell axons or axon collaterals (Lynch & Awe, 1980). Such reactivation may directly result in psychological-behavioral recovery, as noted by Lynch, Gall, and Cotman (1977). The phenomenon of new sprouting from the brain cell axons and the conditions that can enhance this process hold great promise for demonstrating a distinct physiological basis for central nervous system recovery processes. The partial damage of neurons sometimes produces increased sensitivity in these neurons to both intrinsic inputs or extrinsically applied pharmacological agents (Sharpless, 1975; Yarborough & Phillips, 1975). The presence of this supersensitivity could compensate for the apparent loss of brain cell mass or functional ability—by having the remaining (usually redundantly) brain cell field become more responsive to stimuli (an *internal* substitution mechanism)—thus leading to psychological-behavioral recovery.

ACTIVATION–RECONSTRUCTION–RECOVERY

As previously noted, animals that have been reared in stimulus-rich environments display significant biochemical and anatomical changes in their brains. These findings appear to be a consequence of prolonged arousal of the central nervous system (Walsh & Cummins, 1975); electrophysiological evidence for increased neurological activation—following sets of enriched developmental experiences—has been documented by the finding of shorter evoked potentials in enriched young rodents (Maillous, Edwards, Barry, Roswell, & Ackorn, 1974). The neurological arousal response to enriched sets of extrinsic experience apparently stimulates a variety of neurochemical processes in the brain (Ferchmin, Eterovic, & Caputto, 1970). In addition, the apparent transformation of enhanced electrical activity into neurochemical synthesis has also been documented. For example, the RNA content of the Purkinje cells in different areas of the cerebellum was noted to increase after prolonged extrinsic stimulation of touch, position, and vestibular exercises in animals (Jarlstedt, 1966). Further, the effects of nerve cell stimulation on transmitter levels (e.g., acetylcholine), following extrinsic stimulation, have been found to increase the synthesis of RNA (Gistger, 1971); and acetylcholine activation (peripheral) has accelerated the incorporation of radioactively tagged isotopes into brain stem nuclei (Singh & Sung, 1972). The latter phenomenon, as noted by Goldman (1976), demonstrates the transsynaptic induction of a neurotransmitter-synthesizing enzyme. This finding has important implications for understanding the control of postsynaptic cells by presynaptic activity (and the conversion of biochemical to electrical activation phenomena).

The influence of brain cells on the biochemical activity of their target cells (i.e., a cell from the cortex of the brain that eventually fires into a spinal cord pool of peripheral nerve cells) has been referred to as nutritive or *trophic* influences. The activation of central nervous system nutritional responses has been extensively studied. The trophic models include the activation of enzymes by neotransmitters, hormones, or psychoactive drugs to increase the cellular concentrations of carbohydrates and proteins. In turn, these events lead to the increased synthesis of messenger RNA (Uphouse & Bonner, 1975). For example, the trophic induction of the enzyme ornithine decarboxylase increases the synthesis of the polyamines such as spermidine. In turn, spermidine has been shown to stimulate RNA polymerase from brain cell nuclei (Singh & Sung, 1972), which results in enhanced synthesis of messenger RNA. Interestingly, the polyamines (e.g., putrescine and spermidine) are potent stimulators of protein synthesis and appear to assume a major role in cellular growth and differentiation (Russell, 1973; Tabor & Tabor, 1976); hence they are directly related to possible brain tissue recovery mechanisms.

Thus, enriched sets of extrinsic experiences during development or growth stimulate nutritive-trophic responses in brain tissue, and these responses are the physiological basis of underlying psychological-behavioral recovery from brain impairment. The following section examines how the stimulation of trophic responses could influence the proposed physiological mechanisms of recovery, with special emphasis on diaschisis.

Since enriched experience results in the stimulation of nutritive-trophic response in brain tissue, it follows that the condition of diaschisis after birth damage could be reversed by such experiences. Similarly, the reversal of diaschisis could also be explained by the nerve cell supersensitivity (Stavraky, 1961) secondary to injury that was also previously noted. The recovery effects also involve the increased synthesis of structural proteins and the sprouting of axon collaterals into areas of central nervous system damage (Lynch & Awe, 1980). Further, the synthesis of neurotransmitters is also increased and may aid in the development of the nerve cell supersensitivity.

Developmentally, all of these considerations shed additional light on the effects of early versus later sets of developmental experiences (with or without brain impairment). For example, young children have a higher rate of synthesis of brain RNA and proteins. In contrast, the slower rate of RNA synthesis in older animals has been suggested to be due to an age-dependent decrease in brain RNA polymerase activity. Beyond neurochemical factors are the considerations first, that brain impairments in infancy may show more recovery than in comparable impairments in adulthood, because infants might be less vulnerable to the secondary effects of brain injury (e.g., the physical size of the brain impairment and its allied effects); and second, that the relative immaturity of the central nervous system in infancy may have a major influence on the course of future development. Indeed, it is clear that at birth there may actually be an excess of nerve cells in many areas of the brain (Purpura, 1981).

As implied by the foregoing discussion, the trophic response hypothesis can easily be extended to account for the impact of experiences on the unimpaired as well as the impaired brain. While it is beyond the scope of this chapter to develop this concept fully, brief mention should be made of its further applicability to normal development by again utilizing the visual system for illustration. One of the physiological consequences of monocular vision deprivation during sensitive periods of development is that it reduces the population of visual cortical neurons that can be driven binocularly. Thus, sensory loss through one eye renders these neurons hypofunctional or depressed, in that they no longer respond equally well to stimuli through either eye. This hypofunctional visual status in the deprived eye can be activated by drugs; this task was accomplished via intravenous injections of bicuculline (a γ-aminobutyric acid (GABA) receptor antagonist) to visually deprived animals (Duffy, Snodgras, Birchfiel, & Conway, 1976). The loss of responsiveness could be due to depressed activity of the enzyme, choline acetyltransferase, in the lateral geniculate bodies and superior colliculi, and may be pharmacologically responsive to treatment intervention. With regard to the role of the environment, there is ample evidence that some of the effects of selective visual stimulation and/or visual deprivation can be reversed by extensive visual experience (Grob-

stein & Chow, 1975), just as the effects of other (less specific) brain impairments can be ameliorated by more global interactions with the environment. It is possible, then, that the potent effects of experience and those of drugs (like bicuculline) are meditated by common neuronal mechanisms. These and similar challenges to neuroscience research have suggested a major change in the priorities for these research efforts (Sperry, 1981), wherein the complexities can be more directly studied.

SUMMARY

In summary, the mechanisms by which primates cope with brain impairment may be manifested in widely different ways in various species. Just as vertebrates differ from invertebrates in the capacity for regeneration of severed nerve cells, it is possible that primates differ from rodents in the capacity for forming collateral sprouts throughout postnatal and adult life. Plasticity in primates may involve nerve cell redundancy, and resourceful use of intact structures is implied by the apparently greater dependence of functional restitution upon environmental stimulation in primates. In all of these various species-typical responses to brain impairment, perhaps the lowest common denominator for maintaining the structural and functional integrity of the damaged brain is the trophic response. Further investigation of the trophic response and its role in the recovery of function could reap further dividends in producing new therapies for current states of human brain dysfunctioning or clinical diseases. Concurrent with such understanding, there must also be a focus on the specific (i.e., enhanced environmental stimuli) activation of the impaired individual. These extrinsic factors are both necessary and appear to act *both* interdependently and in concert with ongoing intrinsic attempts to positively alter impaired brain functioning. Further understanding of these recently explored interactions between the intrinsic and extrinsic determinants of brain functions and allied behavioral repercussions will greatly enhance

our current ability to mitigate or reverse the effects of brain impairments.

REFERENCES

Blakemore, C. Developmental factors in the formation of feature extracting neurons. In: F.O. Schmitt & F.G. Worden (eds.), *Third study program*. Cambridge, MA: M.I.T. Press, 1974.

Chow, K.L., Riesen, A., & Newell, F.W. Degeneration of retinal ganglion cells in infant chimpanzees reared in darkness. *Journal of Comparative Neurology*, 1957, *107*, 27–42.

Duffy, F.H., Snodgrass, S.R., Birchfiel,J.L., & Conway, J.L. Bicuculline reversal of deprivation amblyopia in cat. *Nature*, 1976, *260*, 256–257.

Ferchmin, P.A., Eterovic, V.A., & Caputto, R. Studies of brain weight and RNA content after short periods of exposure to environmental complexity. *Brain Research*, 1970, *20*, 49–57.

Gistger, V. Triggering of RNA synthesis by acetylcholine stimulation of the postsynaptic membrane in a mammalin sympathetic gaglion. *Brain Research*, 1971, *33*, 139–146.

Glassman, R.B. Recovery following sensorimotor cortical damage: Evoked potentials, brain stimulation and motor control. *Experimental Neurology*, 1971, *33*, 16–29.

Goldberger, M.E. Recovery of movement after CNS lesions in monkeys. In: D.G. Stein, J.J. Rose, & N. Butters (eds.), *Plasticity and recovery of function in the central nervous system*. New York: Academic Press, 1971.

Goldman, P.S. Maturation of the mammalian nervous system and the ontogeny of behavior. In: J.A. Rosenblatt, R.A. Hide, E. Shaw, & C. Beer (eds.), *Advances in the study of behavior*, Vol. 7. New York: Academic Press, 1976.

Goldman, P.S., & Mendelson, M.J. Salutary effects of early experience on deficits caused by lesions of frontal association cortex in developing rhesus monkeys. *Experimental Neurology*, 1977, *57*, 588–602.

Greenough, W.T., Fass, B., & DeVoogd, T.J. The influence of experience on recovery following brain damage in rodents: Hypotheses based on development research. In: R.N. Walsh & W.T. Greenough (eds.), *Environments as therapy for brain dysfunction*. New York: Plenum Publishing Corp., 1976.

Grobstein, P., & Chow, K.L. Receptive field development and individual experience. *Science*, 1975, *190*, 352–358.

Harrell, L.W., Raubeson, R., & Balagura, S. Acceleration of functional recovery following lateral hypothalamus damage by means of elec-

trical stimulation in lesioned areas. *Physiology and Behavior*, 1974, *12*, 897–899.

Hebb, D.O. *The organization of behavior*. New York: John Wiley & Sons, 1949.

Jarlstedt, J. Functional localization in the cerebellar cortex studied by quantitative determinations of Purkinje cell RNS. I. RNA changes in rat cerebellar Purkinje cells after proprio- and exteroceptive and vistibular stimulation. *Acta Physiologica Scandinavia*, 1966, *67*, 243–252.

Levitan, I.B., Mushyinski, W.E., & Ramirez, G. Effects of an enriched environment on aminoacid incorporation into rat brain subcellular fractions *in-vivo*. *Brain Research*, 1972, *41*, 498–502.

Lynch, G., & Awe, J.A. Micro-surgical repair of peripheral nerves. *Irish Medical Journal*, 1980, *73*, 206.

Lynch, G., Gall, C., & Cotman, C.W. Temporal parameters of axon "sprouting" in the brain of the adult rat. *Experimental Neurology*, 1977, *54*, 179–183.

Maillous, J.G., Edwards, H.P., Barry, W.F., Roswell, H.C., & Ackorn, E.G. Effects of differential rearings on cortical evoked potentials of the albino rat. *Journal of Comparative Physiological Psychology*, 1974, *87*, 475–480.

Meyer, J.S., Shinohara, Y., Kanda, T., Ericsson, A.D., & Kok, N.K. Diaschisis resulting from acute unilateral cerebral infarction—quantitative evidence for man. *Archives of Neurology*, 1970, *23*, 241–247.

Meyer, P.M., Horel, J.A., & Meyer, D.R. Effects of dl-amphetamine upon placing responses in neodecorticate cats. *Journal of Comparative Physiological Psychology*, 1963, *56*, 402–404.

Mishkin, M. Perservertion of central sets after frontal lesions in monkeys. In: J.M. Warren, & K. Akert (eds.), *The frontal granular cortex and behavior*. New York: McGraw-Hill Book Co., 1964.

Mistretta, C., & Bradley, R. Effects of early sensory experience on brain and behavioral development. In: G. Gottlieb (ed.), *Studies on development of behavior and the nervous system, Vol. IV: Early influences*. New York: Academic Press, 1978.

Pettigrew, J.D. The effect of visual experience on the development of stimulus specificity by kitten cortical neurons. *Journal of Physiology*, 1974, *237*, 49–74.

Purpura, D. Neuropathological aspects of developmental disabilities. Paper presented at meeting honoring the International Year of the Disabled, Tokyo, Japan, September 1981.

Rosenzweig, M.R. Effects of environment on development of brain and behavior. In: E. Tobach, L. Aronson, & E. Shaw (eds.), *The biopsychology of development*. New York: Academic Press, 1971.

Rosenzweig, M.R., Bennett, E.L., & Diamond, M.C. Cerebral effects of differential environments occur in hypophysectomized rats. *Federation Proceedings*, 1970, *29*, 264–265.

Rosenzweig, M.R., Krech, D., Bennett, E.L., & Diamond, M.C. Effects of environmental complexity and training on brain chemistry and anatomy. *Journal of Comparative Physiological Psychology*, 1962, *55*, 429–437.

Russell, D.H. (ed.). *Polyamines in normal and neoplastic growth*. New York: Raven Press, 1973.

Rutter, M. Psychological sequelae of brain damage in children. *Journal of the American Psychiatric Association*, 1981, *32*, 1553–1554.

Schapiro, S., & Vukovich, K.R. Early experience effects upon cortical dendrites: A proposed model for development. *Science*, 1970, *167*, 292–298.

Sharpless, S.K. Supersensitivity-like phenomena in central nervous system. *Federation Proceedings*, 1975, *34*, 1990–1997.

Singh, V.K., & Sung, S.C. Effect of spermidine on DNA-dependent RNA polymerases from brain cell nuclei. *Journal of Neurochemistry*, 1972, *19*, 2885–2888.

Sperry, R.W. Cerebral organization and behavioral science. *Science*, 1961, *133*, 1749–1757.

Sperry, R.W. Changing priorities. In: W.M. Cowan, Z.W. Hall, & E.R. Kandel (eds.), *Annual review of neuroscience*. Palo Alto, CA: Annual Review, 1981.

Stravraky, G.W. *Supersensitivity following lesions of the nervous system*. Toronto: University of Toronto Press, 1961.

Tabor, C.W., & Tabor, H. 1, 4-diaminobutane (putrescine), spermidine, and spermine. *Annual Review of Biochemistry*, 1976, *45*, 285–306.

Teuber, H.L. Recovery of function after lesions of the central nervous system: History and prospects. *Neurosciences Research Program Bulletin*, 1974, *12*, 197–209.

Uphouse, L.L., & Bonner, J. Preliminary evidence for the effects of environmental complexity of hybridization of rat brain RNA to rat unique DNA. *Developmental Psychobiology*, 1975, *8*, 171–178.

Walsh, R.N., & Cummins, R.A. Mechanisms mediating the production of environmentally induced brain changes. *Psychological Bulletin*, 1975, *82*, 986–1000.

Walsh, R.N., & Greenough, W.T. (eds.). *Environments as therapy for brain dysfunction*. New York: Plenum Publishing Corp., 1976.

Ward, A.A., & Kennard, M.A. Effect of cholinergic drugs on recovery of function following lesions of the central nervous system. *Yale Journal of Biology and Medicine*, 1942, *15*, 189–228.

Will, B.E., Rosenzweig, M.S., Bennett, E.L., Herbert, M., & Morimoto, H. Relatively brief environmental enrichment aids recovery of learning capacity and alters brain measures after postweaning brain lesions in rats. *Journal of Comparative Physiological Psychology*, 1977, *91*, 33–50.

Yarborough, G.G., & Phillips, J.W. Supersensitivity of central neurons—a brief review of an emerging concept. *Canadian Journal of Neurological Sciences*, 1975, *2*, 147–152.

Curative Aspects of Mental Retardation:
Biomedical and Behavioral Advances
edited by Frank J. Menolascino, M.D., Ronald Neman, Ph.D., and Jack A. Stark, Ph.D.
Copyright 1983   Paul H. Brookes Publishing Co., Inc.   Baltimore · London

chapter 8

The Cell Biology of Neuronal Plasticity

Implications for Mental Retardation

GARY LYNCH, PH.D.
University of California
Irvine, California

RELATING THE CELL BIOLOGY of the brain to specific behavioral operations represents one of the most challenging issues facing neurobiology. Part of the difficulty can be traced to the extreme complexity first of behavior and then of the brain itself; behavioral neuroscientists attempt to explain one intricate set of phenomena by the occurrence of brief operations in an enormously elaborate collection of circuitries. The difficulties attendant to establishing causal relationships of this type are, if not overwhelming, at least intimidating.

The history of research into the neuronal origins of learning (or disturbances in learning) illustrates these points. Learning presumably is the consequence of subtle, semi-permanent changes in the characteristics of brain systems, but there are vast numbers of possible cellular explanations for these changes as well as sites at which they might occur. Beyond this lie the psychological issues of what has been learned and when—two questions that are not easily answered at least in animal studies. In addition, learning has sensory, motor, and affective con-

comitants, and these can be expected to confuse attempts to establish isomorphisms between behavioral and neuronal changes.

The above considerations have led a number of investigators interested in the cell biology of learning to begin searching the nervous system for "plastic" properties that seem to be reasonable candidates for a memory mechanism. If such properties could be found, then it might be possible to investigate whether they actually accompany learning. The hallmark of learning is persistence, and therefore the question becomes one of finding effects that occur relatively quickly and yet persist indefinitely. Since the business of brain cells seems to be communication with other brain cells, synaptic transmission has become a focal point in the study of neuroplasticity. It has been known for some time that neuromuscular transmission experiences an augmentation following periods of intense activity (e.g., Weinrich, 1971) but the transient nature of this phenomenon makes it an unlikely candidate for a memory mechanism. Recent studies of hippocampal synapses have uncovered the existence of a much more persistent form of potentiation following repetitive stimulation: this effect, called long-term potentiation (LTP) is induced by very brief trains of stimulation and can last for days or even weeks (Bliss & Gardner-Medwin, 1973; Bliss & Lomo, 1973). Given that it possesses the properties of rapidity and persistence, LTP represents a plausible model with which to search for cellular mechanisms that might be used in learning; the first part of this chapter is concerned, then, with the possible substrates of the long-term potentiation effect.

The mature hippocampus, in addition to its capacity for achieving lasting physiological change, as evidenced by the LTP studies, also possesses a surprising ability to build new synaptic connections (see Lynch, Gall, & Dunwiddie, 1978, for a review). While the extent to which growth and reorganization occur in hippocampus during behavior is unknown, the anatomical plasticity inherent in this and other structures in the mammalian brain certainly suggests a means by which the central nervous system might produce lasting modification of behavior. Therefore, investigations into the neurobiology of growth in the adult nervous system may prove relevant to the biology of memory. This topic is also briefly reviewed in later chapters in this book, particularly Chapter 12.

LONG-TERM POTENTIATION OF POSTSYNAPTIC RESPONSES IN HIPPOCAMPUS: LOCUS OF THE EFFECT AND SOME STRUCTURAL CORRELATES

The hippocampal formation receives the great majority of its afferent input from the entorhinal cortex, an extensive region occupying much of the posterior-medial surface of the rodent cerebral hemisphere. The fibers from this cortical region form a thick bundle of axons, the perforant path, which ends chiefly in the dendritic field of the dentate gyrus granule cells (see Figure 1).

Bliss and Lomo (1973) and Bliss and Gardner-Medwin (1973) made the remarkable observation that repetitive stimulation of this pathway, even for a few seconds, produced a stable enhancement of the postsynaptic potential generated by subsequent single pulse stimulation. This long-term potentiation effect has now been found in many regions of hippocampus (Douglas & Goddard, 1975; see Lynch et al., 1978, for a review; Schwartzkroin & Wester, 1975) and is illustrated in Figure 2.

Long-term potentiation presumably represents the end-point of a sequence of reactions set in motion by repetitive stimulation. Before considering what these reactions might be, it is necessary to identify where they are occurring and significant progress has been made in resolving this question. Several experiments have provided evidence against the idea that the axons undergo any changes as a result of the brief, high frequency stimulation (Dunwiddie, Madison, & Lynch, 1978) while other work argues strongly against the hypothesis that the target cells experience any generalized alterations (Dunwiddie & Lynch, 1978). This evidence together suggests that a modification of some aspect of the synaptic connection—the presynaptic bouton, postsynaptic spine, or the synaptic zone itself—is responsible for potentiation (see Lynch et al., 1978, for a review).

There are, of course, a vast array of potential substrates for the effect. Changes in the structure of the synaptic connection are tempting candidates because of the extreme stability of the LTP effect, and studies have been conducted to test this possibility. Work from one laboratory (Fifkova & Van Harreveld, 1977; Van Harreveld & Fifkova, 1975) using a rapid fixation procedure has provided evidence that high frequency stimulation of the perforant path induces a swelling of the dendritic spines and that this effect is restricted to the regions in which the entorhinal fibers terminate. It was not possible in this laboratory research to determine if the stimulation induced LTP, and so the relationship of the reported swelling to potentiation is uncertain. Work from the present author's laboratory using two hippocampal preparations, anesthetized rats, and *in vitro* slices, indicates that LTP in the pyramidal

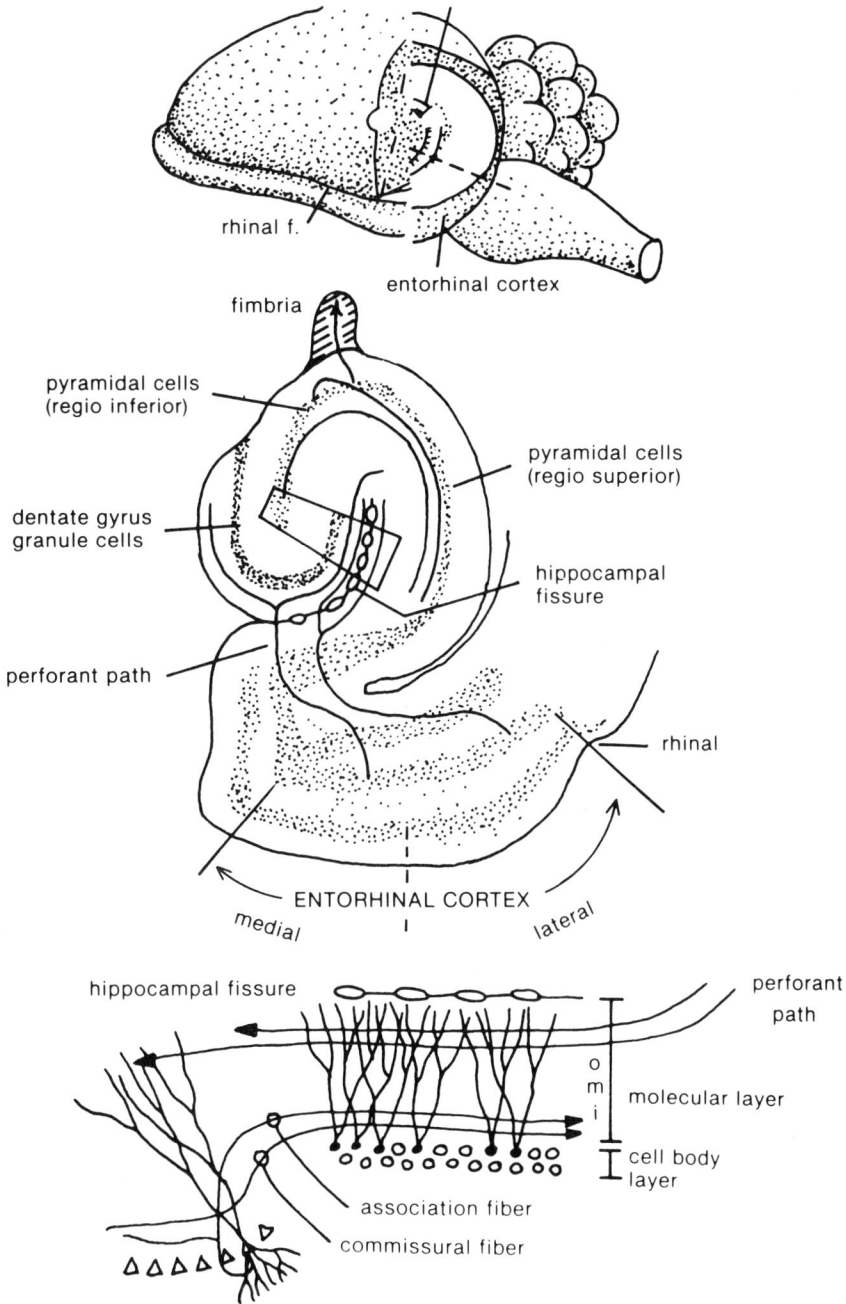

Figure 1. Aspects of the hippocampal formation. The upper panel indicates the position of the hippocampus in a rodent brain. The middle figure provides the location of pathways and structures in the hippocampal formation that are discussed in the text. The bottom drawing is an enlargement of the zone located in the area within the oblong box in the middle figure, and illustrates in further detail one of the areas used in studies of anatomical and physiological plasticity.

cells is accompanied by two very different types of structural changes: 1) an increase in the number of synapses made on the shafts of dendrites, and 2) a change in the shape of the dendritic spines (Lee, Oliver, Schottler, & Lynch, 1981; Lee, Schottler, Oliver, & Lynch, 1980) (Figure 3).

The first result was arrived at simply by

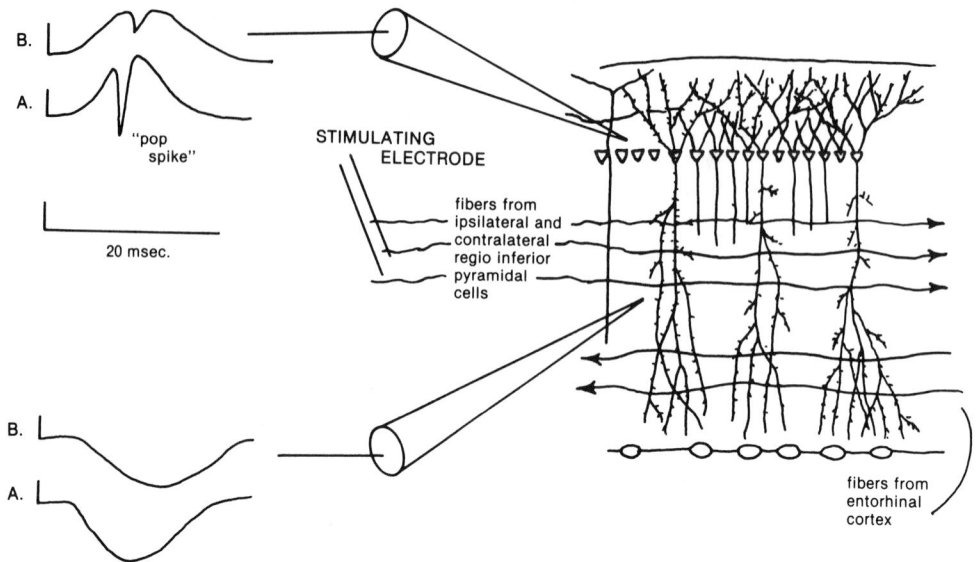

Figure 2.   Schematic illustration of a long-term potentiation experiment. A stimulating electrode is placed in the trajectory of the fibers from both sides of the regio inferior pyramidal cells; these fibers generate the great majority of all synapses in the dendritic zones of regio superior pyramidal cells (see Figure 1 for the location of these regions). Two extracellular recording micropipettes are used: one in the zone where the synapses are located, and the second in the layer of cell bodies that generate the dendrites. When single pulses are delivered to the stimulating electrode, a monophasic negative potential is produced in the synaptic zone; this is the extracellular reflection of current flowing into a sizeable number of dendritic processes. The cell body electrode records a positive response which is presumably due to current flowing out of the somata of the neurons whose dendrites have been activated; the cell body response also exhibits a sharp negative deflection. This is the population spike and is due to the action potentials ("spikes") generated by the pyramidal cell bodies (Andersen, Bliss, & Skrede, 1971). After testing for 15 to 30 minutes to ensure that the various responses are quite stable, 3 or 4 brief (0.5 seconds) trains of high frequency (200 per second) stimulation are delivered to the stimulating electrode after which testing is resumed using widely spaced single pulses. As a result of the high frequency stimulation, the subsequent responses to single pulses (A) are considerably increased. Thus the slope and peak height of the dendritic potential are greater and, as shown by the increased height of the population spike, a greater number of cells are driven to discharge. Once induced, these increases are extremely stable and persist for hours using *in vitro* slices or for days or even much longer in chronically implanted animals (see Lee, Oliver, Schottler, & Lynch, 1981, for a recent review and examples of the physiology). Note that the great majority of the dendrites in the target fields of the stimulated fibers arise from pyramidal cells (which are studded with fine spines) but then an occasional dendrite enters the field from a nonpyramidal cell.

counting (in a "blind" fashion) the numbers of the various types of synaptic contacts found in the dendritic regions exhibiting long-term potentiation. It was found that the incidence of synapses formed with dendritic spines was virtually identical in rats (and tissue slices) that received long trains of low frequency stimulation (which did not produce any detectable physiological effects) and in those in which LTP had been produced by 1-second bursts of 100 s^{-1} stimulation. The frequency of synaptic specializations on the primary shafts of the dendrites, however, was increased by 30% (in anesthesized rats) to 50% (in "slices") in the potentiated groups

compared to their controls. There are two interpretations of this effect: 1) The shape or size of synapses were somehow altered such that an increased number of synapses were detected by electron microscopy, or 2) Additional synapses of this type were constructed or assembled within several minutes of the stimulation train. If the postsynaptic densities of the shaft synapses were lengthened by stimulation, it is possible, perhaps likely, that a greater percentage of the population of these would be noted and counted during the analysis of the electron micrographs; however, careful measurements of this variable indicated that an increase in

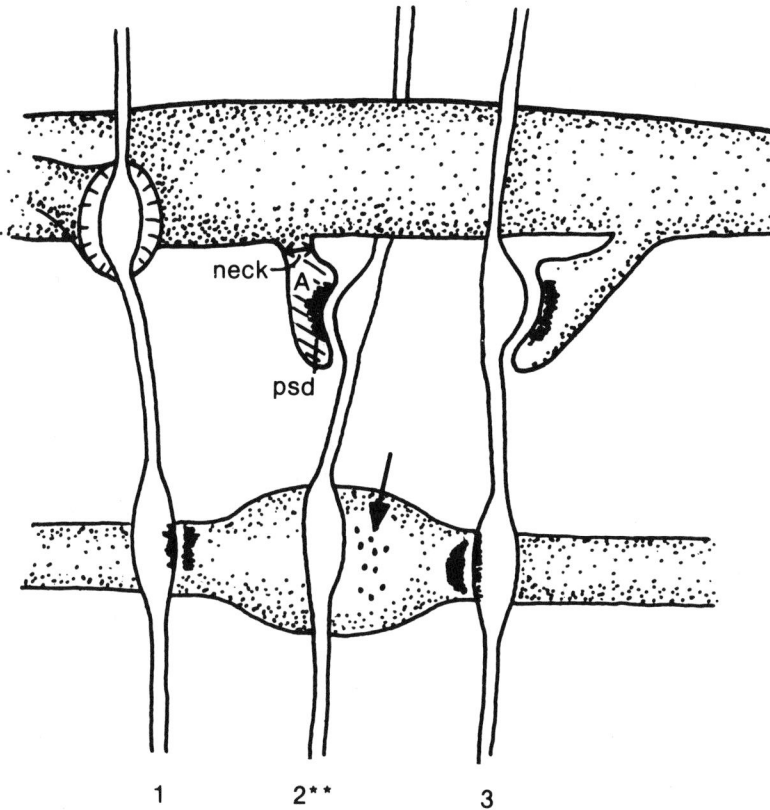

Figure 3.   The effects of repetitive stimulation on dendritic ultrastructure. Shown are an aspinous dendritic process and a dendritic branch possessing three spines. Synapses on the former are "shaft" contacts while the latter has spine synapses. It must be emphasized that the shaft category is much less frequent than the spine variety (about 1:40). Three axons (1, 2, 3) are shown making connections with both dendrites; only the middle axon is activated by the stimulating electrode (not shown). Following high frequency stimulation two changes were noted: 1) The number of "shaft" synapses per unit area was increased, and 2) measurements of the postsynaptic dendrites, the area of the spine, and the width of its neck were less variable. These data suggest that new contacts form between the stimulated fiber and the dendritic shaft (arrow) while the target spine becomes "rounded." Note that the presence of the nonactivated fibers and spines complicates evaluation of the quantitative data since measurements are made on both repetitively stimulated contacts as well as those generated by axons that were not driven by the stimulating electrode.

length had not occurred (Lee et al., 1981; Lee et al., 1980). In light of this, it is more likely that the increase in the number of shaft contacts in the potentiated groups was due to addition of new synapses of this category to the existing population.

Shaft synapses represent only a small percentage (2%–3%) of the total population of contacts in the hippocampus, and thus the increases described above would have very slight effects on the density of synapses in the potentiated zones. Furthermore, there was a marked tendency for shaft synapses to cluster along single dendritic processes; it was not uncommon to find 5 to 6 contacts on one long primary shaft. This raises the possibility that many, and perhaps most, of the shaft synapses are located on a particular and somewhat infrequent type of hippocampal neuron—the interneurons that extend long straight dendritic trees into the zones used in the above-described studies (Lorente de No., 1934) come to mind as one possibility. Therefore, given the small size of the increase in synapses relative to the total population, and the somewhat restricted location of the synaptic type involved, it seems unlikely that the shaft-synapse effect is the substratum of LTP.

This, of course, opens the question of what the physiological consequences of the increases might be, but this can be more profitably discussed once efforts to identify the location of shaft synapses in hippocampus are completed.

The evidence that high frequency stimulation produces a change in the shape of the dendritic spines is somewhat indirect. Measurements were made of the area subsumed by the spines, the length of their postsynaptic densities, and the width of the spine necks; the mean values for each of these were found not to be significantly different between control and potentiated groups. (There was a tendency for the medians to increase, but this did not reach statistical significance.) However, the coefficient of variation as well as the degree of "skewedness" of the within-animal (or slice) distributions for these measures were significantly reduced in the preparations that exhibited long-term potentiation (Lee et al., 1981; Lee et al., 1980). The fact that the distributions for three separate measures of the spine exhibited the same change greatly increases confidence in the general conclusion that the spines were more homogeneous in the potentiated animals. The simplest interpretation of this effect is that a sizable subgroup of the spines in the potentiated groups had changed their shapes such that random measurements through them were less variable; this could be accomplished, for example, by a shift from an ellipsoidal to an ovoidal shape by the "potentiated" spines. The results could not be accounted for by a generalized swelling (increased volume) of the spines, since this would certainly not cause a reduction in the variability of the distribution of measurements.

A change in the shape of the dendritic spines provides a plausible explanation for long-term potentiation, since such effects could act to increase the efficiency of the "coupling" between the site of the excitatory postsynaptic potential and the primary dendrite. Unfortunately, given that so little is known about LTP as well as shape change, tests of the hypothesis that the latter is responsible for the former will necessarily be restricted to attempts to correlate the two phenomena across a variety of experimental manipulations. Experiments are now in progress to determine if there is a correspondence between the time courses of long-term potentiation and the alterations in spines. Future work will measure the effects of treatments that block the induction of LTP upon the structural alterations produced by brief bursts of high frequency stimulation.

POSSIBLE "INTERMEDIATE" MECHANISMS IN THE PRODUCTION OF LONG-TERM POTENTIATION

If we assume that a structural change is at the basis of LTP, the question arises of how such effects could be produced within minutes and by relatively brief stimulation periods. Research into the biochemical processes that act as intermediates between the stimulation train and the final adjustment (structural or otherwise), which is the substratum of LTP, has only recently been undertaken and while nothing conclusive has emerged, the results thus far obtained have been suggestive.

Long-term potentiation is difficult to induce when extracellular levels of calcium are reduced (Dunwiddie & Lynch, 1979); under these conditions transient forms of synaptic facilitation are readily obtained, but the nondecremental LTP response occurs only infrequently. It is possible that this suppression is due to a reduced amount of transmitter released per stimulation pulse or, alternatively, it may indicate that calcium itself participates in the triggering of LTP. There is some evidence that calcium accumulates in nerve terminals during repetitive stimulation, and studies of hippocampal dendrites suggest that calcium invades the dendrites of the regio superior pyramidal cells during synaptic activation (Wong, Prince, & Basbaum, 1979). Calcium is an attractive candidate for the triggering of structural changes, since it exerts very potent effects on cytoskeleton (e.g., microtubules, actin filaments) and cell membranes and presumably these elements are involved both in synapse formation and shape change.

Perhaps related to this, and to the induction of LTP, are recent studies showing that even relatively modest levels of calcium (10–50 μM) produce an increase in the number of glutamate binding sites in hippocampal membranes (Baudry & Lynch, 1979b). This effect was partially irreversible since it persisted even after the calcium treated membranes were placed in low calcium medium; it is also of interest that the effects of calcium on glutamate binding sites were much less pronounced in cerebellar membranes (Baudry & Lynch, 1980a).

There is a substantial body of data suggesting that glutamate, or a closely related compound, is the transmitter of several hippocampal pathways, including those studied in the earlier described experiments on long-term potentiation (Nadler, Vaca, White, Lynch, & Cotman, 1976; see Storm-Mathisen, 1977, for a review; Wieraszko & Lynch, 1979). The hippocampus contains both sodium dependent and independent binding sites for glutamate, and there is reason to believe that the latter are located on postsynaptic membranes (Baudry & Lynch, 1979a,1981). Therefore, the observed effects of calcium on the number of sodium independent sites suggest that the cation regulates some aspect of the postsynaptic membrane or of the proteins related to it. Since the ultrastructural changes that accompany LTP (increased number of "shaft" synapses and alterations in the shape of spines and their postsynaptic densities) undoubtedly involve lasting modification of membranes, it is not unreasonable to hypothesize that the potentiation effect is produced by a mechanism analogous to that responsible for the calcium-induced persistent increase in glutamate binding sites. This idea is summarized in Figure 4 (see also Baudry & Lynch, 1980b).

Experiments attempting to identify the process through which calcium influences glutamate sites in hippocampal membranes have been in progress for a few years. Pharmacological studies have provided evidence that an enzymatic process is involved in the effect (Baudry & Lynch, 1980a); further definition of this process may permit tests of whether it is activated by repetitive stimulation.

GROWTH RESPONSES IN THE MATURE HIPPOCAMPUS

From the experiments described in the above section it appears that brief periods of intense activity produce structural changes in hippocampal synaptic anatomy. Other lines of work have led to the conclusion that the mature hippocampus possesses a far greater degree of anatomical plasticity than was detected in the stimulation experiments. Removal of one afferent of a dendritic field causes the remaining undamaged inputs to generate new terminals that form synapses with the denervated regions, resulting in the replacement of lost contacts. The target dendrites lose spines and postsynaptic densities following lesions of their afferents, but these reappear as the "sprouting" by neighboring fibers continues to develop (Lee, Stanford, Cotman, & Lynch, 1977; McWilliams & Lynch, 1979; Parnavelas, Lynch, Brecha, Cotman, & Globus, 1974). The growth response to partial deafferentation begins at about 5 days after lesions (Lynch, Gall, & Cotman, 1977) and continues at a steady pace (at least in terms of reinnervation) for several weeks (McWilliams & Lynch, 1979; Matthews, Cotman, & Lynch, 1976).

The significance of growth for the ongoing activities and functions of hippocampus is uncertain. There is evidence that degeneration and axonal growth occur in the vestibular nucleus of intact adult rats (Sotelo & Palay, 1971), and it is possible that sprouting is simply an exaggeration of a process that normally replaces lost synapses, spines, etc. Studies using environments of varying "richness" or complexity, as well as learning paradigms (Greenough, 1976, for an excellent review), have found that these variables influence the length of dendritic branches and numbers of spines in the cortex of adult rodents. Thus, growth may well be part of the brain's response to changing circumstances and it is conceivable that this is mediated by the same processes that underlie sprouting.

One factor that seems to argue against this hypothesis is the 5-day delay between the lesion and the onset of growth. While there is no a priori reason to assume that growth initiated by environmental circumstances does not require several days to get underway, at an intuitive level at least it seems unlikely that the brain's reaction to events would occur several days after the events had passed (it is possible that behaviorally induced changes in brain structure represent the final step of a series of processes—''consolidation''—that require several days to reach completion). In any case, the 5-day lag in sprouting may not reflect the time required to mobilize growth so much as the time needed to remove barriers to that growth. An intense astroglial hypertrophy begins to develop within hours of denervation, and the onset of sprouting corresponds reasonably well with the period at which this starts to subside (Rose, Cotman, & Lynch, 1976). Thus, it is possible that the intact axons react quickly to lesions of their neighbors but attempts at reinnervation are hindered for several days by the glial cells (see Lynch & Gall, 1979, for a review).

Almost nothing is known of the processes responsible for postlesion growth in the hippocampus or elsewhere in brain. However, it has been established that the response is much more vigorous in its extent and rate in immature (14 days postnatal) rats than it is in adult rats (Gall & Lynch, 1978; Lynch, Stanfield, & Cotman, 1973). Also, recent work suggests that in terms of the pace of reinnervation, the transition takes place quite gradually (Mc-Williams & Lynch, 1982, unpublished data). There are two general classes of explanation for these age-related changes in the sprouting response: 1) factors (e.g., glia) are added to the neuropil that retard postlesion growth, and 2) the fibers themselves change such that growth responses are altered. It is, of course, possible that both types of change take place.

The response of axons to lesions undergoes marked changes with age—in younger rats

the degenerating fibers rapidly disappear from the neuropil while in the adult they become electron-opaque and can persist as degenerating debris for weeks or months. This suggests that fibers do undergo pronounced changes in their structure and/or biochemistry during the time period in which sprouting becomes progressively more restricted. The question of what regulates axonal (and dendritic) growth in the adult may ultimately relate to the more basic problem of what is the nature of maturation; it is an intriguing possibility that sprouting and other forms of growth in the adult represent a transient and local reversal of the conditions that caused the nervous system to cease incremental growth.

CONCLUSION

It is evident from the above that the hippocampal region of the brain possesses capacities for lasting physiological and structural changes, and it is hypothesized here that one of these effects might occur during learning. Tests of this hypothesis are certain to be difficult. It may prove possible to first establish if cells in the hippocampus or related structures exhibit high frequency firing during training and, second, to test, at least in a crude fashion, for changes in synaptic efficiency following such bursts. The changes in shaft synapses and dendritic spine variability also represent new types of structural change, the occurrence of which might fruitfully be searched for after various types of environmental and behavioral manipulations. However, the greater value of the long-term potentiation effect and the sprouting phenomena may not be as candidates for correlates of learning (or some aspect of behavior related to learning), but rather as experimentally tractable yet plausible models with which to investigate the cellular processes that control physiological and structural plasticity. That is, the functional and anatomical changes described above suggest the existence of potent biochemical mechan-

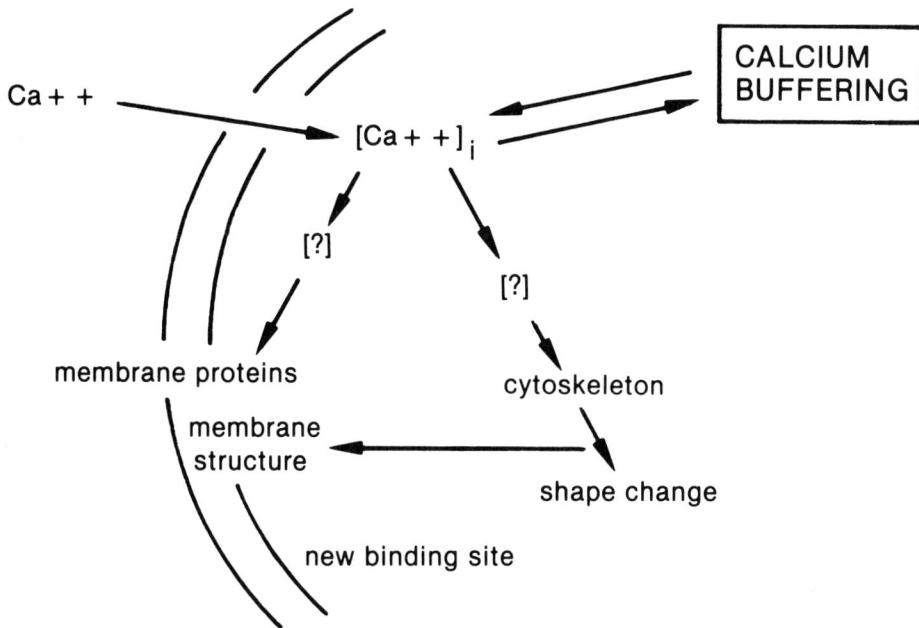

Figure 4. Hypothesis concerning the role of calcium in modifying the dendrite. According to this model, high frequency synaptic activation causes a transient increase in local calcium concentrations (either by influx from outside the cell or by an effect on buffering organelles); this in turn activates an unknown intermediate process that influences the membrane and cytoskeletal constituents. Change in these two results in membrane effects (e.g., uncovering of binding sites) and prepares the way for local shape changes.

isms of a nature and type that may prove to be quite different from those well-studied processes associated with chemical transmission and the regulation of membrane physiology. Thus, more molecular analyses of potentiation and sprouting could uncover the existence of phenomena that by their very natures and prior association with neuronal plasticity, will compel us to consider them as possible substrates of learning and learning disorders. If so, we will have taken a step toward investigating the impairments in central nervous system operation that must underlie some types of mental retardation.

REFERENCES

Andersen, P., Bliss, T. V. P., & Skrede, K.K. Unit analysis of hippocampal population spikes. *Experimental Brain Research*, 1971, *13*, 208–221.

Baudry, M., & Lynch, G. Two glutamate binding sites in the rat hippocampal membranes. *European Journal of Pharmacology*, 1979a, *57*, 283–285.

Baudry, M., & Lynch, G. Regulation of glutamate receptors by cations. *Nature*, 1979b, *282*, 748–750.

Baudry, M., & Lynch, G. Regulation of hippocampal glutamate receptors: Evidence for the involvement of a calcium-activated protease. *Proceedings of the National Academy of Sciences (U.S.A)*, 1980a, 77, 2298–2302.

Baudry, M., & Lynch, G. An hypothesis regarding the cellular mechanisms responsible for long-term synaptic potentiation in the hippocampus. *Experimental Neurology*, 1980b, *68*, 202–204.

Baudry, M., & Lynch, G. Characterization of two ³H-glutamate binding sites in rat hippocampal membranes. *Journal of Neurochemistry*, 1981, *36*, 811–820.

Bliss, T., & Gardner-Medwin, A. Long-lasting potentiation of synaptic transmission in the dentate area of the unanesthetized rabbit following stimulation of the preforant path. *Journal of Physiology*, 1973, *232*, 357–374.

Bliss, T., & Lomo, T. Long-lasting potentiation of synaptic transmission in the dentate area of the anaesthetized rabbit following stimulation of the perforant path. *Journal of Physiology*, 1973, *232*, 331–356.

Douglas, R., & Goddard, D. Long-term potentiation of the perforant path-granule cell synapse in the rat hippocampus. *Brain Research*, 1975, *86*, 205–215.

Dunwiddie, T., & Lynch, G. Long-term potentiation and depression of synaptic responses in the hippocampus: Localization and frequency dependency. *Journal of Physiology*, 1978, *276*, 353–361.

Dunwiddie, T., & Lynch, G. The relationship between extracellular calcium concentration and the induction of hippocampal long-term potentiation,. *Brain Research*, 1979, *169*, 103–110.

Dunwiddie, T., Madison, V., & Lynch, G. Synaptic transmission is required for initiation of long-term potentiation. *Brain Research*, 1978, *150*, 413–417.

Fifkova, E., & Van Harreveld, A. Long-lasting morphological changes in dendritic spines of dentate granular cells following stimulation in the entorhinal area. *Journal of Neurocytolgy*, 1977, *6*, 211–230.

Gall, C., & Lynch, G. Rapid axon sprouting in the neonatal rat hippocampus. *Brain Research*, 1978, *153*, 357–362.

Gall, C., McWilliams, R., & Lynch, G. Accelerated rates of synaptogenesis by "sprouting" afferents in the immature hippocampal formation. *Journal of Comparative Neurology*, 1980, *193*, 1047–1062.

Greenough, W. Enduring brain effects of differential experience and training. In: M. Rosenzweig & E. Bennett (eds.), *Neural mechanisms of learning and memory*. Cambridge, MA: M.I.T. Press, 1976.

Lee, K., Oliver, M., Schottler, F., & Lynch, G. Electron microscopic studies of brain slices: The effects of high frequency stimulation on dendritic ultrastructure. In: G. Kerkut & H. Wheel (eds.), *Electrical activity of isolated mammalian CNS preparations*. New York: Academic Press, 1981.

Lee, K., Schottler, F., Oliver, M., & Lynch, G. Brief bursts of high frequency stimulation produce two types of structural change in rat hippocampus. *Journal of Neurophysiology*, 1980, *44*, 247–258.

Lee, K., Stanford, E., Cotman, C.W., & Lynch, G. Ultrastructural evidence for bouton proliferation in the partially deafferented dentate gyrus of the adult rat. *Experimental Brain Research*, 1977, *29*, 475–485.

Lorente de No., R. Studies on the structure of the cerebral cortex. II. Continuation of study on the ammonic system. *J. fur Psychologie und Neurologie* (Leipzig), 1934, *46*, 13–147.

Lynch, G., & Gall, C. Organization and reorganization in the central nervous system: Evolving concepts of brain plasticity. In: F. Falkner & J.M. Tanner (eds.), *Human growth: A comprehensive treatise*. New York: Plenum Publishing Corp., 1979.

Lynch, G., Gall, C., & Cotman, C.W. Temporal parameters of axon "sprouting" in the brain of the adult rat. *Experimental Neurology*, 1977, *54*, 179–183.

Lynch, G.S., Gall, C., & Dunwiddie, T. Neuroplasticity in the hippocampal formation. In: M.A. Corner (ed.), *Progress in brain research*. Amsterdam: Elsevier Scientific Publishing Co., 1978.

Lynch, G., Stanfield, B., & Cotman, C. Development differences in postlesion axonal growth in the hippocampus. *Brain Research*, 1973, *59*, 159–168.

McWilliams, R., & Lynch, G. Terminal proliferation in the partially deafferented dentate gyrus: Time course for the appearance and removal of degeneration and the replacement of lost terminals. *Journal of Comparative Neurology*, 1979, *187*, 191–198.

Matthews, D.A., Cotman, C.W. & Lynch, G. An electron microscopic study of lesion-induced synaptogenesis in the dentate gyrus of the adult rat. II. Reappearance of morphologically normal synaptic contacts. *Brain Research*, 1976, *115*, 23–41.

Nadler, J.B., Vaca, K.V., White, W.F., Lynch, G.S., & Cotman, C.W. Aspartate and glutamate as possible transmitters of excitatory hippocampal afferents. *Nature*, 1976, *260*, 538–540.

Parnavelas, J., Lynch, G., Brecha, N., Cotman, C., & Globus, A. Spine loss and regrowth in the hippocampus following deafferented hippocampus. *Nature*, 1974, *248*, 71–73.

Rose, G., Cotman, C.W., & Lynch, G. Hypertrophy and redistribution of astrocytes in deafferented hippocampus. *Brain Research Bulletin*, 1976, *1*, 87–92.

Schwartzkroin, P., & Wester, K. Long-lasting facilitation of synaptic potential following tetanization in the *in vitro* hippocampal slice. *Brain Research*, 1975, *89*, 107–119.

Sotelo, C., & Palay, S. Altered axons and axon terminals in the lateral vestibular nucleus of the rat: Possible example of axonal remodeling. *Laboratory Investigation*, 1971, *25*, 653–673.

Storm-Mathisen, J. Localization of transmitter candidates in the brain: The hippocampal formation as a model. *Progress in Neurobiology*, 1977, *8*, 119–181.

Van Harreveld, A., & Fifkova, E. Swelling of dendritic spines in the fascia dentate after stimulation of the perforant fibers as a mechanism of post-tetanic potentiation. *Experimental Neurology*, 1975, *49*, 736–749.

Weinrich, D. Ionic mechanisms of post-tetanic potentiation at the neuromuscular junction of the frog. *Journal of Physiology* (London), 1971, *212*, 431–446.

Wieraszko, A., & Lynch, G. Stimulation-dependent release of possible transmitter substances from hippocampal slices studied with localized perfusion. *Brain Research*, 1979, *160*, 372–376.

Wong, R.K.S., Prince, D.A., & Basbaum, A.I. Intradendritic recordings from hippocampal neurons. *Proceedings of the National Academy of Sciences (U.S.A.)*, 1979, *76*, 986–990.

Curative Aspects of Mental Retardation:
Biomedical and Behavioral Advances
edited by Frank J. Menolascino, M.D., Ronald Neman, Ph.D., and Jack A. Stark, Ph.D.
Copyright 1983   Paul H. Brookes Publishing Co., Inc.   Baltimore · London

chapter 9

Current Uses of Peripheral and Central Nervous System Transplants and Their Future Potential for Reversing Mental Retardation

A.K. OMMAYA, M.D., F.R.C.S., F.A.C.S.
National Institute of Neurological and Communicative Disorders and Stroke
National Highway Traffic Safety Administration
George Washington University Medical Center
Washington, D.C.

T HIS CHAPTER MIGHT APPROPRIATELY be subtitled, "Rebuilding the Brain," although this is not to say that we are anywhere near rebuilding the brain when it has been damaged or not developed, but there *is* hope that we can. In this regard, one is reminded of the story of a scholar who did a favor for a king, and the king offered him a reward. When the scholar asked for 100 gold coins, the king asked him if that was all he wanted. He answered, "Can there be any more than 100?" The point is that we sometimes unconsciously restrict our own capabilities to grasp a situation. There is currently cause for optimism in the field of mental retardation (an optimism that has been described as optimistic skepticism). Although one should never overstep the bounds of reality, certain scientific possibilities do exist for making advances.

Mental retardation is a description that covers a wide variety of disorders, as Holmes et al. (Holmes, 1972) have demonstrated in their excellent compendium of diseases. Anyone who has tried to establish a medical diagnosis for mentally retarded individuals knows how frustrating the process can be (Holmes, 1972). Mental retardation can also be viewed as a group of states that reflect blocks of varying levels of the central nervous system, not only within the organization of the central nervous system itself, but of the input and the output of the system. There is a vital need for diagnostic precision in the great number of individuals on whom a diagnosis is not known. Although the diagnostic clarification difficulties in this field have improved measurably in the past decade, much remains a mystery. In most series of disorders, a large proportion (about 75%–90%) fall into the categories of mild, familial, or "physiological" retardation. In the majority of these patients there is no significant brain pathology, although the concept of "biochemical lesions" without correlated anatomical lesions is well recognized. The remaining 10%-25% of patients with consistently associated brain pathology often have diffuse abnormalities rather than well-localized lesions, a feature that is probably also true of cases with "physiological" retardation who have biochemical "lesions."

In spite of such inauspicious factors in the treatment outlook it is important to review what is known about the scientific efforts aimed at the regeneration of improved function in a damaged and defective nervous system. The work in this area is at present advancing significantly, both at the biochemical-metabolic and the brain–spinal cord levels of study. This chapter highlights these two areas.

GENERAL APPROACHES

The effort to understand the cause of mental retardation can involve basically two research approaches. First, there are ongoing and long-standing classical research programs and scientific procedures aimed at narrowing the cause of the symptom of mental retardation in a given individual down to one cause. It is rare that we are fortunate enough to find *one* cause or condition in such cases, however, because mental retardation is often a multifactorial condition with many types of interacting causes. The second approach is just as important and may be applicable now: i.e., attempt to understand the unique features of the central nervous system in a given retarded individual, thereby allowing us to intervene therapeutically and, it is hoped, improve the ability of this defectively formed nervous system to communicate with the environment.

Among the unique features of the central nervous system usually are, first, a basic structural redundancy. There seem to be *more* structures in the brain than are being used at any one time. In addition, there is plasticity in the nervous system, a good example being in learning to write with one's hand—a pretty good job can still be done at writing with one's nose! The ability to transfer learning

from one part of the body to another is a remarkable achievement for the nervous system. Two other unique features of the nervous system are its reintegrative and regenerative capacities. It seems that the nervous system, when damaged or abnormally formed, will try to reassemble itself into some form that resembles the original. A good analogy here is the holograph picture. A holograph plate may be taken and cut into many pieces; one of these small pieces can then be used to regenerate the original picture—although with much less detail and quality. That the nervous system possesses capacities for reintegration and regeneration is certain; how to take advantage of them is not yet known. Recent research findings show that regeneration in the mammalian nervous system is not an impossible goal.

In considering the ongoing search for causes in mental retardation, a few will be touched upon here. The work of Roscoe Brady in enzyme replacement therapy in inborn errors of metabolism is encouraging because it is based on a clear understanding of an enzymatic defect in a specific group of conditions that cause the symptom of mental retardation. In Tay-Sachs disease, one of the factors that has prevented the application of enzyme therapy has been the blood-brain barrier. Recently, Brady and his colleagues have developed a technique that can harmlessly change the vulnerability of the blood-brain barrier and allow the enzyme being used for treatment to enter the blood stream. This treatment-curative technique is now being tested in a group of patients. Similarly, the applied clinical research of Dean Murray in England on Hunter's disease shows that the subcutaneous implantation of cultured skin fibroblasts can induce the excretion of mucopolysaccharides to correct the enzyme deficit in this disease. Recent observations on Down syndrome indicate that the genetically determined accumulation of aluminum in the brain may be somewhat analogous to that found in senility, and the possible enzymatic clues to the causes of such abnormal accumulation now are being sought.

SPINAL CORD AND BRAIN REGENERATION: GENERAL ASPECTS

Our understanding of the unique features of the central nervous system has always profited from the field of neurosurgical interventions. First, with regard to the general concept of reintegration, there is good evidence that when the nervous system is damaged, it tends to reconstruct itself along the same plan that it uses in its own development (i.e., ontogeny). For example, if there is a small area of damage in the hypothalamus of an animal, the pattern of recovery from the defects follows the same sequence as developing functions in an infant animal. This has also been found in humans; if a hemiplegic limb is observed in its recovery—the development of the way the limb grasps and moves—the pattern of recovery proceeds in exactly the same manner as the development of early movements in infants. The drive to develop the same kind of function is always there; the recovery-cure problems constitute the blocks to full recovery. Recent research suggests that there are higher levels of inhibition in the system that may be blocking the recovery. The recent work with the cerebellar stimulator in cerebral palsy is still at an early stage, and it is perhaps too early to give any definitive answer to this problem. But one can say that such stimulation-induced improvements in spasticity (which then allows recovery with retaining of the ability to move) permit us to consider whether the removal of the inhibitory effects from other parts of the brain may be a key factor in allowing the recovery to occur.

The other aspect of reintegration of the nervous system is not simply *ontogenetic* as described earlier—in other words, recovery along the lines determined by the development of the individual—but it may also be along a *phylogenetic* scale. This idea has originated from observations on patients who have suffered severe head injuries. In the course of their recovery, which often takes months, one sees a replay of behavior patterns that seem to follow repeatable sequences. The first behaviors are extremely reflex, the sort of behavior that Paul MacClean has described in his hypothesis of the evolution of organization of the brain as "reptilian," i.e., predictable reflex behaviors with apparently limited learning capacity. This type of behavior seems to be related to the brain stem and the basal ganglia—the central core of the brain—which has its own chemical nature. This primitive reptilian type of behavior is then dominated very quickly by limbic behavior, in which the patient starts developing emotional overactivity, hypersexuality, voracious appetite, and a tendency to put everything into the mouth. Limbic behavior is followed by a labile affect and then by the slow recreation of intellectual behavior representing possible reintegration of the neocortex, the most advanced development in MacClean's truine-brain hypothesis. It may be that if these types of behavior could be understood at each level, we could use the behaviors to make maximum communicative ability possible in patients who may be retarded at these various levels. This is one approach that remains to be exploited. One of the interesting avenues of neurosurgical biological techniques now being developed is aimed at improving brain function not by stimulation or surgical removal, but by direct addition of an exogenous functioning tissue that can provide factors deficient in the brain (Ommaya, 1979).

REPAIR AND REGENERATION: SPECIFIC DIMENSIONS

Ramon y Cajal, a pioneer in the field of repair and regeneration, as well as in so many areas related to the nervous system, stated in the 1928 revision of his classic book *Degeneration and Regeneration of the Nervous System:* "[T]he regenerative process of the white matter which is so remarkably faint and sluggish under ordinary conditions can be powerfully stimulated by means of active or trophic substances liberated by the mesodermic scar and diffused in the spinal wounds and their edges." Cajal also pointed out in the same work that little stab wounds of the spinal cord did not stimulate regenerative efforts, while major traumatic wounds did, and that the regenerative process was vigorous in younger animals. Cajal and his pupil Tello explored experimentally the use of sciatic nerve grafts into the spinal cord and brain and in a few suitable cases were able to show sprouting of central nervous fibers using the sheath cell components of the graft as a guidance system. The search for the neurotropic or "neuroregenerative factors" from such mesodermic sources then began, culminating in the discovery of nerve growth factor of Levi-Montalcini and Hamburger (1953), and of a neurotropic polypeptide by Liu, Balkovie, Sheef, and Zacks (1981), which appears to be the neurotropic factor of Cajal. What stops the central axon sprouts from reaching their synaptic destinations if such neurotropic factors can be provided, e.g., by Schwann cells, at the site of injury? In experiments by Aguayo (in press) and colleagues, mammalian optic nerve (central nervous system) grafts were placed between cut ends of the sciatic nerve. The actively regenerating peripheral neurons avoided the central nervous system graft, seeing instead the connective tissue sheath of the optic nerve. Could it be that neuroglial or other cells in the central nervous system graft antagonize the positive tropism already present (Windle, 1980)? This antagonistic mechanism as suggested by Windle is very likely to be a major cause of failure of central nervous system regeneration in addition to various technical aspects of neural grafting. Thus Kao (1974) and Kao, Chang, and Bloodworth (1977) have shown that microneurosurgical reconstruction of the crushed spinal cord in dogs using peripheral nerve grafts can be facilitated by two technical improvements: 1) careful sub-pial microsurgical technique, and 2) delaying the graft for 1 week after the initial crush-severance of the spinal cord in order to allow removal of necrotic tissue by a spontaneous self-limiting process the authors call "lysosomal spinal cord autotomy" completed in the first week after trauma. Kao et al. (1977) have shown that such technical

improvements do allow the grafted nerves to adhere to the spinal cord stumps and enable significant axonal regrowth across the graft but have not been able as yet to show significant functional improvement correlating with axonal regrowth. Two recent attempts at replication of Dr. Kao's work have been carried out in rats by J. Cubitt at Dr. Lloyd Guth's laboratory and in rhesus monkeys by Dr. Carrie Walters working in my own laboratory. In the rat, to date, no evidence of functional recovery or histological axonal crossing over the cord transaction has been noted (Cubitt, personal communication). In the rhesus monkey, Dr. Walters and I have tested Dr. Kao's technique of microsurgical delayed grafting in the crushed spinal cord using autologous peripheral nerve with and without adjuvant treatment using pulsed electromagnetic radiation with the Diapulse device. The latter modality had been claimed by Dr. Wilson to facilitate rapid wound healing and encourage axonal regeneration across the hemisected spinal cord of cats. The Diapulse device produces a pulsed electromagnetic radiation in the 27.12 megacycle band at a peak output of 975 watts, with a 25.3 average wattage for 65 microsecond pulses at 900 microsecond intervals. This treatment is given for 30 minutes twice a day for 1 month. In 2 of 10 monkeys, we were able to find definite evidence of neural signal processing across the graft, with scanty axonal growth across the site of the delayed peripheral nerve graft. The signal processing did not, however, reach the cortex and there was no functional improvement in the paraplegic animals. It should also be noted that these two somewhat positive results for axonal regeneration across a transected cord shared only one common factor: Both had received the pulsed radio-frequency Diapulse therapy after cord crush and delayed removal of the debris. However, only one of these two had also received a peripheral nerve graft. Thus, axonal regrowth across a transected cord does not require a peripheral nerve graft, but further experiments are obviously needed (Walters, Ommaya, Rigamonti, et al., 1981).

The early work on biological transplants

into the central nervous system was initially brought to the attention of the scientific community by the late Dr. Hans Teuber, a pioneer neuropsychologist who pointed out in observations still unpublished that certain limbic brain structure can affect permanent implants of cells secreting various types of transmitters, and that such grafts will function. The implications of such a combination of biological and pharmaceutical approaches are indeed extremely important. Dr. Ulf Stenevi (1980), working in Sweden, has developed a technique for transplanting embryonic rat CNS tissue to the brain of adult rats, with a 70%–90% survival rate for the graft. His group claims that embryonic CNS tissue can promote regeneration of axotomized central neurons and serve as a bridge for the regenerating axons across a tissue defect. In the septohippocampal system of rats, Stenevi has shown that embryonic transplants form extensive and reciprocal connections with the denervated regions of the host brain and, in some cases, the distribution of these connections mimic very closely the original innervation patterns (Stenevi, 1980).

Probably the most significant and clinically relevant recent contribution to the use of brain grafts and neural regeneration is that from the laboratory of Dr. Richard Jed Wyatt at the National Institute of Mental Health (NIMH) unit in St. Elizabeth's Hospital in Washington, D.C. A recent paper by Drs. M.J. Perlow and Wyatt from this unit, in collaboration with Dr. B.J. Hoffer from the University of Colorado and Drs. A. Seiger and L. Olson from the Karolinska Institute of Stockholm, Sweden, reported the first successful reversal of an induced neurological disorder in rats (caused by a well-defined biochemical defect) by transplanting to the anatomical site of the defect, fetal brain tissue containing neurons capable of producing the biochemical factor missing in the neurologically ill rats (Perlow, Hoffer, Seiger, Olson, and Wyatt, 1979). This demonstration of the functional potential of brain grafts was carried out as follows: Rats were given unilateral injections of 6-hydroxydopamine into the substantia nigra, which, in one week,

caused degeneration of local dopamine-containing neurons and also of their axonal terminals in the corpus striatum, with resultant severe reduction of dopamine in the ipsilateral corpus striatum. Behaviorally, these rats showed marked rotational movements opposite to the side of the lesion when given the dopamine receptor agonist apomorphine systemically. This was probably due to a supersensitivity of striatal neurons to dopamine, as shown by increased dopamine receptor sites, increased activity of dopamine-stimulated adenylate cyclase, and decreased threshold of caudate nucleus neurons to locally applied dopamine agonists. Two to 4 months after the initial lesions were produced and the rotational behavior to apomorphine injection fully established, grafts of fetal rat midbrain containing the substantia nigra were obtained and injected into the lateral ventricle ipsilateral to the side of the initial lesion. Control injections of sciatic nerve grafts were used in different animals. Rats receiving the midbrain grafts showed significantly better recovery from rotational behavior than the control rats. Moreover, histochemical studies showed excellent survival and growth of the brain tissue grafts with invasion of the adjacent caudate nucleus by the substantial nigra-containing brain grafts and no evidence of tissue rejection for up to 2 months.

In a further study by Freed, Perlow, Karoum, Seiger, Olson, Hoffer, and Wyatt (in press), from Dr. Wyatt's laboratory, additional rats treated as above were studied for 6–10 months after grafting to determine if the grafts would be rejected or survive permanently. They were able to confirm such long-term survival of the grafts histochemically, behaviorally, and biochemically. Concentrations of dopamine increased in adjoining parts of the caudate nucleus, and although the brains of host animals showed the expected changes of aging after 8–10 months, the grafts showed no such aging change or other sign of deterioration. The authors concluded that embryonic brain grafts can become permanent functional constituents of the brains of host animals, at least for this species (rat) and at this location (substantia nigra—caudate nucleus vicinity). The application of such a technique to analogous human diseases, e.g., parkinsonism, was recognized by Freed et al. (in press), and a preliminary report of such an application has been made by Backland.

In a recent chapter in the book *Functional Neurosurgery*, I emphasized the significance of what may be called the biological techniques now available to the neurosurgeon (Ommaya, 1979). Peripheral nerve grafts can serve as a source of Schwann cells for myelinization of experimentally demyelinated portions of the central nervous system, as first demonstrated by Blakemore (1977). Central nervous system grafts from embryonic sources can provide functional support to neurotransmitter deficient areas, as demonstrated by Wyatt and his colleagues (Freed, in press; Perlow et al., 1979) and by Bjorklund (1980, in press) in Sweden.

What are the barriers to the application of such techniques in the human? First of all, obviously, such transplantation techniques are well suited to the correction of a focal deficit, but may not be of much benefit in diseases with diffuse pathology or a multifocal dysfunction. Second, certain obstacles to axonal growth must be overcome; for example, regeneration or elongation of the transected mammalian central nervous system axon requires that the axon must break through its own myelin sheath without rupturing the terminal club, as is the case in the transected goldfish optic nerve. This suggests the need for some method to demyelinate the myelin sheath of the transected axon at its tip. Lysolecithin has been used *in vivo* by Dr. Blakemore and Drs. Borustein and Baine (1980, in press) are currently investigating the use of antiwhite matter serum to inhibit oligodendroglial differentiation and myelinogenesis "*in vitro.*" A further obstacle is the marked glial proliferation at the site of neural injury, which acts as a "scar" to block the pathways for regenerating axons to travel to their synaptic destination. Brockes (1980, in press) and colleagues have recently reported the purification of a brain tissue mitogen (from bovine pituitary gland and brain tissue) that stimulates Schwann cell and astrocyte division but is inactive on oligodendroglia and macrophases. Reir (1980) has suggested that the presence of numerous gap junctions between the astrocytic processes forming mammalian "scars" (which are absent in the easily regenerated Xenopus spinal cord wounds) may be critical.

SUMMARY

Clearly, considerable basic work remains to be done. However, it is also evident that some applications of techniques to human situations are on the horizon. Thus, the possibility of using embryonic brain grafts to correct such relatively well-defined disorders as parkinsonism is close to clinical application. In order to facilitate both the basic research and its subsequent clinical applications, the following observations are pertinent.

Current research in brain transplantation is poorly coordinated and suffers severely from a lack of continuity, often due to interruptions in fiscal support and in the lack of continuous availability of qualified investigators at one location for more than 2 to 3 years. Thus, there is a need for a modest but well-organized program to focus on the potential applications of emerging basic data as well as to coordinate existing data and to serve, as well, as a center for obtaining fiscal support. Because four of the major groups working in neural regeneration in the United States are located in the Baltimore-Washington, D.C. area, the possibility of developing a program center in that locality, and of ensuring coordination, is enhanced. Ideally such a center should have ready access to hospitals as well as laboratory facilities and should have greater flexibility than is currently available in such well-established entities as the National Institutes of Health.

In addition, at this stage of scientific-governmental research cooperation, there is some reason for optimism. Recent significant developments at the scientific organization level have encouraged cooperation among facilities that are at present very difficult to pull together. In many agencies and universities throughout the country, work is proceeding on the nervous system, in the treatment of diseases of the nervous system, in fundamental investigations of the nervous system, and in aspects of the management problems of handicapped and retarded individuals. Often, however, it is the case that an important breakthrough at one level cannot be transmitted to the next level, in terms of transfer of the technology, for reasons that are not logical or scientific. Recognizing this, the Committee on Science and Technology of the United States Congress convened a panel on research on handicapped individuals. At the committee's first session in 1978, a report was published recommending the creation of a "National Council for Research on the

Handicapped" to coordinate the multiplicity facilities for handicapped persons, including, of course, retarded citizens. The problem remained, however, of making this recommendation a reality. The convening of the White House Conference on the Handicapped represented a big step forward in the recognition of handicapped persons' needs and led to an exchange of ideas between the White House and Congress. It is hoped that soon the momentum generated from that conference will lead to legislation sponsoring the creation of a National Council. Such a council would fulfill a crucial need. As we all know, one of the factors that most seriously hampers our ability to use the human resources and scientific knowledge that we have is the absence of a broadly based organization that can transfer latest research findings into practical applications.

REFERENCES

Aguayo, A.J. Axonal regeneration into glial and Schwann cell transplants. *Proceedings of the 5th Biennial Conference on the Regeneration of the Central Nervous System,* in press.

Bjorklund, A. Reconstruction of brain circuitries by neural implants. *Proceedings of the 1st International Symposium on Spinal Cord Reconstruction,* 1980.

Blakemore, W.F. Remyelination of CNS axons by Schwann cells transplanted from the scientific nerve. *Nature,* 1977, *266,* 68–69.

Blakemore, W.F. Unpuslished observations.

Borustein, M.B., & Baine, C.S. Alterations of myelogenesis in tissue culture by anti-CNS antiserum. *Proceedings of the 1st International Symposium on Spinal Cord Reconstruction,* 1980.

Brockes, J.P. The identification and purification of cultured rat Schwann cells and control of Schwann cell proliferation in vitro. *Proceedings of the 1st International Symposium on Spinal Cord Reconstruction,* 1980.

Freed, W.J., Perlow, M.J., Karoum, F., Seiger, A., Olson, L., Hoffer, B.J., & Wyatt, R.J. Restoration of dopaminergic function by grafting of fetal rat substantia nigra to the caudate nucleus: Long-term behavioral, biochemical and histochemical studies. *Experimental Neurology,* in press.

Holmes, L.B. *Mental retardation. An atlas of diseases with associated physical abnormalities.* New York: MacMillan Publishing Co., 1972.

Kao, C.C. Comparison of healing process in transected spinal cords grafted with autogenous brain tissue, sciatic nerve and nodose ganglion. *Experimental Neurology,* 1974, *44,* 424–439.

Kao, C.C. Functional recovery of contused spinal cords repaired by delayed nerve grafting. *Proceedings of the American Association of Neurology Surgeons,* 1977, Article 7.

Kao, C.C., Chang, L.W., Bloodworth, J.M.B. Jr. Axonal regeneration across transected mammalian spinal cords: An electron microscopic study of delayed nerve grafting. *Experimental Neurology,* 1977, *54,* 591–615.

Levi-Montalcini, R., & Hamburger, V. A diffusible agent of Mouse Sarcoma producing hyperplasia of sympathetic ganglia and hyperneurolization of viscera in the chick embryo. *Journal of Comparative Zoology,* 1953, *123,* 238–288.

Liu, H.M., Balkovie, E.S., Sheef, M.F., & Zacks, S.I. Production *in vitro* of a neurotrophic substance from proliferative neurolemma-like cells. *Experimental Neurology,* 1981, *64,* 271–283.

Ommaya, A.K. Frontiers of functional neurosurgery in biomedical research. In: T. Rasmussen & R. Marino (eds.), *Functional neurosurgery.* New York: Raven Press, 1979.

Perlow, M.J., Hoffer, B.J., Seiger, A., Olson, L., & Wyatt, R.J. Brain grafts reduce motor abnormalities produced by destruction of nigrostriatal dopamine. *System. Science,* 1979, *204,* 643–647.

Ramon y Cajal, S. *Degeneration and regeneration of the nervous system.* London: Oxford University Press, 1928.

Reir, P.J. Axonal penetration of transplanted astrocytic scar tissue in amphibians and mammals. *Proceedings of the 1st International Symposium on Spinal Cord Reconstruction,* 1980.

Stenevi, U. Use of embryonic CNS transplants to promote briding of regenerating central axons across lesions in the brain and spinal cord. *Proceedings of the 1st International Symposium on Spinal Cord Reconstruction,* 1980.

Walters, C., Ommaya, A.K., Rigamonti, J., & Kao, C.C. Regenerative potential of transected monkey spinal cord treated with peripheral nerve grafting and pulsed electromagnetic radiation. In: R. Becker (ed.), *Tissue regeneration and regrowth.* New York: Raven Press, 1981.

Windle, W.F. Recollections of research in spinal cord regeneration. *Proceedings of the 1st International Symposium on Spinal Cord Reconstruction,* 1980.

Curative Aspects of Mental Retardation:
Biomedical and Behavioral Advances
edited by Frank J. Menolascino, M.D., Ronald Neman, Ph.D., and Jack A. Stark, Ph.D.
Copyright 1983   Paul H. Brookes Publishing Co., Inc.   Baltimore · London

chapter 10

A Possible Role for Pyruvate Dehydrogenase in Modulation of Synaptic Efficacy

MICHAEL D. BROWNING, PH.D.
Yale University School of Medicine
New Haven, Connecticut

THE SEARCH FOR CURES FOR mental retardation is an extremely ambitious project and, as evidenced by the wide variety of approaches described in this book, the search takes numerous directions. The approach employed in the work described in Chapters 7–9 is based on the assumption that progress can be made in the search for cures for mental retardation by studying the adaptive capability of the brain. One obvious area of importance in such studies is the ability of the brain to recover from damage. Chapter 7 reviewed the parameters of central nervous system recovery and how and why it occurs in young and older animals. Chapter 8 reported on studies with rats in which, following certain types of experimentally-induced brain damage, a dramatic growth is seen in the undamaged neurons. Chapter 9 demonstrated an even more remarkable finding, that it is possible in some cases to transplant brain tissue into an adult mammalian brain and obtain functional growth of the transplant. In the present author's view, it is reasonable to expect that as we progress in comprehending the capacity of the brain for growth and reor-

ganization, we will move closer to understanding conditions that will support the active recovery from the effects of brain damage.

Although brain damage of some type is likely to be a component of many forms of mental retardation, little if any specific organic damage is detected in most of the less severe cases of retardation. Thus, for approximately 75% of all retarded individuals, there is no known evidence of brain damage other than certain demonstrable cognitive and developmental disabilities. One might conclude from this fact that there are no organic defects in mildly retarded individuals. However, such a conclusion is premature, particularly since our knowledge of the brain is most limited when it comes to understanding the organic bases of cognitive abilities. This author would argue that our inability to identify organic bases for most mild or moderate forms of retardation may be due, in many cases, to our inability to detect mild or moderate organic defects. One point that should not be overlooked in this discussion, particularly with regard to the search for cures

119

for mental retardation, is that prospects for cure or amelioration of organic defects will probably be best in those individuals who suffer from only mild organic defects. There are, therefore, compelling reasons for continuing to ask the question, do organic defects underlie some forms of mild or moderate retardation? In order to address this question intelligently, we need to make substantial progress in our understanding of the basic organic components of cognitive processes. For the past several years, Drs. Gary Lynch, Thomas Dunwiddie, Michel Baudry, William Bennett, and this author at the University of California at Irvine, have been actively involved in studying a brain process called long-term synaptic potentiation, which is thought by many to be a likely candidate as a neural building block or substrate of learning. In this chapter, work is discussed that may be pertinent to the search for cures for mental retardation, not because it pertains to the ability of the brain to recover from damage, but rather because it pertains to the basic processes in the brain that underlie cognition and that, when defective, could result in cognitive impairment.

LONG-TERM SYNAPTIC POTENTIATION

Our interest in long-term synaptic potentiation (LTP) was due in part to the suggestion made by D.O. Hebb (1949) that if one wanted to identify processes that subserved learning, then one should search for a synaptic circuit that changed in strength after a brief period of use. For some time, considerable effort was devoted to attempts to find such a circuit, but to little avail. However, in 1973, Bliss and Lomo demonstrated that a brief pulse of high frequency stimulation in the hippocampus (a brain region that has classically been thought to be important for learning and memory) was followed by a significant and long-lasting increase in the strength of the synaptic circuits that had been stimulated. Given the importance of this LTP as a candidate for the neural substrate of learning, our group has been particularly interested in examining the

biochemical basis of this process. However, before describing these biochemical studies, a brief description of this long-term synaptic potentiation is appropriate.

To produce LTP, a stimulating electrode is placed where it can activate one of the major synaptic circuits in the hippocampus. A recording electrode is then placed where it can record the evoked potential which reflects the amount of synaptic current produced by the stimulus. One stimulus is then delivered each second until a stable baseline response is obtained and held for 30 minutes. Then a brief (1 sec) burst of high frequency (100 pulses/sec) stimulation is delivered. This high frequency stimulation mimics the frequency of nerve firing that is commonly seen in the hippocampus. Then testing is resumed with single pulses delivered at one pulse per second. Immediately following the cessation of the high frequency stimulation, the single stimulus produces a much larger evoked potential than it had produced in the stabilization period prior to the high frequency stimulation (Figure 1). Thus, the synaptic circuit has been strengthened or potentiated.

PROTEIN PHOSPHORYLATION AND LTP

We chose to focus, in our studies of the biochemical basis of LTP, on a process known as protein phosphorylation. A protein becomes phosphorylated when an enzyme transfers phosphate from ATP to the protein. The reaction can be reversed by another enzyme that removes the phosphate from the protein. The addition of the charged phosphate to a protein changes the structure of the protein and consequently changes its activity. It is widely thought that protein phosphorylation is one of the primary means of protein regulation in mammalian metabolism. There are a number of other reasons, however, why protein phosphorylation is thought to be significant in the key synaptic events of nerve cells in the brain. First, these phosphorylated proteins, as well as the enzymes that control the phosphorylation process, are all present in high concentrations in

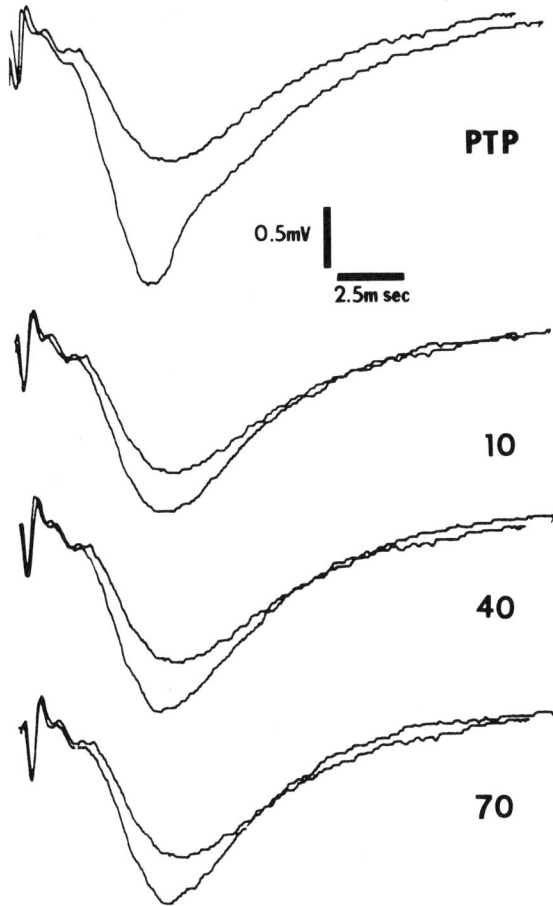

Figure 1.   A time course of the effect of high frequency stimulation on the excitatory postsynaptic potentials recorded in the zone of termination of the Schaeffer collateral-commisural projection to the CA1 pyramidal cells. The upper two superimposed traces depict control responses obtained during the 30 minute stabilization. PTP denotes the short-term potentiation detected immediately following the cessation of stimulation. Note the increase in both the slope and amplitude of the potentiated response compared to the superimposed control. Subsequent records were taken at the time points indicated; note that the magnitude of the potentiated response is constant for all but the initial period following stimulation (Lynch, Browning, & Bennett, 1979).

synaptic regions (Johnson, Maeno, & Green-gard, 1971; Maeno & Greengard, 1972; Maeno, Johnson, & Greengard, 1971). Second, agents known to influence phosphorylation also appear to have effects on synaptic events (see Greengard, 1978, for pertinent review). Therefore, our group chose to attempt to determine in one particular instance, namely, the induction of long-term synaptic potentiation, whether there was any effect on the phosphorylation of specific proteins. We first produced LTP by delivering a brief burst of high frequency stimula-tion to a specific region in the hippocampus. Next, we isolated the synaptic regions from the stimulated and the control (or unstimu-lated) tissue, and then incubated these synaptic regions in presence of radioactive ATP. Thus, when a protein became phosphory-lated, it also became radioactively labeled. We then separated the proteins from each other on acrylamide gels, and exposed these gels to X-ray film. The radioactive proteins then exposed the X-ray film so we could determine which of the proteins were phosphorylated. We then compared the pat-

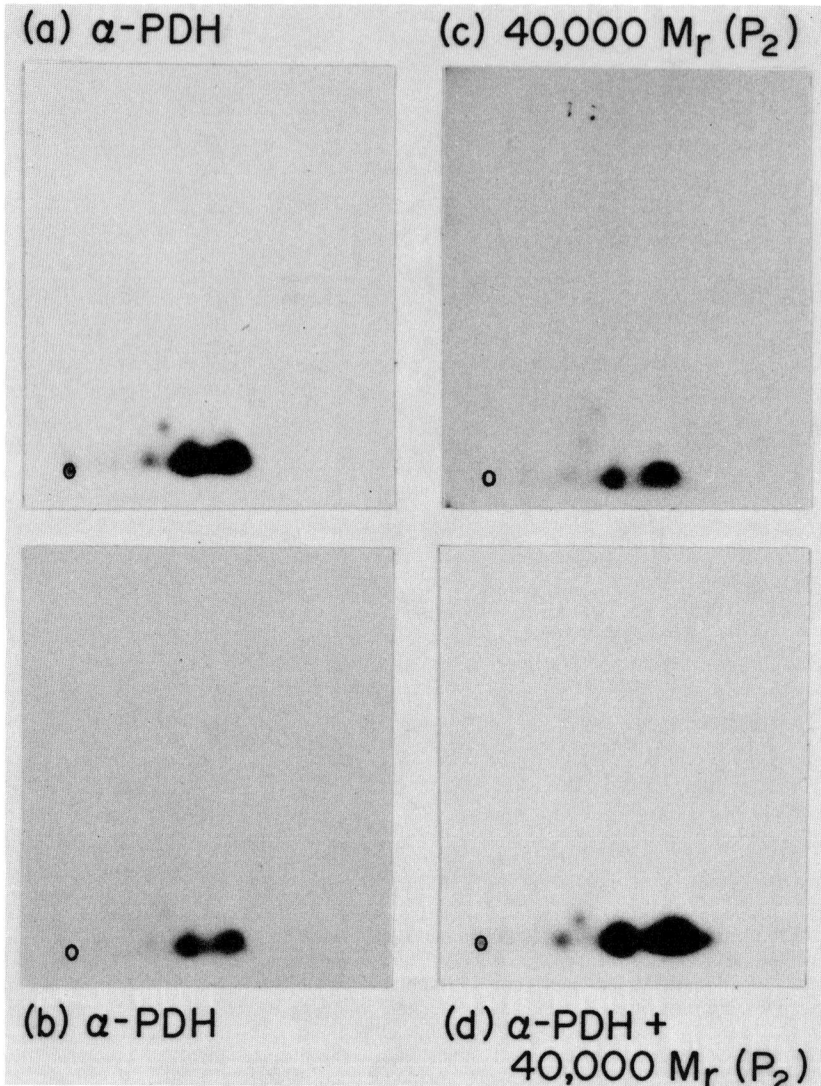

Figure 2.   Polyacrylamide gel depicting the effects of repetitive stimulation on phosphorylation of specific proteins. Symbols: +, stimulated sample; C, control sample. *Left:* The protein staining pattern obtained with Coomassie blue in the 7.5% to 20% gel. *Right:* Autoradiograph showing the bands that incorporated radioactive phosphate. The molecular weight estimations were based on comparisons with the mobilities of standards of known molecular weight. Molecular weight values shown indicate bands in which significant stimulation-dependent changes in phosphorylation were observed (Browning et al., 1979).

tern of phosphorylation in a stimulated fraction with that of the control or unstimulated fraction.

As shown in Figure 2, stimulation produced a marked effect on the phosphorylation of a number of proteins, with the most dramatic effect being an alteration in the phosphorylation of a protein with a molecular weight of 40,000 (Browning, Dunwiddie, Bennett, Gispen, & Lynch, 1979). This find-

ing suggested to us the exciting possibility that the phosphorylation of this protein might in some way be involved in the effect produced by this high frequency stimulation, namely, in the increase in the strength of the synaptic circuit.

To determine whether the change in the phosphorylation of this protein was related to the increase in synaptic strength or was merely a consequence of electrical stimulation, we performed two sets of controls in which we stimulated the hippocampus without producing changes in synaptic strength. We first delivered 100 pulses at a low frequency; such stimulation does not produce LTP and it has no effect on the phosphorylation of the 40,000 dalton protein. We next delivered 100 pulses at high frequency (100 pulses/sec), but under conditions that block the production of LTP (i.e., when calcium was not available, Dunwiddie, Madison, & Lynch, 1978). Such stimulation did not produce LTP and had no effect on the 40,000 dalton protein. It appears, therefore, that the change in the phosphorylation of the 40,000 dalton protein is related to the potentiating nature of the stimulation.

IDENTITY OF THE 40,000 DALTON BRAIN PROTEIN

Given the potential importance of this protein to LTP, we have been particularly interested in establishing its identity. As a first step in characterizing this protein, we examined its subcellular distribution. These studies demonstrated that the protein was concentrated in mitochondria, which are known to be densely packed in synaptic regions. It is well known that the α-subunit of pyruvate dehydrogenase (PDH) is the predominant mitochondrial phosphoprotein with a molecular weight of 40,000 (Hughes & Denton, 1976). Therefore we compared the 40,000 dalton brain protein with highly purified PDH (Linn, Pelley, Pettit, Hucho, Randall, & Reed, 1972), which was a gracious gift of Dr. Tracy Linn. The two proteins exhibited identical pharmacological properties (Browning, Bennett, Kelly, and Lynch, 1981a). We then used the two-dimensional tryptic fingerprint technique to compare the proteins. The proteins were first broken down into specific fragments by trypsin. These fragments were then compared in a two-dimensional analysis (Figure 3), which revealed that the two proteins gave identical patterns. It appears, therefore, that the 40,000 dalton brain protein is in fact the α-subunit of PDH.

RELATIONSHIP OF PYRUVATE DEHYDROGENASE TO LTP

Pyruvate dehydrogenase is part of a multienzyme complex that converts pyruvate and coenzyme A to acetyl-CoA. The activity of this enzyme, which occupies a pivotal position in brain metabolism (McIlwain & Bachelard, 1971) is controlled by phosphorylation (Linn, Pettit, & Reed, 1969a; Linn, Pettit, Hucho, & Reed, 1969b). Therefore, changes in PDH phosphorylation could lead to significant changes in neural metabolism, and these could in turn lead to changes in the strength of synaptic circuits. Production of ATP and calcium sequestration are two of the primary functions of mitochondria. Since it is widely recognized that calcium plays an essential role in synaptic transmission, we were interested in determining whether phosphorylation of PDH could lead to alterations in the ability of mitochondria to regulate calcium in the synapse. We found (Browning, Baudry, Bennett, & Lynch, 1981b) that the phosphorylation of PDH did in fact significantly alter the ability of mitochondria to take up calcium. These data have led us to the following working hypothesis:

1. High frequency stimulation produces an increase in the phosphorylation of PDH.
2. This phosphorylation inhibits PDH (Linn et al., 1969a,b) and consequently mitochondrial calcium uptake is inhibited.
3. Inhibition of mitochondrial calcium uptake results in an increase in calcium in the synapase. This increase leads directly to an increase in the strength of the synaptic circuit, perhaps by directly causing increased neurotransmitter release (Alnaes & Rahamimoff, 1975).

SIGNIFICANCE FOR THE SEARCH FOR CURES FOR MENTAL RETARDATION

The final question to be addressed is obvious: What is the significance of these results for the search for cures for mental retardation? First, it must be emphasized that these studies

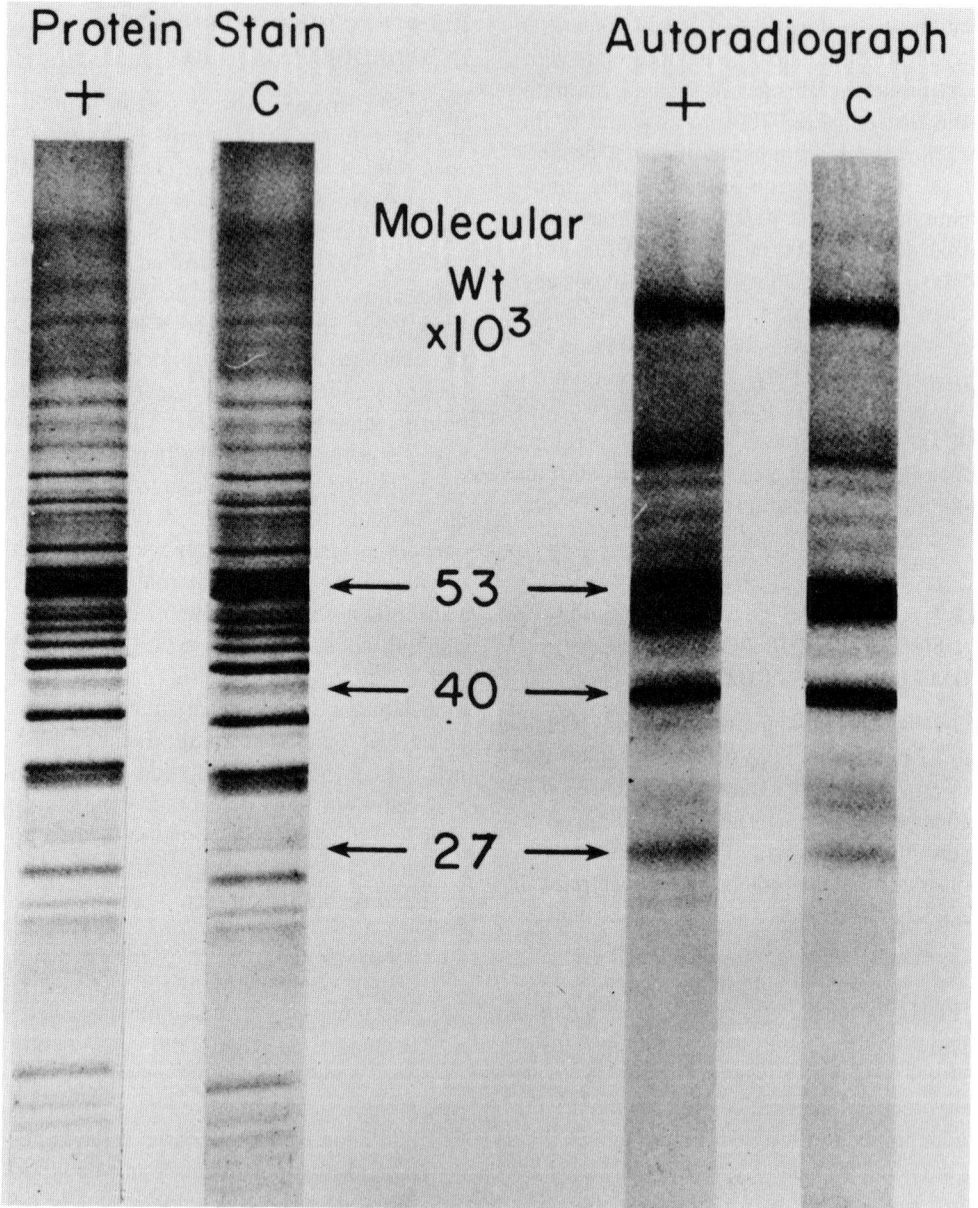

Figure 3.   Two-dimensional tryptic peptide map autoradiograms of the ^{32}P-labeled α-subunit of PDH and the 40,000 M_r brain protein. The pyruvate dehydrogenase complex and a P_2 fraction from brain were phosphorylated with endogenous kinases and electrophoresed in a one-dimensional polyacrylamide slab gel. The 40,000 M_r brain phosphoprotein and the α-subunit of PDH (α-PDH) were located by autoradiography, cut from the gel, and subjected to tryptic digestion followed by electrophoresis and chromatography. (a) ^{32}P-labeled tryptic peptides of the α-subunit of PDH; total radioactivity 1,000 dpm. (b) Same as in (a); total radioactivity 400 dpm. (c) Tryptic peptides of ^{32}P-labeled 40,000 M_r protein from a P_2 fraction; total radioactivity 400 dpm. (d) Equivalent amounts (400 dpm/sample) of (b) and (c) were mixed prior to application to the TLC plate. The open circle at the bottom left corner of each autoradiogram indicates the origin. Electrophoresis was carried out in the horizontal dimension from left (anode) to right (cathode). Chromatography was in the vertical dimension and the front traveled to within 2 mm of the upper edge of each autoradiogram (Browning et al., 1981a).

represent only preliminary investigations into the biological bases of learning. Enormous strides must still be taken to determine whether this alteration in the strength of synaptic circuits is indeed related to learning, and further, whether changes in the phosphorylation of PDH are causally related to changes in synaptic strength. However, a recent report by Morgan and Routtenberg (1981) has shown changes in PDH phosphorylation in rats during training in a passive avoidance paradigm. Thus, in at least one specific context, correlations have been found between the phosphorylation of PDH and learning. It should also be noted that we are not the first to suggest the possibility of a relationship between PDH and mental retardation. Blass, Cederbaum, Kark, and Rodriquez-Budelli (1978) reported severe neurological impairment and mental retardation as a characteristic clinical finding in 35 patients with profound deficiencies in PDH (10%–50% of normal levels). Blass and Gibson (1978) go on to discuss how changes

in PDH could have severe consequences for neural function given the importance of glucose metabolism in the brain. We concur with these authors. However, the data we have presented here indicate that a particular neural capability, namely, the ability to modify the strength of synaptic circuits as a result of experience, may be particularly dependent upon the minute-to-minute activity of PDH. Thus, even subtle changes in PDH or in the enzymes that control its phosphorylation, might be expected to exert significant effects on this particular aspect of neural function.

Much work remains to be done. However, as mentioned earlier, there are compelling reasons for continuing to probe the biological mechanisms of cognitive processes. This author would argue that such studies are essential components of any search for cures of mental retardation. For as we progress in understanding these mechanisms, we will move closer to ameliorating at least some forms of mental retardation.

REFERENCES

Alnaes, E., & Rahamimoff, R. Role of mitochondria in transmitter release from motor terminals. *Journal of Physiology* (London), 1975, *248*, 285–306.

Blass, J., & Gibson, G. Studies of the pathophysiology of pyruvate dehydrogenase deficiency. *Advances in Neurology*, 1978, *21*, 181–194.

Blass, J., Cederbaum, S., Kark, R., & Rodriquez-Budelli, M. Pyruvate dehydrogenase deficiency in 35 patients. *Monographs of Human Genetics*, 1978, *9*, 12–15.

Bliss, T.V.P., & Lomo, T. Long-lasting potentiation of synaptic transmission in the dentate area of the anesthetized rabbit following stimulation of the perforant path. *Journal of Physiology*, 1973, *232*, 331–356.

Browning, M., Dunwiddie, T., Bennett, W., Gispen, W., & Lynch, G. Synaptic phosphoproteins: Specific changes after repetitive stimulation of the hippocampal slice. *Science*, 1979, *203*, 60–62.

Browning, M., Bennett, W., Kelly, P., & Lynch, G. Evidence that the 40,000 Mr phosphoprotein

influenced by high frequency synaptic stimulation is the alpha subunit of pyruvate dehydrogenase. *Brain Research*, 1981a, *218*, 255–266.

Browning, M., Baudry, M., Bennett, W., & Lynch, G. Phosphorylation-meditated changes in pyruvate dehydrogenase activity influence pyruvate-supported calcium accumulation by brain mitochondria. *Journal of Neurochemistry*, 1981b, *36*, 1932–1940.

Dunwiddie, T., Madison, D., & Lynch, G. Synaptic transmission is required for initiation of long-term potentiation. *Brain Research*, 1978, *150*, 413–417.

Greengard, P. Phosphorylated proteins as physiological effectors. *Science*, 1978, *199*, 146–152.

Hebb, D.O. *The organization of behavior*. New York: John Wiley & Sons, 1949.

Hughes, W., & Denton, R. Incorporation of ^{32}P into pyruvate dehydrogenase phosphate in mitochondria from control and insulin treated adipose tissue. *Nature* (London), 1976, *264*, 471–473.

Johnson, E., Maeno, H., & Greengard, P. Phosphorylation of endogenous protein of rat brain by cyclic adenosine 3′,5′-monophosphate-dependent protein kinase. *Journal of Biological Chemistry,* 1971, *246,* 7731–7735.

Linn, T., Pettit, F., & Reed, L. α-Keto acid dehydrogenase complexes. X. Regulation of the activity of the pyruvate dehydrogenase complex from beef kidney mitochondria by phosphorylation and dephosphorylation. *Proceedings of the National Academy of Sciences* (Washington), 1969a, *62,* 234–241.

Linn, T., Pettit, F., Hucho, F., & Reed, L. α-Keto acid dehydrogenase complexes. XI. Comparative studies of regulatory properties of the pyruvate dehydrogenase complexes from kidney, heart and liver mitochondria. *Proceedings of the National Academy of Sciences* (Washington), 1969b, *64,* 227–234.

Linn, T., Pelley, J., Pettit, F., Hucho, F., Randall, D., & Reed, L. α-Keto acid dehydrogenase complexes. XV. Purification and properties of the component enzymes of the pyruvate dehydrogenase complexes from bovine kidney and heart. *Archives of Biochemistry and Biophysics,* 1972, *148,* 327–342.

Lynch, G.S., Browning, M., & Bennett, W. Biochemical and physiological studies of synaptic plasticity. *Federation Proceedings,* 1979, *38,* 69–72.

McIlwain, H., & Bachelard, H. *Biochemistry and the central nervous system* (4th ed.). Edinburgh: Churchill-Livingstone, 1971.

Maeno, H., & Greengard, P. Phosphoprotein phosphatases from rat cerebral cortex: Subcellular distribution and characterization. *Journal of Biological Chemistry,* 1972, *247,* 3269–3273.

Maeno, H., Johnson, E., & Greengard, P. Subcellular distribution of adenosine 3′, 5′-monophosphate-dependent protein kinase in rat brain. *Journal of Biological Chemistry,* 1971, *246,* 134–140.

Morgan, D., & Routtenberg, A. Brain pyruvate dehydrogenase: Phosphorylation and enzyme activity altered by a training experience. *Science,* 1981, *214,* 470–471.

Curative Aspects of Mental Retardation:
Biomedical and Behavioral Advances
edited by Frank J. Menolascino, M.D., Ronald Neman, Ph.D., and Jack A. Stark, Ph.D.
Copyright 1983   Paul H. Brookes Publishing Co., Inc.   Baltimore · London

Conclusion

FRANK J. MENOLASCINO, M.D.
University of Nebraska Medical Center
Omaha, Nebraska

T HE FOUR CHAPTERS IN THIS SECTION focused on the potential for regeneration of the central nervous system.

In Chapter 7, Dr. Frank J. Menolascino integrated what is currently known about the various processes of recovery in the central nervous system. He noted that a body of professional literature documents the nature and extent of recovery processes that occur following damage to the brain. The presence of many important allied variables (e.g., age of the organism, presence or absence of previous training experience in the area of later brain impairment, the complexity of the interactive variables noted) was underscored. Dr. Menolascino also cautioned that one must not view these potentials for recovery as isolated variables, since they are clearly interrelated.

In Chapter 8, Dr. Gary Lynch noted that Chapters 1–3 of this volume concentrated on sets of strategies for examining problems in understanding mental retardation. Rather than examining the genetic factors or the brains of persons who exhibit this disorder, he emphasized another type of strategy, namely, to study the nervous system for the memory mechanisms or learning mechanisms that underlay the symptom of mental retardation. Learning has several peculiar problems, but the most striking one is that it is very persistent throughout a lifetime. Memory is a similar process, and it has led many people to look into the brain for mechanisms for structural growth and change. One way in which to approach the central nervous system is as a system of circuitries, and memory can be viewed as a lasting change that reorganizes the brain's function and/or structure. For the past several years Dr. Lynch and his collegues have been examining the phenomenon called "nerve cell sprouting," which occurs when one removes one set of inputs to the brain's structure and observes the remaining inputs to that structure. These studies have convinced him that even the mature brain has a remarkable capacity for forming new axon terminals and synapses after it has been injured—a selective form of brain cell regeneration takes place at the brain's most crucial site, with this increase in terminals and synapses developing from the new sprouting. The major difficulty Dr. Lynch encountered in his studies was that the nerve cell sprouting began about 5 days after a lesion; that is, 5 days after one input would be removed, the second (new one) would begin the growth phase, and its attachment would also begin growing. The 5 days seemed quite a long period, since learning happens rather quickly. So Dr. Lynch looked at a second type of phenomenon in the search for what might be a logical mechanism for learning. This second phenomenon (as noted by Dr. Browning in Chapter 10) is called "long-term synaptic potentiation." Long-term potentiation of nerve cells was discovered in the hippocampal formation of the rabbit in the middle 1970s. It was found that, following the delivery of a brief train of electrical stimulation to the hippocampal formation (at a high frequency), subsequent testing of that circuit showed that it was much stronger. What was remarkable about this effect is that once it was induced, this long-term potentiation effect persisted indefinitely. In other words, it appeared that given a few seconds of usage, it was possible to induce an increase in the strength of a synaptic circuit that would last for days, weeks, or even months. Subsequent experiments have borne out the idea that, indeed, the strength of synaptic connections in this brain region can be changed with very brief periods of intense usage. The mechanism in the hippocampus seems ideal for a substrate of memory: it develops rather quickly and it certainly lasts for a long period of time. So Dr. Lynch's strategy was to try to find out what is causing the effect: What intermediate mechanisms are being triggered by that brief train of high frequency stimulation?

A second question to be answered is, What is the final nervous system effect—what *is* going on in the brain that could be triggered in a minute or two and could last for weeks or months, perhaps forever? Dr. Lynch's work strongly suggests that in fact there is a structural effect, that it is induced by the high frequency stimulation, and that it resembles new nerve-cell sprouting. Chapter 8 summarized the data regarding the structural sprouting changes as the basis of the long-term potentiation effect—stressing the biochemical mechanisms that are triggered by the high frequency stimulation that actually produces the structural sprouting changes (and hence produces the lasting change in the brain cell synaptic strength). The ultimate goal of this aspect of Dr. Lynch's research is to find out if there is a particular piece of chemistry responsible for this dramatic change in brain structure and function. If so, these same biochemical mechanisms should indeed be triggered in these same synapses when a rat is learning.

Dr. Lynch noted that the hippocampus has a "disreputable" career as to its involvement in memory, but that the bulk of the current human data certainly indicates that the hippocampus plays a major role in memory (especially in information coding, and in the retrievability of information). He also noted that he and his colleagues are trying some pharmacological manipulations of this potentiation effect and that they have had some success in manipulating specific mechanisms of the brain to test their effect on the animal's capacity to store information. Thus, Dr. Lynch's research has major relevance to the possible neurophysiological basis for producing changes in the memory and learning capabilities of mentally retarded individuals. Electrical and biochemical changes that can greatly facilitate learning in general are a major treatment prospect. Further, the actual sprouting phenomenon itself—and its specific induction—can have major curative possibilities in posttraumatic causes of mental retardation. It should also be emphasized that Dr. Lynch's experimental studies have clearly shown both the marked interdependence of the electrical stimulation and the necessity for adequate calcium concentrations in the immediate area of the dendritic sprouting phenomena. His comment that the drug trifluoperazine (Stellazine) blocks the potentiation effect (possibly by interfering with the buffering of the calcium level) clearly shows that the *combined* effects of electrical and biochemical approaches to the brain mechanisms that underlie memory and learning are sensitive to a wide variety of stimuli. This line of research holds great possibilities for the activation—by extrinsic modalities—of the basic mechanisms that underlie nerve cell functioning and, by implication, the mass action of the brain in phenomena such as learning and memory.

It is clear that we are beginning to more fully understand the growth potential inherent in central nervous system recovery—a topic that Dr. A.K. Ommaya addressed in Chapter 9. As Dr. Ommaya noted, there are many possibilities for helping selected groupings of mentally retarded or brain impaired persons via current neurosurgical techniques. Neurosurgical techniques in themselves, of course, are not the answer to these challenges. Dr. Ommaya likes to relate his father's advice when he told him that he wanted to become a surgeon and a specialist in the neurosciences. His father responded, "You have to be very careful when you become a specialist because you tend to become very good at a few techniques, and it can be very much like the man who becomes an expert with the hammer. After awhile every problem begins to look like a nail."

In 10% to 25% of mentally retarded individuals, there is distinct and recognizable brain pathology; the allied problem is that these findings do not usually indicate a localized disturbance. Rather, the disturbance tends to be a diffuse type of disorder at a number of locations in the central nervous system. There are basically inauspicious factors that make surgical treatment not very effective, because surgical treatment is usually applied to localized corrections of "brain machinery" wherein we can detect something wrong with the machinery at one specific point. Dr. Ommaya noted that the great scientist Ramon y Cajal in his work on degeneration and regeneration of the central nervous system, discovered that the degenerative process of white matter (which is so remarkably faint and sluggish under ordinary conditions) can be partially stimulated by means of active substances liberated by the scar and diffused in the spinal wounds in the edges. Also, that little stab wounds of the spinal cord do not stimulate this regenerative effect, whereas major traumatic wounds do; and that this process was much more vigorous in the younger animals than in the older animals. For years these findings have been elaborated upon without too much more evidence of further basic or applied research advances. But it does suggest that the problem may well be quantitative and not significantly qualitative (i.e., in terms of allowing what seems to be a natural capacity to be enhanced upon). Recent experimental neurosurgical studies have shown that the use of sciatic nerve grafts into the spinal cord and the brain in a few suitable cases have produced sprouting of the central nervous system fibers, using the underlying components of the graft as a guidance system for the regenerative process.

The search for a possible neurotropic or neuroregenerative factor(s) (i.e., chemical compounds that can stimulate nerve cell regeneration) has been active and has culminated in a manner of different research directions. One direction has involved work with a compound termed "nerve growth factor," and more recently the finding of a substance that appears similar to the neurotropic factor formerly described by Cajal. The question now is, what stops the central axon sprouts from reaching their synaptic destinations if such neurotropic factors are available? We do not know the answer to this question at this time, and a complicating factor appears to be that the neurobiology of the other cells in the central nervous system—immediately around the lesion—often antagonizes the positive effects of the sprouting process that is already present. In other words, one has to also look for antineurotropic factors as well as neurotropic factors. These two fundamental processes were reviewed by Dr. Ommaya as a prelude to discussing neurosurgical technical aspects that suggest that important technical advances have been made to enhance the possibility of the presence of new pathways in the spinal cord after it has been severed. The severed neurons are capable of axonal sprouting, and these axons can find and make proper synaptic connections across some of the areas that have been severed. Advances in microneurosurgery, and the major finding that delayed grafting in the spinal cord allows the removal of necrotic (i.e., dead) tissues so that more optimal conditions are created that permit the graft to "take," as it were, indeed represent technical advances. But it appears that such technical improvements by themselves are really not the answer, because functional improvement, correlated with the evidence of axon regrowth, does not occur in regards to producing any significant synaptic connections beyond the severed gap. Dr. Ommaya enumerated many of the technical problems that are now becoming more clearly understood, and stated that more specific treatment interventions can soon be undertaken. For example, the delayed grafting, the use of allied Diapulse electrical stimulation, and the use of myelin grafts—from peripheral nerves—taken together seem to hold promise for making reconnection both above and below a severed section of spinal cord.

Of major significance for the possibility of curative approaches in mental retardation is Dr. Ommaya's (personal communication, 1981) statement:

> Paradoxically, the research work in the attempts to functionally reconnect a severed spinal cord is dealing with problems in the grafting area and floundering for lack of the right data. It is an area of the nervous system that is in a sense far simpler than that of the central nervous system (i.e., the brain). The paradox is that the current work in the central nervous system appears to be much more promising.

Dr. Ommaya has reported that Dr. Ulf Stenevi (1980), working in Sweden, has developed a technique for transplanting embryonic rat (CNS) tissue to the brain of adult rats, with a 70%–90% survival rate for the graft. His group claims that embryonic CNS tissue can promote regeneration of axotomized central neurons and serve as a bridge for the regenerating axons across a tissue defect. In the septohippocampal system of rats, Stenevi has shown that embryonic transplants form extensive and reciprocal connections with the denervated regions of the host brain and, in some cases, the distribution of these connections mimic very closely the original innervation patterns.

Further, Chapter 9 reported on recent studies that combine behavioral evidence with histochemical and neurological evidence to show that it may be possible, at least in localized deficits of the central nervous system, to restore function. Experiments have recently been accomplished wherein a lesion was made on one side of the substantia nigra (site of Parkinson's disease in the human) and the damaged area of specific chemical activity (dopaneuregic system) was then reinforced by a graft of substantia nigric embryonic tissue to a region (i.e., the nearby brain lateral ventricle). The lateral ventricle appears to be a very good site if one wants to see the effects of a brain graft that may develop synaptic connections with the cortex; these brain grafts also produce some functional secretions (i.e., neurotransmitters are produced by the graft tissues). By placing the fetal graft in the region of the lateral ventricle, researchers have been able to show that this graft *also* apparently reversed a neurological behavioral disorder that was present. Specifically, these grafts of brain tissue have been able to correct parkinsonism-like disorders in rats and are most significant because they strongly suggest that if the problem in the central nervous system can be well defined in terms of the anatomy and biochemistry of its loci functions, then this focal deficit can be repaired by the utilization of a fetal tissue graft. The possibility for major improvement or cure *is* here! Indeed, some earlier similar studies were the result of research by W.F. Blakemore (see references, Chapter 9) that showed it was possible (in a model of experimental demyelinization of the rat and also the rabbit, using radiation therapy) that areas of demyelinized spinal cord could be remyelinized by placing portions of the sciatic nerve on top of the demyelinized area. The Schwann cells of the graft acted both to direct and to accomplish the remyelinization process. That past study was the first significant use of nervous system graft.

The scientists involved in the brain-grafting studies are from different disciplines—anatomists, neurosurgeons, psychiatrists, neuroscientists, etc.—so this type of work obviously requires a multidisciplinary team and is not done easily by one person working in isolation. One might then ask, "What are the barriers to the application of such techniques to the human?" First of all, it is obvious, as previously noted, that the transplantation techniques are well suited to the correction of a highly localized deficit, but are not of much use in diseases with widespread symptoms, or in those with multilocated functional causes of disturbance. Unless one can show that the diffuse disorder is secondary to some kind of specific biochemical disorder originating from one site, then the process will not be helpful.

The other marked obstacle is an old one: proliferation of the brain's glial cells at the site of injury where axonal sprouting occurs. If this proliferation of glial cells were synchronized in a manner that allowed the axonal sprouting to proceed slightly ahead of it, then it would not be such an inhibiting factor to nerve cell regeneration.

A fund of research is accumulating on these challenging problems of central nervous system regeneration. The work so far is more applicable to local or specific types of brain diseases or disorders like Parkinson's disease. But a number of accomplishments must occur almost simultaneously, however, before significant progress can result. One necessary step is that the exact nature of the brain impairments of patients with mental retardation must be defined much more clearly. Infants and children with these problems should be studied using the growth potential techniques to look at the important factor of input. It should be kept in mind that the nervous system is an interactive system. In other words, if the machinery is there, an identical or almost identical situation can be produced that looks like a case of mental retardation by distorting the input, as by distorting the existing machinery. Of course, if both of these factors are abnormal—if the machinery is ''bad''— normal input will not be provided. Specifically, we need data on how children with these problems process data. What is it in their processing that is abnormal, and how does this type of defective nervous system handle information? These data can be obtained by modern techniques using computerized evoked responses, as well as with the more recent techniques of positron emission tomography. These and similar diagnostic techniques will increasingly yield more vital data on the specific anatomical localization of functioning areas of the brain and permit the expanded use of curative neurosurgical techniques—including the grafting of brain tissue to correct a previously impaired, malformed, or subtly malfunctioning area (or specific areas) of the brain that underlie the memory and learning processes in the human.

Curative Aspects of Mental Retardation:
Biomedical and Behavioral Advances
edited by Frank J. Menolascino, M.D., Ronald Neman, Ph.D., and Jack A. Stark, Ph.D.
Copyright 1983   Paul H. Brookes Publishing Co., Inc.   Baltimore · London

section III

EFFORTS TOWARD
ENHANCING BRAIN FUNCTION

Introduction

JACK A. STARK, PH.D.
University of Nebraska Medical Center
Omaha, Nebraska

O NE OF THE AVENUES OF EXPLORATION toward the goal of curing the symptom of mental retardation is the use of pharmacological agents to enhance learning processes. The use of such agents poses methodological problems that researchers should be aware of, as Dr. Frank J. Menolascino has noted in Chapter 11. A psychiatrist who has been actively involved in the field of mental retardation, Dr. Menolascino has focused particularly on the possible role of pharmocological agents in improving human memory and learning. Chapter 11 discusses the types of drug models used in the assessment of purported memory and learning enhancers; the fallacy of the "magic bullet theory"; the nature of drug effects and experimental variables; environmental problems; limiting conditions both in the subject who is taking the drug and in the drug itself; recurrent challenges of using assessment techniques; controls; and other dimensions aimed at assuring valid research findings on this topic.

Drs. Abba J. Kastin and Curt A. Sandman, in Chapter 12, present an overview of neuropeptides, with a special emphasis on their possible roles in mental retardation. Neuropeptides are strings of amino acids occurring naturally in the brain and elsewhere in the body that represent a major research periscope for future curative research approaches in mental retardation. They affect brain functioning and resultant behavior in dramatic ways—for example, they can obtund consciousness by their excessive action in body water retention or function as the body's self-manufactured "opiate" for stopping pain. An additional major effect of many of these peptides is their reported ability to enhance human memory and learning processes. Because of their profound effects on the central nervous system, one could envision the use of peptides in virtually all aspects of mental retardation, including diagnosis and treatment. Drs. Kastin and Sandman review three recent key clinical studies with mentally retarded adults (enrolled in vocational settings) that strongly indicate that certain learning deficits traditionally thought irreversible in retarded persons were modified in a positive fashion using the melanocyte stimulating peptide. It is still too early to determine the extent of the potential of this neuropharmacological approach in mental retardation. Yet, sufficient basic animal research and clinical human research data already exist to justify a rapid expansion of this research effort. Truly, this relatively new field of research has major implications for producing cures of the symptom of mental retardation.

In Chapter 13, Dr. Kenneth L. Davis evaluates recent major studies on neurotransmitters and allied central nervous system (CNS) enzymes and notes the future curative role of these pharmacological agents in reversing mental retardation. Both neurotransmitters and allied CNS enzymes play an influential role in information processing and memory retention in the brain.

135

Recent clinical trials with specific nerve cell transmitters (e.g., acetylcholine or choline substrate) on patients with senile dementia (i.e., Alzheimer's disease) have had favorable results. Specifically, it has been known for some time that the level of acetylcholine—a major nerve impulse transmission agent between nerve cells in the brain—decreases after the age of 40. Reasoning that this decrease was directly applicable to the clinical finding of presenile dementia (i.e., before age 60), Dr. Davis and his colleagues began to utilize pharmacological agents that would complement the amount of acetylcholine that was available. Utilizing the drug physostigmine—which accelerates the action of acetylcholine—they noted markedly improved memory and intelligence in these severely handicapped elderly citizens. It is a short step from this dramatic finding to the consideration of similar pharmacologically accelerated help for mentally retarded citizens who display similar memory and/or learning problems much earlier in life. Although little such research has been done with mentally retarded individuals, it is increasingly viewed as realistic to suppose that such neurotransmitter deficiencies can figure prominently in mental retardation at all chronological age levels, and especially early in life.

In Chapter 14, Dr. Curt A. Sandman (a research colleague with Dr. Kastin) presents additional data on two specific neuropeptides that may well prove relevant in mental retardation. In addition, he presents a behavioral strategy to assess the effects of peptides in particular, and drugs in general in the treatment of mental retardation. Dr. Sandman's excitement is based on a firm belief that peptides influence behavior and hold the key to understanding physiological imbalance in the neurochemical system. Thus, unlike extraneous drugs, peptides could become useful in the replacement and repair of a deficient system.

Curative Aspects of Mental Retardation:
Biomedical and Behavioral Advances
edited by Frank J. Menolascino, M.D., Ronald Neman, Ph.D., and Jack A. Stark, Ph.D.
Copyright 1983   Paul H. Brookes Publishing Co., Inc.   Baltimore · London

chapter 11

Methodological Considerations in Evaluating Memory and Learning Enhancers

FRANK J. MENOLASCINO, M.D.
University of Nebraska Medical Center
Omaha, Nebraska

As NOTED IN THE PREFACE to this book, the Association for Retarded Citizens (ARC) and a number of professional organizations have recently underscored that many of the diseases that can produce the symptom of mental retardation can be cured, and, moreover, that many diseases once considered incurable are now curable as result of new treatments. It is not surprising, therefore, that laypersons as well as many professionals look forward to the discovery of a cure for the symptom of mental retardation. This hope often takes the form of a search for another "wonder drug," particularly among persons who perceive mental retardation as a "disease." After the administration of such a wonder drug such persons envision, for example, an 8-year-old, severely retarded, nonverbal, and nonambulatory child suddenly start talking, walking, and doing the things one would expect the average 8-year-old to do. Yannet (1957) has labeled the idea of such a potential drug cure of mental retardation as "the magic bullet theory."

Without explicitly articulating the magic bullet theory, a researcher may adopt an ex-

perimental design that clearly implies it. Thus, a number of the glutamic acid studies reviewed by Vogel, Broverman, Draguns, and Klaiber in 1966 had placed retarded subjects on the experimental drug for such short periods of time (e.g., 1 to 2 months) that effects upon global intelligence would have had to be remarkable in order to reach statistical significance. In 1967, Burns, House, Fensch, and Miller conducted a study on the effects of a single dose of magnesium pemoline on learning. The relevant question here is not so much whether drug effects were actually reported, but why the investigators chose to adopt designs that would assess only quick and dramatic effects, and not the gradual effects that are developmentally equally important. The use of adult subjects rather than children also carries with it the flavor of "magic bullet" expectations. Children generally are believed to be much more plastic than adults, and significant increases in their rate of development are easily perceived. In adults, however, a drug effect is difficult to envision except in terms of either performance enhancement or the complete remission of the signs and symptoms of mental retardation (i.e., a cure).

THEORETICAL MODELS

The field of mental retardation has witnessed many attempts to improve cognitive functioning by means of drugs, and a number of models of drug action can be discerned. These attempts can be classified as arising from three theoretical models:

1. *The unblocking model.* Within this model, drugs are employed to treat conditions that interfere with the full use or development of intelligence. Examples are the allaying of anxiety by means of tranquilizers and the control of seizures with anticonvulsants. Especially in psychiatrically oriented circles, the term "unblocking" may be encountered in this connection.

2. *The energizing model.* This model implies the use of drugs to stimulate the central nervous system in an effort to improve alertness and/or performance, thereby hoping to maximize those intelligence-related behaviors that might not be fully utilized even by a well-functioning person. Amphetamines and strychnine have been used in this fashion, as reviewed by Freeman (1966).

3. *The direct action model.* The unblocking model and the energizing model are employed simply as indirect drug effects. However, some drugs are employed in the hope that they will affect cognitive processes directly. Within the "direct action model," drugs can be perceived as having a number of possible modes of action. In 1949, Zimmerman, Burgemeister, and Putnam posited a somewhat vaguely conceptualized improvement in higher cognitive processes. A recent and more sophisticated conceptualization envisions improvement in learning and memory processes. Glutamine and glutamic acid (Louttit, 1965; Vogel, Broverman, Draguns, & Klaiber, 1966), vitamins (House, Wilson, &

Goodfellow, 1964), sickle-cell treatments (Goldstein, 1956), and combination treatments such as Turkel's (1963) "U Series" of 49 drugs and the megavitamin therapeutic regimen (Harrell, Capp, Davis, Peerless, & Ravitz, 1981) have been used within the framework of the direct action model.

While none of the pharmacological agents previously mentioned has been conclusively demonstrated to improve the intelligence or the intellectual development of retarded individuals, some of the so-called replacement therapies that aim at the amelioration of specific metabolic syndromes associated with retardation have been effective. For instance, thyroid preparations have been shown to be effective in selected cases of hypothyroidism. Several other metabolic disorders, such as phenylketonuria, are treated dietetically and with great success (Menolascino & Eggers, 1981). Though many investigators appear to view replacement therapies as essentially constituting "unblock," agreement as to the most appropriate model or mode of drug action in these therapies is lacking. On one point only has there been widespread agreement: The success of replacement therapies appears to be correlated negatively with subject's age (i.e., the older the subject, the less successful the therapy).

It is crucial that researchers be aware of certain other concepts and attitudes that can affect drug study designs in subtle and/or detrimental ways. For example, a curious phenomenon can be discerned in the way people view attempts to improve the intelligence of retarded versus nonretarded individuals. A "pill" to enhance the intelligence of a college student would be expected to improve his learning, memory, and general performance. A moderate and gradually accumulating effect would be considered desirable and quite acceptable. However, with a retarded person, a drug is often scorned if it produces anything less than a complete and perhaps even a rapid "cure"—unless it produces "normality."

Recently, the hope to enhance intelligence

chemically has been rekindled by reports that RNA and drugs believed to facilitate the metabolism of RNA in the brain (e.g., magnesium pemoline) result in improved retention and perhaps even increased acquisition in both animals and human. Other potentially intelligence-enhancing or development-enhancing drugs on which there has been widespread publicity include 5-hydroxytryptophan. Experiences with above drugs have now moved into the classical arena of everyday medicine, the special education classroom, and the vocational training center (Freeman, 1966), with both the media and working scientists increasingly voicing optimism about the future of such drug applications. In 1968, Krech testified favorably about such drug trials before a congressional committee. Pauling (1968) also forecasted an era of ''orthomolecular psychiatry'' wherein drugs would play a large role in behavior maintenance and enhancement. And in 1967, Arthur Koestler joined the ranks of prominent writers anticipating a drug-based utopia with the publication of *The Ghost in the Machine*.

More recently, the 1970s witnessed major pharmacological advances, particularly in cardiovascular and anticonvulsant medications. It is now certain that the 1980s and 1990s will be highlighted by diagnostically aided, computer-assisted technology. This process will particularly allow the fields of immunology and genetics to develop recombinant DNA technology to turn the body's own immune system into a storehouse for preventing and reversing disease processes.

The question of the possible cure of mental retardation by pharmacological agents inevitably continues to attract high interest. In assessing drug effectiveness studies, it may be timely at this point to recall errors made by past researchers in the hope that they are not repeated.

METHODOLOGICAL CONSIDERATIONS

This chapter restricts discussion to only those studies that employ the use of a placebo in a control group and exhibit other features of

well-designed drug experiments. While there may be a need for uncontrolled exploratory work, the power of the placebo effect has been so convincingly demonstrated that no drug should be accepted as possessing development-enhancing properties unless it has undergone the most rigorously controlled tests.

In addition, this chapter is not particularly concerned with pharmaceutical agents that result in improved performance, such as central nervous system stimulants or agents that alleviate such secondary conditions as hyperkinesis, seizures, or emotional disturbance that interfere with intellectual efficiency and/or development. Rather, this chapter focuses primarily on drugs purported to directly improve cognitive functioning or development. When speaking of drug effectiveness studies, it is this type of drug efficacy to which we refer.

General Considerations

The first goal of a study designed to assess a drug's ability to accelerate development should be the exploration of whether or not the drug has any developmental effect. To demonstrate such an effect is not easy without administering tests of sophisticated and advanced hypotheses or comparing several unproved drugs at the same time. Since such procedures are difficult and demand time, money, and other resources, experiments should be designed to maximize discernment of a potential effect. Above all, the study should constitute a fair test of the drug. Many past studies have failed in this regard, and whatever the merit of the drug may have been, such studies were simply irrelevant. The history of the mental retardation field contains instances in which respected and qualified workers enthusiastically embraced belief in the curative action of a drug that was later generally rejected as ineffective, even though neither the original positive, *nor* the later negative, studies may have constituted adequate tests of the drug's potential effects. Freeman pointed out in 1966 that after 25 years of work with glutamic acid and its derivatives, and 30 years with amphetamines, we still do not possess adequate empirical evidence regarding the behavioral effects of those drugs.

Failure to consider certain principles and facts of child development and experimental design account for many erroneous or unpromising research strategies. Much of the rest of this chapter will concern itself with such flawed practices.

Fallacy of the Magic Bullet Theory

One essential consideration is that mental retardation is not a disease, and that the magic bullet model is inappropriate to the drug treatment of mental retardation. Recall the example of the severely retarded 8-year-old. Even if it were possible to restore him to normal learning capacity instantaneously, he would, in all likelihood, have to pass through the developmental stages every normal child goes through. There is reason to believe that some behavior skills, such as those in the areas of speech, language, and perceptual development, may rarely, if ever, be mastered unless they are acquired during sensitive, or prior to critical, periods of development. Thus, instead of having a magic bullet effect, a development-enhancing drug is more likely to work gradually, additively, directionally, and selectively.

Definition of Drug Effect

Once emancipated from the magic bullet model, we can address ourselves more productively to the question of when a drug (or any treatment) can be considered effective. One orientation encountered in the field of mental retardation is that if a treatment does not cure, or at least result in spectacular effects, it is not worth pursuing. It is important to remember that even a small change in behavior or in the rate of development can have major implications for the ultimate functioning of the individual, as well as in terms of social and management costs. Being, or not being, toilet trained, for example, can mean a difference of 2 hours work per day to a parent, which in turn, can mean the difference between the child remaining in the home

or being placed in an institution at great cost to the child, his family, and society as a whole. Since relatively small developmental changes in just one behavioral area can have significant implications for care and management, the efficacy of a drug should not be assessed by its ability to "cure," but on the basis of whether it has any effect that would not have been achieved, or not achieved as efficiently, without its being administired.

Nature of the Experimental Variable

A common error in the conceptualization of drug effects, and consequently in the design of relevant experiments, is associated with failure to appreciate the nature of intellectual growth. Some traditional theories of child development have held that behavior unfolds automatically, like a predictable sequence of development in an embryo; one only need sit back and wait for certain behaviors to emerge at specific, almost predetermined ages. Such theories also usually saw little advantage in developmental exercises, drills, activities, etc.

Today a different view prevails. While it is granted that there is a genetic upper limit to development, it is generally believed that a child's current developmental stage is a better predictor of the next milestone to be attained than is his or her chronological age. A child who holds up his head, turns, crawls, stands with support, and walks while being held by one hand is generally ready to learn to walk unsupported, no matter whether he is 8 or 28 months old. However, it is also generally believed that a normally endowed child can become retarded if his or her perceptual, motor, linguistic, and social world is severely restricted. Ordinarily, we would not expect an otherwise normal 3-year-old child to walk if he or she had never been allowed to leave the crib.

Adherence to most contemporary theories and facts of child development would thus lead us to postulate that the effectiveness of a drug in accelerating development cannot be demonstrated, or only very poorly so, unless the child is exposed to a favorable environment and to experiences that are stimulating and appropriate to his or her developmental level. This means that drug effect must be tested at the interface of readiness and experience. Indeed, the entire concept that the drug is the experimental variable in drug effect studies should be abandoned. It is, rather, the interaction between drug and experience that should be considered the crucial experimental variable.

Since any factor that jeopardizes the drug-experience interaction may invalidate the study as a fair test of drug potential, we must clearly identify the factors that have their locus in the subject, the drug, or in the structure that governs the interaction between the mediated subject and his or her environment. Each of these limiting factors is discussed below.

Limiting Factors in the Environment

Lack of Appropriate Developmental Stimulation   A common feature of drug studies such as those that involved glutamic acid was the use of perceptually and socially deprived subjects. Thus, residents of institutions appear to have been the main subjects to date for many drug effectiveness studies in mental retardation. Retarded individuals living at home in a stimulating environment and engaged in intensive developmental programs would have constituted a more appropriate subject population.

Environmental Effects   If institutional or deprived subjects are used, but are placed in stimulating environments for the purpose of a drug study, a special problem must be kept in mind. Not only can an ordinary placebo effect be expected in the control group, but a genuine and substantial acceleration of development can be anticipated due to the nonspecific environmental treatment component. Thus, the experimental subjects must not only improve greatly, but must improve significantly more than the control subjects who may improve significantly themselves.

Limiting Factors in the Subject

Subject Handicaps   Certain conditions within a person can constitute limits to the drug-experience interaction. Emotional disturbance, severe seizures, sensory impairment, and orthopedic, aesthetic, and health handicaps are such conditions. It follows, therefore, that an optimal subject group, at least during early phases of research with a drug, should be free of such limiting factors.

Optimal Subject Functioning   Conceivably, some drugs might have an effect only in persons who previously have not functioned near their capacity, while little or no effect might be observed on those persons who are already functioning near their maximal limit. A drug effect that can be conceived rather readily on the theoretical level is one that would counteract or dissipate neural inhibitory processes. Thus, it is possible that some drugs may be more effective in retarded individuals than in normal persons, and the use of retarded subjects may be a better strategy than the use of normal or even superior subjects such as college students. An analogous phenomenon has been reported in mice, where maze-dull strains profited more with Metrazol injections than maze-bright ones. More importantly, the optimal dosage was found to be higher in dull than in bright strains of mice, although the drug can have learning-inhibitory effects when administered to maze-bright strains in too high dosages.

Subject Age   The subject's age must be considered to be a limiting factor in drug studies. The rate of mental development is generally accepted to be a positive decelerating function that flattens out in the mid-teens. There is strong reason to believe that most of the growth potential that is not realized during childhood is lost and cannot be recaptured even with intensive stimulation in adulthood. It follows, therefore, that the younger the child, the more effective a drug-experience interaction should be in promoting development. Conversely, this interaction should decline in effectiveness as the child gets older.

Younger Subjects and Assessment Techniques   The use of younger subjects carries with it the dilemma of limitations in assessment techniques for children of low mental age. Instruments and techniques designed to assess global development are wholly in-adequate for children below a mental age of 2 years. Even between mental ages 2 to 5, there are few global tests available, and some of these leave much to be desired. Tests of part or underlying functions of intelligence (e.g., attention, learning, memory) are even more problematic for this mental age range. This means that even with 8- to 10-year-old chil-dren, we would have great difficulties if their IQs were below 40–50. The crux of the prob-lem, then, is to locate a group young enough to profit considerably from a drug-experience interaction, yet whose mental age is high enough to permit application of appropriate available assessment techniques. Until more and better techniques applicable to subjects of lower mental age are developed, we propose that the optimal solution to the dilemma is to use mildly retarded (IQ 50–80) children aged 5 to 10.

Limiting Factors in the Drug

An agent may have toxic or other undesirable side effects, or may be difficult to administer. Further, potentially effective drugs may be effective only if they are available to the nervous system during the learning process, in which case drug administration must be planned with drug characteristics in mind. For instance, a potentially effective drug may be rapidly absorbed and metabolized. An experimental design involving drug admin-istration upon rising at 6 AM, and upon re-tiring at 9 PM may not constitute a fair test of that drug because the child may not be ex-posed to highly stimulating activities until midmorning, and to none at all at night. One must thus decide whether to administer timed release capsules or frequent doses. For this reason, the drug absorption rates should be considered carefully.

The need to give drugs in dosages large enough to be effective creates problems in research, since many drugs given in active dosages have side effects that may reveal the identity of experimental subjects in studies with double- or triple-blind controls, thereby destroying the utility of these controls. To combat this, some drug studies employ a uniform dosage for all experimental subjects, hoping that drug effectiveness, if any, will manifest itself sufficiently in at least enough subjects to yield a statistically significant group difference. Such a design preserves technical purity, but has at least two draw-backs: It may require a large sample before an effect can be accepted as having been ade-quately demonstrated, and it ignores certain pharmaceutical facts. Thus, the common dos-age may be set too low to have a positive and measurable effect on most subjects, or it may be so high as to produce toxic effects that can lead to loss of subjects, or to their identifi-cation by the personnel involved. Only a few subjects are likely to receive a dose optimal to them, that is, a dose individualized to their tolerance, sensitivity, metabolic rate, etc.

This dilemma was highlighted in a review of the literature on the effect of glutamic acid on cognitive behavior (Vogel et al., 1966). The reviewers concluded that current evi-dence factors a positive effect. However, embarassingly, the positive evidence came mostly from studies that were either uncon-trolled or that used individual dosaging tech-niques, which make a double-blind or triple-blind design virtually impossible to maintain. On the other hand, the negative evidence was derived primarily from controlled studies util-izing uniform dosages. A crucial question thus arises: Are the positive results due to the powerful effects of individualized dosaging, or are they due to a placebo effect resulting from loss of subject identity that might have occurred during dosage determination?

Some researchers have attempted to solve the dilemma by separating the clinical man-agement of the subject from the evaluation of drug effect. However, the light of past expe-rience raises serious doubts about the ade-quacy of such a technique in maintaining rigorous blind conditions.

Other Experimental Design Considerations

A research design must be efficient as well as appropriate. First, drug effectiveness studies, by their very nature, must be longitudinal: Experimental and control groups are assessed; a treatment is administered, and then both are reassessed. A statistical design typical for such a study is variously referred to as "repeated measurements of several independent groups" or a "mixed factorial Type I" design. In such a design, the crucial statistical test of the drug-experience effect is not of the difference between groups after treatment, but of the statistical interaction between groups and time, i.e., the differential rate of change.

Second, the efficiency of an experiment is generally related inversely to its duration. Given a potential effect, the design that permits the most rapid demonstration of this effect is, other things being equal, the most efficient. The adequacy, appropriateness, and efficiency of a drug experiment can be affected by many variables, discussed below.

Sample Size In regard to sample size, recall that the larger the experimental and control groups, the less of a difference between their criterion score means is usually required for statistical significance. Taking into account a gradually additive drug effect over time, larger groups will usually permit a shorter study. One can estimate the approximate minimal duration of an adequate experiment for various assumed improvement rates if one knows the distribution of the "before" scores. Conversely, if one decides to run a study for a given period of time, for example, 1 year, one can estimate the approximate minimal change needed for statistical significance.

Controls The history of medicine and of psychology, and of the management of retarded individuals specifically, underscores the imperativeness of rigorously controlled studies of a new treatment before it is accepted as effective. If one views retardation as a static, hitherto "incurable" condition that will yield only to a magic bullet therapy, then controls may appear unnecessary because no improvement would be expected unless the magic bullet were found, in which case the expected effectiveness of the drug improvement would be self-evident. For instance, Zimmerman, Burgemeister, and Putnam (1949) omitted a placebo control group in their glutamic acid study on the assumption that their retarded subjects were incapable of responding to placebo effects.

The tighter the control variables are, and the more sources of error variance that are eliminated, the more efficient a design becomes. For this reason, matching of subject pairs, though more difficult, appears preferable to equation of subject groups. When groups are merely equated (often erroneously referred to as matched), the means of the equated variables are essentially identical, but there may not be a 1:1 correspondence or relevant characteristics between pairs of subjects, and error variance is likely to be higher.

Diagnostic Homogeneity The above considerations underline the desirability for homogeneity of certain variables. However, some investigators commit an error in strategy by pursuing homogeneity of variables that should not be homogeneous. For instance, researchers characteristically aspire to constitute subject groups with the same clinical diagnoses (e.g., Down syndrome). Thus, in their review of glutamic acid studies with retarded persons, Astin and Ross (1962) expressed preference for diagnostic (mostly etiological) homogeneity. Such diagnostic homogeneity is appropriate when there is reason to believe that the drug treatment is of greater benefit in one syndrome than in others. If there is no reason for making such an assumption, however, diagnostic homogeneity is at best irrelevant and wasteful; at worst, it may be destructive to the experiment, for at least two reasons. First, in some syndromes where biochemical function is disturbed, the drug may be metabolized in atypical fashion and thus may not act as it ordinarily would. Rogers and Pelton (1957) have raised the question of whether certain types of retarded persons are capable of metabolizing glutamic acid in the usual manner. Second, in other syndromes, the structure of the brain may be characteristically atypical, and those areas in or upon which the drug ordinarily acts may be impaired. In either instance, there is an increased likelihood that a general effect that might have been observed in a diagnostically heterogeneous group may not take place or may not become measurable. Thus, the experiment would not constitute a fair test for the drug, and might lead to its premature rejection.

Shortcomings of Criterion Measures A common, but questionable, feature of drug and other treatment studies has been reliance on assessment of global or very complex behavior. The use of intelligence tests, such as the Stanford-Binet Intelligence Scale and the Wechsler Intelligence Scales, is an example of such an approach, and may have been a poor strategy. Global intelligence reflects years of learning and experience, and is modified relatively slowly. Lengthy experiments are likely to be necessary to demonstrate changes adequately. A more promising strategy appears to be the assessment of behavior processes that underlie global intelligence, such as arousal, perception (e.g., attention), learning, and retention. For instance, it is conceivable that within a few days or weeks a drug could have measurable effects on vigilance, conditioning speed, or short-term memory, while it might take months or years before such effects are translated into statistically significant improvements on global IQ tests. This point is particularly important if, as reasonably suggested by Krech (1968), drugs are more likely to have selective effects on specific cognitive processes.

If underlying processes do not show any change, no change is likely to occur on the global level. On the other hand, once underlying processes have shown improvement, then it is timely to design "second generation" experiments that may involve more global measures.

Personnel Variables One problem in the design of drug and other treatment studies that is rarely mentioned is the fact that the before-and-after measurements are often made by technicians or other personnel who do not possess a high degree of competence assessment experience. For instance, a junior psychologist may be hired to give intelligence tests to subjects before and after administration of the treatment. The examiner, however, may only have had experience in testing a small number of individuals using the particular test involved. Thus, he or she may improve in competence during the "before" assessment, and may obtain systematically higher or lower scores on the "after" assessments solely on the basis of his or her increased skills. "Improvement" then may be ascribed erroneously to the treatment, and "loss" to detrimental drug effects or to subject characteristics.

To summarize, each of the above-noted factors can, if not correctly addressed, vitiate an otherwise excellently intended and careful approach toward a research effort. As previously described, however, these factors *can* each be assessed and controlled. The reader should note that both Chapters 12 and 13 in this book, which deal with specific drug treatment studies, take these factors into account.

CONCLUSION

In conclusion, returning to the distinction made earlier between direct and indirect effects of pharmacological agents, it is conceivable, in light of this chapter's discussion, that this distinction may have limited utility. The differences between such potential agents may lie not so much in their effects as in their mode of action—at least so long as children are used as subjects, and so long as they are exposed to intensive environmental enrichment while on the drugs. It should be emphasized that no stand was taken in this chapter in regard to two issues relevant to drug research in retardation: 1) What is the theoretical likelihood that intelligence in retarded individuals can be significantly improved by a pharmacological agent? and 2) What emphasis should be given to research of this nature within a global research strategy in mental retardation and/or pharmacology? This author's position is that if studies of the intelligence-enhancing effects of pharmacological agents are to be conducted, they should be designed so as to represent an adequate, fair, and efficient test of such an effect.

REFERENCES

Astin, A.W., & Ross, S. Glumatic acid and human intelligence. *Psychological Bulletin,* 1962, *57,* 429–434.

Burns, J.T., House, R.F., Fensch, F.C., & Miller, J.C. Effects of magnesium pemoline and dextroamphetamine on human learning. *Science,* 1967, *155,* 849–851.

Freeman, R.D. Drug effects on learning in children: A selective review of the past thirty years. *Journal of Special Education,* 1966, *1,* 17–44.

Goldstein, H. Sickle-cell therapy in children. *Archives of Pediatrics,* 1956, *73,* 234–249.

Harrell, R.F., Capp, R.H., Davis, D.R., Peerless, J., & Ravitz, L.R. Can nutritional supplements help mentally retarded children? An exploratory study. *Proceedings of the National Academy of Sciences,* 1981, *78,* 574–578.

House, M., Wilson, H.D., & Goodfellow., H.D.L. Treatment of mental deficiency with α-tocopherol. *American Journal of Mental Deficiency,* 1964, *69,* 328–329.

Koestler, A. *The ghost in the machine.* New York: MacMillan Publishing Co., 1967.

Krech, D. The chemistry of learning. *Saturday Review,* January 20, 1968, 48–50, 68.

Louttit, R.T. Chemical facilitation of intelligence among the mentally retarded. *American Journal of Mental Deficiency,* 1965, *69,* 495–501.

Mead, M. *And keep your powder dry.* New York: William Morrow and Co., 1942.

Menolascino, F.J., & Eggers, M.L. *Medical dimensions of mental retardation.* Lincoln, NE: University Press, 1981.

Pauling, L. Orthomolecular psychiatry. *Science,* 1968, *160,* 265–271.

Rogers, L.L., & Pelton, R.B. Effects of glutamine on IQ scores of mentally deficient children. *Texas Reports on Biology and Medicine,* 1957, *15,* 84–90.

Turkel, H. Medical treatment of mongolism. In: O. Stur (ed.), *Proceedings of the Second International Congress on Mental Retardation,* August 14–19, 1961. Basel, Switzerland: S. Karger, 1963, 409–416.

Vogel, W., Broverman, D.M., Draguns, J.G., & Klaiber, E.L. The role of glutamic acid in cognitive behaviors. *Psychological Bulletin,* 1966, *65,* 367–382.

Yannet, H. Research in the field of mental retardation. *Journal of Pediatrics,* 1957, *50,* 236–239.

Zimmerman, F.T., Burgemeister, B., & Putnam, T.J. The effect of glutamic acid upon the mental and physical growth of mongols. *American Journal of Psychiatry,* 1949, *105,* 661–668.

Curative Aspects of Mental Retardation:
Biomedical and Behavioral Advances
edited by Frank J. Menolascino, M.D., Ronald Neman, Ph.D., and Jack A. Stark, Ph.D.
Copyright 1983   Paul H. Brookes Publishing Co., Inc.   Baltimore · London

chapter 12

Possible Role of Peptides in Mental Retardation

ABBA J. KASTIN, M.D.
Veterans Administration Medical Center
Tulane University School of Medicine
New Orleans, Louisiana
CURT A. SANDMAN, PH.D.
University of California, Irvine
Fairview Hospital
Costa Mesa, California

PEPTIDES ARE STRINGS OF AMINO ACIDS found throughout the brain and elsewhere in the body. When injected, they affect the brain and behavior in dramatic ways. Their role in mental retardation is unknown, but because of their profound effects on the central nervous system (CNS), one could envision the use of peptides in all aspects of mental retardation including diagnosis, treatment, and in better understanding the underlying mechanisms.

For example, it is conceivable that altered levels of one or more endogenous peptides exist in mentally retarded individuals or even in their parents. If it were possible to detect this by a simple blood test, treatment with peptides as replacement before conception, during pregnancy, or early in life could potentially reverse the debilitating effects of this possible imbalance. If the diagnosis is made at birth, then perhaps treatment with peptides during critical periods of development of the brain could have permanent beneficial effects. Even if treatment were required on a daily basis, as in diabetes mellitus, long-

acting analogues of the peptides might make it possible for a single daily administration to suffice. It already appears that some improvement can occur after peptide treatment in certain cases of mental retardation, indicating that some aspects of the disorder may be reversible.

At present, much of the work being done on the appliction of peptides to the symptoms of mental retardation is speculative. This chapter reviews most of the peptides known to affect the brain. Where possible, clinical studies are emphasized. Though it is impossible to define completely the role of peptides in mental retardation, this review and the speculative findings described make clear that neuropeptides can represent a new approach to mental retardation.

MELANOCYTE-STIMULATING HORMONE (MSH)

Melanocyte-stimulating hormone (MSH) is the peptide that stimulates color change in lower vertebrates such as the frog and lizard.

Although MSH has no physiological role in pigmentation of mammals, it is present in the human brain (O'Donohue & Jacobowitz, 1979; Parker & Porter, 1979). In a series of animal experiments with MSH beginning in 1963, a large number of controlling mechanisms were found in the rat, for a pituitary hormone with no known function (Kastin, Olson, Schally, & Coy, 1979; Kastin, Sandman, Stratton, Schally, & Miller, 1975). Guided by our continual amazement at the efficiency of the body, we accordingly began to question the function of MSH. Influenced by the knowledge that melanocytes are of neural crest origin and that an adaptive role of MSH in humans might involve the brain, the first clinical study of the effects of MSH on the CNS was begun more than a decade ago. This initial study found some nonspecific changes in the electroencephalogram (EEG) in half of the subjects studied (Kastin, Kullander, Borglin, Dyster-Aas, Dahlberg, Ingvar, Krakau, Miller, Bowers, & Schally, 1968). Subsequent studies of the EEG changes in animals after injection of MSH have confirmed the initial clinical findings (Denman, Miller, Sandman, Schally, & Kastin, 1972; Sandman, Denman, Miller, Knott, Schally, & Kastin, 1971; Urban, Lopes da Silva, Storm van Leeuwen, & DeWied, 1974).

The second clinical study of the CNS effects of MSH used more specific measurements that resulted in findings of relevance to mental retardation. In addition to significant improvement after MSH in the Benton Visual Retention Test, somatosensory-evoked potentials were measured under conditions of attention and relaxation (Kastin, Miller, Gonzalez-Barcena, Hawley, Dyster-Aas, Schally, Velasco-Parra, & Velasco, 1971). Changes in the electrical activity of the brain were greatly facilitated by administration of MSH, particularly when the subject was attending to the task. No substantial changes in plasma cortisol levels were found, in contrast to studies with ACTH in which the effects of ACTH itself on the CNS are confounded by the changes induced by the cortisol released by ACTH.

In a pilot study published at the same time in 1971, we studied a 14-year-old boy with a mild cognitive deficit (IQ 80) associated with cerebral palsy. After an infusion of α-MSH, he showed a marked improvement in a test of visual spatial perception involving analysis and synthesis, but there were no controls (Kastin et al., 1971).

Several other studies in normal subjects, usually university students, showed that the active core of MSH, namely the 4–10 sequence shared with ACTH, also improved attention. Thus, in studies performed in a "double-blind" fashion in which neither experimenter nor subject knew whether peptide or placebo was administered, improvement in the Benton Visual Retention Test was usually observed (Kastin et al., 1971; Miller, Harris, Kastin, & Van Riezen, 1976; Miller, Kastin, Sandman, Fink, & Van Veen, 1974; Sandman, George, Nolan, Van Riezen, & Kastin, 1975). In this test, the subjects are briefly shown pictures of geometrical forms that they are asked to reproduce almost immediately. Tests of simple verbal memory did not seem to be improved by the MSH peptide (Kastin et al., 1971; Sandman et al., 1975) unless the test had a strong visual content (Miller, et al., 1976) and involved no delay in the time for recall (Miller, Groves, Bopp, & Kastin, 1979).

One study found that MSH/ACTH 4–10 increased the threshold for detection of visual stimuli, but enhanced the discrimination of stimuli once the threshold had been exceeded (Sandman, George, McCanne, Nolan, Kaswan, & Kastin, 1977). This was consistent with the idea that attention involves the exclusion of extraneous distractions so that the subject can attend to the relevant information. It was further illustrated by the more rapid shift to related, or intradimensional, stimuli in subjects tested with MSH/ACTH 4–10 than in shifts to unrelated, extradimensional material (Sandman et al., 1975; Miller et al., 1976). A more recent and clear demonstration that attention rather than memory is improved by MSH/ACTH 4–10 was provided by a study using the Sternberg item recognition task involving reaction to a single test digit in memorized sets of increasing size (Ward, Sandman, George, & Shulman, 1978). At all set sizes, MSH improved reaction time compared to that seen after administration of the vehicle solution. It also appears that the personality of the subject may determine the type of reaction to MSH/ACTH 4–10, since a recent study found the best improvement in extroverted as opposed to introverted male students (Breier, Kain, & Konzett, 1979).

In 1976 these studies were extended to mentally retarded subjects, a group in which impaired attention is a well-documented symptom (Zeaman & House, 1963). Twenty moderately retarded adult men, between 20 and 42 years of age, were recruited from sheltered workshops. Half the subjects received MSH/ACTH 4–10 and half a vehicle control solution of physiological saline (Sandman, George, Walker, Nolan, & Kastin, 1976). In addition to the Benton Visual Retention Test, in which significant improvement was found, the subjects also received other tests. The results were consistent with an improvement in attention. In the orienting response, a significant decrease in heart rate, a finding observed with attention, was found when a slide was changed to a different color on the 13th presentation. No such response was observed in the subjects receiving the vehicle solution as a control. In the concept formation task, the subjects given the peptide performed better than the controls on all shifts (reversal, intradimensional, and extradimensional) of a visual discrimination series. A refined analysis of the extradimensional shift into its subproblem components indicated that subjects given the peptide performed the changed and unchanged components with equal probability. The men receiving the vehicle solution solved the unchanged problem with significantly greater ease than the changed problem (Sandman et al., 1976). This pattern suggested that the MSH/ACTH 4–10 fragment selectively improved dimensional attention (Tighe, Glick, & Cole, 1971).

Several tests from the Halstead-Reitan neuropsychological battery were also used in the Sandman et al. (1976) study of mentally retarded individuals. In the Trails B test, the subject is required to work two sets of information simultaneously by alternatively connecting a series of points in order of numbers and letters; for example, 1 should be connected to A, A with 2, 2 with B, etc. Another test required the subject to listen to and compare two rhythms. Subjects receiving the peptide made fewer errors in these two tests.

In several tests less related to attention in this neuropsychological battery, MSH had no effect (Sandman et al., 1976). No significant improvement was found in the finger-tapping test in which the subject was required to depress a lever as fast as possible. Another test that did not reveal any difference between groups was the tactile recognition test, in which the subject was required to note which of his fingers were touched by the experiment and what number was written on his hand in the absence of visual cues. A related test of astereognosis, in which a subject was required to identify a geometric shape placed in one hand and point with the other hand to a match from a set of four visually presented geometric forms, also did not show improvement, but a ceiling effect may have contributed to the results, since all subjects performed well in the pretest situation in this test. These results firmly established the potential utility of an MSH-like peptide as a somewhat selective treatment for disorders of attention. Two studies, described below, have subsequently confirmed this.

A study of mentally retarded individuals, similar in design to the Sandman et al. (1976) study described above, was conducted with an analogue of MSH/ACTH 4–10. This altered peptide was 1,000 times more potent than MSH/ACTH 4–10 in an animal model involving the conditioned avoidance response, and it was assumed that it would also be more potent in the human being (Greven & DeWied, 1973). This assumption placed undue emphasis on the conditioned avoidance response, as both animal (Beckwith, Sandman, Hothersall, & Kastin, 1977) and human (Miller, Fischer, Groves, Rudrauff, & Kastin, 1977) studies have shown. Nevertheless, the analogue has the advantage that it can be given by mouth and has been found effective in maintaining concentration in normal subjects (Gaillard & Varey, 1979). During the first session, all 24 mentally retarded subjects received placebo; during the second session, one-third of the subjects received placebo, one-third a small dose, and one-third a dose four times larger. As before, the tests included the orienting response, Trails B test, concept formation task of visual discrimination, and Benton Visual Retention Test. Although none of the results were as robust as with the parent MSH/ACTH 4–10, the results suggested improvements in all but the orienting response (Walker & Sandman, 1979). However, it now appears that an inverted-U function represents the dose relationship, so that the most effective dose may not have been used.

The same analogue was used with a similar population of mentally retarded individuals in a third study that examined for the first time interpersonal and environmental awareness (Sandman, Walker, & Lawton, 1980). The environment consisted of a sheltered workshop for mentally retarded adults who were paid a wage based on their productivity in bending electrical resistors to fit a mold. The task involved the monotonous and repetitious turning of leads, bending, cutting, and inspecting, although only one step was assigned for any given day of the test.

The design of the experiment included a placebo week, 2 weeks of peptide (different doses each week), and a final placebo week. As in all of our experiments, the experimenters were unaware of the treatment received by the subjects. Different doses (0, 5, 10, and 20 mg) of the analogue were used. The subjects were observed during the morning hours for 5 consecutive days for each of the 4 weeks. Samples of interpersonal behavior were measured every 15 minutes and productivity was examined every 30 minutes.

An influence of the peptide on productivity

was observed. There was a complex relationship between dosage and difficulty of the task. The first step of the process was the easiest and only involved making turns in the resistors. The second step required smaller, more discrete bends in the leads. The third step required cutting the leads to a prescribed length. The fourth, most complex step, involved inspecting the resistors and making decisions as to whether they met the quality criteria established by the workshop. The results clearly indicated that 10 mg of the peptide enhanced all but the first step of the process. Conversely, 20 mg depressed performance on each step. The influence of 5 mg was mixed, enhancing performance of the complex task and impeding performance of tasks requiring less precision.

Different profiles of behavior also were related to the doses of the peptide analogue. Striking increases in self-stimulation (touching self, lip smacking, etc.) were apparent for all doses. Treatment with the peptide resulted in greater interpersonal communication and gregariousness than during the placebo treatment. In this regard, some studies of MSH peptides in normal individuals have reported decreased anxiety (Miller et al., 1974; Sandman et al., 1975). Concentration scores were also greater in the retarded individuals during treatment with the peptide. There were indications that the effects of 1 week of treatment with the peptide may have persisted for at least another week. Although rats given MSH show increased gregariousness (Beckwith, O'Quin, Petro, Kastin, & Sandman, 1977), this is the first report in human subjects of a peptide affecting interpersonal behavior.

The findings of this study indicate that an analogue of an endogenous peptide can facilitate interpersonal and environmental awareness. The converging array of results suggest that peptide fragments related to ACTH and MSH have a beneficial influence on behavior without known side effects. Thus, the therapeutic use of these substances in groups with deficits in interpersonal and environmental awareness is encouraged by our findings.

All three studies with mentally retarded individuals indicate that certain deficits, traditionally assumed to be irreversible, may be influenced by peptides. This applies particularly to the influence of MSH and its active fragments on the process of attention. However, it is likely that the degree of attention-deficiency in mentally retarded patients differs with the individual. Thus, some patients show greater improvement after MSH than others. Although the MSH peptides may not be therapeutically practical in mental retardation, studies with them have emphasized that at least some of the brain changes are not permanent. Perhaps endogenous peptides in the normal human being are involved in a dynamic balance that may be imbalanced in mental retardation and altered by appropriate treatment.

Thus, evidence gathered in human studies over the past decade indicates that the heptapeptide shared by LPH, ACTH, and MSH (Met-Glu-His-Phe-Arg-Trp-Gly) possesses striking behavioral properties. Although improved memory and increased motivation are constructs proposed to account for the experimental behavioral changes observed, the most consistent laboratory as well as clinical findings support the idea that these peptides enhance attention. For instance, rats injected with MSH or its behaviorally active core reliably perform a reversal shift of the black-white discrimination problem more efficiently than animals receiving a vehicle solution (Beckwith, Sandman, Hothersall, & Kastin, 1976; Sandman, Alexander, & Kastin, 1973; Sandman, Beckwith, Gittis, & Kastin, 1974; Sandman, Miller, Kastin, & Schally, 1972). Since improved performance of the reversal shift has been suggested to relate to increased dimensional or selective attention (Mackintosh, 1965, 1969), these early findings in rats injected with MSH are consistent with the above attentional hypothesis.

Several other lines of evidence obtained in animals encouraged us to believe that individuals suffering from attentional deficits might benefit from treatment with MSH and related molecules. Sandman et al. (1976)

reported that the influence of MSH on attention was most pronounced when the rats were tested while housed under conditions of constant illumination, which inhibit endogenous MSH release. These housing conditions generally resulted in inferior performance, but treatment with MSH restored the attentional behavior to a level similar to that observed when animals were housed in constant darkness. In a related study, Sandman et al. (1973) found that the learning behavior of attentionally deficient albino rats was more profoundly affected by MSH than was the behavior of the relatively attentive pigmented rats. These findings strongly suggested that genetically impaired animals could benefit from treatment with MSH and its fragments.

There is another group of studies with potentially great pertinence to mental retardation. These involve injection of newborn rats during the first week of life with MSH. Infant rats receiving MSH only during the first week of life react differently from control rats injected with diluent when tested as adults (Beckwith, O'Quin, Petro, Kastin, & Sandman, 1977; Beckwith, Sandman, Hothersall, & Kastin, 1977). Considering that we have shown both in rats (Kastin, Nissen, Nikolics, Medzihradszky, Coy, Teplan, & Schally, 1976) and man (Ashton, Millman, Telford, Thompson, Davies, Hall, Shuster, Thody, Coy, & Kastin, 1977; Redding, Kastin, Nikolics, Schally, & Coy, 1978) that the half-time disappearance of MSH is only a few minutes, the long duration of effects is striking. Previously, we thought that we had made a startling finding in showing that MSH could alter the EEG of adult rats several hours after injection (Sandman et al., 1971). But to have an effect persist for months, which represents a good portion of the rat's life span, is even more striking. In addition, these studies showed that male and female rats respond differently on some of these tests (Beckwith, O'Quin, Petro, Kastin, & Sandman, 1977; Beckwith, Sandman, Hothersall, & Kastin, 1977).

It is conceivable that work with peptides will alter our view of brain-behavior relations, and the clinical utility could be dramatic. For instance, early analysis of peptide levels in some bodily fluid may be a biological marker of mental deficiency. If a deficiency is found, it might not be necessary for the infant to receive treatment the rest of his or her life, but rather, be carefully treated only during the stage of critical development. Although such speculations are romantic and may be over-simplified, the results found with peptides do offer some hope for new approaches to mental retardation.

MSH RELEASE INHIBITING
FACTOR NUMBER 1 (MIF-1)

Even though MSH is the only peptide that has been tested in patients with mental retardation, it can be seen that the rationale for doing so resided in this peptide's previously demonstrated ability to improve the process of attention. Thus, studies with other known peptides may demonstrate effects on processes that may also be pertinent to mental retardation. Several investigations have been performed with the peptide MIF-1 (MSH release inhibiting factor number 1). Under some circumstances, MIF-1 inhibits the release of MSH from the pituitary, but in most behavioral situations it exhibits similar rather than opposing actions to MSH, thereby emphasizing that it is probably not the physiological inhibitor of MSH release (Kastin, Sandman, Miller, & Schally, 1976).

MIF-1 constitutes the last three amino acids of the hormone oxytocin, and enzymes have been found in the hypothalamus that split from oxytocin (Walter, Griffiths, & Hooper, 1973). A large series of studies in animals have confirmed the specific effects of MIF-1 and other peptides on the brain (Kastin, Olson, Schally, & Coy, 1979). Its mechanism of action remains a mystery (Kastin, Ehrensing, Coy, Schally, & Kostrzewa, 1979).

The principle of extra-endocrine or extra-pituitary effects of hypothalamic peptides was first shown with MIF-1 in the dopa-potentiation test. The pituitary gland as well

as other endocrine organs was not required for the behavioral excitation in this test involving treatment with a monoamine oxidase inhibitor, dopa, and peptide (Plotnikoff, Kastin, Anderson, & Schally, 1971; Plotnikoff, Minard, & Kastin, 1974). Similar observations were made in the oxotremorine test, where MIF-1 reversed the tremors induced by oxotremorine even without the presence of the pituitary and when administered by several routes (Plotnikoff & Kastin, 1974a; Plotnikoff, Kastin, Anderson, & Schally, 1972). These results have been confirmed by several other groups (Castensson, Sievertson, Lindeke, & Sum, 1974; Huidobro-Toro, Scotti de Carolis, & Longo, 1974; Voith, 1977). MIF-1 also reversed the sedation induced by the rauwolfia derivative deserpidine in rats and monkeys (Plotnikoff, Kastin, Anderson & Schally, 1973). As with the dopa-potentiation test (Plotnikoff et al., 1971), this effect showed a diminishing response with higher doses so that a bell-shaped or inverted-U pattern appeared. This has been found in animals with MIF-1 by other investigators as well (Bjorkman & Sievertson, 1977; Crowley & Hydinger, 1976).

MIF-1 has been shown to be inactive in many other systems. At the doses used in the tests just summarized, it was ineffective in reversing the behavioral actions of serotonin, in changing general motor activity by itself or that induced by methamphetamine, in protecting against convulsions induced by four different methods, in changing cardiac output, heart rate, aortic or left ventricular pressures, or renal blood flow (Plotnikoff & Kastin, 1974b). Since renal blood flow is sensitive to dopaminergic effects, the results indicate a lack of peripheral effect of MIF-1 on dopaminergic receptors. In addition, MIF-1 did not block adrenergic, cholinergic, or histaminergic receptors in the cardiovascular system or inhibit ganglionic transmission in anesthetized dogs (Plotnikoff & Kastin, 1974b).

Despite the fact that under certain conditions MIF-1 inhibits the release of MSH from the pituitary, under normal conditions this apparently does not occur. Several behavioral tests have shown similar actions for MIF-1 and MSH, although higher doses of MIF-1 were used. Perhaps the most intriguing action of MIF-1 is that resembling an endogenous naloxone or opiate inhibitor in some but not all conditions (Olson, Kastin, LaHoste, Olson, & Coy, 1979). Van Ree and DeWied (1976) found that MIF-1 facilitates morphine dependence. These results contrast with those of Walter, Ritzmann, Bhargava, and Flexner (1979) who reported that MIF-1 blocks development of physical dependence. Our data (Olson, Kastin, LaHoste, Olson, & Coy, 1979) support the latter paper.

Clinical studies of MIF-1 have focused upon Parkinson's disease and mental depression. Most of the patients with Parkinson's disease seem to have improved after receiving MIF-1, particularly in conjunction with dopa, but the extent varies from study to study (Kastin & Barbeau, 1972; Kastin, Olson, Schally, & Coy, 1979). Because some of the animal models in which MIF-1 is effective are also sensitive to tricyclic antidepressants as well as known antiparkinsonian agents, MIF-1 was tried in mental depression. As in some of the animal studies, small but not large doses seemed to result in substantial improvement (Ehrensing & Kastin, 1974, 1977, 1978). Similar results were reported for improvement in the mood of patients with Parkinson's disease (Fischer, Schneider, Jacobi, & Maxion, 1975; Gerstenbrand, Binder, Kozma, Pusch, & Reisner, 1975; Gerstenbrand, Poewe, Aichner, & Kozma, 1979; Schneider, Fischer, Jacobi, & Reh, 1978).

In studies of MIF-1 in laboratory animals and human beings, the actions of MIF-1 persist for several hours. Yet this tripeptide is found in blood for only a few minutes after injection in the rat (Redding et al., 1973) and man (Redding, Kastin, Gonzalez-Barcena, Coy, Hirotsu, Ruelas, & Schally, 1974). Moreover, rat plasma, and to a lesser extent human plasma, rapidly degrades MIF-1 (Redding et al., 1973; Redding et al., 1974; Walter, Neidle, & Marks, 1975).

By whatever means MIF-1 exerts its central effects, it is obvious that it does not do so by persisting in intact form in the blood. The action could occur primarily in the periphery, perhaps by changing peripheral levels of the peptides or other substances, in the circumventricular areas or pituitary where retrograde flow into the CSF would render it less subject to enzymatic activity than in the blood, or by altering the permeability of the blood-brain barrier to other substances. Alternatively, an active fragment or a small amount of intact peptide may be sufficient to induce its effects.

The effects of MIF-1 in both animal and clinical studies would seem to be most easily explained by a potentiation of the effects of dopa. Numerous laboratory studies have been performed in an attempt to determine whether this presumed action occurs by increased synthesis, decreased degradation, effects on the rate-limiting enzyme involved in dopamine synthesis (tyrosine hydroxylase), increased conversion from dopa to dopamine by an effect on the enzyme dopa decarboxylase, or uptake of dopamine by striatal synaptosomes. No consistent effect has been found (Kastin, Schally, & Kostrzewa, 1980). This could be explained by experimental error, lack of effect in the striatal region primarily investigated, involvement of a secondary substance(s), removal of an inhibitory control of dopaminergic or nondopaminergic nerves, differences in pathological states like parkinsonism, or a direct action on a specific MIF-1 receptor. Once the mechanism has been determined, a more focused approach both in the laboratory and clinic can be expected. However, examination of the spectrum of effects produced by this interesting peptide need not await such a discovery.

THYROTROPIN RELEASING HORMONE (TRH)

Another tripeptide active in the same animal system of dopa-potentiation in which MIF-1, tricyclic antidepressants, and antiparkinsonian agents are active is thyrotropin releasing hormone (TRH). Although not effective in Parkinson's disease (Chase, Woods, Lipton, & Morris, 1974), there appears to be a small group of depressed patients who may respond to TRH (Furlong, Brown, & Beeching, 1976). In general, most clinical studies of the therapeutic role of TRH in mental depression are negative. Yet there continue to be a few positive reports. A possible explanation, therefore, is that there is a small subgroup of TRH-sensitive depressed patients.

Thus, TRH may illustrate a principle concerning the clinical application of peptides that may eventually be pertinent to mental retardation. As mentioned, the only peptide so far tried in mental retardation is MSH, and that is because we have shown both in humans and rats that MSH may help mentally retarded individuals only to the extent that attention is involved. Similarly, TRH may help depressed patients only to the extent that some process not yet identified is involved. The number of cases involving this unknown factor probably represents a smaller percentage of the total population of depressed patients than attentional deficits represent in mental retardation. Mental depression, like mental retardation, is undoubtedly composed of many diverse mental processes that are involved to varying extents in the disorder. Although the yield for treatment of depression with TRH is small, that is no reason to abandon the search for the mechanisms involved or to abandon clinical trials of peptides in depression.

The trials of TRH and MIF-1 in mental depression and Parkinson's disease were largely based upon results of a single animal system in which known antidepressant and antiparkinsonian agents were shown to be effective. Fortunately, the peptides seemed to work in the same system. However, it would have been just as logical to suppose that a new class of compounds like peptides would not work in the same systems devised for an older class of compounds even though the same

clinical disorder is considered. Otherwise an investigator could be caught in a vicious circle and never find a new approach to any disease process. Obviously what is needed are new animal models for disorders like mental depression and retardation. In order for such a model to be effective, however, one must already have a treatment for the clinical disorder. Again, therefore, one is in a vicious circle for which there is no readily apparent solution.

If there is no animal model for mental retardation sensitive to only peptides, for example, and if such a model would be dependent upon already having a therapeutically active agent, the animal work would be of little promise. There are some ways out of such circular reasoning. These solutions are unlikely to be endorsed by the scientific community as a whole, nor will they find easy funding. A partial answer could involve considering the clinical work already done with MSH and theorizing that any system in which MSH is effective could serve as a model for mental retardation. This is hardly satisfactory. Another solution that might more likely result in an answer would involve trying a series of naturally occurring peptides and their analogues in mental retardation. This ''shotgun'' approach has definite drawbacks from the point of view of theory, efficiency, and ethical considerations. However, if thorough tests for adverse side effects were made, accidental findings in a screening procedure might be the only way certain effects of peptides, that perhaps do not fit in any current theoretical framework, could emerge. It is amazing how little the scientist is aware of the vast number of therapeutically effective drugs on the market whose primary use was first found by accidental trial in the human being.

The preceding discussion is related to the questionable therapeutic usefulness of TRH in mental depression and of MSH in mental retardation. Of relevance to the proposal for clinical screening is that there was also an incidental finding in the early trials of TRH in depression that has been confirmed by a majority of investigators (Ehrensing & Kastin, 1977). This unexpected finding, a blunted TSH response to TRH, has been considered to be of diagnostic and prognostic usefulness of the disorder. The response was not predicted and, even today, almost a decade later, the full explanation of the phenomenon is lacking. Why the pituitary of certain depressed patients releases less thyrotropin (TSH) after being stimulated by the hypothalamic hormone primarily involved in stimulating its release is only suspected, not proven, but may involve cortisol and somatostatin. Further unexpected findings can be anticipated as trials with peptides continue.

Thus, the studies with TRH in depressed patients, unsatisfactory as they were, would seem to illustrate a number of ways in which peptides might eventually help mental retardation. First, the peptide could be therapeutically useful in all patients with this disorder under appropriate conditions. Second, the peptide could be therapeutically useful in only a certain number of mentally retarded individuals. Third, the hormonal response of a subgroup of mentally retarded individuals to the peptide might serve the same diagnostic purpose as the response to TRH serves in depression. Fourth, the response to a peptide, either therapeutic or hormonal, might be prognostic for the same or other treatments.

A final apparent application of TRH to principles that might be involved in mental retardation comes exclusively from some early studies in animals that paralleled those done with MSH. Newborn rats treated during the first week of life with TRH and then tested in a maze as adults ran the maze faster and with fewer errors than infants injected with a placebo (Stratton, Gibson, Kolar, & Kastin, 1976). Infant rats treated with TRH were less emotional and more active in an open field both as infants and adults, but brain weights did not differ (Stratton et al., 1976). Since the effects of a single injection of TRH only persist for a few hours at the most in adults, it

is obvious that some permanent effect must have occurred in the organization of the brain. One should carefully consider the implications of this for human beings.

ENKEPHALINS AND ENDORPHINS

The enkephalins and endorphins are peptides found in the brain that exert morphine-like actions. Although they, like all the brain peptides except MSH, have not been tried in mental retardation, they illustrate at least three principles that might be applicable to the disorder.

The first point is that the actions of a peptide need not be confined to the function by which it was first described. In the case of the brain opiates, they were discovered and initially studied for their morphine-like properties. That they exerted no analgesic effects when given peripherally led the discoverers to discount this route of administration without considering that the brain opiates were peptides. Like other peptides, they could be expected to share general properties that include multiple and independent actions. It was only when specific behavioral actions after peripheral administration were examined that the phenomenon of a behavioral/narcotic dissociation for the opiate peptides was observed (Kastin, Olson, Schally, & Coy, 1979; Kastin, Scollan, King, Schally, & Coy, 1976). Thus, it has not been ruled out that peptides such as enkephalin, endorphin, and TRH that are already known to exist in the brain could play a role in mental retardation or other disorders.

The second point is that some indirect evidence already exists to support a clinical trial of enkephalin in mental retardation. Unfortunately, the evidence is based on the somewhat weak reasoning discussed in a previous section of this review. This reasoning involves animal models of mental retardation. We have discussed the difficulties with these. One of the possibilities was to examine the laboratory situations in which a compound already known to be effective in mental retardation is active. Since MSH has shown some promise in clinical trials of mental retardation, one could examine a learning task in which MSH was effective. The complex maze is the first task to which MSH was shown to affect the rate of acquisition in a learning problem (Stratton & Kastin, 1975). Hungry rats receiving MSH ran the maze faster and with fewer errors than rats given the control solution. In essentially the same task, enkephalin has shown the same results (Kastin, Scollan, King, Schally, & Coy, 1976). Since both MSH and enkephalin improve learning in this situation in the laboratory with rats, it would appear that these peptides may share some properties. The relationship of enkephalin to mental retardation is unknown, but its administration by the peripheral route, rather than by central injections directly into the brain, should obviate any potential problems associated with analgesia or narcotic addiction.

The third principle derived from study of the enkephalins and endorphins that might be applicable to mental retardation is also based upon animal experimentation. It resembles a point already made for MSH since the experiments are conceptually similar. Rats injected during pregnancy or infancy with β-endorphin showed effects lasting into the adult stage of life. Two different experiments were performed. In the first, rats injected during the first week of life were tested for analgesia as adults 3 months later. At that time, they showed a significant elevation in threshold for painful thermal stimuli, much as would be expected if they had been injected centrally less than an hour previously (Sandman, McGivern, Berka, Walker, Coy, & Kastin, 1979). Even more surprising was that the classical opiate antagonist, naloxone, was ineffective in reversing this analgesia. The second experiment resembled the first, with two major exceptions: pregnant rats received the injections from days 7 to 21 of gestation and the rats were tested for other behaviors besides analgesia as infants and adults. During infancy, rats injected with β-endorphin opened their eyes later and were less active

(McGivern, Sandman, Kastin, & Coy, 1979). The adults injected while *in utero* were also significantly less active than controls as shown in the open field and in a passive avoidance situation and spent less time in contact with litter mates (McGivern et al., 1979). Thus, prenatal exposure to β-endorphin can blunt perceptual thresholds, motor activity, and social behavior. This insensitivity to environmental stimulation and the developmental, emotional, and cognitive deficits displayed are not the type of results desired for treatment of mental retardation, and should serve to severely temper any such clinical experiments. However, these results could conceivably contribute to an explanation of certain defects in infants. For example, it is known that many forms of developmental disabilities seem to be related to difficulties in labor. It is now reported that levels of β-endorphin in the amniotic fluid are elevated during fetal distress (Gautray, Jolivet, Veilh, & Guillemin, 1977). Of course, many substances are released in stress and a causal relationship is far from clear. Nevertheless, some peptides like MSH, TRH, and enkephalin seem to have beneficial effects when injected into newborn rats, whereas others like β-endorphin seem to exert different effects under the experimental conditions tested.

In this regard, MSH and its 4–10 core as well as β-endorphin are contained in the LPH molecule. Furthermore, these two peptide groups appear to have some reciprocal actions. Since the MSH/ACTH group stimulates cognitive performance, whereas the results of our developmental studies indicate β-endorphin disrupts learning, it is possible that these two peptide groups are self-regulatory; perhaps they act in opposition to influence behavior. Thus, the MSH/ACTH peptides may be likely candidates for reversing the "retardation" observed after treatment with β-endorphin. The application of this approach to problems of retardation, especially in cases of self-abuse such as the Lesch-Nyhan syndrome, awaits further laboratory study.

Other effects of enkephalins and endorphins continue to be described. Although worthwhile information can be obtained by central administration directly into the brain or its ventricles, studies performed by the peripheral route of administration would seem more readily applicable to any potential use in mental retardation. In 1977, only two more studies were reported. In one of these, enkephalins were found to attenuate carbon dioxide–induced amnesia for an avoidance response (Rigter, Greven, & Van Riezen, 1977). Since the opiate antagonist naloxone failed to prevent this reduction in amnesia, additional evidence for the dissociation of narcotic and behavioral effects was provided. This study also illustrates that memory impairment need not be irreversible and that peptides hold promise in this regard. That same year saw the report of the controversial study of improvement in schizophrenia after β-endorphin (Kline, Li, Lehmann, Lajtha, Laskie, & Cooper, 1977). Largely because of the lack of controls in that study, a great deal of additional work will need to be done in human beings that might have been avoided had a more carefully designed study been performed. This same danger should be avoided in clinical studies with mental retardation. Despite the ethical issues involved in withholding valuable treatment from a patient, one cannot assume a treatment to be valuable until carefully controlled studies have been performed. Such an approach will facilitate the more rapid availability of such compounds for general use.

By 1978, many studies supported our concept of the multiple independent activities of brain opiates. One such study, a year earlier, used a system in which reversal of immobility is tested (Porsolt, Lepichon, & Jalfre, 1977). Several compounds, especially Met-enkephalin, reduced the immobility of the rats confined to an inescapable situation in water (Kastin, Scollan, Ehrensing, Schally, & Coy, 1978). An enkephalin analogue with little narcotic activity produced similar results in contrast to analogues with potent analgesic effects that were essentially inac-

tive behaviorally. The same sort of bell-shaped, inverted-U dose-response relationship described for MIF-1 was observed in this test. Other studies in 1978 of CNS effects of peripherally administered opiate peptides were done in several other species. These included goldfish (Olson, Kastin, Michel, Olson, Coy, & Montalbano, 1978; Olson, Kastin, Montalbano-Smith, Olson, Coy, & Michel, 1978), monkeys (Mello & Mendelson, 1978; Olson, Olson, Kastin, Castellanos, Kneale, Coy, & Wolf, 1978), cats (Catlin, George, & Li, 1978), and chickens (Panksepp, Vilberg, Bean, Coy, & Kastin, 1978). In rats, both we and DeWied reported different behavioral effects with different endorphins (DeWied, Kovacs, Bohus, Van Ree, & Greven, 1978; Veith, Sandman, Walker, Coy, & Kastin, 1978). However, DeWied et al. (1978) postulated that a compound closely related to γ-endorphin was a natural neuroleptic. In 1979, two other groups reported evidence against that postulate (LeMoal, Koob, & Bloom, 1979; Weinberger, Arnsten, & Segal, 1979). The results of the LeMoal et al. (1979) paper support findings that peripheral administraion of brain opiates can result in central effects not related to their narcotic activity. Other studies reported in 1979 showed facilitation of learning of a discrimination reversal task for a reward of food in rhesus monkeys (Olson, Olson, Kastin, Green, Roig-Smith, Hill, & Coy, 1979) and added evidence for a non-narcotic component to tonic immobility in chickens (King, Castellanos, Kastin, Berzas, Mauk, Olson, & Olson, 1979).

Two analogues of opiate peptides were tried in 1979 in schizophrenic patients with promising results (Nedopil & Ruther, 1979; Verhoeven, Van Praag, Van Ree, & DeWied, 1979). Although more work must be done with these, schizophrenia and mental retardation share some similarities. In addition to attentional deficits in some individuals with both disorders, both disorders undoubtedly represent a large number of subgroups different not only in etiology and manifestations, but perhaps also in their responses to new therapeutic agents. Thus, as may be the case with TRH and mental depression, therapeutic responses to these agents may also result in better knowledge of the disease process itself.

DELTA SLEEP-INDUCING PEPTIDE (DSIP)

Delta sleep-inducing peptide (DSIP) was isolated from dialysates of cerebral venous blood taken from rabbits in which sleep was induced by electrical stimulation of the thalamic area of the brain (Schoenenberger & Monnier, 1977). Injection of this nonapeptide enhanced the slow-wave (delta) and spindles EEG pattern that differed greatly from the pattern of arousal seen after i.c.v. injection of dialysates taken from awake rabbits. Like most of the other peptides described in this review, there is little obvious relationship to mental retardation. However, some of the studies conducted with DSIP may have implications for this disorder.

First, DSIP may have a function other than sleep. Although few negative studies of DSIP inducing sleep have been published, skepticism is plentiful among researchers on this point. As pointed out below, these doubts may be misguided, but they serve to illustrate the following point: If a peptide can be isolated from brain tissue or in the case of DSIP, its effluent, on the basis of a test or function not readily reproduced, it is possible that its primary function is different. Therefore, it could be possible that a peptide already isolated for other purposes might play a role in mental retardation. In turn, this emphasizes the need both for a suitable animal model for mental retardation in which to test already existing brain peptides and for the screening of nontoxic peptides in mentally retarded individuals. Both considerations will be unpopular; screening, even in animals, is unappealing since it does not provide sufficient intellectual challenge to most scientists, and clinical screening additionally raises ethical issues. Given the potential benefits of peptide therapy, if the toxic effects are minimized,

the cost/benefit ratio involved in performing the clinical studies might be rather favorable.

A second speculative way in which DSIP could conceivably be relevant to mental retardation is through an influence on sleep, although the relationship of sleep to the disorder is obscure. Several studies have now shown an increased duration of sleep in the rabbit, cat, and rat after DSIP (Kafi, Monnier, & Gallard, 1979; Monnier, Dudler, Gachter, & Schoenenberger, 1977; Polc, Schneeberger, & Haefely, 1978; Schoenenberger & Monnier, 1977). In only one study was increased rapid eye movement (REM) sleep found, and whether this represents a species effect in cats has not been determined (Polc et al., 1978). In rabbits and, to a lesser extent rats, the predominant effect of DSIP on sleep is enhanced delta (slow-wave, non-REM) sleep (Kafi et al., 1979). Even if the major cause of mental retardation is unrelated to sleep, it is possible that a peptide involved in its cause could have a minor effect on sleep.

A third speculation is that studies performed with peptides having no apparent relationship to mental retardation may be applicable to peptides later determined to be involved in the disorder. For example, a chance observation with DSIP has permitted investigation of a phenomenon pertinent to other brain peptides. A rabbit injected with DSIP in an effort to stimulate antibody formation did so to a greater extent than has occurred with other brain peptides. This rabbit produced an antibody against 8 of the 9 amino acids of DSIP. This fortuitous occurrence then permitted an investigation of whether an essentially intact peptide, in this case DSIP, could penetrate the blood-brain barrier. Small amounts were found to do so (Kastin, Buchanan, Schally, & Coy, 1979). This does not imply an exclusive way for peripherally administered peptides to exert their central effects, but does show, under the limitations of the experiment, that at least small amounts of peptides can enter the brain in an intact form. If a peptide(s) were shown to have therapeutic value in mental retardation, such considerations might aid in devising more potent analogues and routes of administration as well as provide a better understanding of its actions.

Studies with DSIP have also confirmed patterns demonstrated with the other brain peptides discussed. These include a bell-shaped, inverted-U dose response curve for sleep, the effectiveness of the peripheral route of administration, and a delayed and prolonged time course after administration (Kafi et al., 1979; Monnier et al., 1977; Polc et al., 1978).

OTHER BRAIN PEPTIDES

The potential of the peptides already discussed for application to the problem of mental retardation could also apply to other peptides already known to exist, as well as to others that undoubtedly will continue to be described. Luteinizing hormone-releasing hormone (LH-RH) is the hypothalmic hormone that controls reproduction in the human being. It appears to exert a direct stimulatory effect on CNS processes that govern sexual behavior in rats, but until now this has not been well documented in humans (Kastin, Coy, Schally, & Zadina, 1980). LH-RH serves to illustrate another limitation, namely, that animal studies are not always directly transferable to clinical studies. This does not mean that animal studies are not usually of value, but it supports the suggestion that a nonspecific screening of naturally occurring brain peptides for effects on mental retardation might not be as unreasonable as it may initially sound to most investigators.

Vasopressin, like MSH, has been considered primarily a pituitary peptide. A series of studies by DeWied have indicated that vasopressin may have a role in improving memory (DeWied & Bohus, 1966). Although analogues would probably be required to avoid the known effects of vasopressin on blood pressure and water retention, the potential for mental retardation is obvious.

Another peptide well studied from an endocrine point of view is somatostatin. In addition to inhibiting the release of growth hormone, it also affects insulin, glucagon, and gastrin release and has been found in the pancreas and gut. Similarly, some hormones originally considered to be exclusively gut hormones have not been found in the brain. These include vasoactive intestinal peptide and cholecystokinin. The latter may be a satiety peptide that tells an individual whether he or she has had sufficient food. The potential for obese subjects is being studied. The lack of exclusivity between gut and brain widens the number of peptides that might be considered to play a role by absence, excess, or relative imbalance in mental retardation and other CNS disorders.

Another group of peptides more clearly functions as neurotransmitters. These include substance P and neurotensin. Although these can exert functions outside of the brain, as the other peptides undoubtedly also do, they may be involved in the normal functioning of the brain and thereby involved in mental retardation as well. Some of the potential interplay on the brain may be illustrated by the interplay on blood sugar: substance P and neurotensin tend to elevate blood sugar, whereas somatostatin would tend to lower elevated levels of sugar.

There may also be a group of rather specific peptides. Several years ago, Ungar described a peptide involved in dark avoidance and two others for blue or green avoidance (Ungar, 1974). Although there has been considerable controversy about these peptides, they may deserve some attention. Other peptides were originally found by Erspamer's group in frog skin. One might imagine literally thousands of peptides for specific functions, but any given peptide probably has multiple functions dependent upon such factors as its entry into the brain; its degradation in blood, CSF, or cell; its binding with specific receptors; its alteration of receptor state or number; its interaction with other peptides and neurotransmitters, etc. Moreover, we would envision a rather limited number of precursor peptides that could give an almost unlimited number of functions by minimal alterations in a small sequence, somewhat as has been shown with MSH/ACTH (Sandman, Beckwith, & Kastin, 1980).

CONCLUSION

Peptides offer a new approach to both diagnostic and treatment considerations of mental retardation. Unfortunately, it is still too early to determine whether the potential of this new approach will be fulfilled. Speculations concerning the measurement of peptide levels to determine an imbalance or treatment with peptides at a gestational, newborn, or adult stage are all premature. Yet, enough animal and clinical data already exist to justify expansion of these efforts to help—and conceivably cure—the symptom of mental retardation.

REFERENCES

Ashton, H., Millman, J.E., Telford, R., Thompson, J.W., Davies, T.F., Hall, R., Shuster, S., Thody, A.J., Coy, D.H., & Kastin, A.J. Psychopharmacological and endocrinological effects of melanocyte stimulating hormones in normal man. *Psychopharmacology*, 1977, *55*, 165.

Beckwith, B.E., O'Quin, R.K., Petro, M.S., Kastin, A.J., & Sandman, C.A. The effects of neonatal injections of α-MSH on the open field behavior of juvenile and adult rats. *Physiological Psychology*, 1977, *5*, 295.

Beckwith, B.E., Sandman, C.A., Hothersall, D., & Kastin, A.J. The influence of three short chain peptides (α-MSH, MSH/ACTH 4–10, MIF-I) on dimensional attention. *Pharmocology, Biochemistry and Behavior*, 1976, *5* (Suppl. 1), 11.

Beckwith, B.E., Sandman, C.A., Hothersall, D., & Kastin, A.J. Influence of neonatal injections of α-MSH on learning, memory and attention in rats. *Physiology and Behavior*, 1977, *18*, 63.

Bjorkman, S., & Sievertson, H. On the optimal dosage of Pro-Leu-Gly-NH₂ (MIF) in neuropharmacological tests and clinical use. *Naunyn-Schmiedeberg's Archives of Pharmacology*, 1977, *298*, 79.

Breier, C., Kain, H., & Konzett, H. Personality dependent effects of the ACTH 4–10 fragment on test performances and on concomitant autonomic relations. *Psychopharmacology*, *1979, 65*, 239.

Castensson, S., Sievertson, H., Lindeke, B., & Sum, C.Y. Studies on the inhibition of oxotremorine induced tremor by a melanocyte-stimulating hormone release-inhibiting factor, thyrotropin releasing hormone and related peptides. *FEBS Letters*, 1974, *44*, 101.

Catlin, D.H., George, R., & Li, C.H. β-endorphin: Pharmacologic and behavioral activity in cats after low intravenous doses. *Life Sciences*, 1978, *25*, 2147.

Chase, T.N., Woods, A.C., Lipton, M.A., & Morris, C.E. Hypothalamic releasing factors and Parkinson's disease. *Archives of Neurology*, 1974, *31*, 55.

Crowley, T.J., & Hydinger, M. MIF, TRH and simian social and motor behavior. *Pharmacology, Biochemistry and Behavior*, 1976, *5* (Suppl. 1), 79.

Denman, P.M., Miller, L.H., Sandman, C.A., Schally, A.V., & Kastin, A.J. Electrophysiological correlates of melanocyte-stimulating hormone activity in the frog. *Journal of Comparative Physiological Psychology*, 1972, *80*, 59.

DeWied, D., & Bohus, B. Long-term and short-term effects on retention of a conditioned avoidance response in rats by treatment with a long acting pitressin and α-MSH. *Nature*, 1966, *212*, 1484.

DeWied, D., Kovacs, G.L., Bohus, B., Van Ree, J.M., & Grevan, H.M. Neuroleptic activity of the neuropeptide β-LPH (Des-Tyr¹) γ-endorphin (DT-γ-E). *European Journal of Pharmacology*, 1978, *49*, 427.

Ehrensing, R.H., & Kastin, A.J. Melanocyte-stimulating hormone-release inhibiting hormone as an antidepressant: A pilot study. *Archives of General Psychiatry*, 1974, *30*, 63.

Ehrensing, R.H., & Kastin, A.J. TRH: Clinical investigations for nonendocrine actions in man. In: L. Martini & G.M. Bresser (eds.), *Clinical neuroendocrinology*. New York: Academic Press, 1977.

Ehrensing, R.H., & Kastin, A.J. Dose-related biphasic effect of Prolyl-Leucyl-Glycinamide (MIF-I) in depression. *American Journal of Psychiatry*, 1978, *135*, 562.

Fischer, P.A., Schneider, E., Jacobi, P., & Maxion, H. Effect of melanocyte-stimulating hormone-release inhibiting hormone (MIF) in Parkinson's syndrome. *European Neurology*, 1975, *12*, 360.

Furlong, F.W., Brown, G.M., & Beeching, M.F. Thyrotropin-releasing hormone: Differential antidepressant and endocrinological effects. *American Journal of Psychiatry*, 1976, *133*, 1187.

Gaillard, A.W.K., & Varey, C.A. Some effects of an ACTH 4–9 analogue (Org. 2766) on human performance. *Physiology and Behavior*, 1979, *23*, 79.

Gautry, J.P., Jolivet, A., Veilh, J.P., & Guillemin, R. Presence of immunoassayable β-endorphin in human amniotic fluid: Elevation in cases of fetal distress. *American Journal of Obstetrics and Gynecology*, 1977, *129*, 211.

Gerstenbrand, F., Binder, H., Kozma, C., Pusch, S., & Reisner, T. Infusion-therapie mit MIF (melanocyte-inhibiting factor) beim Parkinson syndrom. *Wein. Klin. Wochenschift*, 1975, *87*, 822.

Gerstenbrand, F., Poewe, W., Aichner, F., & Kozma, C. Clinical utilization of MIF-I. In: R. Collu, A. Barbeau, J.R. Ducharme, & J. G. Rochefort (eds.), *Central nervous system effects of hypothalamic hormone and other peptides*. New York: Raven Press, 1979.

Greven, H.M., & DeWied, D. The influence of peptides derived from corticotrophin (ACTH) on performance. Structure activity studies. In: E. Zimmerman, W.H. Gispen, B.E. Marks, & D. DeWied (eds.), *Drug effects on neuroendocrine regulation. (Progress in Brain Research*, 1973, *39*, 429.) Amsterdam: Elsevier Scientific Publishing Co.

Huidobro-Toro, J.P., Scotti de Carolis, A., & Longo, V.G. Action of two hypothalamic factors (TRH, MIF) and angiotensin II on the behavioral effects of L-dopa and 5-hydroxytryptophan in mice. *Pharmacology, Biochemistry and Behavior*, 1974, *2*, 105.

Kafi, S., Monnier, M., & Gallard, J.M. The delta-sleep inducing peptide (DSIP) increases duration of sleep in rats. *Neuroscience Letters*, 1979, *13*, 169.

Kastin, A.J., & Barbeau, A. Preliminary clinical studies with L-Prolyl-L-Leucyl-Glycine amide in Parkinson's disease. *Canadian Medical Association Journal*, 1972 *107*, 1079.

Kastin, A.J., Coy, D.H., Schally, A.V., & Zadina, J.E. Dissociaton of effects of LH-RH analogs on pituitary regulation and reproductive behavior. *Pharmacology, Biochemistry, and Behavior*, 1980, *13*, 913.

Kastin, A.J., Ehrensing, R.H., Coy, D.H., Schally, A.V., & Kostrzewa, R.M. Behavioral effects of brain peptides, including LH-RH. In: L. Zichella & P. Pancheri (eds.), *Psychoneuroendocrinology in reproduction*. Amsterdam: Elsevier Scientific Publishing Co., 1979.

Kastin, A.J., Kullander, S., Borglin, N.E., Dyster-Aas, K., Dahlberg, B., Ingvar, D., Krakau, C.E.T., Miller, M.C., Bowers, C.Y., &

Schally, A.V. Extrapigmentary effects of MSH in amenorrheic women. *Lancet*, 1968, *1*, 1007.

Kastin, A.J., Miller, L.H., Gonzalez-Barcena, D., Hawley, W.D., Dyster-Aas, K., Schally, A.V., Velasco-Parra, M.L., & Velasco, M. Psycho-physiologic correlates of MSH activity in man. *Physiology and Behavior*, 1971, *7*, 893.

Kastin, A.J., Nissen, C., Nikolics, K., Medzihradszky, K., Coy, D.H., Teplan, I., & Schally, A.V. Distribution of ³H-α-MSH in rat brain. *Brain Research Bulletin*, 1976, *1*, 19.

Kastin, A.J., Nissen, C., Schally, A.V., & Coy, D.H. Additional evidence that small amounts of a peptide can cross the blood-brain barrier. *Pharmacology, Biochemistry and Behavior*, 1979, *11*, 717.

Kastin, A.J., Olson, R.D., Schally, A.V., & Coy, D.H. CNS effects of peripherally administered brain peptides. *Life Sciences*, 1979, *25*, 401.

Kastin, A.J., Sandman, C.A., Miller, L.H., & Schally, A.V. Some questions related to MSH. *Mayo Clinic Proceedings*, 1976, *51*, 632.

Kastin, A.J., Sandman, C.A., Stratton, L.O., Schally, A.V., & Miller, L.H. Behavioral and electrographic changes in rat and man after MSH. In: W.H. Gispen, Tj. B. Van Wimersma Griedanus, B. Bohus, & D. DeWied (eds.), *Hormones, homeostatis and the brain*. Amsterdam: Elsevier Scientific Publishing Co., 1975.

Kastin, A.J., Schally, A.V., & Kostrzewa, R.M. Possible aminergic mediation of MSH release and of the CNS effects of MSH and MIF-I. *Federation Proceedings*, 1980, *39*, 2931.

Kastin, A.J., Scollan, E.L., Ehrensing, R.H., Schally, A.V., & Coy, D.H. Enkephalin and other peptides reduce passiveness. *Pharmacology, Biochemistry and Behavior*, 1978, *9*, 515.

Kastin, A.J., Scollan, E.L., King, M.G., Schally, A.V., & Coy, D.H. Enkephalin and a potent analog facilitate maze performance after intraperitoneal administration in rats. *Pharmacology, Biochemistry and Behavior*, 1976, *5*, 691.

King, B.M., Castellanos, F.X., Kastin, A.J., Berzas, M.C., Mauk, M.D., Olson, G.A., & Olson, R.D. Naloxone-induced supression of food intake in normal and hypothalamic obese rats. *Brain Research Bulletin*, 1979, *11*, 729.

Kline, N.S., Li, C.H. Lehmann, H.E., Lajtha, A., Laskie, E., & Cooper, T. β-endorphin induced changes in schizophrenic and depressed patients. *Archives of General Psychiatry*, 1977, *34*, 1111.

LeMoal, M., Koob, G.F., & Bloom, F.E. Endorphins and extinction: Differential actions on appetitive and adverse tasks. *Life Sciences*, 1979, *24*, 1631.

McGivern, R.F., Sandman, C.A., Kastin, A.J., &

Coy, D.H. Behavioral effects of prenatal administration of β-endorphin. Abstract, Tenth International Congress of the International Society of Psychoneuroendocrinology, Park City, Utah, 1979, p.41.

Mackintosh, N.J. Selective attention in animal discrimination learning. *Psychological Bulletin*, 1965, *64*, 124.

Mackintosh, N.J. Further analysis of the overtraining reversal effect. *Journal of Comparative Physiological Psychology Monograph*, 1969, *17*(No. 2, Pt. 2).

Mello, N.K., & Mendelson, J.H. Self-administration of an enkephalin analog by rhesus monkey. *Pharmacology, Biochemistry and Behavior*, 1978, *9*, 579.

Miller, L.H., Fischer, S.C., Groves, G.A., Rudrauff, M.E., & Kastin, A.J. MSH/ACTH 4–10 influences on the CAR in human subjects: A negative finding. *Pharmacology, Biochemistry and Behavior*, 1977, *7*, 417.

Miller, L.H., Groves, G.A., Bopp, M.J., & Kastin, A.J. A neuroheptapeptide influence on cognitive functioning in the elderly. *Peptides*, 1979, *1*, 55.

Miller, L.H., Harris, L., Kastin, A.J., & Van Riezen, H. A neuroheptapeptide influence in attention in man. *Pharmacology, Biochemistry and Behavior*, 1976, *5*, 17.

Miller, L.H., Kastin, A.J., Sandman, C.A., Fink, M., & Van Veen, W.J. Polypeptide influence on attention, memory, and anxiety in man. *Pharmacology, Biochemistry and Behavior*, 1974, *2*, 663.

Monnier, M., Dudler, L., Gachter, R., & Schoenenberger, G.A. Delta sleep-inducing peptide (DSIP): EEG and motor activity in rabbits following intravenous administration. *Neuroscience Letters*, 1977, *6*, 9.

Nedopil, N., & Ruther, E. Effects of the synthetic analogue of methionine enkephalin FK 33,824 on psychotic symptoms. *Pharmakopsychiatrie*, 1979, *12*, 277.

O'Donohue, T.L., & Jacobowitz, D.M. Studies on α-melanotropin in the central nervous system. In: R.F. Beers, Jr. & E.G. Basset (eds.), *Polypeptide hormones*. New York: Raven Press, 1980.

Olson, G.A., Olson, R.D., Kastin, A.J., Castellanos, F.X., Kneale, M.T., Coy, D.H., & Wolf, R.H. Behavioral effects of D-Ala²-β-endorphin in squirrel monkeys. *Pharmacology, Biochemistry and Behavior*, 1978, *9*, 687.

Olson, G.A., Olson, R.D., Kastin, A.J., Green, M.T., Roig-Smith, R., Hill, C.W., & Coy, D.H. Effects of an enkephalin analog on complex learning in the rhesus monkey. *Pharmacology, Biochemistry and Behavior*, 1979, *11*, 341.

Olson, R.D., Kastin, A.J., LaHoste, G.J., Olson, G.A., & Coy, D.H. Possible non-narcotic component to action of opiate peptides on tonic immobility. *Pharmacology, Biochemistry and Behavior*, 1979, *11*, 705.

Olson, R.D., Kastin, A.J., Michel, G.F., Olson, G.A., Coy, D.H., & Montalbano, D.M. Effects of endorphin and enkephalin analogs on fear habituation in goldfish. *Pharmacology, Biochemistry and Behavior*, 1978, *9*, 111.

Olson, R.D., Kastin, A.J., Montalbano-Smith, D., Olson, G.A., Coy, D.H., & Michel, G.F. Neuropeptides and the blood-brain barrier in goldfish. *Pharmacology, Biochemistry and Behavior*, 1978, *9*, 521.

Panksepp, J., Vilberg, T., Bean, N.J., Coy, D.H., & Kastin, A.J. Reduction of distress vocalization in chicks by opiate-like peptides. *Brain Research Bulletin*, 1978, *3*, 663.

Parker, C.R., & Porter, J.C. Subcellular localization of immunoreactive α-melanocyte stimulating hormone in human brain. *Brain Research Bulletin*, 1979, *4*, 535.

Plotnikoff, N.P., Kastin, A.J. Oxotremorine antagonisms by Prolyl-Leucyl-Glycine amide administered by different routes and with several anticholinergics. *Pharmacology, Biochemistry and Behavior*, 1974a, *2*, 417.

Plotnikoff, N.P., & Kastin, A.J. Pharmacological studies with a tripeptide, Prolyl-Leucyl-Glycinamide. *Archives Internationales de Pharmacodynamie et de Therapie*, 1974b, *211*, 211.

Plotnikoff, N.P., Kastin, A.J., Anderson, M.S., & Schally, A.V. DOPA potentiation by a hypothalamic factor, MSH release-inhibiting hormone (MIF). *Life Sciences*, 1971, *10*, 1279.

Plotnikoff, N.P., Kastin, A.J., Anderson, M.S., & Schally, A.V. Oxotremorine antagonism by a hypothalamic hormone, melanocyte-stimulating hormone release-inhibiting factor, MIF, *Proceedings of the Society for Experimental Biology and Medicine*, 1972, *140*, 811.

Plotnikoff, N.P., Kastin, A.J., Anderson, M.S., & Schally, A.V. Deserpidine antagonism by a tripeptide, L-Prolyl-L-Leucylglycinamide. *Neuroendocrinology*, 1973, *11*, 67.

Plotnikoff, N.P., Minard, F.N., & Kastin, A.J. DOPA potentiation in ablated animals and brain levels of biogenic amines in intact animals after Prolyl-Leucylglycinamide. *Neuroendocrinology*, 1974, *14*, 271.

Polc, P., Schneeberger, J., & Haefely, W. Effect of the delta sleep-inducing peptide (DSIP) on the sleep-wakefulness cycle of cats. *Neuroscience Letters*, 1978, *9*, 33.

Porsolt, R.D., Lepichon, M., & Jalfre, M. Depression: A new animal model sensitive to anti-depressant treatments. *Nature*, 1977, *266*, 730.

Redding, T.W., Kastin, A.J., Gonzalez-Barcena,

D., Coy, D.H., Hirotsu, Y., Ruelas, J., & Schally, A.V. The disappearance, excretion, and metabolism of tritiated Prolyl-Leucyl-Glycinamide in man. *Neuroendocrinology*, 1974, *16*, 119.

Redding, T.W., Kastin, A.J., Nair, R.M.G., & Schally, A.V. The distribution, half-life, and excretion of ^{14}C and [^{3}H]-labeled L-Prolyl-L-Leucyl-Glycinamide in the rat. *Neuroendocrinology*, 1973, *11*, 92.

Redding, T.W., Kastin, A.J., Nikolics, K., Schally, A.V., & Coy, D.H. The disappearance and excretion of labeled α-MSH in man. *Pharmacology, Biochemistry and Behavior*, 1978, *9*, 207.

Rigter, H., Greven, H., & Van Riezen, H. Failure of naloxone to prevent reduction of amnesia by enkephalins. *Neuropharmacology*, 1977, *16*, 545.

Sandman, C.A., Alexander, W.D., & Kastin, A.J. Neuroendocrine influences on visual discrimination and reversal learning in the albino and hooded rat. *Physiology and Behavior*, 1973, *11*, 613.

Sandman, C.A., Beckwith, B.E., Gittis, M.M., & Kastin, A.J. Melanocyte-stimulating hormone (MSH) and overtraining effects on extra-dimensional shift (EDS) learning. *Physiology and Behavior*, 1974, *13*, 163.

Sandman, C.A., Beckwith, B.E., & Kastin, A.J. Are learning and attention related to the sequence of amino acids in ACTH/MSH peptides? *Peptides*, 1980, *1*, 277.

Sandman, C.A., Denman, P.M., Miller, L.H., Knott, J.R., Schally, A.V., & Kastin, A.J. Electroencephalographic measures of melanocyte-stimulating hormone activity. *Journal of Comparative Physiological Psychology*, 1971, *76*, 103.

Sandman, C.A., George, J., McCanne, T.R., Nolan, J.D., Kaswan, J., & Kastin, A.J. MSH/ACTH 4–10 influences behavioral and physiological measures of attention. *Journal of Clinical Endocrinology and Metabolism*, 1977, *44*, 884.

Sandman, C.A., George, J.M., Nolan, J.D., Van Riezen, H., & Kastin, A.J. Enhancement of attention in man with ACTH/MSH 4–10. *Physiology and Behavior*, 1975, *15*, 427.

Sandman, C.A., George, J.M., Walker, B., Nolan, J.D., & Kastin, A.J. The heptapeptide MSH/ACTH 4–10 enhances attention in the mentally retarded. *Pharmacology, Biochemistry and Behavior*, 1976, *5*(Suppl. 1), 23.

Sandman, C.A., McGivern, R.F., Berka, C., Walker, M., Coy, D.H., & Kastin, A.J. Neonatal administration of β-endorphin produces "chronic" insensitivity to thermal stimuli. *Life Sciences*, 1979, *25*, 1755.

Sandman, C.A., Miller, L.H., Kastin, A.J., &

Schally, A.V. A neuroendocrine influence on attention and memory. *Journal of Comparative Physiological Psychology*, 1972, *80*, 54.

Sandman, C.A., Walker, B.B., & Lawton, C.A. An analog of MSH/ACTH 4–9 enhances interpersonal and environmental awareness in mentally retarded adults. *Peptides*, 1980, *1*, 109.

Schneider, V.E., Fischer, P.A., Jacobi, P., & Reh, W. Der eniflub von MIF (melanozyteninhibierender faktor auf psychomotorik und stimmungsverhalten von Parkinsonkranken. *Arzeimittel Forschung Research*, 1978, *28*, 1296.

Schoenenberger, G.A., & Monnier, M. Characterization of a delta-electro-encephalogram (-sleep)-inducing peptide. *Proceedings of the National Academy of Sciences (U.S.A.)*, 1977, *74*, 1282.

Stratton, L.O., Gibson, C.A., Kolar, K.G., & Kastin, A.J. Neonatal treatment with TRH affects development, learning, and emotionality in the rat. *Pharmacology, Biochemistry and Behavior* 1976, *5*(Suppl. 1), 65.

Stratton, L.O., & Kastin, A.J. Increased acquisition of a complex appetitive task after MSH and MIF. *Pharmacology, Biochemistry and Behavior*, 1975, *3*, 901.

Tighe, T.J., Glick, J., & Cole, M. Subproblem analysis of discrimination-shift learning. *Psychomic Science*, 1971, *24*, 159.

Ungar, G. Molecular coding of memory. *Life Sciences*, 1974, *14*, 595f.

Urban, T., Lopes da Silva, F.H., Storm van Leeuwen, W., & DeWied, D. A frequency shift in the hippocampal theta activity: An electrical correlate of central action of ACTH analogues in the dog? *Brain Research*, 1974, *69*, 361.

Van Ree, J.M., & DeWied, D. Prolyl-Leucyl-Glycinamide (PLG) facilities morphine dependence. *Life Sciences*, 1976, *19*, 1331.

Veith, J.L., Sandman, C.A., Walker, J.M., Coy, D.H., & Kastin, A.J. Systemic administration of endorphins selectively alters open field behavior of rats. *Physiology and Behavior*, 1978, *20*, 539.

Verhoeven, W.M.A., Van Praag, H.M., Van Ree, J.M., & DeWied, D. Improvement of schizophrenic patients treated with Des-Tyr^1-γ-endorphin (DT-γ-E). *Archives of General Psychiatry*, 1979, *36*, 294.

Voith, K. Synthetic MIF analogues. II. DOPA potentiation and fluphenazine antagonism. *Arzeimittel Forschung Research*, 1977, *27*, 12, 2290.

Walker, B.B., Sandman, C.A. Influences of an analog of the neuropeptide ACTH 4–9 on mentally retarded adults. *American Journal of Mental Deficiency*, 1979, *83*, 346.

Walter, R., Griffiths, E.C., & Hooper, K.C. Production of MSH-release-inhibiting hormone by a particulate preparation of hypothalami: Mechanisms of oxytocin inactivation. *Brain Research*, 1973, *60*, 449.

Walter, R., Neidle, A., & Marks, F.N. Significant differences in the degradation of Pro-Leu-Gly-NH₂ by human serum and that of other species. *Proceedings of the Society for Experimental Biology and Medicine*, 1975, *148*, 98.

Walter, R., Ritzmann, R.F., Bhargava, H.N., & Flexner, L.B. Prolyl-Leucyl-Glycinamide, cyclo (leucylglycine), and derivatives block development of physical dependence on morphine in mice. *Proceedings of the National Academy of Sciences*, 1979, *76*, 518.

Ward, M.M., Sandman, C.A., George, J.M., & Shulman, H. MSH/ACTH 4–10 in men and women: Effects upon performance of an attention and memory task. *Physiology and Behavior*, 1978, *22*, 669.

Weinberger, S.B., Arnsten, A., & Segal, D.S. Des-tyrosine¹-γ-endorphin and haloperidol: Behavioral and biochemical differentiation. *Life Sciences*, 1979, *24*, 1637.

Zeaman, D., & House, B.J. The role of attention in retardate discrimination learning. In: N.R. Ellis (ed.), *Handbook of mental deficiency*. New York: McGraw-Hill Book Co., 1963.

Curative Aspects of Mental Retardation:
Biomedical and Behavioral Advances
edited by Frank J. Menolascino, M.D., Ronald Neman, Ph.D., and Jack A. Stark, Ph.D.
Copyright 1983   Paul H. Brookes Publishing Co., Inc.   Baltimore · London

chapter 13

Central Cholinergic and Adrenergic Transmission and Memory

KENNETH L. DAVIS, M.D.
Bronx Veterans Administration Medical Center
Bronx, New York
Mt. Sinai School of Medicine of the City University of New York
New York, New York

THIS CHAPTER REVIEWS DATA that now suggest a possible treatment for some patients with Alzheimer's disease. In so doing, it is hoped that the research strategy that has evolved for the study of Alzheimer's disease may serve as a model for the investigation of those subtypes of mental retardation that have not been associated with histopathological abnormalities, but may be the result of an abnormality in a putative neurotransmitter.

CENTRAL CHOLINERGIC TRANSMISSION AND MEMORY

Numerous studies have indicated that aging is associated with decreasing activity of central cholinergic mechanisms and that this loss is magnified in patients with senile dementia. Specifically, alterations in central cholinergic enzyme activity have been demonstrated to occur in human beings with increasing age. The enzymes that synthesize and degrade acetylcholine, namely choline acetyltransferase (CAT) and acetylcholinesterase (AChE), are found in reduced concentrations

in brains of patients with senile dementia as compared to normal brains (Davies & Maloney, 1966; Perry, Perry, Blessed, & Tomlinson, 1977; Perry, Perry, Blessed, & Tomlinson, 1978; White, Hiley, Goodhart, Carrasco, Keet, Williams, & Bowen, 1977). In a study of 28 patients dying of nonneurological causes, measurement of CAT and AChE activities in 56 different brain areas was performed (McGeer & McGeer, 1976). In these normal subjects CAT activity measured in cortical areas was found to be decreased from 40% to 60% as age increased from 20 to 50 years (McGeer & McGeer, 1976). The septal areas and amygdala showed the greatest reduction in CAT activity, while the extrapyramidal system was least affected. AChE activity showed a similar though less consistent change over all subjects with increasing age. The activity of AChE was most diminished in cortical regions. CAT activity has also been determined in normal subjects dying with nonneurological diseases between the ages of 63 and 98. No further decreases in CAT activity were found in this age group (Bowen, Smith, White, & Davison, 1976).

165

A more extensive and severe loss of CAT activity occurs in patients with Alzheimer's disease. CAT activity was measured in postmortem sections of parietal gray matter and caudate nucleus from patients with a diagnosis of Alzheimer's type senile dementia. The diagnosis of Alzheimer's disease was confirmed by histopathological analysis. It was found that CAT activity in cortical sections was significantly lower for patients with Alzheimer's disease than in age-matched normal subjects (Perry et al., 1977). Postmortem analysis of three more series of patients with Alzheimer's disease reported similar findings (Davies & Maloney, 1966; Kuhar, 1976; White et al., 1977). These studies found that CAT activity was markedly reduced in the amygdala, hippocampus, and cortex of Alzheimer's patients when compared to age-matched controls. The degree of decrease in CAT activity was greatest in brain areas with the most neurofibrillary tangles. Those brains of subjects with prominent cerebrovascular disease did not demonstrate a significant reduction in CAT activity. In mixed cases of cerebrovascular disease and neuronal degeneration with senile plaques and neurofibrillary tangles there was considerable variability in CAT activity, implying a heterogeneous pathogenesis (White, et al., 1977). A more recent study has shown that CAT and AChE activities decrease significantly as the number of senile plaques increases (Perrry, Tomlinson, Blessed, Berg mann, Gibson, & Perry, 1978). The degree of reduction in CAT activity correlated with the extent of intellectual impairment as measured by a memory information test (Perry, Tomlinson, Blessed, Bergmann, Gibson, & Perry, 1978).

The hypothesis that changes in cholinergic enzyme activity reflect a specific degenerative process is attested to by the finding that glutamic acid decarboxylase was unchanged in the brain areas having the greatest reduction in CAT activity. In addition, preliminary analyses of tyrosine hydroxylase, monoamine oxidase, aromatic acid decarboxylase, and dopamine hydroxylase indi-

cated that the activities of these enzymes were also unchanged (Davies & Maloney, 1966).

Thus, the studies reviewed above suggest an age-related decrease in AChE and CAT, and a further decrement in CAT in brains of patients with senile dementia that is characterized by neuronal degeneration, senile plaques, and neurofibrillary tangles.

In a study of normal elderly subjects between the ages of 65 and 95, muscarinic receptor binding was found to decrease with age (White et al., 1977). However, no evidence for age-related changes in muscarinic binding was found among a group of normal subjects between the ages of 46 to 79 (Davies, 1978). Data from patients with nonvascular senile dementia are also contradictory. Patients with Alzheimer's disease were found to have significantly less muscarinic receptor binding than controls with no evidence of histopathological changes of Alzheimer's disease (Reisine, Yamamura, Bird, Spokes, & Enna, 1978). Two other investigations found no decrease in muscarinic receptor binding (Perry et al., 1977; White et al., 1977). Therefore, it may be only until very late in the disease process that a large loss of muscarinic receptors is apparent.

CAT is believed to be a good marker for cholinergic neurons in some cortical areas. Futhermore, decreased CAT activity is compatible with the findings that nerve terminal abnormalities are associated with senile plaque formation (Gonatas, Anderson, & Evangelista, 1967; Perry, Tomlinson, Blessed, Bergmann, Gibson, & Perry, 1978). Complementing these data are the observations on the effects of bilateral lesions of the hippocampus, a brain region rich in cholinergic neurons. Patients with these lesions were described as unable to learn new information (Scoville & Milner, 1957; Victor, Angevine, Mancall, & Fisher, 1961). Elderly subjects and patients with Alzheimer's disease also have difficulty learning or storing new information into long-term memory (LTM) (Brunig, Holzbauer, & Kimberlin, 1975; Clark & Knowles, 1973).

Animal studies partially confirm these results. Age-related changes in the synthesis and metabolism of acetylcholine due to a reduction in CAT and AChE activities have been reported in rats (Hollander & Barrows, 1968; Kaur & Kanungo, 1970). Chickens also show a loss in cortical CAT activity and an increase in AChE activity with increasing age (Vernadakis, 1973). Another study found decreased CAT activity in the caudate nucleus of rat brain; however, there were no concomitant decreases in the levels of acetylcholine or choline (Meek, Bertilsson, Cheney, Zsilla, & Costa, 1977). This decrement in cholinergic activity appears to be specific. That is, as in humans, no general tendency of all brain enzymes to decrease in activity with increasing age has been found. On the contrary, for example, an increase in brain monoamine oxidase activity with age has been demonstrated in rats (Kark, Kuntzman, & Brodie, 1960).

More definite proof of diminished central cholinergic activity in demented and nondemented elderly people would be a demonstration of reduced levels of acetylcholine and a decreased activity of the rate-limiting step in acetylcholine synthesis, which is probably the high affinity uptake system for choline (Yamamura & Snyder, 1973). Techniques for assaying acetylcholine and choline concentrations in cerebrospinal fluid have only recently been established (Hanin, 1974; Jenden, 1977) and warrant further applications in the attempt to examine the neurochemistry of aging and memory loss.

Numerous clinical studies point toward acetylcholine (ACh) as being a neurotransmitter affecting cognition and involved in senile dementia. Pharmacological agents known to affect central cholinergic mechanisms have been shown to affect memory and cognition in man. Several investigators have studied the effects of the anticholinergic agent scopolamine. Normal subjects given 10 μg/kg of scopolamine intravenously became deficient in their ability to store new information. The retrieval of information stored in LTM before the administration of scopolamine was not affected (Safer & Allen,

1971). Interestingly, scopolamine can produce memory deficits in normal young subjects that do not significantly differ from the memory deficits occurring in a group of elderly subjects between the ages of 65 and 85. Specifically, young normal subjects given 1 mg of scopolamine subcutaneously, and drugfree elderly subjects, showed strikingly similar impairment in performance on tests that measured storage of information in LTM (Drachman & Leavitt, 1974). Both groups showed a mild degree of impairment in the retrieval of information from LTM. Subjects showed a tendency to shift categories during the test such that they often retrieved items or words from a different category to that of the test situation. It is interesting to note that patients with Alzheimer's disease frequently have difficulty recalling lists of names that are representative of a particular class of objects (Pearce & Miller, 1973). The "false positive retrievals" that occur after administration of scopolamine in normal subjects may be analogous to the intrusion errors seen in Alzheimer's patients. Repeated studies have continued to demonstrate that scopolamine in a dose of approximately 1 mg selectively affects the storage of new information into LTM (Crow & Grove-White, 1971; Crow & Grove-White, 1973; Dundee & Pandit, 1972; Hrbek, Komenda, & Macakova, 1974; Hrbek, Komenda, & Siroka, 1971; Ostfeld & Araguete, 1962; Soukapova, Vojtechovsky, & Safratova, 1970). Atropine, another anticholinergic, has been shown to have similar cognitive effects to scopolamine (Ostfeld, Machne, & Unna, 1960).

These human studies with anticholinergic agents support the possibility that cognitive impairment and memory loss in the aged could be a reflection of reduced cholinergic activity. Such reports are consistent with the neurochemical findings of cholinergic neuronal degeneration in people with senile dementia. If, as has been suggested, postsynaptic cholinergic receptors are deficient in senile dementia, cholinergic agonists (cholinomimetics) might be anticipated to benefit demented patients with cholinergic neuron depletion only to the extent that an adequate number of postsynaptic cholinergic receptors remain intact.

Role of Physostigmine

Physostigmine is a cholinomimetic drug that selectively inhibits the activity of AChE in the brain. By blocking such enzymatic activity, the physostigmine enhances the transmission of ACh to postsynaptic cholinergic neurons. The effects of this drug were studied in young normal subjects. Two to three milligrams given intravenously produced a decrement in all aspects of memory (Davis, Hollister, Overall, Johnson, & Train, 1976). In contrast, doses of 1–2 mg produced a slight improvement in memory storage. The effect at 1 mg was greater than for 2 mg (Drachman, 1977). A lower dose of physostigmine, 0.5 mg infused at a constant rate over a 30-minute period, significantly improved long-term memory in normal subjects (Davis, Mohs, Tinklenberg, Pfefferbaum, Hollister, & Koppel, 1978). Improvement was seen in the process of consolidation, which is the process of conversion of registered short-term information into a long-term memory trace.

In another study of long-term memory processes in normal subjects, a dose of 1.0 mg of physostigmine was administered intravenously over a 30-minute period (Davis et al., 1978). Testing of word recall was done twice during the infusion when the actual dose of physostigmine was either 0.3 mg or 1.0 mg. Subjects recalled more items after receiving 0.3 mg and 1.0 mg of physostigmine than placebo; however, the difference was only significant for the 1.0 mg dose (Davis et al., 1978). A second long-term memory task was used to test the effect of physostigmine on storage (Buschke, 1973; Buschke & Fuld, 1974).

The task was performed by subjects after they received 0.5 mg of physostigmine or placebo. Subjects recalled significantly more words on the physostigmine day than on the placebo day (Davis et al., 1978). Thus, a relatively low dose of physostigmine sig-

nificantly improved the ability of normal subjects to both store and retrieve information from LTM. When these results are compared with the effects of 2.0 mg of intravenous physostigmine, they suggest a curvilinear relationship between the dose of cholinomimetic and its effect on LTM.

Corroboration of the action of low-dose physostigmine as a cholinomimetic to improve LTM has been reported. A double-bind, placebo-controlled crossover study was conducted with normal subjects aged 21–30. Subjects received 4.0 mg of the muscarinic agonist arecoline in two subcutaneous injections of 2.0 mg or a placebo. Following 4 mg of arecoline, subjects learned a list of 10 familiar objects in significantly fewer trials than they did following placebo (Sitaram, Weingartner, & Gillin, 1978). Higher doses of arecoline have been found to impair aspects of human memory (Franks, Trouton, & Lavery, 1958; Sitaram et al., 1978). Thus, the curvilinear relationship between dose of physostigmine and its effect on LTM apparently exists for another cholinomimetic with a different mode of action.

Physostigmine has also been shown to alleviate memory deficits produced by the anticholinergic scopolamine (Mewaldt & Ghoneim, 1979) and centrally acting anticholinergic drugs used in Parkinson's disease (Granacher & Baldessarini, 1975). These studies suggest that a small increment in central cholinergic activity can significantly facilitate long-term memory functioning.

A case report lends credibility to these studies (Peters & Levin, 1977). A 20-year-old woman, with a profound memory deficit that was secondary to an attack of herpes simplex encephalitis she had sustained 2 years earlier, was administered varying doses of physostigmine and placebo in a double-blind manner. On three separate trials following a dose of 0.8 mg of physostigmine given subcutaneously, there was a significant improvement in the ability to store new information in LTM from short-term memory (STM). Retrieval from LTM was also improved (Peters & Levin, 1977). Both lower and higher doses of physostigmine did not produce this effect.

A natural extension of these studies would be to investigate the effects of cholinomimetic agents in demented and nondemented elderly people.

Since physostigmine improves memory in a narrow dose range, and the dose that improves memory may vary across subjects, in order to study this drug's effect in elderly patients, a design that calls for the comparison of several doses of physostigmine on memory within the same subject seems optimal. Using such a paradigm, we have studied 9 elderly patients: three nondemented elderly women, two men and one woman with Alzheimer's disease, two men with probable Alzheimer's disease, and one man with Huntington's disease. Initially each patient received saline and 0.125 mg, 0.25 mg, and 0.5 mg of physostigmine over a 30-minute period on 4 separate days. The order of infusions was randomized and the study was double-blind. For nondemented patients a verbal learning task was used (Buschke, 1973), but for demented patients a simpler picture recognition task (Shepard, 1967) was used. After the fourth infusion, the dose at which the subject responded best was determined by an investigator blind to the drug condition. On 2 subsequent days the dose that produced the best learning performance and the saline infusion were repeated. When the initial four infusions were given, no patient performed best during the saline infusion. When the optimal dose of physostigmine and the saline dose were replicated, all nine patients again performed significantly better during the physostigmine infusion than during the saline infusion.

In a study of five patients with Alzheimer's disease, physostigmine in doses of 0.4 mg to 0.8 mg administered subcutaneously failed to produce memory facilitation (Peters & Levin, 1979). However, when combined with lecithin, a compound that produces an increase in brain levels of ACh in rats (Hirsch & Wurtman, 1978), physostigmine enhanced memory storage and retrieval (Peters & Levin, 1979) suggesting that a combination of cholinergic agonist and precursor may be a promising strategy for memory improvement. Another case report of a 42-year-old man with familial Alzheimer's disease showed that 1 mg of physostigmine, administered subcutaneously, was able to reduce the number of intrusion errors (Smith & Swash, 1979). Alzheimer's patients have consistently demonstrated a higher proportion of intrusion errors on memory tests than do age-matched controls (Miller, 1978).

Effects of Choline

There are a number of uncontrolled studies of the clinical effects of choline in patients with Alzheimer's disease. In one study, patients were treated for 2 weeks with 5 grams of choline per day, and then for 2 more weeks with 10 g of choline per day. Psychometric testing revealed no significant improvement. The staff, however, reported that patients were more manageable while they received choline (Boyd, Graham-White, Blackwood, Glen, & McQueen, 1976). In 2 of the 7 patients, psychometric testing demonstrated some improvement, which appeared to occur within 24 hours of receiving 5 g of choline. Another uncontrolled study found that a positive effect of 8 g of choline was confined to those patients with the shortest history of dementia (approximately 2 years) (Spillane, Goodhart, White, Bowen, & Davidson, 1977).

Recently, two studies of the effects of choline on memory in normal subjects were completed. In one investigation, subjects received either a single oral dose of 10 g of choline or placebo. In this double-blind randomized study, choline significantly reduced the number of trials required to learn a list of words. Furthermore, on a selective reminding task, subjects were able to store and retrieve more of the difficult words after the ingestion of choline (Sitaram, Weingartner, Caine, & Gillin, 1978). In the other study of the effects of choline on memory, normal subjects received 16 g of choline in four divided doses. In this double-blind study, subjects' ability to store information in LTM while taking choline was not significantly enhanced over when they received placebo (Davis, Mohs, Tinklenberg, Hollister, Pfefferbaum, & Koppel, 1980). However, as has been shown with other cholinomimetics previously described, the dose of drug is crucial. Therefore, individual dose response curves are needed to help establish whether choline can improve memory within individuals before generalization from single dose studies are made.

There is a massive amount of literature on the effects of cholinergic manipulation on memory in animals. Changes in brain ACh levels in subhuman species can influence memory processes. Several factors confound the interpretation of these data. For example, tasks designed to measure memory changes are not standardized and the cholinergic system affects so many aspects of behavior in addition to memory that learning studies can be readily contaminated. Cholinergic agents affect appetitive behavior and nociception, and thus interfere with reward or punishment motivation (Karczmar, 1976). In a similar fashion, interference with the motor system in animals can influence results on learning tasks without affecting the memory process. Finally, most studies investigating anticholinergic agents utilize scopolamine. This drug differs from other anticholinergics in that it produces a significant sedation, which may interfere with the memory process.

Despite these complications, some generalizations that are relevant to the cholinergic underactivity hypothesis of memory impairment can be made. Small doses of anticholinesterases appear to facilitate maze learning, while larger doses decrease the speed with which animals learn to traverse mazes. Systemically administered anticholinergic agents also interfere with maze learning (Kintgen & Apprison, 1976). These results are remarkably consistent with the human studies described previously. However, few conclusions can be reached from the animal studies employing operant behavior paradigms or avoidance tasks, except that agents affecting the cholinergic system can significantly influence the outcome of these investigations.

Various doses of physostigmine and scopolamine have been administered to normal adult rhesus monkeys. Scopolamine produced a specific inability of the monkeys to learn new information. This deficit could be reversed by physostigmine. A dose of 0.1 mg/kg of physostigmine improved the ability of half the monkeys to learn a new task. However, when a larger dose of 0.4 mg/kg (Bartus, 1979) was administered, the monkey's performance was worse than baseline drug-free conditions. These results are strikingly similar to the results of the studies reviewed in humans.

Neurochemical studies, pharmacological studies with anticholinergic drugs, preliminary work in humans with physostigmine and choline, and maze studies in animals all implicate central cholinergic activity in memory. The effect seems to be especially localized to the storage, or acquisition, of new information into LTM. These investigations, however, are not specific to patients suffering with senile dementia. Rather, they point out that diminished cholinergic activity occurs in the normal aging process; and that this reduction is magnified in nonvascular forms of senile dementia. The therapeutic implications of these findings are that administration of cholinomimetics in elderly patients with memory impairment should be tested. Several methodological issues need to be addressed in designing studies to explore cholinergic treatment for memory loss. First, there appears to be a curvilinear relationship between cholinomimetics and the effects on LTM. The "therapeutic window" for the cholinomimetics to improve memory is quite small. Second, because elderly people of different ages and patients with Alzheimer's disease can have very different basal levels of central cholinergic activity, the therapeutic dose could range widely from patient to patient. Thus, many patients may be unresponsive to individual doses of cholinomimetic. Third, there is no method to conclusively diagnose Alzheimer's disease before autopsy; therefore not all people with "dementia" may have a cholinergic underactivity. The cognitive impairment that accompanies senile dementia must ultimately be reflected at the neurochemical level, where pharmacological maneuvers may improve functioning.

CENTRAL ADRENERGIC TRANSMISSION AND MEMORY

Recent neurochemical studies demonstrate that significant changes in central catecholaminergic activity occur in physiological aging. For example, investigations of the related enzyme systems have shown a decrease in the activity of tyrosine hydroxylase (TH), the rate-limiting enzyme involved in the synthesis of dopamine (DA) and norepinephrine (NE), with increasing age. In a study of caudate enzymes in eight human accident victims ranging in age from 5 to 57 years, a significant decline in TH activity was found as age increased (McGeer, McGeer, & Wada, 1971). This pronounced reduction in TH activity was greater and more clearly correlated with age than changes in cholinergic enzyme activity, suggesting that there was a specific change in the DA system in the caudate and not a general degeneration of cells. Similarly, the enzyme responsible for the conversion of L-dopa to dopamine, L-dopa decarboxylase, was found to be reduced in activity with increasing age (Bowen, White, Flack, Smith, & Davison, 1974; Lloyd, Farley, Deck, & Honykiewicz, 1974). In cortical as well as subcortical brain structures, patients with senile dementia showed a further reduction in the activity of L-dopa decarboxylase.

The appearance of extrapyramidal symptoms in patients with Alzheimer's disease (Pearce, 1974) and the gradual worsening of intellectual functioning in patients with Parkinson's disease (Celesia & Wanamaker, 1972) suggest an overlap of these diseases. Decreases in DA activity in the caudates of Parkinson's patients have been demonstrated (Hornykiewicz, 1964) indicating some similarity in striatal pathologies in patients with Parkinson's disease and senile dementia. Furthermore, reductions in the levels of homovanillic acid (HVA), the primary metabolite of DA, have been found in the cerebrospinal fluid of patients with Parkinson's disease and in dementia disorders of the Alzheimer type (Gottfries, Gottfries, & Roos, 1970; Gottfries & Roos, 1969). These data are consistent with postmortem examinations of patients with senile and presenile dementia that show that the levels of HVA in the neostriatum are significantly reduced (Adolfsson, Gottfries, Oreland, Roos, & Winblad, 1978; Gottfries et al., 1969). As HVA is the primary metabolite of DA, this finding may represent a general decrease of DA released in the neostriatum. However, it is also possible that increased levels of HVA could reflect increased breakdown of dopamine. In fact, studies of the enzyme monoamine oxidase (MAO), an enzyme that provides the principal route of inactivation of MAO in hindbrain in man with increasing age (Gottfries, Oreland, Winberg, & Winblad, 1975; Robinson, Davies, & Nies, 1972). The concentration of HVA found in the caudate nucleus and putamen of patients with senile dementia was found to correlate positively with the degree of mental deterioration; HVA levels correlated better with the degree of dementia than with age (Gottfries et al., 1969).

The increasing incidence of Alzheimer's disease and parkinsonism with age suggests that neurochemical changes in physiological aging may be involved in these observed increases. In fact, DA and NE levels in the brain have been found to decrease with increasing age (Carlsson & Winblad, 1976; Gottfries & Winblad, 1976; Robinson, Sourkes, Nies, Harris, Spector, Bartlett, & Kaye, 1977). These findings are in agreement with the reported decreases in enzyme activity and HVA concentration previously reviewed.

In a postmortem study of 19 patients with Alzheimer type dementias and 40 age-matched controls, levels of amines in the brain and MAO activity in platelets were determined (Adolfsson et al., 1978). A significant decline in DA and NE levels was found in physiological aging. In addition, platelet MAO activity in patients with Alzheimer's disease was significantly higher than in age-matched controls. Finally, compared with aged controls, patients with Alzheimer type dementia showed further reduction in levels of DA and NE in several parts of the brain, though these reductions were only statistically significant for DA in the thalamus and pons, and for NE putamen and cortex frontalis. Interestingly, the degree of intellectual impairment was negatively correlated to the concentrations of NE, i.e., the more demented the patient, the less NE was found in the brain. Berger, Escourolle, and Moyne (1976) have reported that in two cases of patients with Alzheimer's disease there was a complete absence of the noradrenergic-like fibers usually seen in the cortex.

In a recent report of 11 cases of Alzheimer's type dementia (Yates, Allison, Simpson, Maloney, & Gordon, 1979), concentrations of DA in the caudate nucleus and substantia nigra of these patients were not significantly different from aged controls, suggesting that there is no loss of dopamine neurons in those brain areas in Alzheimer's patients. In light of the findings (Adolfsson et al., 1978; Gottfries, et al., 1969) that reduced levels of HVA appear in the caudate nuclei from cases of senile dementia of the Alzheimer type, Yates et al. (1979) suggest that a reduction in DA released by nerve stimulation may underline this disorder, rather than a reduced capacity of the tissue to synthesize and/or store DA. Yates et al. (1979) further hypothesize that if a decrease in physiological activity in the nigro-striatal DA system exists in Alzheimer's dementia, then this phenomenon could be related to the observed loss of Ch activity, as evidenced by decreased levels of CAT in the caudate nucleus of Alzheimer's patients. Specifically, animal studies demonstrate that in the caudate nucleus Ch

dendrites may act presynaptically on DA-containing terminals, thus controlling release (Hattori, McGeer, & McGeer, 1979).

Numerous clinical studies have been undertaken to investigate the effects on cognitive functioning of drugs that are known to affect central adrenergic activity. Though these investigations report a wide variety of results, few studies have systematically directed attention to performance on memory tasks. Patients with Parkinson's disease have been observed to undergo varying degrees of intellectual degeneration, similar to the cognitive deficits reported in senile dementia (Riklan & Levita, 1969). L-Dopa, the immediate precursor of the catecholamines, including DA and NE, has been the most effective and commonly employed drug in the treatment of Parkinson's disease. Many investigators have examined the effects of L-dopa on concurrent dementia in parkinsonism. However, research on the cognitive effects of L-dopa in these patients has often been conducted as a secondary undertaking to therapeutic treatment.

In Parkinson's patients, intellectual functioning has been shown to improve with L-dopa administration (Beardsley & Puletti, 1971; Boshes & Arbit, 1970; Loranger, Goodell, Lee, & McDowell, 1972; March, Markham, & Asel, 1971; Meier & Martin, 1970), worsen (Lee, 1970; Sacks, Kohn, Messekoff, & Schwartz, 1972), or remain the same (O'Brien, Digiacomo, Fahn, & Schwartz, 1971; Parkes, Marsden, & Rees, 1974).

L-Dopa

Stemming from the results of studies on L-dopa and cognitive effects in Parkinson's patients, several investigators have sought to study L-dopa's effects on patients with senile dementia of the Alzheimer type. The results have not been encouraging. Van Woert, Yahr, Heninger, Rathey, and Bowers (1970) treated three Alzheimer's patients with L-dopa for 2 months. No significant changes or improvement based on clinical evaluation or psychiatric rating were found. In fact it was suggested that patients with senile dementia may have worsened on L-dopa. In a recent double-blind placebo-controlled study of the 18 patients with presenile dementia, 6 months' treatment with levodopa produced no significant effect in cognitive functioning (Kristensen, Olsen, & Thielgaard, 1977). Memory tasks employed in this study showed that on verbal tests the placebo group performed slightly better than the L-dopa group on retest. On visual tests the L-dopa group performed better. However, these differences were small and without statistical significance.

In a study of nine patients with senile dementia and extrapyramidal signs, L-dopa produced mixed results. In doses ranging from 1,000 to 3,750 mg/day, L-dopa treatment yielded pronounced intellectual and motor improvement in three patients, moderate improvement in two, and equivocal improvement in four (Drachman & Stahl, 1975). Increase in cognitive performance by L-dopa has been explained by some on the basis of increased arousal (Riklan, 1972).

Further investigation of a dopaminergic deficit in Alzheimer's disease has been explored. Since it is thought that mesocortical DA neurons may degenerate in Alzheimer's disease, an investigation of the effects of bromocriptine, a direct DA agonist, was undertaken to determine whether this drug would have an advantageous and selective effect on mesocortical and mesolimbic systems by stimulating dopaminergic responses (Phuapradit, Philips, Lees, & Sterm, 1978). In this single-blind study of nine patients with early presenile dementia, treatment was begun with 2.5 mg daily and increased by 2.5 mg increments every 4 days. After 8 weeks, bromocriptine failed to improve cognitive disabilities.

Thus, manipulation of the adrenergic system in patients with varying forms of dementia and cognitive disability provides varying results. Though intellectual functioning appears to be improved in a proportion of this population, these investigators have focused on nonspecific memory processes.

More specific aspects of memory functioning have been investigated in a population of depressed patients. Oral doses of 5–6 g/day of L-dopa were shown to improve learning and memory functioning in these patients. They performed better on verbal learning tasks designed to measure the process of information transfer from short-term to longer-term storage (Henry, Weingartner, & Murphy, 1973; Murphy, Henry, & Weingartner, 1972). This improvement in memory is most likely a reflection of a return toward premorbid cognitive function from the depressed state (Henry et al., 1973). On the other hand, intravenous L-dopa was not effective in improving verbal learning and memory tasks. In fact, patients demonstrated reduced learning during intravenous L-dopa as compared to placebo infusions (Henry, Buchsbau, & Murphy, 1976).

Amphetamine

Studies of central adrenergic manipulation with amphetamine and its analogues and the effects on memory processes have been conducted in normal human subjects. Amphetamine releases endogenous stores of CAs from presynaptic NE terminals and inhibits their reuptake (Glowinski, Axelrod, & Iversen, 1966). It also acts as a direct agonist on postsynaptic NE receptors (Smith, 1965). Amphetamine affects the DA system, too. Increased release and inhibition of uptake of DA in addition to inhibition of MAO in DA pathways are effects of amphetamine (Garattini, Jori, & Samanin, 1976).

When investigating the effects of amphetamine on memory processes, an important consideration must be noted. Amphetamine produces cortical arousal or activation. Increased arousal may be reflected in consolidation in memory tasks, and therefore better scores on delayed tests of recall (Hurst, Radlow, Chubb, & Bagley, 1969; Walker & Tarte, 1963). Weiss and Laties (1962) found under normal conditions that amphetamines did not enhance intellectual functions. However, in instances where performance is impaired by boredom or fatigue, amphetamine was able to improve intellectual performance. These findings suggest that amphetamine affects systems other than strictly memory, and these effects limit the interpretation one can make with regard to enhancement of memory.

In a study of the effects of methamphetamine on memory, 70 college-age subjects learned and recalled a series of word lists prior to injection of drug. Following injection, the subjects were tested for free recall and recognition of the words. In addition, they completed a short-term digit recall task. Methamphetamine had no effect on recall or retrieval of information learned prior to the injection. Methamphetamine did produce subjective arousal and a small improvement in the recall of words learned after the injection while the subject was still under the influence of the drug. The increase in the number of words recalled was accompanied by a six-fold increase in the number of intrusions (words recalled that were not on the original word list) as compared to controls (Mewaldt & Ghoneim, 1979). These data are difficult to interpret and further illustrate the nonspecificity of the mode of action of methamphetamine.

Finally, the effects of methylphenidate, another drug that increases central CA activity, on test performance in cognitively impaired elderly subjects was investigated (Crook, Ferris, Sathananthan, Raskin, & Gershon, 1977). In this double-blind, placebo-controlled study neither 10 mg nor 30 mg of methylphenidate, administered orally, improved cognitive performance as measured by the WAID or Guild Memory Test.

There are numerous reports of the effects of adrenergic manipulation on memory in animals. Changes in central NE and DA levels can influence memory processes. Several methodological considerations make the interpretation of these data difficult. For example, modes of drug administration differ, doses vary from study to study, paradigms testing memory changes are not standardized, and adrenergic systems affect many aspects of behavior that may contaminate

memory studies. Most studies have employed amphetamine or amphetamine-like compounds. Amphetamine produces improvement in learning; however, this may relate to its ability to decrease fatigue or induce arousal (Weiss & Laties, 1962). In addition, animal studies utilizing reward-punishment tasks may be confounded by findings that suggest that the pathways of brain reward may function additionally as pathways of memory consolidation (Routtenberg, 1979). These observations show that when something is learned, activity in the brain-reward pathways may facilitate the formation of memory. In fact, electrical stimulation of brain-reward regions that are rich in CA pathways, during the course of learning a simple task, disrupts the ability of the animal to remember the task 24 hours later (Routtenberg, 1979).

Despite these complications, some generalizations relevant to adrenergic mechanisms in memory can be made. Disruption of DA pathways in rat brain interfere with learning (Routtenberg & Holzman, 1973). Furthermore, inhibition of CA synthesis via α-methylparatyrosine (AMPT) impairs delayed-response performance in cats (Kitsikis & Roberge, 1973) whereas administration of L-dopa to DA-deficient cats produces significant improvement in delayed-response performance (Kitsikis, Roberge, & Frenette, 1972).

More evidence implicating CAs in memory storage includes the effect of reserpine, a drug that depletes intraneuronal stores of CAs via blockade of uptake systems, to impair memory consolidation of active avoidance tasks. This action is also reversible by administration of L-dopa (Dismukes & Rake, 1972). β-Adrenergic blockage in the amygdyla of rats has been shown to disrupt long-term memory functioning in a passive-avoidance task (Gallagher, Kapp, Musty, & Driscoll, 1977).

SUMMARY

The critical question for investigators in the field of mental retardation is: To *what* extent are the effects of physostigmine and arecoline in normal young subjects and in patients with Alzheimer's disease generalizable to mental retardation? The answer to this question necessitates speculation. Obviously the prerequisite to a rationale pharmacology is an understanding of the neurochemistry and neurophysiology of cholinergic neurons in a large number of subtypes of mental retardation. It would not be altogether surprising, given the involvement of acetylcholine in memory, for some of the subtypes of mental retardation that have not been found to be associated with a neuroanatomical abnormality to have an abnormality in some aspect of cholinergic neurotransmission. Thus, acetylcholine synthesis, CAT, cholinergic receptors, and the high affinity choline uptake system could all be essential areas of investigation. However, a neurochem-

ically based approach to the pathophysiology and psychopharmacology of mental retardation should not be limited to only one neurotransmitter. It is entirely possible, even likely, that other putative neurotransmitters are functioning abnormally in some subtypes of mental retardation. Thus, the challenge to the field of mental retardation is to utilize those neurochemical techniques that are now being employed so fruitfully in the elaboration of the mechanisms underlying Alzheimer's disease, and that have been utilized so successfully in understanding Parkinson's and Huntington's diseases, to elucidate the neurochemical bases of some forms of mental retardation. This, it seems, would be a first step in developing an effective and helpful pharmacology for selected groups of mentally retarded individuals, particularly among individuals with Down syndrome.

REFERENCES

Adolfsson, R., Gottfries, C.G., Oreland, L., Roos, B.D., & Winblad, B. Reduced levels of catecholamines in the brain and increased activity of monoamine oxidase in platelets in Alzheimer's disease: Therapeutic implications. In: R. Katzman, R.D. Terry, & K.L. Bick (eds.), *Alzheimer's disease: Senile dementia and related disorders. Aging,* Vol. 7. New York: Raven Press, 1978.

Bartus, R.T. Aging in the rhesus monkey: Specific behavioral impairments and effects of pharmacological intervention. Paper presented at the XI International Congress of Gerontology, Tokyo, 1979. *Excerpta Medica,* 1978.

Beardsley, J.V., & Puletti, F. Personality (MMPI) and cognitive (WAIS) changes after levodopa treatment: Occurrences in patients with Parkinson's disease. *Archives of Neurology,* 1971, *25,* 145.

Berger, B., Escourolle, R., & Moyne, M.A. Catecholamine axons of human cerebral cortex: Histofluorenice study of cerebral biopsies including two cases of Alzheimer's disease. *Revue Neurologique* (Paris), 1976, *132,* 183.

Boshes, B., & Arbit, J. A controlled study of the effect of L-dopa upon selected cognitive and behavioral functions. *Transactions of the American Neurological Association,* 1970, *95,* 59.

Bowen, D.M., Smith, C.B., White, P., & Davison, A.N. Neurotransmitter-related enzymes and indices of hypoxia in senile dementia and other abiotrophies. *Brain,* 1976, *99,* 459.

Bowen, D.M., White, P., Flack, R.H.A., Smith, C.B., & Davison, A.N. Brain decarboxylase as indices of pathological change in senile dementia. *Lancet,* 1974, *1,* 1247.

Boyd, W.D., Graham-White, J., Blackwood, G., Glen, I., & McQueen, J. Clinical effects of choline in Alzheimer senile dementia. *Lancet,* 1976, *2,* 711.

Brunig, R.H., Holzbauer, I., & Kimberlin, C. Age-word imagery and delay interval: Effects on short term and long term retention. *Journal of Gerontology,* 1975, *30,* 312.

Buschke, H. Selective reminding for analysis of memory and learning. *Journal of Verbal Learning and Verbal Behavior,* 1973, *12,* 543.

Buschke, H., Fuld, P.A. Evaluating storage, retention and retrieval in disordered memory and learning. *Neurology,* 1974, *24,* 1019.

Carlsson, A., & Winblad, B. Influence of age and time interval between death and autopsy on dopamine and 3-methoxytyramine levels in human basal ganglia. *Journal of Neural Transmission,* 1976, *38,* 271.

Celesia, G.G., & Wanamaker, W.M. Psychiatric disturbances in Parkinson's disease. *Disease of the Nervous System,* 1972, *33,* 557.

Clark, L.E., & Knowles, J.B. Age differences in dichotic listening performance. *Journal of Gerontology,* 1973, *28,* 173.

Crook, T., Ferris, S., Sathananthan, G., Raskin, A., & Gershon, S. The effect of methylphenidate on test performance in the cognitively impaired aged. *Psychopharmacology*, 1977, *52*, 251.

Crow, T.J., & Grove-White, I.G. Differential effect of atropine and hyoscine on human learning capacity. *British Journal of Pharmacology*, 1971, *43*, 464.

Crow, T.J., & Grove-White, I.G. An analysis of learning deficit following hyoscine administration to man. *British Journal of Pharmacology*, 1973, *49*, 322.

Davies, P. Regional distribution of muscarinic acetylcholine receptors in normal and Alzheimer's type dementia brain. *Brain Research*, 1978, 138, 385.

Davies, P., & Maloney, A.J. Selective loss of central cholinergic neurons in Alzheimer's disease. *Lancet*, 1966, *2*, 1043.

Davis, K.L., Hollister, L.E., Overall, J., Johnson, A., & Train, K. Physostigmine: Effects on cognition and affect in normal subjects. *Psychopharmacology*, 1976, *51*, 23.

Davis, K.L., Mohs, R.C., Tinklenberg, J.R., Hollister, L.E., Pfefferbaum, A., & Koppel, B.S. Cholinomimetics and memory: The effect of choline chloride. *Archives of Neurology*, 1980, *37*, 49.

Davis, K.L., Mohs, R.C., Tinklenberg, J.R., Pfefferbaum, A., Hollister, L.E., & Koppel, B.S. Physostigmine: Improvement of long term memory processes in normal humans. *Science*, 1978, *201*, 272.

Dismukes, R.K., & Rake, A.V. Involvement of biogenic amines in memory formation. *Psychopharmacologia*, 1972, *23*, 17.

Drachman, D.A. Memory and cholinergic function. In: W.S. Fields (ed.), *Neurotransmitter function*. New York: Stratton Intercontinental Medical Book Corp., 1977.

Drachman, D.A., & Leavitt, J.L. Human memory and the cholinergic system. *Archives of Neurology*, 1974, *30*, 113.

Drachman, D.A., & Stahl, S. Extrapyramidal dementia and levodopa. *Lancet*, 1975, *1*, 809.

Dundee, J.W., & Pandit, D.K. Anterograde amnesic effects of pethidine hyoscine and diazepam in adults. *British Journal of Pharmacology*, 1972, *44*, 140.

Franks, C.M., Trouton, D.S., & Lavery, S.G. The inhibition of a conditioned response following arecoline administration in man. *Journal of Clinical and Experimental Psychopathology*, 1958, *19*, 226.

Gallagher, M., Kapp, B.S., Musty, R.E., & Driscoll, P.A. Memory function: Evidence for a specific neurochemical system in the amygdyla. *Science*, 1977, *198*, 523.

Garattini, S., Jori, A., & Samanin, R. Interactions of various drugs with amphetamine. *Annals of the New York Academy of Sciences*, 1976, *281*, 409.

Glowinski, J., Axelrod, J., & Iverson, L.L. Regional studies of catecholamine in rat brain. *Journal of Pharmacology and Experimental Therapeutics*, 1966, *153*, 30.

Gonatas, N.K., Anderson, A., & Evangelista, I. The contribution of altered synapses in the senile plaque: An electron microscopic study in Alzheimer's dementia. *Journal of Neuropathology and Experimental Neurology*, 1967, *26*, 25.

Gottfries, C.G., Gottfries, J., & Roos, B.E. The investigation of homovanillic acid in the human brain and its correlation to senile dementia. *British Journal of Psychiatry*, 1969, *115*, 563.

Gottfries, C.G., Gottfries, J., & Roos, B.E. Homovanillic acid and 5-hydroxyindoleacetic acid in cerebrospinal fluid related to rated mental and motor impairment in senile and presenile dementia. *Acta Psychiatrica Scandinavica*, 1970, *46*, 99.

Gottfries, C.G., Oreland, L., Winberg, A., & Winblad, B. Lowered monomine oxidase activity in brains from alcoholic suicides. *Journal of Neurochemistry*, 1975, *25*, 667.

Gottfries, C.G., & Roos, B.E. Homovanillic acid and 5-hydroxyindoleacetic acid in the cerebrospinal fluid of patients with senile dementia, presenile dementia and Parkinsonism. *Journal of Neurochemistry*, 1969, *16*, 1341.

Gottfries, C.G., & Winblad, B. Post-mortem investigation of human brains with special reference to monoamine metabolism: Methodology. Paper presented at the CINP Congress, Quebec, Canada, 1976.

Granacher, R.P., & Baldessarini, R.J. Physostigmine: Its use in acute anticholinergic syndrome with antidepressant and anti-Parkinson drugs. *Archives of General Psychiatry*, 1975, *32*, 375.

Hanin, I. *Choline and acetylcholine: Handbook of chemical assay methods*. New York: Raven Press, 1974.

Hattori, T., McGeer, P.L., & McGeer, E.G. Dendro axonic neurotransmission II. Morphological sites for synthesis, binding and release of neurotransmitters in dopaminergic dendrites in the substantia of nigra and cholinergic dendrites in the neostriatum. *Brain Research*, 1979, *170*, 71.

Henry, G.M., Buchsbau, M., & Murphy, D.L. Intravenous L-dopa plus carbidopa in depressed patients: Average evoked response, learning and behavioral changes. *Psychosomatic Medicine*, 1976, *38*, 95.

Henry, G.M., Weingartner, H., & Murphy, D.L. Influence of affective states and psychoactive drugs on verbal learning and memory. *American Journal of Psychiatry*, 1973, *130*, 966.

Hirsch, M.J., & Wurtman, R.J. Lecithin consumption increases acetylcholine concentrations in rat brain and adrenal gland. *Science*, 1978, *202*, 223.

Hollander, J., & Barrows, C.H. Enzymatic studies in senescent rodent brains. *Journal of Gerontology*, 1968, *23*, 174.

Hornykiewicz, O. Biochemical and neurophysiological correlation of centrally acting drugs. *Proceedings of the 2nd International Pharmacological Meeting*, Prague, August, 1963. Elnsford, N.Y.: Pergamon Press, 1964.

Hrbek, J., Komenda, S., & Macakova, J. The effect of scopolamine (0.6 mg) and physostigmine (0.1 mg) on higher nervous activity in man followed up during five hours after application. *Activitas Nervosa Superior* (Prague), 1974, *16*, 213.

Hrbek, J., Komenda, S., & Siroka. A. On the interaction of scopolamine and physostigmine in man. *Activitas Nervosa Superior* (Prague), 1971, *13*, 200.

Hurst, P.M., Radlow, R., Chubb, N.C., & Bagley, S.K. Effects of D-amphetamine on acquisition, persistence and recall. *American Journal of Psychology*, 1969, *82*, 307.

Jenden, D.J. Estimation of acetylcholine and the dynamics of its metabolism. In: D.J. Jenden (ed.), *Cholinergic mechanisms and psychopharmacology*. New York: Plenum Publishing Corp., 1977.

Karczmar, A. Central actions of acetylcholine cholinomimetics and related drugs. In: A.M. Goldberg & I. Hanin (eds.), *Biology of cholinergic function*. New York: Raven Press, 1976.

Kark, N., Kuntzman, R., & Brodie, B.B. Storage, synthesis and metabolism of monoamines in the developing brain. *Journal of Neurochemistry*, 1960, *9*, 53.

Kaur, G., & Kanungo, M.S. Alterations in the activity and regulation of cholinesterase of the nervous tissue of rats of varying ages. *Indian Journal of Biochemistry*, 1970, *7*, 122.

Kintgen, J.N., & Apprison, M.H. Behavioral and environmental aspects of the cholinergic system. In: A.M. Goldberg & I. Hanin (eds.), *Biology of cholinergic function*. New York: Raven Press, 1976.

Kitsikis, A., & Roberge, A.G. Behavioral and biochemical effects of α-methylparatyrosine in cats. *Psychopharmacology*, 1973, *31*, 143.

Kitsikis, A., Roberge, A.G., & Frenette, G. Effect of L-dopa on delayed response and visual discrimination in cats and its relation to brain chemistry. *Experimental Brain Research*, 1972, *15*, 304.

Kristensen, V., Olsen, M., & Thielgaard, A. Levodopa treatment of presenile dementia. *Acta Psychiatrica Scandinavica*, 1977, *55*, 41.

Kuhar, M.J. The anatomy of cholinergic neurons. In: A.M. Goldberg & I. Hanin (eds.), *Biology of*

cholinergic function. New York: Raven Press, 1976.

Lee, J.E. The outpatient management of Parkinson's disease with levodopa. *Clincal Medicine*, 1970, *7*, 21.

Lloyd, K.G., Farley, I.J., Deck, J.H.N., & Hornykiewicz, O. Serotonin and 5-hydroxyindoleacetic acid in discrete areas of the brain stem of suicide victims and control patients. *Advances in Biochemical Psychopharmacology*, 1974, *11*, 387.

Loranger, A.W., Goodell, H., Lee, J.E., & McDowell, F. Levodopa treatment of Parkinson's syndrome: Improved intellectual functioning. *Archives of General Psychiatry*, 1972, *26*, 163.

McGeer, E., & McGeer, P.L. Age changes in the human for some enzymes associated with metabolism of catecholamines, GABA, and acetylcholine. In: J.M. Ordee & R.R. Brizee (eds.), *Neurobiology of aging*. New York: Raven Press, 1976.

McGeer, E.G., McGeer, P.L., & Wada, S.A. Distribution and tyrosine hydroxylase in human and animal brain. *Journal of Neurochemistry*, 1971, *18*, 1647.

March, G.G., Markham, C.M., & Asel, R. Levodopa's awakening effect on patients with Parkinsonism. *Journal of Neurology, Neurosurgery and Psychiatry*, 1971, *34*, 209.

Meek, J.L., Bertilsson, F., Cheney, D.L., Zsilla, G., & Costa, E. Aging induced changes in acetylcholine and serotonin content of discrete brain nuclei. *Journal of Gerontology*, 1977, *32*, 192.

Meier, M.J., & Martin, W.F. Intellectual changes associated with levodopa therapy. *Journal of the American Medical Association*, 1970, *213*, 465.

Mewaldt, S.P., & Ghoneim, M.M. The effects and interactions of scopolamine, physostigmine, methamphetamine on human memory. *Pharmacology, Biochemistry and Behavior*, 1979, *10*, 205.

Miller, E. Retrieval from long term memory in presenile dementia: Two tests of an hypothesis. *British Journal of Social and Clinical Psychology*, 1978, *17*, 143.

Murphy, D.L., Henry, G.M., & Weingartner, H. Catecholamines and memory: Enhanced verbal learning during L-dopa administration. *Psychopharmacologia*, 1972, *27*, 319.

O'Brien, C.P., Digiacomo, J.N., Fahn, S., & Schwartz, G.A. Mental effects of high dosage levodopa. *Archives of General Psychiatry*, 1971, *24*, 61.

Ostfeld, A.M., & Araguete, A. Central nervous system effects of hyoscine in man. *Journal of Pharmacology and Experimental Therapeutics*, 1962, *137*, 133.

Ostfeld, A.M., Machne, X., & Unna, K.R. The

effects of atropine on the electroencephalogram and behavior in man. *Journal of Pharmacology and Experimental Therapeutics*, 1960, *128*, 265.

Parkes, J.D., Marsden, C.D., & Rees, J.E. Parkinson's disease, cerebral arteriosclerosis, and senile dementia. *Quarterly Journal of Internal Medicine*, 1974, *43*, 49.

Pearce, J. Mental changes in Parkinsonism. *British Medical Journal*, 1974, *2*, 445.

Pearce, J., & Miller, E. *Clinical aspects of dementia*. Bailiere Tindall, 1973.

Perry, E.K., Perry, R.H., Blessed, G., & Tomlinson, B.E. Necropsy evidence of central cholinergic deficits in senile dementia. *Lancet*, 1977, *1*, 189.

Perry, E.K., Perry, R.H., Blessed, G., & Tomlinson, B.E. Changes in brain cholinesterases in senile dementia of Alzheimer type. *Neuropathology and Applied Neurobiology*, 1978, *4*, 273.

Perry, E.K., Tomlinson, B.E., Blessed, G., Bergmann, K., Gibson, P.H., & Perry, R.H. Correlation of cholinergic abnormalities with senile plaques and mental test scores in senile dementia. *British Medical Journal*, 1978, *2*, 1457.

Peters, B.H., & Levin, H.S. Memory enhancement after physostigmine treatment in the amnesic syndrome. *Archives of Neurology*, 1977, *34*, 215.

Peters, B.H., & Levin, H.S. Effects of physostigmine and lecithin on memory in Alzheimer disease. *Annals of Neurology*, 1979, *16*, 219.

Phuapradit, P., Philips, M., Lees, A.J., & Sterm, G.M. Bromocriptine in presenile dementia. *British Medical Journal*, 1978, *1*, 1052.

Reisine, T.D., Yamamura, H.I., Bird, E.D., Spokes, E., & Enna, S.J. Pre and postsynaptic neurochemical alterations in Alzheimer's Disease. *Brain Research*, 1978, *159*, 477.

Riklan, M. Levodopa and behavior. *Neurology* (Minneapolis), 1972, *22*, 43.

Riklan, M., & Levita, E. *Subcortical correlates of human behavior*. Baltimore: Williams & Wilkins Co., 1969.

Robinson, D.S., Davies, J.M., & Nies, A. Aging, monoamine and monoamine oxidase levels. *Lancet*, 1972, *1*, 290.

Robinson, D.S., Sourkes, T.L., Nies, A., Harris, L.S., Spector, S., Bartlett, D.L., & Kaye, I.S. Monoamine metabolism in human brain. *Archives of General Psychiatry*, 1977, *34*, 89.

Routtenberg, A. The reward system of the brain. *Scientific American*, 1979, *239*, 154.

Routtenberg, A., & Holzman, N. Memory disruption by electrical stimulation of substantia nigra, pars compacta. *Science*, 1973, *181*, 83.

Sacks, O.W., Kohn, M.S., Messekoff, C.R., & Schwartz, W.D. Effects of levodopa in parkinsonian patients with dementia. *Neurology* (Minneapolis), 1972, *22*, 516.

Safer, D.J., & Allen, R.P. The central effects of scopolamine in man. *Biological Psychiatry*, 1971, *3*, 347.

Scoville, W.B., & Milner, B. Loss of recent memory after bilateral hippocampal lesions. *Journal of Neurology, Neurosurgery and Psychiatry*, 1957, *20*, 11.

Shepard, R.N. Recognition memory for words, sentences, and pictures. *Journal of Verbal Learning and Verbal Behavior*, 1967, *6*, 156.

Sitaram, N., Weingartner, H., Caine, E.D., & Gillin, J.C. Choline: Selective enhancement of serial learning and encoding of low imagery words in man. *Life Sciences*, 1978, *22*, 1555.

Sitaram, N., Weingartner, J., & Gillin, J.C. Human serial learning: Enhancement with arecoline and choline and impairment with scopolamine. *Science*, 1978, *201*, 274.

Smith, C.B. Effects of d-amphetamine upon brain amine content and locomotor activity in mice. *Journal of Pharmacology and Experimental Therapeutics*, 1965, *147*, 96.

Smith, C.M., & Swash, M. Physostigmine in Alzheimer's disease. *Lancet*, 1979, *1*, 42.

Soukapova, B., Vojtechovsky, M., & Safratova, V. Drugs influencing the cholinergic system and process of learning and memory in man. *Activitas Nervosa Superior* (Prague), 1970, *12*, 91.

Spillane, J.A., Goodhart, M.H., White, P., Bowen, D.M., & Davidson, A.N. Choline in Alzheimer's disease. *Lancet*, 1977, *2*, 826.

Van Woert, H., Yahr, M., Heninger, G., Rathey, V., & Bowers, M.H. L-dopa in senile dementia. *Lancet*, 1970, *1*, 573.

Vernadakis, A. Comparative studies of neurotransmitter substances in the maturing and aging central nervous system of the chicken. *Progress in Brain Research*, 1973, *40*, 231.

Victor, M., Angevine, J.B., Mancall, E.L., & Fisher, C.M. Memory loss with lesion of the hippocampal formation: Report of a case with some remarks on the anatomical basis of memory. *Archives of Neurology*, 1961, *5*, 244.

Walker, E.L., & Tarte, R. Memory storage as a function of arousal and time with homogenous and heterogenous lists. *Journal of Verbal Learning and Verbal Behavior*, 1963, *2*, 113.

Weiss, B., & Laties, V.G. Enhancement of human performance by caffeine and the amphetamines. *Pharmacological Reviews*, 1962, *14*, 1.

White, P., Hiley, C.R., Goodhart, M.H., Carrasco, L.H., Keet, J.P., Williams, I.E.I., & Bowen, D.M. Neocortical cholinergic neurons in elderly people. *Lancet*, 1977, *1*, 668.

Yamamura, H., & Snyder, S.H. High affinity transport of choline into synaptosomes of rat brain. *Journal of Neurochemistry*, 1973, *21*, 1355.

Yates, C.M., Allison, Y., Simpson, J., Maloney, A.F.J., & Gordon, A. Dopamine in Alzheimer's disease and senile dementia. *Lancet*, 1979, *2*, 851.

Curative Aspects of Mental Retardation:
Biomedical and Behavioral Advances
edited by Frank J. Menolascino, M.D., Ronald Neman, Ph.D., and Jack A. Stark, Ph.D.
Copyright 1983   Paul H. Brookes Publishing Co., Inc.   Baltimore · London

chapter 14

The Effects of
Neuropeptides on Behavior

Implications for Mental Retardation

CURT A. SANDMAN, PH.D.
University of California, Irvine
Fairview Hospital
Costa Mesa, California

THIS CHAPTER DESCRIBES neurochemical changes relating to human behavior and the implications of these research findings on mental retardation. Chapter 12 indicated that a variety of peptides have effects on the brain and behavior. Chapter 13 presented information that drugs which influence acetylcholine also influence behavior. This chapter focuses on two peptides, MSH and β-endorphin and proposes a behavioral strategy to assess the effects of peptides in particular, and drugs in general. Dr. Abba J. Kastin (co-author of Chapter 13) and this author share a bias with regard to our research of peptides and not other drugs. It is clear that a number of drugs influence and even have ameliorative effects on behavior. However, the study of peptides is particularly interesting because peptides are endogenous substances and it is conceivable that an influence on behavior of this class of molecules suggests physiological imbalance of this neurochemical system. Thus, unlike drugs, treatment with peptides may ultimately be construed as direct replacement or repair of a deficient system.

The classical approach to brain-behavior relationships is that function or abilities are localized in structures of the brain. The wealth of data from this orientation has guided conventional physiological psychology for years. Application of this view to clinical problems, such as frontal lobotomy as a treatment for schizophrenia, has not fared well. An alternative view is that processes (such as chemical flux) in the brain may influence behavior. Ultimately, a synthesis of these paradigms needs to be implemented. Some of the structural changes that have been suggested by the work of Gary Lynch and colleagues (Lynch, Gall, & Dunwiddie, 1978) on neural plasticity may be mediated by chemicals such as peptides (see Chapter 8). Thus, the search for chemical changes in specific structures may be fruitful.

From Table 1, it is apparent that peptides have an effect on behavior. These effects are extra-endocrine, and certainly would not have been viewed as conventional 5 years ago. The peptides this chapter concentrates on are the MSH/ACTH fragments and the endorphins. Table 1 lists normative views with respect to

Table 1. Reported effects of several peptides on behavior

Peptide	Function
Scotophobin	Causes fear of darkness
ACTH fragments	Improve attention and memory, reduce anxiety, increase social contact
MSH	Improves attention
Vasopressin	Enhances memory
Luteinizing hormone	Increases libido
Endorphins	Causes analgesia, decreases sensitivity
MIF	Decreases parkinsonian tremor, reverses affective disorder

the influence of these substances on behavior. Findings in this regard are controversial, and our understanding of these substances will be revised as research progresses.

There are many interesting relationships among peptides and perhaps the most interesting is that fragments of MSH and ACTH and the endorphins are contained in the LPH molecule. Further, the LPH molecule is contained in an even larger fragment, the 31 K precursor glycoprotein described by Mains, Eipper, and Ling (1977). The initial interest in studying these peptides was rationalized teleologically. The fact that these molecules were contained in the same molecule portended functional significance. Two hypotheses for examining the MSH and endorphin-like relationships were obvious: 1) These two peptides (and perhaps others in the precursor) share redundant functions, or 2) These peptides have reciprocal or modulating influences. As outlined in Table 2, the literature

Table 2. Suggestive evidence of relationship between MSH/ACTH fragments and endorphin/enkephalin molecules

MSH/ACTH fragments	Endorphin/Enkephalin
Behavioral Effects	
1. Improve acquisition of maze	Improve acquisition of maze
2. Delay extinction of avoidance learning	Delay extinction of avoidance learning
3. Facilitate reversal learning	Delay reversal learning
4. Reverse amnestic treatment with prior administration	Attenuate amnestic treatment before or after ECT
5. Increase exploratory activity	Decrease exploratory activity
6. Increase gregariousness	Decrease gregariousness
7. Increase sexual activity	Decrease sexual activity
8. 4-10 has no effect on grooming	Increase grooming behavior
9. Increase self-stimulatory behavior	Decrease self-stimulatory behavior
10. Accelerate eye-opening in newborn	Retard eye-opening in newborn
Opiate-Related Effects	
11. Hyperalgesia	Analgesia
12. Attenuate morphine-induced analgesia	Addiction and tolerance
Electrophysiological Effects	
13. Increase early components of AEP	General suppression of AEP
14. Abolish elliprogenic spiking in nucleus gigantocellularis produced by β-endorphin	Initiate spiking in nucleus gigantocellularis
15. Increase spinal-neuron excitability	Decrease spinal-neuron excitability

tended to suggest support for a reciprocal influence between them.

In addition to developing the theme of a modulating or reciprocal relationship between MSH and β-endorphin, this chapter also introduces the suggestion that attentional processes are affected primarily. Evidence from a number of studies we have done with animals, normal volunteers, and patient groups suggests that attentional processes were augmented after treatment with the MSH/ACTH fragment (Sandman & Kastin, 1981). This chapter will not review all of this research. Although there is some debate regarding our interpretation of the results, the fact that there are behavioral effects of these peptides is undisputed. Our interpretation is that MSH/ACTH improves attentional processes and that β-endorphin (and possibly other endogenous opioids) restrict attention.

MSH/ACTH FRAGMENTS

Among the tasks employed in our search are the: 1) learning of a maze for the reward of food; 2) active and passive avoidance learning; 3) learning a visual discrimination to avoid shock; 4) reversal shift of the visual discrimination; 5) open field activity; 6) social behavior in the open field; and 7) lever pressing for the reward of food. The constellation of results suggests that MSH/ACTH peptides influence the perceptual/attentional functioning of the organisms (Sandman & Kastin, 1981; Sandman, Kastin, & Miller, 1977).

In several studies (Sandman, Alexander, & Kastin, 1973; Sandman, Beckwith, Gittis, & Kastin, 1974; Sandman, Beckwith, & Kastin, 1980; Sandman, Miller, Kastin, & Schally, 1972) rats were trained with a two-choice visual discrimination problem to avoid shock by running to a white door. After the animals acquired the response, the task was reversed so that the simultaneously available black door was the correct response. An attentive animal solved the reversal problem faster that an unattentive animal, because it learned about the dimension of brightness during the original problem and not only that

white was correct. Thus, when the problem was changed, the attentive animal tested values on the dimension of brightness (black-white) rather that irrelevant dimensions (e.g., in this case spatial localization).

Treatment of rats with MSH had no appreciable effect on original learning. However, rats treated with MSH required approximately 50% fewer trials to solve the reversal learning problem. We have concluded from these data, as well as from data gathered in other paradigms, that the MSH/ACTH peptide enhanced attentional processes.

In a recent study we (Sandman, Beckwith, & Kastin, 1980) compared the influence of MSH/ACTH 4-10, α-MSH (1-13), β_p-MSH (1-18), β_h-MSH (1-22), and ACTH (1-24) on learning and attention. This study was designed to evaluate the thesis that redundant chemical information was stored in these related molecules.

The results indicated that the speed of learning the original problem diminished with administration of compounds of increasing molecular weight. Learning of the initial stage of learning was enhanced significantly with administration of MSH/ACTH 4-10. Except for ACTH 1-24, all of the other peptides also improved learning, though acceptable levels of statistical significance were not achieved. Thus, with respect to initial learning, these related peptides appear to share redundant functions.

However, the structure-activity relationships were much different for reversal learning. Maximal enhancement of reversal learning (an index of attention) was achieved only with administration of α-, β- and (human) β-MSH. Thus, when plotted according to molecular weight, a significant quadratic relation with learning (attention) was apparent.

The results of the early phases of the learning process (original learning) are in agreement with the conclusions of DeWied and Bohus (1966). If behavioral information was coded redundantly in these related molecules, a monotonic relationship was predicted between performance and molecular weight. Our findings are consistent with this analysis. However, the results of the reversal learning problem indicated that only compounds with MSH-like configurations improved attention. These findings suggested that attention may be influenced by a particular peptide sequence. Thus, the fit of MSH-like molecules with their putative receptors may initiate and maintain discrete behavioral patterns related to attention.

STUDIES IN NORMAL HUMAN SUBJECTS

In a series of early studies, the effects of MSH/ACTH 4-10 were studied on a number of behavioral parameters in normal volunteers. Among the most reliable findings were increased visual retention, decreased anxiety, and enhanced visual discrimination (Miller, Kastin, Sandman, Fink, & van Veen, 1974; Sandman, George, Nolan, van Reizen, & Kastin, 1975). Several parameters were not affected by the peptide, including short-term memory for digits, measures of emotionality, reaction time, and verbal memory. Several studies were initiated in our laboratory to examine the primary processes affected by the peptide.

The first study was designed to test the influence of MSH/ACTH 4-10 on perceptual threshold (Sandman, George, McCanne, Nolan, Kaswan, & Kastin, 1977). Infusion of MSH/ACTH 4-10 raised the threshold for detection and impaired the subject's ability to report accurately the presence of a stimulus. However, discrimination of stimuli improved when subjects were administered the peptide. These results suggested that MSH/ACTH 4-10 facilitated stimulus processing or selective attention, whereas simple intake or detection of threshold stimuli was impaired. Conceivably, the peptide raised the absolute threshold for stimuli and thus functioned as a filtering mechanism to protect the organism from distracting "perceptual noise." However, when stimuli were above the threshold, the processing of information was facilitated.

A recent study in our laboratory (Ward, Sandman, George, & Shulman, 1979) was designed to test the influence of MSH/ACTH 4-10 on attention and memory with the item

recognition test. In this test subjects are given various amounts of information to memorize and are then presented "individual stimuli" (probes). The subjects must decide if the probes are members of the memorized set or not. Reaction time is measured as a reflection of cognitive processing required in this task. Typically the slope of reaction time reflects the demands of memory load on reaction, with reaction time increasing linearly with increased load. The intercept relates, in a general sense, to attentional processes. Treatment of subjects with MSH/ACTH 4-10 exerted a clear influence on the intercept but no effect on the slope. This finding was interpreted as evidence that the primary influence of MSH and ACTH fragments was on attention.

In addition, we recently completed a research project on the effects of ACTH/MSH fragments on the cortical-evoked potential of normal humans (an excellent measure of attention). This study presents some possibilities for understanding the effects of peptides on behavior, and it might be a useful tool for examining the effects of peptides in mentally retarded individuals. In this completely crossed, double-blind study, we used an orally administered analogue of ACTH 4-9. This fragment is supposed to be 1,000 times more potent than ACTH 4-10 in some systems, but it appears somewhat less potent in other systems. We administered it in four doses, of 0, 5, 10, and 20 mg, or a positive control of 10 mg of d-amphetamine. The positive control was included because many researchers have assumed that peptides produce generalized arousal similar to amphetamine. Our view is that peptides produce specific effects and not general arousal associated with an amphetamine-like effect. Visual evoked potentials were measured in the left and right hemisphere immediately, at 1 hour, 2 hours, and 4 hours after receiving the peptide. The ACTH analogue increased area-under-the-curve measures in the left hemisphere of females and in the right hemisphere in males. This is consistent with the sexually dimorphic effects we have reported previously (Veith, Sandman, George, & Stevens, 1978). Another finding of interest was the dose relationships. A clear increase in area was observed for the 5 and 10 mg doses, but the effect of 20 mg was decreased and similar to d-amphetamine. These preliminary findings indicated that the cortical-evoked response was sensitive to the influence of peptides and further support the notion that the dose of peptide does not produce a linear effect on the electrical activity of the brain.

STUDIES OF
MENTALLY RETARDED SUBJECTS

Three studies have been completed on the influence of MSH/ACTH fragments in mentally retarded persons. In the first study (Sandman, George, Walker, Nolan, & Kastin, 1976), 20 mentally retarded men were injected with 15 mg of MSH/ACTH and then given tests similar to those administered to normal volunteers. Treatment with the peptide resulted in a significant orienting response to novel stimulation (deceleration of heart rate). In addition, the peptide treatment improved learning of intradimensional and extradimensional shifts in a concept learning paradigm, which is consistent with findings from studies of animal learning and human volunteers. In addition, visual retention, spatial localization, and matching auditory patterns were improved in the mentally retarded subjects after administration of MSH/ACTH 4-10.

In a second experiment (Walker & Sandman, 1979), the influence of an orally administered analogue of MSH/ACTH 4-9 was examined in a group of retarded adults with many of the same tests as in the 1976 study. Three doses (0, 5, and 20 mg) were evaluated. The results indicated significant improvement in measures of attention (in the concept formation tests), but the effects were not as dramatic or pervasive as in the initial study. A number of factors may account for the attenuated effects, including reduced potency of the analogue, route of administration, etc.; however, a subsequent study suggested that the choice of doses may have been unfortunate.

In the third study, four doses (0, 5, 10, and 20 mg) of the ACTH 4-9 analogue were examined in retarded clients while they performed their day-to-day activities (Sandman, Walker, & Lawton, 1980). The clients were paid a wage to bend leads of an electrical resistor to fit a mold. There were four graded steps in the process that varied in difficulty from the bending of resistors to quality control inspection. During the course of the study the clients performed the same task each day. The peptides were administered in the morning every day for 2 weeks. Placebo weeks preceded and succeeded the treatment weeks. Observations of productivity and of social behavior were done at regular intervals during the morning hours.

The dose of the peptide interacted with the difficulty of the task to produce distinctive curves. The high dose, 20 mg, interfered with productivity of each task. A dosage of 5 mg had mixed effects, enhancing performance only for the more complex tasks. A 10-mg dosage improved productivity in all but the easiest task.

These data provided support for the hypothesis that the MSH/ACTH 4-9 analogue exerted an influence on perceptual/attentional mechanisms in a dose-dependent manner. Further, since performance was disrupted by extraneous movement, lack of coordination, or inattention to detail, these data may be construed as ecological validation that MSH/ACTH 4-9 influenced attentional processes, which facilitated performance.

Other data collected in this study indicated that the peptide might also influence social behavior in a dose-dependent way. The evidence suggested that patient-patient and patient-supervisor contact increased during treatment, especially with 10- and 20-mg doses. Self-stimulation also increased during treatment with the peptide. These data are in agreement with the reports of Beckwith, O'Quin, Petro, Kastin, and Sandman (1977), in which rats increased contact time after injections with MSH.

A curious pattern emerged from this study. Increased productivity coupled with greater interpersonal awareness and self-stimulation was evident, especially at the 10-mg dose. Apparently, when the clients worked after treatment with this dose of peptide, they did so with greater concentration and intensity. These data are consistent with earlier findings that normal and retarded subjects evidence enhanced orienting responses to novel stimuli and also retained the ability to discriminate relevant from irrelevant information after treatment with MSH/ACTH fragments. However, these findings (consistent with earlier data, Sandman, Beckwith, & Kastin, 1980) indicated that some behaviors are related linearly to dose while others, specifically measures of attention, have a curvilinear relation with dose of the peptide.

DEVELOPMENTAL STUDIES USING MSH-LIKE PEPTIDES

The influence of early treatment with MSH-like peptides on later behavior has been investigated in several studies. The rationale of this approach is that the brain and endocrine system are not fully developed in immature organisms and may be extremely pliable. The relevance of this approach is clear. Early diagnosis of mental retardation may be countered with endogenous substances having the capacity to alter the brain and behavior. Thus, administration of peptides at early stages of development may result in structural changes that are reflected in permanent alterations in behavior. Although this reasoning has been explored favorably with some substances, relatively little developmental work has been done with MSH, ACTH, and their fragments.

In a series of studies (Beckwith, Sandman, Hothersall, & Kastin, 1977; Sandman & Kastin, 1981), we reported that MSH treatments administered postnatally between days 2–7, resulted in significant improvement in learning of adult rats. Consistent findings have been generated with the visual discrimination

procedure. Rats treated as infants with MSH performed the discrimination and reversal problem more accurately than rats treated with placebo. However, this result pertained only to the male animals. There was no effect of MSH on the learning performance of female rats (Beckwith, Sandman, Hothersall, & Kastin, 1977; Champney, Sahley, & Sandman, 1976).

In a study of social behavior (Beckwith, O'Quin, Petro, Kastin, & Sandman, 1977), infant rats were again treated with MSH between the ages of 2–7 days and then observed in the open field when they were adults. Pairs of rats of the same sex were placed in the open field for 5 minutes and the time in contact with one another was measured. The findings indicated that females treated with MSH as infants spent the greatest amount of time in contact with each other. Treatment of infant male rats with MSH also increased contact time as compared to control animals, but the effect was not as great as for female rats. These complex findings indicated that early treatment with MSH influenced social behavior in a sexually dimorphic manner.

Thus, animals treated with MSH during critical stages of development display enhanced adaptive behaviors throughout their life span. These findings may be of physiological significance, since MSH apparently has a major role during early development. MSH stimulates fetal growth and brain development in the immature organism (Swaab, Boer, Boer, Dogterom, van Leevwen, & Visser, 1978). Maternal blood levels of MSH may be related to the onset of labor. The levels rise during the initiation of labor, remain elevated until birth, and then they return to normal levels (Clark, Thody, Shuster, & Bowers, 1978). It is conceivable that the fetus is exposed to high levels of MSH just prior to birth. As we shall see, there is a remarkable parallel for MSH with β-endorphin in the normal birth process. However, the effects of a traumatic birth may have a disorganizing influence on the biochemical balance, which may reflect permanent changes in the developing fetus.

ENDORPHINS

Embedded in the C-terminal of the LPH molecule is β-endorphin, occupying positions 61–91. The discovery of the analgesic properties of these related molecules catalyzed enormous interest in the study of peptides. We now know that many peptides possess analgesic properties, some with even greater potency than the endorphins. Thus, even though it is now considered somewhat of an epiphenomenon, injections of the endorphins into the ventricles or into discrete areas of the brain can produce profound analgesia. However, peripheral administration of endorphins of their potent D-Ala-2 analogues does not result in analgesia.

A growing number of studies indicate that β-endorphin has extraopiate effects. In addition to the analgesia after central administration, a number of behavioral responses not directly associated with analgesia have been reported. For instance, intracerebral injection of opioid peptides increased grooming behavior (Gispen, Reith, Schotman, Weigant, Zwiers, & DeWied, 1977), decreased electrically induced self-stimulation (Stein & Belluzzi, 1978), depressed levels of sexual activity of male rats in the presence of estrous females (Meyerson & Terenius, 1977), stimulated penile erection and spontaneous seminal emission (Walker, Brentson, Sandman, Coy, Schally, & Kastin, 1977), and increased food intake in rats (Belluzzi & Stein, 1978). All of these effects are reversible by the opiate antagonist, naloxone.

Peripheral administration of opioid peptides also results in a number of behavioral responses. Kastin, Scollan, King, Schally, and Coy (1976) reported that small doses (80 μg/kg) enhanced maze learning of hungry rats. In a later series of studies, DeWied, Bohus, Van Ree, and Urban (1978) reported that Met-enkephalin (related to endorphin) was as potent as MSH/ACTH 4-10 in affecting passive and active learning.

Among the most striking reports of the multiple independent actions of peripheral administration of endorphin is that of Veith,

Sandman, Walker, Coy, and Schally (1978). The different effects of α-, γ-, and β-endorphin on the behavior of rats were examined in the open field. Veith, Sandman, Walker, Coy, and Schally (1978) reported that each of these peptides exerted specific, nonoverlapping effects. Treatment with α-endorphin typically produced penile erection and spontaneous seminal discharge—an effect interpreted as relating to pleasure. Administration of γ-endorphin increased defecation and diminished exploratory behavior. Peripheral administration of β-endorphin resulted in increased grooming. Just as with the MSH/ACTH-like peptides, these data suggested that peptides of the endorphin family, which share in amino acid core, exerted discrete and specific influences on behavior.

DEVELOPMENTAL STUDIES USING β-ENDORPHINS

Several factors converged to suggest that the effects of exposure to β-endorphin early in life would have profound influence on the organism. First, previous studies (reviewed above) suggested that early exposure to MSH/ACTH fragments results in a permanent change in behavior. Second, Gautray, Jolivet, Veilh, and Guillemin (1977) reported that β-endorphin was elevated in the amniotic fluid during fetal distress, a condition that can result in profound physical and cognitive impairment. Third, in the rat it is known (Simon & Hiller, 1978) that opiate receptors continue to proliferate during the first 21 days of life and mature by about 140 days of age. Fourth, hypoxia in pregnant animals, a major cause of retardation, results in elevated levels of β-endorphin in the amniotic fluid (Wardlaw, 1981). Thus, sufficient inferential information suggested that exposure to opiate peptides early in life has significant influences on the brain and behavior.

In the first direct experiment of the effects of β-endorphin on development (Sandman, McGivern, Berka, Walker, Coy, & Kastin,

1979), infant rats were injected with 50 μg (β-endorphin or a vehicle control) subcutaneously (s.c.) each day from day 2 through 7 of life. The rats were then tested for analgesia at age 90 days. The results indicated that early exposure to β-endorphin permanently increased the threshold for thermal, but not shock-induced, pain.

In the second study, fetal exposure to β-endorphin was evaluated by injecting pregnant rats with either β-endorphin or a vehicle solution. Pregnant rats were injected subcutaneously every other day, from day 7 through day 21 of pregnancy. The male offspring were cross-fostered and studied longitudinally from birth through 180 days. Preliminary findings after injection of radioactive β-endorphin into separate rats suggested that appoximately 5% of the radioactivity may pass the placental barrier and enter the fetal brain.

The results indicated that early, *in utero* exposure to β-endorphin retarded aspects of development. The rats given the peptide were delayed significantly in eye opening, were less active during early life, and failed to exhibit the normal pattern of activity later. By day 40 through maturity, the rats exposed to β-endorphin *in utero* evidenced a significant weight gain.

Behavioral tests indicated that rats exposed to β-endorphin *in utero* appeared less responsive to environmental stimulation than the animals in the control group. The startle response is measured by assessing the animal's somatomuscular reaction to a very loud (60 dB) tone. The response of rats exposed to β-endorphin was attenuated by more than a factor of 3 as compared with animals given the control solution.

Two tests of learning also distinguished the rats exposed *in utero* to β-endorphin from those exposed only to the vehicle solution. Rats exposed to β-endorphin took significantly longer than control animals to re-enter a chamber in which they had received shock 24 hours earlier. There were no differences between groups during initial learning of a visual discrimination problem; however, the rats treated with β-endorphin required significantly more trials than controls to learn the reversal shift.

Surprisingly, there were no differences between the rats exposed *in utero* to β-endorphin or to vehicle solution on the tail flick test. However, the rats exposed to β-endorphin were significantly more sensitive to analgesic doses of morphine than the control animals. Thus, an interesting pattern emerges, suggesting a critical period effect of the peptides on behavior. Rats treated neonatally with β-endorphin evidence increased their threshold for painful stimuli, but rats exposed prenatally do not. However, prenatal exposure to β-endorphin increases rats sensitivity to morphine as adults.

OPIATE ANTAGONISTS AND SELF-ABUSE

Among the most dramatic behaviors observed in institutionalized patients, especially retarded persons, is self-inflicted abuse. The estimates of occurrence of this behavior among retarded individuals range from 10% to 20% of the institutionalized population. The etiology of this observation is unknown but a common explanation is that it is an "attention-getting" behavior. Many "therapies" are directed either at 1) not paying attention to the client during a self-abusive episode in the hope that it will "extinguish" or 2) punishing the client with electric shock during the early stage of an abusive episode in order to abort the behavior. Punishment can control this behavior, but the effect is transient and tends to return when the client is removed from a highly contingent environment.

One may think of self-abusive behavior as an extreme form of stimulation. If the perceptual/attentional field of a client were restricted (as in analgesia), perhaps the attempt to achieve some degree of stimulation would become exaggerated and expressed as self-abuse. What about pain in these clients? The anecdotal reports are mixed, but the consensus of our staff was that most of the self-abusive clients do not show reactions commensurate with the damage they inflict.

Since we have shown that β-endorphin restricts attention and perception and that self-abusers may suffer from such restrictions of environmental impact, we hypothesized that self-abuse may be maintained by endogenous opioids. Thus, an opiate antagonist, such as naloxone, may attenuate this behavior. In a preliminary study we observed two self-abusive clients after double-blind administration of naloxone or a placebo. The clients were videotaped and independent observers tallied self-abusive episodes as well as other behaviors.

Treatment with naloxone eliminated self-abuse in one client and attenuated it 58% in the second client. In addition, a self-clasping behavior often associated with self-abuse was greatly attenuated in one client. The effects of naloxone only lasted 90 minutes, but the effects observed during this period were clinically significant.

More recently, with Barron-Quinn, the response to medication was surveyed in self-abusive clients; clients evidencing stereotypy; clients with both behaviors; and clients matched demographically and intellectually, but without these behaviors. Remarkably, we have found that about 50% of the clients with self-abuse and/or stereotypy have "paradoxical" responses to hypnotic, sedative, or narcotic medication. Although future research will provide greater resolution of the mechanisms involved, it appears that at least a subgroup of self-abusive clients may have a significant biochemical imbalance.

CONCLUSIONS

Two major conclusions may be derived from this review. The first conclusion is that peptides of the LPH chain modulate attentional/perceptual functions. The second conclusion is that there may be a reciprocal relationship among fragments of the LPH chain. These conclusions would seem to have major implications for mental retardation. Clearly, one of the major problems among retarded citizens is an attentional/perceptual deficit. The evidence suggests that ACTH/MSH fragments improve attention. Indeed, the greatest improvement was reported with retarded clients treated with these fragments. Conversely, it appears that β-endorphin may produce deficits in attention or perception. Developmental studies indicated that β-endorphin is elevated during pregnancy, but excessive levels are present in conditions such as hypoxia, acidosis, and fetal distress. Further, pharmacological elevation of amniotic fluid levels of β-endorphin results in delayed development. Other evidence indicates that during normal birth, elevation of MSH may parallel the elevations of β-endorphin. Hence, in the normal birth process, free from excessive pain and trauma, a balance of these peptides is present. If the MSH peptides "modulate" the endogenous opiates, the influence of endorphin may be mitigated during a normal birth process. However, in a traumatic pregnancy or birth, perhaps only endorphin is elevated. Left unchecked, the intrauterine environment becomes toxified by a 10- to 20-fold increase in endorphin. It is tempting to speculate that β-endorphin may be of etiological significance in some cases of developmental disability. If this is true, and the reciprocal or modulating relationship between β-endorphin and MSH is validated, perhaps some developmental disorders related to traumatic pregnancy or birth will be prevented by treatment with peptides. Since attention to task and problem solving are two key deficiencies in mentally retarded persons, the possibility of reversing (or curing) these two key components of sensory and learning activities may also directly/indirectly affect the symptoms of mental retardation. The brain's own chemical products may prove to be self-correcting factors that can dramatically change or reverse the brain's own structured or functional deficiencies.

REFERENCES

Beckwith, B.E., O'Quin, R.K., Petro, M.S., Kastin, A.J., & Sandman, C.A. The effects of neonatal injections of α-MSH on the open field behavior of juvenile and adult rat. *Physiological Psychology*, 1977, *5*, 295–299.

Beckwith, B.E., Sandman, C.A., Hothersall, D., & Kastin, A.J. The influence of neonatal injections of α-MSH on learning, memory and attention in rats. *Physiology and Behavior*, 1977, *18*, 63–71.

Belluzzi, J.D., & Stein, L. *Neuroscience Abstracts*, 1978, 405.

Champney, T.F., Sahley, T.C., & Sandman, C.A. Effects of neonatal cerebral ventricular injections of ACTH 4–9 and subsequent adult injections on learning in male and female albino rats. *Pharmacology, Biochemistry and Behavior*, 1976, *5*, 3–10.

Clark, D., Thody, A.J., Shuster, S., & Bowers, H. Immunoreactive α-MSH in human plasma in pregnancy. *Nature*, 1978, *273*, 163–164.

DeWied, D., & Bohus, B. Long-term and short-term effects on retention of a conditional avoidance response in rats by treatment with a long acting pitression and α-MSH. *Nature*, 1966, *212*, 1484–1488.

DeWied, D., Bohus, B., Van Ree, J.M., & Urban, I. Behavioral and electrophysiological effects of peptides related to lipotropin (β-LPH). *Journal of Pharmacology and Experimental Therapeutics*, 1978, *204*, 570–580.

Gautray, J.P., Jolivet, A., Vielh, J.P., & Guillemin, R. Presence of immunoassayable β-endorphin in human amniotic fluid: Elevation in cases of fetal distress. *American Journal of Obstetrics and Gynecology*, 1977, *129*, 211–212.

Gispen, W.H., Reith, M.E., Schotman, P., Weigant, V.M., Zwiers, H., & DeWied, D. CNS and ACTH-like peptides: Neurochemical response and interactions with opiates. In: L.H. Miller, C.A. Sandman, & A.J. Kastin (eds.), *Neuropeptide influence on the brain and behavior*. New York: Raven Press, 1977.

Kastin, A.J., Scollan, E.L., King, M.G., Schally, A.V., & Coy, D.H. Enkephalin and a potent analog facilitate maze performance after intraperitoneal administration in rats. *Pharmacology, Biochemistry and Behavior*, 1976, *5*, 691–695.

Lynch, G., Gall, C., & Dunwiddie, T.V. Neuroplasticity in the hippocampal formation. In: M.A. Corner, R.E. Baker, N.E. van de Poll, D.F. Swaab, & H.B.M. Uylings (eds.), *Maturation of the nervous system, progress in brain research*. Amsterdam: Elsevier Scientific Publishing Co., 1978.

Mains, R.E., Eipper, B.A., & Ling, N. Common precursor to corticotropins and endorphins. *Proceedings of the National Academy of Sciences*, 1977, *74*, 3014–3018.

Meyerson, B.S., & Terenius, L. β-endorphin and male sexed behavior. *European Journal of Pharmacology*, 1977, *42*, 191–192.

Miller, L.H., Kastin, A.J., Sandman, C.A., Fink, M., & van Veen, W.J. Polypeptide influences on attention, memory and anxiety in man. *Pharmacology, Biochemistry and Behavior*, 1974, *2*, 663–668.

Sandman, C.A., Alexander, W.D., & Kastin, A.J. Neuroendocrine influences on visual learning in the albino and hooded rat. *Physiology and Behavior*, 1973, *11*, 613–617.

Sandman, C.A., Beckwith, B.E., Gittis, M.M., & Kastin, A.J. Melanocyte-stimulating hormone (MSH) and overtraining effect on extradimensional shift (EDS) learning. *Physiology and Behavior*, 1974, *13*, 163–166.

Sandman, C.A., Beckwith, B.E., & Kastin, A.J. Are learning and attention related to the sequence of amino acids in ACTH/MSH peptides? *Peptides*, 1980, *1*, 277–280.

Sandman, C.A., George, J., McCanne, T.R., Nolan, J.D., Kaswan, J., & Kastin, A.J. MSH/ACTH 4–10 influences behavioral and physiological measures of attention. *Journal of Clinical Endocrinology and Metabolism*, 1977, *44*, 884–891.

Sandman, C.A., George, J., Nolan, J.D., van Reizen, H., & Kastin, A.J. Enhancement of attention in man with ACTH/MSH 4–10. *Physiology and Behavior*, 1975, *15*, 427–431.

Sandman, C.A., George, J., Walker, B.B., Nolan, J.D., & Kastin, A.J. Neuropeptide MSH/ACTH 4–10 enhances attention in the mentally retarded. *Pharmacology, Biochemistry and Behavior*, 1976, *5*, 23–28.

Sandman, C.A., & Kastin, A.J. The influence of fragments of the LPH chain on learning memory and attention on animals and man. *Pharmacology and Therapeutics*, 1981, *13*, 39–60.

Sandman, C.A., Kastin, A.J., & Miller, L.H. Central nervous system actions of MSH and related pituitary peptides. In: L. Martini & G.M. Besser (eds.), *Clinical neuroendocrinology*. New York: Academic Press, 1977.

Sandman, C.A., McGivern, R.F., Berka, C., Walker, J.M., Coy, D.H., & Kastin, A.J. Neonatal administration of β-endorphin produces "chronic" insensitivity to thermal stimulus. *Life Sciences*, 1979, *25*, 1755–1760.

Sandman, C.A., Miller, L.H., Kastin, A.J., & Schally, A.V. Neuroendocrine influence on attention and memory. *Journal of Comparative Physiological Psychology*, 1972, *80*, 54–58.

Sandman, C.A., Walker, B.B., & Lawton, C.A.

An analog of MSH/ACTH 4–9 enhances inter-personal and environmental awareness in mentally retarded adults. *Peptides*, 1980, *1*, 109–114.

Simon, E.J., & Hiller, J.M. In vitro studies on opiate receptors and their ligands. *Federation Proceedings*, 1978, *37*, 141–146.

Stein, L., & Belluzzi, J.D. Brain endorphins and the sense of well-being: A psychobiological hypothesis. *Advances in Biochemical Psychopharmacology*, 1978, *18*, 299–311.

Swaab, D.F., Boer, G.J., Boer, K., Dogterom, J., van Leevwen, F.W., & Visser, M. Fetal neuroendocrine mechanisms in development and parturition. In: M.A. Corner, R.E. Baker, N.E. van de Poll, D.F. Swaab, & H.B.M. Uylings (eds.), *Maturation of the nervous system, progress in brain research*. Amsterdam: Elsevier Scientific Publishing Co., 1978.

Veith, J.L., Sandman, C.A., George, J., & Stevens, V.C. Effects of MSH/ACTH 4–10 on memory, attention and endogenous hormone levels in women. *Physiology and Behavior*, 1978, *20*, 43–50.

Veith, J.L., Sandman, C.A., Walker, J.M., Coy, D.H. Schally, A.V., & Kastin, A.J. Endorphins: Systemic administration selectively alters open field behavior of rats. *Physiology and Behavior*, 1978, *20*, 539–542.

Walker, B., & Sandman, C.A. Influences of an analog of the neuropeptide ACTH 4–9 on mentally retarded adults. *American Journal of Mental Deficiency*, 1979, *83*, 346–352.

Walker, J.M., Brentson, G.B., Sandman, C.A., Coy, D., Schally, A.V. & Kastin, A.J. An analog of enkephalin having prolonged opiate-like effects *in vivo*. *Science*, 1977, *196*, 85–87.

Ward, M.M., Sandman, C.A., George, J., & Shulman, H. MSH/ACTH 4–10 in men and women: Effects upon performance of an attention and memory task. *Physiology and Behavior*, 1979, *22*, 669–673.

Wardlaw, S.L., Stark, R.I., Daniel, S., & Frantz, A.F. Effects of hypoxia on β-lipotropin release in fetal, newborn and maternal sheep. *Endocrinology*, 1981, *108*, 1710–1715.

Conclusion

Frank J. Menolascino
University of Nebraska Medical Center
Omaha, Nebraska

In Chapter 12, Drs. Abba J. Kastin and Curt A. Sandman began by reviewing current knowledge on the effects of peptides on the brain and pointed out areas of speculative research that might apply to mental retardation, citing both human and animal studies. Drs. Kastin and Sandman described peptides as specific strings of amino acids that are now known to exist throughout the body: in the brain, intestine, and elsewhere. Years ago, there was a great deal of skepticism about whether brain or hypothalamic peptides even existed. Now, however, the existence of the peptides is firmly established, and delineation of their endocrine effects was recognized by two Nobel prizes in 1977. Of great interest to mental retardation is what is called the "extra-endocrine" effects of the hypothalamic peptides. One of these peptides is the melanocyte-stimulating hormone (MSH). The current belief that these peptides and others work on the brain was already noted in tests such as the dopapotentiation test—a neuropharmacological test that essentially looks at increased activities in rats who have been pretreated with an amine-oxidase inhibitor and dopa. On this test, the effects of the MSH tripeptide were exerted regardless of whether the pituitary gland was present or not, and none of the other endocrine glands were necessary for its action. Subsequent to this finding, numerous other peptides have been found to be active on the dopapotentiation test. Most of these peptides are much more potent that the common psychoactive (e.g., tranquilizer) agents now in use. Drs. Kastin and Sandman called attention to two groups of psychoactive agents that have major effects on the central nervous system: Amytriptyline (an effective agent in the treatment of mental depression), and L-dopa (which is helpful in Parkinson's disease).

Since these peptides are naturally occurring substances, the question arises, "How can one use available information to further research?" Should it be used, for example, to explore ideas in mental retardation or in some other clinical challenge?" As Drs. Kastin and Sandman point out, what is required, of course, is an animal model of mental retardation, but this does not exist. Some pharmaceutical companies have in fact set up their own research models, calling them "animal models of human mental depression," or "animal models of Parkinson's disease." There is little research basis for this approach, however, and attempting to judge the effectiveness of models becomes a vicious circle. For example, the dopapotentiation test is called an "animal model" of mental depression and Parkinson's disease because pharmacological agents known to be active (or helpful) in these disorders are active in this particular test. But what if a whole new type of agent arose—similar to a peptide? The agent might initially be thought the answer to mental depression or Parkinson's disease—but when tried on the dopapotentiation test it is found to be ineffective. It probably would never get a clinical trial! The vicious circle is, of

193

course, that the dopapotentiation test is predicated on agents already known to be active, so that all one ends up with—if one uses these current "animal models"—is the "me too" type of drugs. These considerations have pertinence to mental retardation because we still do not know *how* MIF acts in the dopapotentiation test, and yet there are some clinically promising results. In actuality, then, it is not necessary to know the exact mechanism of action or the natural compound of a drug in order to arrive at a therapeutically active agent—even though that is most desirable. The point is that any given peptide is *not* the answer to a given disease: MIF, for instance, is not "the answer" to Parkinson's disease or mental depression, and MSH is not "the answer" to different manifestations of the symptom of mental retardation. The study of peptides does offer, however, a new approach to a wide variety of central nervous system disorders. There are still many unanswered puzzles. For example, when peptides are injected—and at the very time that one sees central nervous system effects or some of the endocrine effects—very little, if any, of these compounds are noted to persist in the blood stream.

MSH, TRH, ENKEPHALINS, AND ENDORHINS

Drs. Kastin and Sandman offered a detailed review of the melanocyte-stimulating hormone (MSH), a peptide with between 13 and 18 amino acids of various forms that has been used in patients with mental retardation. MSH was originally thought to come from the pituitary gland and to cause amphibians like the frog to change color and adapt better to their environment. In the embryo, the melanocyte cells are of neurocrest origin and thus Drs. Kastin and Sandman felt that MSH could produce distinct effects on the central nervous system. Their early studies on animals have been almost identical to those noted subsequently with humans. The administration of MSH appears to increase the ability of the organism, be it rat or human, to pay attention (i.e., increased performance on the Benton Visual Retention Test). The authors have done a number of studies in humans, such as with college students, that found increased visual discrimination at different levels of luminescence (i.e., light). The college students were able to better discriminate whether dots were present on a screen or not. MSH also increased the threshold for detection and discriminaton of whether the dots were paired or not, and focused the process of attention onto a particular area. The authors noted that they did not originally intend to do research on mental retardation and did not even consider that MSH could play a role in mental retardation. When they saw that MSH positively affected the process of attention, and knowing that mentally retarded individuals are widely reported to have attentional deficits, they decided to focus their investigation in this area. Their studies have shown that retarded individuals who are administered MSH show an average of 25% improvement in specific areas, which is statistically significant. Now the question becomes: How does MSH act? Is it improving these mentally retarded individuals (or the college students) by some kind of mechanistic action? The authors' research with regional blood flow studies, evoked potentials, and biogenic amines has shown that MSH focuses its effects in the occipital lobe of the brain. The effects of MSH in rats injected in the first week of life and then tested as adults were also retested—finding similar long-lasting and apparently permanent changes. This is remarkable!

The authors next turned to another peptide that has attracted some attention—TRH, a tripeptide that has three amino acids. Some of its properties and actions are directly referable to mental retardation. First, it seems that there may be a small subgroup of depressed mentally retarded people (and nonretarded depressed people) who respond favorably to TRH. This may well indicate the heterogeneous nature of mental depression and mental retardation. The fact that a subgroup of depressed people responds favorably to this peptide has, unfortunately, not attracted the interest of any pharmaceutical company, however, because of the economic impracticability of catering to a relatively small population. Accordingly, large scale study in this area may be thwarted. Second, studying TRH in mental depression was predicated upon results in an animal model, and we still do not know what animal model should be utilized for mental retardation. Should we, perhaps, screen all mentally retarded individuals for the naturally occurring peptides? Drs. Kastin and Sandman also noted their past experience with the TRH therapeutic effect, in which they found that a significant percentage of depressed people had a blunted thyroid stimulating hormone response following the administration of TRH. This is the normal endocrinological response that is seen in everyone except those with pituitary tumors or hyperthyroidism, but it was *not* seen in depressed people. Thus, this therapeutic "failure" has become an excellent diagnostic and prognostic technique for assessing the presence of depression in the human. It was a completely unexpected finding, yet this happens often in clinical medicine in which a compound used for one purpose is found to have a widely divergent diagnostic or therapeutic application. The current study of peptides could have a similar spinoff effect in mental retardation. For example, a peptide utilized for diagnostic testing of the pituitary gland might be found useful in treating retarded individuals. It is not inconceivable.

The review in Chapter 12 of the peptide studies performed by Drs. Kastin and Sandman is most pertinent to mental retardation. These studies of peptides in newborn rats have not been done elsewhere. Newborn rats were injected in the first week of life with TRH, and the rats were not tested until they were adults. The testing (running in an eight-choice maze) showed that the rats who received TRH as newborns ran the maze faster and with fewer errors *as adults*, while other adult rats who had been treated with TRH only a week before testing showed no effect. This particular peptide apparently has some major effect on the organization of the brain at an early developmental stage. The implication of these studies is that perhaps someday we will have the diagnostic tools—if our pharmacological studies are reflecting what is going on physiologically—to either detect deficiencies or excesses of these naturally occurring peptides, and thereby correct them at an early stage. Even if the mental retardation stems from some other cause, perhaps administration of these peptides could produce dramatic improvements or significantly alter the long-term outcome.

Lastly, Chapter 12 discussed enkephalins and endorphins—the peptides that appear to be the brain's own opiates. When research first suggested the presence of morphine receptors in the brain, this did not make sense, since morphine is a plant. The presence of naturally occurring opiates in the brain has been determined, however, and their peptide structure has been discerned. Interestingly, the pituitary peptide, β-lipotropin has 91 amino acids, and it contains within it the important parts of ACTH and MSH in the active core, as well as *all* of the enkephalins and endorphins. Also, the 61st to 65th position of β-lipotropin includes the enkephalins, and the 61st to 91st β-lipotropin is known as "β-endorphin."

The morphine-like findings produced the initial research-clinical interest in the pain-relieving potential of enkephalins and endorphins. However, it is now accepted that there are behavioral effects of these "brain opiates" that can be dissociated from their pain alleviating effects. Dr. Kastin and colleagues tested a sample of rats as to the effects of enkephalins in a maze test, and rats given enkephalin ran it faster and with fewer errors than rats not getting enkephalin—just as had been noted with MSH. Beyond treatment aspects of this finding, Dr. Kastin noted that since a valid animal model of mental retardation is not currently available, perhaps what we need to do is to take a compound that is active in mental retardation (and MSH appears to be an excellent candidate among the peptides), determine those specific brain systems in which MSH is active, and then reason that another peptide more active in that system might be worth trying in mental retardation. Following this kind of reasoning, the use of the enkephalins in mental retardation could be of great potential in furthering our understanding of behavioral and other central nervous system actions.

A final point mentioned in Chapter 12 and further examined in Chapter 14 by Dr. Sandman is one that continues to bother many professionals in peptide research: How do peptides exert their central action? It could be that they do not even enter the brain, but exert their affects in the peripheral segments of the nervous system. We know that they are rapidly degraded and only a small fragment is active. Or maybe the peptides just increase the permeability of some other amino acids or some other compounds—rather than directly exerting their own action. Over the last few years, accumulating evidence indicates that a very small number of these peptides *do* cross the blood-brain barrier intact. Probably, however, not more than one-tenth of a percent of the L-dopa that is used in the treatment of Parkinson's disease crosses, so it could be that a very small amount is all that is required for a significant effect.

In summary, Chapter 12 reviews what is known about the peptides that have been shown to directly affect the brain and its subsystems (with the addition of vasopressin, which affects memory from different patterns of activity). These are all *naturally occurring compounds,* that in clinical trials have exhibited great pertinence to mental retardation. Drs. Kastin and Sandman have been primarily interested in what they have termed the "multiple independent actions" of the peptides—their endocrine, and extra-endocrine effects. It is these extra-endocrine effects and the presence of amino acid cores in the same molecule that apparently produce significantly changed behavior. The more recent concept of the behavioral/narcotic dissociation of the opiate peptides has also gained their attention. Soon, it is hoped, we will arrive at the stage where we can routinely examine not only the endocrine, but the extra-endocrine effects, and thus be able to administer a blood test to a young couple desirous of having children to see whether they have alterations in their own endogenous peptide levels (or at a later stage via amniocentesis). Further, we should also consider treating these very early diagnosed individuals *in utero*, or at least during the first week of life (as Dr. Kastin has done with newborn and infant animals), rather than only as adults. Thus, the peptides hold great promise for improving the learning and behavioral competence of mentally retarded individuals. We must look beyond the concept of fixed levels of improvement in retarded individuals. The last 5 years have seen an explosion in research concerning peptides that are active in the central nervous system. These findings show great promise in the clinical (i.e., applied research) studies accomplished to date.

TREATMENT MODEL OF ALZHEIMER'S DISEASE

Dr. Kenneth L. Davis, author of Chapter 13, related to me a scientific anecdote about the peptide vasopressin—a peptide of great interest to him because of his ongoing study with the nerve transmitter substance acetylcholine. He notes that there is a breed of rat called the Brattleboro rat that has a vasopressin deficit and also develops diabetes incipitious. It does not learn very well, nor does it retrieve information well. Dr. Davis notes that though he does not like to talk about "animal models of disease," in some ways the Brattleboro rat is a mentally retarded animal. Interestingly, the vasopressin—which in many animal models has been shown to augment the ability of animals to learn tasks and retrieve information from tasks that they have previously learned—is under the control of the neurotransmitter acetylcholine that Dr. Davis addresses directly in Chapter 13.

In Chaper 13, Dr. Davis noted that until recently, the possibility that a drug might be administered to an individual to improve memory was considered a remote possibility. Such claims had been made occasionally, but had rarely withstood rigorous double-blind control studies. It is for these reasons that Dr. Davis became very excited when he noted that upon the administration of physostigmine—a drug that can directly inhibit the enzyme acetyl-cholinesterase and thereby increase brain acetylcholine—he was able, under carefully con-trolled conditions—to greatly improve the ability of normal subjects to learn. The relevance of such work to mental retardation is clear: In the context of a sypmtom (mental retardation) in which there is not a significant drug treatment available, it would seem that the ability to pharmacologically enhance memory is particularly relevant.

Dr. Davis's involvement in the field of memory came about rather accidentally. His initial involvement in attempts to improve memory (especially in patients with Alzheimer's disease) began about 8 years ago. At that time he had become interested in the possible effects of increasing brain acetylcholine levels in patients who displayed mania. His interest in mania stemmed from a 1972 professional report that physostigmine had a major effect in decreasing manic symptoms in manic-depressive mentally ill patients. The possibility was posed that, by changing acetylcholine levels, the noted improvement in manic and normal patients was mediated through changes in the levels of the brain's neurotransmitters. Dr. Davis became actively involved in looking at spinal fluid metabolites of selected neurotransmitters in manic patients, and observing what happened. In fact, what did occur was that when he administered physostigmine to normal people who did not have a mood disorder, he did not produce a change in mood. Far from it, the only real effect produced was that the normal subjects became physically ill. So he concluded that the reported finding of the role of physostigmine in mania was really a result of making manic people physically sick: When they became physically ill, it was not difficult to control their mania! His next study was again performed on manic patients: whether physostigmine could actually reverse manic symptoms in manic-depressive patients. He hypothesized that the subjects would get physically sick and because they got sick they would no longer be manic. To his surprise the manic symptoms decreased before anybody got sick or nauseated! The physostigmine really was accomplishing what colleagues had reported: It did reverse mania. Notable in his future memory studies was the finding that these manic patients, when they received about 1 mg of physostigmine (rather than the 2-mg dosage level that would reverse mania), would frequently say, "You know, Doctor, this is great stuff. You ought to bottle it. My memory has become great—I'm just thinking so much sharper than I ever did before." He initially dismissed such statements as manic euphoria! But the patients kept saying it so repeatedly that he started to listen. Joining with his colleagues in experimental and cognitive psychology, Dr. Davis devised a carefully controlled study to measure whether physostigmine really was improving memory. An initial study of normal young people assessed the effect of physostigmine on one day and saline solution on another day in double-blind research conditions. They received 1 mg of physostigmine by a constant infusion over a 1-hour time period. Tests were administered on both short-term and long-term memory. The results were amazing: Across *all* trials on the physostigmine injection days the subjects learned significantly more information than they did on the saline injection days—and the differences were highly statistically significant. The implications of these findings were obvious and, in an article in the journal *Science*, he and his colleagues concluded that physostigmine should be able to improve the memory capacity of people with Alzheimer's disease (a markedly disabling disorder of late life manifested by severe memory and learning decays).

Dr. Davis has also commented (personal communication, 1981) on why he decided to do further research on Alzheimer dementia and not give physostigmine to persons with mental retardation:

A number of investigators have fairly well established that, as people age, there is a specific loss of cholinergic neurons as reflected by the decrease in an enzyme (acetylcholinesterase) that only lies in cholinergic neurons. This loss of enzyme is much, much greater in Alzheimer's disease so that Alzheimer's disease is a specific lesion—at least from a neurochemical level of choline acetyltransferase—of neurons and that the loss is greatest in the frontal cortex, the temporal areas, and in the hippocampus. We therefore had a specific disease with a specific neurochemical substance involved—which is *not* the case in the vast majority of mentally retarded individuals. I could not find any specific subgroup of the mentally retarded that had such a specific disorder. In other words, I could not find in mental retardation any specific neurochemical deficiency wherein I could propose a rational pharmacological intervention. That work has simply not been done! Instead we turned, therefore, to Alzheimer's disease, and to specific age-related memory deficit.

Dr. Davis's observation and his research on the effectiveness of physostigmine in improving memory in patients with Alzheimer's disease clearly illustrates that the question of whether this drug will (or will not) work in mental retardation revolves around: 1) a relative lack of professional interest in the known biochemical errors in mental retardation (e.g., the inborn errors of metabolism) and the documented finding of Alzheimer lesions in Down syndrome, and 2) the need to take a more aggressive posture toward reversing the memory changes in mental retardation, rather than viewing these deficits as "fixed" phenomena. The latter dimension is analogous to the situation in Alzheimer's disease, since a scant 10 years ago this disorder was literally enmeshed within the vague diagnostic category of "senility"—a category of disorders that have uniformly been viewed as hopeless. Truly, Alzheimer's disease has not changed in the 76 years since it was first described by Dr. Alois Alzheimer—it is our understanding of its mechanisms and the professional posture that it *can* be altered that has changed.

Dr. Davis believes that his physostigmine treatment model of Alzheimer's disease is *directly* applicable to many of the specific disease processes noted in mental retardation. Clearly, the restoration of memory abilities for Alzheimer's patients *has* obvious relevance to the question of whether we can develop a drug that can improve memory in people with mental retardation. If we reflect on the findings of the authors in this volume, it is eye-opening just how histopathologically abnormal many people with mental retardation can be. I would not presume to suggest that some of these people would improve by the above treatment model. Yet, such individuals often have some remaining normal substrate of brain architecture—as pointed out in Chapters 4 and 5. There must be some subgroups of mentally retarded individuals—in fact, I would be surprised if there were not—that we might find who have a cholinergic deficit. After all, acetylcholine is demonstrated abundantly in the literature on animals to affect memory and encoding and retrieval—all processes involved in learning. So I would be surprised if we could not find something to help mentally retarded persons.

In closing, Chapter 13 suggests that future research aimed at the application of the physostigmine treatment approach to mental retardation should include: 1) assessment of the choline acetyltransferase activity, 2) study of the acetylcholine synthesis, 3) study of high affinity choline uptake and, 4) examination of various other parameters of cholinergic functioning in retarded persons. Dr. Davis believes that we should not limit investigations to the acetylcholine transmitter alone, since it is very likely that other neurotransmitter abnormalities are found in some subgroups of people with mental retardation.

On the basis of the above suggested research thrusts, the findings of specific abnormalities would suggest guidelines for designing rational pharmacological approaches. The challenge, therefore, according to Dr. Davis, is to use the neurochemical procedures that have been fruitful and beneficial to create a picture of some forms of the symptom of mental retardation: the pathophysiology of aging (e.g., Alzheimer's disease, Huntington's disease, and certainly Parkinson's disease)—is perhaps the best model. Truly, this research approach suggests that we can find treatment routes to the pharmacology of some of the basic problems of a wide variety of mentally retarded individuals. Such an approach and commitment could also excite other psychopharmacologists and scientists to become involved in similar research endeavors, the ultimate goal being to maximally change the learning and memory potentials of mentally retarded persons.

Curative Aspects of Mental Retardation:
Biomedical and Behavioral Advances
edited by Frank J. Menolascino, M.D., Ronald Neman, Ph.D., and Jack A. Stark, Ph.D.
Copyright 1983   Paul H. Brookes Publishing Co., Inc.   Baltimore · London

section IV

EXTERNAL ENVIRONMENTAL LEARNING ENHANCEMENT

Introduction

JACK A. STARK, PH.D.
UNIVERSITY OF NEBRASKA MEDICAL CENTER
OMAHA, NEBRASKA

D R. EARL C. BUTTERFIELD SUMMARIZES his approach to the opening chapter of Section IV (Chapter 15) by stating, ''. . . this chapter presents an optimistic case for the heady possibility that behavioral science is on the threshold of delivering ways to improve human thinking to the extent that we will be able to claim cures for the cognitive deficits that lead to mental retardation.'' Dr. Butterfield observes that there are barriers to be overcome, but that owing to dramatic progress in the last several years, these barriers do not now look insurmountable. It is our (the editors') conclusion that during the 1980s we will be able to fashion efficient learning environments that will greatly accelerate the acquisition of enhanced levels of global intelligence and social-adaptive behaviors.

In addition, there are many natural research bridges between the *intrinsic* treatments of biochemical replacement/enhancement of neurotransmitters (e.g., via the neuropeptides as reviewed by Drs. Abba J. Kastin and Curt A. Sandman in Chapter 12, increased efficiency of the neurotransmitters as noted by Dr. Kenneth L. Davis in Chapter 13), and the *extrinsic* treatments (provision of human learning environments that can fully help the retarded individual to utilize his or her original/augmented biological equipment). The authors in this volume have stressed the clear and recurrent opportunities that transdisciplinary approaches can provide in describing the dimension of curative goals. Indeed, the possibilities that can result from the orchestration of the recurrent and dynamic interplays between intrinsic biological and extrinsic environmental challenges aimed at the discovery of curative approaches is perhaps the most exciting aspect of this book.

In Chapter 16, Dr. Sidney W. Bijou reviews a well-researched strategy for the prevention of mild and moderate levels of mental retardation in young children. Utilizing a behavioral analysis point of view, the strategy involves modifying (through specific and systematic training) the behavior of parents and teachers in order to provide the young child with more and new opportunities (and incentives) for intellectual and academic achievement. This objective has already been recognized through current programs that integrate ongoing behavioral-educational programs and that have clearly demonstrated replicable success in effecting major changes in parent and teaching practices. The current research results are clear. If these ''special-special'' educational procedures are utilized in very young *mildly* retarded youngsters, they result in a child who, by the end of the fourth grade, demonstrates intellectual and social-adaptive competencies within the normal range of development on objective tests. Dr. Bijou strongly believes that an extension of these research approaches to the basically similar learning problems of *moderately* retarded children will permit such youngsters to function in the upper mild or borderline intellectual levels of development. It should be noted that the results of these ''state of the art'' intervention programs (with mildly retarded youngsters) have often resulted in essentially normal levels of functioning. In this context then, and if the procedures are applied at a young enough age, we *are* now able to cure this very large grouping (75%–85%) of the entire population of mentally retarded individuals! That is, we currently have the behavioral technology and knowledge to move individuals from the ''retarded functioning range'' to an average intellectual and social-adaptive range via environmental enrichment and engineering.

The challenge now becomes one of disseminating these behavioral analytic oriented intervention programs into the mainstream of education so that this secondary prevention (i.e., cure) becomes available to all mildly retarded children who have been and are now viewed as ''forever'' retarded.

Dr. Gershon Berkson, in Chapter 17, presents an environmental approach to curing mental retardation. His analysis embodies an ecological model that seeks to prevent the cumulative deficits in many mentally retarded children. His hypothesis, however, goes beyond the previous authors of this volume who stress early childhood intervention and education, and cites research that demonstrates that prevention of accumulating deficits can be conducted in adolescence and perhaps throughout adulthood. This is especially the case if environmental enrichment is provided that minimizes the disabling effects.

In summary, Chapters 15–17 provide us with a great deal of encouragement that the behavioral sciences can play a major role in the curative aspects of mental retardation in the next two decades.

Curative Aspects of Mental Retardation:
Biomedical and Behavioral Advances
edited by Frank J. Menolascino, M.D., Ronald Neman, Ph.D., and Jack A. Stark, Ph.D.
Copyright 1983   Paul H. Brookes Publishing Co., Inc.   Baltimore · London

chapter 15

To Cure Cognitive Deficits
of Mentally Retarded Persons

EARL C. BUTTERFIELD, PH.D.
University of Washington
Seattle, Washington

HAS BEHAVIORAL RESEARCH provided bases for curing mental retardation by making it possible to teach the skills that add up to intelligence? Not yet is the only realistic answer. Will behavioral research provide such bases soon? Perhaps is probably a more wishful than realistic answer. But wishfulness is sometimes remarkably heuristic, so this chapter presents an optimistic case for the heady possibility that behavioral science is on the threshold of delivering ways to improve thinking to the extent that we will be able to claim cures for the cognitive deficits that lead to mental retardation. I doubt that any behavioral researcher believes that his or her work, or even the combined products of all behavioral researchers, is as close to permitting a behavioral cure of mental retardation as is suggested in this chapter. Nevertheless, this author is comfortable suggesting it because of some promising trends in behavior modification and cognitive development.

For years, behavior modifiers and their basic science colleagues, the behavior analysts, have been the behavioral researchers who are most optimistic about the possibility of making important practical improvements in the behavior of mentally retarded persons. Their optimism is predicated in part on the philosophical belief that any behavior, no matter how complex, can be analyzed into teachable components that can be chained together to create effective performance. Many scientists reject this belief as simplistic and naive, and until recently the rejection could be rationalized by observing that behavior modifiers had not tried to teach retarded people to do anything more "thoughty" than toileting and cleansing themselves. Many behavior modifiers still teach exclusively such nonintellective, though badly

The preparation of this chapter, and the execution of much of the research upon which its ideas are based, was supported by U.S.P.H.S. grants HD-00870 (Donald Baer, Principal Investigator), HD-08911 (John Belmont, Principal Investigator), and HD-13029 (Earl Butterfield, Principal Investigator). I could not have prepared the chapter if I had not had the benefit of exchanging ideas over the years with John Belmont and Donald Baer. Pamela Hudson, Tom Heffernan, and Donn Nielsen assisted in preparation of the manuscript.

needed skills. Nevertheless, the trend now is for behavior modifiers to try to promote intellective skills such as self-management of learning (Bornstein & Quevillon, 1976) and comprehension and production of speech (Guess, Sailor, & Baer, 1974). Many behavior modifiers (see Meichenbaum, 1976) have also abandoned their former refusal to acknowledge the existence of unobservable behaviors, such as thought and the use of grammar.

In addition, behavior modifiers have now accrued enough success at teaching "thoughty" behaviors to make it harder than it used to be to reject their optimistic philosophy. The trend for behavior modifiers to tackle more intellective behaviors is one reason to believe that behavioral research will soon provide ways to cure the cognitive deficits of mentally retarded individuals. Behavior modifiers are not only optimistic, they are among the most resourceful innovators of successful teaching procedures in the behavioral sciences.

An encouraging trend is also well underway in developmental cognitive science. Developmental cognitive scientists, like their basic science colleagues, psychology's general experimentalists, have been committed for years to the belief that cognition cannot be taught. Consequently, their methods have been observational, inferential, and diagnostic, rather than instructional. Many developmental cognitivists still employ such methods exclusively. Nevertheless, the tendency is for more and more developmentalists to employ instructional techniques designed to promote mature thinking by young and retarded children (Belmont & Butterfield, 1977). This trend is another reason to believe that behavioral research will soon provide ways to cure the cognitive deficits of mentally retarded persons, because developmental cognitivists are among the most knowledgeable scientists about what should be taught to make a person intelligent.

Two other trends offer longer-term promise that behavioral cures of cognitive deficits may stem from behavioral research: Speci-

fically, the renewed interest of general experimental psychologists in individual differences in cognition (Carroll & Maxwell, 1979) and the increasing focus of educational psychologists on cognitive processes (Wittrock & Lumsdaine, 1977). The first of these trends, the clarification of individual differences in cognition, is propitious because clarification must eventually lead to improved techniques for reducing those differences, and because general experimental psychologists are among the most effective analysts of complex human behaviors. If general experimentalists give serious attention to individual differences, and some show every indication that they will (Hunt, Frost, & Lunneborg, 1973), we can reasonably expect important clarification of cognitive differences among people. The second trend, the increasing focus on cognitive processes, offers hope because curing the cognitive deficits of mentally retarded people is an educational undertaking. Until recently, educational researchers were insufficiently concerned with cognitive processes to be regarded as allies in the attempt to teach intelligence. Both of these trends must be regarded as promising only in the long term, however, because general experimental psychology and instructional psychology are fields with well-established agendas that for the most part will not produce information to help cure mental retardation.

In sum, this author feels secure in the argument that behavioral research will produce ways to cure cognitive deficits of mentally retarded persons because of four trends in behavioral science. The most comforting trends for the short run are that 1) behavior modifiers are increasingly teaching "thoughty" behaviors, and 2) developmental cognitive psychologists are more often using instructional methods. Long-term optimism is warranted for the trends of 1) general experimental psychologists focusing more often on individual differences in cognition, and 2) educational psychologists focusing more directly on cognitive processes.

Whether trends in scientific subdisciplines

are an adequate basis for predicting or for being optimistic about any sort of progress can surely be argued both ways. In this author's view, the four developments in question may be more reliable indicators of future developments than is sometimes the case, because they represent impressive convergence among formerly disparate viewpoints. Consider the fact that the schism between behaviorists and cognitivists over the nature of language and whether it can be studied experimentally has been mended by both cognitivists who are studying child language (Bricker & Bricker, 1974) and by behavior modifiers who are producing language training programs (Guess et al., 1974). In view of the history of vitriolic dispute across this schism (see Statts, 1974), the convergence of behavior modifiers and cognitivists on the same substantive concerns (described below) and similar instructional methods offers, in this author's opinion, substantial hope that progress will be made toward curing the behavioral aspects of mental retardation. Consider, too, that the differences in focus and method between experimental and differential psychologists have existed since the beginning of scientific psychology. The recent interest of general experimental psychologists in individual differences (Hunt et al., 1973), of differential psychologists in experimental procedures (Jensen, 1979), and of differential psychologists in the interaction of instructional procedures and ability factors (Cronbach & Snow, 1977) represent a rapprochement of revolutionary proportions. Moreover, it is an "alliance" that seems designed to produce progress toward curing cognitive deficits, and, indeed, some progress has already resulted (see Carrol & Maxwell, 1979).

THE STATE OF THE SCIENCES

It would be lovely if the above-noted trends within subdisciplines of psychology would progress straight to a cure for the cognitive deficits of the mentally retarded population. Even this author's most hopeful scenario is not so simple. More deliberate focusing of effort is required than will come from the natural evolution of those trends. Intense attention must be paid to the barriers that separate our present capabilities from what we must attain in order to increase intelligence through training. A prime purpose of a volume such as this is to focus intense attention; the art comes in deciding what to emphasize. Brief consideration of the state of the relevant sciences shows that the barriers have been defined.

Language Training

Fristoe (1976) has determined that more than 200 language training programs have been implemented in our country alone. Of these, perhaps seven have a sufficiently broad scope and are specified in sufficient detail to be considered serious ways to cure general deficits in language use. The seven are the programs by Miller and Yoder (1972a, 1972b, 1974), by MacDonald and colleagues (MacDonald, 1976; MacDonald & Blott, 1974; MacDonald, Blott, Gordon, Spiegel, & Hartman, 1974; MacDonald & Nichols, 1974), by Bricker and colleagues (Bricker, 1972; Bricker & Bricker, 1970; Bricker, Dennison, & Bricker, 1975); by Kent (1974); by Carrier and Peak (1975); by Guess et al. (1974); and by Stremel and colleagues (Stremel, 1972; Stremel & Waryas, 1974). The differences among these programs are real, but their similarities are striking. Nearly all use teaching methods based on principles of operant conditioning and teach grammatical forms identified as developmentally critical by psycholinguistic research. All of the programs employ one teacher per child, and all use regular assessment of children's performance as guides to the next skills to be taught. Despite the substantial amounts of data that have been generated by the use of regular assessment, none of the programs has been analyzed fully enough to allow judgment of which of its techniques are most effective. Consequently, all of the language training programs remain extremely complex and detailed. Moreover, none has been shown to produce effective language use outside of the training environment, even though all have been shown to create important practical improvements in language use by severely and moderately retarded children in the training environment. The complexity and detail of language teaching programs and the failure to have established that they promote language use outside of the training environment are the two main barriers to using these programs to train linguistic aspects of intelligence. These barriers will be discussed more later in the chapter, since they are the same ones identified in other key areas of investigation.

Memory Training

Memory training is not new to developmental psychology (Pyles, 1932), but until recently it was infrequently used (see Belmont & Butterfield, 1977) because few memory tasks were analyzed well enough to allow the design of instructions aimed at the thinking processes responsible for good performance. That changed dramatically after Flavell, Beach, and Chinsky (1966) used lipreading to identify the verbal mediators used by accurate child memorizers as they studied for later recall. By now, many investigators have used various procedures to identify effective elements in the thinking of good memorizers (e.g., Belmont & Butterfield, 1969; Flavell, Friedricks, & Hoyt, 1970; Kellas, McCauley, & McFarland, 1975; Resnick & Glaser, 1976; Rohwer, 1973; Turnure, Buium, & Thurlow, 1976). Thus, armed with an understanding of what good thinking amounts to for particular memory tasks, fair numbers of these investigators have undertaken to train children to produce the good thinking that they do not produce on their own, thereby showing that minutes of instruction can bring ordinary children to levels of performance they would normally achieve only years later (Belmont & Butterfield, 1971; Brown, Campione, Bray, & Wilcox, 1973; Hagen, Meacham, & Mesibov, 1970). Moreover, mildly retarded children can be brought in a few hours to levels of performance that they would never achieve without instruction

(Brown & Barclay, 1976; Butterfield, Wambold, & Belmont, 1973).

The instructions used to secure accurate memory performance from young children and mildly retarded people are simple, and the resulting memory gains swift and dramatic. Despite the simplicity of the instructions, discovering how to fashion them has required long and detailed programs of laboratory analysis of particular memory tasks (see Brown & DeLoache, 1978; Butterfield, Siladi, & Belmont, 1980). The understandings on which the instructions have been based are complex and detailed. The prospect of the huge effort that would be required to produce such understanding for the full range of tasks that would need to be trained in order to raise mentally retarded individuals to normal levels for all varieties of memory functioning has prevented developmental psychologists (see Butterfield et al., 1973) from trying to devise memory training programs analogous to those developed by language trainers. Moreover, even though memory instruction has resulted in swift and dramatic performance gains, those gains have seldom endured or transferred to closely related memory problems.

Having analyzed the thinking required for accurate performance on particular memory tasks, and having instructed children and retarded people to use such thinking when performing memory tasks, researchers have found that the instructed subjects seldom use the effective ways of thinking very long after the instruction or in situations that are not identical to those in which they were taught. Thus, the same barriers that stand in the way of training linguistic aspects of intelligence exist also in training mnemonic aspects of intelligence. The necessary understandings and techniques are too complex and detailed, and the results obtained so far have seldom endured or generalized beyond the training environment.

Piagetian and Other Cognitive Training

Reviews of Piagetian and other intelligence training efforts (see Belmont & Butterfield,

1977; Kuhn, 1974) reveal the same barriers encountered in efforts to train language and memory. Complex and detailed instructional protocols or preliminary analyses are required, and even though the induced performance gains have been impressive, they have seldom generalized. The status of the relevant sciences is thus encouraging with respect to the possibility of teaching intelligence, but two imposing barriers remain to be crossed.

CREATING GENERALIZED INSTRUCTIONAL EFFECTS

To be termed intelligent, a person must behave cognitively in generally effective ways. This is the reason that intelligence training must produce general effects before we will be able to cure the cognitive deficits of mentally retarded persons. All educators acknowledge the necessity of teaching so that learning transfers to diverse settings. Most behavioral scientists who study mentally retarded persons' thinking and learning agree that the test of whether their studies have clarified intelligence is whether the studies lead to instructions that not only raise retarded persons' performance levels, but also transfer widely outside the training environment (see Brown, 1977; Butterfield, 1979; Fisher & Zeaman, 1973). Thus, there are strong scientific, as well as practical, reasons to promote cognitive instructional transfer. Two distinct approaches are being tried. One has grown from the behavior modification literature (see Stokes & Baer, 1977), and the other from the cognitive development literature (see Butterfield, 1979).

Behavioral Approaches [1]

Behaviorism began with the study of simple behaviors of animals. Such study showed that the influence of prior experience upon behavior was mediated by the present environment, so that behavior could be controlled by manipulating the present environment. Therefore, behaviorists came to regard the actions of experimenters as actions of environments. When behaviorists turned their attention to simple behaviors of human students, they thought of teachers' actions as actions of the environment. Thus, both experimenters and teachers were viewed by behaviorists as using conditioning (e.g. contingencies of reinforcement, punishment, and extinction), controlling stimuli, and motivation (deprivation and histories of reinforcement). These actions are called *behavior analysis* when used by experimenters and *behavior modification* when used by teachers.

When behaviorists first extended their approach to complex behaviors, such as language and mathematics, they treated the complex behaviors as if they were simply combinations of simple behaviors. To make this possible, they analyzed the tasks requiring complex behaviors and then used behavioral techniques to teach the simple behaviors revealed by their task analyses. Often, this approach produced the complex behavior that had been analyzed. When it did not, the inference was drawn that prerequisite behaviors were acquired, and rational analysis was employed to identify these prerequisites, which were then taught as any other behavior. Task analysis gradually became an important procedure of behaviorists, and it undermined the idea that all behavior could be controlled by manipulating the present environment. While that idea works for simple animal and human behaviors, it does not work for complex behaviors that depend upon prerequisite learnings. Prerequisites are historical events which indicate that behavior is structured. As this was revealed by task analysis, behaviorists had to abandon the idea that behavior has no inherent structure.

Acknowledging structured behavior is the same as acknowledging rules and processes, since the nature of structured behavior is that

---

[1]The ideas in this section were brought home to me by Donald Baer, to whom I remain indebted.

it is general across stimuli and responses. Thus, the rules of addition, subtraction, multiplication, division, square root extraction, integration, and so on, allow people to make an infinity of responses to an infinity of stimuli. Such general behavior could not possibly be taught by considering every number as a separate stimulus and every sum, difference, root, etc., as a separate response, which is how a behaviorist who did not acknowledge the structure of behavior would need to approach the teaching of mathematics. Acknowledging the structure of behavior required that behaviorists acknowledge the generality of behavior.

Behavior analysts and behavior modifiers knew about generalization before they tried to manage structured behavior, but they did not regard it as a process to be promoted. Generalization was viewed as a passive outgrowth of conditioning, and it has yet to become an object of behavioral analysis. But a behaviorist technology of generalization is now emerging. Stokes and Baer (1977) cataloged seven ways that behavior modifiers promote generalization.

1. Introduce Natural Maintaining Contingencies According to Stokes and Baer, the least direct but most dependable way to insure the transfer of learned responses from a teaching environment to an everyday environment is to teach responses that will be rewarded in the learner's everyday environment. Assuming an environment that rewards intelligent behavior, this can be a simple and expedient approach. Its effectiveness can be enhanced by teaching ways to solicit rewards in the everyday environment. For example, Seymour and Stokes (1976) taught institutionalized delinquent girls to recognize when the quality of their work was good, and to call the attention of nearby adults to their work when it was good, which resulted in fairly consistent reinforcement from an environment that was otherwise not reinforcing to these girls.

2. Train Enough Exemplars When the teaching of one exemplar of a generalizable lesson does not result in generalization,

teaching a few more examples frequently will. Adding additional instructional exemplars promotes generalization both across stimuli, as when teaching a child how to greet any unfamiliar person (Stokes, Baer, & Jackson, 1974), and across responses, as when teaching a child to imitate any action by an adult, to comply with any instruction, or to pluralize any noun. Stokes and Baer (1977) noted that two exemplars are frequently all that are needed to promote generalization across either stimuli or responses.

3. Train Loosely Behavior analysts, and to a lesser extent, behavior modifiers, usually exercise tight control over the stimuli they present and the responses they teach. However, loosening one's training approach by varying stimuli and allowable responses, produces wider generalization of the responses learned (Schroeder & Baer, 1972). Absolute sloppiness will not do, but deliberate variation of learning materials and liberal definition of acceptable responses can promote generalized behavior.

4. Use Indiscriminable Contingencies Stokes and Baer noted that if a child could be taught a response under conditions that prevented the child from discriminating the environment in which he or she would be rewarded from environments in which he or she would not be rewarded, then generalization across environments would be likely, just as generalization across time is likely when learning results from intermittent schedules of reinforcement. Properly programmed delay of reinforcement is one way to make environmental features indiscriminable. A disadvantage of the technique is that while it can promote generalization (Schwartz & Hawkins, 1970), delay of reinforcement slows learning.

5. Use Common Stimuli Teaching in an environment that contains stimuli like those found in the everyday environment can promote generalization to the everyday environment. Even people can be the stimuli common to the teaching and everyday environments. Though Stokes and Baer (1977) did not discuss it, this author cannot help but ask:

What are the conditions necessary to make the learner himself the common stimulus? As is discussed below, this is a behaviorist's form of the main question cognitivists are trying to answer about generalization.

6. Teach Mediators To produce mediated generalizations, one teaches a response that can be used whenever a particular sort of problem is encountered. Language responses are the most often taught mediating responses. For example, Risley and Hart (1968) rewarded young disadvantaged children for reporting at the end of each day what they had been playing with during the day. As days passed these children varied what they played with, in order to be able to report it, so as to earn rewards. Thus, verbal reports led to generalized changes in play. This same technique has been used to promote generalized social interaction (Rogers-Warren & Baer, 1976).

7. Train to Generalize The most direct, though least frequently used, behaviorist approach to producing generalization is to treat generalization as a response, and to reward it directly. For example, Parsonson, Baer, and Baer (1974) had two teachers of retarded children judge all responses of their pupils as appropriate (to be rewarded) or inappropriate (not to be rewarded). The usual approach would have been to focus on a single response in a specified environment. Rewarding or not rewarding all behavior produced generalized results, leading Stokes and Baer (1977) to argue that ''to generalize'' may be treated as an operant and increased by application of standard behavioral principles. Training to generalize is the last approach mentioned by Stokes and Baer.

8. A Direction for the Future Behavior analysts and modifiers have yet to consider that generalization is a process that might be task analyzed, just as the prerequisites to structured behavior have been analyzed. In the past, one might have doubted that such an approach would ever be adopted by behavior analysts, since ''to generalize'' is an unobservable response, and since they have steadfastly resisted analysis of unobservables. However, Baer (1978) has observed that the behaviorists' antipathy for unobservable responses has been breached already by their acceptance of task analysis of prerequisites of structured behaviors. The breach was accomplished by defining a prerequisite as a teaching that is required to make a subsequent teaching succeed. The routines by which the first teaching is accomplished are observable, and they stand as the behaviorists' definition of prerequisites. Having accepted teaching routines as observable analogues of prerequisite behaviors, there should be little resistance from behaviorists to the idea that a teaching routine that promotes generalization makes generalization as observable as are prerequisites. In behaviorist terms, generalization would be defined as a teaching that makes a subsequent teaching generalize. This idea is also discussed later in the chapter in reference to current cognitive approaches to promoting generalization.

Cognitive Approaches

Whereas behaviorists turned their attention to complex behaviors only after a long history of managing simple behaviors, cognitivists began with complex behaviors. They began with the observation that complex behavior consists of consistent patterns of diverse responses to diverse stimuli. They noted that complex behaviors cannot even be described without reference to abstract processing, and their analyses of complex behavior used to be little more than rationally derived descriptions of abstract processes. Usually, the described processes were hypothetical, unobservable, and of unknown and unquestioned origin. Cognitivists called the processes by such names as syntax, rules, and strategies. More often than not, no experimental data were used to establish the validity of the inferred processes. Rather, the cognitivists noted that they themselves used the processes when analyzing the complex behaviors they were trying to explain, and this sufficed as evidence.

During the mid-1960s, cognitivists concerned with child development began to collect data to determine whether children of different ages used the processes that rational analysis attributed to adults. Their methods were sometimes gross and sometimes precise, but the findings were generally the same: Older children, and more intelligent ones, more often used abstract processes. By adding process observation to process analysis, developmentalists importantly augmented the analytic methods of cognitive science. Moreover, their observations led developmental cognitivists to ask whether younger or less intelligent children could be taught to use the processes employed spontaneously by older and more intelligent people. As noted earlier in connection with memory and cognitive training, instruction to promote mature processing worked swiftly and dramatically, but the resulting performance gains seldom generalized.

Cognitivists' consideration of how to promote transfer of training (Borkowski & Cavanaugh, 1979; Brown & Campione, 1978; Butterfield, 1979) highlighted a distinction that is not obvious in behaviorists' considerations. The distinction is between promoting transfer by modifying the method of teaching the to-be-transferred material and promoting transfer by teaching rules or strategies for transferring subsequent teachings, regardless of the method of subsequent teaching. Behaviorists' considerations of promoting transfer have emphasized ways of teaching the to-be-transferred material, even though, as mentioned at the conclusion of the foregoing description of behaviorist approaches to promoting generalization, a future behaviorist direction might well be to define generalization as teaching routines that allow subsequent teaching to generalize. Unlike behaviorists, cognitivists have given explicit consideration to what such teaching should convey. Like behaviorists, they have also discussed ways of teaching the to-be-transferred material.

The distinction between training prerequisites for the transfer of future teachings and teaching for the transfer of a current lesson is based on the idea that there are two levels of cognitive process: a subordinate level and a superordinate level. Subordinate processes operate on environmental information or transformation of it. In Piagetian theory, both concrete and logical operations are subordinate processes. In information processing theory, subordinate processes include, among many others, recognition (matching a representation of incoming information to a representation from long-term memory), labeling (applying a name from long-term memory to a representation of incoming information), rehearsal (repeated labeling), and elaboration (retrieving from long-term memory the diverse sorts of information connoted by a label). A premise of cognitive theory is that different intellectual chores are performed with different combinations of subordinate processes: Any one subordinate enters into the solution of various intellectual problems by being combined with different subordinates. The wider the range of problems to which a particular subordinate applies, the greater its generality.

Superordinate processes operate on subordinate processes rather than on environmental information or its transformations. The role of superordinate processes is to select and coordinate the subordinate processes required to solve particular problems. Superordinates are analogous to the executive programs of a computer. Like executive programs, the superordinates' functions are to select and control subordinate programs that work on information. When a cognitivist talks about training so that a lesson will transfer, he or she means transfer of subordinate processes. When a cognitivist talks about teaching prerequisites to the transfer of future lessons, he or she is talking about teaching superordinate processes. By transfer, a cognitivist means not only the use of a learned subordinate outside of the learning environment, but also the modification of learned subordinates, and the combination of them with other subordinates so as to permit solutions to novel problems. In cognitive theory, adaptability and inventiveness are subsumed under the concept of transfer, and they enter cognitive theory as consequences of superordinate processes, because superordinates are responsible for matching subordinate cognitive processes to problem demands.

1. Teaching Subordinate Processes So They Will Transfer By strategy, a cognitivist means a combination of subordinate processes. In their discussion of how to promote transfer, Borkowski and Cavanaugh (1979) suggest that the instructor begin by identifying strategies that can be applied in various contexts. This is a precondition to prompting transfer, since one should find no transfer of a strategy that works in only one context. It is also a way of insuring that the instructor is training an aspect of intelligence, since intelligent behavior necessarily transcends contextual conditions. Borkowski and Cavanaugh's (1979) second suggestion is to instruct several strategies. When the strategies all apply to the same problem, this is analogous to the behaviorist approach of training several exemplars. Borkowski and Cavanaugh's (1979) third suggestion is to include stimuli in the training environment that are also found in the environments to which transfer is desired. This is the same as the behaviorist prescription of training common stimuli.

Brown and Campione (1978) suggest that generalized effects will result from training processes with transituational generality, whose components are well understood, and that have counterparts in the environment to which transfer is desired. These are the same suggestions as the first and third of Borkowski and Cavanaugh (1979).

Cognitivists have emphasized the importance of two of the methods advocated by behaviorists to foster transfer: train several exemplars, and use common stimuli. The bulk of cognitivists' suggestions are different than behaviorists', and they concern superordinate processes.

2. Teaching Superordinate Processes The preceding section equated Borkowski and Cavanaugh's (1979) suggestion to train several strategies with the behaviorist technique of training several exemplars. This is a valid equation when the several strategies are taught as solutions to a single intellectual problem. But Borkowski and Cavanaugh meant their prescription to cover as well the teaching of how to solve several problems. In fact, they stressed the importance of training children to solve several problems, each with several different strategies, and of making certain that the training also conveyed ways to decide when and how each strategy is appropriate. From a behaviorist viewpoint, such a recommendation seems like an undesirable complication. Behaviorists would rather concentrate on teaching one solution to one problem at a time. From a cognitive viewpoint, simultaneous teaching of several strategies for each of several problems is more likely to result in transfer, because it sets the conditions for also training superordinate functions. In particular, it sets the occasion to teach the child about matching strategies to problem requirements, and about how to select among various strategies that might fit any particular problem. Training in such superordinate decisions is what Borkowski and Cavanaugh (1979) intended to stress as a prime way of promoting generalized use of instructed strategies, and this author would add, as a prime way of leading children to invent their own strategies. Borkowski and Cavanaugh also stressed the desirability of teaching children to analyze the problems they face, to scan their strategic repertoires, and to match the demands of problems with their knowledge of strategies. Each of these sorts of instruction is designed to improve children's superordinate processing, and the assumption is that improving superordinate processing will increase generalized use of cognitive skills. Borkowski and Cavanaugh (1979) also recommended using ways to highlight for children and retarded individuals that using such superordinate processes improves their intellectual performance. A desirable additional step would be to teach children to evaluate for themselves the improvements in their performance that result from managing their own problem solving. Rather than recommend this latter approach, Borkowski and Cavanaugh (1979) suggested that ways be employed to bring superordinate processing under the control of everyday reinforcing events. This is exactly the same as the behaviorist recommendation to introduce natural maintaining contingencies, except that Borkowski and Cavanaugh suggested that the natural maintaining contingencies be applied to superordinate rather than to subordinate processes.

The preceding section noted that Brown and Campione (1978) argued that to promote transfer, one should train processes with transituational generality. This author equated transituational generality with strategies that apply to several problems. In fact, Brown and Campione meant more than that. In addition, they meant the training of superordinate processes, for example, the teaching of retarded children to judge when their study had prepared them to recall material with great accuracy (Brown & Barclay, 1976). Brown and Campione (1978) also argued that children should be taught to appreciate that superordinate processes are reasonable and effective. This is the same as Borkowski and Cavanaugh's (1979) emphasis on highlighting for children and retarded persons that having used superordinate processes improves their intellectual performance.

3. Some Specifics of Superordinate Processing [2] Clearly, Brown and Campione (1978) and Borkowski and Cavanaugh (1979) have concluded that teaching superordinate processes is the way to promote generalized use of cognitive processes. They are not alone. Butterfield and Belmont (1977) and Flavell and Wellman (1977) have reached the same conclusion from analyzing the results of cognitive instructional experiments. So far, only one paper has been very specific about the range of processes that might be trained to

promote transfer (Butterfield, 1979). Part of that paper is paraphrased below.

Figure 1 depicts the results of a rational analysis of the superordinate steps through which a person should progress in order to be an effective problem solver. Having encountered a problem, a person should determine the best possible outcome it allows (Step 1), by asking himself, herself, or others such questions as: "What kind of response would I make if I solved this problem?" and "How many of them would I make if I solved it perfectly?" Faced with a balance problem of the sort studied by Klahr and Siegler (1978), the answer would be "After the experimenter puts weights on both sides of the balance, but before the experimenter releases it so it can tilt, I need to say which side will go down. I can choose only one side, and the best I can do is to pick the side that goes down when he releases the beam." The child might arrive at this answer after simply listening to introductory instructions, or the child might question the experimenter to find out what is expected. In any event, he or she should define the best possible outcome as completely as possible before designing a strategy for the problem. How completely a person's queries of self and others define the best possible outcome will depend upon the person's knowledge of the problem (what to ask), which means that the individual might change his or her definition following some experience with the problem. Accordingly, the step of defining a best outcome should not be a one-time effort, completed only before undertaking the first attempt at problem solution. Rather, prior to each attempt to solve a problem, the person should define as completely as possible what a best outcome would look like.

Figure 1 shows that Step 2 has four parts. Step 2a, Design Strategies, requires people to draw on their knowledge of problems like the one they are facing and to design from their knowledge a reasonable first strategy.

---

[2]The ideas in this section grew from a long collaboration with John Belmont, to whom I remain indebted.

Step Number	Description of Process
Step Number	**Description of Process**
1	Define Best Possible Outcome (Set Goal)
2-A	Design Strategies
2-B	Estimate Outcomes
2-C	Compare Estimates to Goals
2-D	Select Strategy with Smallest Goal — Estimate Discrepancy
3-A	While Implementing Selected Strategy, Note Difference Between Implementation and Design
3-B	Estimate Response Accuracy as if Implementation Were Stopped
3-C	Compare Most Recent Accuracy Estimate to Prior Estimates
3-D	Determine When Accurate Estimates Stop Increasing; then Respond
4-A	Assess Response Accuracy (Outcome)
4-B	Compare Outcome to Estimated Outcome
4-C	Decide Whether Outcome Reached Estimate

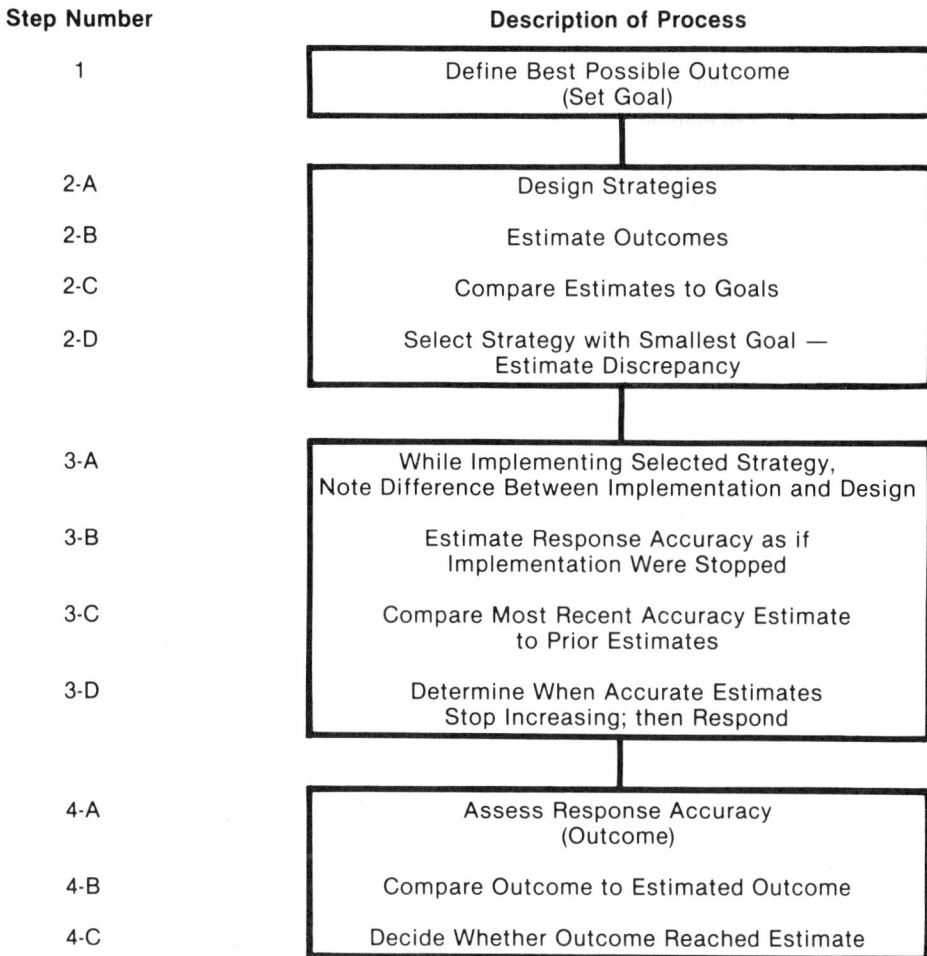

Figure 1.   A rationally derived outline of processes a person should use to solve novel problems.

Having designed a first strategy, the person should estimate the probable outcome of implementing it (Step 2b). The person should ask, "What sort of response(s) is this approach to the problem likely to generate?" For example, when faced with a six-word free recall task, whose best possible outcome is to say all six words in a list, a person might design the strategy of saying each word only once, as it is presented. If a person understands the effectiveness of such an approach, he or she will estimate its probable outcome as about three words—the last three presented. Having estimated the likely outcome of applying one's first strategy (Step 2b), a person should compare (Step 2c) the likely outcome to the best possible outcome (Step 1). If the likely outcome and the best outcome are not the same, a person should design an alternative strategy (return to Step 2a), estimate its likely outcome (Step 2b), and compare it to his or her estimated best outcome (Step 2c). A person should continue this process, keeping track of the discrepancies between likely outcomes and best possible outcomes. Step 2d calls for a decision about which of several strategies should be implemented. The rule is that a person should implement the strategy associated with the smallest discrepancy between its likely outcome and the best possible outcome. Thus, when facing a six-word memory problem, if a person designs no strategy that yields an estimate of more than three words recalled, he or she should use the three-word strategy.

Step 3 concerns strategy implementation. While implementing a strategy, Step 3a calls for monitoring how well the implementation compares to the strategic design. This comparison is necessary to allow modification of the implementation in response to local and unanticipated requirements. For example, when applying a rehearsal strategy to a list of words, difficulties arise when there are acoustic similarities among the words, and a person cannot always know whether there will be such difficulties until implementing the strategy, e.g., rehearsing the words. Monitoring how well the implementation matches one's strategic design is also necessary to noting (Step 3a) whether the implementation and the design are the same, which is required later to decide, in the event of an unsatisfactory outcome, whether the fault lay in the strategy or in its implementation. This matters, because if the fault was only in implementation, then an unsatisfactory result may not call for strategy revision. Step 3b calls for periodic assessment of how accurately a person would be able to respond if he or she stopped implementing his or her strategy. The point is, there must be some basis for deciding whether it is time to stop preparing to respond and to actually respond. The assessment in Step 3b provides the basis for such decisions. Step 3c calls for a person to compare the most recent estimate of probable response accuracy with previous estimates. Notice, the comparison is *not* between how accurately one would respond now and how accurately one believed one's strategy would allow one to respond before one implemented it (Step 2b). The reason is that a failure to accurately implement the strategy or having mis-estimated its likely outcome could result in never approaching the 2b estimate, in which case a person might continue to implement a strategy indefinitely or unnecessarily. Asking

only about whether the strategy is yielding further gains in estimated response accuracy eliminates the possibility of such inefficiencies, as well as the need during implementation to refer further back in memory than to the last estimate of probable accuracy. Comparisons of the most recent to prior response accuracy estimates are used in Step 3d, which calls for a decision about whether further implementation of the strategy will yield a more accurate response. When estimated accuracy ceases to increase, a response should be initiated.

Following a response, outcome is assessed (Step 4a). That is, a person asks, "How accurate was my response?" There are problems for which assessing outcome accuracy is not simple, but many problems do allow straightforward accuracy judgments. Thus, a child might count how many words he or she recalls and assess how confident he or she is that each came from the list to be recalled. Or, a child might compare the direction in which the balance beam tilts with his or her prediction of which way it should go. In this latter case, Step 4a includes Step 4b, which calls for the person to compare response accuracy to the estimate made (Step 2b) of the strategy's likely outcome. This latter comparison is not a necessary part of the solution of a current problem, but combined with Step 4c, it provides feedback about an important part of the solution process, namely, estimating outcomes (Step 2b). Increasing how accurately a person estimates outcome should improve how well the person solves future problems, and especially those of the class just encountered.

Several of the steps provide information that can be critical to designing and refining problem solutions. Consider that during a first effort to solve a problem a person estimates the best possible outcome (Step 1), the likely outcome of implementing a strategy (Step 2b), and the obtained outcome of implementation (Step 4a). When the time comes to try another problem of the same sort (which may be right away) a person will already have compared his or her obtained outcome to estimated outcome. This can tell a person whether he or she has a good appreciation of the processes from which his or her first strategy was assembled. If the obtained outcome is far from the estimate, a person can infer that something is awry with his or her first approach. He or she will know that the first strategy does not do what he or she expects, so that he or she should probably design another strategy. If the estimated and obtained outcomes do match, then comparing the obtained to the best possible outcome will tell a person whether to be satisfied with the first strategy. If the obtained and best possible outcome are discrepant, then another strategy is called for, even though the first one may have done exactly what was expected. Another source of information comes from comparison of the planned strategy with its implementation. Difficulties in implementation are often cues to how to design a better strategy, and such difficulties should have been noted during prior implementations (Step 3a). For example, when learning long lists of words, an effective general strategy is to attend successively to small groups of them, and to rehearse each group before attending to other items. But if one tries too large a group, one will have forgotten its first items before returning to rehearse the whole group. Noting this during the implementation can be a clue to revise the strategy to use smaller attention-rehearsal groups.

The hypothesis that follows from cognitivists' emphasis on superordinate processing is that training the use of processes like those outlined in Figure 1 will result in broad transfer of subsequently instructed subordinates. It will promote the adaptive modification of known problem solutions to meet changed environmental demands, and it will increase children's and retarded individuals' invention of effective strategies for novel problems that yield to conscious analysis. When considering the behaviorist approach of using common stimuli to promote transfer, the question was asked above: "What are the conditions necessary to make the learner himself the common stimulus?" It seems that this is the behaviorist form of the question that cognitivists answer when they say that training superordinate processes will produce transfer. The conditions are that the learner understand the sorts of superordinate processes outlined in Figure 1 and use those processes whenever he or she encounters a novel problem—whereas behaviorists think of environmental events as controlling behavior. There is truth in both views, but when one entertains the possibility that a person can be a stimulus for his or her own behavior, one must mean that internal events and states can be stimuli for a person's behavior. No doubt behaviorists will want to interpret internal events and states in terms of the teaching required to produce general behavior. This is acceptable to cognitivists, because if those internal states are to have educational importance, the cognitivist must think about teaching them too.

Reconciling and Integrating Behavioral and Cognitive Approaches

The burgeoning behavioral technology for promoting generalization (Stokes & Baer, 1977) focuses almost exclusively upon ways of teaching that will promote the transfer of specific lessons. The most advanced cognitive analyses of how to promote transfer focus predominately upon teaching superordinate processes as prerequisites to transfer of simultaneously or subsequently taught specific lessons, i.e., subordinate processes (Borkowski & Cavanaugh, 1979; Brown & Campione, 1978; Butterfield, 1979). A likely reason for the differing emphases of cognitivists and behaviorists is that cognitivists have concentrated on complex behaviors and have been more influenced by computer science (see Lachman, Lachman, & Butterfield, 1979). Therefore, cognitivists have been drawn to the distinction between subordinate and superordinate processes. Behaviorists, coming from their tradition of dealing with simple behaviors and of regarding complex behaviors as concatenations of simple behaviors, have not been drawn to this distinction. A reason to believe that the behavioral and cognitive approaches will nevertheless converge on similar ways of promoting transfer is that the teaching of superordinates is directly analogous to the teaching of prerequisites for complex behavior. In the words of this author's favorite behaviorist:

> The essence of a behaviorist task analysis is not to infer what a successful student does to be successful, but rather to demonstrate what to teach to a student first so that otherwise unsuccessful teaching will now work. Similarly, the essence of cognitive task analysis is to demonstrate what rule, strategy, process, etc. may be taught to subjects so as to accomplish a generalized complex pattern of behavior .... The two approaches are virtually identical (Baer, 1978, p. 10).

This is not to suggest that either approach, the behavioral or cognitive as it is now practiced, will prevail over the other. Rather, this author believes that some lessons will generalize better if they are taught by behaviorists' methods, and other lessons will generalize better if they are taught during or after instruction in superordinate processing. Consider the limits of cognitivists' ideas about superordinate processes. The scheme outlined in Figure 1, like all notions about superordinates, probably applies only to problems that yield to deliberate strategic analysis, and for which there is time for reflection and the planning of solutions. Understanding spoken discourse is not such a task, nor is using one's knowledge of grammar while talking, or even while writing. Such examples could be multiplied, and for all of them instruction in the superordinates so far identified by cognitivists would do little to promote generalized skill. Conversely, learning to calculate torque and to recognize when such calculations might be useful is not a skill that behaviorist approaches can promote efficiently. Nor is learning to extract and extrapolate the regularities in a letter sequence (ABXBCY__ __ __) likely to yield

to behavioral techniques as fully and rapidly as to cognitive methods. Yet, to cure the cognitive deficits of mentally retarded people, we must teach general versions of all these skills, and many more.

ECONOMICS OF CURING COGNITIVE DEFICITS

The first barrier standing between present practices and ways to cure the cognitive deficits of mentally retarded persons is the incompleteness of our understanding about how to produce generalized improvements in thinking. The second barrier is the complexity of the techniques so far developed to train aspects of intelligence. The two barriers are related, even though the first is technical and the second is economic. If intelligent people did fewer things well, we would not need to teach retarded persons so that our lessons transfer. We could analyze all of the skills used by intelligent people and teach the skills to the retarded population. But lives are too short and resources too limited for this approach. Until we can teach basic skills so that they generalize, curing cognitive deficits of mentally retarded individuals will be an economic impossibility, especially since teaching basic skills that generalize will probably not suffice. In addition, we will probably need to teach retarded persons how to modify skills they already possess to meet the varying demands they face, and we will need to teach them how to invent solutions to the new problems they encounter.

Two examples should bring the economic issues into sharp focus. One concerns memory training for mildly retarded persons. The other concerns language training for severely retarded people. It took Dr. John Belmont, myself, and many colleagues 7 years to analyze a simple memory problem thoroughly enough to raise retarded adolescents' performance to the level of uninstructed normal adults. Even allowing for the fact that we were learning how to perform such analyses as we went (see Butterfield, Siladi, & Belmont, 1980), this is an unacceptably long time (10^5 too much?), if the approach to curing mental retardation is to be teach-a-task-at-a-time. It is especially long because the instruction we devised after 7 years produced neither enduring nor general improvements in memory. It took 3 more years to effect minimally satisfactory transfer, which we did by combining subordinate and superordinate instruction (Belmont, Butterfield, & Borkowski, 1978).

Guess et al., (1974, pp. 541–542) have provided an economic analysis of language training programs. Their key point is that to be used by anyone other than a highly trained specialist, training programs must be spelled out step-by-step. When this is done for programs that start with mute and uncomprehending retarded persons and end with the persons understanding and speaking meaningful sentences, the length and complexity of the programs is so great that it is impossible to believe that any service agency would employ them. Some economies might be worked by further analysis of the training programs, which probably contain unnecessary steps that could be eliminated. But implementing entire programs for analytic purposes is prohibitively expensive for most investigators and their funding agencies. Thus, two classes of economic impracticality stand in the way of curing the cognitive deficits of mentally retarded people: The economics of improving techniques and of importing effective techniques into service settings.

Improving Techniques

Experience with both behavioral and cognitive analyses of intelligent behavior and how to teach it has shown that a dauntingly complex and wide range of research approaches is required (see Butterfield et al., 1980). To document a theoretical understanding of an intellectual development of even the narrowest sort, to show how to raise young and retarded persons' performance to levels attained by older normal people, and to promote the generalization of a single intellectual skill require the use of observational, experimental instructional, and psy-

chometric methods. Few laboratories have the range of personnel required to provide expertise in all of these methods. The result is that all of the research strategies required for a complete analyses of how to train any aspect of intelligence have seldom been brought to bear upon any aspect of intelligence.

The modal behavioral laboratory is directed by a university professor who devotes only part of his or her time to research. The modal laboratory is staffed by part-time assistants, who are usually full-time graduate students. The bulk of the work in such laboratories is designed as much to meet the academic and professional needs of graduate students and their professors as to meet the rigorous requirements of curative research. These academic and professional needs include the requirement that projects last no longer than about a year, because students need to move ahead and to move on. Mastering a wide range of sophisticated approaches in such a short time is out of the question, which is part of the reason that most laboratories specialize in one problem or one approach to one problem. Specializing in one problem means per force a lack of attention to the generality of a behavior or process. Because advancing through faculty ranks requires demonstrated originality, most university professors do not collaborate with one another. Doing so dilutes any claim they might make to originality. Successfully completing a graduate program also requires demonstration of originality, so students' needs sometimes militate against doing closely related pieces of research within a laboratory. A laboratory with a part-time director and only part-time help cannot justify large grant requests, and very few universities provide sufficient financial support for the conduct of complex research. A result is that most behavioral laboratories contain few pieces of sophisticated equipment, and most of these are highly specialized, outdated, and unsuited to more than one sort of research. This lack is offset by the huge computers that most universities make available to their faculty, because huge computers are good only for handling data. The greatest value of sophisticated equipment is not its data handling capabilities, but the control of experimental events and the precision of measurement it allows. These functions are not served by large, multiuser computers.

The point is that the requirements of intelligence training research exceed the economic resources of most university laboratories. This author knows of only three laboratories in this country that approximate the range of skills and technologies required to perform all of the sorts of experimentation that will be required to produce generalized improvements in cognition. All three are located in research centers or institutes that hold large federal grants designed to promote collaborative research among investigators whose primary and often full-time purpose is to conduct mission-oriented research on cognitive development. Federal support for these kinds of programs is being reduced, not increased. New ways are needed to finance behavioral research if we are going to train intelligence soon.

Introducing Techniques into Service Settings

The educational establishment has developed ways, including certification, continuing education, and categorical classes and programs, to introduce improved methods of teaching into the public schools. When effective ways are developed to cure cognitive deficits of mentally retarded persons enrolled in public school programs, the techniques will begin to find their way to most of the needy students. I do not suggest that the process will be fast nor efficient, but improved techniques do find their way into school programs.

The trend toward deinstitutionalization may or may not continue. Whether it does or not, more and more mentally retarded persons will be served in programs outside of the public schools. Community-based programs are too new in this country for one to judge how quickly they might adopt new teaching methods as they arise, nor do I know the economic realities of such programs. I suspect they are financially strained, and that special kinds of help will be required if they are to integrate new teaching procedures.

Institutional programs are notoriously conservative and slow to change, and no effective ways have been found to substantially improve them without massive financial and other investments, which are difficult to defend and to continue, except by court order. Court orders cause other problems that make this author doubt their utility.

Perhaps it is too soon to give serious thought to implementing intelligence training in service settings, inasmuch as we have work to do before we have effective intelligence training programs. But, eventually, thought will need to be given to that end.

REFERENCES

Baer, D.M. Generalized language and thought in the mentally retarded. U.S.P.H.S. Grant Application, HD-13029, 1978.

Belmont, J.M., & Butterfield, E.C. The relations of short-term memory to development and intelligence. In: L. Lipsitt & H. Reese (eds.), *Advances in child development and behavior,* Vol. 4. New York: Academic Press, 1969.

Belmont, J.M., & Butterfield, E.C. Learning strategies as determinants of memory deficiencies. *Cognitive Psychology,* 1971, *2,* 411–420.

Belmont, J.M., & Butterfield, E.C. The instructional approach to developmental cognitive research. In: R. Kail & J. Hagen (eds.), *Perspectives on the development of memory and cognition.* Hillsdale, NJ: Lawrence Erlbaum Associates, 1977.

Belmont, J.M., Butterfield, E.C., & Borkowski, J.G. Training retarded people to generalize memorization methods across memory tasks. In: M.M. Gruneberg, P.E. Morris, & R.N. Sykes (eds.), *Practical aspects of memory.* London: Academic Press, 1978.

Borkowski, J.G., & Cavanaugh, J.C. Maintenance and generalization of skills and strategies by the retarded. In: N.R. Ellis (ed.),

Handbook of mental deficiency, psychological theory, and research. Hillsdale, NJ: Lawrence Erlbaum Associates, 1979.

Bornstein, P.H., & Quevillon, R.P. The effects of self-instructional package on overactive preschool boys. *Journal of Applied Behavior Analysis,* 1976, *9,* 179–188.

Bricker, D. Imitative sign training as a facilitator of word-object association with low-functioning children. *American Journal of Mental Deficiency,* 1972, *76,* 509–516.

Bricker, W.A., & Bricker, D.D. A program of language training for the severely handicapped child. *Exceptional Children,* 1970, *37,* 101–111.

Bricker, W.A., & Bricker, D.D. An early language training strategy. In: R.L. Schiefelbusch & L.L. Lloyd (eds.), *Language perspectives: Acquisition, retardation and intervention.* Baltimore: University Park Press, 1974.

Bricker, D., Dennison, L., & Bricker, W.A. Constructive interaction-adaption approach to language training. MCCD Monograph Series, No. 7, Mailman Center for Child Development, University of Miami, Miami, FL, 1975.

Brown, A.L. Knowing when, where, and how to remember: A problem in metacognition. In: R. Glaser (ed.), *Advances in instructional psychology.* Hillsdale, NJ: Lawrence Erlbaum Associates, 1977.

Brown, A.L., & Barclay, C.R. The effects of training specific mnemonics on the metamnemonic efficiency of retarded children. *Child Development,* 1976, *47,* 70–80.

Brown, A.L., & Campione, J.C. Memory strategies in learning: Training children to study strategically. In: H. Pick, H. Leibowitz, J. Singer, A. Steinschneider, & H. Stevenson (eds.), *Application of basic research in psychology.* London: Plenum Publishing Corp., 1978.

Brown, A.L., Campione, J.C., Bray, N.W., & Wilcox, B.L. Keeping track of changing variables: Effects of rehearsal training and rehearsal prevention in normal and retarded adolescents. *Journal of Experimental Psychology,* 1973, *101,* 123–131.

Brown, A.L., & DeLoache, J.S. Skills, plans and self-regulation. In: R. Siegler (ed.), *Children's thinking: What develops.* Hillsdale, NJ: Lawrence Erlbaum Associates, 1978.

Butterfield, E.C. *Instructional techniques that produce generalized improvements in cognition.* Paper presented at the Congress of the International Association for the Scientific Study of Mental Deficiency, Jerusalem, Israel, August, 1979.

Butterfield, E.C., & Belmont, J.M. Assessing and improving the executive cognitive functions of mentally retarded people. In: I. Bialer & M. Sternlicht (eds.), *The psychology of mental retardation.* New York: Psychological Dimensions, 1977.

Butterfield, E.C., Siladi, D., & Belmont, J.M. Validating theories of intelligence. In: H. Reese & L. Lippsitt (eds.), *Advances in child development and behavior.* New York: Academic Press, 1980.

Butterfield, E.C., Wambold, C., & Belmont, J.M. On the theory and practice of improving short-term memory. *American Journal of Mental Deficiency,* 1973, *77,* 654–669.

Carrier, J.K., & Peak, T. *Non-SLIP (Non-speech language initiation program).* Lawrence, KS: H & H Enterprises, 1975.

Carroll, J.B., & Maxwell, S.E., Individual differences in cognitive abilities. *Annual Review of Psychology,* 1979, *30,* 603–640.

Cronbach, L.J., & Snow, R.E. *Aptitudes and instructional methods.* New York: John Wiley and Sons, 1977.

Fisher, M.A., & Zeaman, D. An attention-retention theory of retardate discrimination learning. In: N.R. Ellis (ed.), *International review of research in mental retardation,* Vol. 6. New York: Academic Press, 1973.

Flavell, J.H., Beach, D.R., & Chinsky, J.M. Spontaneous verbal rehearsal in a memory task as a function of age. *Child Development,* 1966, *37,* 283–299.

Flavell, J.H., Friedricks, A.G., & Hoyt, J.D. Developmental changes in memorization processes. *Cognitive Psychology,* 1970, *1,* 324–340.

Flavell, J.H., & Wellman, H.M. Metamemory. In: R. Kail & J. Hagen (eds.), *Perspectives on the development of memory and cognition.* Hillsdale, NJ: Lawrence Erlbaum Associates, 1977.

Fristoe, M. Language intervention systems: Published programs in kit form. In: L.L. Lloyd (ed.), *Communication assessment and intervention strategies.* Baltimore: University Park Press, 1976.

Guess, D., Sailor, W., & Baer, D.M. To teach language to retarded children. In: R.L. Schiefelbusch & L.L. Lloyd (eds.), *Language perspectives—Acquisition, retardation and intervention.* Baltimore: University Park Press, 1974.

Hagen, J.W., Meacham, J.A., & Mesibov, G. Verbal labeling, rehearsal, and short-term memory. *Cognitive Psychology,* 1970, *1,* 47–58.

Hunt, E., Frost, N., & Lunneborg, C. Individual differences in cognition: A new approach to intelligence. In: G.H. Bower (ed.), *The psychology of learning and motivation,* Vol. 7. New York: Academic Press, 1973.

Jensen, A.R. *Reaction time and intelligence.* Paper presented at NATO Conference on Intelligence and Learning, York, England, July 1979.

Kellas, G., McCauley, C., & McFarland, C.E. Developmental aspects of storage and retrieval. *Journal of Experimental Child Psychology,* 1975, *19,* 51–62.

Kent, L. *Language acquisition program for the severely retarded.* Champaign, IL: Research Press, 1974.

Klahr, D., & Siegler, R.S. The representation of children's knowledge. In: H.W. Reese & L.P. Lipsitt (eds.), *Advances in child development and behavior,* Vol. 12. New York: Academic Press, 1978.

Kuhn, D. Inducing development experimentally: Comments on a research paradigm. *Developmental Psychology,* 1974, *10,* 590–600.

Lachman, R., Lachman, J., & Butterfield, E.C. *Cognitive psychology and information processing: An introduction.* Hillsdale, NJ: Lawrence Erlbaum Associates, 1979.

MacDonald, J.D. Environmental language intervention: Programs for establishing initial communication in handicapped children. In: F. Withrow & C. Nygren (eds.), *Language curriculum and materials for the handicapped learner.* Columbus, OH: Charles E. Merrill Publishing Co., 1976.

MacDonald, J.D., & Blott, J.P. Environmental language intervention: The rationale for a diagnostic and training strategy through rules, context, and generalization. *Journal of Speech and Hearing Disorders,* 1974, *39,* 244–256.

MacDonald, J.D., Blott, J.P., Gordon, K., Spiegel, B., & Hartman, M. An experimental parent-assisted program for preschool language-delayed children. *Journal of Speech and Hearing Disorders,* 1974, *39,* 395–415.

MacDonald, J.D., & Nichols, M. *Environmental language inventory.* Columbus, OH: The Nisonger Center, Ohio State University, 1974.

Meichenbaum, D. Cognitive factors as determinants of learning disabilities: A cognitive functional approach. In: R. Knights & D. Bakker (eds.), *The neuropsychology of learning disorders: Theoretical approaches.* Baltimore: University Park Press, 1976.

Miller, J.F., & Yoder, D.E. A syntax teaching program. In: J. McLean, D. Yoder, & R. Schiefelbusch (eds.), *Language intervention in the retarded: Developing strategies.* Baltimore: University Park Press, 1972a.

Miller, J.F., & Yoder, D.E. *The Miller-Yoder test of grammatical comprehension.* Madison, WI: The University Book Store, 1972b.

Miller, J.F., & Yoder, D.E. An ontogenic language teaching strategy for retarded children. In: R.L. Schiefelbusch & L.L. Lloyd (eds.), *Language perspectives—Acquisition, retardation, and intervention.* Baltimore: University Park Press, 1974.

Parsonson, B.S., Baer, A.M., & Baer, D.M. The application of generalized correct social contingencies: An evaluation of a training program. *Journal of Applied Behavior Analysis,* 1974, *7,* 427–437.

Pyles, M. Verbalization as a factor in learning. *Child Development,* 1932, *2,* 108–113.

Resnick, L.B., & Glaser, R. Problem-solving and intelligence, In: L. Resnick (ed.), *The nature of intelligence.* Hillsdale, NJ: Lawrence Erlbaum Associates, 1976.

Risley, T.R., & Hart, B. Developing correspondence between the nonverbal and verbal behavior of preschool children. *Journal of Applied Behavior Analysis,* 1968, *1,* 267–281.

Rogers-Warren, A., & Baer, D.M. Saying and doing: The verbal mediation of social behaviors. *Journal of Applied Behavior Analysis,* 1976, *9,* 335–354.

Rohwer, W.D. Elaboration and learning in childhood and adolescence. In: H.W. Reese (ed.), *Advances in child development and behavior,* Vol. 8. New York: Academic Press, 1973.

Schroeder, G.L., & Baer, D.M. Effects of concurrent and serial training on generalized vocal imitation in retarded children. *Developmental Psychology,* 1972, *6,* 293–301.

Schwartz, M.L., & Hawkins, R.P. Application of delayed reinforcement procedures to the behaviors of an elementary school child. *Journal of Applied Behavior Analysis,* 1970, *3,* 85.

Seymour, F.W., & Stokes, T.F. Self-recording in training girls to increase work and evoke staff praise in an institution for offenders. *Journal of Applied Behavior Analysis,* 1976, *9,* 41.

Statts, A.W. Behaviorism and cognitive theory in the study of language: A neopsycholinguistics. In: R.L. Schiefelbusch & L.L. Lloyd (eds.), *Language perspectives—Acquisition, retardation and intervention.* Baltimore: University Park Press, 1974.

Stokes, T.F., & Baer, D.M. An implicit technology of generalization. *Journal of Applied Behavior Analysis,* 1977, *10,* 349–367.

Stokes, T.F., Baer, D.M., & Jackson, R.L. Programming the generalization of a greeting response in four retarded children. *Journal of Applied Behavior Analysis,* 1974, *7,* 599–610.

Stremel, K. Language training: A problem for retarded children. *Mental Retardation*, 1972, *10*, 47–49.

Stremel, K., & Waryas, C. A behavioral-psycholinguistic approach to language training. *American Speech and Hearing Monographs*, 1974, *18*, 96–124.

Turnure, J., Buium, N., & Thurlow, M.L. The effectiveness of interrogatives for promoting verbal elaboration productivity in young children. *Child Development*, 1976, *47*, 851–855.

Wittrock, M.C., & Lumsdaine, A.A. Instructional psychology. *Annual Review of Psychology*, 1977, *28*, 417–460.

Curative Aspects of Mental Retardation:
Biomedical and Behavioral Advances
edited by Frank J. Menolascino, M.D., Ronald Neman, Ph.D., and Jack A. Stark, Ph.D.
Copyright 1983   Paul H. Brookes Publishing Co., Inc.   Baltimore · London

chapter 16

The Prevention of Mild and Moderate Retarded Development

SIDNEY W. BIJOU, PH.D.
The University of Arizona
Tucson, Arizona

T HE PREVENTION OF RETARDATION is usually thought of as a biomedical problem involving surgery, drugs, and diets that forestall severe and profound retardation. For example, a report by the California Association for the Retarded titled *Prevention: An Agenda for Action* (1979), lists the following causes of retardation: childhood accidents, drugs, alcohol, toxic substances, genetic disorders, high risk women and infants, lead poisoning, metabolic disorders, nutritional deficiencies, Rh blood disease, rubella, and other infectious diseases. Disadvantageous sociocultural conditions that require psychoeducational intervention are not mentioned.

Prevention programs that do recognize the need for both biomedical and psychological procedures tend to designate medical intervention as *primary* prevention and psychoeducational intervention as *secondary* prevention.

It is unfortunate that most prevention strategies tend to ignore the full range of antecedent conditions that retard development and, in the few that do take such conditions into account, a distinction between primary and secondary prevention rests on biomedical criteria.[1] Such practices assume a kind of mental development in which deficiencies in the body cause deficiencies in the mind (or in intelligence). These notions are incompatible with a naturalistic philosophy of science theories of development (e.g., Bijou & Baer, 1978; Kantor, 1959; Skinner, 1953, 1974). This view holds that human development results from successive changes in the relationships between the behavior of a biological human being (that has evolved from the interaction between genetic processes and the biological environment) and the environment (that consists of organismic and sociocultural conditions), and that retarded development is the consequence of restrictions brought about by limitations in organismic (biomedical

---

[1]In the mental health field, the distinction between primary and secondary prevention is based on objectives rather than presumed etiology. Primary prevention is aimed at lowering the rate of new cases of mental disorders in a population, and secondary prevention, at preventing existing mild disorders from becoming acute or prolonged (Ansbacker, 1978; Cowen, 1978).

pathology) and sociocultural conditions. According to this view, the relative importance of biomedical pathology and of sociocultural handicaps in retarding development cannot meaningfully be ranked as primary or secondary, since *any* condition that decelerates development may be viewed as a cause. One could say, however, that biomedical pathologies dominate in about 15% to 20% (about 200,000 persons) of the total cases in the United States while sociocultural handicaps are paramount in about 80% to 85% (4,200,000 persons) of the total cases in this country. The former are usually the severe forms of retardation; the latter are the milder categories. To be realistic as well as humanistic, prevention programs should be directed at all levels of retardation—mild, moderate, severe, and profound—and should include all biomedical and psychoeducational techniques that have been demonstrated to reduce or eliminate the restricting conditions of development.

This chapter concerns the prevention of mild or moderate retarded development in sociocultural disadvantaged, non-organically impaired children. That is to say, it deals with the psychoeducational procedures for reducing or eliminating sociocultural conditions that restrict development. The discussion is in three parts: The first part describes the rationale for the prevention program, which is founded on the behavior analysis theory of retarded development; the second part details the prevention program; and the third outlines the steps required to activate the program.

BEHAVIOR ANALYSIS THEORY

The concept of retarded development[2] does not require a special theory. It is an integral part of a behavior analysis theory of human development (Bijou, 1963, 1969; Bijou & Baer, 1978). In order to understand the behavioral treatment of retardation and the

techniques involved in the prevention program it implies, we offer a brief statement on the background of the approach, an outline of the theory itself, and an exposition of retarded development.

Background

Behavior analysis has its historical moorings in learning and conditioning research (Keller, 1973). For this reason, it is usually classified as a learning theory, one that attempts to explain all psychological phenomena simply in terms of learning principles. But behavior analysis is not a learning theory. It is a *complete system of psychology* in that it has the essential elements of a scientific system; namely, 1) an articulate philosophy of science (Kantor & Smith, 1975; Skinner, 1974), 2) a general theory of behavior (Kantor, 1959; Skinner, 1953), 3) a core research (single subject) methodology (Sidman, 1960), and 4) an applied approach based upon the concepts and principles of the theory (Bijou, 1970; Kazdin, 1975).

General Theoretical Formulation

Psychological behavior (organized as a personality) evolves from interactions between an individual and his or her environment. Psychological development consists of progressive changes in interactions between a biological individual and the successive changes in his or her ever-changing environment. Hence, development depends on the specific ways in which past and present organismic, physical, and sociocultural events alter behavior, transforming a person from complete helplessness to relative independence.

The individual, conceptualized as a unique biological structure with the capacity for activities characteristic of his or her species, including all the intricacies of verbal behavior, is in continuous interaction with stimuli that constitute the environment. The unique biological makeup of an individual

---

[2]The term "retarded development" is used instead of "mental retardation" because it is more descriptive of the condition (Bijou, 1966; Bijou & Donitz-Johnson, 1981).

results from a combination of genetic history and personal history.

The environment is conceptualized functionally as the stimuli that interact with an individual. Some of the stimuli originate from the individual's external environment (physical and sociocultural stimuli), some from his or her own behavior (stimuli generated by behavior), and some from biological functioning (organismic stimuli). The individual is not only the source of all psychological behavior, but is at the same time the source of the organismic part of the environment. He or she is, of course, also a source of stimulation for the social and physical environment. Thus, the relationship between the individual and the environment is *reciprocal*: The environment changes the individual and the individual changes the environment.

Stimuli, whether internal or external, are described in terms of 1) their physical dimensions, such as intensity and duration of a child's cry, and 2) their functional dimensions, such as a mother's succoring reaction to a cry. The functional dimensions of stimuli in turn fall into: a) *specific functions*, such as the reinforcing function (which strengthens or increases the probability of occurrence of the preceding behavior under similar conditions), and the discriminative (cue) function (which sets the occasion for behavior that has been consequated in the past); and b) the *setting conditions*, such as deprivation of food (an organismic condition) or a prolonged anger reaction (an emotional condition).

An individual's genetic endowment is such that some classes of his or her behavior are influenced primarily by *preceding* stimulation (respondent or reflex interactions), some by *consequent* stimulation (operant interactions, which include verbal, social, intellectual, motor, and academic behaviors), and some by both preceding and consequent stimulation, as for example, sphincter reactions. Stimuli may, of course, be related to the simultaneous occurrence of both respondent and operant behavior, as in emotional reactions.

Progressive Changes in Respondent Interactions

The number and kinds of preceding stimuli that elicit respondent behavior are modified through *classical or Pavlovian conditioning*, which follows this formula: A stimulus that initially has no power to elicit respondent behavior (neutral stimulus) may acquire this power (conditioned stimulus) if it is consistently associated with a stimulus that has the power to elicit respondent behavior (unconditioned eliciting stimulus). The functional power acquired through conditioning may be weakened or eliminated by discontinuing the association of the stimuli by repeatedly presenting the conditioned stimulus without the eliciting stimulus (respondent extinction).

Conditioned respondent behavior may be elicited by a stimulus that resembles the conditioned stimulus (respondent generalization). Stimuli that have acquired the functional power to elicit respondent behavior because of their resemblance may lose that power by differential conditioning, that is, by the continued pairing of the unconditioned stimulus with the conditioned stimulus while presenting the generalized stimulus without the unconditioned stimulus (respondent discrimination).

Progressive Changes in Operant Interactions

With progressive interactions, operant behavior changes in form, i.e., manual, locomotor, and verbal skills, become increasingly complex and the preceding controlling situations (cues) change with the maturation and cultural practices. These transitions come about through consequent stimuli, some of which strengthen new forms of operant behavior or new cue relationships while others weaken or eliminate old forms of behaviors and well-established preceding occasions. Two classes of consequent stimuli *strengthen* operant interactions: 1) *positive* reinforcers, i.e., organismic, physical, or sociocultural stimuli that are added to the situation, and 2) *negative* reinforcers, i.e., organismic, physical, or sociocultural aversive stimuli that are *removed* from the situation. And three classes of consequent stimuli *weaken* operant interactions: 1) the *addition* of aversive stimuli ("punishment by hurt"), 2) the *removal* of positive reinforcing stimuli ("punishment by loss"), and 3) *no change* in the situation (extinction).

Reinforcing stimuli are also categorized on the basis of whether their origin is innate (primary) or acquired (secondary). Innate reinforcers, which are built into the individual as a consequence or his or her genetic history, are further subdivided into appetitional (those that maintain the functioning of the body: air, food, water) and ecological (those that stem from interactions with the physical environment or the physical aspects of the social environment, such as movements, sounds, or changes in light intensity). Acquired reinforcers, on the other hand, develop their functional power either through a history of functioning as a discriminative stimulus or a history of conditioning (pairing) with innate reinforcers. Their acquired reinforcing function can, of course, be eradicated by terminating either their discriminative function through nonreinforcement, or their conditioned function through cessation of pairing with the innate reinforcers.

In all strengthening and weakening procedures, whether deliberate, as in teaching and training, or natural, as in free play and exploration, the functional power of consequent stimuli changes with the *setting condition* in effect at the time. Resting, for example, is reinforcing after a period of vigorous or prolonged activity (the setting condition of fatigue) and praise is most reinforcing when given by an esteemed person (the setting condition of a positive social reinforcement history). Thus, the power of a consequent stimulus is dependent upon the prevailing circumstance.

Setting events contribute to the specificity of the reinforcing function of stimuli. *Specific* reinforcers strengthen a specific class of behaviors and acquire their function under only one kind of setting condition. For example, coming in from the rain (operant behavior) is negatively reinforced by the termination of the rain falling on one's head (aversive stimulus). *Generalized* reinforcers, such as money, approval, and attention, strengthen many behaviors and acquire their generalized property through a history with a variety of setting conditions.

As noted above, one aspect of development involves operant behavior coming under the control of a succession of preceding situations (cues or discriminative stimuli) for positive and negative reinforcers. In other words, preceding situations or aspects of preceding situations, such as the color or form of an object, come to control an individual's operant behavior because in the past they have been followed by certain kinds of consequences. These preceding stimuli increase the probability of occurrence of operant behavior. Thus, the question "How old are you?" sets the occasion for the listener to say "Four," although he or she may not make that response because "Everybody asks the same question."

Stimuli that resemble discriminative stimuli acquire the power to increase the probability of occurrence of the response in the original situation. Stimuli that acquire discriminative functions for operant behaviors through their resemblance may lose them through differential training, that is, by reinforcing operant behavior to the discriminative stimulus and not reinforcing or punishing it in the presence of the generalized discriminative stimulus.

The maintenance of learned operant behavior ("memory") depends upon reinforcement history, i.e., the *schedule of reinforcement*. Behavior reinforced on a continuous schedule, or every time it occurs, results in a regular pattern of responding. When the behavior is no longer reinforced, it weakens relatively quickly, although there tend to be irregular recurrences of the response during this extinction process. Behavior reinforced on an intermittent schedule based either on the amount of response output (fixed or variable ratio schedules) or the time between reinforcements (fixed or variable interval schedules) tends to weaken more slowly when no longer reinforced. Fixed schedules tend to slow down responding after a reinforcement and to accelerate responding prior to reinforcement, while variable schedules tend to generate steady and even performances. Schedules of intermittent reinforcement may be combinations of both ratio and interval schedules, including increasing and decreasing ratios and intervals over the period of training. The various schedules of reinforcement not only maintain learned behavior in a variety of ways, they also generate individual characteristic ways of responding to situations, often referred to as personality traits.

Progressive Changes in Complex Interactions

Most human behavior consists of complex interrelationships of respondent and operant behavior occurring in sequential interactional units. A class of operant behavior (such as opening a box) may produce stimuli with a reinforcing function (the sight of an assortment of candy), a discriminative function (the candy sets the occasion for selecting a piece and putting it in one's mouth), and an eliciting function (salivating). Candy in the mouth is a discriminative stimulus for chewing (operant behavior), for reaching for another piece of candy (operant behavior), and so on.

Some operant behaviors (drinking cocktails) generate stimuli that have an immediate reinforcing function (feeling good) and a remote aversive function (hangover), and some (taking a cold shower) are followed by stimuli with the reverse relationship, an immediate aversive effect (cold water on a warm body) and a remote reinforcing effect (feeling fresh, clean, and cool). Situations with such multiple response consequences may lead to conflict and to self-management practices. In self-management practices the individual arranges part of his internal and external environment to increase the probability of con-

tingencies that are more reinforcing over extended periods.

Situations that require operant behaviors, in the form of a skill or knowledge, that are not available to the individual at the moment, require *problem-solving* (and thinking) behaviors. In problem-solving behavior, as in self-management, the individual engages in behavior aimed at changing his environment so as to facilitate the occurrence of a response that will be reinforcing, in this case, reaching a solution. Problem solving extends from pedestrian solutions to everyday routine problems to novel solutions to problems in the arts, sciences, and humanities. The latter type of problem solving is usually referred to as *creative behavior*.

RETARDED DEVELOPMENT

As stated earlier, human psychological development consists of progressive changes in interactions between a biologically maturing individual and the physical, sociocultural, and organismic conditions that constitute his or her evironment. Such progressions may be slow, normal, or rapid, depending upon *developmental opportunities* provided by 1) the biological makeup of the individual (which includes normal biological variations among individuals) as well as biomedical pathologies, and 2) environmental conditions. Slow or retarded progressions can be traced to *restrictions* in developmental opportunities induced by anatomical and/or physiological impairments, sociocultural handicaps, or both. The more extreme the restrictions and handicaps, the slower the development (Bijou & Donitz-Johnson, 1981).

The concept of developmental opportunities requires some elaboration since it is a pivotal concept in the discussions to follow. By developmental opportunities are meant natural or contrived situations in which a developing person interacts and, as a consequence of which, he or she extends or maintains motor and self-help skills, knowledge, communication-socialization abilities, and motivational hierarchy. Such situations consist of 1) a stimulating condition, 2) a response to the stimulating condition, and 3) a consequence. (See previous section on changes in operant interactions.) It should be emphasized that developmental opportunities do not refer simply to stimulating conditions. Mere stimulation does not accelerate development; the individual must take some action in relation to the stimulation. It should also be emphasized that for a situation to be a developmental opportunity, the individual must have the necessary behavioral equipment and the behavioral repertoire to make the required response. If he or she cannot respond, the situation is not functional for that individual. Finally, developmental opportunities include response consequences that 1) extend his or her behavior repertoires, 2) weaken nonfunctional behavior, or 3) escape or avoid conditions detrimental to development.

Following is a brief review of how biomedical pathologies and sociocultural handicaps curtail developmental opportunities.

Biomedical Pathologies

Biomedical pathologies such as injuries, microcephaly, Down syndrome, phenylketonuria, cerebral agenesis, and so on, restrict developmental opportunities and severely retard development in two ways. The first, of course, pertains to physiological alterations in *response equipment*. If an individual cannot respond to stimuli for *any* reason, his or her potential for normal psychological development is reduced. For example, in a group of infants blind from birth, it was found that while neuromuscular maturation and postural achievements were within the normal range, self-initiated mobility, locomotion, and exploratory behavior were delayed (Adelson & Fraiberg, 1974). Similarly, a study of deaf boys with impaired static equilibrium showed increasing locomotor incoordination as they grew older (Boyd, 1967).

The second way in which biomedical pathologies restrict opportunities for development relates to impairment in the *internal sources of stimulation*, i.e., stimulation from glands, muscles, viscera, and physiological connecting systems. Individuals so afflicted are not exposed to all aspects of the organismic component of their environment and are deprived of opportunities to react to them.

There is a paucity of literature on the pathological functioning of intero- and proprioceptors. It is therefore difficult to document the role of these conditions in retarding development. The following may be instructive: Clinical studies of children who do not respond to noxious stimuli such as hot objects, blows to the body, pin pricks, and the like, have shown that these children have to be protected and helped to avoid the physical damage that could be wrought by such stimuli. Whether the absence of pain stimulation in these cases has led to retarded development is difficult to determine, since the essential follow-up data are not available.

Biomedical Pathologies Together with Certain Forms of Social Practices

When biomedical pathologies include physical and/or behavioral stigmata, parents and others tend to treat a child as permanently ill. Such treatment often means that the child is given less responsibility, has fewer limits imposed on his or her behavior, and is frequently indulged in capricious whims (Shere, 1956). It may also mean extended time away from school and peer activities because of medical examinations and special treatment regimens (Richardson, 1969). There is, furthermore, the probability of exposure to educational programs designed for a sick rather than a physically impaired child (Stinson, 1974).

Restrictions in developmental opportunities may also result when a physically stigmatized or behaviorally deviant infant or child is treated as peculiar or undesirable. Some parents are likely to give little attention to infants who are impaired, unresponsive, unattractive, or irritable, and such isolation tends to deprive them of essential social experiences (Cleland & Clark, 1966; Mercer, 1974; Richardson, 1969). Peers, too, are apt to reject and respond negatively to physically handicapped and educationally deviant children (Force, 1956; Iano, Ayers, Heller, McGettigan, & Walker, 1974). The same is true of teachers and recreational personnel. A study has shown that teachers and recreation workers tend to treat handicapped children in a stereotyped and inhibited fashion and to terminate their contacts more quickly with a handicapped than with a nonhandicapped person (Kleck, Ono, & Hastorf, 1966). All of these avoidance types of social reactions undoubtedly contribute not only to developmental retardation but to the high incidence of behavior disturbance found among the physically impaired (Waldrop, Pedersen, & Bell, 1968).

Sociocultural Handicaps

Sociocultural handicaps, such as socioeconomic poverty, abusive child treatment, parental indifference, and family practice in conflict with the cultural norms, limit opportunities for learning and adjustment.

Poverty With poverty comes marginal physical living conditions, a paucity of books and play materials, and haphazard family routines. Marginal physical living conditions have been shown to be related to, among other things, poor home-teaching practices (Radin & Weikart, 1967); and a meager supply of toys, books, and play equipment is related to low performance on intelligence tests (Bradley & Caldwell, 1976a, 1976b; Elardo, Bradley, & Caldwell, 1975, 1977).

Socioeconomic poverty is also accompanied by limited social support for social behavior including all forms of verbal behavior and play. The lack of social support is associated with mothers' absences from the home, minimal verbal interaction (Hess & Shipman, 1965; Lewis & Wilson, 1972), and ineffective home-teaching techniques (Brophy, 1977; Karnes, Studley, Wright, & Hodgins, 1968; Wilton & Barbour, 1978).

Finally, socioeconomic family poverty seems to generate negative parental attitudes toward intellectual and educational achievement in their children. Parents in economic despair tend not to have high educational aspirations for their children nor are they prone to reinforce academic achievement (Heber, 1978; Kagan & Freeman, 1963; Radin & Weikart, 1967).

Child Abuse There is substantial evidence that child abuse—strong and/or frequent aversive child-rearing practices—can result in behavior disturbances *and* retarded development. Child-rearing practices centering on punishment and strict discipline establish escape and avoidance behavior that, like biomedical anomalies and socioeconomic handicaps, foreclose occasions for acquiring skills and knowledge. And a child retarded because of physical or social handicaps may be further retarded by excessive parental punishment (Burgess & Conger, 1978; Pavenstedt, 1965).

Parental or Child Care Indifference The previous section on poverty noted that low family social interactions tend to develop meager social-verbal skills, which are central to school achievement and to performance on intelligence tests. In this section, our concern centers on the effects of low social interactions in nonpoverty families and in child care institutions.

Studies of parent-child relationships in the home have repeatedly shown that the extent of the mother's involvement with her infant is the most consistent predictor of scores on developmental scales (Bradley & Caldwell, 1976a, 1976b; Elardo et al., 1975). Infants who have received less verbal-social attention from their mothers tend to score lower on scales of intelligence (Beckwith, 1971); mothers who only routinely handle their babies have infants who spend a significantly greater amount of time crying (Ourth & Brown, 1961), while responsive mothers tend to rear responsive infants (Osofsky, 1976). Maternal involvement and responsivity also relate to the language development of children (Elardo et al., 1977). Children with high verbal fluency come from families with high interactions and have mothers who encourage good speech (Jones, 1972). Low verbal children are more likely to have been punished for poor speech and to have had relatively few interactions with their mothers (Wulbert, Englis, Kreigsmann, & Milk, 1975).

Studies of child care practices in institutions indicate that such institutions are deprived environments, generating retarded development in motor, language, and intellectual abilities (Yarrow, 1961). And studies comparing child-rearing in families with child-rearing institutions indicate that children raised in families develop better language repertoires (Lyle, 1960) and engage in more social play (Collard, 1971). Furthermore, institutionally reared babies tend to engage in a great deal of repetitive play (Collard, 1971)—a characteristic often considered to be inherent in retardation.

Parental Practices in Conflict with Cultural Norms Parents often reinforce behaviors that conflict with mainstream society. Such practices may occur unwittingly in the sense that parents or caregivers are not aware that their practices do, in fact, support maladjustive and antisocial behaviors. They may also occur wittingly when parents or caregivers wish to perpetuate and cherish behaviors, motivations, and attitudes regardless of whether or not they conflict with social norms. This is often the case among ethnic or minority groups intent on preserving their customs and life-styles (Marjoribanks, 1972). Conflicting practices are likely to occur when a minority group disapproves of certain forms of behavior associated with the majority culture (Deutsch, 1960), and when the goals of individual achievements conflict with ethnic values that classify such achievements as appropriate only when they are for the good of a larger social body, such as the family or the tribe (Ramirez & Price-Williams, 1976). The behaviors that evolve from both unwitting and witting social practices may compete successfully with culture

norms and in so doing reduce the child's opportunities to develop highly functional behaviors.

PREVENTION OF RETARDATION

According to our analysis of human development, severe and profound retardation is a function of limited opportunities originating primarily in biomedical pathologies (and often exacerbated by social practices), whereas mild and moderate retardation is a function of limited opportunities stemming primarily from sociocultural handicaps. The strategy for the prevention of severe and profound retardation must be founded on research findings from the biomedical sciences; the strategy for the prevention of mild and moderate retardation must be founded on knowledge from the behavioral sciences.

Those concerned with the prevention of mild and moderate retardation must address two questions: Have there been sufficient advances in the behavioral sciences to warrant a program of prevention at present? If so, what is the nature of such a program? The answer to the first question is definitely, "Yes." During the past 15 years there have been significant advances in knowledge of mild and moderate retardation in the fields of education, child rearing, medicine, pediatrics, community work, criminology, and business and industry (Kazdin, 1979). Most advances have been concerned with remediation. The answer to the second question is that a program for the prevention of retardation will have to consist of parent training in child-rearing practices, compensatory preschool, and special elementary instruction, all welded together by theory and technique to form a unified approach.

Parent training, which begins upon the children's enrollment in the preschool at the age of 18 months, teaches the parents behavioral management techniques that will enhance their child's development in skills, knowledge, and motivation hierarchies. The preschool component provides social and preacademic opportunities for normal development and prepares the child for successful participation in the first grade; the special elementary school program helps the child to master the use of language and basic academic skills—reading, arithmetic, and writing—and to acquire the motivation to apply these skills with little or no assistance.

Sufficient research has been done on parent training programs, preschool compensatory programs, and special elementary instructional programs to indicate cogent formats, although such formats have not as yet been systematically integrated to form a workable program to help prevent mild or moderate retardation.

The Parent Training Program

Parent training programs, which have proliferated during the past 15 years, fall into two main categories: how-to books and multimedia packages, and face-to-face instructional programs. How-to books and multimedia packages have always been popular, particularly among middle-and upper-socioeconomic parents. However, relatively few of these materials have been assessed for their utility in furthering the development of children; and those that have been evaluated have been found to be of little value when used without professional assistance (Bernal & North, 1978).

From the research to date it is clear that the present training aspect of a prevention program must be of the face-to-face instructional variety and must have realistic observable objectives, explicit teaching methods, and procedures for monitoring progress that provide a guide for continually modifying materials and/or practices. The Portage Project (Shearer & Shearer, 1976) meets these requirements. Launched in 1969 by a grant from the Bureau of Education for the Handicapped, U.S. Office of Education (now the office of Special Education Programs), the Portage Project was established to develop, implement, and demonstrate a model program serving young handicapped children in a rural area. In 1970, 205 children and their

families were provided services through federal, state, and local funding. The major components of the model include:

1. An educational program that takes place in each enrolled child's home and is implemented by home teachers on a weekly basis.
2. Assessment using the Portage Checklist, plus any other assessment instruments necessary to plan a curriculum.
3. Implementation of the behavioral teaching model.
4. Curriculum planning with the expectation that children will achieve weekly prescribed goals.
5. Weekly staff meetings for problem solving and curriculum modification (Shearer & Shearer, 1976).

The Portage data show that the average Cattell Infant Scale and Stanford-Binet Intelligence Scale IQ of the children upon enrollment was 75. After an 8-month period of training there was an average gain of 18.3 IQ points—raising the average IQ to 93—and a mental age score gain of 15 months (Shearer & Shearer, 1976). Furthermore, a comparison of the Portage children with those attending local classroom programs for culturally and economically disadvantaged preschoolers showed a significant difference in favor of the Portage children in terms of their mental age and IQ scores (Cattell Infant Scale, Stanford-Binet Intelligence Scale, and Gesell Developmental Schedule), as well as in their language, academic, and socialization skills as measured by the Alpern-Boll Developmental Profile (Peniston, 1972).

The Portage Project has been approved for dissemination and replication by the Joint Dissemination Review Panel established by the Bureau of Education for the Handicapped. At present, there are 60 replication sites in the United States, one in England, one in Wales (Revill & Blunden, 1979; Smith, Kushlick, & Glossop, 1977), and one in Peru (Bluma, Shearer, Frohman, & Hilliard, 1979). The Portage Project materials have been translated and adapted for Spanish-speaking and French populations, and for the Japanese.

Because this Project was designed to be a self-sufficient, home-based program, certain modifications are necessary for its integration into a compensatory preschool and in special elementary school programs. In the prevention program proposed here, the home teacher: 1) teaches one or both parents techniques to improve their child's skills and knowledge in an individualized curriculum similar to the Portage curriculum (self-help, socialization, language and communication, motor, and cognitive or preacademic behavior) and coordinates the home program with the preschool curriculum; 2) helps the parents to provide and develop motivation for academic achievement; 3) encourages the parents to use their newly acquired skills in dealing with the other children in the home; and 4) weans the parents from the supervision and assistance provided by him or her.

The specific activities of the home teacher include:

Orienting the parents to the intervention program. The home teacher presents and discusses with the parents and interested members of the immediate family the home training, preschool, and elementary school procedures, elaborating on the printed orientational information provided them at the time of their recruitment into the program. Introductory remarks include an explanation of how the parents should work with their child, both at home and in the preschool, and later, in the elementary school. The parents are also assured that the home teacher will help them through all phases of the program and that they will eventually be able to carry on without the teacher's assistance.

Administering the inventories. The home teacher initiates the parent training program before, or at the same time, that the child is enrolled in the preschool. He or she begins by administering the Portage Parent Inventory (Boyd, Stauber, & Bluma, 1977) to each parent, and the Portage Checklist (Bluma, Shearer, Frohman, & Hilliard, 1976a) to the child. The Parent Inventory provides infor-

mation on the teaching competence of the parent in terms of his or her skills to instruct the child, to consequate correct and incorrect responses, and to record progress. Results of the Parent Inventory serve as a baseline for a parent's progress in learning the techniques of behavioral teaching. The results of the Portage Checklist indicate the child's competencies in socialization, motor development, self-help, cognitive skills, and language and communication.

Setting teaching goals, assigning teaching tasks, and recording progress. On the basis of the Portage Checklist, the teacher selects one or two of the child's low competency items for the parent to begin to emphasize. Using the *Portage Guide to Early Education* (Bluma et al., 1976b), he or she sets the teaching goal or goals and demonstrates the teaching procedures that will help the child attain such goals. He or she also shows the parent how to record the child's progress. When the parent's performance indicates that the parent can carry out the teaching model acceptably, the teacher prescribes the training schedule to be followed for the next several days. The teacher also suggests routines in the home that promote pleasant and profitable parent-child working relationships.

Teaching effective teaching techniques. The teacher's demonstrations of teaching procedures use techniques that have been derived from applied behavior analysis involving the four-term contingencies of cuing, responding, consequating, and managing setting factors (Bijou, 1977). The same techniques are used by the teachers in the preschool and special elementary school programs.

Revising and extending the teaching program. In the next home visit the teacher reviews the parent's work and the records. If information from both sources indicates that the child has made little or no progress, the teacher revises the program, models the revised version, observes the mother's performance on the revised teaching procedure, and assigns the revised task. If, on the other hand, the information indicates that progress has been satisfactory, the teacher introduces the next task in the sequence and again models the teaching technique, gives the parent practice until the parent is proficient, and assigns that task for the next week. This procedure is continued and more tasks are added as progress is accelerated. Thus, within a month, a child may be working simultaneously on three tasks, such as socialization, self-help, and preacademics.

When problem behaviors such as non-attending behavior or negativistic behavior interfere with learning, the teacher institutes programs specially designed to weaken or eliminate them. The techniques the parent learns for dealing with interfering behaviors become part of the parent's child-rearing repertoire.

The home teacher enhances the child's opportunities for learning by supplying books, toys, educational materials, and play equipment and, using programming techniques, shows the parents how the materials can be used to augment the child's activities to produce not only additional skills and knowledge but enjoyment and satisfaction as well. The teacher also arranges trips, outings, and other activities to acquaint the child and his or her family with community resources, facilities, and civic practices. Throughout these interactions and in the teaching of the modified Portage curriculum, the home teacher shows the parents how to develop the child's motivation for academic achievement, an objective similar to that advocated by Jesse Jackson in a 1978 article in *Time* magazine entitled "Education: Learning to Excel in School."

Coordinating program components. The home teacher coordinates the parent-training activities with the preschool and elementary school programs in order to integrate and generalize learning from all three sources. Coordination of activities with the preschool includes emphasizing training that is common to both settings (e.g., toilet training), extending home programs into the preschool (e.g., properly washing one's hands and face), and extending preschool programs into

the home (e.g., further experiences in generalizing colors). Interrelating activities with the elementary school program involves providing information to the parents about the changing school goals and programs and showing them how they can enchance their child's academic progress.

The home training program is designed to wean the parents from the teacher's assistance by giving them more opportunities to make their own decisions and solve their own problems. The teacher's visits become less and less frequent, although he or she maintains active contacts with the parents until their child has completed the fourth grade and has acquired mastery of the basic academic skills.

The Preschool Program

The compensatory preschool component of the prevention program is based on four models: 1) the preschool for handicapped children developed at the University of Illinois at Urbana-Champaign (Bijou, 1972) and at the University of Arizona (Bijou, 1977); 2) the preschool for young deviant children at the University of Kansas (Baer, Rowbury, Baer, Herbert, Clark, & Nelson, 1976); 3) the classroom for severely and profoundly retarded children in Corvallis, Oregon (Fredericks, Baldwin, Grove, Riggs, Furey, Moore, Jordon, Gage, Leval, Alrik, & Waldow, 1977); and 4) the nursery school for Down syndrome babies at the University of Washington, Seattle (Hayden & Haring, 1976). The programs in Corvallis and Seattle have been approved for dissemination by the Joint Dissemination Review Panel of the U.S. Offfice of Education, Bureau of Education for the Handicapped.

The preschool program coordinates its activities with the parent training program described above and the elementary school program described in the next section. Specifically, the aims of the preschool are to carry forward and expand upon the work of the home teacher and to provide the child with social experiences and preacademic and academic activities that will help him or her acquire the skills and knowledge expected of normal preschool children in our society.

The two-part curriculum, for children from ages 2 to 6, includes the usual kindergarten activities so that the children will be prepared for the first grade of the elementary program. Part One covers the typical preschool activities—free play, storytime, show and tell, music and rhythms, snack, rest, and toileting. Part Two emphasizes individualized teaching (in one-to-one and small group situations) in self-care skills, language development and facilitation, and preacademic skills and knowledge. The program has the following features:

Initial assessment. A child's competencies upon enrollment at age 2 are ascertained through a criterion-referenced inventory administered either by the home teacher or the head preschool teacher. The inventory is also given at yearly intervals to assess progress.

Setting goals and preparing curricula. Initial goals, derived from the inventory, are the basis for preparing the initial individualized curriculum. The number of goals, hence the number of programs, in a child's curriculum may vary, but increases as the child advances in the preschool.

Each item in the curriculum is tailored to the child's unique development, taking into account language competence and the kinds of contingencies that are meaningful (functional) to him or her.

Teaching the curriculum and recording performance. Teaching the curriculum subjects, as well as treating interfering problem behaviors, is based on the application of behavior principles (Bijou & Baer, 1978). In essence, this entails managing 1) the conditions that precede responses, such as instructions and prompts, 2) the conditions concurrent with responses, such as setting factors, and 3) the conditions that follow responses. The latter requires selecting functional reinforcers, pairing them with the child's productions so as to develop intrinsic reinforcers for school activities, and scheduling the reinforcers so that they encour-

age independence and perseverance. Each child's response on each curriculum item is recorded by either the teacher or an aide on the child's individual record forms, which are kept on a clipboard.

Revising programs and attaining ultimate academic and social goals. A child's performance on the programmed tasks is assessed weekly, or more often if necessary, in a progress review conference. If progress has been unsatisfactory, the program is modified, and the child's performance on the modified program is reviewed the following week. This systematic correcting procedure is continued until the child makes reasonable progress.

When a goal is attained, it is replaced by the next higher goal in the curriculum. Ultimate goals are tied to social and academic requisites for the first grade. If a child attains all the anticipated goals before the end of the preschool program, additional goals are set to extend his or her competencies into the first grade. In this intervention strategy there is no concern for "over-preparing" a child, for the first grade curriculum is individualized and the content is simply a continuation and extension of the items that constituted the preschool compensatory program.

The Elementary School Program

The elementary school component of the intervention has the objective of teaching the social and academic skills and knowledge (language, reading, spelling, and arithmetic, and conceptual and problem-solving skills that constitute intelligent behavior) to a level at which they are intrinsically (automatically) reinforcing, and therefore serviceable for advancement in academic, recreational, and vocational endeavors. To accomplish this above primary objective, the special elementary program begins in the first grade and continues through the fourth grade, at which point the child has learned to work fairly independently, an expectation assumed by most teachers of "normal" children. Academic progress is measured by achievement tests, such as the Metropolitan Achievement

Test; changes in motivation for school work and in self-concept are assessed by criterion-referenced and norm-referenced tests.

The elementary school component is a variation of the Direct Instruction Model developed by Englemann and Becker:

> The major goal of the Direct Instruction Model is to improve the basic education of children from economically disadvantaged backgrounds and thus increase their life options . . . . The model emphasizes small-group, face-to-face instruction by a teacher using carefully sequenced, daily lessons in reading, arithmetic, and language. These lessons utilize modern learning principles and advanced programming strategies (Becker, Englemann, & Thomas, 1975a, 1975b). Each set of lessons has been meticulously field-tested to determine that low-performing children will achieve the program objectives under carefully monitored conditions (Becker, 1977, p. 521).

The model was one of eight programs in the Follow Through research in which provisions were made for the children to learn, in addition to basic academic skills, "arts, crafts, social skills, and values in ways designed to suit local conditions. It was further stressed that instructional methods led to a service of personal competence and a positive attitude toward self" (Becker, 1977, p. 522).

In the follow-up study, over 8,000 children from low-income families in 20 communities across the country participated in the Direct Instruction Model at a given time. Some had entered the program at kindergarten and some at first grade; all terminated at the end of the third grade. The findings on a group of over 5,000 showed, among other things, that the children performed at about or above the national average in reading, spelling, mathematics, and language according to scores on the Metropolitan Achievement Test and the Wide Range Achievement Test; that significant gains in IQ were maintained throughout the period of the study; and that there were significant increases in measures of self-esteem and intellectual responsibility. The results also showed, and from the point of view of this proposal it is important, that

low IQ students (IQ under 80) made substantial gains (Becker & Carnine, 1981).

There is considerable controversy over the Follow Through research. Some claim that the results of the research were inconclusive—that none of the eight models was differentially significant (Abt Associates, 1977; House, Glass, McLean, & Walker, 1978). On the other hand, Becker and Carnine (1980, 1981) maintain that the evaluation method used by Abt Associates underevaluated the differences, that the Direct Instruction Model was clearly superior to the others, and that the results are all the more impressive when one takes into account the serious problems in research design involving the composition of the groups and the absence of standards for model implementation. Bereiter and Kurland (1978) also disagree with the conclusion of the House et al. (1978) evaluation. They note the shortcomings of the Follow Through research design: limited range of outcome measures, lack of comparable control groups, and lack of comparable training at all sites of the model, and state:

> The two high-scoring models according to our analysis are Direct Instruction and Behavior Analysis. The two low-scoring are ECD Open Education and Responsive Education. If there is some clear meaning to the Follow Through results, it ought to emerge from a comparison of these two pairs of models. Distinctive characteristics of the first pair are easy to name: Sponsors of both the Direct Instruction and Behavior Analysis models call their approaches "behavioral" and "structured" and both give a high priority to the three R's. ECD and Responsive Education, on the other hand, are avowedly "child-centered." Although most other Follow Through models could also claim to be child-centered, these two are perhaps the most militantly so and most opposed to what Direct Instruction and Behavior Analysis stand for (pp. 26–27).

In the proposal presented here, there is a variation on the Direct Instruction Model relating to staff. Six teachers are required: two for two first grade classes of 15 children each, two for two second-grade classes of 15 each, one for one third-grade class of 30, and one for one fourth-grade class of 30. This decreasing ratio of teachers to students is entirely feasible, since the children would have learned to work independently and resourcefully throughout the earlier years. There are, in addition, 10 aides: two to assist each first and second-grade teacher, and one each for the third and fourth-grade teachers. As in the preschool, teachers and aides are trained and supervised by the principal investigator.

The salient features of the elementary school program are as follows:

Initial assessment of competencies. Upon the child's entrance to school, the teacher assesses his or her competencies using criterion-referenced tests. The teacher also reviews the preschool reports, especially for information about the child's hierarchy of functional reinforcers and his or her academic work repertoires, e.g., how long he or she can work constructively without supervision, proficiency in various kinds of problem-solving tasks, differential behaviors toward reading and arithmetic, and whatever else might be gleaned from the records.

Preparing the individualized curriculum. A child is placed in the Distar reading, arithmetic, and language programs (Becker et al., 1975b) according to his or her performance in each subject on the criterion-referenced test. The remainder of the child's curriculum is made up of the traditional elementary subjects and activities.

Teaching techniques. Initially, the teacher divides the class into small groups and gives instructions from scripts; guides and facilitates responding in unison; controls the pacing of learning; corrects errors; and praises correct responses. Built into this type of teaching are techniques that continue to train the child to work independently. Most children can be expected to move from the group-teaching situation to working independently in from 2 to 3 months and to continue doing so until the end of the fourth grade.

Monitoring individual progress, revising programs, and assessment. The teacher monitors performance weekly by means of

tests and revises a child's programs according to the findings. As the child progresses, only biweekly testing is generally necessary. In the course of the four elementary grades, the child moves through the three currently available levels of Distar reading, arithmetic, and language, plus a year of an advanced academic program—all of which have included supplementary activities geared to developing writing and spelling skills. Completion of this 4-year program should enable almost all of the children to handle with confidence the work they will encounter in a regular fifth-grade class.

STEPS TO ACTIVATE THE PROGRAM

The proposed prevention program calls for a three-stage operation. Stage I includes a series of short-term studies devoted to 1) modifying and extending the materials and procedures of the Portage parent training program, the behavior analysis preschool model, and the Direct Instruction model; 2) coordinating the practices in all three models so that the techniques and procedures are consistently and competently applied; and 3) incorporating findings from recent research literature that relate to parent training, compensatory preschool education, and early elementary education. Stage II involves a pilot study focusing on one full-scale, full-term investigation with 30 children and their families, and a cohort group. The economic status of the families in both groups will be required to meet the U.S. Office of Economic Opportunity (OEO) poverty guideline for low income and will have to have at least one mildly or moderately retarded child over the age of 6, and one child under the age of 2 without known physiological impairment, the latter of whom will be the candidate for admission to the prevention program. The children in both groups will be formally evaluated upon enrollment and at yearly intervals both during the study and after completion of the study.

The Stage II study will be prepared to deal

with the problem of dropouts in both groups. Since the study will be based on individual research designs, the number of dropouts would affect both the number of replications possible and the smooth operation of an intervention program in which teachers are assigned to a set number of parents and a set number of children in each class. In order to keep the total number of subjects in a study as close as possible to 30, up to 35 children could be enrolled at the beginning in the hope that the number of dropouts would not exceed the average. Another possibility is to replace dropouts with comparable families and children from a waiting list.

The Stage II study will also have to deal with certain ethical problems. One problem pertains to securing informed consent from participants, i.e., making certain that the parents in the prevention program understand the nature of the parent-training and educational programs before agreeing to participate. Needless to say, there will be simple and full explanations as to the purpose of the study, the way in which parents and teachers will work together during the 8- or 9-year period of the investigation, and the inconveniences, if any, and benefits involved. Parents having reservations on any grounds should not be accepted into the project.

Another ethical problem is that of benefits to the cohort group. Parents and children in the cohort group will not benefit directly from the periodic testing they will receive; on the other hand, they will suffer no harm. Some might argue that in a sense the cohort group is deprived of the benefits of the treatment, but inasmuch as the stated purpose of the study is to *demonstrate empirically* that mild and moderate retarded development can be prevented by combining the three specified programs, this argument cannot be considered too seriously. To offset this objection, however, there is the possibility of offering the cohort group a remedial program at the end of the study.

There is perhaps a third ethical problem. Over the past 10 years, each of the three programs described in this study has demonstrated on a large-scale basis that the development of retarded children can be accelerated. Unfortunately, when the children in these programs were sent to regular school, the gains they had made were, for the most part not maintained, and in some cases there was considerable "back-sliding." This discontinuity in progress is attributable mainly to the fact that the receiving teachers (those in whose classes the children were placed subsequent to their attendance in one of the programs) were not trained in the teaching techniques that had helped the children to succeed earlier. What is needed now—and an ethical problem arises if it is not provided—is the demonstration that mild and moderate retardation can be prevented by combining the three models described here.

Suppose the data on the Stage II study were equivocal. This outcome is highly improbable, first, because of the demonstrated effectiveness of the component parts of the program, and second, because the program involves a self-correcting procedure. In other words, the monitoring system is of such a nature that plateaus in progress are quickly identified and modifications in procedures and materials are quickly instituted.

In Stage III, the actual pilot prevention program is replicated in various parts of the country. These programs will begin about 3 years after completion of the Stage II pilot study and will include only enrolled children and their families. Cohort groups will be unnecessary.

Finally, a comment on budget is necessary. A program of this kind requires a substantial budget for teaching personnel and materials for an 8- to 9-year period. Funding agencies generally prefer to support research and demonstration projects for 3 years or less. Although short-term funding is satisfactory for fulfilling the objectives of many programs, this is not true for intervention programs whose aim is to bring about meaningful and lasting changes in the social environment, i.e., in the day-to-day behavior of children, parents, and teachers. For such programs, long-term support is a necessity.

Funding agencies are more likely to support long-term projects if proposals include a system of accountability. In this proposed prevention program, a report would be submitted at 2-year intervals describing in quantitative terms the children's progress. Since fine-grain monitoring of each child's progress on each instructional program is a cardinal and constant feature of all aspects of the intervention strategy, biannual accountability would present no problems. Although the cost of this program might be considered high, it cannot begin to approach the staggering cost of supporting mildly and moderately retarded individuals throughout their lives.

SUMMARY

A strategy for preventing mild and moderate retardation in young children, from a behavior analysis point of view, involves modifying through systematic training the behavior of parents and teachers in order to provide children with more and new opportunities and incentives for intellectual and academic achievement. This objective can be attained through a program that integrates three behavioral programs that have clearly demonstrated their effectiveness: the Portage Project for training parents to train their handicapped child in the home, the behavior analysis preschool model for compensatory education for the handicapped, and the Direct Instruction Model for comprehensive educational intervention with the disadvantaged.

A prevention program is described showing how the three programs, each somewhat altered, will be integrated to effect substantial changes in parent and teacher practices so that by the completion of the fourth grade the children involved will be able to demonstrate on objective tests intellectual, personal, and academic competencies within the normal range of development.

The first stage of the present program consists of a series of short-term studies aimed at fusing the three programs into a unified prevention strategy; the second stage consists of a long-term (8 to 9 years) study designed to demonstrate the effectiveness of the unified approach. The third stage consists of replications of the prevention program in various parts of the country.

The proposed research will require a substantial budget over a long period, but such support cannot be considered a high-risk investment because each component of the intervention strategy has already demonstrated its effectiveness in accelerating development among retarded children. Although it may be difficult to estimate the ultimate benefits to children and their families, it is clear that such a program will allow most of the children to participate in the mainstream activities of their peers. That outcome alone cannot help but enrich the lives of the children and strengthen their functioning in society.

REFERENCES

Abt Associates. *Education as experimentation: A planned variation model,* Vol. 4. Cambridge, MA: Abt Associates, 1977.

Adelson, E., & Fraiberg, S. Gross motor development in infants blind from birth. *Child Development,* 1974, *45,* 114–126.

Ansbacker, H.L. What is positive mental health? In: D.G. Forgays (ed.), *Primary prevention of psychopathology.* Hanover, NH: University Press of New England, 1978.

Baer, D.M., Rowbury, T., Baer, A.M., Herbert, E., Clark, H.B., & Nelson, A. A program test of behavior technology: Can it recover deviant children for normal public schooling? In: T.D. Tjossem (ed.), *Intervention strategies for high risk infants and young children.* Baltimore: University Park Press, 1976.

Becker, W.C. Teaching reading and language to the disadvantged—what we have learned from field research. *Harvard Educational Review,* 1977, *47,* 418–543.

Becker, W.C., & Carnine, D.W. Direct instruction: An effective approach to educational intervention with the disadvantaged and low performers. In: B.B. Lahey & A.E. Kazdin (eds.), *Advances in clinical and child psychology*. New York: Plenum Publishing Corp., 1980.

Becker, W.C., & Carnine, D.W. Direct instruction: A behavioral theory-based model for the comprehensive educational intervention with the disadvantaged. In: S.W. Bijou & R. Ruiz (eds.), *Behavior modification: Contributions to education*. Hillsdale, NJ: Lawrence Erlbaum Associates, 1981.

Becker, W.C., Englemann, S., & Thomas, D.R. *Teaching 1: Cognitive learning and instruction*. Chicago: Science Research Associates, 1975a.

Becker, W.C., Englemann, S., & Thomas, D.R. *Teaching 2: Cognitive learning and instruction*. Chicago: Science Research Associates, 1975b.

Beckwith, L. Relationships between attributes of mothers and their infants' IQ scores. *Child Development*, 1971, *41*, 1083–1097.

Bereiter, C., & Kurland, M. *Were some Follow Through models more effective than others?* Paper presented at meeting of American Educational Research Association, Toronto, March 30, 1978.

Bernal, M.E., & North, J.A. A survey of parent training manuals. *Journal of Applied Behavior Analysis*, 1978, *11*, 533–544.

Bijou, S.W. Theory and research in mental (development) retardation. *Psychological Record*, 1963, *13*, 95–110.

Bijou, S.W. A functional analysis of retarded development. In: N.R. Ellis (ed.), *International review of research in mental retardation*, Vol. 1. New York: Academic Press, 1966.

Bijou, S.W. The mentally retarded child. In: *Readings in educational psychology today*. Del Mar, CA: CRM Books, 1969, 121–128.

Bijou, S.W. What psychology has to offer education—now. *Journal of Applied Behavior Analysis*, 1970, *3*, 65–71.

Bijou, S.W. The technology of teaching young handicapped children. In: S.W. Bijou & E. Ribes-Inesta (eds.), *Behavior modification: Issues and extensions*. New York: Academic Press, 1972.

Bijou, S.W. Practical implications of an interactional model of child development. *Exceptional Children*, 1977, *44*, 6–14.

Bijou, S.W., & Baer, D.M. *Behavioral analysis of child development* (rev. ed.). Englewood Cliffs, NJ: Prentice-Hall, 1978.

Bijou, S.W., & Donitz-Johnson, E. Interbehavior analysis of developmental retardation. *Psychological Record*, 1981, *31*, 305–329.

Bluma, S.M., Shearer, M.S., Frohman, A.H., & Hilliard, J.M. *Portage guide to early education: Checklist*. Cooperative Educational Service Agency 12, Box 564, Portage, WI 53901, 1976a.

Bluma, S.M., Shearer, M.S., Frohman, A.H., & Hilliard, J.M. *Portage guide to early education: Manual* (rev. ed.). Cooperative Educational Service Agency 12, Box 564, Portage, WI 53901, 1976b.

Bluma, S.M., Shearer, M.S., Frohman, A.H., & Hilliard, J.M. *Guia Portage de educacion pre-escolar*. Cooperative Educational Service Agency 12, Box 564, Portage, WI 53901, 1979.

Boyd, J. Comparison of motor behavior in deaf and hearing boys. *American Annals of the Deaf*, 1967, *112*, 598–605.

Boyd, R.D., Stauber, K.A., & Bluma, S.M. *Portage parent program*. Cooperative Education Service Agency 12, Box 564, Portage, WI 53901, 1977.

Bradley, R.H., & Caldwell, B.M. Early home environment and changes in mental test performance in children from 6 to 36 months. *Developmental Psychology*, 1976a, *2*, 93–97.

Bradley, R.H., & Caldwell, B.M. The relation of infants' home environment to mental test performance at 54 months: A follow-up study. *Child Development*, 1976b, *47*, 1172–1174.

Brophy, J.E. Mothers as teachers of their own pre-school children: The influence of socioeconomic status and task structure on teaching specificity. *Developmental Psychology*, 1977, *13*, 242–248.

Burgess, R.L., & Conger, R.D. Family interaction in abusive, neglectful, and abnormal families. *Child Development*, 1978, *49*, 1163–1173.

California Association for the Retarded. *Prevention: An agenda for action*. (rev. ed.). California Association for the Retarded, 1225 Eight St., Suite 312, Sacramento, CA 95814, 1979.

Cleland, C.C., & Clark, C.M. Sensory deprivation and aberrant behavior among idiots. *American Journal of Mental Deficiency*, 1966, *71*, 213–225.

Collard, R.R. Exploratory and play behaviors of infants reared in lower and middle-class homes. *Child Development*, 1971, *42*, 1003–1015.

Cowen, E.L. Demystifying primary prevention. In: D.G. Forgays (ed.), *Primary prevention of psychopathology*. Hanover, NH: University Press of New England, 1978.

Deutsch, M. Minority group and class status as related to social and personality factors in scholastic achievement. *Monographs for the Society for Applied Anthropology*, No. 2, 1960.

Education: Learning to excel in school. *Time*, 1978, *2*, 45–46.

Elardo, R., Bradley, R., & Caldwell, B.M. The relation of infants' home environment to mental test performance from six to thirty-six months: A longitudinal analysis. *Child Development*, 1975, *46*, 71–76.

Elardo, R., Bradley, R., & Caldwell, B.M. A longitudinal study of the relation of infants' home environment to language development at age three. *Child Development*, 1977, *48*, 595–603.

Force, D.G. Social status of physically handicapped children. *Exceptional Children*, 1956, *23*, 104–107.

Fredericks, H.D., Baldwin, D.N., Grove, D.N., Riggs, C., Furey, V., Moore, W., Jordon, E., Gage, M., Leval, L., Alrik, G., & Waldow, M. *A data based classroom for the moderately and severely handicapped* (2nd ed.). Monmouth, OR: Instructional Development Corp. (P.O. Box 361, 97361), 1977.

Hayden, A.H., & Haring, N.G. Early intervention for high risk young children: Programs for Down syndrome children. In: T.D. Tjossem (ed.), *Intervention strategies for high risk infants and young children*. Baltimore: University Park Press, 1976.

Heber, F.R. Sociocultural mental retardation: A longitudinal study. In: D.G. Forgays (ed.), *Primary prevention of psychopathology*. Hanover, NH: University Press of New England, 1978.

Hess, R.D., & Shipman, V.C. Early experience and the socialization of cognitive modes in children. *Child Development*, 1965, *35*, 869–886.

House, E.R., Glass, G.V., McLean, L.D., & Walker, D.F. No simple answer: Critique of the "follow through" evaluation. *Harvard Educational Review*, 1978, *28*, 128–160.

Iano, R.P. Ayers, D., Heller, H.B., McGettigan, J.F., & Walker, V.S. Sociometric status of retarded children in an integrative program. *Exceptional Children*, 1974, *40*, 267–271.

Jones, P.A. Home environment and the development of verbal ability. *Child Development*, 1972, *43*, 1081–1086.

Kagan, J., & Freeman, M. Relation of childhood intelligence, maternal behaviors, and social class to behavior during adolescence. *Child Development*, 1963, *34*, 899–911.

Kantor, J.R. *Interbehavioral psychology*. (2nd rev. ed.). Bloomington, IN: Principia Press, 1959.

Kantor, J.R., & Smith, N.W. *The science of psychology: An interbehavioral survey*. Chicago, IL: Principia Press, 1975.

Karnes, M.B., Studley, W.M., Wright, W.R., & Hodgins, A.S. An approach for working with mothers of disadvantaged preschool children. *Merrill-Palmer Quarterly*, 1968, *14*, 174–184.

Kazdin, A.E. Behavior modification in applied settings. Homewood, IL: The Dorsey Press, 1975.

Kazdin, A.E. Fictions, factions, and functions of behavior therapy. *Behavior Therapy*, 1979, *10*, 629–654.

Keller, F.S. *The definition of psychology* (2nd ed.). New York: Appleton-Century-Crofts, 1973.

Kleck, R., Ono, H., & Hastorf, A.H. The effects of physical deviance upon face-to-face interaction. *Human Relations*, 1966, *19*, 425–436.

Lewis, M., & Wilson, C.D. Infant development in lower-class American families. *Human Development*, 1972, *15*, 112–127.

Lyle, J.G. The effect of an institution environment upon the verbal development of imbecile children. *Journal of Mental Deficiency Research*, 1960, *4*, 14–23.

Marjoribanks, K. Ethnic and environmental influences on mental abilities. *American Journal of Sociology*, 1972, *78*, 323–337.

Mercer, R.T. Mothers' responses to their infants with defects. *Nursing Research*, 1974, *23*, 133–137.

Osofsky, J.D. Neonatal characteristics and mother-infant interaction in two observational situations. *Child Development*, 1976, *47*, 1138–1147.

Ourth, L., & Brown, K.B. Inadequate mothering and disturbances in the neonatal period. *Child Development*, 1961, *32*, 287–295.

Pavenstedt, E. A comparison of the child-rearing environments of upper-lower and very low-lower class families. *American Journal of Orthopsychiatry*, 1965, *35*, 89–98.

Peniston, E. *An evaluation of The Portage Project*. Unpublished manuscript, The Portage Project, Cooperative Educational Service Agency No. 12, Portage, WI 53901, 1972.

Radin, N., & Weikart, D. A home-teaching program for disadvantaged preschool children. *The Journal of Special Education*, 1967, *1*, 183–190.

Ramirez, M., & Price-Williams, D.R. Achievement motivation in children of three ethnic groups in the United States. *Journal of Cross-Cultural Psychology*, 1976, *7*, 49–60.

Revill, S., & Blunden, R. A home training service for preschool developmentally handicapped children. *Behavior Research and Therapy*, 1979, *17*, 207–214.

Richardson, S.A. The effect of physical disability on the socialization of a child. In: D.A. Goslin (ed.), *Handbook of socialization theory and research*. Chicago, IL: Rand McNally & Co., 1969.

Shearer, D.E., & Shearer, M.S. The Portage Project: A model for early childhood intervention. In: T.D. Tjossem (ed.), *Intervention strategies for high risk infants and young children*. Baltimore: University Park Press, 1976.

Shere, M.O. Socio-emotional factors in the family

of twins with cerebral palsy. *Exceptional Children*, 1956, *22*, 196–199, 206–208.

Sidman, M. *Tactics of scientific research.* New York: Basic Books, 1960.

Skinner, B.F. *Science and human behavior.* New York: Macmillan Publishing Co., 1953.

Skinner, B.F. *About behavior.* New York: Alfred A. Knopf, 1974.

Smith, J., Kushlick, A., & Glossop, C. *The Wessex Portage Project: A home teaching service for families with a preschool mentally handicapped child.* Research Report No. 125, Health Care Evaluation Research Team. Dawn House, Sleepers Hill, Winchester, Hants, England, June 1977.

Stinson, M.S. Relations between maternal reinforcement and help and the achievement motive in normal-hearing and hearing-impaired

sons. *Developmental Psychology,* 1974, *10*, 348–353.

Waldrop, M.F., Pedersen, F.A., & Bell, R.Q. Minor physical anomalies and behavior in preschool children. *Child Development,* 1968, *39*, 391–400.

Wilton, K., & Barbour, A. Mother-child interaction in high-risk and contrast preschoolers of low socioeconomic status. *Child Development,* 1978, *49*, 1136–1145.

Wulbert, M., Englis, S., Kriegsmann, E., & Milk, B. Language delay and associated mother-child interactions. *Developmental Psychology,* 1975, *11*, 61–70.

Yarrow, L.J. Maternal deprivation: Toward an empirical and conceptual re-evaluation. *Psychological Bulletin,* 1961, *58*, 459–490.

Curative Aspects of Mental Retardation:
Biomedical and Behavioral Advances
edited by Frank J. Menolascino, M.D., Ronald Neman, Ph.D., and Jack A. Stark, Ph.D.
Copyright 1983   Paul H. Brookes Publishing Co., Inc.   Baltimore · London

chapter 17

Developmental Teaching Enhancement of Intelligence

Avoiding the Cumulative Deficit

GERSHON BERKSON, PH.D.
University of Illinois at Chicago
Chicago, Illinois

S EVERAL STUDIES (FISHER & ZEAMAN, 1970) on the prevalence of mental retardation have shown that mild mental retardation tends to increase with age until age 15 and then gradually declines, as demonstrated in Figure 1. A number of explanations for this increase and decrease have been proposed (Gruenberg, 1963), but the most widely accepted idea is that variation in the criteria for adaptation accounts for varying prevalence rates (Kott, 1968; Lemhau & Imre, 1969; Taylor, 1965). If one carries this thinking a bit farther, one can easily see that a cure for mental retardation can arise, not only as the result of changing the individual's characteristics, but also from changing the nature of the environment, i.e., an ecological approach.

The focus of Chapters 15 and 16, by Drs. Earl C. Butterfield and Sidney W. Bijou, respectively, has been on ways in which environments can be enriched so that mentally retarded individuals are no longer considered "retarded." Dr. Bijou discussed the multifaceted contributions to an individual's

development, stressing that normal development results from the interaction of many variables organized through time. He emphasized the important point that this interaction involves reciprocity between the individual and his or her environment. The result of this reciprocity is the emergence of new behaviors. In essence, if we view human development only in terms of single isolated variables acting at one time only, we neglect a basic assumption of developmental biology—that the interaction of many variables, organized over time and in intricate ways, produces changes having emergent properties. These emergent properties are not necessarily anticipated from the particular variables one may have focused on initially.

Dr. Bijou further noted that a child, whether normal or retarded, undergoes a series of events each of which offer the child an opportunity to grow. Sometimes, however, the opportunities do not occur at the right time, and the consequence is a deficit whose effect(s) accumulates over the developmental history of that person. For instance, the intel-

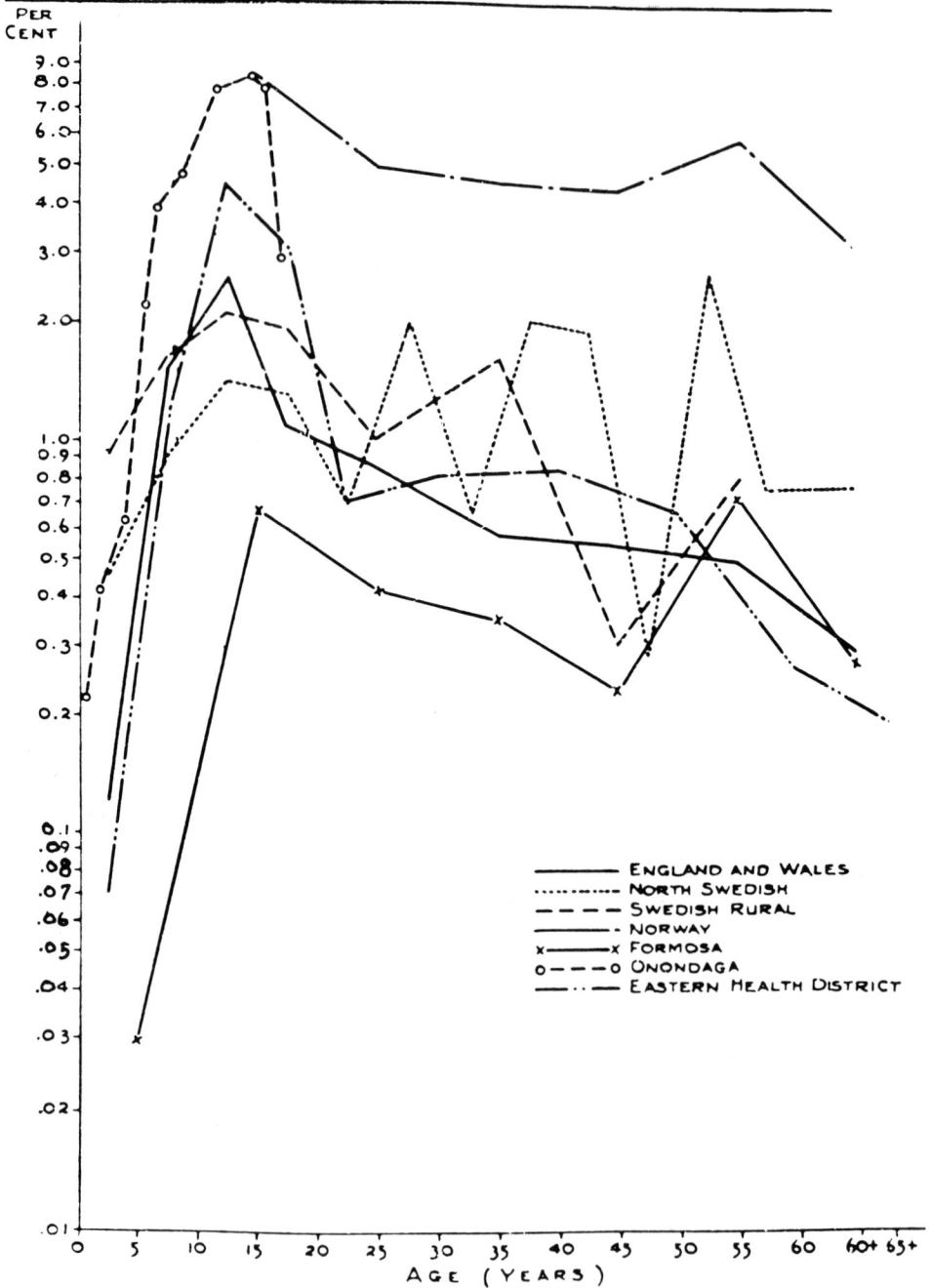

Figure 1. Prevalence of mental retardation by age. (Reprinted by permission from: Gruenberg, E.M. Epidemiology. In: H.A. Stevens & R. Heber (eds.), *Mental Retardation*. Chicago: University of Chicago, 1963.)

ligence quotient, instead of staying relatively static, may decline with the age of the child, perhaps to the point where the child becomes retarded.

TOWARD PREVENTING
A CUMULATIVE DEFICIT

The early education programs that Dr. Bijou analyzed have demonstrated that one can utilize techniques to prevent this cumulative deficit. There is also a possibility that we can increase the rate of individual development using these procedures, but there is not yet sufficient empirical data to demonstrate this. What has been clearly demonstrated, however, is the programs' ability to prevent a cumulative deficit in many children.

While research findings from early intervention programs reveal that mental retardation is not always inevitable and that the prevention of the cumulative deficit is possible, the specific definition of these programs needs refinement. We also need to know whether these early intervention programs have long-term success. Research on the Head Start and Follow Through programs in the late 1960s and early 1970s demonstrated that a child may show improvement in an early intervention program, only to enter a regular school system where the early education is not supported, with the result that the development of the cumulative deficit resumes.

On the other hand, it may not always be necessary to provide effective programs *early* in development. Feuerstein and Karasilowsky (1972) have shown that intervention even during adolescence can compensate for educational social disadvantage. Therefore, if a child has not had the benefits of an early intervention program, there is still an opportunity for change later on. A great deal more research is needed that is directed at determining what kinds of skills must be learned and at what various times during development.

In Chapter 15, Dr. Butterfield emphasized that we determine what the nature of human intelligence is by introducing the crucial test: Can human intelligence be altered? Dr. Butterfield is engaged in pursuing the answer to whether we can remove people from the area under the mental retardation prevalence curve *permanently*. He believes that by providing retarded individuals with training in general skills that are adaptive in a wide variety of environments (i.e., that can then integrate more refined skills), retarded persons can be helped to be less disabled. The work of the last 15 years has shown that we can help a retarded person to behave normally for a brief period of time by teaching him or her a specific skill. The effects of such teaching last but ''a moment'' however—while the person is in a special testing situation—for when the individual is tested in another place, he or she once more behaves in a retarded manner. A major challenge for mental retardation and developmental psychologists over the next 10 years is to learn to teach retarded individuals in ways whose effects are not only specific, but so that transfer and generalization skills are also provided. It is a significant goal to strive for, yet one can share Dr. Butterfield's optimistic outlook for the success of these endeavors.

The teaching of individual skills is important too, however. After all, what parents of a mildly retarded child would not be reasonably happy if their child could do a fairly restricted task in a competitive employment setting, or if the child is taught the living skills necessary for residing independently in the community. If retarded persons can perform productive work for which they are paid, and if they live in a relatively natural environment as a member of the community with their friends, they are in a real sense only minimally disabled.

Learning technologies can accomplish these tasks now for many retarded persons. Yet one of the most discouraging things that we experience when we visit early education programs is that although the techniques are available for teaching ''thoughty behaviors'' via specific skills, the techniques are not generally being used because the program teachers themselves are not skilled in using them. This is the perennial problem of disseminating research findings.

In summary, Drs. Butterfield and Bijou have understood the major point that mental retardation is not a static condition. Modern training techniques do work. There is increasing acceptance of the view that these considerations fully employ the posture of the cure of mental retardation.

REFERENCES

Feuerstein, R., & Karasilowsky, D. Interventional strategies for the significant modification of cognitive functioning in the disadvantaged adolescent. *Journal of American Academy of Child Psychiatry,* 1972, *11,* 572–582.

Fisher, M.A., & Zeaman, D. Growth and decline of retardate intelligence. In: N.R. Ellis (ed.), *International review of research in mental retardation.* New York: Academic Press, 1970, 151–191.

Gruenberg, E.M. Epidemiology. In: H.A. Stevens & R. Heber (eds.), *Mental Retardation.* Chicago: University of Chicago, 1963.

Kott, M.G. Estimating the number of retarded in New Jersey, *Mental Retardation,* 1968, *6,* 28–31.

Lemhau, P.V., & Imre, P.D. Results of a field epidemiologic study. *American Journal of Mental Deficiency,* 1969, *73,* 859–863.

Taylor, J.L. *Mental retarded prevalence in Oregon.* Portland, Oregon: State Board of Health, 1965.

Curative Aspects of Mental Retardation:
Biomedical and Behavioral Advances
edited by Frank J. Menolascino, M.D., Ronald Neman, Ph.D., and Jack A. Stark, Ph.D.
Copyright 1983   Paul H. Brookes Publishing Co., Inc.   Baltimore · London

Conclusion

FRANK J. MENOLASCINO, M.D.
JACK A. STARK, PH.D.
University of Nebraska Medical Center
Omaha, Nebraska

IN CHAPTER 15, DR. EARL C. BUTTERFIELD INITIALLY discussed how we might recognize that we had cured a mentally retarded person. Convinced that we can move closer to curing mentally retarded people, he stated that we need to directly attend to the question of, how would a cure of the symptom of mental retardation be defined? A major problem here is that there is heated disagreement among psychological theorists of intelligence over what constitutes normal intelligence. However, there are two dimensions of intelligence about which there is no dispute. One is that intelligence develops with age: People tend to become more and more intelligent (especially early in life). A cure process must therefore promote normal development—such as bringing retarded children to perform at the levels of nonretarded children. The second dimension is that intelligent behavior is a part of *general behavior*, and that intelligence manifests itself in a wide variety of behavioral phenomena. It will not suffice to teach retarded persons to be "super memorizers" of a particular sort. Nor will it be enough to teach them how to use only part of the spoken language system—or to solve only certain problems. Before we can legitimately claim a cure, we must promote effective *general behavior*.

With those two key ideas in mind, Dr. Butterfield reviewed research efforts focused on promoting "thoughty behaviors"—a global sign of intelligence—in mentally retarded people, and discussed areas that have yet to be conquered in the efforts to cure the symptom of mental retardation. Some examples of "thoughty behavior" can be provided by dividing cognition globally into specific kinds of behavior: 1) Language behavior is clearly a primary element: People need to be able to use essentially the full range of language that normal adults do to be considered intelligent in the language domain. 2) Memory is also generally regarded as important. For example, following a lecture, the usual listener will have formed some idea of the gist of the message that the speaker was trying to convey. Being able to extract the gist of the message is an important indication of memory, but one would not be expected to be able to remember word-for-word the lecture. There are some conditions, however, under which more complete recall is regarded as intelligence—for example, a physician would be expected to know all of the symptoms of particular kinds of diseases, not just some of them. Thus, in special circumstances a relatively complete detailed recall is an indication of intelligence. 3) In the problem-solving domain, an intelligent person is one who can arrive at a solution even though he or she has not formerly been taught the solution. The individual is equipped with some general knowledge of problem solving that will allow him or her to figure out the details of a new or novel problem. Consider, for instance, a simple physics problem involving a balance beam. Few college graduates who have had courses in the physical sciences could currently recall the details of the calculation of torque in order to predict which side of a balance scale would go up or down in a given problem. However, most of them faced with a balance beam weighted in different ways would be able to figure this out relatively quickly. 4) Noticing regularities in environmental stimulation is another kind of example of "thoughty behavior"; it is tested on intelligence tests by "series completion problems" (e.g., if one were to ask, "Tell me what comes next," and then say, "ABX, BCY," before very long the intelligent listener would say "CDZ"—having noticed the regularities in the previous items). Accordingly, such phenomena as figuring out several principles such as the physical principles involved in the calculation of torque, noticing regularities in problems and continuing them, recognizing the conditions under which relatively complete recall of material is required, and doing what is necessary to produce that complete recall—are the types of phenomena that Dr. Butterfield meant by his term "thoughty behaviors."

PROMOTING "THOUGHTY BEHAVIOR"

Over the last 15 years, research psychologists have devoted much attention to teaching people how to accomplish "thoughty behaviors." The people they teach are either young, normal children who cannot be reasonably expected to have acquired the understanding yet, but who are expected to acquire same later, or retarded persons who do not have the understanding yet, and are not expected to acquire it later. Preliminary research results indicate that retarded persons can be taught "thoughty behaviors" quickly and effectively! For example, Dr. Butterfield noted that in a matter of hours a mildly retarded child (or young adolescent) can be instructed to perform "thoughty behavior" or tasks at least as well as an uninstructed normal adult. In short, a mildly retarded person can be taught strategies that normal adults use, so that he or she can, for example, calculate torque, recognize when it is appropriate to do so, and derive the right answers to balance beam problems. The same can be done with the task of recalling lists, though it is a little harder. Such instruction is facilitated by analytically oriented psychologists who, given a problem that will yield to rational analysis, can in a relatively short period of time figure out the intellectual components necessary to solve that problem and design ways of teaching them to retarded or young normal children so that they will be developmentally advanced on that item.

Such accomplishments would seem to suggest that great progress is being made toward teaching intelligence. However, the *other* test of whether one has taught intelligence is whether the person behaves in generally effective ways, and, as Dr. Butterfield points out in Chapter 15, young children—or mildly retarded people—who have been taught "thoughty behaviors" generally *do not maintain* the use of these behaviors for a long period of time, and seldom transfer them to situations that are only superficially different from the training environment. To amplify this second point, Dr. Butterfield noted that his former colleagues at the University of Kansas and other behaviorally oriented researchers around the country have, for a number of years, worked to design programs for moderately and severely retarded children who at the time they entered the program did not speak and showed little evidence of any language comprehension. It has been shown that such children can, after months of specific instruction, be brought to the point of comprehending and using well-formed, simple instruction. These programs have been applied largely to institutionalized populations, and some of the scientists who have performed the special instructions have followed the children back to the units where they live, and asked, "Are the children using the linguistic tools that we have taught them in their everyday surroundings?" By and large, the answer is, "No." A child who will use effective language with his instructors will *not* be found to use that language in his or her other everyday living environments. Even closer tests of transfer, or tests of generality, frequently fail. Dr. Butterfield mentioned the balance beam problem, and noted that one can assess a child's ability to solve balance beam sorts of problems either with a physical apparatus that the child can manipulate and put weights on and move around, or with a paper and pencil test that represents the balances in different amounts of weights. A child can be trained with either of those kinds of materials so that he performs exceedingly well. However, the child will not transfer the same principles taught him or her on paper to the mechanical version, or vice versa. Thus, a large problem in the instruction of intelligence is promoting the *generalized* use of those ''thoughty behaviors'' that we can now teach.

There has been some success in promoting generalized use of instructed behaviors, and there is an interesting characteristic of these successes. A distinction has been noted between ways of thinking that give one a solution to a problem like calculating torque, and ways of thinking that help one decide what approaches should be used to solve a problem. One can conceive of a problem-solving strategy that will work in any situation, and distinguish that from the particular strategies one needs to think about to perform well in particular situations.

A few studies have managed to promote reasonable transfer, have taught some aspects of generalized problem solving, as well as the specific mechanisms required to solve the problems that they are teaching. For example, by teaching in such a way that a retarded child is specifically asked to pay close attention to whether his study is doing him any good, instructions can teach a retarded child to assess for himself whether he is learning the items. The child can be asked to assess how ready he is to recall the material that he is studying, or simply shown how to study the material. If one adds special instruction methods pertaining to attending to a child's ongoing questioning of whether the study is doing him any good, the child will be far more likely to utilize that method in other unrelated procedures. Recent research has shown this approach to be effective, in the sense that following the ''special study instruction'' retarded children can recall more items after an equal amount of study than normal adults! A year later these same children—who had been taught both a method and an approach to assessing whether it was working for them—were examined again. An interesting finding was that these children had remembered the method and had used it in similar tests. One year is a long intervening period in such an experiment, and the ability to demonstrate the continued use of the learning strategy was significant. Of equal interest, however, was the sustained improvement in a substantially different kind of task: reading a story and extracting the gist of the message. The children's ability to remember these stories was also markedly improved a year later for those children who had been given instruction in how to evaluate whether their ways of studying were working. This study showed substantial evidence of generalization, especially generalization across a wide range of skills and over a period of 1 year.

The research hypothesis in the above-noted studies is that if one can analyze those strategic skills (methodology) that people use to solve particular problems, the methodology could then be systematically broken down into discrete facets and taught as successfully as we teach problem solutions or content. In this manner, general increases in global intelligence could result. As Dr. Butterfield noted, learning theory research is on the verge of doing just that. There is reason to be optimistic that for such ''thoughty behaviors,'' we will, in the next several years be able to promote generalized improvements in mildly retarded citizens' ways of thinking. This type of research is one of two current approaches to the problem of how to promote generalized improvement in thinking. It is an approach that stems directly from what is called developmental cognitive psychology. In short, developmental cognitive psychologists draw a distinction between what they call *subordinate* mechanisms of thought, which are mechanisms for operating on information and solving particular problems, and what they call *superordinate* mechanisms of thought, which are mechanisms for devising and selecting the use of subordinate mechanisms. The bulk of current research in this area shows that directing instructional effort at *superordinate* mechanisms of thought holds substantial promise for improving generalized thinking (and hence decreasing the handicap of mental retardation).

Another very different approach to essentially the same problem of improving "thoughty behaviors" has emerged from behavioral psychology. While the cognitivist's approach has been to ask, in effect, "What do we have to teach in order to facilitate subsequent teachings and generalize teaching to other settings?" and to answer that we have to teach some *superordinate* ways of thinking in a more generalized mode, behavioral psychologists have tended to ask, "How should we teach the specifics that we are now teaching so that youngsters will generalize?" (rather than, "Are there ways of teaching specific lessons so that they will generalize?"). Recall the previous situation in which learning techniques were successful in teaching previously mute, severely retarded people to use simple sentences in the special teaching environment, but not in their everyday, institutionalized environments. The question behavioral psychologists would ask is, "What can we do in the process of teaching to remedy that serious transfer of learning deficit (i.e., from one interpersonal/environment setting to another) in our teaching techniques?" One approach that has been used with some success is to ask, "One of the reasons that behaviors I have taught do not transfer is that in that other environment there are not people (or events) that help to maintain the newly taught behaviors." In the previous example, an analysis of the problem might be as follows: "The attendants who are responsible for taking care of the children provide no occasions in which it makes sense for the children to talk, nor do they expect them to talk, and they do not provide social feedback for them if they do talk."

Accordingly, one approach to producing generalization of learning, from a behavioral psychologist's point of view, would be to directly and specifically intervene in the many external environments wherein the child will interact. The teaching focus is placed on events and/or transactions that will encourage the use of the behaviors that were taught in another environment. Behaviorists call this technique the introducing of natural maintaining contingencies, "natural" in the sense that they are occurring in the everyday world. Another approach is to utilize many different ways of helping the retarded person to think better—to teach them to use a variety of ways of thinking—conveyed a number of times in a number of distinctively different problems and environments. Having received training in several different ways of thinking promotes generalized use of newly learned information. An additional technique is to arrange the primary teaching environment so that it has distinct features similar to the other interpersonal/physical environments to which behavior transfer is desired; the behavior is thus more likely to transfer. Currently, there are about half a dozen similar teaching techniques designed to produce the above-noted transfer of learning that we call generalization.

In summary, Dr. Butterfield synopsized the two current, substantially different approaches in research psychology to the problem of learning "thoughty behaviors." Researchers on both sides are optimistic that their side will succeed, and one can ask: "Can these seemingly separate approaches both be right?" Dr. Butterfield believes the answer is, "Yes." He noted that the cognitive approach is designed especially for the kinds of behaviors that yield to time-consuming thought (such behaviors are designed for deliberate problem-solving efforts). By implication, the cognitive approach will probably not help much that class of "thoughty behaviors" that we all do without deliberate thought (e.g., like composing a well-formed sentence, or conveying the gist of an idea). The behavioral psychologist's approach, on the other hand, does not work particularly well with problems that yield to deliberate thought, but the approach has accrued some successes in the class of behavior that includes those natural and rapid acts that people do. Until relatively recently, there was little basis for communication among the research psychologists who were using these two seemingly different approaches.

Behavioral psychologists, over the last 10 or 15 years, have tackled progressively more complex behaviors (historically, they worked with relatively simple responses, reflecting the fact that their approach grew out of animal experimentation). As behavior modification grew and became a kind of applied arm of behavior analysis, the behavioral scientists found themselves in schools, clinics, and institutions for retarded persons where they were asked to improve performances that were substantially more "thoughty" than the ones they had previously tackled. These sets of experiments have given them some common ground with their more cognitively oriented research colleagues. The former trend within the cognitive area was quite similar: In the past, cognitively oriented psychologists regarded themselves as only naturalistic observers of how people think. However, starting about 15 years ago, their belief system changed substantially as a result of their practical success in attempting to teach children to do things that adults do. Their role as teachers who could take their observations and improve how children think brought them closer to what behavior modification people had been doing all along. So the two fields, because of different kinds of trends, have merged to the point that it is possible for a thoroughly behaviorally oriented psychologist such as Dr. Donald Baer to recently conclude that current cognitive development techniques are absolutely identical to current behavioral techniques for purposes of analyzing and/or altering behavior.

Thus, there are many sources of optimism in this field of endeavor. One is the successes that have occurred in efforts to instruct "thoughty behaviors" in mentally retarded persons. Another is the recent major change in methods of the various schools of thought regarding how to accomplish such instruction. Within the next decade we can fully expect the combined efforts of the behavioral and cognitive approaches to move us further toward the goal of curing the underlying faulty thinking-learning mechanisms that comprise the symptom of mental retardation.

A PSYCHOEDUCATIONAL PREVENTION PROGRAM

In Chapter 16, Dr. Sidney W. Bijou initially focused on the relationship between biomedical research and the total functioning of the individual interacting with the external environment, and stressed his concept of "developmental opportunities." He used the term "environment" to mean the external as well as the internal environment. Further, he focused on high-level functioning retarded individuals (i.e., mildly retarded persons who comprise 80% to 85% of the mentally retarded population) because this group can be identified more readily as the group that is socially-economically disadvantaged and is for the most part non-organically involved. He proposed that a prevention program for this upper level of the mentally retarded population be primarily psychoeducational in nature, that it should be an intervention program, and that it should extend over a rather long time period (e.g., 8 years' duration).

Chapter 16 was organized in three parts. The first provided a rationale for a prevention program, the second described the component parts of such a program, and the third briefly reviewed what has yet to be done to make such a program reality. The program rationale is based on a behavior analysis (or behavior modification) approach. Dr. Bijou utilizes the term "behavior analysis" rather than behavior modification, and his view of a behavioral approach is very close to B.F. Skinner's behavior modification. He reviewed retarded development and why it is relatively practical to proceed on the basis of behavior analysis in terms of educating a young mildly retarded individual. From the viewpoint of a behavioral psychologist, human psychological development consists of progressive changes in interactions between a biologically maturing individual and the physical, sociocultural, and organismic conditions that constitute his or her environment. These progressions may be slow, normal, or rapid—depending on the developmental opportunities provided by 1) the biological makeup of the individual, and

2) external environmental conditions. Slow or retarded progression may be traced to restrictions in developmental opportunities induced by anatomical or physiological impairments, sociocultural handicaps, or, in most cases, both factors. The more extreme the impairments, whether biomedical or sociocultural, the more severe the level of mental retardation.

The concept of developmental opportunities underscores the provision of meaningful contacts with the environment so as to affect certain kinds of developmental changes. Injury to the central nervous system is conceptualized as restricting the development of the organism— restricting his or her opportunities to interact. One kind of restriction, obviously, is any impairment in the special sensory or other response equipment. Such impairments to the organism result in developmental restrictions because the affected individual is not capable of responding in the usual way. Further, the individual may not be able to have (or capitalize upon) the opportunities for development as other individuals do. The latter aspect—ability to respond to the opportunities for development—is more difficult to document since it typically involves individual clinical cases. For example, if an individual child does not have the ability to respond to painful stimuli, it may be necessary to safeguard such a child's development until he or she is old enough to be told (or instructed) that there are kinds of stimuli that will have to be avoided or reported to others. Prior to the ability to understand (or be instructed) about the dangers of pain stimuli, such children have to be protected so that they do not damage their tongue or injure a limb, for example. The point is that if the intrinsic equipment is in any way impaired, through biological malfunctioning or damage, developmental progress is also impaired.

As to sociocultural handicaps, Dr. Bijou noted that many categories of sociocultural conditions that restrict development have been identified. Clearly, socioeconomic poverty is one set of conditions that can greatly restrict developmental opportunities. Studies of children living under extremely deprived conditions have reported sufficient data to demonstrate that such children do not have the opportunities to learn as other children do, and do not have adequate relationships with their parents to be encouraged to learn, to achieve, or to gain support for accomplishing developmental tasks. Another set of conditions that can greatly restrict developmental opportunities is abusive child care practices. The professional literature clearly documents not only physical injury to children, but also that child abuse curtails the opportunity for development and for a sense of identity with other children. A third category is apparent indifference and lack of concern for child care, growth, and development. To a large extent, we have undergone a period in which we have found that child care practices have been less than ideal as to the kind of emotional and social support that normal children must have to grow in normal ways. Extended to families, these data clearly show indifference, or lack of concern for the development of individual children by the family unit. The final category that promotes sociocultural handicaps is family practices that are in conflict with the culture—involving many problems in which subcultures and minority cultures have strong interests in maintaining their culture and their modes. Often, a great deal of conflict is created in children regarding what the families want versus what the outside societal group expects. In brief, these internal-external developmental and biological vicissitudes, when present, do not give a child an opportunity to grow in a normal way.

Given the above view of the sociobehavioral rationales for retarded behavior, Dr. Bijou's position is that we can currently take mildly retarded individuals and try to arrange a developmental program whereby these sociocultural dimensions are either minimized, reduced, or eliminated. Specifically, this proposed prevention-cure program would focus on a type of Head Start program, the importance of preschool education, and the significance of parent training. At present, there are programs existing in each of these areas that have clearly demonstrated that they are effective—and, for the most part, technologically speaking, we know how to remediate their deficits.

Dr. Bijou's thesis is that we are ready now to move from remediation, at least in this particular area, to prevention and cure. The program would include selecting what has been demonstrated to be the most effective *parent training program*, what has been the most effective *preschool program*, and the most effective "follow through" early grade school educational program. Exposing all retarded children to a combination of these three specific training programs early in life will, in Dr. Bijou's opinion, prevent the occurrence in most instances of mild retardation.

Each of these three programs has been effective in its own way. In the critical parent training area of a prevention program—making the parents aware, giving them information, and helping them with their own problems (rather than taking their problems away)—there is a model called the Portage Project. The Portage Project, which has been in operation now for about 10 years, has been well accepted in this country, and is now being accepted in many other countries. Basically, it is a simple program, and perhaps that is why it is so effective. In this training program a trained teacher identifies a family with a retarded child, asks the family whether they want service, and if they do, the service is provided without charge. The teacher assesses the child herself, not by means of an intelligence test, but by what is called a criterion-referenced test (i.e., a test of developmental competence based on criteria references rather than age norms). The test asks what the individual can do. Usually, competence is measured in five areas: motor skills, self-help skills, socialization skills, preacademic, and cognitive skills. (Incidently, in South American countries—Peru, particularly—wherein the Portage Project was piloted and adopted, there were three added dimensions—nutrition, safety, and hygiene.)

After the teachers assess the children, they select from the information obtained (including a report from the parents), a baseline of the current level of performance. The highest point that the child can accomplish in each of the above-mentioned competence areas is utilized as a start for the beginning of education, or as the beginning for training. The teacher also teaches or demonstrates to the parents how they can help their child in these various specific development areas: The teacher models for the parents and shows them directly how to teach a series of simple training techniques. This method, in a sense, is self-correcting—a technique of prescribing a treatment, keeping records, and closely monitoring the program's progress. It is a very simple kind of "pedagogy," but well-founded from the point of view of what we know about the learning process of mildly retarded individuals.

Dr. Bijou noted that another needed prevention component is a model, developmentally oriented preschool program such as that of Dr. Alice Hayden for very young Down syndrome children at the University of Washington in Seattle.

Another model preschool program is the one researched by Dr. Donald Baer at the University of Kansas-Bureau of Child Research, which has a similar format. These programs have clearly indicated that young handicapped children, between the chronological ages of 2 and 5 years, can make excellent progress at their level of competence.

A major difficulty that one encounters in a prevention-cure program of this type is that when the children leave preschool and go to the normal kindergarten (or a special kindergarten or the first grade), the receiving teacher is not obliged to adhere to the earlier utilized training procedures (neither is he or she generally trained to use comparable teaching or programming procedures). As a consequence, mildly retarded children, by-and-large, do not continue to make significant development progress. Thus, every effort must be made to try to maintain the kinds of gains achieved in the earlier years of developmental stimulation of the child. If such gains are not maintained by the teacher in each succeeding class, the gains either remain static or regress; these children will be shunted aside and their teachers will tend not to do programming according to the child's competence. Thus, the third program of prevention that Dr. Bijou recommended for young mildly retarded children is known as the Follow Through program. Follow Through is a national program that was completed 6 years ago (1977) and comprised eight different "Follow Through" models that were in operation at the same time. The thrust, by the Bureau of Education for the Handicapped, attempted to document which model was the most effective in treating socially disadvantaged children in the early years in school. The Follow Through program developed from earlier Head Start programs, at a time when there was controversy over whether Head Start should be funded on a larger scale. Some professionals argued that the data from Head Start showed that the involved children did not continue to make gains after they had left Head Start, and that it was "a waste of money" because these children could not really be educated in any long-term productive way: they would just slip back to where they were before the Head Start training experience. Another view was that unless there were actual follow-through attempts to continually maintain the child's motivation and to closely monitor the programming and the teaching techniques utilized, then these children would not be able to maintain their relatively new developmental advances. The main findings in this research over the past 10 or 15 years (interestingly, excellent studies, behavioral or cognitive, have really only emerged since then) have clearly shown that remediation via the Follow Through studies—again from a behavioral point of view—have demonstrated themselves to be very effective.

Accordingly, Dr. Bijou suggests that the time has come to sythesize these recent findings and actively consider the possibilities for preventing and curing mild retardation. He strongly advocates that the three programs (i.e., parent training, preschool, and Follow Through) be integrated into a prevention-cure program in which three aspects follow the *same* set of principles and the *same* technology. He conceives of this challenge as proceeding in three stages. The *first stage* would take these three aspects of early childhood education and develop an integrated model: It would determine the necessary material, do the adequate teacher training, etc. Integrating these three components would not be difficult because they each have the same kind of rationale and use the same kind of teaching techniques. The *second stage* would actually implement the program on a continual basis for a period of 8 years. The program should start when the child is 2 years of age, and continue until he or she completes the fourth grade. Dr. Bijou believes that the Follow Through program ended a little too early (i.e., when the children were in the third grade), and that it was not adequate to provide the children with the basic academic skills that would be self-motivating or automatically reinforcing. (In other words, a child must attain a certain level of reading or a certain level of mathematic skills to enable him or her to automatically read for the sake of enjoyment, at which time the training becomes automatically reinforcing. By stopping short of this projected time period, one faces the possibility of losing many skills because the individual has not achieved the end goal.) Thus, the *third stage* would, after it had been demonstrated that the two previous programs were operational, strongly focus on monitoring and documenting developmental progress.

In closing, Dr. Bijou noted that perhaps it is not realistic—in terms of how much money it will cost to accomplish the proposed three stage program—to expect to obtain support for a long-range program such as his proposal at this particular time. Nevertheless, the professional community *is* ready to make this kind of contribution to preventing mild mental retardation. It *is* ready to intervene and to help parents, teachers, and the general community in its efforts to improve the general opportunities for learning and to reduce the possibility of retarded development in a large segment of our child population.

In Chapter 17, Dr. Gershon Berkson added perspective to Chapters 15 and 16 by focusing on the ways in which Drs. Butterfield and Bijou, respectively, have suggested that we can remove retarded people from the area under the developmental curve, thereby promoting a cure and preventing mental retardation from occurring. Dr. Berkson, too, is optimistic about the long-term contributions of behavior technologies in promoting the cure of mental retardation, and strongly urged more effective dissemination of research findings.

Curative Aspects of Mental Retardation:
Biomedical and Behavioral Advances
edited by Frank J. Menolascino, M.D., Ronald Neman, Ph.D., and Jack A. Stark, Ph.D.
Copyright 1983   Paul H. Brookes Publishing Co., Inc.   Baltimore · London

section V

CURATIVE ASPECTS OF MENTAL RETARDATION
Future Prospects

Introduction

JACK A. STARK, PH.D.
FRANK J. MENOLASCINO, M.D.
University of Nebraska Medical Center
Omaha, Nebraska

T HE OBJECTIVES OF THIS FINAL SECTION of the book are to provide the reader with an opportunity to share in the "dialogue" that the contributing authors engaged in in Chapter 18, as well as to provide, in Chapter 19, a discussion of future directions and critical content areas not included in this book.

Chapter 18 offers some insight into the difficulty that we have in understanding the terminology, concepts, and technology in various disciplines. Since certain portions of this book are rather technical, Chapter 18, by featuring concrete questions and answers to material covered in earlier chapters, should provide the reader with some additional understanding.

Having participated in Chapter 18's "dialogue," the editors of this book cannot help but feel that we and our colleagues are often limited by our own lack of creative thinking. It would seem that we are deeply entrenched in the traditional research methodology of *heuristic investigation*. That is, we collect data and information and build upon previous research to advance the field one small notch further. This research process is necessary, but can often lead to a lack of creative breakthroughs in the field—via a major leap in knowledge which frequently happens by accident. For example, Dilantin (diphenylhydantin) was originally developed as a cardiovascular medication and discoveries were later made that (as is the case in many medications) it was effective in the control of another disorder (in this case, epilepsy). It would also appear that our traditional research approaches can be traced to our emphasis on deductive reasoning, in which facts and figures are collected from the world in general and specific deductions made therefrom. Science has tended to proceed in this manner ever since the influence of the 16th-century empiricists. Unfortunately, we have not emphasized inductive reasoning, which involves a more creative process on the part of an investigator and in which research findings are referred to to verify one's creative hypotheses. Nevertheless, some of the best medical and behavioral research has been conducted in this latter fashion.

Those participants who contributed to the dialogue, and in many instances contributed chapters, represent some of the best minds in their respective fields. But most impressive is their creative talents, as they seem to possess what psychologists label as *gestalt,* the ability to see the whole picture. Their general concensus was that we may be entering a new technological era in which creativity will be a *sine qua non* if we are to fashion the essential concepts, theories, models, and equipment to achieve what we now know to be possible—cure(s)!

Chapter 19 focuses on the five major biomedical and behavioral components of the book and on future directions for consideration. In addition, areas not touched upon in this volume are addressed and implications raised regarding future hypotheses and prospects for finding additional cures to mental retardation.

Curative Aspects of Mental Retardation:
Biomedical and Behavioral Advances
edited by Frank J. Menolascino, M.D., Ronald Neman, Ph.D., and Jack A. Stark, Ph.D.
Copyright 1983   Paul H. Brookes Publishing Co., Inc.   Baltimore · London

chapter 18

A Dialogue
with the Authors

FRANK J. MENOLASCINO, M.D.
University of Nebraska Medical Center
Omaha, Nebraska

R ARELY IS THE READER AFFORDED the opportunity to sit in on a unique process in which some of the world's renowned scientists discuss the latest advances in a specific area, in this case the biomedical and behavioral aspects of mental retardation. This chapter records a dialogue among the authors who have contributed to this volume. The reader will note that throughout this chapter constant reference is made to the importance of inter- and intra-disciplinary collaboration bringing multidisciplinary approaches to the diagnosis and treatment of mental retardation. These scientists have all recognized the need for greater understanding and for bridging gaps between other disciplines. The conversations recorded here demonstrate that perhaps our greatest limitation to finding cures for mental retardation is our sometimes narrow focus on only our own areas of specialization. In the course of reading the discussion of issues one cannot help but appreciate the complexity of the challenge in finding "cures" in mental retardation.

The setting for this dialogue was a remote ocean resort that afforded the opportunity for the contributors of this volume to share and be challenged in their findings with invited guest scientists. The author of this chapter served as moderator and "devil's advocate" in posing the questions and directing the course of discussion.

This chapter's format consists of questions posed to the volume contributors and other invited scientists, followed by their reactions. Marginal notes indicating subject areas are included to assist the reader.

GENETIC AND DEVELOPMENTAL
ASPECTS OF MENTAL RETARDATION

Genetic Aspects of Mental Retardation

Comment: Though scientists must not view the cure of diseases that can produce the symptom of mental retardation in a cavalier fashion, they must also not become too obsessed with what is not known. For example, it

GENETICS

is time to assume a hopeful posture toward curative approaches such as the information Dr. Milunsky [Chapter 1] reviewed on the currently available medical and surgical treatments for genetic disorders—treatments that were just not possible 10 to 15 years ago!

Dr. Milunsky: Yes, we do have, in some selected instances, the where-with-all to effectively treat—cure, if you will—some genetic disorders both before and after birth. But we have a long, long way to go!

Question: If you *do* diagnose in a fetus, via amniocentesis, a neurotube disorder—such as a meningomyelocele wherein the cord herniates out of the spinal column—I would raise the question, "Why not do intrauterine surgery?"

Dr. Milunsky: A recent article in the *Journal of the American Medical Association* reviewed ongoing attempts to surgically correct neurotubal malformations such as a meningomyelocele *in utero*. Clearly, we are making great progress! Eventually we will be able to surgically remove the fetus from the uterus via cesarian section surgery, surgically correct the neurotube defect, and return the fetus to the uterus. This was viewed as medical science fiction just 5 years ago, yet I think that this is an example of one of the negative postures we have taken toward the possibilities of cure. In other fields of medical endeavor we have reexamined types of interventions. For example, a decade ago there was the fixed view that physicians should never put a scalpel to the living heart. Obviously, that view has changed to the point wherein a wide variety of cardiac procedures are routinely accomplished. But, currently we still do not want to put a scalpel to a pregnant uterus to perform a preventive or curative procedure on the impaired fetus. It may have to do with our continuing scientific posture against seeking cures. Lest I be too critical, beyond attitudinal dimensions, we must focus on the issue of whether we are asking the correct questions and whether we currently have the equipment and technology that is needed to effectively cure some of the underlying causative mechanisms in mental retardation.

Question: Dr. Milunsky raised questions in my mind as to cost-effectiveness in general regarding the treatment or prevention of genetic disorders—especially the cost of curing or preventing the inborn errors of metabolism, the alpha feto protein work, or just general aspects.

Dr. Milunsky: I think you are asking more than you are saying. Unfortunately, we live in the real world, and we must realize that though there are both financial and humanistic reasons to justify the screening efforts for the inborn errors of metabolism—it would be much cheaper if we had mass screening efforts such as in the regional multi-state metabolic screening laboratories for the assessment of all newborns. Similarly, the impact of alpha feto protein screening in all high risk pregnancies—if utilized on a national scale—will truly be cost beneficial. We will soon begin to stress more fully the possibility of wide-range genetic screening that can be utilized as a national model of care for all pregnancies.

Comment: One of the limitations here may not be the lack of scientific knowledge, but the financial where-with-all and national priorities. Dr. Williams commented on high incidence of hydrocephaly—two to three per 1,000 births—as well as that of Down syndrome—one in 600 pregnancies. Maybe we should take a different view than we have in the past. Rather than screen for the inborn errors of metabolism that have a very low frequency, maybe we should screen for the far more frequent disorders that cause the symptom of mental retardation, and focus on the possible curative postures therein.

Question: A basic question to Dr. Gerald [Chapter 2], and I question if it is too basic: Are there multiple genes controlling a given enzyme?

Dr. Gerald: Yes. For instance, take lactic acid dehydrogenase, which is a widely recognized enzyme. In general it is the product of two or more polypeptide chains, and thus it is a multiple chain enzyme. On the contrary, there are genes that produce their own specific enzymes, such as G6PD [glucose-6-phosphate dehydrogenase], which is a single chain enzyme and not a multiple chain enzyme. Perhaps about half of all enzymes are multi-chain enzymes.

GENETIC
RESEARCH

Question: In regard to Down syndrome, how much do we know about the contents of chromosome 21? There are certain components of chromosome 21 that are known, such as the superoxidase enzyme that you mentioned. How much do we know about the particular zone of the long arm of chromosome 21 that you referred to?

Dr. Gerald: There are several other enzymes that have been identified on chromosome 21. Their specific localization with reference to what I was calling the Down syndrome phenotype zone has not yet been accomplished but, again, the answers will come from research currently in progress.

Question: When you have three gene alleles producing an enzyme, is transcription under substrate controls?

Dr. Gerald: Let me answer in "English"! The question refers to my comments that the genes in Down syndrome are being produced in three copies instead of two, and I discussed their protein products. Of course, it is not a direct step from gene to protein product. The gene makes a copy of itself in RNA. This RNA is called messenger RNA categorically, and the messenger RNA is used as the model from which you then make the protein. Your question, I gather, is that you want to know whether or not there is an excess amount of messenger RNA—or just an excess amount of protein—when we have the trisomy of chromosome 21. There actually is only one paper on that topic, and that paper was directed to chromosome 21. The researchers literally measured messengers produced by the genes of chromosome 21 in cells that are trisomic, as opposed to those that are normal. They found that the messenger RNA attributable to trisomic chromosome 21 cells was literally 150% of that found in cells with only two chromosomes 21.

Question: The amount of the product, then, is, in terms of a normal cell, not going to be appropriate to the substrate conversation? Will it meet the needs of that enzyme?

Dr. Gerald: Well, the question really is, "How much of an enzyme do you have in a cell?" Do you have enough enzyme to do its job, a phenomenon that technically we call feedback control of the level of an enzyme? Or is there something intrinsic about the synthetic machinery for the enzyme that is the primary determinant? It appears at the present time that it is not a feedback regulatory mechanism that controls the level; rather, it is the amount of machinery that you have present to accomplish the control functions. Though that may sound surprising, it does not account for the fact that an individual who is a heterozygote for PKU [phenylketonuria] has a reduced amount of the enzyme for PKU (i.e., the phenoalanine-hydroxy-lates in their liver cells) and so it is those individuals who are heterozygotes for deficiency states who, in general, have only half of the necessary enzyme available. Now we are adding to that story: Those individuals who have 150% of the machinery tend also to have 150% of the product. Thus, feedback regulation certainly is important, but it does not seem to be as major a determinant as we had suspected in the past.

Question: If that is the case, then the outlook for enzyme therapy is not very good.

Dr. Gerald: Well, that topic is still being actively explored. All of the information needed to answer that question is not in at this time. So, I would say that the topic is still an open question.

Comment: I would like to make a comment about our national problem in interesting young people in the scientific study of mental retardation—in the genetic challenges or any other areas. Money is not the sole problem. At this time, the major problem appears to be one of inspiring people so that they are eager to accept the challenge of research. There really is a shortage of people who are interested in doing such research, and money is not the major problem.

Dr. Harrod: I think that is a profound observation, and I mean that sincerely. We have all lived in times of excellent funding in the past. But the issue of inspired leadership and professional models is totally different, and is a vital link between our past, current, and future research efforts.

Question: What would you do to change that?

Dr. Ommaya: I think it would take a major scientific training evolution. It is a very complex problem that tends to be the result of economic and social factors in the U.S., but there has also been a distinct lack of leadership in society in general and in the scientific community as well. This is a major dilemma, for it leads to a narrowing of our scientific vision, and to settling for lesser objectives. It takes a great deal of courage, in all segments of society, and equally so to the scientist, to explore the nontraditional paths of scientific inquiry.

Question: I was interested in Dr. Harrod's comment [Chapter 3] about parents asking during an interpretation interview concerning the results of their child's genetic survey, "What does all of this mean?" When you get into associated psychological problems in the child, there is obviously always a danger of trying to link a learning disability or a behavioral disorder with some sort of genetic disorder. Because it isn't preordained that these psychological problems are attached to any specific kinds of genetic disorders, that could be very ticklish, couldn't it?

GENETIC COUNSELING

Dr. Harrod: I think that was part of the problem Dr. Gerald alluded to regarding the difficulties in genetic screening of sex chromosome disorders. Some of the general public-professional flap that came about as a result of that activity (e.g., the importance of the XXY syndrome in individuals who commit murder) remains with us. The end result is that part of the information that we direly need about the natural history of those disorders we may not ever be able to obtain from patients who are being so labeled. Thus, we are going to have continuing major difficulties in trying to find out exactly how much of a given condition is due to the abnormal chromosomes and how much of it is due to inappropriate psychosocial-educational expectations.

Dr. Menolascino: That is a very good point, Dr. Harrod. We will fail to remember Dr. Benjamin Pasamanick's spectrum of reproductive causality, if we are not careful. If you are strictly clinical genetics-oriented, you tend to look at all handicaps as being caused by some sort of a genetic dosage kind of thing. The wide variety of other causative agents—such as posttraumatic, postinfectious, or major psychosocial factors—that can produce a learning disability may be easily overlooked. Excessive focus on genetic mechanisms may divert our clinical attention from adverse role modeling within the family and, in regard to treatment, mask the need for applying special educational and psychosocial techniques for correcting learning disabilities.

Question: Dr. Milunsky reviewed studies that showed that in people who were told that they were high-risk for a future abnormal pregnancy, about half of them seemed to respond to this genetic counseling information by definitive changes in their reproductive family planning, while about half did not. The question I have is whether we have any scientific notion of what the distinction between those two groups could be?

Dr. Milunsky: A number of studies have illuminated this area, and have focused on the narrowing of health belief models; that is, cases based on the kinds of health attitudes that people develop toward genetics and prevention. The studies have pointed out the obvious: that it is the perception of susceptibility, the perception of burden, and the perception of benefit that underlie the decision-making process in these kinds of reproductive decisions. Also, it is the mix of those perceptions and the educational level of the individuals, and the degree of directiveness of many counselors—that cause families sometimes to arrive at the strangest kinds of conclusions. For example, I have known couples who go along with a 50% risk in having a future abnormal baby, because they had arrived at the genetic counselor's office with the impression that their risk of having a subsequent child with the same defect was 100%. They walked out of the office almost "happy" with the idea that the risk was "only 50%"! This was not so bad, they said. So, the perception of risk is extremely different among individuals as to its effect on their idea of what is good and bad, and in terms of an optimistic or pessimistic view in particular families of having a future defective child.

Question: The reason I asked the question was that I received the impression from your chapter that you felt that genetic counseling was something that is being reduced in its influence. Did I perceive that correctly?

Dr. Milunsky: No, I think the perception is an individual thing. What I am trying to communicate is that genetic counseling has a limited opportunity for prevention because it provides the parents with decision-making opportunities but doesn't direct them or force them (as it should not) into a particular line of action.

Question: Scientists have always had the ability to prevent certain diseases, and a recurrent blindspot is the one that the possession of facts will change another person's behavior in a significant way. In this case, the issue is whether the health perception model is being incorporated into the genetic counseling methods so that perhaps a longer-term relationship with the parents will perhaps affect their reproductive behaviors. Parents' perceptions must be looked into at the beginning—before the genetic counseling information is presented—and then followed up over a long period of time.

Dr. Milunsky: I think there is much work to be done on that subject. In fact, one of the group of factors is based on prenatal diagnosis that begins with this period as the key to the whole subject of counseling effects. However, the instant that "at risk" parents acknowledge that they really need genetic counseling, they tend to retreat from the specifics of the topic and fall back on myth and folklore.

Question: Pursuing this same line, geneticists have persistently urged that all physicians be aware of genetics. In fact, some scientists believe that the family physician or practitioner should become a geneticist. Do we know of the relative effectiveness of a family practitioner or pediatrician doing ongoing counseling with the family, versus a single visit to a genetic counseling center to obtain specific genetic information? Do we know the relative effectiveness of the different groups and different kinds of contacts?

Dr. Harrod: No, these studies have not been accomplished to the best of my knowledge. We have pushed for a greater awareness of genetics and genetic counseling by the pediatrician and family physician. One model that seems to be effective is that of graduate or postgraduate training programs in genetic counseling for family physicians—who then train other colleagues in their own geographed areas on this topic.

Brain Development and Function: Relationships to Mental Retardation

Question: In regard to a hypothesis about the early nerve cell migration [Chapter 4], what is the mechanism that underlies this movement; that is, what provokes the cells of the embryo to move?

BRAIN CELL
DEVELOPMENT

Dr. Caviness: We do not know what provokes the cells to move. We can only observe that they do, and observe that for some reason they are able to select their ultimate site of placement. As to the reason or specific mechanism that they do this, we have no information about that at all.

Question: To what extent can amniocentesis detect the existence of malformed brains in the fetus?

Dr. Caviness: Many of the major malformations probably can be detected. Certain of the malformations, such as forms of hydrocephaly wherein the cerebrospinal fluid is leaking, are clearly detectable by amniocentesis.

Question: In the fetal alcohol syndrome, there has been described an ectopic brain malformation. Can such malformations be detected prenatally?

Dr. Caviness: I don't know for certain. It has been suggested that it might be picked up by ultrasound. These are very slight brain malformation findings, and one might not even note them with the naked eye.

Question: Are we lacking objective measures to prove that a fetal alcohol syndrome really is present?

Dr. Caviness: It could be argued that there is some question here. There is the initial work of Dr. Kenneth Lyons in San Diego, and some of the clinical research as to follow-up studies. It all does fit the Lyons' criteria for maternal alcoholism as a major causative agent. The key findings seem to be the type of facial configuration of the individual and, of course, the history of maternal alcoholism. It has only been within the last decade that we have delineated the fetal alcohol syndrome, and there is currently very little available as far as follow-up. It is critical to point out, as far as treatment, that the important variable is the timing of the insult. A great deal of the AAMD [American Association on Mental Deficiency] diagnostic system utilized in mental retardation, as we all know, is that if you can find a distinct cause, fine, otherwise what you attempt to say, in very broad terms is, is it of prenatal origin? paranatal? or postnatal? I think just being able to fix the timing of the phenomenon gives us an idea where our prevention or treatment would be maximally effective. On the point of making sure that we professionally consider both the mother and fetus together, I think of the vitamin B_{12} disorder (Murphy's disease) wherein we are beginning to treat pregnant women while they are carrying their baby. This is a treatment approach—in the prenatal timing sequence—which shows that we can cure some disorders prior to birth!

Question: Dr. Purpura, you spoke about the axon tubules and transport therein [Chapter 5]. Have you looked at the cross-section of the axon structure and its allied cilium structures? And do any of the patients wherein you have seen the rosary effect on their axons have any history of a respiratory disease as a complication?

Dr. Purpura: I reviewed with you my findings of some neurons with only a few dentrites left. I have examined many postmortem brain specimens from the Letchworth Village Collection [in Thiels, New York], and done some Golgi strain preparations on them—all you typically see are just the cells with a few projections to suggest where the dendrite tree has been in place. It is as if all of the axon's major dendritic systems had died a long time ago; they have been stripped away at some point before death.

NEUROLOGICAL
DEVELOPMENT

Dr. Paul Adams: I would caution against making quick assumptions about the relation of possible causes to a particular malformation. It is always a delight to hear Dr. Purpura because he is one of the few people in the country who can combine neurophysiological studies with neuro-cytological studies. He is going to proceed to look, I hope, at the function of the cortices before they are biopsied. He is using a methodology that is extremely capricious, and he knows this as well as anyone. In the first place, no one yet knows why the Golgi preparation works on certain neurons and not others. If I had to make a guess, Dr. Purpura, it would be that it is related in some way to a fixation artifact in which pressures are exerted against the unfixed cortex that causes dark staining of certain neurons; this has been suggested by the comparison of profused material versus immersion material. One of the best examples of a tragic mistake that was made in not recognizing these histological staining peculiarities in biopsied brain material was that of Dr. Carl Hebane (many years ago) when he decided to look at sections of the cortex of schizophrenic patients. He had persuaded a neurosurgeon move brain biopsy material, and to his astonishment he found that many of the cells were very dark, and that there was an apparent deficiency in the amount of RNA present in these cells. He quickly concluded that this was the pathology of schizophrenia—not knowing something that had been known to histopathologists for generations: that whenever you press on the cortex of the brain with your thumb (or make a scalpel incision) you create dark cells. Dr. Hebane just had not made the proper controls for his study! This entire incident has now vanished, but it was an extremely interesting lesson. I would suggest that a worthwhile study for Dr. Purpura would be to examine the brain tissue conditions more carefully under which Golgi stain positivity occurs; I think it is still an open question. The second part of my concern with Dr. Purpura's findings relates to the possible change in spines and the morphology of dendrites on the pyramidal cells he has studied. I think that is an extremely interesting development and, again, one has to be awfully careful to have the proper controls to know that some of these dendrites, bereft of spines, are not due to a staining defect related in some way to the biopsy procedure itself, or to postmortem incomplete fixation and distortion.

Lastly, I would comment that we are in great need of new methodologies and technologies in the field of neuropathology. Here we are looking at a cerebral cortex with its billions of neurons, organized in very special ways within the cortex, and organized in very special ways with various thalamic nuclei, and we can say, ''Well, we have made a microscopic section and the ordinary light in microscope does not show any pathology.'' But there are many questions that could be asked where one would not expect that type of microscopic study to show the abnormality. One thing that is very simple to check is a brain that is 10% smaller than normal; one may find that there is nevertheless a 50% reduction in the number of neurons that should be present. So, the simple matter of quantitation of the different cell types in a given area at the cerebral cortex, their relationships to one another and to the number of thalamic nuclei, would be of vast importance as a fundamental step. I have often thought that if one could not ascertain the numeration of total cortex cells, one ought to work on the thalamic nuclei because they are all confined within a single space, and one can make rather exact computations therein. Yet, this thalamic methodology is not being used anywhere in the world, as far as I know. Also, I think that there is a possibility of going back to the Ayres-Shoday method of neuropile complexity; we have heard nothing of this method in recent years. Dr. Ayres showed very early that the number of dendritic crossings and the spatial relations of neurons in the developing brain were thrown off by thyroid deficiency; there was a volume published on this matter by Dr. Shoday. So here is a methodology that is in need of further application.

NEURO-
PATHOLOGY

One always has to study specific disease processes and cannot expect to find a pathology that is going to be informative if it is common to many diseases. Otherwise, it is always going to be end-stage pathology, so to speak. This is one of the major problems with understanding the rosary effect that Dr. Purpura described. In order to get at the pathogenesis of the change that leads to this end-stage, one has to focus on a particular disease process, learn all you can about it, and then find some way of translating this into an experimental animal model where you can get more data. I would suggest that that is going to be the approach in the future. We can talk, Dr. Menolascino, about cure, but we are really taking great license with that term. What we are talking about is learning about disease, and finding a way of intercepting it before it wrecks the nervous system.

Dr. Menolascino: I do not agree. I am of the opinion that, in many ways, we have become too obsessed with neuropathology—past and present. At the turn of this century the French school of neuropathology reduced all forms of mental retardation to a pathological classification: every retarded citizen had, literally, a "hole in his head"—the porencephaly that Dr. Williams discussed [Chapter 6] or a vague, "Something is wrong with his brain." Precious little has come from these old "insights" during the last fifty years. Five years ago, a colleague in New York state, Dr. George Jervis, at the occasion of his retirement, commented to me—because I have long had an interest in Down syndrome—that there is *no* distinctive neuropathology in Down syndrome. Send the brain of the deceased child with Down syndrome to the pathology laboratory unmarked as far as the clinical history or diagnosis, and the neuropathologist will maybe comment about some minor diminution of weight in the cerebellum and less prominent gyrae, and that is all! If the individual was over age 35, perhaps some senile plaques or neurofibrils will be noted. I want to repeat: No distinct neuropathology is noted in Down syndrome. So we must look not at just fixed neuropathology—but at functional CNS parameters.

Dr. Adams: Well, those brains of Down syndrome have not been looked at by the right methods.

Dr. Menolascino: That's a good question, but some colleagues would maybe say, "That is the narrow neuropathologist speaking," and that we should look into scientific topical areas beyond neuropathology as having more relevance to the etiology of Down syndrome. I would agree that we need, as Dr. Purpura pointed out, many new sets of questions to ask—not just the old research approaches or methods. On another topic, I was impressed with the studies reported by Dr. Williams (Chapter 6) on the major neurophysiological changes noted in pregnant monkeys (with the monkey fetus hooked up to the physiologically monitoring equipment mentioned by Dr. Williams). When you physiologically stress a pregnant mother monkey while she is restricted to a chair, the changes that are recorded from the monitored monkey fetus are those that can produce major neurophysiological and neuropathological changes. Herein one may be able to provide a hard scientific basis for the residuals of repeated maternal abuse, and, indirectly, fetus/infant abuse. Similarly, these are the very types of research which, if we had talked about them 10 years ago, we would have been called quacks.

Dr. Adams: Yes, but grandmothers have known this type of finding for generations.

Dr. Menolascino: Agreed. But they apparently haven't told anyone! Otherwise how do you explain that the diagnosis of child abuse has only been formally recognized in organized medicine for the last 15 years? Surely pathologists had examined such battered mothers or their battered infants-children before that time. I do not intend to be critical, only to point out that we have a series of medical blinders that seem to hold us to entrenched ideas concerning the causalogy factors in mental retardation—and our traditional methods of exploring these topical areas, in my opinion, remain equally constructed. That professional posture is specifically the issue that Dr. Adams and myself are both addressing!

Comment: When Dr. Williams discussed hydrocephaly, I must admit that I did not realize the incidence was so high: 3 per 1,000 live births. I think it is an area in which I wholeheartedly agree that we know precious little about the underlying mechanisms such as spinal fluid dynamics.

Dr. Williams: Yes, we still have only fragmentary information about hydrocephaly. There have been some attempts to control the excess production of cerebrospinal fluid by pharmacological agents to excrete the excess cerebrospinal fluid—rather than neurosurgery. Also, we still do not have a good technique for assessing which child with hydrocephaly at birth will or will not do well.

Question: Dr. Purpura, would you comment on the postnatal development of the pyramidal cells?

POSTNATAL CELL DEVELOPMENT

Dr. Purpura: Well, the laying down of the number of neurons is a prenatal event and it mostly occurs in the cortex. The subsequent and final development of the dendritic system of the pyramidal cells does begin antenatally, but is carried on in terms of the final extent of the branching pattern (which as started antenatally) in the postnatal period. Eventually, by about the second year postnatally, one reaches the maximum number of synapses in the brain. The remarkable thing, it seems to me, is that there is a *reduction* in the number of synapses from about 11 to 12 years onward, according to the studies that have been done. There is, in fact, an overproduction of synapses in the early stages of postnatal development by the counts that have been made—such as the studies in the frontal cortex by Dr. Peter Hukenmacher. I want to make clear that there is an additional volume of dendrites added in the postnatal period, which may go on for the first year or two, at the most. Beyond that time period, the weight of the brain is a direct function of the increase in lipid content through myelin and glial cell development. In brief, a significant amount of all the synapses that are made, are made prior to the sixth month postnatally.

May I also make a reply to Dr. Adams? He knows as well as I do that we are always worried about the Golgi method. The reason I literally sat on the findings that I have presented—for 7 years—was that I wanted to wait until we had sufficient electron microscopy data to back up our findings. I also wanted to be certain that our findings were not a fixation artifact in relation to the varicose formation that produces the "rosary" effect. In fact, we now have the electron microscopy studies completed in the fixation stage, and it is done within a few seconds—from the surgeon right into the staining process! So there is *not* a question what we see as the varicosities can be due to an artifact in the fixation process that *would* influence significantly the electron microscopy findings I have reported. Second, the preservation of organelles in the dendrite absolutely rules against this being a natural or, specifically, an artifical aspect of the method we utilize. That is one thing I am absolutely certain about! Whether it is or is not an artifact of the disease process we are studying is another matter, but it is not the laboratory methodology that produced these varicosities. In regard to Dr. Adams' other questions of dendritic spine changes that occur in relation to postmortem material, there is no question that these can be certainly artifactual. But when we viewed the same picture in the electron microscopy that we see in the Golgi, I think that was the time when I became alert to the full significance of our findings.

Dr. Adams: Except, Dom, that the electron microscopy is always done on biopsy material.

Dr. Purpura: Yes, it has to be.

Question: So it has to have an artifact component to the tissue you study.

Dr. Purpura: Yes, there might be some swelling of the tissues, since we do not get quick-freezing of the specimens. There would be some swelling of the tissues, but it's not different from anything else we have seen in our control studies in normal cat brain or rat brain.

Dr. Bijou: I would like to just take off for a little bit from something that Dr. Purpura and Dr. Williams shared with us. Dr. Purpura said he was interested in the brain. I presume that is partly because it is the seat of the mind. Dr. Williams said that in some cases, at least, there are malformed brains that are at least relatively intact, and at least the gross function of the child is relatively normal. Now, in the last 10 years, there has been an explosion of research on the psychological development of newborns and infants—extending through the first year. This research has provided many techniques and a mass of knowledge about how the mind grows, at least in the first year. This research has provided us with many kinds of objective assessments of the behavior of the child that the clinicians are viewing, and so we talk about developmental milestones. In many ways these developmental milestones are still very crude measures. So we have excruciatingly beautiful techniques for the measurement of the structure of the brain, but the brain is still being assessed as to its functional (behavioral) capacities by very crude behavioral methods. The point I want to stress is that we need somehow to distinguish the probable diseases that, when they strike the brain, result in major developmental deficits in the child, from those disease processes whose residuals are going to produce areas that are relatively intact. We need to better assess this latter infant and give him or her appropriate tests of behavioral functions. If we do that for a long enough time period, it may be that ultimately we will have a *functional* understanding of the underlying neuroanatomy and neurophysiology of the brain during the first year, or the first few years of life. Then we could more meaningfully correlate the neuropathological data with the behavioral data. Now, this idea is an old idea since it was very common in the 1930s, but I believe that we need to come back to it.

EXTERNAL
VS.
INTERNAL
ENVIRONMENT

Dr. Menolascino: That is very intriguing. You know, when Dr. Purpura discussed the disease progeria, his illustrations took me back to the cover of an issue of *Science* about 2 years ago. The cover displayed two examples of a similar type of neuron in the crayfish: one from a group that was raised in a dark cavern, and one from crayfish raised in the light. The first showed a neuron that looked like an early sapling with very little roots, and the other one—from the enriched environment-treated crayfish—had a rich, dense kind of root structure. The picture reminded one of the rich branching of the dendrites versus the neurons with a paucity of branching. It makes you wonder. We keep talking about the crucial role of extrinsic (i.e., external environmental) factors. The concept of the plasticity of the central nervous system—and its response to external enrichment tactics—has not really "taken hold" in the field of neuropathology. Drs. Caviness, Purpura, and Williams have addressed, and I think correctly so, the role of intrinsic factors. But the questions raised by Dr. Bijou (Chapter 16) directly focus on postnatal factors. It makes me question if we all have focused too specifically on the growth of the major cell bodies *prenatally,* and not sufficiently on the factors that effect *postnatal* growth of these cells. That sounds like a truism, but I want to repeat that I think we get stuck with certain kinds of ideologies. Perhaps we should focus more attention on the factors—postnatally—that spur the growth of the pyramidal cells as to their ultimate form and allied richness of their dendrites.

Dr. Purpura: I agree, and would also like to answer Dr. Bijou's question since it is a very important point about development. One of the dimensions we are stressing is that the majority of the morphological brain machinery that is present early in life is functional machinery—if you can assume that synapses are there for a purpose and that they are not silent. There is a good deal of information that strongly suggests that if a synapse is there morphologically, it is probably not silent, and is ready to work and be put to use. Therefore, the "problem" with the newborn baby is not the baby's problem. *It is ours to communicate with him or her.* We must develop better systems to communicate with babies—never mind going after dolphins or various other mammals for studying this external developmental challenge. By trying to develop ways to communicate more effectively with newborn infants, I am convinced that we will find a huge repertoire of behavior similar to the preliminary recent studies that are trying to find out just what the baby is really thinking—even though it cannot communicate via formal language. I think that newborn babies' morphology really shows that he or she is further advanced than we had imagined. Their brain weight belies the extent to which their brain's organization is ready to go, ready to be put into operation, and validated by function—which is a major principle of very early brain functions: Validate me and I'll be fine. Use me and everything will be fine. Don't use me and things will happen. Wrongly as well as rightly. Plasticity is a two-way street, you know. It can so happen that things are good or, conversely, you can get the occurrence of inhibiting events in which plasticity works against the developing nervous system.

Question: Dr. Purpura, are you saying that object permanence is adherent in the structure of the child at birth and that the majority of the central nervous system connections are there?

Dr. Purpura: Yes. The synapses are there and they have got to be there for some purpose! Indeed, the number of synaptic connections that are present in the newborn period—I would say, offhand, perhaps 30%–50% of the ultimate total—are sufficient to really do the job. That is in the normal infant. The other challenge is to use modern research methods. In this regard, we have been particularly interested in using the computer graphic analysis method for studying the developing dendritic systems. You cannot do concentric circles anymore. You have got to have computer methods that will do the full graphics of the structure of the axon and its synapses: branch points, the angles, the whole thing. Several such studies are underway in laboratories across the world—there are only about two or three such laboratories that are really developing methods to do the quantitative study of the morphology of the human cortex at different developmental stages. We have completed several such studies in our laboratory, and they have shown quite remarkable findings, ones that we never would have expected! For example, at a recent national neuroscience meeting, one of my associates reported that if you closely look at two babies of the same gestation age—but who have had different clinical histories (e.g., one being in an intensive care unit for about 5 weeks before death due to intercurrent problems, and another born just at that time and surviving just a few days before death)—you will note on the Golgi histological picture alone that there were not any differences in their two brains. However, if you do a computer study of the actual branch points of the axon synapses, angles, and terminal portions in about 20 neurons in a well-localized area of each of the brains, then you find that the baby who had the extrauterine experience in the intensive care unit had dendritic development that is accelerated over that of the other child. Now the number of cases is only two, but it is intriguing that *unless* you do the proper kind of statistical analysis—similar to that which is now being utilized by colleagues who use computer graphic methods—you will miss quantitative data that could be very important in evaluating what it is about the environment that is going on, and exactly what is happening to the baby. So I wanted to indicate that there are new methods, and everybody is certainly trying to "get with it" as to advanced neuropathology techniques in this area of research.

Dr. Adams: Yes, Dr. Purpura, we do not have to affix ourselves to just postmortem neuropathology, we can—must—do much, much more in utilizing the recently available modern techniques in this area of endeavor.

Dr. Menolascino: I agree! The new technology is slowly evolving, and we must fully utilize it to explore the full range of potential causes of the symptom of mental retardation so as to clarify areas for potentially curative approaches to the causative factors of mental retardation.

EFFORTS TOWARD
UNDERSTANDING AND REPAIRING BRAIN FUNCTION

Question: Dr. Lynch, is the long-term potentiation (LTP) effect [Chapter 8] a quantitative one, and does it bear some orderly quantitative relationship to either the frequency or the duration of stimulus, or do you see actually a threshold at its induction?

Dr. Lynch: No, it bears an orderly relationship. We did an experiment wherein we took 100 pulses and just put them in at different frequencies. When the frequencies get to be about 15 per second, you start to induce the effect. But you go on getting more of it when you get to 100 pulses/s or 200/s. You get a much more robust effect.

Question: The shape of the curve suddenly goes up then, is that right?

Dr. Lynch: That's right, it does. It goes from nothing to something, and then there is another leap when you get to the very high frequencies. Now there is a complication in this experiment that we are gradually unraveling: Lower frequency stimulations in the 6/s to 10/s range seem to induce more generalized effects in target cells. So it may be acting against potentiation. We cannot rule that out, but my current impression is certainly that you go from nothing to something and then jump at the very high frequencies.

Question: If the change in the dendritic spine configuration is isomorphic with the LTP, then one would project a parallel change in these quantitative parameters. Have you seen that?

Dr. Lynch: No, we have not. Obviously, in these two experiments we try to optimize the conditions for finding an effect. Now that we have all of our data computerized, we are going back to see if the drug has blocked structural changes and if the changes you are referring to occur or not.

Question: How many animals have you looked at so far?

Dr. Lynch: In the *in vivo* experiment, there were 20 experimentals and 11 controls. And in the hippocampal slice experiment we started off with 5 animals.

Question: Would you suppose that this is the same as Goddard's kindling effect?

Dr. Lynch: It could be. Dr. Goddard thinks that, and it is possible that it is the same basic phenomenon.

Question: Has Dr. Goddard done any studies of this sort—morphological studies—that you know about?

Dr. Lynch: On the kindling effect, yes, but he had no luck with them. I think the reason is that the cell populations he studies are dispersed over a large cortical area. The problem with doing this kind of research is that the effects that I have shown you could be much, much larger than what you regularly see because our potentiated neuronal spines are presumably being diluted by the spines that are not innervated by the axons we are driving. Of course, it is virtually impossible to get 100% of the synapses stimulated at the same time. In Dr. Goddard's case, he was too far in the other direction. The kindling synapses constituted a population that was too small for him to see an effect when you do electron microscopy. But he did try and he had generally negative results. He went through the same experiences we did, including 3½ years of electron microscopy studies.

Question: Is there generally a place in the neocortex (not just the hippocampal region) that you see this potentiation phenomenon?

Dr. Lynch: I don't think anyone systematically has tried to study the neocortex for this phenomenon.

Comment: Well, I think many people have stimulated any variety of areas of the neocortex, and it never seems to show up. In 1959 when I did similar research, one of the reasons was to show that the hippocampus effect was unique and that it did not occur in any neocortical surface.

Dr. Lynch: Is that right? Which study was that?

Comment: On the origin of brain waves—the issue of the evoked potential in the cat.

Dr. Lynch: And you did test for the neocortex?

Comment: Yes—the neocortex showed nothing.

Dr. Lynch: We find the mechanism we described is very well-developed in the hippocampus. Perhaps it is a biochemical reaction that is noted in some regions of the cortex and not in the cerebellum or in the brain stem. In other words, the effects of calcium on the cell membrane may vary from one brain region to the next. If we are right in saying that calcium is causing these effects, it may be that there is an enzyme present in one region and not in other regions. But your observation is correct: I know of no reports of the presence of long-term potentiation effects outside of the hippocampus.

NEURONAL
PLASTICITY

Question: Well, maybe there is something very peculiar to the extraordinary synapses that hit those spines; you know that the size of those spines is virtually not seen in neocortical pyramidal cells. But it does emphasize the importance of that spine neck. What bothers me is that the minimal change that might occur in the spine neck might be biophysically significant in terms of its effects on the PSP in the shaft. There is a point at which it doesn't really pay to have a spine that is not doing anything. Obviously you get the full injected current at some very critical points. It may be that at that point the spine is not useful at all in terms of what it is supposed to be doing, so I don't know. The other thing that bothered me is if that little interneuron is the spineless element that is picking it up, do you see any potentiation of the IPS beads that are part of the circuit that you are hitting?

Dr. Lynch: No. You see increased potentiation, but let me hasten to add that that is hardly surprising because you are driving more pyramidal cells. Now, there is a form of feed-forward inhibition in this circuit that numerous people have been talking about very recently. That spine in the neuron is in an ideal position to do that; the dendrite is going up into the shape of the collateral zone. So it may be possible to test the feed-forward inhibition and see if you can potentiate it. Nobody has tried that yet. But that certainly would be the prediction. I should also emphasize again that we have only done quantitative studies. I have no idea of what is the actual size of the change or what the nature of the change would be in those forms that are actually potentiated.

Question: Do I understand that you have modified calcium levels and altered this effect?

Dr. Lynch: Yes. If you take calcium down to about the 1 millimolar level and raise magnesium by an equivalent amount, you cannot induce this effect. Or if you do induce it, it is very weak.

Question: If you did that later, would it reverse?

Dr. Lynch: No. As a physiologist, I could not resist the question of what happens if you stop all synaptic activity in an experiment? We put the potentiation in, removed all of the calcium, raised to a high level of magnesium, and absolutely no synaptic transmission occurred. Then we waited a half hour, restored synaptic transmission, and the first thing to reappear was the potentiation. We had two inputs, one potentiated and one not, so we compared them against each other: they both go out and they come back and the potentiated one is still as potentiated as it was when it went in.

Question: As a calcium regulator, do you see this as in ionophere?

Dr. Lynch: No.

Question: Or something that depends upon internalization of calcium?

Dr. Lynch: It would have to depend upon internalization of calcium. It is a protein with a molecular weight of about 18,000. It binds the calcium and it undoubtedly is responsible for an enormous number of calcium effects inside cells. The muscle regulatory calcium unit is probably the calcium regulator. And the evidence is fairly good that the drug Stellazine binds the calcium regulator.

Question: I want to bring us back to the "why" of sprouting, and ask Dr. Ommaya [Chapter 9] a question. What troubles me about brain graft experiments is that they use the reversal of the supersensitivity model to make their statement about the functioning of the whole graft tissue. Now, it could be that if the receptor site of graft proliferation occurred after the degeneration somehow was reversed—by a factor related to the transplant of the fetal tissue—then the same result would occur without there really being intact nervous tissue transmission. The question that I ask is, does anyone in the current research group on the topic of brain grafts know whether the grafts are responsive to stimulation?

CELL
SPROUTING

Dr. Ommaya: No, they have not studied the stimulation aspects as of this time. What they are doing is using other parts of fetal brain. This question came up quite early in their discussions, and in their experiments they are using fetal tissues from three sources of the brain—not just the substantia nigra. The point of the impediments to the sensitivity of the grafts has been brought up, and the researchers are currently testing the same, but the data is not in yet.

Question: Can they be sure that the tissue that survives in the graft is from the donor and not the host?

Dr. Ommaya: The data on that looks something like this: In the histology study of the grafted tissue, it remains intact. There is still tissue—a lump of tissue that is growing there—stuck on to the cortex nucleus. The histochemistry would suggest that the source of the dopamine is from the neurons in this grafted tissue. So, unless there is a budding of tissue from the cortex nucleus, it would be difficult to explain that it is the graft that is the active agent. I don't know how else one would prove it.

Question: In your experiment with the monkeys where you crushed their spinal cords, in those where you did see some regeneration, could it be that you did not completely crush that cord?

TISSUE
REGENERATION

Dr. Ommaya: Yes. But this possibility has been worked out in controlled experiments, and we have ruled it out. One never knows for sure, of course, even though the crushing is done under the microscope, and the actual surgery wherein we open up the cord is done under the microscope (under 40 power). We then remove, with the suction, all the dead debri until we can see just the spinal artery and the pier. And we see no fibers whatsoever. Now, it is always an open question, of course, as to whether a few shreds of cord get stuck in the pier and so some axons may have been left.

Question: You said that reciprocal synaptic relations had been reestablished in the crushed cords, but I'm not aware that it has been proven that there is invasion into the new graft from the host's mature tissue growing into it. As to the reciprocal tissue, they can't get the host's mature neurons to innervate the new graft and develop synaptic relations. In other words, are hippocampal neurons able to sprout into a new septal region graft?

Dr. Ommaya: Yes. There is a claim that Dr. Spinelli has made at a scientific meeting, and I sent him the same question—as you just stated—and asked him to send me a copy of his recent paper. I have not been impressed by his data on this question to date.

Question: With regard to the substantia nigra grafting, I gather that the new projection of the substantia nigra is a well-formed growth that has a logically ordered projection as to its functional ability?

Dr. Ommaya: Yes.

Question: One would wonder if this spatial ordering of a projection has any dependence upon its spatial ordering. If one grafts, does one reproduce this relationship, or can one restore function without restoring the spatial order of the projection? Can one reproduce the effect of grafting by simply bathing the area chemically? To transmit a substance, one does not have to reproduce the substance, suggesting that the spatial order of the projection may have nothing to do with this function.

CELLULAR GRAFTS

Dr. Ommaya: That is a very interesting point because I was talking to Dr. Richard Wyatt, and I said, "The implants are a significant discovery, but it is not fantastic. These rats still look very abnormal. I mean, they are still sick—they are not normal rats. They are still not doing well." And the same thing happens when you give dopamine. You know it is rather like a poor result with a Parkinson's patient—you do not get complete recovery. So I think that the recovery of spatial orientation after grafting may be a quantitative matter. But it doesn't seem that high doses of dopamine completely obliterate the syndrome either.

Question: But do they do as well as the transplant?

Dr. Ommaya: They seem to do as well as the transplant. Could I just make a statement on that? If you look at the histophorence data of the Swedish group, they do in fact claim the histophorence developed in the cortex, which is the same region that we see the innervation normally as the casual factor; the histophorence is not all over the place. It tends to want to go to the region of the cortex that normally is innervated by the graft factor, as opposed to the other neurons that tend to go more directly into the mid-brain circuits. Thus, the transplant *is* working in a manner that is remarkably similar to the original tissue.

Question: Parallels of excitation, contractions, and the coupling and uncoupling of the muscle are obviously very crucial. How important is adenosine triphosphate to all of this activity?

Dr. Browning: The mitochondria, which buffer calcium, do not use ATP; they help make ATP. The mitochondria apparently either make ATP or sequester calcium. So when the mitochondria start sequestering calcium, their ATP production shuts down. Now, in the cells' other organelles such as the plasma membrane and the endoplasma particulum, these organelles use ATP produced by the mitochondria to sequester calcium, and, in the case of the plasma membrane to transport it. So ATP is an essential component of

BRAIN CELL FUNCTIONING

this process of normal calcium sequestration. Certainly in terms of the phosphorylation,the enzymes that are involved in phosphorylation have a much higher affinity for ATP than many of these calcium buffering systems. So, you would see changes in the calcium buffering before you would see changes in phosphorylation.

Question: In other words, in order for the terminals to continue to work, ATP has to be available some of the time, and you are looking at a long-lasting structural change that is not true in muscles. The confirmational change in muscle can be seen in 40 seconds.

Dr. Browning: The change that I was discussing in terms of calcium is not long lasting.

Question: Well, in the muscle, you know, one might presume that actomyosin filaments and elements are important in this context, but in the muscle, once the calcium goes back, the confirmational change occurs. That is not true here apparently.

Dr. Browning: I am saying that this would actually initiate the change. Under normal conditions the synapses cannot change shape because the cytoskeleton keeps it rigid. All that may happen is that when you elevate the calcium, you disinhibit the terminal. Other factors could be invoked to explain the change in shape.

Question: But did one see a big change in the morphology of the presynaptic terminal in the previous studies? You said no.

Dr. Browning: I will ask Dr. Lynch.

Dr. Lynch: No, we didn't see any big change.

Question: So this is really something that involves, perhaps, the release of the transmitter, rather than a morphological change in the dimensions of the presynaptic terminal?

Dr. Browning: It certainly would involve, at the least, the transmitter. One problem in our studies is that we have no clearer evidence that the phosphorylation change and the calcium change are exclusively at the presynaptic terminal. We use this site method as a model. The change could be exclusively in the postsynaptic cell, as well. There is no firm reason for localizing it only presynaptically. We just do not know!

Question: What specifically do you think is the fate of the phosphorylated 40,000 protein, and what role do you think it plays in the modulation of synaptic transmission?

Dr. Browning: What I think is happening is that as you change the phosphorylation, I think you inhibit the facility of this calcium buffering system to sequester the calcium. That particular effect lasts as long as the protein is phosphorylated, and that signal decays simply because a phosphatase removes the phosphate from the protein. So the short one-second signal that initiated these events decays, probably because the phosphatase removes the phosphate from the protein.

Question: It bears no relation to receptive sites on the surface of the membrane itself?

Dr. Browning: Well, the status of the receptive sites is a different question. What Dr. Lynch was talking about in terms of the calcium effects on the receptor sites could very well be an effect on the postsynaptic site. I do not think it is exclusively presynaptic and have no evidence that it is. So, a calcium effect on the postsynaptic site could, in fact, produce the definitive calcium effect that we have noted.

Question: Yes. I may be a bit obtuse. I really am having trouble with this concept of synaptogenesis. We have heard two different types of experiments. One in which a set of neurons is stimulated, rather unnaturally at a high frequency . . .

Dr. Browning: Well, it's not really unnatural . . .

Question: Well, now let me finish . . .

Dr. Browning: Okay.

Question: —and where that set of neurons and their excitability is altered for a long time. And another set of experiments where a lesion is made and, presumably, there would be some regenerative phenomenon without growth of axon and new synapses formed. Now, can you clarify these two problems?

Dr. Browning: I agree they are very different. In terms of lesion response, and also the synaptogenesis in the animal model, we are suggesting a possible correlation. I have no other evidence, except that we have shown that when you change the phosphorylation of this protein, you *do* change the ability of this system to buffer calcium. Now, I have no idea, at this point, whether the change that we see in the phosphorylation is related to the nature of the lesion, *or* if it is related to the altered nature of the synaptogenesis in the experimental animal that has caused it all. I am presenting that data because we are interested in the possibility—since we had observed this synaptogenic response in the stimulation dependent situation—of whether this effect might occur in other synaptogenic contexts. I have no evidence that the two phenomena are actually related.

Question: I want to be a heretic. Tell me how this data applies to mental retardation.

Dr. Browning: Well, it applies, I think, to the search for cures of the symptom of mental retardation. And the reason is that if normal cognitive functioning—or if Dr. Lynch [Chapter 8] is correct when he suggests that this long-term potentiation phenomenon is, in fact, a substrate of memory and learning processes—then synaptogenesis obviously is a very important component of our ability to learn and remember. So consequently, being able to understand the mechanisms of learning and remembering may prove very important to those who seem to be defective, or have deficits, in their learning and memory. Furthermore, in instances where there is brain damage, it is conceivable, I suppose, that if one understood the synaptogenic process well enough, that one could actually restructure the brain, whether it be a graft, or by induction of new synaptogenic response via a compensatory mechanism.

APPLICATION TO MENTAL RETARDATION

Question: Would you synopsize via a drawing what you just said?

Dr. Browning: Well, basically what I was trying to say was that if we hope to change the ability of these synaptic terminals to release transmitters, one of the problems with doing the phosphorylation studies the way we do them is that it is difficult at times to know which way the process goes: we can only go by what we see and detect as a change in the phosphorylation. What I am suggesting is that as you change the phosphorylation of this 40,000 protein, you appear to change the ability of the hippocampal system to release its transmitters. If you increase the release of an excitatory transmitter, you obviously can produce a potentiating situation. If you decrease the release, it is an inhibitory situation. I do not mean to suggest that this effect can be clinically produced by flooding the systems with γ-aminobutyric acid (or the 40,000 protein, or high levels of calcium, etc.). However, we can cure the symptom of mental retardation if we can definitively alter the nerve transmission potential of a key part of the brain that is involved in storing information about the world outside. I *do* suggest that this total mechanism, via further research—and eventually a future series of carefully conducted clinical studies—*does* hold the potential for significantly altering the capability of the brain to function more efficiently.

EFFORTS TOWARD ENHANCING BRAIN FUNCTION

Question: Pharmacological dogma always dictates that one follow some sort of Koch's postulate. Namely, you must identify the compound, you must test it individually (controlling all others), and you must be able to replicate some sort of behavior and isolate the compound as the major variable involved. I think that that has been the major value of most pharmacological work that has been done. Well, now we know that presumably these 20 or more neuropeptide agents—which Drs. Kastin and Sandman have [Chapter 12] described—have certain metabolic and possibly nerve transmitter actions, and so now the pharmacological dogma is to test them against known transmitters. For example, one tests endorphin against the actions of known nerve transmitters such as acetylcholine and norepinephrine as to various test data. But it so happens that if they are *all* present then they might be modulating each other. In fact, Dr. Kastin, you and Dr. Sandman presented a series of seven compounds that look like a spectrum, and you broke them up into individual colors, when in fact they may be multi-active so that each of their individual actions may therefore have different actions when two or three of them are combined—as would be a natural interactive type of function in the central nervous system. So one wonders: *How* would you go about trying to find out if, in fact, several of these neuropeptides are operating together? By looking at different combinations and getting different kinds of effects? It may be that our pharmacological postulates have to be changed in relation to the old way in which we identified and characterized single well-known, rapidly acting, and chemically clear actions of drugs on the membranes of the nerve cells in the central nervous system.

Dr. Kastin: Exactly. That is a very good point, Dr. Purpura. We have never been bothered much by dogma in my group, and so it does not concern me from that aspect. But the point you raise is excellent since we are finally just at that stage where we are beginning to look at *interactions* of the various peptides on the central nervous system. As I said, initially there was a question: Do these peptides exist? Then, if they do exist, do they have central nervous system actions? Yes, they do and we now are just at the point that you aptly described. We are beginning to find some examples of these interactions. For example, by themselves the MIF and MSH peptides have no effect on motor activity. But if you give them along with apomorphine—

PHARMACO-
LOGICAL
ASPECTS

at low doses, not high ones—you can get some motor effect. Similarly, if you also give amphetamine you can also get some motor effects. So we are beginning to look at this interaction. Now that is just with those two peptides, and I will get back to your point. I already pointed out, in terms of mechanisms of action, we are not seeing any really explainable actions for most of the biogenic amines. I showed you the data on MSH, but in terms of looking at most of the findings with norepinephrine and serotonin, we are not finding much. Some research groups are finding effects, but we have not been able to replicate same. Some people are finding explanations that would explain our own work beautifully, and I would love to be able to confirm it, but we have not been able to! Now we are getting to a more complex stage of evaluation, and it is not like our simple endocrine testing wherein one could simply observe the effects of taking out the pituitary gland, or removing the pituitary gland's target organs. Instead, these peptides are found all over the brain, and so we are getting into a situation that you undoubtedly must have found yourself. It would have been nice if one part of the brain affected learning and mental retardation, and another part of the brain did this, and another part of the brain did that . . . just purely a set of actions on structural localization. However, as is well known, these simple positions are no longer tenable. We have *concurrent systems* running through the central nervous system, and they greatly interact with each other. Now, I do not see any easy way to answer your question physiologically, but pharmacologically we could. The rationale, though open to much criticism, would be that pharmacologically we would just exaggerate the normal physiological tendencies. So we must always test a number of substances and evaluate our findings on a number of theories. You could do it either way: give all 20 peptides at once and start observing the effects produced when you start taking one away at a time, *or* you have an initial effect with one peptide and you just add one more at a time. But even that approach, you know, is really going to be impractical considering that the known peptides also interact with the known biogenic amines. Anyway, I think the point you raise is excellent, and one of the scientific services that the peptides are going to perform for all fields is just as you say: They are going to dramatically change the way we look at any number of complex interactions in the central nervous system. I wish we had a clear answer for the dilemma you have proposed.

ENDOCRINE
SYSTEM

Question: A couple of developmental questions. First, are there any single gene mutations known in the human species that specifically knock out certain of the peptides that have a general distribution in the brain, or perhaps knock out their functions?

Dr. Kastin: None that I know of.

Question: Second, could you say something about the ontogeny (i.e., the origin and development) of these substances? When do they appear in the brain, where do they appear early in the brain, or where and when do receptors appear in pace with the developmental profile?

Dr. Kastin: Actually, your question is one that I asked about 12 years ago, and we published it at about that time. I was doing one of our first studies in Sweden. Dr. David Engbar is an excellent electroencephalographer, and we showed some of the *first* effects of peptides on the central nervous system. While working on this study I was contacted by a colleague who pointed out that he had available a series of young aborted human fetuses. So we measured MSH in the fetus and at *every* early fetal stage there was MSH in the pituitary gland of all of these fetuses. Indeed, there was more MSH than can be accounted for by the instrinsic MSH-like activity of ACTH (which we also measured). So, at least we do have this developmental data in the human. Replication studies (in the rat) of this finding in blood, pituitary, and brain also show that there are some differences, but MSH seems to be present from a very early age. Now you can ask, what about phylogeny? And this permits me to make a very interesting point about MSH. For most of these peptides, they seem to be present in just about every species. There are some small differences when you look at some of the actions, but MSH is very interesting because α-MSH is present in the pituitary of just about every species you look at *until* you get to the human being, and then there is no α-MSH in the pituitary gland of the human (and none in the blood). Yet, all of the other species have it. So you could say that is a good argument that MSH is like the appendix—it has no purpose whatsoever! Recently, α-MSH has been found in the human brain and the cerebrospinal fluid, and what this suggests, at least for someone who might be inclined to reason teleologically (as I am) is that MSH—if you permit this sort of familiarity—is so important to the individual that even though it has lost its pituitary function and its pigmentary function and is not necessary in the periphery of the nervous system, it is *still* persisting in the human brain. It is a little more complicated because we used to think that there was a 22-amino-acid form of MSH, but it turns out that that was an artifact of laboratory extraction. So, biogenetically, it seems that peptides were important and, like MSH, probably had some other function, though it was an adaptive function for the lizard or chameleon to be able to change color and adapt to the environment. You can say, well, if humans are going to use MSH adaptively, how would they do so? I would answer: Probably some process involving the brain. This is speculative, but it might be that way.

In terms of the last part of your question concerning receptors, Dr. Caviness, work on peptide receptors is really in its infancy, to use a developmental term. I do not know of anyone who has done a developmental study on the *receptors* in this area of scientific endeavor. There has not been much interest and as far as I know, developmental studies are the only ones that have been done with peptides. Indeed, at the present time, the only developmental studies in terms of administering peptides at an early stage have been our studies. In other words, there apparently is not any major current interest in this area, but we are hoping that our work will generate some additional studies in this exciting field.

Question: One of the points you made was that this was an endogenous (i.e., produced by the body) peptide. Did you assess the dose given in terms of what level you might be inducing?

Dr. Sandman: You mean what does the brain "see"?

Question: Right. For example, when you administer 5 milligrams?

Dr. Sandman: As Dr. Kastin suggested, only a small percentage is thought to pass the blood-brain barriers, so when you put 5 mg in the human for instance, the brain may be "seeing" extremely small quantities. In the rat, our studies have shown that very, very little actually goes into the brain. There has also been some debate whether the peptides even act at the central nervous system level; they could act via the peripheral nervous system. There are a couple of hypothesis. For example, Bloom and McGaw have suggested that these peptides may have central nervous system effects, but some of these effects are not seen when some of the peripheral organs are removed. It is a good question. I think, as Dr. Kastin suggested, that we have not yet evolved to that level of understanding wherein we can definitively answer such questions. Some of the possible mechanisms for looking at the effects of these peptides have been clearly suggested by the other contributors to this volume. Our research group has been remiss in not looking at cell growth in various parts of the cortex after neonatal and *in utero* exposure to developmental insults. It is something that has been clearly suggested by Drs. Caviness and Purpura.

Question: Do you claim that MSH and β-endorphin are both antagonistic, even though they both are derived from the same molecule?

Dr. Sandman: No. We have some evidence that, in some behavioral systems, they indeed attenuate one another. The studies are proceeding right now, in a number of laboratories, to look at the possible reversibility of behavioral deficits as a function of *in utero* exposure to β-endorphin—either by simultaneous treatment with MSH *in utero*, or neonatal treatment— which is more exciting to us—with MSH.

Question: After you produce the dull rat that you mentioned *(in utero)*, can you do something neonatally to reverse it?

Dr. Sandman: To directly answer your question, yes. We suspect that these peptides can be antagonistic to one another, and therein lies great potential for the future treatment or cure efforts in mental retardation.

Question: I am not familiar with the literature, but one of the hypotheses to explain the use and efficacy of transcutaneous electrical nerve stimulation units is that it does facilitate the production of endorphins at the junctures. Do you have any information as to the role of peptides secondary to transcutaneous electrical nerve stimulation?

Dr. Sandman: Well, our suspicion is that any kind of stress, physical stress in particular (including electrical stimulation), can produce a pituitary cocktail. Everything just streams out of the pituitary and it is rather nonselective in global response.

Question: Yes. I guess my question was whether there were behavioral data that you had associated with this electrical stressor?

Dr. Sandman: No, with the technique of transcutaneous electrical stimulation, specifically.

Question: It is bewildering, isn't it, that one gets a profound change in the function of the animal, and yet there is no change in the brain receptors? I assume that what you mean by that is that there is no change in their structure or their density.

Dr. Sandman: Yes, at this point it is awfully crude; we took a shot in the dark. The distribution of β-endorphin in the brain would suggest that we look at the arc of the nucleus, and not at the whole brain. A small effect in the arc could be highly significant, but would have been lost by the techniques that we used. We just took an initial shot in the dark to explore this area.

Question: One really needs a way of looking at the function of a defined system, don't you think?

Dr. Sandman: Yes.

Question: Is it possible that you might be looking at a sort of phenomenon wherein you block a system by giving a drug, and then recreate the ability to get a response by the local infusion of a drug (this research technique has been done with noradrenalin). Here at least one can reduce a complex pharmacological phenomenon through the function of an identifiable system. It would seem that this would be a lovely paradigm by which to examine the effect of these peptide loads, these world series doses of peptides that you seem to administer. Can you use such a model?

Dr. Sandman: Yes, but we would need a specific target behavior to do that.

Question: Which target behavior has a nervous system analogy?

Dr. Sandman: I did not mention it, but there are some beginnings from Dr. Stan Watson's work on the chemical anatomy of those parts of the central nervous system that would be involved when you use a specific peptide. In the arc of the nucleus, there are cells that contain both MSH and β-endorphin, and it appears that that area is the only area wherein the β-endorphins tend to function most effectively. There has been some beginning work, but we have a long way to go.

Question: Two parts of one question. Why do you think that mentally retarded individuals have better control over their peripheral autonomic nervous system than nonretarded individuals? And what implication does that have for the education of retarded individuals?

IMPLICATIONS

Dr. Sandman: The latter part of that question is intriguing. I have a crackpot idea about it: I think that when we currently assess intelligence or the mind (which ought to be defined in some equation that includes brain and body, not just the brain!), all of the testing materials—and all of our research focus—tend to deal exclusively with the *central nervous system* aspects of the functioning of the mind. We tend to have a total disregard for the autonomic nervous system (i.e., the *peripheral* central nervous system). We do not have many tools to study the autonomic nervous system; we have some, but they are expensive and esoteric. It is conceivable that too much scientific preoccupation has been placed on the central nervous system—upon verbal skills and all of that type of behavior—and this elitism has prevented us from dealing more directly with the autonomic nervous system. It is clear that some of the current anecdotal data may, at some future date, be formalized. For example, it is anecdotally said that artists cannot communicate very well with verbal skills, and they are often construed as people who ''think with their hearts''—especially if you look at the language we typically use to describe their work. I do not think that that analogy is totally ''off the wall'' with respect to the kind of phenomena I am suggesting. How could it be used to educate the retarded? I think that colleagues who have extensive experience and contacts with developmentally disabled individuals must become more creative. It seems to me that one simple idea is that any kind of self-control—any kind of competence with a skill—might be programmed so that this competency could generalize to other areas of a developmentally disabled person's control over his or her environment. Another creative approach is that you could pharmacologically create a physical-metabolic state in which the organism is more receptive to information.

Question: I have been sitting here listening to all the discussion about how animal models are a problem and so forth, and thinking that perhaps genetics has something to offer in this area—especially if we stop talking about mentally retarded persons as a large amorphous group who have this "problem" in functioning intellectually. We should specifically look at the subgroups such as the different (and specific) genetic categories, and the many different syndromes wherein we have, if not a full causative explanation for the retardation, at least some firm assumptions of the nature of timing of the causative agents. We *do* have ample evidence to state that specific categories or subcategories of retarded people *do* have a similar problem or set of problems. I think we could then get some of the behavioral people to look at some of those specific subgroups as to see just *what* the deficit is in a particular genetic disorder, for example. At that point, we might find experimental subjects that would be much better choices than the kind of source we have now. For example, if you presented a paper at a meeting and in that paper you said, "Well, I took some rats." And somebody from the audience asked, "Where did you get the rats?" And you said, "Well, I went out and trapped them behind the barn," they would laugh at you! But if you talk about, "Well, we went out and we took a group of mentally retarded clients . . . ," you have the *same* sort of heterogeneity. We need to think about more specific subgroupings of the retarded persons, and not the usual nonspecific mixing together of retarded persons from widely varying causes of the retardation aspect under study.

Dr. Sandman: We have strain differences in rats. We also have housing condition differences that are probably much more significant than strain differences. With respect to directly what you are talking about, a major flaw in the study [Chapter 14] I presented is that there is no homogeneity of the causes of retardation in that sample. It *is* a heterogeneous sample, and in other ways I am sure we lost resolution because it was not defined more clearly. It has been already suggested that maybe there are endocrine disorders that are directly related to mental retardation syndromes, and perhaps the endocrine-type peptides would be more effective therein.

Dr. Berkson: It should be said that during the '60s there were a great many studies like yours that were reviewed by Dr. John Belmont (in 1971). The general conclusion of the review was that, in fact, there are very few behavioral differences between subgroups among the mentally retarded as to causology. Now that finding does not sound quite right at first, but if you think about the sum of genetic defects, the disabilities that do or do not become expressed, and individual differences then even within a specific genetic group there are tremendous differences in people with the same genetic cause to their retardation. In fact, what you usually result with at the end of such studies are large heterogeneous groups wherein there may be very few specific subgroup differences. If somebody does embark upon that diagnostic clarification trip again, he or she should use different behavioral assessments—not just the focus on physical assessments that has repeatedly been done in the past.

Dr. Menolascino: I don't follow your comment.

Dr. Berkson: Well, if the suggestion is being made that the behavioral professionals should take subgroups among the mentally retarded
persons—defined by specific causes of their mental retardation—and compare them with respect to their behaviors, and if we are implying that that
task would be an easy one, I think that would be an error. Such studies, in
fact, have been done repeatedly by many people without positive results.
Maybe we have had an incorrect view of the behaviors of retarded individuals, so that we have not used our data as a valid assessment tool. If a new
behavioral categorizing of specific subgroups is to be accomplished, it ought
to be done with new concepts about the types of behavior to be studied.

Dr. Menolascino: New concepts such as—?

Dr. Berkson: I have no idea. Personally, I would not recommend
any further such studies, since they are rather fruitless undertakings.

Dr. Menolascino: But you are posing a dilemma in many ways: We
are talking about a heterogeneous class of active compounds, and there is a
marked heterogeneity of the diagnostic causes of retardation (i.e., the
350-plus causes of the symptom of mental retardation that are subsumed into
the eight diagnostic categories of the diagnostic system of the American
Association on Mental Deficiency [AAMD] that is currently utilized in the
field of mental retardation), and a wide variety of behaviors have been
described in retarded individuals. So the heterogeneity becomes progressively more compounded, and where do we go from there? Any way out
of that dilemma?

Dr. Berkson: Well, it is a very important issue because the etiological (i.e., causes) categories listed in the classification system of the American Association on Mental Deficiency are viewed by many professionals as
not being of much use. These current AAMD diagnostic categories are not
very predictive at all as to their outlining expected behaviors in individual
retarded persons. Also, the currently utilized social-adaptive scales, as
behavioral classifications are too gross and hence outmoded. So the current
classification system utilized for the diagnosis of the different disorders that
produce the symptom of mental retardation has some prize problems.

Dr. Sandman: I think you are misinterpreting what we may have
been saying. We talked about subgroups and we are saying that we expect
that there will be subgroups. The subgroups that you cannot detect by
present methods, either by etiologies or anything else you mentioned, may
only be detected as we have the new tools—such as possible peptide
response differences in the different subgroups. Accordingly, our current
causology-behavior description may only be a reflection of needed diagnostic changes as our knowledge has, and will continue, to expand.

Dr. Berkson: No, I was responding to the suggestion that genetic
subclassifications might be a useful dimension of the research sample
selection. It is a very obvious suggestion, and it has been an important one
for the last 15 years.

Dr. Sandman: Well, let me add that I am not taking a strict behavioral point of view. We are talking about the modification of behavior by
a peptide, and I think it is very conceivable that some disorders are likely to
respond to a peptide as a function of one kind of nervous system disorder,
and another disorder will not respond because the elements are not common.

With respect to behavior, I think our studies reflect your sentiment completely. We tested the same behaviors in rats and in our heterogeneous human population because the peptide *was* sensitive in the populations we were looking at. We took a specific behavior and stayed with it; basically, a behavior that required an intradimensional shift. It is conceivable to me that, using a peptide as an intrinsic marker, you can categorize a population behaviorally and then look at the effects of all kinds of data. It might turn out that the chemical variables *are* the important variables for outlining both causes and future treatment interventions. Further, at that point it could turn out that factors are operative that are currently unknown to all of us.

Dr. Berkson: Along that line, and with all due respect to Dr. Sandman, I think if one risks some intuitive notions based on the subjects' data, it may be that taking a better look at extinction curves—as opposed to mylonic curves—may offer some productive way to tell the specific behavorial differences involved.

Dr. Sandman: I agree completely. We have looked at habituation in the orientation sequence, and tried to fully develop that model because it is particularly applicable in retarded persons. We have also developed all of the comparative age norms (with normal and retarded individuals) for these peptides. For similar reasons, as you expressed, I agree completely. I think that *is* the way to go.

Question: It has been reported for some years (e.g., the earlier work of Dr. George Jervis and others) that there are similar signs of Alzheimer's disease cell pathology in middle-age Down syndrome individuals. Accordingly, Dr. Davis, would you comment whether the physostigmine which seems to improve memory in Alzheimer's disease individuals [Chapter 13] should *also* work in Down syndrome?

DOWN SYNDROME

Dr. Davis: I do not know whether the neurofibrillary tangles and the senile plaques that occur in Alzheimer's disease are specific for just *that* disease. We know they exist in Down syndrome, and we know they exist in many people who are not demented. I would like to see somebody study the brain of people with Down syndrome, and look specifically for the choline acetyltransferase abnormalities. However, I think that a reasonable approach to the treatment of Down syndrome—certainly one that could be justified on the basis of our data and the presence of neurofibrillary tangles and senile plaques—would be to study some young Down syndrome individuals who are not badly afflicted, infuse a little physostigmine and see what happens.

Question: Would you like the answer to your question?

Dr. Davis: Yes.

Comment: We have had a number of biopsy cases on a variety of severely retarded persons and also studied the cholinergic transferase in their receptors. We have not found any significant changes in those retarded children who were very severely retarded.

Dr. Davis: So then your biopsy studies do not show a cholinergic abnormality.

Dr. Menolascino: How about Down syndrome?

Dr. Paul Adams: We do not biopsy routinely any Down syndrome children—the condition is too obvious.

Dr. Menolascino: Well, without biopsy, how about the assessment of the brain in Down syndrome after death?

Dr. Adams: We rarely do that and, to the best of my knowledge, the acetylcholine studies have not been done after death.

Dr. Menolascino: It hasn't been done in Down syndrome?

Dr. Adams: Right, because you have got to do frozen brains in order to do the study; therefore you are not going to do them. You see?

Dr. Menolascino: Are you saying it is too technical to accomplish?

Dr. Adams: No, we just don't do these procedures in Down syndrome in this country.

Dr. Menolascino: Yes, but can they be done?

Dr. Adams: In the question of Down syndrome, when I said it can't be done, at least it can't be done under all the current ethics.

Dr. Menolascino: Wait a minute—

Dr. Adams: Well, yes, we could get autopsy material and that can be frozen very rapidly. We could then do assay methods. But will there be a defect that we can measure?

Dr. Menolascino: That was the question originally asked—we do not know if there will or will not be a defect. I also asked whether Down syndrome people should be candidates for biopsy—like those that have been done in Scotland for Alzheimer's? The same kind of diagnostic studies would be done as have been done on old folks—studies that would attempt to clarify if these individuals have an acetylcholine deficit that could then be treated with physostigmine.

Question: Who should select which Down syndrome person to study as to postmortem examination, and who wants to do this type of work?

Dr. Menolascino: I would think that both parents and professionals would want to see these pathology studies done on a large scale basis—if there is a realistic possibility that we can eventually learn more and thus help Down syndrome people.

Question: Dr. Davis, I think it would be useful, regarding Alzheimer's disease, if you could give some idea of how many years in relative memory—or memory improvement—are equivalent to the reversal effects you have noted in using physostigmine in your research samples of Alzheimer's patients.

Dr. Davis: I do not know! The effect that we are dealing with here is a transient one, and the therapeutic window is so short that the only time we have is the time in which to administer tests that we know to be sensitive to cholinergic manipulation—namely, tests that measure the ability of a subject to encode or learn information. I do not know how much those effects would relate on a global memory level. We do not have any scales that I believe are very good in measuring the role of memory in regards to global behavior.

Comment: No, there *must* be a paramount developmental study of memory changes—over time—that are similar to the sort seen in Alzheimer's.

MEMORY DEFICITS

Dr. Davis: Let me give you some idea of what happens. When you do these intravenous studies with physostigmine, the subjects, at best—especially those who have had Alzheimer's less than 2 years—have a eureka experience that is hard to deny. Both the subject and the experimenter are aware of it, and anybody else in the room is aware of it. The subject usually comes out, afterwards, and says—even days later—and these are very demented people . . . "I want that stuff in my arm." Or another subject said, "I want to go back to that doctor who made me think better."

Question: I have another question. In the first experiment, you described three different examples of memory changes—including long-term memory [Chapter 13]. I want to ask, did you not find any effect on the Sternberg Test?

Dr. Davis: On the Sternberg Test there was no effect. There was no effect in attention, short term memory, or on the digit span. The effect we have found on memory retrieval in normals, we have never been able to show in any of the elderly people. So we have narrowed down our evaluation focus to just modifications of the Bushky Test.

Question: What kinds of variations in the Bushky Test have you looked at? Stimulus material variations, imagery, or what?

Dr. Davis: Well, what we do in the Bushky Test with these very demented people is have them perform at about the only level they can respond at. Most of these people are so demented that they can do little more than recognize whether they have seen a picture before. What is critical in all of these studies is to establish a paradigm in which people can actually show improvement—and this is virgin territory, because for the most part, the past studies that have been done in Alzheimer's disease have used inappropriate measuring devices to assess pharmacologically mediated changes.

Question: Well, you understand the import of my question. That unless you produce effects that are clearly demonstrable in well people in general, then cognitively speaking, any claims for a possible extension of improvement in mental retardation would have to be looked at skeptically.

Dr. Davis: I make no claims about specific results in mental retardation, but it *is* intriguing to note the marked similarities between my studies on Alzheimer's and the reported memory deficits in mentally retarded individuals.

Question: Was the physostigmine given in I.V. bullets, or by continuous intravenous infusion, and how long did it last?

Dr. Davis: Continuous infusion was utilized, and the effect usually is worn off within 20 minutes after giving the drug.

Question: What do you think the physostigmine is working on? After all, there are numerous neurons that have been destroyed that are cholinergic, and do you think it is really acting as an anticholinesterase agent?

Dr. Davis: Yes, I think it is acting as an anticholinesterase agent, and I think that is why we see a difference in those people who have been demented for less than 2 years versus those who have had Alzheimer's for more than 2 years. It is obviously not the treatment strategy of choice, but then no one would have thought that the L-dopa precursor should have been effective in Parkinson's disease—which primarily wiped out the presynaptic dopaminergic neuron—yet it appears that what cells were left in Parkinsonism *were* able to synthesize more. I think what happens is that what little acetylcholine *is* left is kept around longer and is more fully utilized.

There comes a point where even that little amount is probably not there. The optimal treatment strategy is a pharmacological receptor agent that could be orally administered. We have done some oral studies with physostigmine. It is a short-acting drug, but you can still get absorption and some minimal effects by oral administration.

Question: What vital functions did you assess during your studies? For example, cerebral profusion, blood pressure . . .

Dr. Davis: Blood pressure, heart rate, and what we were looking for was no change because of the potential danger of the drug. We usually administer a peripheral cholinergic agent to see what it will do to block the side effects. What happens under the conditions in which we have administered the drug is that the peripheral effects are hardly noted at all.

Comment: The Atkinson short-term/long-term memory model is more controversial than I think you have indicated. Now one dimension that is not controversial is the distinction between learning and performance. If these studies showed a performance effect and not a learning effect, it is important, because it might be that the effect you are getting is not related through a learning variable, but something that is related to the eureka experience. In other words, you may have a motivational variable that might be skewing your research data.

Dr. Davis: I think what argues against the nonspecificity of our findings is that if we had had a performance effect, we should have seen it on the Sternberg Test and we should have seen it on other tests. Since we only found this specifically in one area of memory, it would seem to me that we are dealing with a specific effect. One other important point is that with cholinergic administrations in animals (e.g., the use of scopolamine in humans) the effect is again limited to just that part of memory that we are improving here—a total reversal effect that shows the specificity of our findings.

EXTERNAL ENVIRONMENTAL LEARNING ENHANCEMENT

Question: Dr. Butterfield, are you certain that the transfer of learning research studies that you reviewed [Chapter 15] were well-controlled ones?

Dr. Butterfield: Yes, these studies were done by experienced researchers who utilized excellent research designs. For example, in the follow-up studies, the examiners did not know which students had been taught in a special way and which ones had not. The people who did the training were typically not the people who did the testing. The environment, however, was substantially and deliberately the same. So there were bases for environmentally mediated transfer. There are about half a dozen studies that together show that substantial transfer of learning can be obtained; none of them is absolutely or perfectly controlled, but as a group they are quite compelling.

Question: Two questions. First, in the group of retarded persons, what was the upper chronological age range in which you were able to accomplish sentence structure?

Dr. Butterfield: The upper chronological age range was in the

LEARNING
RESEARCH

20–25-year group. Now, that is not work that I have personally done; I am reporting on the work of other researchers, and you need to understand that the behavior modification researchers who have done that work pay relatively less attention to—or give relatively less importance to—the subjects' characteristics, like chronological age, than some of the rest of us do. Their argument is that the important factor is the functional level of the subject, and the functional level of these people was such that they would start out with language skills less than that of a typical 2-year-old, and end up with language skills like that of a 4- or 5-year-old individual.

Question: The second part of my question: Let us say we are going to set up a research design with children whose chronological ages range from 3 to 12 years. What absolute minimum measures of cognitive function would you need to measure to assure that these environmental techniques have or have not produced significant findings?

Dr. Butterfield: That is a very difficult question. The question boils down to, from my way of thinking, how widely do you have to sample in the domain of intellectual behaviors in order to be satisfied that some treatment that you administer has, in fact, influenced intelligence? Well, one simple answer is to administer a good standardized intelligence test. A virtue of the standardized intelligence test is that it ranges widely in the behaviors that it samples. Further, in the developmental literature there are good measures of language functioning, various kinds of memory, and various kinds of problem-solving techniques. Accordingly, the minimum measures that you need to sample, it seems to me, are in the following areas: Creating solutions to new problems, using linguistic skills, and being able to extract and remember information. It would also depend very heavily on the kinds of retarded persons you were starting with. For example, in mildly retarded children of chronological ages 8 to 10 years, I think we could do a good job of creating for you a set of experimental measures so that if your treatment were able to improve performance on all of them, then hardly anybody would say that you had not made an important impact on intelligence.

Question: I infer from your comments that it is very important that one is careful in the selection of tests.

Dr. Butterfield: I know what you are getting at. There is substantial debate about bias in global intelligence tests. Some people argue that global intelligence tests are strongly biased against large segments of the population. Other people are not so concerned about same. I think that it depends on what your purposes are in using an intelligence test, whether you have to attend seriously to the fact that intelligence tests do have some kinds of biases in them. If you are using a global intelligence test as a research tool to ask, ''Have I probably made an important impact on global intelligence?'', then I think you can be relatively less concerned about the bias. If you are using intelligence tests for the purposes of educational programming, then you have to be terribly concerned about the bias. But as a research tool, as a dependent measure for asking the general question, ''Have we influenced intelligence?'', I would not unduly worry about the biases.

Question: We have heard a great deal of discussion from the biomedical people, and now we are concentrating on some of the behavioral aspects. You outlined the sort of historical mergers that have recently

INTELLIGENCE

occurred between the cognitive and behavioral people in two major areas of psychology. Do you see, looking ahead, a greater merger between the two major areas of biomedical and behavioral research—looking at, for example, the behavioral effects on a retarded person of a drug as a potential memory and/or learning enhancer—such as a neurotransmitter of peptide? Is there a way that we are going to get a closer working relationship between these two groups?

Dr. Butterfield: The question is, if I have anything to say about the likelihood of biomedical research working constructively with behaviorally oriented researchers, toward the challenge of creating cures for the symptom of mental retardation. I really want to punt! I don't know, but I will observe that we have already seen many examples of the blending of behavioral and biomedical approaches. Now, how likely it is that there will be more of that sort of blending, I don't know. I would predict that if there are increasing professional transactions on common areas of research interest among a reasonably wide range of professional research paths, then you *will* find a fair number of psychologists becoming interested and wanting to know more about these areas of research and becoming actively engaged.

Question: I am very curious, Dr. Bijou [Chapter 16]. You are dealing with a large population of children whose nervous systems would be undergoing prodigious maturation over a period of 8 years—the length of the national prevention-cure program that you recommend. You are applying a rather complex methodology of instruction. How will you ever know whether any given method applied at any given time is really more effective or efficient than any other? I am always reminded of the attempts in New England to teach a foreign language to children starting at age 6; the children received language instruction for the next 4 years. They later discovered that 1 year of instruction at the at the age of 14 was worth about 4 or 5 years of instruction at an earlier time because the nervous system wasn't ready to cope with a second language earlier in life. What are going to be your controls? Your methodology? How will you know whether you can get the same results starting at 6 years or 8 years of age? Or whether to use this method or that method of instruction?

Dr. Bijou: Well, I don't suppose there is going to be a clear way of knowing. The basic hypothesis is that you have to have a supporting environment to get development going at a normal rate, and most of this early support is in the home: in the behavior of parents and siblings in relation to the child. Even if a study came along and reported that these children can advance by starting them at age 6—rather than at age 2—I would be skeptical about the study, because I think it is important that changes start earlier than age 6. I think that attitudinal and motivational changes must begin very early in a child's life so that the early instruction can be maintained in the home. This early learning is very important, and Dr. Butterfield referred to the lack of generalization in many experimental efforts; we run into that problem all the time. But we know that we can improve generalization, for example, or learning of one sort or another by simply arranging the environment to support the learning. Again, I do not think in terms of the role of the nervous system of the individuals as the biomedical scientists do. Rather, I think in terms of a total functioning

EARLY
INTERVENTION

organism and in terms of what the young child needs to initiate and maintain the kinds of instruction he is getting from home and the school—the kind of motivation he is getting. Now we do know that this group of disadvantaged mildly retarded children, if left the way they are going now, will continue to be retarded. That is certain, since the research is clear on this topic. We know that the method discussed *is* effective in the same sense of individual achievements of individual children as compared to children who do not get similar kinds of individual training. Again, I would be skeptical about cutting off the time elements (earlier versus later time for initiating educational interactions) because of the notion that *early* support in family relationships is extremely important for early-later learning attainments.

Dr. Menolascino: May I take a swing at that question? You asked specifically about the acquisition of a second language. I have two brothers who came from Italy when I was 4 years old. I speak Italian fluently, and as my paisano friends know, I also have (fortunately or unfortunately) all of the hand gestures. If I had waited until 14 years of age to learn the Italian language, this might not be so, since I can readily pick out the people who learned Italian at age 14: The *total* language expression (verbal and nonverbal) and comprehension are simply not there! I think one of the key parts of language acquisition is the developmental embedding of a language beyond the mechanics of the grammar—into the thinking-feeling-understanding aspects and its resultant finer nuances of same. Similarly, you can tell those colleagues who took German during their premedicine years: They speak in a stilted and minimally involved way. But the finer nuances— I think we come to them by the developmental mode of early imprinting via family-instructional-cultural reinforcements. The breadth of that type of developmental learning seems to be intimately involved with the psychosocial and familial motivational aspects of learning as a major foundation. Am I off base?

Dr. Bijou: I agree with Dr. Menolascino wholeheartedly and what he was saying about language is also true of skiing. You can readily tell one who learned to ski as a child versus someone who learned to ski as an adult, there *are* major differences!

Question: I am not sure if what I am going to say is a question, or more of a comment, but I would like to have seen some tables of data in the chapters by Drs. Bijou and Butterfield. For example, I would like to have seen some data that gave measures of performance by any set of criteria Drs. Bijou and Butterfield wished to have proposed; measures that would have permitted comparisons, or comparisons of a normal individual over time, and a normal individual who had been exposed to a variety of ways of improving his or her level of adaptation. Or beyond tables of data, descriptions of the exact nature of the adaptations noted in handicapped children who had been specially educated. From the viewpoint of the biologist, I have the feeling that the developmental process presents a very heterogeneous range of problems to the educator. Perhaps that is the nature of handling the external phenomena that eminates from the generalized functions of the central nervous system and the developmental problems noted by Dr. Purpura. There are going to be developmental problems wherein massive sectors of the brain, or perhaps systems, are involved. One would

BIOLOGICAL
DEVELOPMENT

wonder from the viewpoint of the biology of developmental process that perhaps these different structural problems of the nervous system are going to present different problems or different potentialities. Therefore, how can you present a uniform set of measures to assess development that stems from a wide variety of "non-uniform" brains? One would wonder, *if* there *were* adequate measures of adaptation, that comparing the cures of adaptation would permit us to see that, in fact, one kind of brain is going to do it one way, and *other* kinds of brains are going to do it in other ways. Is there a uniform approach or strategy to optimize the adaptation? It is really difficult for me to know what you are specifically talking about!

Dr. Bijou: Well, the comment is a very good one. I have presented the specific data in Chapter 16, but the other point you are making is a good one: You are talking about the way the brain functions. For example, you are right: Different individuals behave differently in learning situations. For example, educators like to talk about those who are good with visual stimulation versus those who are good with auditory stimulation. And they say this factor has to be taken into account in the teaching situation. Absolutely right! If you have a technique that adjusts the material to the child's competence, then baseline where it is—rather than where you "think" he or she ought to be—or on the basis of an IQ test or something of that sort. Second, we must utilize a teaching technique that closely observes the child and is guided by the child's behavior—so that if you are working with a child, and he is not making progress, you must ask yourself, "Am I using the techniques that are appropriate for him? Maybe I ought to get off the visual and get on to auditory." You must actively and continuously question yourself: "If this child is not making progress in a week or two, then I will have to move to another technique." Don't stay with the nonhelpful techniques! That is the essential dimension of any good educational approach. You initially should not have any preconceptions that a child ought to learn this way or that way because of his or her "damaged brain" or "damaged parents" (etc.). That would be the idea. I think your point is well taken, but with a flexible teaching device that always embodies watching the child and not the principle, so to speak, then you are in a position to make changes on the basis of the child's performance.

EDUCATIONAL ASPECTS

Question: Then you use a criterion of success that permits comparison of the individual to himself?

Dr. Bijou: Right. Within himself: It is his own developmental curve—that is, progression of his own curve. If he doesn't make progress, then you examine your program, you examine your technique, and you have a whole range of options to move around until you get one that works. This approach is the essence of the individualized treatment prescription for any needy child.

Dr. Menolascino: I just want to comment. I think a fascinating observation is that the medical model always shows on tables of data or slides the "before" and "after" results. In the psychosocial model, one rarely sees data about "before" and "after" considerations. The only major study in mental retardation on this topic that utilized this "before" and "after" device was the Milwaukee Study of Rick Heber. We have also raised the brain *versus* the total organism-environment tautology. Lastly,

MODELS OF RESEARCH

we may also narrow our scientific research vision on *either* intrinsic or extrinsic dimensions—as noted by Dr. Sandman when he wondered if we may not be giving too much attention to the *central* nervous system versus the *peripheral* nervous system; we tend to show "prejudice" against the basic phenomena of the peripheral nervous system via our "obsession" with the central nervous system and its functions.

Dr. Butterfield: I was aware during the compilation of this volume that there were going to be presented a variety of substantially different approaches. Well, I didn't add a single table to my chapter because, in effect, I can assure you that my results are true. I could have added 700 tables of data that would have shown you in excruciating detail the controls that are necessary. But, you know, you would have gotten out of those 700 tables about as much as I visually got out of the biomedical tables and slides, which is precious little. Except that I do appreciate that my biomedical colleagues have great enthusiasm for highly sophisticated techniques, and biomedical studies are working over a wide range of scientific topics. But it seemed to me that the purpose of a volume of this sort is to focus on the general strategic levels that influence the many potential pathways to curing the symptom of mental retardation. Accordingly, it is the *ideas* that are important, not the details!

Comment: One of the reasons why many of us show tables of data or slides is because currently we do not really have a way of approaching a universal professional discourse, where we start with a great conceptualization that one has really thought about over the years. Accordingly, I speak for many neuroscientists who have gotten into the habit of trying to stay away from the generalizing principles because they do not aid our current level of data-based research findings. Now, let me address another key issue, because we are trying to *bridge the gaps:* I wonder how we get so constrained in *only* the universes that we work in every day. Let me illustrate by referring to material presented by Drs. Kastin and Sandman [Chapter 12] on the retarded persons who were being given the 5 mg of the ACTH 4–9 fragment. They showed behavioral increase in performance, I would say. At the 10-mg dosage level the performance was still peaking, but at the 20-mg dosage level there was a decrease in performance. The interpretation based on that particular constraint about pharmacology is the biphasic mechanism: You give a little of something, that is good; you give a little more of that *same* something, and that is bad. Could it not have been that at the 20-mg dosage level, the people who were doing that performance suddenly started to realize how really devastatingly boring this all is—that they had attained a level of thought (perhaps for the first time!) of what in the world am I doing here? In that kind of universal professional discourse you start getting a totally different kind of interpretation of behavioral effects than the pharmacologists' constant appeal: That a little acetylcholine depolarizes and a lot more will make you totally unable to respond. Those are the usual principles that we go on in terms of drug therapies. So maybe we have all gotten into areas that maybe we did not anticipate we would be, and for a short period of time we—like the retarded citizen who improved on the peptides—come to the "eureka" insight of learning to change, and start viewing our old singular approaches as very boring. We neuroscientists often get stuck in *our* way of interpreting *our* data and selecting or ignoring the work of others that we do not understand—perhaps for fear that it questions our own narrowness.

Dr. Menolascino: Dr. Purpura, your superb comments and reflections regarding professional growth and the quest for a common forum for universal professional discourse remind me of the cartoon byline, "Ideology aside—what do you *really* believe?"

Question: After reviewing the wide variety of exciting contributions to this volume, one suddenly finds out how "retarded" we are about the research efforts of others in very closely allied fields! I would like to ask a question of Dr. Bijou in regard to his chapter contribution [Chapter 16]. In reference to your Peruvian experience, Dr. Bijou, you stated that the Portage Project there had to introduce other assessment techniques, and one of them was nutrition. You made a reference that the focus on nutrition was not necessary here in our country. My question is, do you believe that we don't need excellent nutrition in the furtherance of the development of retarded children (or any children!) of our country?

Dr. Bijou: That is an excellent point; I do not believe that it is not necessary in our country. What happens here, again taking the Portage model I was talking about, is that the teacher *does* devote a good deal of time to nutrition, health, and sanitation, but it is only indirectly built into the program. However, in Peru the hunger-nutrition problem is so devastating and so prior to everything else, that the teacher has to *start* by directly addressing these topics. They have had to provide help with sanitation and nutrition *before* they can begin educating, since these were the essential first tasks to do. So it was just a matter of how much attention had to be given to these matters.

Question: I want to pose a question to Dr. Berkson about the incidence of mental retardation data being reviewed from Dr. Alfred Greunberg [Chapter 17]. In the northern Swedish group, why is there a peak in the incidence? What is going on sociologically there? Is that a reality or not?

Dr. Berkson: It is probably a statistical reliability problem since that particular survey had a very small sample size.

Question: But the data in the Aberdeen study showed part of the incidence curve as being very smooth—not the curve noted in the northern Sweden sample.

Dr. Berkson: The Aberdeen study was not a summary study, but a longitudinal study. That is quite different from the northern Sweden data, which was all from cross-sectional studies, and those particular cross-sectional studies had different ends at different times.

Comment: Your discussion [Chapter 17] pointed out that we are each tending to look at the same thing within our own set of skills and our own learning sets. For example, the structuralists tend to look primarily at neurochemical substances or anatomical sites. There is a pressing need for cooperative and collaborative efforts all along the line, and I'm thinking primarily of attempting to coordinate the behavioral and biomedical endeavors.

Dr. Berkson: Yes, I think there have been some very impressive

BEHAVIORAL
STRATEGIES
AND
THEIR
IMPACT

collaborative efforts, like the studies on the interactions of pharmaceutical substances and behavior. I would like to point out, too, that by manipulating the environment, specifically by manipulating the consequences of behavior—or the lack of same—that we can produce all kinds of things. We can produce ulcers. We can produce a lack of functional vision in animals. We can produce obesity. We can produce a loss of general function that is similar to retardation by changing some of the behavioral aspects. I would like to submit that one other avenue of pursuing our goal is to take a look not just at the behavioral concomitants of biological or naturally occurring chemicals, but the reverse. Let's take a look at some changes, biomedical changes that are concomitant to particular kinds of behavioral experiences. I think we need to go in both directions if we are going to make a quantum step forward in the field of mental retardation.

Question: Do the behavior modification techniques *only* work with the mildly mentally retarded, as Dr. Bijou suggested?

Dr. Berkson: No, the research data are also very clear that the same techniques *do* work for the moderately and the severely retarded. [Dr. Bijou agreed with the answer.]

Dr. Ommaya: There is a fundamental problem that I would like someone to comment upon. In former studies on animal intelligence, it has been noted that the animal can tell that his master is going to take him for a walk, but he cannot tell if his master is going to take him for a walk tomorrow. Why not? Much of our current discussion reminds me of our attempts to teach sign language to subhuman primates. The chart graphing shows that it works well, but is it *really* very far removed from the famous studies on the training of horses? In other words, the problem seems to be how to detect differences between itonic and superitonic thinking. Perhaps we should be focusing on trying to modify abstract inner thought because if *that* can be modified, then one can possibly start teaching skills in an environment that those individuals who are incapable of superitonic thinking can be able to function in because there is a fundamental cutoff in the way animals think: they do not think superitonically. There must also be a limit to the kinds of manipulations you can make with the thinking of retarded individuals. I think this issue has to be solved and maybe some focusing should perhaps be aimed at what is superitonic thinking.

Dr. Berkson: Is superitonic thinking the same phenomenon that Dr. Butterfield termed "superordinate"?

Dr. Butterfield: That particular term, superitonic, is not one that is in my repertoire. But the idea of being able to go beyond the perceptional controls of the immediate environment certainly is an important one. In fact, we would normally not call a person intelligent unless he or she was able to do that. When I spoke about *superordinate* kinds of processes, I think I was talking about much the same thing as the superitonic thinking phenomenon. We *are* focusing on it. In the current state of the art, those sorts of functions are not assessed directly, they are assessed indirectly and largely by measurements of whether the child was taught a specific thing and then can (or will) modify and apply it in a different environment. There are not assessment devices that I know of, or the kind that you were calling for, as yet to measure these phenomena. However, there is some promising and interesting work with young children on what is called metacognition to assess what they know about thinking as opposed to what they know about the environment. Whether teaching metacognition will be useful is still an empirical question.

Dr. Ommaya: There are sometimes assumptions that make the problem more complex than need be, whereas a simple discrimination process may be present. There is a past research study of the chimpanzee, wherein a pear was buried under a marked spot and the ground was cleared off so it could not be guessed where the pear was except for the marked spot. The researcher showed one chimpanzee a picture of the pear and where he had buried it; he then took this chimpanzee back to the cage. The researcher then released a *second* chimpanzee from the same cage, and this second chimpanzee went directly to the place where the pear was buried and dug it up. Now, would we assume that the first chimpanzee ''told'' the second one where the pear was?

Dr. Butterfield: Now the assumption that animals and humans are different from each other assumes that there is some sort of a straightforward or simple gap. In fact, what happens in evolution is the building of one more stage of complexity: one more ''thoughty'' thing in animal intelligence. That would mean to me that the suggested attempts to simply discriminate between itonic and superitonic properties would merely have to be something that would have to do with an *order of complexity,* and you don't need to worry too much about the question of itonic and superitonic thinking because what you want to do, in fact, is to make a person's behavior as general as possible across as large a variety of situations as possible. Accordingly, the second chimpanzee could have been ''told'' about the first pear, sniffed it out, whatever. Probably the best test of that—or any—task is to release him into a variety or normal or unnatural environments and find out how he reacts.

Dr. Bijou: I can't help but deduct that we are looking unduly for something that exists specifically within the organisms here, and we are not paying enough attention to the idea that whatever is taught must be supported and maintained by the environment. Even memory functions to test our ability to be supported by environments: We forget when the environment doesn't support us, we remember when it does. To say a dog doesn't know if he is going to go for a walk tomorrow is simply to say that he has not been exposed to the right variables. If he could be exposed to the thinking of his master, he would know whether he was going for a walk or not. He can respond to the relative clues, *if* you give them to him. If they're not there, he cannot do it.

ENVIRONMENTAL INFLUENCES

Dr. Ommaya: But that is the fundamental difference between the human and the nonhuman.

Dr. Bijou: Well, it is not so fundamental. I think that Dr. Butterfield would agree with my idea of environmental support; at least that was the direction of his last comments.

Dr. Butterfield: Yes. Now if the dog were exposed to the same variables that the master is exposed to, the chances are that he would know that he is going for a walk tomorrow. But the issue really gets into the domain of volition—on the part of the master—and we go beyond qualitative-quantitative thinking processes. The question becomes irrelevant to our discussion of superordinate thinking.

Dr. Bijou: Well, what we do in rearing children is not to teach them how to tell time early on; we teach them events. For example, they learn these events: When the clock looks like "that" it is time to go and eat. Or when the teacher looks like "this" it is time to do that. You teach them events and through these events they later learn time.

Dr. Ommaya: Yes, but it is the initial theory that is very important—such as the fact that the human mind does deviate from an expected schedule of behavior is very important. It is important that when you cannot free yourself from time-blocking, then you do become very predictable and become like an amoeba.

Dr. Bijou: I think what Dr. Ommaya is saying is that children of a certain level of intelligence never acquire any sense of time. We have tested that again and again. Even severely retarded children can, more or less, equate a sense of temporal order, if not a specific time sequence. They read environmental effects that occur in and around a daily schedule of activities very well.

Question: Yes, but the question is why?

Dr. Bijou: I don't know. It may have to do with a synthetic level of functioning in the nervous system—such as the child's reading of a pattern of recurring behaviors (i.e., habits), etc.

Dr. Butterfield: I just want to comment that using the analogy of the symbolic communication in chimpanzees—when we are ostensibly dealing with mild, moderate, and severe forms of mental retardation—is rather somewhat farfetched and dehumanizing. We are talking at a level far beyond the question of relationship between symbolic communication in humans and symbolic communication in animals. We are talking about people who use language, who use symbols, some of whom can write, and all of whom can respond to a wide range of verbal and visual stimuli. Thus, the analogy is false. We must remember that the Down syndrome person thinks, understands words, understands the sequence of sounds and syllables, etc., at a far different type and level of discourse than the kind of sign language that one notes with animals. I just want to emphasize that we are talking about mild and moderately retarded individuals, wherein one can have significant impact by well-thought sequences of education and training.

Dr. Menolascino: My sincere thanks to all of the authors of this volume for the foregoing dialogue concerning their scientific research efforts and hopes—and the obvious opportunities for significant cross-fertilization these efforts present as we continue the quest for curative approaches to the multi-faceted symptom of mental retardation.

Curative Aspects of Mental Retardation:
Biomedical and Behavioral Advances
edited by Frank J. Menolascino, M.D., Ronald Neman, Ph.D., and Jack A. Stark, Ph.D.
Copyright 1983   Paul H. Brookes Publishing Co., Inc.   Baltimore · London

chapter 19

Future Prospects for
Curing Mental Retardation

Frank J. Menolascino, M.D.
University of Nebraska Medical Center
Omaha, Nebraska
Ronald Neman, Ph.D.
Association for Retarded Citizens
Arlington, Texas
Jack A. Stark, Ph.D.
University of Nebraska Medical Center
Omaha, Nebraska

It has been said that nature alone performs miracles; scientists merely exploit them. If this is true—and the authors believe it is—we are most assuredly accelerating the rate of exploitation. Scientific advances in aviation, for example, have led us in the past 50 years from a single engine airplane to a space shuttle program. Similarly, in the area of mental retardation, although research and discovery have not progressed as rapidly, we too may be entering the age of "light speed." We have also witnessed a spin-off effect, in which the mental retardation field, like so many other health-related areas, has certainly benefited from the knowledge gleaned from space programs, computer technology, basic and applied biomedical research, as well as contributions from the behavioral sciences.

What is amazing about the findings and predictions of the contributing authors of this book is their claim that the goal of "cure" of

mental retardation is not only possible, but possible in many areas within our lifetime. After decades of resigning ourselves to the "irreversibility" of mental retardation, the concept of "cure" is difficult for many of us to comprehend.

THE CONCEPT OF CURE

The first reaction of most health care professionals to the concept of cure for mental retardation is that individuals who postulate such an idea must be either naive or seeking publicity for a sensationalized "medical model."

"Cure," afterall, is a word fraught with emotion, and a term that scientists and clinicians alike prefer to avoid, particularly those who view the symptom(s) of mental retardation as a "given"—and, at best, difficult to treat and devoid of curative possibilities. The thinking, for example, is that all of the enriched environments in the world will not alter a severely damaged brain. The word "cure," from the Latin word *cura,* means to treat or make better, and its historical association with reversibility has resulted from medical treatment of disease through surgery, medication, or specific therapies. As this book demonstrates, when the modern concept of cure is viewed in relationship to the primary, secondary, and tertiary prevention aspects of mental retardation, cure can also be seen as the reversibility process of early secondary prevention approaches.

Mental retardation is a symptom that is caused by numerous diseases; the disease process, though very complex, can be approached either functionally or organically. The authors of this book have many reasons to be optimistic about future scientific developments that will effect an increasing number of cures for the symptom of mental retardation. The intentions of the authors are not to raise false hopes through the prediction of quick cures for the majority of today's mentally retarded individuals. The authors merely wish to draw attention to significant scientific developments from a multidisciplinary point of view and to demonstrate the cumulative impact that these will have on mentally retarded individuals and their families within the next 3 decades. As the data converge from such diverse scientific disciplines as neuropathology, behavioral science, biochemistry, psychiatry, neurosurgery, genetics, and endocrinology, they indicate—in overwhelming fashion—that we are on the brink of startling breakthroughs that can lead to "curing" many of our current and future mentally retarded citizens.

Scientific Advances

Time has a way of solidifying scientific assumptions and turning them into "facts." Indeed, the "fact" of irreversibility in mental retardation has been with us so long it has generated an almost automatic counter-reaction: reluctance to accept the possibility of cures, and suspicion of those who claim

advances (or even the possibility of advances) in this area. There is, of course, precedence for these attitudes. Historically, ideas and proposals that conflict with established beliefs have often been greeted with reservation, fear, or skepticism. For example, Louis Pasteur, discoverer of the rabies vaccine, was ejected from the French Academy of Sciences in 1867 when he proposed the "radical" theory that germs cause diseases. Then there was the German physicist who, with the advent of the railway, argued that trains traveling at speeds in excess of 20 miles per hour would rupture the blood vessels of the passengers. Our own century is not without its skeptics. Not long ago some authorities claimed that pilots who attempted to break the sound barrier might be "turned into jelly."

Interestingly, many of the contributing authors to this book were skeptical at first about the concept of cure as applied to mental retardation. It is perhaps difficult to appreciate how the initial attitude of careful skepticism evolved into cautious optimism and scientific excitement in Chapter 18's dialogue, initiated at the "Mental Retardation: The Search for Cures" conference in 1980 (see Themes and Overviews). During the dialogue, one is conscious of the participants' gradual acceptance of the basic concepts herein and of their realization and acknowledgment for the first time that "cure" was an attainable goal in the field of mental retardation.

As a result of the dialogue and exchange, five recurrent research themes have been identified. The first involved the pressing need to support *both* basic and applied research across a variety of disciplines in order to provide an interdisciplinary approach to the challenge of cure. The second stresses the need to enhance support of basic research in this country and to take steps to make the research field an attractive career possibility. The third research theme strongly urges researchers to find new models for conducting research as well as new theoretical designs and techniques. Many health care professionals, for example, feel that the development of "software" strategies has not kept pace with the proliferation of technology, i.e., hardware, so that new hardware devices are not being used to the best advantage. The fourth theme involves the need for creativity and for innovative ways of approaching and conducting research in finding cures for mental retardation. The fifth and perhaps most important, research-related message is the need for interdisciplinary communication that, by providing cumulative knowledge from a wide variety of fields, can have a greater impact on curative aspects. Not only were each of the investigators/contributors to this volume encouraged in their own effort by knowing that other researchers were attacking similar types of problems in their own disciplines, but the group as a whole was provided new energy and an enhanced sense of unity in working toward a common goal.

A major aim of this book is to stimulate ongoing discussion of curative research in mental retardation. As such, there are numerous research pathways that can be followed: The first pathway is the *traditional approach* in which one specializes in a highly focused field guided by the standard techniques of science and research. A second pathway might be labeled that of *serendipitous adventure:* One may frequently uncover basic insights and discoveries with "unscientific" luck seeming to play a large role. One particularly successful researcher in the "serendipitous adventure" mode was Dr. Hans Selye, the eminent endocrinologist who conducted the seminal research on stress. The third type of research pathway might be labeled that of *scientific dogmatism.* According to this approach, which has played a conspicuous role in scientific research, certain researchers remain dogmatic in their adherence to their doctrines, refusing to consider alternatives and rejecting criticism beforehand. Some have virtually spent a lifetime adhering to unproved assumptions. Whether or not their theories and/or results ultimately prove to be correct, this approach

has served a useful purpose in stimulating research methodology and the accumulation of additional knowledge, though it may sometimes work against the freedom of research. On the positive side, one is reminded of the work of Isaac Newton, whose scientific dogma, based on his recognized authority, was unconditionally accepted by his followers and resulted in the laws of mechanics and gravitation. Newton's work is a splendid example of dogma that has been justified by centuries of research and that is still basically valid, although certainly changed by Einstein's theory of relativity. Another example is the dogma cited by astrologists who maintained that lunar craters were volcanos; this belief was held by the scientific establishment for many years and ultimately disproved; however, this did not detract from the valuable contribution of scientists' observations. The fourth approach can be described as a *slow ripening of fundamental insight,* as demonstrated, for example, in Darwin's life works. Although Darwin recounted spontaneous flashes of insight—as can all scientists—his ultimate contribution, *Origin of the Species,* was essentially the result of 20 years of hard labor, scrutinizing the evidence of his thoughts, discussion, and observations.

The Growth and Development of Curative Research

Under typical conditions, the growth and development of scientific achievements has been demonstrated to follow an exponential function, doubling every 10 to 15 years. This function applies to the number of publications, the number of individuals engaged in a particular field of study, as well as other parameters such as the degree of technological development and research dissemination. The recent rapid growth of researchers in and around the field of mental retardation has meant that about one-half of all mental retardation researchers worldwide have worked for less than a dozen years. In addition, on a quantitative basis, one-half of our total accumulated knowledge of mental retardation research findings are the result of

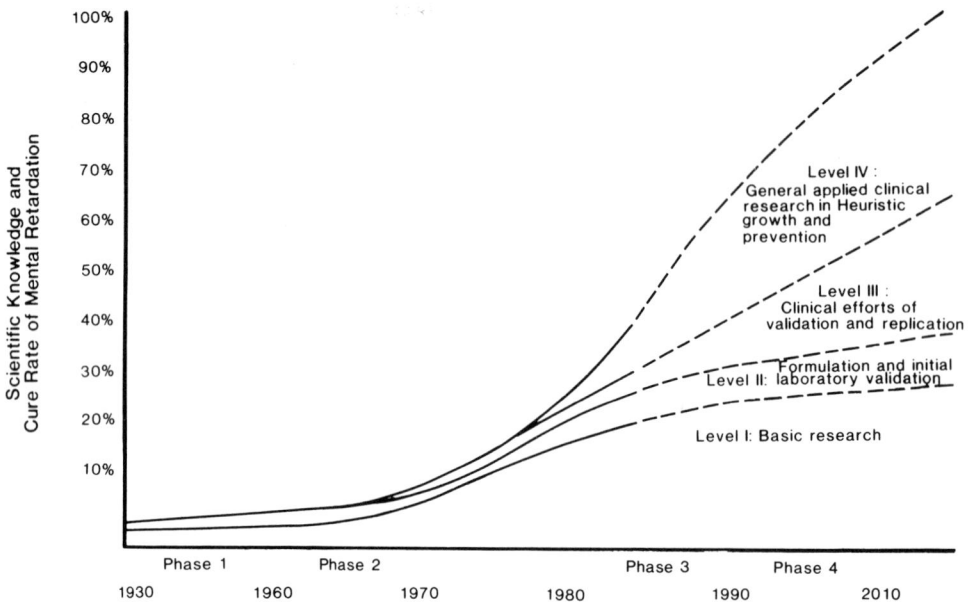

Figure 1. Growth and development of research on curative aspects of mental retardation as a function of scientific knowledge.

research done in the last decade. Obviously, such a collection of information is difficult to integrate, particularly when it stems from multiple disciplines from both biomedical and behavioral science.

Figure 1 broadly illustrates the growth and development of research on the curative aspects of mental retardation as a function of scientific knowledge. The y-axis contains the percentage of "cure rate" based upon the scientific knowledge available at that time. The x-axis chronologically lists the periods during which significant events occurred that resulted in an increase in the cure rate as a function of the incremental research findings. As noted above, there tends to be a doubling of knowledge every 10 to 15 years until we ultimately reach the upper limits of a field of study, in this case, "cure," at which time growth is not as graphically dramatic due to the mathematical principles of diminishing returns involved in calculating growth.

Research Phases

Figure 1 depicts the chronological dimensions of research growth and development represented via major phases. The first phase

is represented by a major breakthrough in the prevention of mental retardation via the discovery of phenylketonuria by Fölling (1939). In addition, this 30-year period was marked by continued biomedical research findings such as genetic abnormalities in Down syndrome, maple syrup urine disease, and galactosemia. Phase 2, 1960–1975, was marked by the rapid emergence of behavioral technology through the introduction of behavior modification technology and its application to mentally retarded individuals. This growth was spurred by B.F. Skinner's publication in 1953 of his landmark book, *Science in Human Behavior,* which provided a model for understanding human behavior that could be applied to diagnosing and changing the behavior of mentally retarded persons. Major credit also must be given to Sidney Bijou, the behavioral scientist primarily responsible for taking the basic behavioral principles and applying them to the mentally retarded population with significant success. Largely owing to Bijou's work in the 1960's, and publications by his colleagues in behavioral analysis in the 1970s, we now have access to some 1,000 behavioral principles and techniques, utilizing such principles as shaping, fading, intermittent reinforcement, backward/forward chaining, and task analysis. Biomedical achievements also began to increase during Phase 2 due to advances in diagnostic and laboratory techniques through computer technology. For example, brain and whole-body scanners, along with genetic evaluations made by the cell sorter, would be impossible without computerization, which often involves the analysis of over one million bits of data per patient.

In Phase 3, 1975–1990, the phase we are now in, we are beginning to see a convergence and marriage between the biomedical and behavioral sciences. Technological advancement is of considerable assistance to both fields and we are also understanding more fully the complexity of the nature/nurture controversy and that one area has an inexorable impact upon the other—thus forcing researchers to work more interdisciplinarily.

Phase 4, 1990–2010, would seem to represent an even more sophisticated technological period in which 5th-and 6th-generation computers will enable us to prevent and reverse some conditions and symptoms that we now label as mental retardation.

Levels of Research

The growth and development of research has often been termed a heuristic process, that is, the gradual building of knowledge based upon previous findings. If we analyze the field of mental retardation and the progress of basic curative discoveries, we find that this stepwise growth is also true of mental retardation. As shown in Figure 1, Level 1 represents basic research, in which animal research has been gradually expanding and contributing to our knowledge and understanding of disease entities and behavioral anomalies. Level II represents the second step in formulating research via the initial discoveries and breakthroughs in a specific field. Level III demonstrates the validation and replication of studies, procedures that

have proved important in eliminating placebo effects and sensationalized ''cures.'' Level IV represents applied clinical research and continues the heuristic growth process leading toward an even greater cure rate in the area of mental retardation. Each of these levels thus provides a building block for understanding, preventing, reversing, and ameliorating the symptoms that produce mental retardation. In summary, Figure 1 graphically provides an understanding of the chronological process of research phases, their interaction with levels of research, and their end results in the curative process.

Theoretical Model

In the introduction to this book, cures for mental retardation were seen as significantly increasing the level of global intellectual and social-adaptive functioning. Curative intervention was viewed as an additive component that increases the individual's level of functioning beyond the mental retardation range. In Chapter 17, Dr. Gershon Berkson discusses this phenomenon in terms of removing the individual from under the ''curve'' of mental retardation. This additive process serves as an inherent basis for the theoretical model of cures in mental retardation. For example, at the primary prevention level, the additive process acts to prevent the mental retardation condition from ever occurring, i.e., rubella vaccination. At the secondary prevention level, a very early diagnosis and reversal to a normal state is the goal, for example, in screening for PKU. At the tertiary prevention level, the additive process minimizes the residual disability, i.e., through infant stimulation.

Perhaps the best method to explain this prevention-addition-removal process is through the following formula:

Theoretical formula of cure =
$$C + F (P_1, P_2, P_3 + T)$$

In this formula, C represents the cure ratio or the number of individuals who are removed from the ''curve'' and who no longer meet the criterion of a definition of mental retardation. The cure ratio, C, then, is a function, F, of primary (P_1), secondary (P_2), and tertiary (P_3) prevention as described above. The "output" (C) is dependent upon the "input" of $P_{1, 2, 3}$ plus the *intensity* of treatment (T). Thus, the output can be increased by more intensive treatment (higher T) via more staff, resources, equipment, funding, or by an increase of *scientific knowledge* via prevention at each level, or both. This theoretical model of "cure," with almost infinite variation, is empirically implementable in a wide variety of allocation decisions. This chapter does not attempt to describe the numerous variations or discuss in detail how to implement this model. Rather, mention of the model here is intended to functionally demonstrate the reality of curative prospects over the next three decades given the anticipated improvements in scientific knowledge and our commitment to treatment.

Perhaps the best example of the cure model is found in the use of production theory in the field of agriculture. The two major premises of improving agricultural production consist of additive procedures to increase yield and prevention techniques to avoid loss. Similarly, in mental retardation this process (formula) involves the additive procedure of intensifying *treatment* and the use of preventive techniques discovered through research.

Consider an acre of land and its yield capability. The yield or production rate (cure rate in mental retardation) is contingent upon the intensity of intervention, what one does to improve the soil, and the available knowledge on the best methods to prevent crop loss. Ongoing agricultural research provides the technological base for treatment procedures and serves as a stable variable in the following examples. Along with this knowledge base, then, the *intensity* of a farmer's intervention determines the yield, as seen below:

Level 1—Dry Land Farming = 10% of potential yield (30 bu. per acre)

Level 2—Irrigated Land Farming = 20% of potential yield (60 bu. per acre)

Level 3—Irrigation and Fertilization Farming = 30% of potential yield (90 bu. per acre)

Level 4—Irrigation + Fertilization + Contour Plowing and Crop Rotation = 40% of potential yield (120 bu. per acre)

Level 5—Irrigation + Fertilization + Contour Plowing and Crop Rotation + Genetically Enriched Seeds = 100% of potential yield (300 bu. per acre)

In the above example, Level 4 represents the current knowledge base of what constitutes the most productive rate, on the average, when extensive treatment is available. Level 5 demonstrates that we have not reached the full potential for production based upon such potentially promising areas as genetic recombinant DNA research in the production of "super" seeds that are also disease resistant.

The analogy between agricultural production theory and cure ratio in mental retardation becomes more closely linked when we analyze the mental retardation cure rate in third world countries. Certainly the knowledge base in third world countries is available, if pursued, but the intensity of intervention is considerably less in these countries than in the United States. The result in agriculture is lowered yields in farming, and, in mental retardation higher incidence of disability, primarily due to poor nutrition.

Tables 1–3 serve as final examples of the *process* we are suggesting in our efforts to "cure" mental retardation. This intervention process toward cure is best demonstrated through an incremental additive process and through a primary, secondary, or tertiary prevention process.

Cost-Benefit Analyses

It is beyond the scope of this chapter, and of even perhaps one book, to fully analyze the cost-benefit ratio of finding cures for mental retardation. The instrumental work of R.W. Conley in his book *The Economics of Mental Retardation* points out the billions of dollars spent yearly to prevent mental retardation as well as to treat some six million members of our society. Average affected individuals' annual costs range from $5,000 for home care to $30,000 for institutional care for more

Table 1. Physical disability—Spinal cord injury

Intervention	Treatment	Level of recovery
Level 1	Traditional Supportive Care	0% Total Paralysis
Level 2	Intensive Emergency Care (Mandal Injection, Prosthetic Protection)	25% Recovery
Level 3	Intensive Emergency Care + Corrective Surgery	50% Recovery
Level 4	Intensive Emergency Care + Corrective Surgery + Electrical Nerve Stimulation	75% Recovery
Level 5	Intensive Emergency Care + Electrical Nerve Stimulation + Transplant Grafting	100% Recovery

Table 2. Sociocultural retardation

	Prevention/Intervention
Primary	Neonatal monitoring and nutritional supplementation of the mother
Secondary	Medical intervention via medication, i.e., blood level of toxic agents
Tertiary	Environmental enrichment and early childhood stimulation

Table 3. Down syndrome

	Prevention/Intervention
Primary	Genetic defect correction via use of prenatal chromosomal alteration
Secondary	Brain dysfunction correction via postnatal enzyme replacement
Tertiary	Computer-assisted instruction and one-on-one instruction

severely handicapped persons. Such figures underscore that the benefits of research and screening for conditions that we can prevent, such as PKU, far outweigh the monetary costs involved.

Rather than analyze the financial cost-benefit findings of curative research, the authors of this chapter wish to stress the importance of this thrust toward ''cure'' on the philosophical and political as well as economic levels. The cartoon in Figure 2 best captures the relevance of this goal, as well as the public's attitude toward resource allocation.

CURATIVE ASPECTS: THEMES

Genetics

Chapters 1, 2, and 3, by Drs. Aubrey Milunsky, Park Gerald, and Mary Jo Harrod,

Figure 2. (Adapted by permission of American Psychological Association, copyright 1981.)

respectively, focused on current and future genetic research and the potential for curing the symptoms of mental retardation. The importance of genetic research is obvious from the statistics alone. It is now estimated that 20%, or 45 million people in our population, have a genetically determined or associated disorder. Prenatally, approximately 30%–40% of all spontaneously aborted embryos/fetuses have a chromosomal abnormality. Perinatally, a little more than 1 in every 200 live-born babies has a chromosomal abnormality, the most frequent of which is trisomy 21 in Down syndrome, occurring in about 1 in 700 live births. At least 5% of all these live-born infants have a severe recognizable condition at birth and could have a genetically determined implication. Postnatally, in infancy, the consequences of complications of genetic malformation are the leading cause of death under the age of 12 months, and the second cause of death to children under the age of 5 years (Laxova, 1981).

Dr. Harrod, in Chapter 3, offers a systematic program for the prevention of genetic disorders via genetic screening and counseling. In another direction, Dr. Milunsky, in Chapter 1, notes the era of "new genetics" and its relationship to the "cure" of mental retardation. He points out that there are 30–40 inborn errors of metabolism that can now be prevented or reversed. Perhaps even more exciting than these findings, however, is the potential for prenatal diagnosis and the reversal of genetic disorders during pregnancy. Experimental results are extremely encouraging as to the prospects of intrauterine treatment of inborn errors of metabolism as a major deterrent in preventing and reversing mental retardation symptoms. Dr. Milunsky argues strongly in favor of gene therapy in establishing prenatal diagnosis during the embryonic phase of pregnancy. It is through the active intervention of gene therapy, he says, that we may succeed in applying future technological refinements that will enable the reversal of mental retardation during the gestational period.

The era of new "genetics" discussed by

Dr. Milunsky is carried further in Chapter 2 by Dr. Gerald, who discusses a strikingly new concept of reversing mental retardation through the treatment of genetic disorders after birth. Dr. Gerald challenges the *fait accompli* attitude that genetic disorders at birth that cause mental retardation cannot be reversed, i.e., trisomy 21 (Down syndrome). In his investigation of gene dosage studies, Dr. Gerald provides support to the notion that postnatal actions of genes may contribute to the morbidity of patients with chromosomal abnormalities. He further states that blocking or altering the genetic activity should ameliorate the patient's morbidity, and he offers encouraging information on how we can apply such genetic intervention to Down syndrome, and more specifically, to the disorder to which he has devoted a great deal of research—the fragile-X syndrome.

Certainly, progress in genetic engineering has been spectacular in recent years. Not only are bacteria being programmed to produce medically useful compounds such as insulin and growth hormone, but normal genes have been transferred successfully into mammalian cells, thus curing individual cells in tissue culture of genetic defects (Anderson, Killos, & Sanders-Hagigh, 1980; Pellicer, Robins, & Wold, 1980). Following, in greatly simplified form, are the steps involved in this gene therapy:

1. Identify the defective gene through chromosomal analysis.
2. Identify the defective protein or enzyme in the gene and its amino acid sequence via the use of a protein sequencer and the cell sorter, and analysis.
3. Isolate a normal gene for matching.
4. Build a matching nucleotide by recombinant DNA procedures, which involve fractionation and the combining of matched nucleotides.
5. Probe to locate, isolate, and purify the gene via molecular cloning of normal gene or matching with bacterium such as *E. coli*.
6. Develop the genes by reinsertion of defi-

cient gene or production of a vaccine, that sends messages to the defective organ to behave differently.

For example, Drs. C. Thomas Caskey and John Brennand, researchers at the Howard Hughes Medical Institute at Baylor College of Medicine in Houston recently reported what appears to be the first successful cloning of a gene directly related to an X-linked disease, Lesch-Nyhan syndrome. This syndrome is a relatively rare condition that causes severe mental retardation and a tendency toward self-mutilation. It may be inherited or may occur spontaneously through mutation, and is untreatable at this time. Lesch-Nyhan develops when a gene on the X-chromosome fails to produce the adequate amount of the enzyme HPRT (hypoxanthine prosphoribosyltransferase) that is from a chromosomal region believed to be near the site of genes related to fragile-X syndrome, a form of mental retardation affecting males. In a milder form, HPRT deficiency can lead to gouty arthritis and serious kidney damage.

The achievement of Drs. Caskey and Brennand may lead to a better understanding not only of the Lesch-Nyhan syndrome, but of the fragile-X syndrome as well. New data reported in the March, 1982, issue of *Proceedings of the National Academy of Sciences,* in an article by Drs. Caskey and Brennand, described the successful gene cloning procedure using cultured nerve cells from mice. Although laboratory mice are not human, procedures using them offer a hopeful model on cloning the gene in man. The fact that this research successfully zeroes in on a genetic area and perhaps on the development of tools to help facilitate studies of fragile-X is significant, although very substantial breakthroughs are still many steps away. More broadly speaking, Dr. Caskey, who heads the genetics section at Baylor, noted that the development offers several opportunities from a medical standpoint. "First, it provides a chance to better understand, at a molecular level, a human heritable disease that can occur by mutation," he said. "That

will be very valuable new information on how mutations produce disease."

Developmental Processes and Their Interaction with Disease Processes

In the introduction to Section I, Dr. Frank J. Menolascino notes that the era for the scientific study of the biological basis (with an emphasis on the central nervous system) of the symptom of mental retardation has truly arrived. Chapters 4 through 10, with the exception of Chapter 9, focus on the *understanding, development,* and *functioning* of the brain. Drs. Verne Caviness, Dominick Purpura, and Roger Williams (Chapters 4, 5, and 6, respectively) provide valuable insight into the brain's development and functioning at the embryonic and fetal stages. By knowing the exact stage at which trauma occurs—and thereby understanding the causative factors—we can develop intervention strategies to prevent or reverse the damaging effects.

The studies of the early development and subsequent functioning of the central nervous system—as noted by Drs. Caviness, Purpura, and Williams—have provided firm evidence over the past two decades that points to a neurobiological basis for many causes of mental retardation. This realization has sparked an emphasis on more rigorous neurochemical and genetic research.

As previously noted, we know that normal central nervous system development essentially depends on chemical factors that are expressed throughout the various stages of nerve cell maturation. For example, if one studies genetic causes of mental retardation, one must look at aberrant biochemistry, since it is the basis for genetic disease that is expressed behaviorally. All genetic diseases, whether manifested physically or behaviorally, have abnormal biochemical reactions at their core. This modern view of causality in mental retardation includes three basic questions whose answers have produced the current/future development of causative models: What are the normal stages of central nervous system development? Where in these developmental stages is it likely that central nervous system damage could be expressed—physically or behaviorally? What neurochemical factors are particularly important?

Since mental retardation represents a clinical disturbance that may or may not have defined central nervous system abnormalities, it can result from disturbances in the early, middle or late stages of central nervous system development. For example, it is in the late stage of central nervous system development that neurochemical factors are most important in defining and facilitating a person's ultimate developmental potential. As Drs. Caviness and Purpura noted, brain development at each of its major stages can go awry and produce distinctive resultant derangements of brain structure or function. Interruption of neurolation—the development and folding of the neural tube to form the basic structures of the brain—is a profound failure of brain development producing lethal results in infants born with this malformation.

Histogenesis—the formation of neurons, glial, and ependymal cells—is the second phase of brain development, and it can be intimately affected by hundreds of chemical compounds. Glycolipids and glycoproteins, in particular, seem to be important in the formation of nerve cells because they regulate the differentiation of these cells into their final structure. Although glycolipid and glycoprotein disorders usually produce observable anatomical abnormalities, the consequences of interrupted histogenesis depend on when it occurs and how much of the germinal ridge is involved; nearly always, the brain structures fail to mature.

During the brain maturation phase of cell migration—the third phase—the cells leave the germinal ridge and migrate to their final places in the developing brain. As noted by Dr. Caviness, glial cells are critical in determining the outcome of this process because of their role in making a structural core in which the migrating neurons can move, and because of the chemicals they secrete. The exact chemistry and diseases of the glial cells are not yet understood; in rats, genetic diseases known to affect the glial cells tend to inhibit nerve cell migration and result in undeveloped areas of the brain. An exciting current/future curative possibility here is the question of whether substance P can reverse the degeneration—or lack of development—of these neurons in early neonatal life. This reversal has been successfully accomplished through the use of substance P in newborn rats. If this same reversal can be duplicated in human newborns, then exciting vistas are present for major alterations of currently "untreatable" malformations of the central nervous system at the very beginning of human life.

During the fourth stage of nerve cell differentiation, the cells have arrived at their final positions within the brain and begin to develop even further dendrites and axons, establishing multiple communications with other nerve cells. The establishment of this cell-to-cell communication system is the critical element in central nervous system function. The consequences of interrupting this particular developmental stage can range from subtle to catastrophic depending on how and when it happens and the extent to which the cell-to-cell communication systems are disrupted. An example of this complex communication system, as noted by Dr. Purpura, is the Purkinje cell; it receives thousands of communications from other neurons—communications that it integrates into a single axon responsible for output. If the Purkinje cell is maldeveloped, it can disrupt communications in the central nervous system and thus produce minor to catastrophic results. The impact of interruption of this fourth stage of cell differentiation may well explain many causes of mental retardation that do not have obvious signs of brain impairment (e.g., mild retardation). Interruption of cell differentiation may not involve the total central nervous system, but only very special areas of the brain. For instance, the mental functions of processing of incoming information, sensory modalities transfer, and language-symbol acquisition could become impaired if there is interference with the final maturation of the nerve cells in the cortex of the brain.

Current/future research indications strongly suggest that three types of causes—viral, genetic and metabolic—tend to interfere most often with cell differentiation. Genetic factors impair nerve cell development because they ultimately determine the final nature of the development of the nerve cell structure. Formation of the dendrites of the nerve cells is particularly important because without the establishment of adequate communications with other nerve cells, the individual nerve cell itself cannot develop—even if its own genetic material is optimal. Beyond genetic factors, metabolic factors can also greatly affect cell differentiation, such as in phenylketonuria (PKU), wherein the defect in phenylalanine hydroxylase enzyme permits the accumulation of toxins that this enzyme usually metabolizes. It is thought that the mental retardation noted is damage inflicted by the excessively accumulated toxin in developing nerve cells. Lastly, agents such as viruses can also disrupt nerve cell differentiation, and this observation supports the clinically noted finding that viruses such as rubella often produce symptoms of mental retardation. Clearly, the recent understanding of the basic disease mechanisms in these three

categories of *major* causes of the symptom of mental retardation—viral, genetic, and metabolic—has provided an excellent scientific platform for further refinement of our focus on possible treatment (i.e., curative) interventions. In other words, in each of these major areas of known causative mechanisms, we currently have workable prototypes for presenting and/or curing a great number of the disease states that were viewed as ''unknown-untreatable'' only a decade ago.

Toward a Physiological Basis of Learning

Of the many outstanding findings presented in this book, one of the most impressive regarding future applications is the work conducted by Drs. Gary Lynch and Michael Browning (Chapters 8 and 10). Based on their research, it would appear that for the first time we now have a *physiological* basis for and understanding of how learning occurs. The implication of this finding is enormous. Obviously if we can understand the physiological basis (i.e., the how) of learning, then we ought to be able to better correct or increase our learning capacity, thus removing or reversing the symptoms of mental retardation.

Figure 3 demonstrates how we learn via a

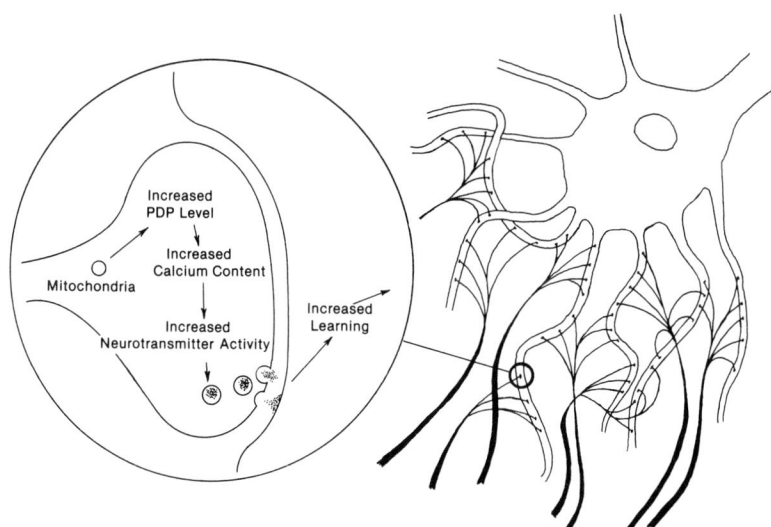

Figure 3.   Cellular biological explanation of the learning process.

cellular biological explanation. The enzyme pyruvate dehydrogenase (PDH) found in cellular structures called mitochondria, enhances the transmission of nerve and brain signals and appears to be a critical component in the learning process (Editor, *Science*, 1982). As neural impulses travel across synaptic endings via neurotransmitters, the activity is controlled by the calcium level. PDH seems to directly control the calcium content and thereby the neurotransmitted activity of learning (Browning, Baudry, Bennett, & Lynch, 1981). Additional research by Morgan and Routtenberg (1981) clearly demonstrates distinct changes in the level of PDH in the frontal cortices of rats as a direct result of learning. The implications of this research are that we are rapidly elucidating the biochemical and neurophysiological basis of learning. It should be a short step for us to soon be able to increase learning by altering the source, amount, and activity of the high-energy phosphates like PDH—via medications—in mentally retarded individuals.

Central Nervous System Transplants

In Chapter 9, Dr. A.K. Ommaya reports his and other investigators' research efforts in the area of central nervous system transplants. The initial findings of nerve cell regeneration in animals and the very preliminary experimental efforts with humans are indicative of a new era of neurology and neurosurgery that has profound implications for individuals with brain damage. Dr. Ommaya's research focuses on neurosurgical techniques to "fuse" severed spinal cords via a myelin sheath graft. Using both injections of sciatic nerve grafts and electromagnetic radiation with diapulse therapy, he feels there is just cause for optimistic skepticism in this expanding field.

Figure 4 illustrates a second topic discussed in Chapter 9—brain grafts and neural regeneration. It has been demonstrated that embryonic brain tissue injected into the brain of a rat will grow and become neurochemically active via nerve cell transmission. The same principle is being applied successfully

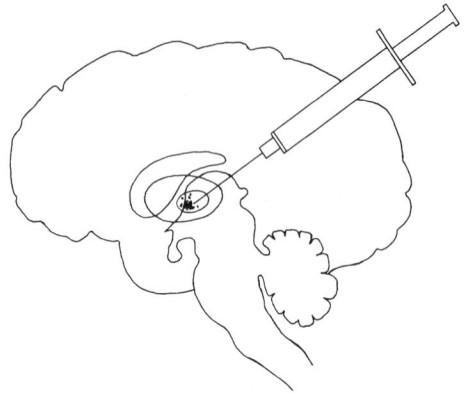

Figure 4. Cellular implant in the brain for neuronal regeneration, sprouting, and functioning.

in humans via implants for Parkinsonism, and there is potential for other organ cellular implants (i.e., insulin-producing cells injected into the pancreas).

Pharmacological Enhancement of Brain Function

Section III of this book analyzes ways of evaluating memory and enhancing learning, with a particular emphasis on neuropeptides—brain chemicals that affect functioning and resultant behavior. The concept of pharmacological agents to enhance the learning processes in mental retardation is not new. It perhaps symbolizes our society's obsession with the use of pills to cure our problems. Dr. Menolascino, in Chapter 11, dispels some of the fallacies surrounding this "magic bullet theory" and provides insight into the complexity of conducting effective pharmacological research.

Unlike extraneous, synthetically produced drugs, neuropeptides could become useful in the "metabolic repair" of a deficient system. Researchers are increasingly learning more about the body's own natural ability to suppress pain, moods, hunger, motivation, and drive. Drs. Abba Kastin and Curt Sandman, in Chapters 12 and 13, respectively, focus primarily on three neuropeptides—thyrotropin releasing hormone (TRH), melanocyte stimulating hormone (MSH), and adrenocortical stimulating hormone (ACTH).

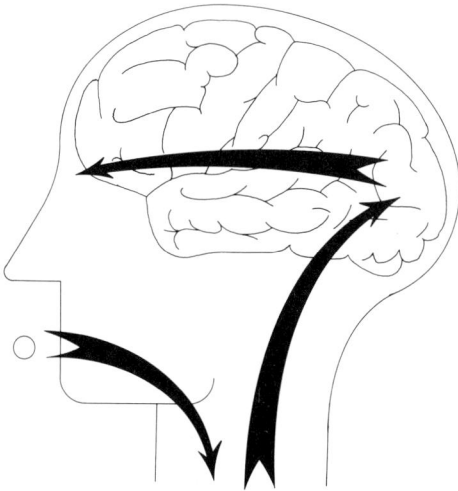

Figure 5. Neuropeptide ingestion and improvement in memory and visual perception and attention.

Their research in endocrinology and pharmacology demonstrates the importance of these peptides in both the *diagnosis* and *treatment* of mental retardation. For example, in their preliminary research, these peptides, as demonstrated in Figure 5, have proven successful in increasing the visual perception and attention of mentally retarded individuals in vocational settings.

The most recent research by Dr. Kenneth Davis, Chapter 14, demonstrates the ability to temporarily alter the memory and learning abilities of patients with Alzheimer's disease by selectively increasing the efficiency of a major neurotransmitter in the brain: acetylcholine. His specific research is summarized in Figure 6.

Although Dr. Davis's research has focused on a selective aspect of acetycholine metab-

olism (i.e., the lengthening of the effectiveness of acetylcholine by the use of the drug physostigmine to extend the action of the enzyme choline acetyltransferase), it is important to further illustrate how *other* portions of acetylcholine metabolism may also be altered in an effort to benefit individuals with impaired memory and/or learning. Figure 7 outlines the process by which acetylcholine is metabolized and its role as a central nervous system neurotransmitter.

This figure illustrates what has been heralded as a revolutionary concept in modern nutrition: how a basic ingredient of the diet (phosphatidylcholine) can, if ingested in adequate amounts, begin to function as a central nervous system facilitator (i.e., as a drug rather than as the classic nutrient). In other words, increasing the amount of choline (a substrate) while simultaneously altering an enzyme system (i.e., the work of Dr. Davis via the relative blocking of the enzyme choline acetyltransferase through administration of physostigmine) can produce a markedly synergistic enhancement on the role of acetylcholine as a neurotransmitter. This relationship between substrate (the dietary source of choline), enzyme action, and the electrical enhancement at the brain cell synapses is illustrated in Figure 8.

As discussed above, these treatment interventions can be utilized with mentally retarded persons who have similar neurotransmitter deficits (i.e., Down syndrome adults). Figure 9 illustrates the clinical neurophysiological findings that are noted when choline -> acetylcholine enriched diets are utilized in such patients.

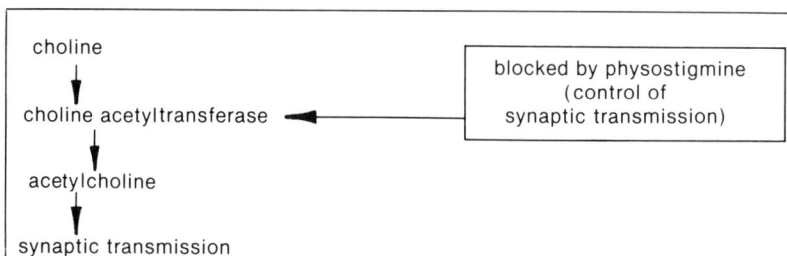

Figure 6. Enhancement of acetylcholine.

Lecithin (as phosphatidylcholine from the **diet**)

Fatty Acid

Fatty Acid

Metabolic Degradation

Choline

Choline Acetyltransferase

Blocked by Physostigmine

Acetylcholine

Cholinesterase

Choline

Recycling of Choline

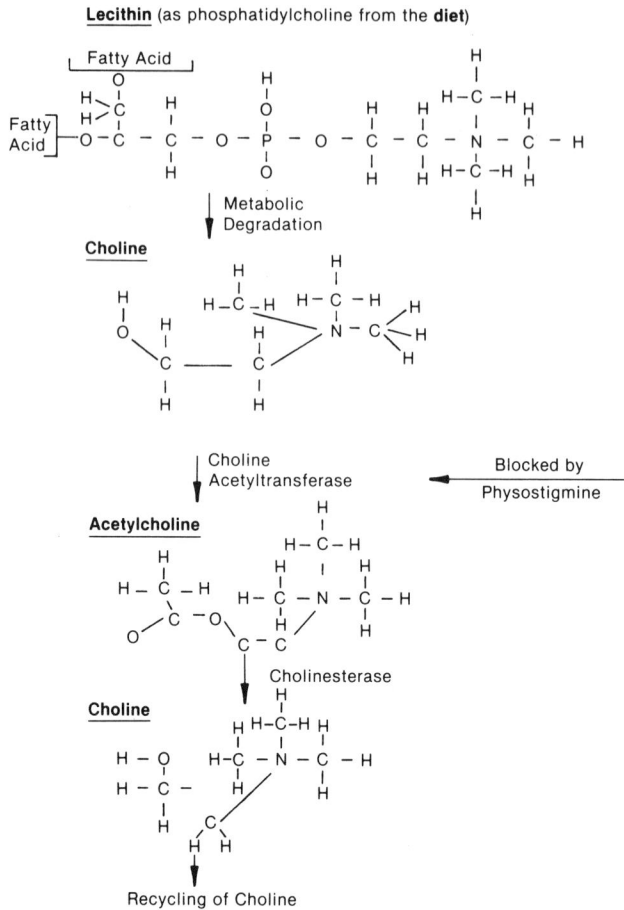

Figure 7. Source and action of acetylcholine.

This particular curative vista of altering the amount of neurotransmitter availability and its functional efficiency holds exciting promise for maximizing the biochemical and neurophysiological basis of memory-learning efficiency. One such possibility is the combination of the above-noted nerve cell–to–nerve cell transmission efficiency mechanism with the intracellular changes noted in the previous work of Drs. Lynch and Browning on PDH.

The Environment and Its Impact

Readers of this book may question the comparatively less attention given to behavioral, as opposed to the biomedical aspects of mental retardation. Nevertheless, the editors are acutely aware of the fact that the majority of mentally retarded individuals (75%–85%) are functioning in the mild to moderate range of retardation; and that they, as such, are primarily influenced by the external environment comprised of the social, cultural, and educational aspects each individual experiences.

In Chapter 16, Dr. Sidney Bijou provides an excellent and comprehensive review of the impact of the environment on mildly and moderately retarded children. His evaluation of the contributions of behavioral analysis in training parents, teachers, and mentally retarded children demonstrates that this behavioral technology has been extremely effective in ameliorating and preventing mental retardation. Although the development of new surgical techniques and medications is exciting to consider, it is still the task of "environ-

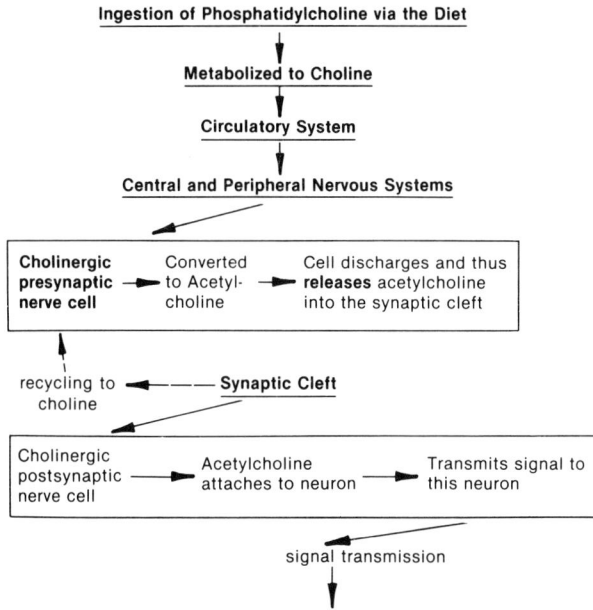

Figure 8. Metabolic, biochemical, and neurophysiological aspects of memory/learning enhancement via acetylcholine.

mentalists'' (teachers, parents, peers) to improve the overall functioning of the majority of mentally retarded individuals by optimizing the environment.

Dr. Gershon Berkson, in Chapter 17, further elucidates behavioral approaches in his analysis of an ecological model. Dr. Earl Butterfield (Chapter 15) also supplies evidence of the importance of environmental enhancement on the level of functioning of the mentally retarded person. Dr. Butterfield's memory model (see Figure 10) provides a cognitive-behavioral explanation of the cognitive deficits of mentally retarded

Figure 9. Neurophysiological model for acetylcholine-enhanced functioning of the central nervous system.

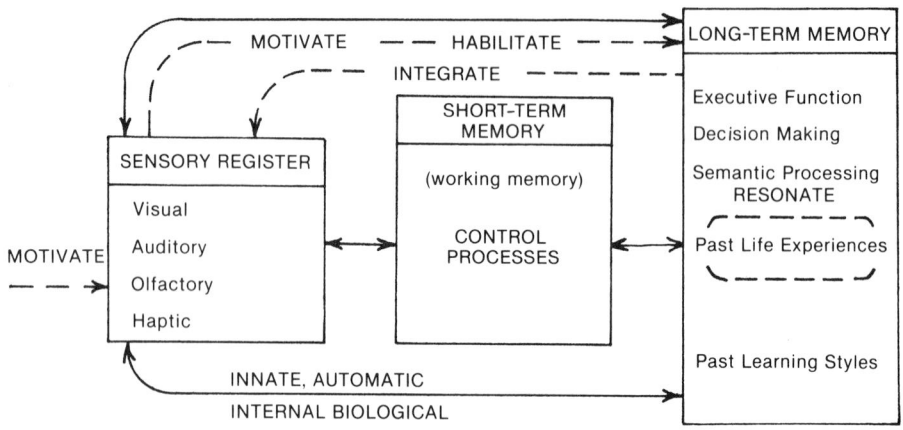

Figure 10. Memory model for cognitive impairment and integrative therapy. (Provided by E. Butterfield.)

persons, thus offering an additional explanation of a behavioral basis in brain functioning that compliments the biochemical process as discussed by Dr. Gary Lynch and his colleagues. The model illustrates the integrative aspects of short- versus long-term memory and the interaction of the external-psychosocial component with the internal-biological component.

PREVENTION

Throughout this volume the concept of "cure" has been applied to and used synonymously with prevention. Although cure has been directed toward primary, secondary, and tertiary prevention, most of the emphasis has been on the secondary prevention component, or the aspect of reversibility. It is important to at least touch upon the significance of preventive programs and their impact on "curing" mental retardation. In 1977, a major national report entitled *Preventing Mental Retardation: More Can Be Done* (1977) noted that the (then) current "state-of-the-art" in the prevention of mental retardation was fragmented and, while promising much, delivered little. This is still true today. The report also described the problem of major time lags between the development of new knowledge of mental retardation and its application in the field. The lack of and

inconsistent use of federal funds seems to be the major culprit in the development and delivery of a national preventive program in mental retardation.

In the United States eight major areas of focus in the prevention of mental retardation are currently being implemented, albeit with some major gaps: 1) comprehensive prenatal care (including recent increased attention to high-risk pregnancies) and prenatal nutrition; 2) infectious diseases, both pre- and postnatal; 3) chromosome disorders; 4) metabolic diseases (such as inborn errors of metabolism); 5) internal (i.e., Rh blood incompatibility) and external (i.e., blood poisoning) intoxications; 6) adverse early childhood experiences within the family; 7) childhood accidents; and 8) infant screening devices for physiological deficits such as neurotube disorders.

The discussion below of some of the previously mentioned preventive efforts is designed to demonstrate the importance of such procedures in working toward the goal of "cure." First, a brief mention of lead toxicity. National statistics show that we use some 1.3 million tons of lead annually, with 600,000 tons released into the environment. According to the President's Committee on Mental Retardation (1973), it was reported that 4% of preschool children have excessive levels of lead in their blood. Clearly, a lead poisoning prevention program is necessary.

Vitamin Therapy

Recently, considerable attention has been given to the early research efforts of Harrell and associates (Harrell, Capp, Davis, Peerless, & Ravitz, 1981), whose research findings offer strong support for the view that "nutritional" therapy can significantly improve intellectual functioning in mentally retarded children. Harrell and her co-workers found, for example, an average IQ gain of nearly 16 points among subjects given vitamin and mineral supplements for an 8-month period, and a 20-plus point gain for two subjects. In two other cases, children were removed from special education classes and reassigned to regular classrooms as a result of the progress they made. According to the noted psychologist, Edward Zigler, if results obtained in the Harrell et al. (1981) study can be verified by independent investigators, such findings would constitute one of the most significant breakthroughs ever made in the treatment of mentally retarded persons (Associated Press, 1981). Current efforts are underway around the country to replicate Dr. Harrell's study and to evaluate these initial findings. If these findings prove at least partially worthwhile, they will represent a major leap forward in developing cures for the 75%–85% of retarded persons who are mildly retarded as a result of behavioral/environmental influences.

Infectious Diseases

The third and final area of curative/preventive efforts to be focused on here is that of infectious diseases. The development of new diagnostic and treatment technologies provides optimism for major developments in this topical area via avoidance of an infectious disease. As an example of the possibilities for curative approaches, the magnitude and mechanism of cytomegalovirus in causing mental retardation will be briefly discussed as a current/future research frontier. Cytomegalovirus (CMV) is probably the most common *infectious* cause of mental retardation in infants and young children. It is second only to Down syndrome when one considers all of the specific biological causes of mental retardation. The CMV virus is a member of the herpesvirus family, the outstanding characteristics of which are 1) the capacity to enter a latent state in the body's cells (i.e., remain alive but not cause disease symptoms) and 2) to be reactivated later in life. Other members of the herpesvirus family, which are common and well known, are 1) herpes simplex virus, which causes cold sores and can be reactivated by such physical irritants as sunlight, and 2) varicella zoster virus, an agent causing chicken pox in childhood and that, when reactivated in adults, can cause the painful eruption known as shingles.

On the basis of recent studies, we know that 1% of all newborn infants around the world are infected with CMV. This represents a very large number of infected babies: with the annual U.S. birth rate at 4,000,000, it becomes apparent that 40,000 CMV-infected babies are born each year in the United States. Fortunately, only 10% of these 40,000 (or 4,000) CMV-infected newborns are noted to be retarded in early infancy. However, we know that this 10% figure is falsely low, because when the known CMV-infected babies—who had appeared normal at birth—are reexamined carefully upon entry to kindergarten, one finds lower IQs and more deafness than would have been projected in a control population of non-CMV-infected children.

Generally, CMV has been thought to cause birth defects when the pregnant woman experiences a symptomless CMV infection during the first 3 or 6 months of pregnancy. Consequently, the mental retardation has been attributed to brain damage that takes place during early pregnancy in a manner similar to the way the German measles (i.e., rubella) virus exerts its damaging effect. However, because of the general characteristics of the herpesvirus described above, some research groups (Bray, Bale, Anderson, & Kern, 1979) have questioned whether this virus can behave like other so-called "slow viruses" and either produce progressive brain damage in young infants, or be somehow reactivated and cause retardation in older infants and children. Bray and his colleagues, during the last decade, have identified CMV-infected young babies who, though they appeared relatively normal in the newborn period, have subsequently exhibited progressive destructive changes in their brain. If these observations are confirmed and extended by others, it may eventually help to account both for otherwise unexplained brain defects that may have been assumed to be caused by an obscure disorder of congenital origin, and for the appearance of mental retardation and other signs of brain damage in babies who had appeared normal at birth.

The above serve to highlight the importance of a virus such as CMV as a cause of mental retardation that though acquired before birth, may express its symptoms (including mental retardation) at a delayed time. It also underscores the need to study the full spectrum of diseases caused by viruses, such as CMV. Certainly, more vigorous efforts are warranted, either in developing a preventive vaccine (such as that for rubella), or in developing antiviral drug treatments. Neither approach will be easy. For one thing, viruses such as the human CMV tend to be very host-specific (i.e., so far laboratory workers have been unsuccessful at infecting an animal or an animal's cells with this human strain of virus), so vaccine development is moving slowly. This problem may be circumvented, however, with the development of new and ingenious techniques, such as was the case in poliomyelitis. Regarding development of an array of effective antiviral drug treatments, not only has progress been slow in this field for *all viruses,* but when a pregnant woman becomes infected she has no symptoms and, consequently one does not, at present, know when to treat her. Given sufficient attention to the problem, however, ways will eventually be found to either prevent or treat the infected person, whether the person be a pregnant mother or an infected symptomatic (or nonsymptomatic, i.e., having delayed onset) infant.

FUTURE DIRECTIONS

In 1972, the President's Committee on Mental Retardation (PCMR) identified as a national goal the reduction of mental retardation by 50% before the end of the century, and the substantial improvement in the level of functioning of most mentally retarded individuals.

Menolascino and Strider (1981) have outlined a number of national guidelines that have evolved for the effective prevention of mental retardation. They reviewed the following key components: 1) assure immunization for all infants and preschoolers; 2) expand the current programs of Rh screening to include mandatory marriage license recording of blood typing and also include RhoGAM availability for treatment (and cure!) in the affected mothers; 3) extend the lead poisoning prevention program for rapid screening of mass populations, active treatment of those currently ill, and spurred national development of rigid lead control measures; 4) establish at least one regional intensive care unit in each state for highly "at-risk" newborns; 5) establish state (or regional) genetic and/or metabolic laboratories to screen more extensively for inborn errors of metabolism, lead poisoning, and hypothyroidism; 6) extend the current centers and initiate other teenage pregnancy treatment-intervention centers to help manage and/or prevent this major source of high risk pregnancies in our nation; 7) activate and extend local public education programs, especially for primary and secondary school students, in teaching the basic public health elements of the prevention of mental retardation; and 8) extend early intervention educational programs, such as Head Start and Follow-Through, to broaden the understanding of the psychosocial causes of mental retardation. Lastly, the critical need of support for the establishment and extension of local programs to combat child abuse and neglect is noted. However, despite the future prevention vistas noted by Menolascino and Strider, a number of prominent researchers have questioned the feasibility of accomplishing any major prevention goals—including the 50% reduction noted from the PCMR. These experts clearly delineate the biomedical or "organic" mentally retarded population from the behavioral (socio-cultural) "nonorganic" population. Although they feel that the feasibility of accomplishing this goal in the biomedical area exists, they are doubtful about the ability of the behavioral sciences to accomplish this goal—especially with mild to moderately mentally retarded persons. They also point out that what knowledge we have is not *applied knowledge* (Clarke & Clarke, 1977). This theme is further developed by the research analyses of Dr. Edward Zigler (Zigler, 1978), who believes that we do not pay enough attention to this larger (85%) segment of the mentally retarded population and that it will be especially difficult to accomplish this goal—especially since federal funding's emphasis is on biomedical research.

Dr. Hugo Moser (1982) has stated that applying what we now know could reduce the incidence of severe retardation by only 20%–30%, rather than the hoped for 50%. He does, however, provide encouragement for improving our efficacy with the "nonorganic" population, citing the impact of early intervention programs and the surprisingly low incidence of mild levels of mental retardation in Sweden (i.e., .4% in Sweden compared to 2% in the United States). Dr. Moser made a strong appeal for the collaborative efforts of both the biomedical and behavioral sciences in the reduction of mental retardation.

It is the hope and intention of the editors of this volume that this major theme of cooperation between the biomedical and behavioral sciences will indeed become the strategy of future research in mental retardation. Perhaps it is time that those of us in the field rethink the long-held dichotomy between these two scientific thrusts. The goal of reducing mental retardation by 50% at the end of the century is of course unreasonable if we consider only the sociocultural vicissitudes of poverty (i.e., education, housing, employment, etc.). However, based upon findings presented in this volume, it is reasonable to expect that the biomedical sciences will greatly aid the "nonorganic" mentally retarded person and vice versa. For example, medication to chelate toxic lead in the blood, brain cell implants, neuropeptide medication to enhance memory and retention, or vitamin therapy to increase visual attention are all examples of possible ways of enhancing learning abilities with biomedical technology. The opposite is also possible. For instance, the efficacy of biofeedback procedures has been demonstrated to alleviate the key signs and symptoms of hypertension, depression, migraine headaches, and Raynaud's syndrome. This type of treatment intervention represents behavioral strategies that effectively overcome major signs and symptoms of physiological dysfunctioning.

Diagnostic Tools

Both the biomedical and behavioral sciences are witnessing an explosive era of new diagnostic devices that fuel our enthusiasm and hope. Each medical subspecialty—from genetics with its protein sequencer and cell sorter, to microbiology and endocrinology with their computer-assisted staining techniques—has its own high technology to assist it. There are also generic diagnostic tools for both fields. Now that we are just becoming comfortable with the CT (computed tomography) scan, we see the rapid development of the PET (positron emission tomography) scanner that will detect and visualize brain chemistry in action by tracing glucose consumption. In other words, we have arrived at a point wherein there are biomedical markers of *internal* processes that directly demonstrate the effects of external stimulation. Development is also underway with microwave evaluation, which picks up three-dimensional images on a screen for computer analysis. Perhaps even more exciting is the development of the nuclear magnetic resonance scanner (NMR). Within the next decade this experimental device may become the major diagnostic choice for observing physiological processes in action, as it exceeds the capabilities of both the CT scan and the PET scan. Our current "windows to the brain" can even now not only tell us if the brain is altered (i.e., the "old" pathological view) but also what parts have been stimulated during learning (the evolving new direct-observation view of the living brain in action). If, for example, pyruvate dehydrogenase (PDH) proves to be an essential biochemical underlying the process of learning, we could then take a PDH medication to enhance learning or at least maintain its natural level during the presentation of an enriched learning environment (via NMR) to see whether one approach or approaches used in combination could be utilized to improve the level of functioning.

In addition, the sometimes secondary effects of physical disabilities in mental retardation can be debilitating and lead to mild levels of retardation (i.e., visual impairment). The development of artificial organs, laser surgery, and the potential for microchip implantation directly into the brain are examples of ways to ameliorate both organic and nonorganic retardation. Methods such as the later-mentioned microchip placed surgically into the brain, to be programmed by and "interconnect" with the various parts of the brain, no longer seem like science fiction. Indeed, the rapid development of computer-assisted technology with laser imprinted chips will have an enormous impact on our society, particularly in the area of artificial intelligence.

It would appear that the future directions of research on curative aspects of mental retardation (both biomedical and behavioral) will be primarily controlled by political and economic variables and dependent upon the commitment of the federal government to consistently and adequately provide funding to keep pace with the technological advances in our postindustrial society (Plog, 1980).

SUMMARY

No single volume, particularly one that plows new, fertile ground, can hope to cover all of the curative aspects of mental retardation. The challenge of writing and editing this book has been both difficult and enjoyable: difficult, because of the need to investigate the rapid technological advances and research findings from a variety of biomedical and behavioral standpoints; and enjoyable, both because of new knowledge gained and because this knowledge reaffirms the promise of a bright future in our search for cures to mental retardation.

Perhaps this quest for knowledge can best be summarized by the great Swedish chemist, Carl Vilhelm Scheele, who some 170 years ago wrote: "It is the truth we are searching for, and what a delight it is to find" [in translation].

REFERENCES

Anderson, W.F., Killos, L., & Sanders-Hagigh, L. Replication and expression of thymidine, thyamine kinase in human globins microinjected into mouse fibroblasts. *Proceedings of the National Academy of Sciences, U.S.A.,* 1980, *77,* 5399–5403.

Associated Press. Added nutrients visibly smarten retarded young. *Fort Worth Star Telegram,* January 24, 1981, 1.

Bray, P.F., Bale, J.F., Jr., Anderson, R.E., & Kern, E.R. Progressive neurological disease caused by human cytomegalovirus. *Annals of Neurology,* 1979, *6*(2), 158–162.

Browning, M., Baudry, M., Bennett, W.F., & Lynch, G. Phosphorylation-mediated changes in pyruvate dehydrogenase activity influence pyruvate-supported calcium accumulation by brain mitochondria. *Journal of Neurochemistry,* 1981, *36*(6), 1932–1940.

Clarke, A.D.B., & Clarke, A.M. Prospects for prevention and amelioration of mental retardation: A guest editorial. *American Journal of Mental Deficiency,* 1977, *81*(6), 523–533.

Conley, R. W. *The economics of mental retardation.* Baltimore: Johns Hopkins University Press, 1973.

Editor. Enzymes that help you think. *Science Digest*, 1982, *90*(7), 92.

General Accounting Office (GAO). *Federal effort to prevent retardation*. Washington, DC: General Accounting Office, 1977.

General Accounting Office (GAO). *Preventing mental retardation: More can be done*. Washington, DC: U.S. Government Printing Office, 1977.

Harrell, R.F., Capp, R.H., Davis, D.R., Peerless, J., & Ravitz, L.R. Can nutritional supplements help mentally retarded children? An explorative study. *Proceedings of the National Academy of Sciences, U.S.A.*, 1981, *78*, 574–578.

Laxova, R. Genetics: An overview. *Interactions*. Madison, WI: Harry A. Waisman Center on Mental Retardation and Human Development, 1981.

Menolascino, F.J., & Strider, F. Advances in the prevention of mental retardation. In: S. Arieti (ed.), *American handbook of psychiatry* (7th ed.). New York: Human Sciences Press, 1981.

Morgan D., & Routtenberg, A. Brain pyruvate dehydrogenase: Phosphorylation and enzyme activity altered by a training experience. *Science*, 1981, *214*, 470–471.

Moser, H.W. Prevention of mental retardation: A realistic and achievable goal. Paper presented to the President's Committee on Mental Retardation, Atlanta, September 17, 1982.

Pellicer, A., Robins, D., & Wold, B. Altering genotype and phenotype by DNA-mediated gene transfer. *Science*, 1980, *209*, 1414–1422.

Pilmelli, S. A model program for lead screening: International Association on Prevention of Mental Retardation, biomedical causes. Washington, DC: U.S. Department of Health, Education, and Welfare, 1979.

Plog, S.C., & Santamour, M.D. (eds). *The year 2000 and mental retardation*. New York: Plenum Press, 1980.

President's Committee on Mental Retardation. *Islands of excellence*. Washington, DC: U.S. Government Printing Office, 1973.

Zigler, E. National crisis in mental retardation research. *American Journal of Mental Deficiency*, 1978, *83*(1), 1–8.

Curative Aspects of Mental Retardation:
Biomedical and Behavioral Advances
edited by Frank J. Menolascino, M.D., Ronald Neman, Ph.D., and Jack A. Stark, Ph.D.
Copyright 1983   Paul H. Brookes Publishing Co., Inc.   Baltimore · London

Index